THE ANTHROPOLOGY OF DRESS AND FASHION

THE ANTHROPOLOGY OF DRESS AND FASHION

A Reader

**EDITED BY
BRENT LUVAAS AND JOANNE B. EICHER**

BLOOMSBURY VISUAL ARTS
LONDON • NEW YORK • OXFORD • NEW DELHI • SYDNEY

BLOOMSBURY VISUAL ARTS
Bloomsbury Publishing Plc
50 Bedford Square, London, WC1B 3DP, UK
1385 Broadway, New York, NY 10018, USA

BLOOMSBURY, BLOOMSBURY VISUAL ARTS and the Diana logo are
trademarks of Bloomsbury Publishing Plc

First published in Great Britain 2019

Cover design by Liron Gilenberg
Cover images © Brent Luvaas

A catalogue record for this book is available from the British Library.

A catalog record for this book is available from the Library of Congress.

ISBN: HB: 978-1-4742-8258-1
        PB: 978-1-4742-8256-7

Typeset by Integra Software Services Pvt. Ltd.
Printed and bound in India

To find out more about our authors and books visit www.bloomsbury.com
and sign up for our newsletters.

CONTENTS

ACKNOWLEDGMENTS

Producing this reader has been an exercise in collaboration—across distances, theoretical perspectives, and generations. We put it together by email, phone, and the occasional in-person lunch at academic conferences. Picking up a reader such as this one, it is easy to imagine it as a static, bound volume, an inert thing. Its production was anything but. We appreciated how working on this reader helped solidify our collegial relationships, both with each other and the growing number of scholars interested in dress and fashion as objects of anthropological analysis.

We would like to thank all of the contributors to this reader for their valuable and important work in the emerging field of the anthropology of dress and fashion and the anonymous reviewers whose comments we considered, appreciated, and incorporated. We appreciate the early interest anthropologists took in the subject, back at the dawn of our discipline, and the growing interest dress and fashion hold for a new generation of scholars.

All chapters in this book originally appeared in peer-reviewed journals, monographs, and edited volumes and are reproduced here with the permission of their publishers and authors, except in cases where the original text is no longer subject to copyright. We have edited each for length. Many thanks to the publishers and authors who so graciously agreed to let us include their valuable work here.

We would also like to thank Anna Wright at Bloomsbury for initiating this project, and Frances Arnold, Pari Thomson, Faith Marsland, and the rest of the team at Bloomsbury for seeing it through to fruition. Joanne thanks Kathryn Earle, managing director at Bloomsbury, formerly Berg, for her long, sturdy support of the study of dress and fashion and for her publishing prescience. Joanne also appreciates Shirley Ardener, Lidia Sciama, and the late Helen Callaway at the University of Oxford for their recognition of dress as culturally significant. Nicholas Grodsky, our graduate student assistant, deserves special thanks for the many hours he spent in conversation with publishers and authors in order to secure the reprint rights to make this reader possible. Finally, many thanks to Kate Leibfried, who provided sturdy assistance and support for Joanne from the earliest queries about the project through the final stages of publication.

INTRODUCTION

Brent Luvaas and Joanne B. Eicher

When curator and fashion historian Valerie Steele was in graduate school at Yale, she got into a conversation with a history professor about the focus of her dissertation. Instead of hearing the word "fashion" when she described what she did, the professor apparently heard "fascism." "That's interesting," he said. "Italian or German?" There was a long silence, Steele recalls, until she finally figured out what had happened. "Not fascism," she clarified, "fashion." Without saying another word, the professor turned around and walked away (Steele 1991). Fashion, apparently, was not just an inappropriate topic for academic study; it was toxic, something the professor wanted to get away from as quickly as possible.

In much of academia, fashion still triggers that kind of response. Italian versus German fascism? Fine, that's well within the parameters of "serious" academic work. But Italian versus French fashion, let alone heels versus flats? That's another story, altogether. Many academics steer well clear of the subject of what people wear and why, as if they were afraid of being contaminated by the topic's perceived superficiality. These are heady people. They must study heady things.

Anthropology, on the other hand, has never been afraid of dress or fashion. With its holistic, "everything is culture" approach to studying human society, our discipline has long included an attention to the most minute aesthetic details of personal adornment. The earliest anthropological field accounts provide obvious examples. Anthropologists in the nineteenth century fixated on what their subjects were wearing, or just as often, not wearing. Taking their cue from the classic fieldwork guide *Notes and Queries in Anthropology* (first published in 1874), anthropologists documented in laborious—sometimes gratuitous—detail the painful size of lip implants and neck elongation rings, the barely-there ostentation of gourd-made penis sheaths, the elaborateness of ceremonial make-up and tribal tattoos. By 1919, renowned anthropologist Alfred Kroeber (included in this volume) was using the skirt length and garment shoulder size of Western women's gowns as indicators of the arch of cultural change over time (Kroeber 1919). In 1931, Alfred Crawley (included in this volume) was theorizing dress as a fundamental component of social evolution (Crawley 1931). That same year, Ruth Benedict and Edward Sapir (included in this volume) published entries in the *Encyclopedia of the Social Sciences* on "dress" and "fashion" respectively (Benedict 1931; Sapir 1931).

We do not mean to suggest, however, that anthropologists are without ambivalence towards dress and fashion. We identify, with few exceptions, with the left side of the political spectrum and have a tendency to carry a liberal disdain for anything that reads as too explicitly "bourgeois." Carole McGranahan, writing about the fashion sensibilities of anthropologists attending the annual American Anthropological Association meeting, paints a portrait of the attendees as self-conscious misfits in drab earth tones and basic black with a few small items of "anthropological flair" thrown in, usually from the anthropologist's own field site (McGranahan 2013). In self-presentation, we tend to downplay our interest in fashion, careful not to be too ostentatious, making only the slightest nod to it through an ikat scarf or dangling turquoise earrings. And similar to other social scientists, we exhibit a clear preference for research foci with "obvious" social import: structural inequality in the immigration system, the enduring legacy of colonialism in American environmental policy. We, the editors, have heard our share of stories of advisors steering their students away from projects too conspicuously about dress or fashion. We have had our share of colleagues say something to the effect of "how fun!", the condescension audible in their voices, when they hear about the work we are doing. Fashion, apparently, is fine when it is *part* of what we study, but it can be quite a different matter when it is the focus of our study.

As editors of this reader, we have worked actively to thwart that conceit. We, like a growing cohort of like-minded colleagues, see dress and fashion as critical sites of anthropological study. Dress and fashion matter, not just as pieces of a cultural whole but as subjects in their own right, having a significant impact on the way people live, define themselves, and operate within the world around them. Dress is the most visible component of social distinction worldwide (Schoss, Moors, and Marlow—included in this volume), comprising one of the most basic building blocks of inequality (Benedict, Sapir, Turner, Polhemus, and Eicher and Roach-Higgins—included in this volume). Dress distinguishes one ethnic group from another (Renne, Durham, Erekosima and Eicher, and Leshkowich—included in this volume), one social status (Friedman, Jones, and Heath—included in this volume) and religious affiliation (Silverman, Moors, and Tarlo—included in this volume) from another. It helps legitimize colonial regimes (Callaway, and Comaroff and Comaroff—included in this volume), serves to stigmatize the foreign, the minority, and the marginal (Moors, and Tarlo—included in this volume), and can arise as a powerful means by which people throughout the world challenge their status (Jones, Pipyrou, Kondo, Luvaas, and Masquelier—included in this volume), remaking their place in their own societies and on the global stage.

Fashion, likewise, is neither frivolous nor trivial. It matters, has consequence. The textile and apparel industry is one of the world's most profitable, employing millions of people in cities around the world, whether as designers (Kondo, Balasescu, and Philomena—included in this volume), sewers and manufacturers (Moon—included in this volume), intermediaries (Hansen, and Sadre-Orafai—included in this volume), or interlopers of various kinds (Craciun, Skoggard, and Luvaas—included in this volume). Also one of the most environmentally damaging industries (Hepburn—included in this volume), fashion pollutes waterways with dyes, toxins, and synthetic microfibers, and contributes more than its share to carbon emissions. In countries like Indonesia (Jones, and Luvaas—included in this volume), China (Zhao—included in this volume), Japan (Kondo—included in this volume), Iran (Balasescu—included in this volume), the United States (Moon—included in this volume), and Denmark (Riegels—included in this volume), fashion comprises a critical component of the national economy. It is part of larger processes of modernization and development (Leshkowich, Schoss, and Jones—included in this volume), operating hand in hand with infrastructure, education, and the loosening of trade restrictions in defining a nation's place on the global stage. Fashion links nations together across sites of manufacture, disposal, and trade (Hansen, Luvaas, Skoggard, and Keet—included in this volume). By creating transnational ties and dependencies, fashion helps construct, and reconstruct, the world order. This is why the Danish and Chinese governments invest so much money in fashion and why Jakarta Fashion Week is sponsored by the British Council, the Thai Ministry of Commerce, and the Embassy of India, along with a plethora of other state and corporate entities. In short, fashion is not peripheral to the larger interests of anthropology. Fashion is, and ought to be, front and center.

Fortunately, we are not the first anthropologists who have felt this way. Well-known names paved the road before us, contributing books and significant articles on the topic. Justine Cordwell and Ronald Schwarz, for instance, put together the edited volume *Fabrics of Culture: The Anthropology of Clothing and Adornment* all the way back in 1973. In 1976, Marshall Sahlins published a structural analysis of the "American clothing system" within his theoretical treatise *Culture and Practical Reason*. Annette Weiner and Jane Schneider organized *Cloth and Human Experience* in 1989. In 1999, Fadwa el Guindi, presented The "Anthropology of Dress" as a chapter in her book *Veil: Modesty, Privacy and Resistance* (el Guindi 1999a), followed by Joanne Eicher's 2000 article with the same title. Eicher reviewed the contributions made to the topic of dress and fashion from the discipline's beginning. For a detailed summary of the work that has taken place in the anthropology of dress and fashion up to the early twenty-first century, we recommend Karen Tranberg Hansen's 2004 review, "The World in Dress: Anthropological Studies of Clothing, Fashion, and Culture" in the *Annual Review of Anthropology* (Hansen 2004b).

In addition, many anthropologists' work was cited in the comprehensive article "Style and Substance: Fashion in Twenty-First-Century Research Libraries" by two librarians, Lindsay M. King and Russell T. Clement (2012), which underscores how the topic of dress and fashion has become interdisciplinary and quickly growing. Several anthropologists have written special focus accounts with selections included in this volume, such as Hansen's work in Zambia (included in this volume). Other notable works in the anthropology of dress and fashion are Emma Tarlo's *Clothing Matters: Dress and Identity in India* (1996); Susanne Küchler with Graeme Were's *The Art of Clothing: A Pacific Experience* (2005); Mukulika Banerjee with Daniel Miller's *The Sari* (2003); Susanne Küchler with Daniel Miller's *Clothing as Material Culture* (2005); and also Daniel Miller with Sophie Woodward on both *Global Denim* (2010) and *Blue Jeans* (2012). Miller's several single and coauthored books on dress and fashion arise from his continuing research focus on consumption and material culture. He would not consider himself a fashion or dress scholar specifically.

We think it is important to point out that in each of these cases, the anthropologists writing about dress and fashion have been part of departments that expected them also to have other foci for their teaching and research. Few anthropologists have been hired to pursue only an interest in dress and fashion, though there are exceptions, like Sandra Niessen, who was affiliated with the Clothing, Textiles and Material Culture Department at the University of Alberta and authored *Legacy in cloth, Batak textiles of Indonesia* (2009). In addition, we have found that these anthropologists' dress and fashion titles are not always listed in their abbreviated bios on university websites, implying that they do not consider the titles to be "front and center" to their own work, or at least feel that they cannot present them as if they were. We hope this volume plays a role in changing that.

THE ANTHROPOLOGY OF DRESS AND FASHION

We endeavored, for this reader, to collect some of the best and most influential English-language work produced so far in the emerging field of the anthropology of dress and fashion. We have only included works written by scholars whom we identified as members of anthropological associations or departments or who refer to themselves as anthropologists. We recognize that "anthropologist" is a complicated, and at times controversial, designation, and our intention was to be as inclusive in our application of that category as possible. Our collection represents a diverse body of scholarship that we think will be useful to our colleagues, students, and other scholars and professionals interested in understanding how and why human beings manipulate and decorate our bodies as we do. We strove to elucidate the social and cultural stakes of the global fashion system today, providing insight into how the fashion industry operates at the ground level, and the various ways in which it intersects with politics, ideology, and other structures of power. Readers interested in reading the entirety of the works selected are encouraged to seek them out in the books and journals in which they originally appeared.

Before moving to the articles directly, a few preliminary statements follow. First, we acknowledge that—strictly speaking—"the anthropology of dress and fashion" does not exist, or at least it does not exist as a formal subdiscipline of anthropology. There are no specific conferences convened for only anthropologists of dress and fashion. We gather instead at a growing number of interdisciplinary conferences in fashion and dress studies. Or we sit in on each other's talks at the larger anthropology conferences. We are a small and scattered group, with no identity cards, and no journal to call our own. The anthropology of dress and fashion, then, is a convenient contrivance, which we as editors are using to distinguish anthropological work on dress and fashion from work in other related disciplines.

Second, there is no clear boundary between the anthropology of dress and fashion and work in those other humanities and social sciences devoted to dress and fashion. Anthropologists who do work on dress and fashion cite sociologists, historians, costume historians, philosophers, semioticians, linguists, fashion journalists, and anyone else found helpful in understanding the complexities of what people wear and why. Members of these other related disciplines also often cite us. We reject traditional disciplinary limitations. Some of us, however, do identify, at least to some degree, with that large and growing multi-disciplinary entity referred to as "fashion studies." Fashion studies is also a convenient contrivance, but it is one that does real cultural work, providing a term of identification for a larger body of scholars and a pool of resources to read and to cite. An anthropology of dress and fashion that only included and cited anthropologists would be a thin and bare scholarship, relying on a select handful of resources. So, anthropologists of dress and fashion speak to a much broader audience than just themselves, and they tend to do so in a vernacular comprehensible to that broader audience. They tend to avoid jargon specific to anthropology. They sometimes write in a more popular or journalistic style than other anthropologists. We believe that to be a strength.

That said, there are certain characteristics—or perhaps we might call them tendencies—that anthropologists who do work in dress and fashion share with one another and which effectively distinguish them from other scholars doing similar work. For one, anthropologists tend to prioritize first-hand engagement with the people we study over textual or visual analysis. The anthropology of dress and fashion, like cultural anthropology more generally, is derived primarily (though not exclusively) from participant-observation. It holds an ethnographic bias, privileging forms of knowledge gained through immersing oneself in a place or culture, typically one other than the anthropologist's own, for a long period of time. Once again, we see this as a strength, and we are not the only ones who see it this way. Scholars in many disciplines have borrowed this commitment to ethnographic fieldwork, and we find it increasingly common among scholars in fashion studies as a whole.

For another, the anthropology of dress and fashion, at least until recently, has tended to focus on non-Western dress and fashion. While other scholars who study dress have tended to cast their sights on European, American, and Australian traditions, anthropologists have sought out people and places left out of the larger scholarly conversation: Kayapo Indians in Brazil (Turner—included in this volume), or middle-class urbanites in Indonesia (Jones—included in this volume). This has always been the strength of anthropology. It provides a comparative model across cultures. And yet, it sometimes does so at the expense of contributing to the larger understanding of Western models of fashion and dress. We devote a few articles in this reader to Western fashion, for example Sophie Woodward's work on jeans in the UK and Daniel Rosenblatt's work on tattooing and body piercing in San Francisco, but generally an anthropological focus on analyzing Western fashion remains an underdeveloped domain. Daniel Miller and his former graduate students in material culture at University College London are a notable exception. We have included some of their work here (Woodward, Miller, and O'Connor—included in this volume). We hope that more work of this kind takes place. Nonetheless, the anthropology of dress and fashion, like every other variety of cultural anthropology, has until recently centered around the first-hand observation of non-Western traditions of dress, and our selection of articles reflects that.

Third, we need to be clear about our terms. "Dress" and "fashion" are not the only terms we might have selected for the title of this reader. We could also have used "style," or "adornment," or "body decoration," or even, as does Polhemus (included in this volume), "anti-fashion." We chose "dress" and "fashion" for a simple reason: they are the terms we employ in our own work. These terms also have played an important role in anthropological work more generally. We define dress rather broadly, following Eicher and Roach-Higgins (included in this volume), "as an assemblage of body modifications and/or supplements displayed by a person in communicating with other human beings" (Eicher and Roach-Higgins 1992: 15). We use this definition for reasons Eicher and Roach-Higgins discuss at length in their contribution to this volume. In short, it enables us to discuss, and include within this volume, a wide range of body modifications and supplements that carry social meaning. In employing the term "fashion," on the other hand, we describe a larger process in which items of dress are systematically replaced by newer items in order to maximize profit. Dress describes social and cultural practices. Fashion describes a particular moment in those practices, inseparable from the profit-incentive of modern industrial capitalism.

We do not pretend that these are the only possible definitions of "dress" and "fashion," nor do we intend to imply that all anthropologists share our definitions. Cultural anthropologists have yet to settle on a common definition of "culture." It is far too much for us to expect them to do so for "dress" and "fashion." The lack of shared definitions, we would suggest, is also a strength in that it demonstrates a continuing dynamism, a field in motion, and a steadfast refusal to settle into permanent or stable meanings. Dress and fashion change. They evolve, though we would never imply that they "progress." The anthropology of dress and fashion, likewise, continually evolves, which is our reason for arranging the chapters in each section of the book according to their date of original publication. We want to enable you, the reader, to see how research on these topics is changing over time, how it builds upon itself, develops, and occasionally circles back around to earlier themes.

Finally, we want to say a few words about who we are and how our backgrounds and research foci influence the readings we have selected. The two of us, Brent Luvaas and Joanne Eicher, represent two different generations in the anthropology of dress and fashion and two different approaches to its study. Brent Luvaas's background is in sociocultural anthropology. Trained in a traditional, four-field anthropology department at the University of California, Los Angeles, in the mid-2000s, his work is about cultural production and how it is impacted by digital technologies. His early research, and first book, centered on a network of do-it-yourself (DIY) clothing designers, zine writers, and indie musicians in Indonesia (Luvaas 2012). Fashion, particularly in the form of streetwear, was a big part of this work. But it was not the only part. He approached fashion and dress in dialogue with music, written discourse, and new media technologies. His most recent work, on street style bloggers, those (largely) amateur photographers who post pictures of "cool-looking" pedestrians from cities around the world on their personal websites, makes fashion central to his analysis (Luvaas 2016). It appears as a system, an industry, and a network of situated social actors in which street style bloggers have no choice but to be engaged. In both these projects, fashion emerges as a force his interlocutors have to contend with. It is both a pleasure and a burden. Luvaas, then, sees fashion from the point of view of a critical outsider.

Starting in 2012, however, Luvaas began to blur the line between critical outsider and active participant. As part of his street style blogger project, he started a street style blog of his own, Urban Fieldnotes (www.urbanfieldnotes. com). The blog, featuring images of stylish pedestrians in Philadelphia, New York, Jakarta, and elsewhere, was profiled in fashion publications including *Nylon, Harper's Bazaar Brazil,* and *Mojeh Magazine.* Luvaas went on to shoot street style features for fashion publications like *Refinery 29, Kenton Magazine*, and *Racked*, and partnered with fashion brands including Uniqlo, Indochino, Members Only, American Apparel, and Century 21 department stores. The experience complicated his relationship with fashion considerably. The readings selected for this volume reflect that complication, pursuing the multiple ways in which people throughout the world become both empowered by and entangled within fashion.

Joanne Eicher's background stems from a combined degree in anthropology and sociology for her graduate degrees at Michigan State University, focusing on cultural meaning and an emphasis on fieldwork. She used this approach as a springboard for her research and courses taught only on dress and fashion in the department of Textiles, Clothing, and Related Arts (later called Human Environment and Design) at Michigan State, which she continued when moving to a sister department, Textiles and Clothing (later folded into the Department of Design, Housing and Apparel) at the University of Minnesota, where she also became director of the Goldstein Museum of Design. Her first book was the first coedited book of readings on dress and fashion (Roach and Eicher 1965) followed by a textbook (Roach and Eicher 1973). Her cross-disciplinary approach arose from participation in the International Textile and Apparel Association, the Costume Society of America, the Textile Society of America, and the Arts Council of the African Studies Association.

After living in Nigeria in the 1960s and collecting material on indigenous dress practices from across the country, she conducted fieldwork among the Kalabari people of the Niger Delta, and as a result identified as an Africanist and interacted with a wide range of scholars in the African Studies Association from various disciplines in organizing panels on dress and fashion over the years. Her research on the Kalabari escalated, as she learned they do not produce their own cloth, instead, as part of the British Commonwealth and as traders, created a distinctive cutwork textile from Indian madras that she and Kalabari colleague called "cultural authentication" (Erekosima and Eicher—included in this volume). The Kalabari wear many imported textiles and dress items and feature them in colorful funeral rites honoring elders (Eicher 2015). Editor-in-chief of the ten volume *Encyclopedia of World Dress and Fashion* (Eicher 2010, 2016), she continues to commission articles annually for the online additions, and is also editor of two Bloomsbury book series, *Dress, Body, Culture*, and *Dress and Fashion Research,* the former reaching seventy-three titles in its twenty-one years from 1997 to 2018, and the latter, ten titles since 2014, of which many were authored by anthropologists.

These two, very different perspectives on dress and fashion are woven throughout this reader, in both the introductions to each section, and the chapters and articles selected for inclusion. Eicher's expertise in world traditions of dress informs the ranges of regions represented and the emphasis of the role of dress in defining ordinary lives and experiences. Luvaas's interest in the global systems of fashion informs the emphasis on power and economics and the critical tone of much of the work included. Not all the authors featured here, however, represent the viewpoints of the editors. We sought to include as broad a range of work in the anthropology of dress and fashion as possible. There are articles, particularly early in the book, that contain viewpoints or statements easily seen as outdated or ill informed. We have included them as part of anthropology's historical record. If we are to progress as a subfield of anthropology, we have to know where we have been. We hope this reader provides you with a sense of where the anthropology of dress and fashion has been and where it is currently going.

PART 1

CLASSIC WORKS IN THE ANTHROPOLOGY OF DRESS AND FASHION

PART INTRODUCTION

Alfred L. Kroeber would never have considered himself a fashion scholar. Nor, for that matter, would have Ruth Benedict, Edward Sapir, Ernest Crawley, or A. R. Radcliffe-Brown. Kroeber, the well-known anthropologist, who trained under Franz Boas and spent much of his career at University of California, Berkeley, was first and foremost a scholar of culture. He was interested in human cultural variation, why it differed from one place to another and how it changed over time. Of particular concern to Kroeber, like other American anthropologists of his day, was the disappearance of culture, whether by colonial conquest or changing traditions. Fashion became emblematic for Kroeber of the structural transformations of culture more generally, and it became a resource for tracking changes in culture across the historical record. Like an archaeologist analyzing the battleship curves in gravestone motifs, Kroeber analyzed the hem lengths of skirts as depicted in women's fashion magazines. They demonstrated, he argued, a predictable pattern of change, something "that resembles what we call law" (p. 17). Kroeber's point in arguing for fashion's law-like quality was not, however, to reduce it to some physical or biological inevitability, but rather to emphasize that like other kinds of laws to which humans subscribe, it is built out of forces social in origin. Like his mentor Franz Boas before him, Kroeber was invested in countering race-based hypotheses, all too common at the time, about why different groups behave as they do. Fashion was one weapon in his culturalist arsenal.

Other prominent anthropologists of the early twentieth century shared Kroeber's interest in fashion as a marker of cultural and historical change. Both Sapir and Benedict wrote about fashion in contrast to dress. For Benedict, dress was a practice distinctive to human beings. Our proclivity for decorating, extending, and modifying our bodies separates us from our closest nonhuman relatives. Lacking in fur, people in temperate climates wear clothing to protect themselves from the elements. In warmer environments, clothing protects from insects and the sun. Nonetheless, Benedict is hesitant to ground the practices of dress in biological necessity, noting that modesty is not a human universal, and that a number of societies have little concern about covering the sex organs, or any other part of the body. Like Kroeber before her, Benedict uses dress as another form of evidence to combat race-based biological determinism. For her, practices of dress are exceedingly variable from place to place. It is only dress itself—loosely defined—that is universal among humans.

Fashion, however, is not. For both Benedict and Sapir, fashion is a historical phenomenon, beginning with modern Western civilization. "Whereas in simpler conditions, even in untouched rural districts of Europe today," writes Benedict, "dress is geographically differentiated, in modern civilization it is temporally differentiated" (p. 24). One style overtakes another. Fashions fade while dress endures.

Sapir links the phenomenon of fashion to "boredom," "restlessness and curiosity" along with "the more vulgar desire for prestige and notoriety" (p. 25). For him, fashion is a game of differentiation, the means by which one class distinguishes itself from another. It is also an enunciation of a particular kind of modern ennui, whereby an individual, sick to death of the persona she has created for herself, strives in vain to find another mask to wear. There is a sense in Sapir's description of fashion, that he reads it as an ailment of contemporary European society, not just a feature. It distinguishes it, unfavorably, from other kinds of people anthropologists traditionally study.

Neither Sapir nor Benedict, interestingly, linked fashion explicitly to the advent of capitalism, as Polhemus and other anthropologists later would. It seemed to spring fully formed out of that nebulous spirit of the times they referred to simply as "modern civilization."

A. R. Radcliffe-Brown, in contrast, took no particular interest in either dress or fashion. But like any good anthropologist of his day, he did make extensive note in his work of how the people he studied ornamented themselves, particularly when it came to traditions and rituals. For Radcliffe-Brown, such ornamentation was "functional," but like Sapir, Benedict, and Kroeber, he did not draw a biological meaning from the term. "The customary regulation of personal ornament," he wrote, "is a means by which the society acts upon, modifies, and regulates the sense of self in the individual" (p. 20). Here, dress serves both social and psychological ends, though for Radcliffe-Brown the social and psychological were mutually constitutive.

Among the classic anthropologists featured in this volume, only Ernest Crawley took extensive interest in the subject of dress specifically. Crawley, an English school teacher, sports journalist, and former clergyman, was a something of an "armchair anthropologist." He occasionally contributed to anthropological journals and was a member of the Royal Anthropological Institute, but he seems to have disappeared into relative obscurity as the discipline gained popularity in the mid-twentieth century. Crawley's posthumously published collection of essays, *Dress, Drink, and Drums: Further Studies of Savages and Sex* (1931), is the first anthropological book we know of to include the term dress in its title. Though not particularly influential to the anthropology of dress and fashion, we have included it here for its historic significance. We were quite surprised to find someone taking dress so seriously so early in the anthropological tradition. Perhaps it should come as no surprise that it came from a part-time scholar with an equal interest in sports, drink, and sex. There is something of a post-Victorian fascination with the "primitive" and "prurient" to Crawley's work. Nevertheless, we admire its pioneering spirit, the way it folds dress into the larger body of anthropological scholarship and takes it seriously as a critical component of human social evolution.

1

THE PRINCIPLE OF ORDER IN CIVILIZATION AS EXEMPLIFIED BY CHANGES IN FASHION

Alfred L. Kroeber

FASHIONS IN DRESS

Twenty years ago the project of inquiring into the principles that guide fashion arose in my mind, and I went so far as to turn the leaves of volume after volume of a Parisian journal devoted to dress. But the difficulties were discouraging. Pivotal points seemed hard to find in the eternal flux. One might measure collars or sleeves or ruffles for some years, and then collars and sleeves and ruffles disappeared. One lady in a plate was seated, another erect, a third in profile, the fourth elevated her arms. If one took as a base the total length of the figure, coiffures fell and rose by inches from time to time, or were entirely concealed by hats or nets. I abandoned the plan as infeasible.

In 1918 I renewed the endeavor, this time with less ambitious scope and greater readiness to seize on any opening. I decided to attempt only eight measurements, four of length and four of width, all referring to the figure or dress as a whole, and to disregard all superficial parts or trimmings. Strict comparability of data being essential, it was necessary to confine observations to clothing of a single type. Women's full evening toilette was selected. This has served the same definite occasions for more than a century; does not therefore vary in purpose as does day dress, nor seasonally like street clothing. The material always remains silk, and there have been no totally new fundamental concepts introduced, such as the shirtwaist and tailored suit. The variations are therefore purely stylistic. And while this range promised to be perhaps somewhat narrower than those of certain other types of women's wear, this was of little moment. If any principle could be determined, it would apply *a fortiori* to the more changeable kinds of clothing.

MEASUREMENTS

The measurements made were the following:

1 Total length of figure from the center of the mouth to the tip of the toe. If the shoe was covered, the lowest point of the skirt edge was chosen. The selection of the mouth obviated all difficulties arising from alteration of hairdress.

2 Distance from the mouth to the bottom of the skirt. This equals the last measurement less the height of the skirt from the ground.

3 Distance from the mouth to the minimum diameter across the waist. This serves as some sort of indication of the length of the "waist" or corsage, that is, of the upper part of the figure. The true waist line of the dress has been disregarded. It would have been much more significant stylistically and probably shown more decided variations; but there are periods when it vanishes. When the waist line is visible and below the minimum diameter of the waist, the distance between the two was also noted.

4 Depth or length of decolletage, measured from the mouth to the middle of the corsage edge in front.

A. L. Kroeber, "On the Principle of Order in Civilization as Exemplified in Changes in Fashion," *American Anthropologist*, n.s., 21 (1919): 262–63.

5 Diameter of the skirt at its hem or base.

6 Maximum diameter of the skirt at any point above the base. In some cases this exceeds the diameter at the bottom. Ordinarily it is smaller, but in some instances nevertheless definitely visible: that is, the skirt swells, constricts, and flares again. This diameter did not prove a generally useful measurement. Whenever it could be taken, the distance from its middle to the mouth was also recorded as a supplementary datum.

7 Minimum diameter in the region of the waist.

8 Width of shoulders, or more accurately, width of the decolletage across the shoulders. In the earlier years of the period covered, the upper edge of the dress frequently passes below the point of the shoulder, across the uppermost part of the arm, as a bertha or slight sleeve. In such cases the measurement was recorded. Of recent years, the corsage often really ends under the arms, being held up in appearance by straps over the shoulders. Here it seemed best to measure the distance between the straps. When however the strap is pushed off the shoulder to fall loosely down the arm, or is wholly wanting, the present measurement had to be omitted.

Ten figures were measured for each calendar year, the first ten suitable for measurement being taken from each volume, so as to ensure random instead of subjective selection. Fashion journals of the middle of the nineteenth century contain fewer illustrations than recent ones. It sometimes happened therefore that only seven or eight toilettes were represented in the numbers from the first of January until summer, when full dress styles suspend seasonally. In such cases the rear end of the volume for the preceding year was drawn upon to supplement the deficiency. An entry like 1857 is thus normally based on plates issued from January to March or April or May of that year, but occasionally would begin in December or even November of 1856. Even at that, insufficiency of material or oversight has resulted in a few years being represented by only nine sets of measurements. Unfortunately also, there is scarcely a year for which ten illustrations could be found in each of which all eight measurements were recordable. A gown may be shown very completely in full face except for one corner of the skirt, which is hidden behind the chair of a seated companion. The basal skirt width can often be pretty well guessed in such cases, and an estimate was generally made; but only actual measurements have been included in the averages discussed. If in the taking of the observations such a deficient figure had been passed over, the next picture might have indeed exhibited the desired skirt width, but failed to show two or three other features; and too firm an insistence on all eight traits would often have yielded only three or four instead of ten measurable illustrations in a year. For instance, there are periods when it was overwhelmingly fashionable to hold the forearm horizontal, or to bring out the convexity of the bust by drawing it in semi-profile. In such years waist diameters are mostly obscured by the arm, and full shoulder widths very hard to get. The consequence of all these little circumstances is that the majority of the eight features observed are represented, year by year, by less than ten measurements, sometimes only by four or five. On the whole, preference was given to observations of the entire figure length, which was to be used as a norm for computations; and to the two next greatest measures, skirt length and width. For these, then, the series of data are fullest.

It must be admitted that ten measures is not a very large maximum from which to derive reasonably true averages in so variable a thing as fashionable dress, where each design strives almost as keenly after distinctiveness as after conformity to the prevailing style. I was conscious of this slenderness of basis. But the measurements as well as the reductions to percentages and averages are time-consuming; and for a preliminary investigation it seemed wiser to obtain a comparatively long series of small groups of measurements than to operate with measurement groups of a size more reliable for averages but covering fewer years. Ten cases from each of seventy-five years would give a better surveying perspective than twenty-five cases continued for thirty years; in addition to which the ten or approximately ten illustrations were rather readily obtainable, whereas it would have been bibliographically exacting to find twenty-five for most of the earlier years.

The outcome vindicated the hazard. The smallness of the series is unquestionably the cause of many of the fluctuating irregularities that appear in the chronologically arranged results. But in the case of every dimension the irregularities are not so great as to prevent recognition of the underlying drifts and tendencies; whereas the period of these tendencies is mostly so long that they would have been very imperfectly determinable, and often not at all, within a compass of only thirty years. In fact it would have been desirable if the range of investigation could have been extended from 75 years to 125. The net result of a larger series of cases would therefore have been a probable smoothing and increased regularity of the plotted curves expressive of the course of fashion; and some segregation of the present irregularities into historically true ones and others that represent only statistical inadequacy. But presumably nothing more would have eventuated from the increase of data.

I may here express my conviction that any farther quantitative investigations that may be undertaken as to the course of stylistic changes should be planned to cover if possible a period of from one to two centuries, whether they concern fashions of dress or of jewelry, silverware, or furniture.

THE DATA OBTAINED

I began the measurements with the year 1844 for the reason that that was the first volume of a fashion journal which I happened to know to be accessible in New York city, where I then was. The journal was the *Petit Courrier des Dames* in the Avery Library of Columbia University. The broken set ended in 1868, and I was driven to the Public Library for continuation. *Harper's Bazar* was available here in complete file to the present, and in it were made the measurements up to 1908. The Parisian journal contained beautiful lithographs only, the American exponent of fashion woodcuts of a horribly crude kind; and I feared at first that the difference in mode of illustration would vitiate comparison, and render wasted the work already done. The American waists seemed at least a quarter thicker,

and all of the proportions clumsier. Juxtaposition of the percentages for adjacent years however proved at once that the difference was only in artistic execution. The American draftsman fell as far short of his French colleague as the American designer was obviously doing slavish imitations of French models. In the same way the introduction, years later, of the zinc-engraved ink drawing, and then of the half-toned wash painting, yielded an entirely new type of fashion plate without in the least affecting the fashions represented.

Still more recently, half-toned photographs of living models suddenly made their appearance, and again I was disconcerted. Surely no dress worn on an actual human frame could be as extreme as the stylistically idealized pictures that had preceded. But again alarm was vain. Fashion journals are conducted to serve a definite practical purpose whose achievement their users can apparently gauge; and the reproduction, whatever its manner, must conform. The appended percentaged comparisons for several years are convincing as to the substantial unity of the data employed.

The chief constant difference of any consequence appears to be the diameter of the waist—dimension 7—which is greater in life. That is, draftsmen of fashion plates pinch this in beyond the cut of actual dresses; and that even when a thick waist is correct, as in these years from 1912 to 1917.

From 1909 to 1918, I had available volumes of *Harper's Bazar* in the Public Libraries of New York and San Francisco; and the fashions for 1919 are taken from the March number of *Vogue*.

It is surprising how poorly equipped in fashion journals the greater institutional libraries of our largest cities are. For those interested in similar researches, I would recommend inquiry at theatrical organizations for data on dress, and files of manufacturers' catalogues for industrial products.

It has not seemed necessary to print my measurements in full. I append those of three years as samples. The complete manuscript data are at the disposal of anyone who may be interested to follow the matter farther.

The absolute numbers were throughout converted into percentage ratios to the length of the entire figure as it has been defined. The percentages for each measure were then averaged for each year. It is these year percentage averages that are brought together in the appended summary tabulation, are plotted in the charts, and are throughout referred to in the discussion that follows.

WIDTH OF SKIRT

Of all the elements of dress examined, that of diameter of skirt yields the most impressive results, especially in graphic plotting. The irregularities of the rhythm of change are also more quickly understood in this point of fashion than for most others. Nevertheless the superiority which skirt width enjoys over other factors as an index of demonstration is more apparent than actual. It is even exceeded by some of them in the wave-length of their periodicity.

The following remarks refer to the diameter of the bottom of the skirt. This is not always the maximum diameter. But on the whole the fashions that narrow the skirt downward are rare; and they disagree among themselves as to the region of the greatest width.

When our record opens in 1844, it finds evening toilettes of moderate skirt width, 57 per cent, of the body length.[1] For several years the proportion fluctuates mildly, gradually rising.

In 1851, having attained a percentage of 61, the width of skirt suddenly begins to mount rapidly and continuously, until the plotted curve skyrockets to the extreme maximum of 116 in 1859. This is the apex of the crinoline hoop skirt fashion, when the flare of the skirt exceeds the height of the person. In eight years the skirt diameter has nearly doubled.

From 1859 on, the history of the skirt may be summarily described as a fifty years' progressive constriction.

The narrowing after 1859 is not as rapid as the widening immediately preceding; but within three years the proportion has fallen from 116 to 96. At this point a new sub-factor enters: the train. The skirt as a whole continues to lose fulness, but the attached train more than compensates for the shrinkage of diameter at its base. The plot therefore shows a checking of the descent, a new rise, and a secondary maximum of 108 in 1865.

The inflated, bell-like hoop skirt and the long-trained skirt are obvious antitheses, structurally as well as stylistically, and must have been felt so at the time. It is interesting that on wider perspective they prove both to have been only surface manifestations of a much more profound though less articulate impulse toward a pyramidal presentation of the figure.

From 1866 the great underlying swing toward narrower skirts continues, until about 1871 the figure has sunk to 75, although trains still rule.

In 1872 begins a second reaction, resulting in another superficial rise in the plot. This is due to the coming in of the "Grecian Bend," famous in the caricature of its day. This specialty however holds its own only four or five years, and by 1877 the proportion is back around 75.

From 1878 to 1881 the general narrowing which is the normal tendency for this era resumes, until in 1881 the percentage sinks to 52—a lower figure than any since the opening of our examination.

In 1881 the first trainless skirts in a dozen years appear, and until 1895 trainless and trained gowns occur side by side in about equal numbers. A skirt that rises well above the ground would ordinarily be narrower than a sweeping one. The inclination to constriction might expectably therefore be accentuated by the partial disappearance of the train; but this is not so. The general tendency of these fifteen years is for the diameter to remain stationary, with fluctuations between 50 and 60.

The period from 1895 to 1907 is one of more violent fluctuations, the limiting percentages almost attaining 70 and 50. The years from 1892 to 1898 show a widening and narrowing whose course looks as if it might constitute a third superficial wave. It is notable that the peak of 68 in 1896 is reached in a trainless year, this type of skirt prevailing also through the recession of 1897 and 1898 back to 53. The sudden widening to 65 in 1899 corresponds with the reintroduction of trains; but the succeeding years, with percentages of 52, 65, 59, and 50, constitute a period of almost exclusively trained skirts. From 1903 to 1907 the fluctuations are less violent, as if the reactionary tendencies that had forced the spasmodic widenings of the preceding decade were becoming exhausted, preparatory to the impending great impulse to constriction.

By 1908, the main sweep of the half century is once more on its way. For the first time in our story the basal diameter falls below 50. The next three years witness the final plunge into the extreme hobble and tube skirt toward which the progress of fashion has been consistently trending for a life time. The violence of this culmination is parallel to that of the inflation which 52 years before marked the end of the half century or more of gradual widening since the days of the Directoire and early Empire,—itself a period of accentuated revulsion from the flaring skirts of Louis XV and XVI. On the chart the recent chasm is as abrupt as the pinnacle of 1859. By 1911 the apogee of slimness is reached: the percentage is only 23—less than half the extremest narrowness attained in sixty preceding years, and but a fifth of the greatest width.

It is perhaps worth noting that trained and trainless skirts prevail side by side during these years.

By 1912 the tide has once more turned—no doubt to continue now for another two or three score years unless the periodicity of the rhythm is accelerated by some unknown new cause or is totally broken off by an alteration of fundamental fashion, such as the substitution of trousers for skirts. As in 1860–62, the recovery is rapid: 23, 27, 34, 29, 46, 49, 56.

1918 and 1919 show a reaction toward narrowness, with percentages of 20 and 33. The former indeed is the lowest figure in the entire series—lower even than the true climax in 1911. The cause is in part a sudden loss of trains in 1918. Compare 1911, 4 trained skirts, 28.7, 6 trainless, 19.5; 1918, 1 trained, 44, 8 trainless, 17.4. On the other hand, there is also a real reaction in this year, as the figures for trainless skirts alone reveal. Thus 1911–14: 19, 20, 20, 13; 1915–17: 35, 49, 37; 1918–19: 17, 18. Perhaps the reconstriction of these last two years may be considered as paralleling the rewidening during 1863–65 after the recession from the peak of 1859.

The complicating factor of trained versus trainless skirts, … which begins with 1863, when trains were reintroduced. It appears that on the whole trains are less favored as a device for attaining width and trainless skirts as a means toward slenderness than might be anticipated. Rather do the proportions for both types of skirts rise and fall together according to the tendency of the time.[2] A train that springs from the waist or hip can indeed be used to give the effect of fulness. But one of equal or greater length that only begins to trail from below the knee allows the lower part of the figure to attain as much slimness as may be sought; and if wrapped around the ankle, may even accentuate the effect of constriction.

The average width of skirt for the 76 years is 65.3. It will be seen that from 1852 to 1878 inclusive this figure is exceeded each year, whereas before and after that period it is never attained, except in 1880 (68) and again in the spasmodic flares of 1896 (68) and 1899 (65). On the plot the horizontal line for this average helps to emphasize the crest and the trough of the great secular wave.

LENGTH OF SKIRT

There is a one sided correlation between width and length of skirt. A short gown may be full or narrow; but a tight one will scarcely extend very near the ground, on account of the inconvenience. A period of decisively close skirts will therefore almost necessarily be a period of short skirts also; but the reverse does not hold.

There is a farther difference. A skirt may be of almost any width or narrowness in a fashion plate or on a posed model. When slenderness is desired, one leg is put behind the other, in a front view, and the dress made to cling to an exaggeratedly slim calf or ankle. In other words, there is no fixed limit of extremity. The possible length of a dress is however automatically cut off when it reaches the ground, or when, in an illustration, it descends far enough to conceal the feet. Yet a gown can shorten indefinitely.

This brings it about that when skirt length attains its maximum, it remains apparently stationary for a time, whereas at its minimum it reaches a climax and quickly descends again. It might be said that fashion clearly tries, and is prevented only by physical impossibility, to draw the bottom of the dress several inches into the ground.

The rhythmic period for skirt length is only a third that for width: about thirty-five years as against a century. …

The curves, allowing for their impinging on the limit, look symmetrical; but if the figures for the seventy-odd years examined are representative, the wave-length of the trait is diminishing and the amplitude increasing. In untechnical language, style alters more rapidly and unrestrainedly on this point as time goes on.

DIAMETER OF WAIST

A first glance at the plot suggests that the greater part of a century has brought little change in the minimum diameter of the fashionable woman's waist; and that change irregularly fluctuating. The only very striking movement is at the end of the plot …. But a grouping of the figures … brings out two definite swings each way.

This might be put as follows in terms of tendency:

Ca. [1844] to 1860, decreasing.

Ca. 1860 to 1874, increasing.

Ca. 1874 to 1882, decreasing.

Ca. 1882 to 1914, increasing.

The durations would be about 16, 14, 8, and 32 years. This does not look very regular.

It must be remembered that the measurement used is the smallest diameter in the waist region, which usually does not coincide with the waist line as the cut of the dress brings it out, and often departs considerably from it. Stylistically this measurement is therefore somewhat arbitrary.

LENGTH OF WAIST

Length of waist, as here defined, is also an arbitrary measurement. It is the distance from the mouth to the middle of the minimum diameter of the waist, not to the formal waist line of the dress, which is sometimes strongly accentuated and at other periods indefinite. Could the height of the waist line have been satisfactorily used, there might perhaps have eventuated a considerably more striking amplitude or decision of rhythm.

As it is, the plot shows a marked shortening or raising of the waist, a still more decisive lowering, and then a sudden sharp rise again, which appears to have reached its consummation and to be hovering before a new decline. The period of waist lengthening extends from about 1867–69 to 1903–04, or approximately thirty-five years. On the assumption that the rhythm is symmetrical, the preceding acme of long-waistedness would fall around 1833. But the figures from 1844 to 1850 are too uniform to allow too much inference. They might, so far as their plot proves anything, come from a middle and more or less halted portion of a long swing toward high-waistedness, or be the end of a briefer tendency toward a drawn-out bust. A carrying of the investigation back some fifty years more would no doubt elucidate these questions.

In any event, the shortening of the waist between 1904 and 1909, which coincides with its enlargement, is a more extreme and rapid movement than any that precede. It can further be noted that the culmination of the previous period of waist shortening, about 1867–69, is also a time of transverse enlargement; or to be accurate, in both cases the acme of shortness is attained while the movement toward thickness is well under way, the peak of this latter falling several years later. The effect on the bodily appearance is however quite different. The earlier high waist was directed toward producing a high and roundedly protruding bust, the later a flat one.

DECOLLETAGE

This is measured from the upper edge of the corsage to the mouth. The plot looks inconclusive; but the figures show the following rhythms:

1844, at 14.6.

Then the corsage rises to 12.7 in 1850.

Exposure increases gradually to 15.2 in 1858.

It decreases again to 11.7 in 1867.

Lowering of the edge progresses to 15.4 in 1880.

Sudden rise to 12.7 by 1882.

Lowering to 15.1 in 1900.

Another sudden rise to 12.5 in 1901.

Lowering, with fluctuations, to 16.2 by 1906.

Rise to 11.7 by 1908.

Lowering to 16.4 by 1916.

Since then a rise seems in progress.

The periods of lowering, or increase of exposure, aggregate nearly three times as long as the rises of the corsage, which come by leaps, especially after 1880:

Decrease of exposure, 6 years; increase 8.

Decrease, 9; increase 13.

Decrease, 2; increase 18.

Decrease, 1; increase, 5.

Decrease, 2; increase, 8.

The cause of this asymmetry is not clear.

The periodicity is also rather irregular as regards duration. It seems to average around fifteen years.

WIDTH OF DECOLLETAGE

This trait appears to have a very long periodicity. The first few years of the record are indecisive: they may represent the end of a period of broadening of shoulder exposure. At any rate by 1851–53 a maximum is reached above 21. From here on a narrowing continues without substantial interruption for more than sixty years.

By 1861 the figure has sunk below 18, by 1869 to 16. An increase to 18.3 in 1873 may be discounted on the ground of being based on only three measurements. By 1876 the percentage has fallen to 13.5, and the plates evince a strong inclination to show the bust in profile; which is likely itself to be a symptom of aversion for expanse of shoulders.

1877 to 1883 are reactionary, with an increase to 17. This wave is however so brief in comparison to the general swing as to be obviously secondary.

From 1883 to 1891 the narrowing continues, reaching the new low record of 12.6. From 1892 to 1897 there occurs another secondary broadening, which however fails to attain 16. From here on the course is fluctuating, but generally downward, as shown by the new low figures around 11 in 1898, 1902, 1906, 1912, 1915, and 1917, and a supreme minimum below 11 in 1918. The broadest decolletage in these last twenty years comes in 1905 and 1914 at 15. These may represent a third and fourth brief superficial rhythm carried on the downward swing of the underlying one.

The general course of this trait is similar to that of basal skirt width, with probability of an even longer period, though a less accentuated amplitude of variation owing to anatomical limitations.

Continuity of movement is particularly impressive when depth and breadth of decolletage are compared together in units of sufficiently large periods to smoothe out the fluctuations due to temporary changes of fashion and the irregularity that is inevitable when small series of figures are employed. It is true that the most striking event in the history of decolletage depth is its increase in recent years, which synchronizes with a decrease in width. Yet it is clear that this is no mere coincidence, but the culmination of a drift that has set for 70 years.

COMPARISON OF THE SEVERAL RHYTHMS

We have, I think, now found reasonable evidence of an underlying pulsation in the width of civilized women's skirts, which is symmetrical and extends in its up and down beat over a full century; of an analogous rhythm in skirt length, but with a period of only about a third the duration; some indication that the position of the waist line may completely alter, also following a "normal" curve, in a seventy-year period; and a possibility that the width of shoulder exposure varies in the same manner, but with the longest rhythm of all, since the continuity of tendency in one direction for seventy years establishes a periodicity of about a century and a half, if the change in this feature of dress follows a symmetrically recurrent plan.

There is something impressive in the largeness of these lapses of time. We are all in the habit of talking glibly of how this year's fashion upsets that of last year. Details, trimmings, pleats and ruffles, perhaps colors and materials, all the conspicuous externalities of dress, do undoubtedly alter rapidly; and it is in the very nature of fashion to bring these to the fore. They are driven into our attention, and soon leave a blurred but overwhelming impression of incalculably chaotic fluctuations, of reversals that are at once bewildering and meaningless, of a sort of lightning-like prestidigitation to which we bow in dumb recognition of its uncontrollability. But underneath this glittering maze, the major proportions of dress change with a slow majesty, in periods often exceeding the duration of human life, and at least sometimes with the even regularity of the swing of an enormous pendulum. The child whose braids hang down her back may be reasonably sure that in the years when her daughters are being born she will wear longer dresses than her mother now goes about in; and that her skirts promise to be wider each successive decade until she is a grandmother. There is something in these phenomena, for all their reputed arbitrariness, that resembles what we call law: a scheme, an order on a scale not without a certain grandeur. Not that the fashion of a future date can be written now. Every style is a component of far too many elements, and in part uniquely entering elements, to make true prediction possible. But it does seem that some forecast can be made for any one basic element whose history has been sufficiently investigated; and that, when the event arrives, if the anticipation be proved to have been more or less erroneous, the source of the aberration may be clear, and the disturbingly injected forces stand revealed as subject to an order of their own.

It is not to be expected that the development and decline of every trait of dress or civilization should follow a normal curve, that is, a symmetrical course. For an element of civilization wholly unrelated to all others, such symmetry could perhaps be anticipated. But completely integral elements are an idea rather than a fact. There must always be some interaction with other factors in the same and cognate phases of culture, and occasional interferences from more remote domains. A certain proportion of features should therefore follow irregular courses, or asymmetrical curves; and in this class it seems that diameter of the waist and depth of decolletage should be placed.

Secondary tremors ruffling the evenness of the great pulsations are at first sight disturbing to the concept of orderliness, but on analysis confirmatory, in that they reveal an increase of the intricacy of the operative forces without diminishing their regularity. In this manner the long range curves for width of skirt and shoulders, each bearing about three superimposed but symmetrical minor crests, add substance to the generic conclusions reached.

Finally, while it would make for the greater simplicity of historical causality if it were found that acmes of fashion came in recurrences of equal periodicity, such regularity can hardly be expected. There is no conceivable reason why there should be anything inherent in the nature of dress tending toward a change from full to narrow and back to full skirts in a century. All historical phenomena are necessarily unique in some degree, in the field of nature as well as of human activity; and a similar rhythm of fashion might well extend over a thousand, a hundred, or ten years in different eras or among separate nations. Again, therefore, there is if not support for the idea of "law," at least no disconcertion in the fact that the past quarter century on the whole evinces distinctly more rapid and extreme variations of fashion than the half century preceding. This is the case for every feature examined except shoulder width.

CONCLUSIONS AS TO CHANGE IN CIVILIZATION

The fact of regularity in social change is the primary inference from our phenomena. The amplitude of the periodicities is of hardly less importance. Their very magnitude dwarfs the influence which any individual can possibly have exerted in an alteration of costume. Were each rhythm confined to a few years, it might be thought that a mind, a particular genius, was its motivating impulse; and the claim would certainly be asserted by those who like to see history as only a vast complex of biographies. But when a swing of fashion requires a century for its satisfaction, a minimum of at least several personalities is involved. No matter how isolating one's point of view, how resistant to a social or super-individual interpretation, how much inclined to explain the general from the particular and to derive the fashions of a world from the one focus of Paris, the fact remains that a succession of human beings have contributed successively to the same end. Once the existence of tendencies or forces transcending the limits of organically inherited personality is thus admitted, the entire field of the history of civilization becomes disputable ground for the two conflicting interpretations. If the major swing of skirt proportions during the nineteenth century is the product, wholly or partly, of super-individual causes, it becomes a valid speculation whether the smaller developments are not also due to similar mechanisms. The re-introduction of the train in 1863, the invention of the Grecian bend in 1872, may now be looked upon as the product of the dress styles that preceded them, or of other cultural factors affecting style, more justifiably than they can be attributed to the talent of a specially gifted mind and hand. The wedge has entered.

It is also evident how little even the intensest individual faculty can have added to the outcome of the greater revolutions, how little hastened their momentum. When a tide sets one way for fifty years, men float with it, or thread their course across it; those who breast the vast stream condemn themselves in advance to futility of accomplishment. A designer born with an inextinguishable talent for emphasizing what we may call the horizontal as opposed to the vertical lines of the figure, and maturing twenty-five years ago, might have possessed ten times the genius of a Poiret or Worth: he would yet have been compelled to curb it into the channels which they followed, or waste it on unworn and unregarded creations. What it is that causes fashions to drive so long and with ever increasing insistence toward the consummation of their ends, we do not know; but it is clear that the forces are social, and not the fortuitous appearance of personalities gifted with this taste or that faculty. Again the principle of civilizational determinism scores as against individualistic randomness.

It would be extravagant to infer that these conclusions deny the validity of superior minds, or even that they tend to minimize the differences between genius and mediocrity. There can be no questioning the universal experience that there are competent individuals and incompetent ones, and that the gulf between their extremes is vast. The existence of varying degrees of intellectual quality does not touch, one way or the other, the finding that there operate super-individual principles which determine the course of social events. The content of history as a sum and in its parts, so far as these have civilizational meaning, is the product of such principles. Whether individual X or individual Y is to have the larger share in bringing one particular product of his culture to fruition, depends on their respective native endowments, plus a greater or less modification by their educations, personal environments, and settings of circumstance. For the career of X, it is obviously of the greatest importance that his heredity and opportunities be more favorable than those of other individuals. On the contrary, given this advantage, it will very little affect his success in life whether his society be moving from polytheism to monotheism, from monarchy to democracy, or democracy to tyranny, from bronze to iron, from the wearing of wide skirts to narrow, or the reverse.

Conversely, so far as these social changes are concerned, it can well be argued on theoretical grounds that the greater or less innate capacity of this or that individual, or of any limited number of individuals, is of negligible consequence. That this factor is actually negligible from the aspect of civilization, the analysis of the data here presented goes to show. In short, monotheism arises, an iron technique is discovered, institutions change, or dresses become full at a given period and place—subsequent to other cultural events and as the result of them, in other words—because they must.

Historians may have been chary of asserting such a principle; but the greatest minds among them have time and again accepted it implicitly, though vaguely. This is as true of Thucydides as of Gibbon, and explains why Herodotus was as much interested in ethnology as in anecdotes, and Tacitus could place a *Germania* beside his *Annals*.

Among the commonalty of men, such a recognition has not obtained, and does not now hold. What above all they are interested in, is their own lives and fortunes, their own feelings and acts, their competitions with other individuals and personal relations to them. Therefore, when they listen to history, or tell it, they look for what history can reflect that is similar; and what it offers of psychology and morality in its biographies, or those of its parts which can be distorted into dramatic crises or romantic tales, they seize with avidity.

The satisfaction of these interests has its justifiable function; only it prevents instead of cultivating an understanding of the workings of civilization. The individualistic view of historical phenomena is in its nature subjective, and its treatment must always remain subjective. To find "law" in the infinite intricacy of millions, of inter-playing personalities is hopeless. We can not even begin to get the facts as they happened. A geologist could as usefully set himself the task of explaining the size and shape of each pebble in a gravel bed. We are but such stones. Being human, we cannot however divest ourselves of inquisitiveness about other human beings as human beings, nor of inquisitiveness into their morality and psychology and of the desire for an aesthetic representation of their actions. Only, the pursuit of such impulses does not lead to knowledge that is scientifically applicable; nor to a comprehension of what lies beyond ourselves as individuals; of that which touches and permeates our lives at all moments, which is the material on which our energies are released, which could not be if we did not exist, but which yet endures before and after, and grows and changes into forms that are not of our making but of its own definite unfolding. Our minds instinctively resist the first shock of the recognition of a thing so intimately woven into us and yet so far above and so utterly uncontrollable by our wills. We feel driven to deny its reality, to deny even the validity of dealing with it as an entity; just as men at large have long and bitterly resented admitting the existence of purely automatic forces and system in the realm that underlies and carries and makes possible the existence of our personalities: the realm of nature. The center of our interests must always be personal. Yet this pivoting has not prevented an increasing realization of objectivity; nor will it prevent the realization that objectivity is to be found on levels beyond us in both directions, instead of one only. The super-organic or superpsychic or super-individual that we call civilization appears to have an existence, an order, and a causality as objective and as determinable as those of the subpsychic or inorganic. At any rate, no insistence on the subjective aspects of personality can refute this objectivity, nor hinder its ultimate recognition; just as no advance in objective understanding has ever cramped the activity of personality.

NOTES

1. Mouth to toe, or to lowest point of skirt if the toe is covered.
2. The numbers are too small for satisfactory graphic plotting, but indicate that with a larger series of cases the lines for trained and trainless skirts would roughly parallel the combined line shown—one above and one below it. At least two times out of three, perhaps oftener, they would move in the same direction.

2

CUSTOMS AND BELIEFS:
Ceremonial

Alfred R. Radcliffe-Brown

We may now return to the question of the meaning of personal ornament in general. It is a commonplace of psychology that the development of the sense of self is closely connected with the perception of one's own body. It is also generally recognized that the development of the moral and social sentiments in man is dependent upon the development of self-consciousness, of the sense of self. These two important principles will help us to appreciate the hypothesis to which the discussion has now led, that in the Andamans the customary regulation of personal ornament is a means by which the society acts upon, modifies, and regulates the sense of self in the individual.

There are three methods of ornamenting the body in the Andamans, (1) by scarification, (2) by painting, and (3) by the putting on of ornaments.

The natives give two reasons for the custom of scarification, that it improves the personal appearance and that it makes the boy or girl grow up strong.

Both these mean that scarification gives or marks an added value. The explanation of the rite would therefore seem to be that it marks the passage from childhood to manhood and is a means by which the society bestows upon the individual that power, or social value, which is possessed by the adult but not by the child. The individual is made to feel that his value—his strength and the qualities of which he may be proud—is not his by nature but is received by him from the society to which he is admitted. The scars on his body are the visible marks of his admission. The

individual is proud or vain of the scars which are the mark of his manhood, and thus the society makes use of the very powerful sentiment of personal vanity to strengthen the social sentiments.

Turning now to the painting of the body, we have seen that the pattern of white clay serves to make both the painted individual and those who see him feel his social value, and we have seen that this interpretation explains the occasions on which such painting is used. To complete the argument it is necessary to consider the occasions on which the use of white clay is forbidden.

Those to whom this prohibition applies are (1) a youth or girl who is akaop, i.e., who is abstaining from certain foods during the initiation period, (2) a mourner, (3) a homicide during the period the isolation, and (4) a person who is ill. All these persons are excluded from full participation in the active social life, and therefore the social value of each of them is diminished. It would obviously be wrong for a person in such a condition to express by decorating himself a social value that he did not at the time possess … All ornament in some way marks the relation of the individual to the society and to that force or power in society to which he owes his well-being and happiness. When painting or ornament is used to give protection, it is, as we have seen, the protective power of the society itself that is appealed to, and what is expressed is the dependence of the individual on the society. When ornament or paint is used for display it is again the dependence on the society that is expressed, though in a different way and on occasions of a different kind. We have seen that scarification is also a means of marking the dependence of the individual on the society, and it is very important to note that the Andamanese sometimes explain it as due to the desire for display and sometimes to the need of protection (enabling the child to grow strong and so avoid the dangers of sickness), showing very clearly that there is some intimate connection between these two motives, or at any rate that one and the same method of ornamentation can satisfy both. There is one further example of red paint, which is combined with the pattern of white clay for purposes of display, and is also constantly used in many ways as affording protection.

We are thus brought to the final conclusion that the scarification and painting of the body and the wearing of most if not all the customary ornaments are rites which have the function of marking the fact that the individual is in a particular permanent or temporary relation to that power in the society and in all things that affect social life, the notion of which we have seen to underlie so much of the Andaman ceremonial.

… In the various methods of ornamenting the body the two chief motives that we have considered are so combined that they can hardly be estimated separately, and it is this mingling of motives that has led us to the final understanding of the meaning and social function of bodily ornament. Each of the different kinds of ornament serves to make manifest the existence of some special relation between the individual and the society, and therefore of some special relation between him and that system of powers on which the welfare of the society and of the individual depends. One of the most important aspects of the relation of the individual to the society is his dependence upon it for his safety and well-being and this is revealed in all painting and ornament worn for protection. But the society not only protects the individual from danger; it is the direct source of his well-being; and this makes itself felt in the customary regulation by which the use of the more important ornaments used for display is confined to occasions on which it is quite clear that his happiness is directly due to the society, such as a dance or feast. Thus the customs relating to the ornamentation of the body are of the kind that I have here called ceremonial. They are the means by which the society exercises on appropriate occasions some of the important social sentiments, thereby maintaining them at the necessary degree of energy required to maintain the social cohesion.

3

DRESS

Ruth Benedict

For the history of dress there are roughly four fields of study: prehuman behavior, archaeology, primitive peoples and modern civilized conditions.

The study of animal behavior emphasizes two facts regarding the origin of clothing. In the first place, human dress, in so far as it is for protection against the elements, has no continuity with any prehuman behavior. Animals in frigid climates grow warm coats, which are transmitted to their offspring by heredity. The opposite technique of invention and traditionally transmitted processes does not occur except in man. In the second place, observation of the higher apes has emphasized the prehuman roots of clothing as self-decoration. Köhler describes the naïve delight of chimpanzees in hanging objects about their bodies and trotting about to display them.

Archaeology reveals nothing about the history of dress until the upper palaeolithic era—which is far removed from earliest man. Clothing is necessarily of perishable materials, but even ornaments of animal teeth, ivory and shells begin to appear only in the Aurignacian period at the same level at which is found the characteristic palaeolithic development of mural drawing and engraving. From this period date also the characteristically distorted nude figurines of the female form, some of which are wearing bracelets although they are not represented with any other clothing. It is obvious, however, that the distortion of these female figurines is in the direction of fertility symbols, and their nudity furnishes no information as to women's daily wear in the Aurignacian period except that bracelets were worn at this period.

The reasons that have led man to clothe himself can therefore be studied chiefly from a comparison of the divergent behavior of now existing peoples. There is a strong association in western civilization between dress and the covering of the sex organs, but most of the literature concerning the origin of clothing has directed its array of facts to demolish the assumption of the primacy of this connection and to point out that dress did not have its origin in a specific instinct of modesty focused on the organs of reproduction.

It is obvious from any study of primitive clothing that this particular function of dress has very often been unknown in other cultures. The habit of complete nudity has a wide distribution in the tropical regions of South America, Melanesia, and Africa. In some cases both men and women are habitually naked, in others only the men, in still others only the women. Even outside of tropical regions habitual nudity is widespread, although a skin may be thrown over the shoulders for protection. Such regions are the Great Basin in North America, California, and Australia. Even in arctic regions, where well tailored clothing is universal, the conventions are often such that both men and women are habituated to indoor nudity like all people so habituated exhibit no shame in uncovering. Nansen describes the inter-crural cord of the east coast of Greenland, the sole covering of the natives when indoors, as being "so extremely small as to make it practically invisible to the stranger's inexperienced eye" (1890: 1:338–39, 2:277–78).

In more extreme instances that may be brought to bear against this theory of the origin of clothing in an

Ruth Benedict, "Dress," in *Encyclopedia of the Social Sciences*, Vol. 5 (New York: Macmillan, 1931), 235–37.

instinct of modesty the very nature of the coverings themselves is the point of the argument. The codpiece which was worn in Europe about 1450 and the custom of the men of certain Papuan tribes who squeeze their members into the opening of a gourd are indicative of the exhibitionist nature of certain forms of dress. Many observers in many parts of the world have commented on the fact that the most obvious function of the genital coverings was to attract attention rather than to divert it.

It is possible therefore to discard the notion that there is a human instinct of modesty that expresses itself in clothing. Modesty is a conditioned reflex and has its roots in the fashion of dress to which any group is accustomed. It is therefore to be expected that, given certain turns of fashion, other regions than the genital will be singled out and this emotion directed elsewhere—to the feet, as among Chinese women of past generations, or to the face, as with Mohammedan women. Native Brazilian women are extremely unwilling to remove their nose plugs and Alaskan women to remove their enormous labrets. Feelings of shame may also be associated with types of behavior not connected with clothing. Perfectly naked savages, for example, show acute feelings of shame at seeing anyone eat in public.

All the other theories of the origin of clothing contain varied amounts of truth. The advocates have erred only in too generalized a support of their particular positions. It is not necessary to deny any of them, once one has granted that human custom has no unique root but in different parts of the world has been the result of quite different circumstances and habits of mind variously interacting.

Thus Frazer and Karsten argue for the origin of clothing in ideas of magic, as, for example, the covering of the organs of reproduction in order to prevent the evil eye being cast upon them. Amulets hung about the neck or inserted in the lip or the nose are the full scope of clothing among some peoples, and in those and similar cases costume can be most pertinently studied in connection with local magical beliefs. In some regions these have had a profound influence upon the development of dress, but it is not necessary to generalize them as the origin of clothing.

The theory that clothing originated in protection against the rigors of climate is defended by Knight Dunlap. To doubt that weather has ever been a factor would be to cast a gratuitous slur on human intelligence and to ignore one of the great differentiations between human and animal behavior. If it were the primary factor, however, the primitive tribes living in the cold climates of the southern hemisphere would have provided for themselves as well as those living in similar climates of the northern hemisphere. But they have not done so. For the freezing weather to which they are seasonally exposed the Australians and the Fuegians do not make themselves clothing but barely protect their shoulders with a skin. Certainly many other motivations have been as potent in the history of clothing as protection against the weather.

Westermarck considers dress under the heading of "Primitive Means of Attraction." He believes that it is fundamentally rooted in the erotic impulses. Instances of this sort have been given above and he presents many others, both of habitual ornamentation of the pubic coverings and of ornamentation worn for particular occasions, such as dances, especially those of a licentious character. The history of clothing in our own civilization is ample evidence of the degree to which one sex dresses for the other, and certainly the often recurring differentiation of the dresses of the two sexes should be studied from this angle.

It does not seem necessary, however, to single out the one trait of display before the opposite sex when dress is so obviously and so often a self-display on all counts. Sex display in dress may hardly appear in a given area, but display of trophies or display of status may be fundamental. Thus on the plains of North America men's dress is a heraldic display of war counts, and on the northwest coast a man's hat will be built up in cumulative units to designate his rank. As an old explorer said of the Fuegians, "although they are content to be naked, they are very ambitious to be fine." This impulse toward decoration is the most constantly recurring motivation in the history of clothing and, as we saw above, the one which is found also among the higher apes.

Modern conditions have introduced only one important factor into human behavior in regard to clothing. In all that has been said above, modern dress like that of any other period is merely one of many possible varieties all illustrative of the general principles. But there is one fundamental difference. Whereas in simpler conditions, even in untouched rural districts of Europe today, dress is geographically differentiated, in modern civilization it is temporally differentiated. This rise of fashion in the field of dress had begun somewhat tentatively between the tenth and the fourteenth century, but it is with the Renaissance that its full and startling effect is first to be gauged. In rural districts dress remained and has remained to the present time a matter of local individuality perpetuated for centuries with great conservatism. The revolutionary rise of fashion had to do only with the urban population and even more specifically with the court. Its onset in the fifteenth century was marked by those peculiarities that have continued to characterize fashion in the modern world: first, the grotesque exaggeration of certain features, in this case notably the hennin (the fantastically elongated head dress that was held on by a chin band); and second, the personal arbitership of the great lady, which is said to have been already a well developed role of Isabelle of Bavaria, wife of Charles VI.

From this period fashion has been of unceasing importance in the field of dress. The latter part of the fifteenth century and the earlier part of the sixteenth show some of the most pleasing of all western European fashions, styles that are best known through the portraits of the Italian Renaissance. In the first half of the sixteenth century the woman's hoop skirt was elaborated, and this returned in extreme forms in the mid-eighteenth and mid-nineteenth centuries, in less extreme form in the mid-seventeenth. In the eighteenth century version in the reign of Louis XVI this was coupled with spectacular display of costly material in garments; clothes became a primary means for the ostentatious exhibition of wealth. The greatest excesses were cultivated in the matter of hairdressing; coiffures were a half yard high and prints show the hairdressers seated on ladders in order to reach the upper tiers of their creations. Nor was there any marked improvement during the nineteenth century. Probably the fashions of the period from 1830 to 1900—the desperately constricted waist, the bustle, and the heavy dragging skirt—were the ugliest and most unhealthful in the history of women's dress in western civilization.

The usual view of fashion is, first, that it is an affair of violent contrasts, each few years' swing of the pendulum reversing that of the preceding; and second, that it is essentially dictated by individual Parisian costumers. Kroeber, however, taking as a test case woman's full dress toilette from 1844 to 1919, has shown that, at least in the measurements he has considered, fashion's vagaries follow definite long time trends. This is clearest in the measurement of the width of the skirt, which for fifty years before 1919 had in spite of incidental variations become progressively more constricted. For almost as long a period previously it had in the same way grown progressively fuller, and its cycle therefore would be about one hundred years. The length of the skirt showed a similar trend. Its cycle for this period was about a third the duration of the width cycle, but even this is too long to be due to the influence of a single gifted designer. Kroeber does not claim universal validity for his examples but draws from them two conclusions: first, in a broader view styles not merely oscillate between two points but work themselves out in cycles of considerable length; second, these cycles are obviously longer than the reign of influence of any one designer and are therefore independent even of the most powerful costumer.

The study of fashion along with a variety of other cultural traits of modern civilization, such as mass production, can derive no assistance from the history of the world before comparatively modern times. Fashion is new in human history and its future course is not known. At present it marks, as Santayana says, that margin of irresponsible variation in manners and thoughts which among a people artificially civilized may so easily be larger than the solid core. It may well be that this swift succession of styles will maintain itself as a fixed characteristic of dress as a culture trait in our civilization.

4

FASHION

Edward Sapir

The fundamental drives leading to the creation and acceptance of fashion can be isolated. In the more sophisticated societies boredom, created by leisure and too highly specialized forms of activity, leads to restlessness and curiosity. This general desire to escape from the trammels of a too regularized existence is powerfully reinforced by a ceaseless desire to add to the attractiveness of the self and all other objects of love and friendship. It is precisely in functionally powerful societies that the individual's ego is constantly being convicted of helplessness. The individual tends to be unconsciously thrown back on himself and demands more and more novel affirmations of his effective reality. The endless rediscovery of the self in a series of petty truancies from the official socialized self becomes a mild obsession of the normal individual in any society in which the individual has ceased to be a measure of the society itself. There is, however, always the danger of too great a departure from the recognized symbols of the individual, because his identity is likely to be destroyed. That is why insensitive people, anxious to be literally in the fashion, so often overreach themselves and nullify the very purpose of fashion. Good hearted women of middle age generally fail in the art of being ravishing nymphs.

Somewhat different from the affirmation of the libidinal self is the more vulgar desire for prestige or notoriety, satisfied by changes in fashion. In this category belongs fashion as an outward emblem of personal distinction or of membership in some group to which distinction is ascribed. The imitation of fashion by people who belong to circles removed from those which set the fashion has the function of bridging the gap between a social class and the class next above it. The logical result of the acceptance of a fashion by all members of society is the disappearance of the kinds of satisfaction responsible for the change of fashion in the first place. A new fashion becomes psychologically necessary, and thus the cycle of fashion is endlessly repeated.

Fashion is emphatically a historical concept. A specific fashion is utterly unintelligible if lifted out of its place in a sequence of forms. It is exceedingly dangerous to rationalize or in any other way psychologize a particular fashion on the basis of general principles which might be considered applicable to the class of forms of which it seems to be an example. It is utterly vain, for instance, to explain particular forms of dress or types of cosmetics or methods of wearing the hair without a preliminary historical critique. Bare legs among modern women in summer do not psychologically or historically create at all the same fashion as bare legs and bare feet among primitives living in the tropics. The importance of understanding fashion historically should be obvious enough when it is recognized that the very essence of fashion is that it be valued as a variation in an understood sequence, as a departure from the immediately preceding mode.

Changes in fashion depend on the prevailing culture and on the social ideals which inform it. Under the apparently placid surface of culture there are always powerful psychological drifts of which fashion is quick to catch the direction. In a democratic society, for instance, if there is an unacknowledged

Adapted from Edward Sapir, "Fashion," in *Encyclopedia of the Social Sciences, vol 6.* (New York: Macmillan, 1931).

drift toward class distinctions fashion will discover endless ways of giving it visible form. Criticism can always be met by the insincere defense that fashion is merely fashion and need not be taken seriously. If in a puritanic society there is a growing impatience with the outward forms of modesty, fashion finds it easy to minister to the demands of sex curiosity, while the old mores can be trusted to defend fashion with an affectation of unawareness of what fashion is driving at. A complete study of the history of fashion would undoubtedly throw much light on the ups and downs of sentiment and attitude at various periods of civilization. However, fashion never permanently outruns discretion and only those who are taken in by the superficial rationalizations of fashion are surprised by the frequent changes of face in its history. That there was destined to be a lengthening of women's skirts after they had become short enough was obvious from the outset to all except those who do not believe that sex symbolism is a real factor in human behavior.

The chief difficulty of understanding fashion in its apparent vagaries is the lack of exact knowledge of the unconscious symbolisms attaching to forms, colors, textures, postures and other expressive elements in a given culture. The difficulty is appreciably increased by the fact that the same expressive elements tend to have quite different symbolic references in different areas.

5

DRESS:
Its origins, forms, and psychology, with special emphasis on the sexual psychology

Ernest Crawley

An analysis of the relations of man's clothing with his development in social evolution will naturally be chiefly concerned with psychological categories. When once instituted, for whatever reasons or by whatever process, dress became a source of psychical reactions, often complex, to a greater extent (owing to its more intimate connexion with personality) than any other material product of intelligence. Some outline of the historical development of dress will be suggested, rather than drawn, as a guide to the main inquiry. For formal, chronological, or regional histories of dress, the reader must look elsewhere.

The practical, or, if one may use the term, the biological uses and meaning of dress, are simple enough and agreed upon. These form the first state of the material to be employed by the social consciousness. Its secondary states are a subject in themselves.

ORIGINS

The primary significance of dress becomes a difficult question as soon as we pass from the institution in being to its earliest stages and origin. For speculation alone is possible when dealing with the genesis of dress. Its conclusions will be probable in proportion as they satisfactorily bridge the gulf between the natural and the artificial stages of human evolution. The information supplied by those of the latter that are presumably nearest to the natural state, to *Protanthropus*, is not in itself a key to the origin of clothing, but, on the other hand, the

mere analogy of animal-life is still less helpful. An animal has a natural covering more efficient for the two uses of protection against the environment and of ornamentation as a sexual stimulus. An animal may become adapted to a change, for instance to an Arctic climate, by growing a thick fur which is white. It may be supposed that, to meet a similar change, man invents the use of artificial coverings. But this old argument is contradicted by all the facts.

It may serve, however, to point by contrast the actual continuity of the natural and the artificial stages, the physical and the psychical stages, of our evolution. If we say that man is the only animal that uses an artificial covering for the body, we are apt to forget that even when clothed he is subject to the same environmental influences as in the ages before dress. Again, there is no hint that the approach of a glacial epoch inaugurated the invention of dress. But it is an established fact that the survivors of immigrants to changed conditions of climate and geological environment become physically adapted by some means of interaction, and in certain directions of structure, which are just coming to be recognized. The British settlers in North America have assumed the aboriginal type of the Indian face and head; migrants from lowlands to uplands develop round-headedness; from the temperate zone to the tropics man develops frizzly hair, and so on. The most obvious of these natural adaptations, physiologically produced, to the environment, is pigmentation. The skin of man is graded in colour from the Equator to the Pole. The deeper pigmentation of the tropical skin

---

Adapted from Ernest Crawley, *Dress, Drinks, and Drums: Further Studies of Savages and Sex* (London: Methuen & Co., Ltd., 1931).

is a protection against the actinic rays of the sun; the blondness of northern races, like the white colour of Arctic animals, retains the heat of the body.

If we followed the analogy of the animal, we should have to take into account the fact that a mechanical intelligence enables it to obviate certain disadvantages of its natural covering. The animal never exposes itself unnecessarily; its work, in the case of the larger animals, is done at night, not in the glare of the sun. Automatically it acquires an artificial covering in the form of shelter. If man in a natural state followed a similar principle, he would be at no more disadvantage than is the animal. A similar argument applies to the other use mentioned above, namely, sexual decoration. What these considerations suggest is that man was not forced by necessity to invent. The reason is at once deeper and simpler. Again, we get the conclusion that one primary use and meaning of dress is not so much to provide an adaptation to a climate as to enable man to be superior to weather; in other words, to enable him to move and be active in circumstances where animals seek shelter. The principle is implicit in the frequent proverbial comparison of clothing to a house.

Dress, in fact, as a secondary human character, must be treated, as regards its origins, in the same way as human weapons, tools, and machines. Dress increases the static resisting power of the surface of the body, just as tools increase the dynamic capacity of the limbs. It is an extension (and thereby an intension) of the passive area of the person, just as a tool is of the active mechanism of the arm. It is a second skin, as the other is a second hand.

Further, if we take an inclusive view of evolution, admitting no break between the natural and the artificial, but regarding the latter as a sequence to the former, we shall be in a position to accept indications that both stages, and not the former only, are subject to the operation of the same mechanical laws, and show (with the necessary limitations) similar results. These laws belong to the interaction of the organism and the environment, and the results are found in what is called adaptation, an optimum of equilibrium, a balanced interaction, between the two. In this connexion we may take examples from two well-marked stages in the evolution of our subject, the one showing a deficiency, the other a sufficiency, of the artificial covering of the body. A good observer remarks of the Indians of Guiana, not as a result of habituation, but as a first impression of their naked forms, that "it is a most curious but certain fact that these people, even as they wander in the streets of Georgetown, do not appear naked."[1] The other case is that of the Chaco Indians: "The Indian is perfectly suited to his environment; even his picturesque costume and the ornamental painting with which he adorns his body is in perfect harmony with his surroundings. The colours blend so beautifully that there is no doubt whatever that the Indian has, in a very great degree, the idea of fitness and harmony."[2]

If we qualify in the last sentence the word "idea" by the adjective "unconscious," we shall have a sound explanation of a very remarkable phenomenon. The point of the phenomenon is that the evolution of man's artificial covering maintains a balance or harmony with the environment, particularly in respect to light, just as was the case with the naked Indian skins, arrived at just as mechanically, but through the unconscious reaction of the retina. Thus there is a real continuity between the adaptive colour of the chameleon, and similar cases of so-called protective coloration (which is primarily merely a mechanical attuning to the environment), and the harmony which human dress may show with its surroundings. The selective process has not been conscious, but neither has it been accidental. It is the result of law. Equally unconscious in its first stages was the adaptation of dress to temperature.

This brings us no nearer to the origins of dress, though it clears the ground. Still further to simplify speculation, we may notice some prevalent hypotheses on the subject. Dress being a covering, it assumes, when instituted, all the applicable meanings which the idea of covering involves. But it by no means follows that all of these, or even any, were responsible for its original institution.

There is, first, the hypothesis that clothing originated in *the decorative impulse*. This has the merit of providing a cause which could operate through unconscious intelligence, automatic feeling. Stanley Hall found that of the three functions of clothing whose realization and expression he investigated in a *questionnaire*— protection, ornament, and Lotzean self-feeling—the second is by far the most conspicuous in childhood. The child is not consciously aware of sex, otherwise this statistical result might be brought into line with the sexual ornamentation of animals. And though it is not always safe to press any analogy between the civilized child and the savage, the savages known to science are, as a rule, very fond of finery, absolutely, and not always in relation to the other sex. The natural man will undergo any trouble, any discomfort, in order to beautify himself to the best of his power. Dandies, Im Thurn remarks, are about as frequent among the Indians as in civilized communities.[3] At Port Moresby, in New Guinea, young men actually practise tight-lacing, to be smart and fashionable.[4] In these spheres, indeed, it is chiefly the young, if not mere children, who express the impulse to decoration. Of the Dayaks of Borneo a good observer has remarked that a "love of finery is inherent in the young of both sexes; the elderly are less fond of it and often dress very shabbily, and save up their good clothes for their offspring."[5]

It is in accordance with the rule among animals that among primitive peoples the male sex chiefly assumes decoration. Ornaments among the Indians of Guiana are more worn by men than by women. The stock ornamentation is paint; scented oils are used as vehicles.

> A man, when he wants to dress well, perhaps entirely coats both his feet up to the ankles with a crust of red; his whole trunk he sometimes stains uniformly with blue-black, more rarely with red, or he covers it with an intricate pattern of lines of either colour; he puts a streak of red along the bridge of his nose; where his eyebrows were till he pulled them out he puts two red lines; at the top of the arch of his forehead he puts a big lump of red paint, and probably he scatters other spots and lines somewhere on his face.

Down is often used with red paint.[6]

But this analogy is not to be pressed, though it is sound as far as it goes. It applies, that is, up to a certain point in social evolution. Beyond that point the balance inclines the other way, and for the last five hundred years of European civilization decorative dress has been largely confined to women. During a previous period of some centuries—to be regarded as one of unstable equilibrium—not only did the curve of luxury in dress reach its highest point, but there were attempts—spasmodic, it is true—to put down any tendency towards such luxury on the part of women, prostitutes being excepted. The previous stage—one of very considerable length—is still that of Islām; its significance and origin will concern us later. Its chief feature was the principle that female dress should be not ornamental, but protective—of the rights of the husband. Thus we may infer that, in the latest stage, woman as a sex has not only gained freedom, and the right to fascinate, previously possessed by the courtesan alone, but has also shifted the equilibrium of sex to a more permanent and efficient position. The story of woman's unconscious struggle for a monopoly of beauty in dress thus illustrates an important social movement.

In practical investigation it is difficult to say where clothing ends and ornament begins, or, on the previous hypothesis, where clothing springs out of ornament. Since either may obviously develop into the other when both are instituted, it is idle to examine such cases. Cases where one or the other is absolutely unknown might serve, but there are no examples of this. If an instance, moreover, of the presence of clothing and entire absence of ornament were observed, it would be impossible to argue that clothing cannot be subject to the decorative impulse. In any case, there is the self-feeling, satisfaction in individuality, to be reckoned with, for the impulse to finery is only one phase of it.

The supporters of the ornamentation hypothesis of the origin of dress have an apparently strong argument in the Brazilians and the Central Australians. These peoples possess no clothing in the ordinary sense of the term. But they wear ornament, and on special occasions a great deal of it. Brazilian men wear a string round the lower abdomen, the women a strip of bark-cloth along the perineum, tied to a similar abdominal thread. This is sometimes varied by a small decorative enlargement. The Central Australian man wears a waist-string, to which is tied a pubic tassel. Corresponding to the last in the case of the women is a very small apron. Leaving the waist-string out of account, we have remaining the question of the erogenous centre. In both the decoration hypothesis and the concealment hypothesis this centre is the focus of speculation. If the Australian tassel of the male sex and the leaf-like enlargement of the Brazilian woman's perineal thread are considered superficially, they may appear to be, if not ornaments, at least attractions. But if this be granted, it does not follow that we have here the first application of the idea of dress.

It would be impossible to make out a case to prove that these appurtenances can ever have satisfied the idea of *concealment*, as on the next hypothesis is assumed. This hypothesis is to the effect that male jealousy instituted clothing for married women. Ratzel observes that if clothing was originally instituted for purposes of protection only, the feet and ankles would have been protected first. Clothing, he holds, stands in unmistakable relation to the sexual life. "The first to wear complete clothes is not the man, who has to dash through the forest, but the married woman." The primary function of her dress is to render her unattractive to others, to conceal her body from other men's eyes. In the lower strata of human evolution he considers that dress as a protection from rain and cold is far less common.[7]

But if we may argue from the practice of existing savages, this hypothesis cannot hold even of the origin of female clothing. Only by straining can it be applied to that of men. It is certainly a *vera causa*, at a certain stage in barbarism (the stage when wives became "property"), of the customs of shrouding and veiling woman, and of confiscating all a maiden's ornaments and finery when she became a wife. But it does not explain the origin of the small apron worn in very early stages, or of the mere thread in the earliest, and we cannot deny these articles a place in the category of dress.

A frequent corollary of such views is that modesty is a result, not a cause, of clothing (so Sergi). But, as Havelock Ellis observes, "many races which go absolutely naked possess a highly developed sense of modesty."[8] Andamanese women

> are so modest that they will not renew their leaf aprons in the presence of one another, but retire to a secluded spot for this purpose; even when parting with one of their *bōd*-appendages [tails of leaves suspended from the back of the girdle] to a female friend the delicacy they manifest for the feelings of

the bystanders in their mode of removing it almost amounts to prudishness.[9]

Yet they wear no clothing in the ordinary sense. The Guiana Indians, when they want to change their single garment, either retire from sight or put the new over the old, and then withdraw the latter.[10] Modesty is "in its origins independent of clothing; … physiological modesty takes precedence of anatomical modesty; and the primary factors of modesty were probably developed long before the discovery of either ornaments or garments. The rise of clothing probably had its first psychic basis on an emotion of modesty already compositely formed of" these elements.[11]

This last statement, of course, cannot hold of the ultimate genesis of clothing. But, once instituted, it was sure to coincide with emotions of modesty. The general connexion between modesty and dress is a subject of little importance, except in so far as it has involved the creation of false modesty, both individually and socially. Modesty, where there is dress, tends to be concentrated upon it mechanically. When clothing is once established, the growth of the conception of women as property emphasizes its importance, and increases the anatomical modesty of women. Waitz held that male jealousy is the primary origin of clothing, and therefore of modesty. Diderot had held this view. Often married women alone are clothed. It is as if before marriage a woman was free and naked; after marriage, clothed and a slave. "The garment appears—illogically, though naturally—a moral and physical protection against any attack on his [the husband's] property."[12]

But the fact of dress serving as concealment involved the possibility of *attraction by mystery*. Even when other emotions than modesty, emphasized by male jealousy, intervene, they may work together for sexual attraction.

> The social fear of arousing disgust combines easily and perfectly with any new development in the invention of ornament or clothing as sexual lures. Even among the most civilized races it has often been noted that the fashion of feminine garments (as also sometimes the use of scents) has the double object of

concealing and attracting. It is so with the little apron of the young savage belle. The heightening of the attraction is indeed a logical outcome of the fear of evoking disgust.[13]

Similarly we find in the most primitive clothing a curious interchange of concealment, protection, decoration, and advertisement. As has been hinted, when an appurtenance has come to be attached to the sexual area, the resulting psychical reactions are significant. In the previous natural stage there is no artificial stimulus; now there is such an addition to the natural stimulus, first by mere attraction or signification, and later by decoration or veiling. In the mind of the subject also there comes, first, the consciousness of sex, and later the enhancing of self-feeling, which in the case of dress generally, and not merely sexual, is distributed throughout the personality. The subject's material personality is increased by clothing, and his psychical reaction is proportional to this. The result is a rich complex of self-consciousness, modesty, and self-feeling generally, the balance between them varying according to circumstances. But it is highly improbable that such impulses could have led to the invention of dress, much less of mere attachments and appurtenances. Their only means of expression would have been ornament.

Finally, there is the *protection-hypothesis*. Sudden falls in the temperature, rains and winds and burning sunshine, the danger of injuring the feet and the skin of the body generally when in the forest, and the need of body-armour against the attack of insects and of dangerous animals, seem obvious reasons for the invention of dress. But they do not explain the process of invention, which is the main problem. The cloak, the skirt, the apron, cannot have been invented in answer to a need, directly, without any stages. The invention of cloth was first necessary, and this was suggested by some natural covering. The only line of development which seems possible is from protective ligatures. There are numerous facts which apparently point to such an origin of clothing. One of the most characteristic ornaments of savages all over the world is the armlet. It is quite probable that this has an independent origin in the decorative impulse, like the necklace. But here and there we find bands worn round the ankles, knees,

wrists, and elbows, the object of which is clearly to protect the sinews and muscles from strains. The pain of a strained muscle being eased by the grip of the hand, the suggestion of an artificial grip might naturally follow, and system of ligatures would be the result. The Nāgas wear black rings of cane round the knee—as some say, to give strength for climbing.[14] The Malays wear bands and ligatures to protect the muscles and prevent strains, as for instance, round the wrists and below the knee.[15] Ratzel observes that arm-rings may be useful in striking and warding off blows. But the idea of a cestus is unlikely to be the primary motive for ligatures.[16] The Chacos wear anklets of feathers, chiefly to protect their feet against snake-bites.[17]

Wild peoples, in fact, understand quite well the limitations and the capacity of the human organism in respect to the environment. We may credit them with an adequate system of supplying natural deficiencies, and of assisting natural advantages also. For instance, the Malays explain the object of the papoose for infants as being to prevent the child from starting and so straining itself.[18] And it seems probable that there is a connexion between the earlier use of the ligature and the prevalent custom of wearing metal rings or wire as a decoration. Men and women of the Watusi wear round the ankles innumerable coils of iron wire, representing a weight of many pounds. The women wear heavy bracelets of brass.[19] It is possible, also, that in certain cases dress itself might have been developed from the same source. Thus, when we compare the following type of body-dress with the frequent use, in earlier stages, of a pliant bough or cane as a girdle, we can imagine the possibility that the invention of the sheet form of covering might have been delayed by the extension of the bandage form. The garment, termed *lumiet*, of the Sakarang women is a series of cane hoops covered with innumerable small brass links. The series encasing the waist fits close. It sometimes extends right up to the breasts. The Ulu Ai and Ngkari women wear eight to ten parallel rows of large brass rings round the waist. They are strung on rattans, and fixed to a cane network inside them. Dense coils of thick brass wire are also worn on the legs.[20]

But the ligature as a primary stage of sheet-clothing might have developed merely by adding to its breadth.

Given a girdle, we might suppose a natural enlargement of its depth. And among the various bands used by the lowest peoples there is a gradation of the kind. The armlets of the Indians of Guiana are broad cotton bands or string.[21] Yet there is no evidence to show that such a development, from the belt to the kilt, has been the main origin of the skirt form of dress. A skirt supplying its own belt is generally a late modification.

Examination of the earliest peoples inevitably leads to a rejection of the ligature-hypothesis. Every consideration goes to show that the earliest ligature was not intended to support the muscles. It is inconceivable that the use of string in the Guiana example can be intended for such a purpose. In the next place, it must be borne in mind that the chief area of the organism with which dress proper is concerned is the central part of the body, the trunk. Now, the great majority of the lowest peoples known wear no clothes. Shelter is used instead. But there is very commonly a waist-string, and it is more used by men than by women. We assume that the girdle is the point of departure for the evolution of dress, and the mechanism of that departure will be presently discussed. But for the origin of body-clothing it is necessary to find the origin of the girdle. The civilized idea of a girdle is to bind up a skirt or trousers. This is certainly not its object among the earliest peoples, who have nothing to tie up. It might be supposed that the original purpose of the girdle was that of the abdominal belt, useful both as a muscle-ligature and to alleviate the pangs of hunger. But the earliest girdles are merely strings, and string is useless for such purposes. String, moreover, made of grass or vegetable fibre, or animal sinew or human hair, is an earlier invention than the bandage. Its first form was actually natural, the pliant bough or stem.

It is significant that this waist-string is chiefly a male appendage, and that it is worn neither tight nor very loose. Both facts are explained by the purpose for which the string is worn. It is neither a bandage nor a suspender, but a continuous pocket. The savage finds it indispensable for carrying articles which he constantly needs, and which otherwise would encumber his hands. Once fitted with a waist-string, the body, as a machine, is enormously improved, being able to carry the artificial aids of manual operations ready for use as occasion requires, without hampering the work of that universal lever, the band.

We can only speculate vaguely as to the series of "accidents" which led to the idea of the waist-string. It was, no doubt, analogous to the series which ended in the invention of artificial hands in the shape of weapons and tools, but it was certainly much later in time. The varied unconscious ideas of holding, gripping, and encircling, which the muscular experience of the hand imprinted on the brain, might have evolved the principle and practice of a hold-all round the trunk, without the occurrence of any fortunate accidents whatever. The natural position of the hands when at rest would be rejected by unconscious reasoning in favour of a more convenient spot, slightly higher, which would not interfere with the movements of the legs. The downward tapering of the thigh, moreover, renders it impossible to keep a string in position. In this connexion it is worth noting that knee- and ankle-bands are commonly used in various stages of culture for the purpose of holding implements.

The waist-string, therefore, being earlier than clothing proper, and being, as we have suggested, the point of departure for the wearing of coverings, we have next to examine the mechanism of the connexion between them. The use of the string as a holder being given, it would serve not only as a pocket, but as a suspender for leaves or bunches of grass, if for any reason these were required. The point to be emphasized here is that the presence of a suspender would suggest the suspension and therefore the regular use of articles for which there had been no original demand. If, for occasional purposes, a decoration or covering was desired, there was the waist-string ready for use. Central as it was, the decoration or covering would fall below it and be thus applied automatically to the perineal region. Similarly, the hair of the head is a natural holder, though much less efficient, and it is used to support leaf-coverings or flower-decorations.

It is unnecessary to enter upon a description of the various zones of the body which require protection, such as the spine at the neck and in the small of the back, against sun and cold, or the mucous membranes of the perineal region, against insects. The use of clothing of certain textures and colours to maintain a layer of air about the skin at a temperature adapted to that of the body, and to neutralize those rays of light which are deleterious to the nervous system and destructive of protoplasm, is also out of place here. We may note, however, that by unconscious selection the evolution of dress has probably followed a thoroughly hygienic course. But no principles of such hygiene, except the very simplest, can have occurred to primitive man. One of the simplest, however, we may admit for tropical races—the use of a protection against insects. The perineal region is most subject to their attacks when man is naked, owing to the sebaceous character of the surface and its relatively higher temperature. These facts, no doubt, more than anything else, are the explanation of primitive habits of depilation. But depilation is not a complete protection. Something positive is required. The use of bunches of grass or leaves is natural and inevitable, as soon as there is something to hold them, namely, the waist-string. A parallel method is the use of a second string depending from the waist-string in front and behind, and passing between the legs. The Brazilian strip of bast used by women, and the red thread which takes its place in the Trumai tribe, though they attract attention like ornaments instead of drawing attention away, yet, as Von den Steinen also satisfied himself, provide a protection against insects, a serious pest in the forests of Brazil.[22] These inter-crural strings protect the mucous membranes, without, however, concealing the parts, as do leaves and grass. In the present connexion their chief interest is the use made of the waist-string. When cloth was invented the first form of the loin-cloth was an extension of the inter-crural thread. It may be illustrated from the Indians of British Guiana, though it is practically universal, significantly enough, among tropical and sub-tropical peoples. The Guiana man wears a narrow strip, called *lap*; it is passed between the legs, and the ends are brought up at back and front and suspended on a ropelike belt. The women wear an apron, called *queyu*, hung from a string round the waist. Very young children, before wearing a cloth, have a string round the waist. The *lap* is often made of bark, beaten till soft.[23] The *lap* method is employed by the Veddas of Ceylon,[24] and by numerous early races throughout the world.

As the various methods of draping and tying developed with man's familiarity with sheet-dress, the later form of loin-cloth naturally superseded the earlier. A length of cloth passed round the waist and between the legs, the ends depending, was both more convenient and more comfortable. In the first place, it supplied a broader bandage, and being two articles in one, was more easily kept in position. This is the familiar and widely prevalent "loin-cloth." Secondly, it supplied a more efficient method of binding the male organs. There is no doubt that the naked male often finds it desirable, for obvious anatomical reasons which do not trouble the animal (whose organs are practically withdrawn into the perineal surface), to confine these parts. Hence, it may be conjectured, the use of a perineal cloth for men and of a mere apron or skirt for women—a distinction of the earliest date and generally maintained. As showing the practice of such confinement, it is enough to point to a common use of the earlier waist-string. The end of the organ is placed under the string, made tight enough to hold it flat against the abdomen.[25]

The development of the apron and skirt is a simple extension (given the suspensory string and the invention of cloth) of the use of leaves hung from the waist. The frequent use of a rear apron as a sitting mat is a later detail, having no influence upon the skirt, which developed independently. A frequent variation is the fringe. A combination of front and rear aprons no doubt preceded the complete skirt. When the latter was developed, new methods of suspension were adopted, among them being one similar to that of the loin-cloth, the upper edge serving as a bandage. The use of the waist-string by women, for keeping an inter-crural cloth or tampon in place during the periods, may be referred to; but it did not lead to the development of any article of attire. One example of its use, however, is instructive, as showing how a temporary protection may pass into a regular appendage. Among the majority of the Nyasa tribes a woman during her periods wears a small piece of calico corresponding to a diaper. The same is worn after childbirth. This is the case generally in Nyasa-land. But Angoni women "always wear them."[26]

The protection-hypothesis of the origin of dress may thus be adopted, if we qualify it by a scheme of development as suggested above. When once instituted as a custom, the wearing of leaves or bark-cloth upon the abdominal region served to focus various psychical reactions. One of the earliest of these was the impulse to emphasize the primary sexual characters. It is an impulse shown among the great majority of early races in their observances at the attainment of puberty, and it is, as a rule, at that period that sexual dress or ornament is assumed. Among civilized peoples, in the Middle Ages and in modern times, the impulse is well marked by various fashions—the phallocrypt and the tail of the savage having their European analogues. A less direct but even more constant instance of the same recognition is the assigning of the skirt to women as the more sedentary, and trousers to men as the more active sex. The suggestion sometimes met with, that the skirt is an adaptation for sexual protection, need only be mentioned to be dismissed. The central Australian public tassel and similar appendages will here find significance, but it is improbable that such accentuation was their original purpose. Once instituted for protection, the other ideas followed. Another of these, which at once received an artificial focus, was the emotion of modesty. It has been observed among the higher animals that the female, by various postures, guards the sexual centres from the undesired advances of the male. The assumption of a waist-cloth does not actually serve the same purpose, but it constitutes a permanent psychical suggestion of inviolability. Similarly, the use of any appendage or covering involves the possibility of attraction, either by mere notification, by the addition of decoration, or, later, by the suggestion of mystery.

Further than this speculation as to origins need not be carried. The various forms and fashions of dress, and the customs connected with it, will supply examples of the material as well as of the psychological evolution of the subject.

NOTES

1. Sir E. F. Im Thurn, *Among the Indians of Guiana* (1883), 194.
2. W. B. Grubb, *An Unknown People in an Unknown Land: The Indians of the Paraguayan Chaco* ([London: Seeley,] 1911), 55.
3. Im Thurn, [*Among the Indians of Guiana*], 199.
4. A. C. Haddon, *Head-Hunters, Black, White, and Brown* ([London: Methuen,] 1901), 256.
5. [B.] Low [and H. Ling] Roth, "The Natives of Borneo[. Part II]," *Journal of the Anthropological Institute* [*of Great Britain and Ireland*] 22 (1893): 41.
6. Im Thurn, [*Among the Indians of Guiana*], 195 ff.
7. F. Ratzel, *History of Mankind* ([London: Macmillan and Co., Ltd.,]1896–98), 1:93–94.
8. H. H. Ellis, *Studies in the Psychology of Sex* ([London: University Press,] 1897), i. 5.
9. E. H. Man, "The Aboriginal Inhabitants of the Andaman Islands[. (Part II.)]," *Journal of the Anthropological Institute* [*of Great Britain and Ireland*] 12 (1883): xii. 94, 331.
10. Im Thurn, [*Among the Indians of Guiana*], 194.
11. Ellis, [*Studies in the Psychology of Sex*], 1:37.
12. Ibid., 1:41.
13. Ibid., 1:39.
14. T. C. Hodson, *The Nāga Tribes of Manipur* ([London: Macmillan and Co., Ltd.,] 1911), 23.
15. [W. W.] Skeat [and C. O.] Blagden, *Pagan Races of the Malay Peninsula* ([London: Macmillan and Co., Ltd.,] 1906), 1:140.
16. F. Ratzel, [*History of Mankind*], 1:99.
17. W. B. Grubb, [*An Unknown People*], p. 262.
18. W. W. Skeat, *Malay Magic* ([London: Macmillan and Co., Ltd.,] 1900), 335.
19. L. Decle, "The Watusi," *Journal of the Anthropological Institute* [*of Great Britain and Ireland*] 23 (1894): 425.
20. Low [and Ling] Roth, ["The Natives of Borneo,"] 40–41.
21. Im Thurn, [*Among the Indians of Guiana*,] 197.
22. K. Von Den Steinen, *Unter den Naturvölkern Zentral-Brasiliens* (Berlin[: D. Reimer,] 1894), 190 f. For other protective coverings for the organs against insects, see [G. A.] Wilken [and C. M.] Pletye, *Handleiding voor de vergelijkende Volkenkunde van Nederlandsch-Indië* (Leyden[: Brill], 1893), 37–38.
23. Im Thurn, [*Among the Indians of Guiana*,] 194.
24. C. G. Seligmann and B. Z. Seligmann, *The Veddas* ([Cambridge: Cambridge University Press,] 1911), 93.
25. See Wilken [and] Pleyte, [*Handleiding voor de vergelijkende Volkenkunde van Nederlandsch-Indië*,] 38.
26. H. S. Stannus, "Notes on some Tribes of British Central Africa," *Journal of the Royal Anthropological Institute* [*of Great Britain and Ireland*] 40 (1910): 321.

PART 2

THEORIZING DRESS AND FASHION

PART INTRODUCTION

This part of the reader includes significant theoretical work in the anthropology of dress and fashion. The chapters and articles included here continue to be cited in anthropological work written today and have helped shape scholarship in the anthropology of dress and fashion as it is currently understood and practiced. We do not, however, claim that this work is "foundational" to the anthropology of dress and fashion. There is no canon, formal or otherwise, that all anthropologists of dress and fashion read or cite. We believe that is a good thing.

Ted Polhemus is an independent anthropologist, writer, marketing consultant, and photographer, who has been chronicling the stylistic changes in urban youth subcultures since the mid-1970s. His curated exhibition and corresponding book *Streetstyle: From Sidewalk to Catwalk* (1994) were highly influential in shaping the way cultural theorists talked about youth subcultures in the mid-1990s, and his follow-up book *Style Surfing: What to Wear in the Third Millennium* was a key text in the retheorizing of youth subcultures that took place in the United States and the United Kingdom in the late 1990s. Unlike earlier anthropologists featured in this reader, Polhemus would have no qualms about labeling himself as a fashion scholar and seems to take a kind of impish delight in thwarting the conventions and expectations of academic anthropology, an affordance, perhaps, of his outsider status. The Polhemus text included here was taken from his 1978 book *Fashion and Anti-Fashion: An Anthropology of Clothing and Adornment*, originally coauthored with photographer Lynn Proctor then republished (with her permission) as a single-authored publication in 2011. Polhemus, in this book, puts forward a useful distinction between forms of dress (fashion) subject to a continually changing marketplace and forms of dress (anti-fashion), which resist changes in the marketplace for reasons of tradition, religious practice, or countercultural politics.

Terence Turner's "The Social Skin" is one of the most commonly cited articles by anthropologists working in dress and fashion. Written by a scholar well known for his activism and human rights work and focused on the dress practices of Kayapo Indians living in the Amazonian rainforests of Brazil, it is perhaps an unlikely contender for most influential theoretical work in the anthropology of dress and fashion. Nonetheless, the richness of his observations and the profundity of his conclusions, both inspired, in part by the insights of Marcel Mauss's classic essay "Techniques of the Body" (1973) have made a better case for the importance of studying dress than perhaps any other anthropological work. "The surface of the body," wrote Turner, "seems everywhere to be treated, not only as the boundary of the individual as a biological and psychological entity but as the frontier of the social self as well" ([p. 43]). People all over the world, he observed, decorate and manipulate their bodies, and in doing so, they shape themselves as members of society. Dress is not only universal, but crucial to defining a human as a cultural being, establishing one's place in the world and one's orientation to it. No matter how naked a native may appear to an outside observer, she remains garbed in meaning.

Grant McCracken's "Clothing as Language" takes this assumption as its starting point. For him, like Turner, dress matters and holds meaning. And yet, he argues, it is crucial not to confuse the way human beings construct meaning through clothing with the way we construct meaning through language. In this article, the independent anthropologist, who is better known perhaps in the world of marketing than in academia, takes issue with the reduction of clothing to the linguistic metaphor. "Clothing," he claims, "is a very different system of communication, the cultural significance of which cannot be fully assessed until the 'language' metaphor is abandoned or revised" ([p. 52]). Clothing has no syntax, no grammar, no "combinatorial freedom" or "generative potential" ([p. 52]). It is doomed to be perpetually vague in the signals it sends. And yet perhaps, McCracken suggests, it is its very vagueness that makes clothing such a potent communicational medium. He is not altogether clear in what he means by this, but it is easy to imagine. Clothing's open-ended semiotics allows it to spread easily between groups. Styles can mean one thing to one person and another to someone else.

Joanne Eicher and Mary Ellen Roach-Higgins's contribution to this volume provides the influential definition of "dress" that informs this reader along with much of the work in the anthropology of dress and fashion today. For Eicher and Roach-Higgins, dress refers not only to the clothing and ornaments people put on, but also to any kind of modification or supplement to their bodies people may do as social and cultural beings. Like Turner and McCracken, the authors see dress as a communication system and locate its social importance in its ability to communicate, but they are also clear that dress communicates not only to others but to one's self, informing an individual of what kind of person they are, what possibilities are open to them, and what kind of role they can or must play within a particular social milieu.

Daniel Rosenblatt, building on much of this earlier work, demonstrates the potential of dress—in this case tattooing, piercing, and modification of the body—to assert an oppositional identity and reposition oneself within a modern capitalist society. For Rosenblatt, dress does not just place a person within a group. It can also *dis*place them from that group, serving as a strategy of conscious self-alienation on the path to some other, more meaningful and (potentially) fulfilling way of living and being. Tattooing may be on the surface of the skin, but it cuts deep, speaking to the desire of "alternative culture" practitioners to be part of something outside of consumer culture.

Finally, Daniel Miller's "Style and Ontology" disabuses readers of any notion that that which is "superficial" is somehow unimportant or lacking in purpose. Using dress practices in Trinidad as his example, Miller attacks the "depth ontology" ([p. 78]) of contemporary Western societies that assumes that everything that is truly important lies in some imagined interior space, beneath the surface or deep inside. For the people of Trinidad, he claims, there is no difference between the performance you put on for others and who you "really are." Reality, for them, is on the surface.

This, we would argue, may be the defining mantra of the anthropology of dress and fashion today. We are how we dress. How we dress does not reflect some enduring interior state. It does not merely represent who we are. It shapes who we are. Without dress we have no easy, visual means of communicating to others, or defining for ourselves, who we are as social and cultural beings. To modify and supplement our bodies is thus a profound existential act. It makes us. It creates us. It forges us into our future selves, even, at times, entraps us within past versions of our selves. This part of the reader provides a theoretical roadmap for navigating that process.

6

FASHION -V- ANTI-FASHION

Ted Polhemus

The fashion show of the People's Republic of China obliges us to examine and redefine the term "fashion." Although adornment and fashion are often used as synonyms, this is clearly neither accurate nor useful. The time has come to subdivide the generic subject of adornment into two separate types: *fashion* and, on the other hand, *anti-fashion*. The gist of this differentiation is contained in Flügel's distinction, made in 1930, between "modish" and "fixed" types of dress:

> The distinctions here implied are not so much matters of race, sex, or cultural development, but depend rather on certain differences of social organisation. In their actual manifestations, the differences between the two types become most clearly apparent in the opposite relations which they have to space and time. "Fixed" costume [anti-fashion] changes slowly in time, and its whole value depends, to some extent, upon its permanence; but it varies greatly in space, a special kind of dress tending to be associated with each locality and with each separate social body (and indeed with every well defined grade within each body). "Modish" costume [fashion], on the other hand, changes very rapidly in time, this rapidity of change belonging to its very essence; but it varies comparatively little in space, tending to spread rapidly over all parts of the world which are subject to the same cultural influences and between which there exist adequate means of communication. (Flügel 1930: 129–30)

Although fashion and anti-fashion are both forms of adornment, they have little in common other than the general functions discussed in chapter 1 [of the book Fashion and Anti-Fashion]. We can begin to appreciate the specialized functions of each simply by examining two gowns which were in the public eye during 1953: Queen Elizabeth II's coronation gown and one from Dior's 1953 collection. The Queen's coronation gown is traditional, "fixed" and anti-fashion; it was designed to function as a symbol of continuity, the continuity of the monarchy and the British Empire.

Dior's gown also created a stir in 1953, but then Dior had been creating a sensation since 1947, when he boldly launched the "New Look," which defied cloth rationing in favour of longer, fuller, very feminine gowns. And each year Dior created a new New Look. In coronation year, he left behind his "immediately successful 'princess line' with dresses fitted through the midriff, waist unmarked" (Howell 1975: 227) and

> "reintroduced padding over the bust with his 'tulip' line, and captured headlines by shortening his skirts to 16 inches from the ground—still two or three inches below the knee. Women were by now used to wearing skirts almost to their ankles, and were nervous of a change that might date their clothes as suddenly as the New Look did in 1947 …" (Howell 1975: 231).

Likewise, in 1954 Dior changed the "tulip line" into the "H line," and in 1955 replaced the "H line" with the "A line." In this way he captured the essence of fashionable attire: its function as a symbol of change, progress and movement through time. Like any

Adapted from Ted Polhemus, *Fashion and Anti-Fashion*. (London: Thames and Hudson, 1978).

fashionable (modish) garments, Dior's 1953 "tulip line" announced that a new season had arrived. Anti-fashion adornment, on the other hand, is concerned with time in the form of continuity and the maintenance of the status quo. Fashion and anti-fashion are based upon and project alternative concepts and models of time.

In his famous ethnographic study of *The Nuer* (a Nilotic people of the Sudan), E. E. Evans-Pritchard (1968), one of the founding fathers of British anthropology and an opponent of Malinowski's functionalist school, included a chapter dealing with Nuer concepts of time and space. His argument, building upon the ideas of Émile Durkheim, was that these concepts reflect and express the patterns of social organization and relationships which are accepted as correct and proper by the Nuer.

Time, as Evans-Pritchard appreciated, is a socio-cultural concept which reflects and expresses a society's or a person's real or ideal social situation. This principle is clearly echoed in fashion and anti-fashion as alternative models of time. If traditional, anti-fashion adornment is a model of time as continuity (the maintenance of the status quo) and fashion is a model of time as change, then it is appropriate that Queen Elizabeth II should not have chosen a fashionable gown for her coronation. It is rational that she should have worn a gown which proclaims a message of continuity over hundreds of years, a message of timelessness and changelessness. In short, her social, economic and political situation suggests that she should prefer things to change as little as possible, and she expresses this attitude in her dress and adornment—especially at her coronation.

On the other hand, a social climber who is, or would like to be, "On the way up" will use the latest fashions to reinforce and project an image of time as change and progress. His or her fashionable attire constitutes an advertisement for socio-temporal mobility and will remain so as long as he or she stands to benefit from social change rather than from the maintenance of the social status quo.

That form of clothing and adornment which we have identified as fashion has, in fact, always been linked with those situations of social mobility where it is possible to be a social climber. In Europe, up to and including the Early Middle Ages, the rigid feudal system made such mobility highly unlikely and, accordingly, serfs and noblemen each had their own fixed anti-fashion costume. However, well before the Renaissance, a number of elements converged to create a socio-cultural environment suited to the development of changing fashion. The costliness of the Crusades, the population decline brought by the Black Death and other factors had weakened the power of the aristocracy and increased the power of the "lower orders." Frequently the nobility were forced to pay off their debts with money gained by selling serfs their freedom. With the further development of towns and cities, trade, commerce, education and travel created opportunities for these freemen to better themselves and to compete in wealth and power with the aristocracy.

This conflict between the rising bourgeoisie and the landed nobility was often fought with weapons of bodily decoration and adornment. To protect themselves, the nobility enacted sumptuary legislation to ensure the exclusivity of their attire. But these laws were often unenforceable, and furthermore, instead of simply copying the particular fixed costumes of the aristocrats, the rising bourgeoisie increasingly opted for constantly changing fashions.

This system of stylistic mobility—fashion—was an appropriate and logical expression of the social mobility which was implicit in the breakdown of the feudal system. As Flügel commented, "fashion implies a certain fluidity of the social structure of the community. There must be differences of social position, but it must seem possible and desirable to bridge these differences; in a rigid hierarchy fashion is impossible"(Flügel 1930: 140).

The fashion/anti-fashion distinction, therefore, is concerned with changing and fixed modes of adornment respectively. Furthermore, changing fashion "looks" reflect and express changing, fluid situations of social mobility, while anti-fashion styles reflect and express fixed, unchanging, rigid social environments. It is important to emphasize, however, that, as regards both social and stylistic change, we are concerned not with any quantitative, measurable, objective rate of change, but rather with impressions, perceptions, assumptions and the ideology of change and progress.

It has often been pointed out that fashion change, if looked at over a period of centuries, is cyclical, with themes and looks being repeated every few decades. Nevertheless, the impression that each and every new season's fashion is a fresh "New look" is as strong as the impression that anti-fashion styles are traditional and unchanging—even though we know that traditional societies and fixed, anti-fashion costumes must, obviously, undergo gradual evolution over long periods of time. Just as the British monarchy has changed over several centuries, so have the garments and regalia worn at coronations. For example, even a casual glance at the coronation robe which Elizabeth I wore at her coronation in 1559 reveals remarkable differences from that worn by Elizabeth II in 1953 (see Halls 1973: 6). Nevertheless, when we look at pictures of Elizabeth II's coronation, the impression, the atmosphere conveyed by the Queen's appearance is such that we feel that she could almost be wearing the clothes of her namesake.

The same principle applies when we consider the fixed folk costumes of peasant and primitive peoples. For example, Petr Bogatyrev in *The Functions of Folk Costume in Moravian Slovakia* (Czech Republic), while arguing that "the tendency of folk costume is NOT to change—grandchildren must wear the costume of their grandfathers," admits that he is "speaking here of the TENDENCIES of … folk costume. Actually we know that even folk costume does not remain unchanged, that it does take on features of current fashion" (Bogatyrev 1971: 33). He demonstrates how folk costume—especially in those parts of Moravian Slovakia where there is a growing tourist industry—has changed both subtly and dramatically. But this change is clearly differentiated from the phenomenon of fashion change by the attitude of the peasants themselves, who take pride in what they call "our costume" and which they perceive as being absolutely traditional and unchanging. That it does change is to them either unnoticeable or an anathema, and they would not be pleased to be told that their traditional costume isn't what it used to be.

A similar but somewhat more bizarre example of transient anti-fashion costume is to be found in New Guinea. In his definitive study of penis sheaths, the English archaeologist Peter Ucko states that in New Guinea the Telefolmin tribe normally wear as part of their traditional attire penis sheaths made of various types of gourds or large nuts. But now "the occasional individual is to be encountered wearing instead a toothpaste container, a Kodak film container or a cut-open sardine tin … "(Ucko 1969: 39).

Does this constitute a new fashion in penis sheaths? Most probably not. The introduction and development of new technologies should not be confused with true fashion change. Although fashion is not immune to technological advance, it can, and often does, choose to ignore such developments. For example, while fashion in the early 60s delighted in Perspex, Lurex, PVC and various other "space-age" materials, late 60s fashion made a deliberate change of direction back to natural fabrics such as wool and silk—making the "clothes of the future" passé while recycling the clothes and materials of the past as a New Look. Equally, Perspex, Lurex and PVC were technologically available long before they came into fashion. Whether technological advance consists of the introduction of PVC or that of toothpaste tubes, it should not be seen as the same type of phenomenon as fashion change.

Fashion is not simply a change of styles of dress and adornment, but rather *a systematic, structured and deliberate pattern of style change*. This is demonstrated in an essay by the anthropologists Jane Richardson and Alfred L. Kroeber which presents the results of their detailed quantitative analysis of rising and falling hem lengths and other parameters of evening dress design between 1787 and 1936. They show not only that the design of women's fashionable evening dress changes, but that it changes systematically rather than haphazardly, according to what Kroeber calls a "pattern":

Our first finding is that the basic dimensions of modem European feminine dress alternate with fair regularity between maxima and minima which in most cases average about fifty years apart, so that the full wave-length of their periodicity is around a century …

There appear accordingly to be two components in dress fashion. One is mode in the proper sense:

that factor which makes this year's clothes different from last year's or from those of five years ago. The other is a much more stable and slowly changing factor, which each year's mode takes for granted and builds upon. It cannot be pretended that these two factors are definably distinguishable throughout. Behavioristically, however, they can mostly be separated by the length and regularity of the changes due to the more underlying component.(Richardson and Kroeber 1940: 148)

Richardson and Kroeber's findings suggest that fashion functions as a system, an internally determined pattern—a mechanism, a structure, a programme—of change. It is possible that this phenomenon has occasionally occurred in non-Western societies, but there is, as far as I know, no information available to prove or disprove this conclusively. It is unlikely, however, that such a mechanism of deliberate change in clothing and adornment would occur in any traditional primitive or peasant society, where there exists by definition an ideology of the value of tradition and the desirability of cultural stability from one generation to the next—which, of course, is the defining feature of any traditional society.

Only a society organized upon a principle of social and cultural mobility (the rising bourgeoisie) would find a system of structured and deliberate change of dress and adornment to be appropriate, desirable and useful. And while fashion may have developed in conjunction with the rise of the bourgeoisie, once some of these individuals had broken the stranglehold of the landed aristocrats and moved into a newly formed, stable class group (the established bourgeoisie; the landed gentry) they became entrenched as an anti-fashion force.

However, social mobility and fashion, once set in motion, could not be stopped. Great debates have taken place as to whether it is fashion designers, fashion magazines or "the public" who dictate fashion change. One thing is certain, as Richardson and Kroeber's research shows: once the fashion machine was started up, it developed a will of its own, becoming a continuous system of change which operated and continues to operate according to its own internal structure or pattern.

It is true, of course, that wars, depressions and other such events influence the fashion pattern, but, as Richardson and Kroeber point out in their conclusions:

The explanation propounded is not that revolution, war, and sociocultural unsettlement in themselves produce scant skirts and thick and high or low waists, but that they disrupt the established dress style and tend to its overthrow or inversion. The directions taken in this process depend on the style pattern: they are subversive or centrifugal to it. By contrary, in "normal" periods dress is relatively stable in basic proportions and features: its variations tend to be slight and transient—fluctuations of mode rather than changes of style. In another civilization, with a different basic pattern of dress style, generic sociocultural unsettlement might also produce unsettlement of dress style but with quite different specific expressions—slender waists and flaring skirts, for instance, or the introduction or abolition of decolletage. (Richardson and Kroeber 1940: 149–50)

This permits an interesting reappraisal both of fashion and of the relationship of society and culture. Émile Durkheim and Karl Marx shared the belief that what happens on the socio-economic level influences and generates culture (e.g., language, the arts, style/ fashion). According to this view, society is like a group of people holding balloons on strings, the balloons representing culture. The movement of the crowd of people determines the movement of the balloons; the balloons do not move the people.

Basically, of course, this is correct, but our analysis of fashion change causes us to add a footnote to Durkheim and Marx. Aspects of culture such as fashion may become organized as internally integrated cultural systems, and this systematic organization dictates its own rules of change which socio-economic and political change can only "subvert" or "invert," to borrow Kroeber's terms. Thus fashion change occurs not only with reference to social change, but more directly with reference to the internal, structural organization of the *Système de la mode* of fashion (see Barthes 1967)

The introduction of any fashion innovation must respect and relate to the fashion changes which have come before. In this sense, neither designers nor the fashionable are in charge, directing the course of fashion change. Fashion is to a large extent running its own show, and one can only choose to get on or get off the fashion merry-go-round. If, indeed, even this is really a matter of personal choice. At least until very recent times, throughout history and throughout the world, few could be said to exercise personal *choice* over their appearance—and over an inclination towards the "modish" or, on the other hand, the "fixed"; one's socio-cultural situation rather than personality or idiosyncrasy determining your trendy or traditional leanings.

With the exception of the unfashionable (those who can't keep up with fashion change but would like to), *anti-fashion* refers to all styles of adornment which fall outside the organized system of fashion change. The Royal Family, at least in public, wear anti-fashions; Hells Angels, Hippies, Punks and priests wear anti-fashions; Andy Capp and "The Workers" wear anti-fashions. In no case is their dress and adornment caught up in the mechanism of fashion change, neither do they want it to be. Each wears a form of traditional costume which should ideally, like "our costume" of the Slovaks, remain unchanged and unchanging. There wouldn't, for example, be demand for or logic to "this year's New Look" for Hells Angles—a "tribe" so determined to resist change that, like so many of the tribes studied by anthropologists, they inscribe their culture permanently on their skin.

While anti-fashions most certainly do occur within the context of contemporary "Western" society, the most readily identifiable forms are the folk costumes of primitive and peasant peoples. In primitive societies, for example, anti-fashion costume plays an important part as one means whereby a society's way of life— its culture—can be handed down intact from one generation to the next. Social and stylistic changes constitute a threat to the maintenance of a particular way of life and a stable tribal identity. Taking things to an extreme, many tribes incorporate within their anti-fashion adornment permanent body arts such as tattooing, scarification, cranial deformation, circumcision, tooth filling, ear, nose and lip piercing, and so on. These permanent body arts are drastic and traditional methods used in part to hold on to at least the illusion of absolute social and cultural stability—an increasingly difficult task in a world where the changes and transitions begun in our own Middle Ages have become global and pandemic.

Interesting to note, therefore, that so many of the anti-fashion styletribes which have emerged in recent years within our own, rapidly changing world have rediscovered the value of such permanent body arts as tattooing and piercing as effective tools in their own attempts at subcultural stability and as a bulwark against a world where change is forever gathering pace and, in the eyes of many, seems out of control.

7

THE SOCIAL SKIN

Terence S. Turner

Man is born naked but is everywhere in clothes (or their symbolic equivalents). We cannot tell how this came to be, but we can say something about why it should be so and what it means.

Decorating, covering, uncovering or otherwise altering the human form in accordance with social notions of everyday propriety or sacred dress, beauty or solemnity, status or changes in status, or on occasion of the violation and inversion of such notions, seems to have been a concern of every human society of which we have knowledge. This objectively universal fact is associated with another of a more subjective nature— that the surface of the body seems everywhere to be treated, not only as the boundary of the individual as a biological and psychological entity but as the frontier of the social self as well. As these two entities are quite different, and as cultures differ widely in the ways they define both, the relation between them is highly problematic. The problems involved, however, are ones that all societies must solve in one way or another, because upon the solution must rest a society's ways of "socialising" individuals, that is, of integrating them into the societies to which they belong, not only as children but throughout their lives. The surface of the body, as the common frontier of society, the social self, and the psycho-biological individual, becomes the symbolic stage upon which the drama of socialisation is enacted, and bodily adornment (in all its culturally multifarious forms, from body-painting to clothing and from feather head-dresses to cosmetics) becomes the language through which it is expressed.

The adornment and public presentation of the body, however inconsequential or even frivolous a business it may appear to individuals, is for cultures a serious matter: *de la vie sérieuse*, as Durkheim said of religion. Wilde observed that the feeling of being in harmony with the fashion gives a man a measure of security he rarely derives from his religion. The seriousness with which we take questions of dress and appearance is betrayed by the way we regard not taking them seriously as an index, either of a "serious" disposition or of serious psychological problems. As Lord Chesterfield remarked:

> Dress is a very foolish thing; and yet it is a very foolish thing for a man not to be well dressed, according to his rank and way of life; and it is so far from being a disparagement to any man's understanding, that it is rather a proof of it, to be as well dressed as those whom he lives with: the difference in this case, between a man of sense and a fop, is, that the fop values himself upon his dress; and the man of sense laughs at it, at the same time that he knows that he must not neglect it. (cited in Bell 1949, p. 13)

The most significant point of this passage is not the explicit assertion that a man of sense should regard dress with a mixture of contempt and attentiveness, but the implicit claim that by doing so, and thus maintaining his appearance in a way compatible with "those he lives with," he defines himself as a man of sense. The uneasy ambivalence of the man of sense, whose "sense" consists in conforming to a practice he

Adapted from Terence S. Turner, "The Social Skin," in *Not Work Alone: A Cross-Cultural View of Activities Superfluous to Survival*, edited by Jeremy Cherfas and Roger Lewin (Beverly Hills, CA: Sage Publications, 1980), pp. 112–140.

laughs at, is the consciousness of a truth that seems as scandalous today as it did in the eighteenth century. This culture, which we neither understand nor control, is not only the necessary medium through which we communicate our social status, attitudes, desires, beliefs and ideals (in short, our identities) to others, but also to a large extent constitutes these identities, in ways with which we are compelled to conform regardless of our self-consciousness or even our contempt. Dress and bodily adornment constitute one such cultural medium, perhaps the one most specialised in the shaping and communication of personal and social identity.

The Kayapo are a native tribe of the southern borders of the Amazon forest. They live in widely scattered villages which may attain populations of several hundred. The economy is a mixture of forest horticulture, and hunting and gathering. The social organisation of the villages is based on a relatively complex system of institutions, which are clearly defined and uniform for the population as a whole. The basic social unit is the extended family household, in which residence is based on the principle that men must leave their maternal households as boys and go to live in the households of their wives upon marriage. In between they live as bachelors in a "men's house," generally built in the centre of the circular village plaza, round the edges of which are ranged the "women's houses" (as the extended family households are called). Women, on the other hand, remain from birth to death in the households into which they are born.

The Kayapo possess a quite elaborate code of what could be called "dress," a fact which might escape notice by a casual Western observer because it does not involve the use of clothing. A well turned out adult Kayapo male, with his large lower-lip plug (a saucer-like disc some six centimetres across), penis sheath (a small cone made of palm leaves covering the *glans penis*), large holes pierced through the ear lobes from which hang small strings of beads, overall body paint in red and black patterns, plucked eyebrows, eyelashes and facial hair, and head shaved to a point at the crown with the hair left long at the sides and back, could on the other hand hardly leave the most insensitive traveler with the impression that bodily adornment is

a neglected art among the Kayapo. There are, however, very few Western observers, including anthropologists, who have ever taken the trouble to go beyond the superficial recording of such exotic paraphernalia to inquire into the system of meanings and values which it evokes for its wearers. A closer look at Kayapo bodily adornment discloses that the apparently naked savage is as fully covered in a fabric of cultural meaning as the most elaborately draped Victorian lady or gentleman.

The first point that should be made about Kayapo notions of propriety in bodily appearance is the importance of cleanliness. All Kayapo bathe at least once a day. To be dirty, and especially to allow traces of meat, blood or other animal substances or food to remain on the skin, is considered not merely slovenly or dirty but actively anti-social. It is, moreover, dangerous to the health of the unwashed person. "Health" is conceived as a state of full and proper integration into the social world, while illness is conceived in terms of the encroachment of natural, and particularly animal forces upon the domain of social relations. Cleanliness, as the removal of all "natural" excrescence from the surface of the body, is thus the essential first step in "socialising" the interface between self and society, embodied in concrete terms by the skin. The removal of facial and bodily hair carries out this same fundamental principle of transforming the skin from a mere "natural" envelope of the physical body into a sort of social filter, able to contain within a social form the biological forces and libidinal energies that lie beneath.

The mention of bodily hair leads on to a consideration of the treatment of the hair of the head. The principles that govern coiffure are consistent with the general notions of cleanliness, hygiene, and sociality, but are considerably more developed, and accord with those features of the head-hair which the Kayapo emphasise as setting it apart from bodily hair (it is even called by a different name).

Hair, like skin, is a "natural" part of the surface of the body, but unlike skin it continually grows outwards, erupting from the body into the social space beyond it. Inside the body, beneath the skin, it is alive and growing; outside, beyond the skin, it is dead and without sensation, although its growth manifests the unsocialised biological forces within. The hair of the head thus focuses the dynamic and unstable quality of the frontier between the "natural," bio-libidinous forces of the inner body and the external sphere of social relations. In this context, hair offers itself as a symbol of the libidinal energies of the self and of the never-ending struggle to constrain within acceptable forms their eruption into social space.

So important is this symbolic function of hair as a focus of the socialising function, not only among the Kayapo but among Central Brazilian tribes in general, that variations in coiffure have become the principal visible means of distinguishing one tribe from another. Each people has its own distinctive hairstyle, which stands as the emblem of its own culture and social community (and as such, in its own eyes, for the highest level of sociality to have been attained by humanity). The Kayapo tribal coiffure, used by both men and women, consists of shaving the hair above the forehead upwards to a point at the crown, leaving the hair long at the back and sides of the head (unless the individual belongs to one of the special categories of people who wear their hair cut short, as described below). Men may tease up a little widow's peak at the point of the triangular shaved area. The sides of this area are often painted in black with bands of geometrical patterns.

Certain categories of people in Kayapo society are *privileged* to wear their hair long. Others must keep it cut short. Nursing infants, women who have borne children, and men who have received their penis sheaths and have been through initiation (that is, those who have been socially certified as able to carry on sexual relations) wear their hair long. Children and adolescents of both sexes (girls from weaning to childbirth, boys from weaning to initiation) and those mourning the death of a member of their immediate family (for example, a spouse, sibling or child) have their hair cut short.

To understand this social distribution of long and short hair it is necessary to comprehend Kayapo notions about the nature of family relations. Parents are thought to be connected to their children, and siblings to one another, by a tie that goes deeper than a mere social or emotional bond. This tie is imagined as a sort of spiritual continuation of the common physical substance that they share through conception and the womb. This relation of biological participation lasts throughout life but is broken by death. The death of a person's child or sibling thus directly diminishes his or her own biological being and energies. Although spouses lack the intrinsic biological link of blood relations, their sexual relationship constitutes a "natural" procreative, libidinal community that is its counterpart. In as much as both sorts of biological relationship are cut off by death, cutting off the hair, conceived as the extension of the biological energy of the self into social space, is the symbolically appropriate response to the death of a spouse as well as a child.

The same concrete logic accounts for the treatment of children's hair. While a child is still nursing, it is still, as it were, an extension of the biological being and energies of its parents, and above all, at this stage, the mother. In these terms nursing constitutes a kind of external and attenuated final stage of pregnancy. Weaning is the decisive moment of the "birth" of the child as a separate biological and social being. Thus nursing infants' hair is never cut, and is left to grow as long as that of sexually active adults: infants at this stage *are* still the extensions of the biological and sexual being of their long-haired parents. Cutting the infant's hair at the onset of weaning aptly symbolises the severance of this bio-sexual continuity (or, as we would say, its repression). Henceforth, the child's hair remains short as a sign of its biological separation from its parents, on the one hand, and the undeveloped state of its own bio-sexual powers on the other. When these become strong enough to be socially extended, through sexual intercourse and procreation, as the basis of a new family, the hair is once again allowed to grow to full length. For men this point is considered to arrive at puberty, and specifically with the bestowal of a penis sheath, which is ideally soon followed by initiation (a symbolic "marriage" which signals marriageability, or "bachelorhood," rather than being a binding union in and of itself).

The discrepancy in the timing of the return to long hair for the two sexes reflects a fundamental difference in Kayapo notions of their respective social roles. "Society" is epitomised for the Kayapo by the system of communal societies and age-sets centred on the men's house. These collective organisations are primarily a male domain, as their association with the men's house suggests, although women have certain societies of their own. The communal societies are defined in terms of the criteria for recruitment, and this is always defined as a corollary of some important transformation in family or household structure (such as a boy's moving out of his maternal family household to the men's house, marriage, the birth of children, etc.). These transformations in family relations are themselves associated with key points in the process of growth and sexual development.

The structure of communal groups, then, constitutes a sort of sociological mechanism for reproducing, not only itself but the structure of the extended family households that form the lower level or personal sphere of Kayapo social organisation. This communal institutional structure, on the other hand, is itself defined in terms of the various stages of the bio-sexual development of men (and to a much lesser extent, women). All this comes down to the proposition that men reproduce society through the transformation of their "natural" biological and libidinal powers into collective social form. This conception can be found elaborated in Kayapo mythology.

Women, by contrast, reproduce the natural biological individual, and, as a corollary, the elementary family, which the Kayapo conceive as a "natural" or infra-social set of essentially physical relations. Inasmuch as the whole Kayapo system works on the principle of the cooption of "natural" forces and their channelling into social form, it follows that women's biological forces of reproduction should be exercised only within the framework of the structure of social relations reproduced by men. The effective social extension of a woman's biological reproductive powers therefore occurs at the moment of the first childbirth within the context of marriage, husband and household. This is, accordingly, the moment at which a woman begins to let her hair grow long again. For men, as we have seen, the decisive social cooption of libidinal energy or reproductive power comes earlier, at the point at which those powers are publicly appropriated for purposes of the reproduction of the collective social order. This is the moment symbolically marked by the bestowal of the penis sheath at puberty.

The penis sheath, then, symbolises the collective appropriation of male powers of sexual reproduction for the purposes of social reproduction. To the Kayapo, the appropriation of "natural" or biological powers for social purposes implies the suppression of their "natural" or socially unrestrained forms of expression. The penis sheath works as a symbol of the channelling of male libidinal energies into social form by effectively restraining the spontaneous, "natural" expression of male sexuality: in a word, erection. The sheath, the small cone of woven palm leaf, is open at both the wide and narrow ends. The wide end fits over the tip of the penis, while the narrow end has an aperture just wide enough to enable the foreskin to be drawn through it. Once pulled through, it bunches up in a way that holds the sheath down on the *glans penis*, and pushes the penis as a whole back into the body. This obviously renders erection impossible. A public erection, or even the publicly visible protrusion of the *glans penis* through the foreskin without erection, is as embarrassing for a Kayapo male as walking naked through one's town or work place would be for a Westerner. It is the action of the sheath in preventing such an eventuality that is the basis of its symbolic meaning.

Just as the cutting or growing of hair becomes a code for defining and expressing a whole system of ideas about the nature of the individual and society and the relations between the two, so other types of bodily adornment are used to express other modalities of the same basic relationships.

Pierced ears, ear-plugs, and lip-plugs comprise a similar distinct complex of social meanings. Here the emphasis is on the socialisation, not of sexual powers, but of the faculties of understanding and active self-expression. The Kayapo distinguish between passive and active modes of knowing. Passive understanding is associated with hearing, active knowledge of how to make and do things with seeing. The most important aspect of the socialisation of the passive faculty of understanding is the development of the ability to "hear" language. To be able to hear and understand speech is spoken of in terms of "having a hole in one's ear"; to be deaf is "to have the hole in one's ear closed off." The ear lobes of infants of both sexes are pierced, and large cigar-shaped ear-plugs, painted red, are inserted to stretch the holes to a diameter of two or three centimetres (I shall return to the significance of the red colour). At weaning (by which time the child has learned to speak and understand language) the ear-plugs are removed, and little strings of beads like earrings are tied through the holes to keep them open. Kayapo continue to wear these bead earrings, or simply leave their ear-lobe-holes empty throughout adult life. I suggest that the piercing and stretching of these secondary, social "holes-in-the-ear" through the early use of the ear-plugs for infants is a metaphor for the socialisation of the understanding, the opening of the years to language and all that implies, which takes place during the first years of infancy.

The lip-plug, which reaches such a large size among older men, is incontestably the most striking piece of Kayapo finery. Only males have their lips pierced. This happens soon after birth, but at first only a string of beads with a bit of shell is placed in the hole to keep it open. After initiation, young bachelors begin to put progressively larger wooden pins through the hole to enlarge it. This gradual process continues through the early years of adult manhood, but accelerates when a man graduates to the senior male grade of "fathers-of-many-children." These are men of an age to have become heads of their wives' households, with married daughters and thus sons-in-law living under their roofs as quasi-dependents. Such men have considerable social authority, but they wield it, not within the household itself (which is considered a woman's domain) but rather in the public arena of the communal men's house, in the form of political oratory. Public speaking, in an ornate and blustering style, is the most characteristic attribute of senior manhood, and is the essential medium of political power. An even more specialised form of speaking, a kind of metrical chanting known as *ben*, is the distinctive prerogative of chiefs, who are called "chanters" in reference to the activity that most embodies their authority.

Public speaking, and chanting as its more rarified and potent form, are the supreme expression of the values of Kayapo society considered as a politically ordered hierarchy. Senior men, and, among them, chiefs, are the dominant figures in this hierarchy, and it can therefore be said that oratory and chanting as public activities express this dominance as a value implicit in the Kayapo social order. The lip-plug of the senior male, as a physical expression of the oral assertiveness and pre-eminence of the orator, embodies the social dominance and expressiveness of the senior males of whom it is the distinctive badge.

The senior male lip-plug is in these terms the complement of the pierced ears of both sexes and the infantile ear-plugs from which they derive. The former is associated with the active expression and political construction of the social order, while the latter betoken the receptiveness to such expressions as the attribute of all socialised persons. Speaking and "hearing" (that is, understanding and conforming) are the complementary and interdependent functions that constitute the Kayapo polity. Through the symbolic medium of bodily adornment, the body of every Kayapo becomes a microcosm of the Kayapo body politic.

As a man grows old he retires from active political life. He speaks in public less often, and on the occasions when he does it is to assume an elder statesman's role of appealing to common values and interests rather than to take sides. The transformation from the politically active role of the senior man to the more honorific if less dynamic role of elder statesman is once again signalled by a change in the style and shape of the lip-plug. The simplest form this can take is a diminution in the size of the familiar wooden disc. It may, however, take the form of the most precious and prestigious object in the entire Kayapo wardrobe—the cylindrical lip-plug of ground and polished rock crystal worn only by elder males. These neolithic valuables, which may reach six inches in length and one inch in diameter, with two small flanges at the upper end to keep them from sliding through the hole in the lip, require immense amounts of time to make and are passed down as heirlooms within families. They are generally clear to milky white in colour. White is associated with old age and with ghosts, and thus in general terms with the transcendence of the social divisions and transformations whose qualities are evoked by the two main Kayapo colours, black and red. This quality of transcendence of social conflict, and of direct involvement in the processes of suppression and appropriation of libidinal energies and their transformation into social form which constitute Kayapo public life in its political and ritual aspects, is characteristic of the content of the oratory of old men, and is what lends it its great if relatively innocuous prestige. Once again, then, we find that the symbolic qualities of the lip-plug match the social qualities of the speech of its wearer.

Before the advent of Western clothes, Kayapo of both sexes and all ages constantly went about with their bodies painted (many still do, especially in the more remote villages). The Kayapo have raised body painting to an art, and the variety and elaborateness of the designs is apt to seem overwhelming upon first acquaintance. Analysis, however, reveals that a few simple principles run through the variation of forms and styles and lend coherence to the whole. These principles, in turn, can be seen to add a further dimension to the total system of meanings conveyed by Kayapo bodily adornment.

There are two main aspects to the Kayapo art of body painting, one concerning the association of the two main colours used (red and black) on distinct zones of the body, the other concerning the two basic styles employed in painting that part of the body for which black is used.

To begin with the first aspect, the use of the two colours, black and red, and their association with different regions of the body reveal yet another dimension of Kayapo ideas about the make-up of the person as biological being and social actor. Black is applied to the trunk of the body, the upper arms and thighs. Black designs or stripes are also painted on the cheeks, forehead, and occasionally across the eyes or mouth. Red is applied to the calves and feet, forearms and hands, and face, especially around the eyes. Sometimes it is smeared over black designs already painted on the face, to render the whole face red.

Black is associated with the idea of transformation between society and unsocialised nature. The word for black is applied to the zone just outside the village that one passes through to enter the "wild" forest (the domain of nature). It is also the word for death (that is, the first phase of death, while the body is still decomposing and the soul has not yet forsaken its

social ties to become a ghost: ghosts are white). In both of these usages, the term for black applies to a spatial or temporal zone of transition between the social world and the world of natural or infra-social forces that is closed off from society proper and lies beyond its borders. It is therefore appropriate that black is applied to the surface of those parts of the body conceived to be the seat of its "natural" powers and energies (the trunk, internal and reproductive organs, major muscles, etc.) that are in themselves beyond the reach of socialisation (an analogy might be drawn here to the Freudian notion of the id). The black skin becomes the repressive boundary between the natural powers of the individual and the external domain of social relations.

Red, by contrast, is associated with notions of vitality, energy and intensification. It is applied to the peripheral points of the body that come directly into contact with the outside world (the hands and feet, and the face with its sensory organs, especially the eyes). The principle here seems to be the intensification of the individual's powers of relating to the external (that is, primarily, the social) world. Notice that the opposition between *red* (intensification, vitalisation) and *black* (repression) coincides with that between the *peripheral* and *central* parts of the body, which is itself treated as a form of the relationship between the *surface* and *inside* of the body respectively. The contrasting use of the two colours thus establishes a binary classification of the human body and its powers and relates that classification back to the conceptual oppositions, *inside: surface: outside*, that underlies the system of bodily adornment as a whole.

Turning now to the second major aspect of the system of body painting, that is, the two main styles of painting in black, the best place to begin is with the observation that one style is used primarily for children and one primarily for adults. The children's style is by far the more elaborate. It consists of intricate geometrical designs traced in black with a narrow stylus made from the central rib of a leaf. A child's entire body from the neck to below the knees, and down the arms to below the elbows, is covered. To do the job properly requires a couple of hours. Mothers (occasionally doting aunts or grandmothers) spend much time in this way keeping their children "well dressed."

The style involves building up a coherent overall pattern out of many individually insignificant lines, dots, etc. The final result is unique, as a snowflake is unique. The idiosyncratic nature of the design reflects the relationship between the painter and the child being decorated. Only one child is painted at a time, in his or her own house, by his or her own mother or another relation. All of this reflects the social position of the young child and the nature of the process of socialisation it is undergoing. The child is the object of a prolonged and intensive process of creating a socially acceptable form out of a myriad of individually unordered elements. It must lie still and submit to this process, which requires a certain amount of discipline. The finished product is the unique expression of the child's relationship to its own mother and household. It is not a collectively stereotyped pattern establishing a common identity with children from other families. This again conforms with the social situation of the child, which is not integrated into communal society above the level of its particular family.

Boys cease to be painted in this style, except for rare ceremonial occasions, when they leave home to live in the men's house. Older girls and women, however, continue to paint one another in this way as an occasional pastime. This use of the infantile style by women reflects the extent to which they remain identified with their individual families and households, in contrast to men's identification with collective groups at the communal level.

The second style, which can be used for children when a mother lacks the time or inclination for a full-scale job in the first style, is primarily associated with adults. It consists of standardised designs, many of which have names (generally names of the animals they are supposed to resemble). These designs are simple, consisting of broad strokes that can be applied quickly with the hand, rather than by the time-consuming stylus method. Their social context of application is typically collective: men's age sets gathered in the men's house, or women's societies, which meet fortnightly in the village plaza for the purpose of painting one another. On such occasions, a uniform style is generally used for the whole group (different styles may be used to distinguish structurally distinct groups, such as bachelors and mature men).

The second style is thus typically used by fully socialised adults, acting in a collective capacity (that is, at a level defined by common participation in the structure of the community as a whole rather than at the individual family level). Collective action (typically, though not necessarily, of a ritual character) is "socialising" in the higher sense of directly constituting and reproducing the structure of society as a whole: those painted in the adult style are thus acting, not in the capacity of *objects* of socialisation, but as its *agents*. The "animal" quality of the designs is evocative of this role; the Kayapo conceive of collective society-constituting activities, like their communal ceremonies, as the transformation of "natural" or animal qualities into social form by means of collective social replication. The adult style, with its "animal" designs applied collectively to social groups as an accompaniment to collective activity, epitomises these meanings and ideas. The contrasts between the children's and adults' styles of body painting thus model key contrasts in the social attributes of children and adults, specifically, their relative levels of social integration or, which comes to the same thing, their degree of "socialisation."

It may be suggested that the "construction of the subject," is a process which is broadly similar in all human societies, and the study of systems of bodily adornment is one of the best ways of comprehending what it involves. As the Kayapo example serves to illustrate, it is essentially a question of the conflation of certain basic types of social notions and categories, among which can be listed categories of time and space, modes of activity (for example, individual or collective, secular or sacred), types of social status (sex, age, family roles, political positions, etc.), personal qualities (degree of "socialisation," relative passivity or activity as a social actor, etc.) and modes of social value, for example, "dominance" or "beauty." In any given society, of course, these basic categories will be combined in culturally idiosyncratic ways to constitute the symbolic medium of bodily adornment, and these synthetic patterns reveal much about the basic notions of value, social action, and person- or self-hood of the culture in question.

In the case of the Kayapo, three broad synthetic clusters of meanings and values of this type emerge from analysis. One is concerned with the Kayapo notion of socialisation, conceived as the transformation of "natural" powers and attributes into social forms. The basic symbolic vehicle for this notion, after the general concern for cleanliness, is the form of body painting by which the trunk is contrasted with the extremities as black and red zones, respectively. This fundamental mapping of the body's "natural" and "social" areas is inflected, at a higher level of articulation, by hair style. The contrast between long and short hair is used to mark the successive phases of the development and social extension of the individual's libidinous and reproductive powers. Finally, the penis sheath (correlated with the shift to long hair for men) serves to mark the decisive point in the social appropriation of male reproductive powers and, perhaps more important, the collective nature of this appropriation. A second major complex concerns the distinction and relationship between the passive and active qualities of social agency. The basic indicator here is again body painting, in this case the distinction between the infantile and adult styles. This basic distinction is once again inflected by the set composed of pierced ears and ear-plugs, on the one hand, and pierced lips and lip-plugs on the other. This set adds the specific meanings associated with the notions of hearing and speaking as passive knowledge and the active expression of decisions and programmes of action, respectively. Finally, both these clusters are cross-cut by a broad distinction between modes of activity. The most strongly marked distinction here is between secular and sacred (ritual) action, with the latter distinguished from the former by a rich variety of regalia. This distinction, however, may be considered a heightened inflection of the more basic distinction between individual or family-level activities and communal activities, not all of which are of a sacred character. Secular men's house gatherings or meetings of women's societies, for example, may be accompanied by collective painting and perhaps the wearing of simple head-dresses of palm leaves, even though there is no ceremony.

An important structural principle emerges from this analysis of the Kayapo system—the hierarchical or iterative structure of the symbolic code. Each major cluster of symbolic meanings is seen to be arranged in a series of increasingly specific modulations or inflections of the general notions expressed by the most basic symbol in the cluster. A second structural principle is the multiplicative character of the system as a whole. By this I mean that the three basic clusters are necessarily simultaneously present or conflated in the "dress" of any individual Kayapo at any time. One cannot paint an infant or adult in the appropriate style without at the same time observing the concentric distinction between trunk and extremities common to both styles.

The conflation first of the levels of meaning within each cluster, secondly of each cluster with the others, and finally of the more basic categories of meaning and value listed above that are combined in different ways to form each cluster, is what I mean by "the construction of the cultural subject" or actor. (It is sometimes necessary to speak in terms of *collective* subjects, such as the class of young men, or of workers, but for the sake of simplicity I shall leave this issue aside here.) It is, by the same token, the construction of the social universe within which he or she acts (that is, an aspect of that construction). As the Kayapo example suggests, this is a dynamic process that proceeds as it were in opposite directions at the same time, towards equilibrium or equilibrated growth at both the individual and social levels (it goes without saying that in speaking of equilibrium I am referring to cultural ideals rather than concrete realities, either social or individual).

In the Kayapo case, the externalisation of the internal biological and libidinous ("natural") powers of individuals as the basis of social reproduction, and the socialisation of "external" natural powers as the basis of social structure and the social identity of actors otherwise defined only as biological extensions of their parents, are clearly metaphorical inversions of one another. Each complements the other, just as the social values respectively associated with the two aspects of the process, "dominance" and "beauty," complement each other; a balance between the two processes and their associated values is the ideal state of Kayapo society as a dynamic equilibrium. It is also, and equally, the basis of the unity and balance of the personality of the socialised individual, likewise conceived as a dynamic equilibrium.

The point I have sought to demonstrate is that this balance between opposing yet complementary forces, which is the most fundamental structural principle of Kayapo society, is systematically articulated and, as it were, played out on the bodies of every member of Kayapo society through the medium of bodily adornment. This finding supports the general hypothesis with which we began, namely that the surface of the body becomes, in any human society, a boundary of a peculiarly complex kind, which simultaneously separates domains lying on either side of it and conflates different levels of social, individual and intra-psychic meaning. The skin (and hair) are the concrete boundary between the self and the other, the individual and society. It is, however, a truism to which our investigation has also attested, that the "self" is a composite product of social and "natural" (libidinous) components.

At one level, the "social skin" models the social boundary between the individual actor and other actors, but at a deeper level it models the internal, psychic diaphragm between the pre-social, libidinous energies of the individual and the "internalised others," or social meanings and values that make up what Freud called the "ego" and "super-ego." At yet a third, macro-social level, the conventionalized modifications of skin and hair that comprise the "social skin" define, not individuals, but categories or classes of individuals (for example, infants, senior males, women of child-bearing age, etc.). The system of bodily adornment as a whole (all the transformations of the "social skin" considered as a set) defines each class in terms of its relations with all the others. The "social skin" thus becomes, at this third level of interpretation, the boundary between social classes.

That the physical surface of the human body is systematically modified in all human societies so as to conflate these three levels of relations (which most modern social science devotes itself to separating and treating in mutual isolation), should give us cause for reflection. Are we dealing here with a mere exotic phenomenon, a primitive expression of human society at a relatively undifferentiated level of development, or is our own code of dress and grooming a cultural device of the same type?

8

CLOTHING AS LANGUAGE:
An object lesson in the study of the expressive properties of material culture

Grant McCracken

Some years ago a new and influential metaphor captured the attention of the social sciences. This metaphor suggested an essential similarity between language and inanimate objects. Suddenly it became fashionable to talk about the "language" of clothing, the "language" of food, the "language" of houses. This metaphor has helped to point out the symbolic properties of material culture and consumer goods. But it has also created some thoroughgoing misconceptions about what these symbolic properties are and how they operate. This chapter suggests that clothing, one of the most expressive of the product categories, is *not* usefully compared to language. It argues that clothing is a very different system of communication, the cultural significance of which cannot be fully assessed until the "language" metaphor is abandoned or revised.

CLOTHING AS LANGUAGE REQUIEM FOR A METAPHOR

It is characteristic of other studies of clothing to resort to a particular metaphor when talking about the expressive aspect of clothing. Again and again the critical literature suggests that clothing is a kind of language. Thus, Bogatyrev notes the resemblance between Moravian folk costume and language (1971: 84), Turner calls Tchikrin body language a kind of "symbolic language" (1969: 96), Wolf speaks of the "vocabulary" of the symbolic system of Chinese mourning costume (1970: 189), Messing calls the Ethiopian toga a "nonverbal language" (1960: 558), and Nash refers to one aspect of contemporary clothing as a "silent language" (1977: 173). In Sahlins the comparison is a detailed one and includes references to the "syntax," "semantics," and "grammar" of clothing (1976[a]: 179). Neich is still more exacting in his comparison and advocates the use of an "explicitly linguistic model" for the study of New Guinea self-decoration (1982: 214). This tendency to compare clothing to language is not limited to anthropological studies; it exists in the work of other social scientists (Gibbins 1971; Gibbins and Schneider 1980; Holman 1980[a], 1980[b], 1981; Roach and Eicher 1979; Rosenfeld and Plax 1977) as well as those of popular writers (e.g., Lurie 1981).

Plainly, this comparison of language and clothing is not always intended with the same degree of seriousness or conviction. Sometimes it serves only as a rhetorical ornament. Furthermore, even when the metaphor is used more purposefully, it is hard to fault the reflex from which it springs. For it *is* a helpful figure of speech, and it succeeds in illuminating certain properties shared by clothing and language. It is also apparent that the comparison follows the same worthy instinct that has informed so much work and progress in recent anthropology. It continues in the tradition of applying linguistic models to the study of nonlinguistic phenomena (e.g., Lévi-Strauss, 1963).

Adapted from Grant McCracken, *Culture and Consumption II: Markets, Meaning, and Brand Management* (Bloomington, IN: Indiana University Press, 2005).

Still, it must be observed that the metaphor has been used so liberally that it has started to cool and take on the fixity of conventional wisdom. What was once a lively and illuminating suggestion of similarity is more and more a statement of apparent fact. This latter-day development in the history of the metaphor radically changes its value as a rhetorical device and academic instrument. As a "dead metaphor" it now threatens to conceal as much as it once revealed. It now dulls our critical senses as it once stimulated our imaginative faculties.

The time has therefore come to bury this metaphor or rehabilitate it. It is necessary to examine the relationship between clothing and language and determine where the similarities hold and where the differences exist. This new scrutiny of the metaphor promises a clearer idea of the expressive properties of clothing and the other instances of material culture which appear to give voice to culture.

RESEARCH REPORT AND CRITICAL COMMENT

In order to investigate some of the similarities and differences which exist between language and clothing, a study was undertaken in the fall and winter of 1982–83. The purpose of this study was to design a research project which would examine how clothing is "decoded" or interpreted by the observer. A larger study will help to substantiate the findings of this initial project but the pilot gives sufficient data to address the issue raised in this chapter.

It was while examining the twenty-five hours of interview testimony generated by the pilot study that I began to have grave doubts about the wisdom of a thoroughgoing language-clothing comparison. In order to demonstrate this skepticism, it is necessary to resort briefly to the terms and concepts of structural linguistics.

Speech, Jakobson and Halle argue (1956: 58–62), implies the operation of two linguistic principles (cf. de Saussure 1966; Barthes 1967). One of the principles, that of selection, occurs when the speaker selects a linguistic unit from each paradigmatic class to fill each of the corresponding "slots" that make up the sentence.

Each class consists of all of the units that can potentially fill the same slot in a sentence. These units are capable of substitution one for the other and therefore enjoy a relationship of equivalence. But they are also defined by their difference to one another and therefore enjoy a relationship of contrast. The units of each paradigmatic class may be viewed as a vertical plane not altogether dissimilar to the rolling wheel of the slot machine. Any particular unit in a sentence is invisibly attended by all the other units of its class. These units stand ready to take its place and so change the meaning of the sentence. When the speaker employs the principle of selection he evokes one unit from each paradigmatic class and thus exploits the system of contrast that each of these classes represents.

The second linguistic principle, that of combination, occurs when the speaker combines the units selected from the paradigmatic classes into a syntagmatic chain. This chain consists in the various slots for which paradigmatic alternatives exist. Rules of combination specify how units are to be combined into a syntagmatic chain. This is the horizontal plane of language that gives language its linear, discursive aspect. Any syntagmatic chain creates a sequential context which acts on the meaning of each unit as it is entered into speech. The unit, already defined by its paradigmatic relations, undergoes a further process of definition when it is conjoined with other items in a syntagmatic chain.

The code of any particular language consists in a specification of the units of the paradigmatic classes and the rules for their syntagmatic combination. The code establishes how the principles of selection and combination are to be used in any particular linguistic exercise.

Each speaker of a language is both constrained and empowered by the code that informs his language use. He or she has no choice but to accept the way in which distinctive features have been defined and combined to form phonemes. He or she has no choice but to accept the way in which phonemes have been defined and combined to form morphemes. The creation of sentences out of morphemes is also constrained but here the speaker enjoys a limited discretionary power and combinatorial freedom. This discretionary power increases when the speaker combines sentences into utterances. By this stage the action of compulsory rules of combination has ceased altogether. The speaker is no longer constrained but free in his combinatorial activity. Jakobson and Halle refer to this characteristic of language as "an ascending scale of freedom" (1956: 60). At the bottom of the scale the speaker is fully constrained, at the top he or she is completely free. It is this dual character of language that allows it to stand both as a collective and systematic means of communication and as an instrument of endlessly various expressive potential.

This model of language is for present purposes well illustrated by Neich (1982) in his study of self-decoration in Mount Hagen, New Guinea. Neich suggests that we may treat this self-decoration as a code which specifies paradigmatic choices appropriate for syntagmatic combination. The Hagener chooses a decorative unit from each paradigmatic class and combines these in a syntagmatic chain, his clothing outfit. Does the Hagener thus create a message about status and role on formal and informal social occasions? Whether the Hagener is a donor, donor's helper, warrior, etc., can be read by the observer from the decoration of his/her body. For Neich, this decoration demonstrates both principles of language. He argues that the self-decoration of Hageners, examined in the light of a structural linguistic model, reveals a languagelike character, and that we may call it a "semiotic or system of signs" (1982: 217) (cf. Barthes 1967: 111).

My research suggests that the application of the structural linguistic model to clothing is problematical. While clothing does bear a resemblance to language in some respects, it departs from it in a fundamental way. Ironically, when clothing most fully conforms to language and its principles of selection and combination, it fails completely as a semiotic device. Or, to put this another way, when clothing as a code is most like language, it is least successful as a means of communication. There is to this extent a fundamental difference between language and clothing. This difference must be taken into account if we are to make a successful examination of the communicative aspect of clothing.

In examining my research data, I sought to determine how informants interpreted examples of clothing. The external assessment of an internal activity of this sort is of course extremely difficult. The best I could hope to do was to establish a characteristic pattern of interpretation, and hope that this pattern was a reliable guide to the inner activity itself. While this latter assumption is itself problematical, it does seem to me that there is a characteristic pattern, and that this pattern does serve, at least in a negative way, to cast doubt on one of the supposed similarities between language and clothing.

Informants were asked to respond to a series of slides which pictured a variety of instances of contemporary North American clothing. There were three categories of response to these slides. These categories represent levels of relative ease of interpretation.

In the first category of interpretation, informants were swift and sure in their reading of the clothing portrayed. Typically, they delivered their response to the slide almost instantaneously. Selecting a term from our vocabulary of social types, the informant would identify the person pictured as a "housewife," "hippie," "businessman," etc. Sometimes this term would be accompanied by a demographic adjective (e.g., "middle-class," "uneducated," "wealthy").

It is difficult to judge from these external signs just what internal process had occurred. But it did appear unlikely that the informant had performed a "reading" of the clothing portrayed in anything like the terms we associate with language proper.

First, there was no evidence of a linear reading of the clothing outfit. Informants did not appear to begin their interpretive activity with one body slot and work their way through to others. They did not sort through the syntagmatic chain in order to determine how each paradigmatic selection modified the meaning of other selections and the chain itself. They appeared instead to read the clothing outfit before them as an ensemble. It was clear that the outfit was examined to discover the differential effect of its various parts, but the successive combination of these parts did not seem to play an important part in the informant's account of their meaning. The parts of the outfit did not present themselves in a linear way to the informant (for they exist not in sequence but as co-present elements), and the informant did not read them this way.

Instead, clothing presents the parts of its "syntagmatic combination" simultaneously, and it is simultaneously that they are read.

Second, the meaning of the outfits was always rendered in terms of a limited vocabulary of adjectives and nouns. By their own account, informants sought to determine the "look" of the outfit before them. These "looks" did not constitute a set of infinite possibilities but a delimited universe. The informant showed no expectation that the message of a particular clothing outfit would constitute a novel piece of discourse. And more important, he or she showed no evidence of possessing the interpretive resources necessary to deal with such a message. He or she had at his disposal the use of only a limited set of adjectives and nouns that did not allow for novelty.

In the second category, informants experienced hesitation and difficulty in making their interpretation. Unable to make an immediate identification of an outfit, they began a more careful examination of the "body sentence" and its component parts. Often they would deliver comments of the following kind: "Let's see, they're wearing 'x' so they might be 'a,' but they're also wearing 'y' so perhaps they're 'b.'" Typically, the informant would then complain that the parts of the outfit did "not really go together," and that it was therefore difficult to read the individual pictured. This period of hesitation and uncertainty would be resolved by one of two strategies. The informant would either take the most salient item of clothing and offer its meaning as an interpretation of the clothing message, or, he/she would attempt to reconcile contradictory messages with an explanatory vignette (e.g., "Well, he wears that jacket because he used to be a businessman, but it doesn't fit with the pants and shoes because he's lost his job and is on the skids").

This second, more difficult, category of interpretation shows a characteristic similar to the first. Here again, no evidence of a linear reading of the body-sentence presents itself. Despite the fact that the informant was now attending with greater attention to the body-sentence, he was apparently not reading each item of clothing in its syntagmatic relation to other items of clothing. Indeed it appeared that the informant employed his careful reading not to decode a sentence,

but to solve a puzzle. He engaged in a hunt for clues that would allow him to disambiguate a potentially opaque message.

This category of interpretation also allows us to see what becomes of this code when it is confronted with a modestly novel message. The informant did not treat a novel combination of clothing parts as a sentence that could be rendered intelligible by an application of the code. He treated it as a puzzle that could be resolved only by ignoring one of its contradictory elements or by inventing a story that explained the contradiction away. Again, and perhaps here more strongly, we see the informant possessed of limited interpretive resources. A clothing outfit either conformed to one of the terms contained in his limited exegetical set or it remained ambiguous. The exercise of even a small degree of combinatorial freedom by the wearer created not discourse, but confusion.

The third, most difficult, category of interpretation also conforms to the pattern noted here. When confronted with still more anomalous outfits, informants would hesitate, begin their answers by fits and starts, and then give up the interpretive effort altogether, often with an explanation such as: "Oh, he [the person pictured in the slide] could be anyone, I can't read this guy at all." The individual pictured in the slide departed so completely from a prescribed "look" that he was impossible to read even in speculative terms. Thus, when the individual pictured had exercised the combinatorial freedom characteristic of language and begun to group clothing elements in novel combination, the interpreter was least able to make sense of the resulting message. When clothing was most like language, it was least successful as a means of communication.

DISCUSSION

The most apt explanation of this decoding behavior is, perhaps, that we have in clothing a peculiar kind of code. It appears that clothing as a means of communication has no genuine syntagmatic aspect. The code does not provide rules of combination for the manipulation of paradigmatic selections to semiotic effect. The combination of clothing elements is, therefore, not a crucial part of the creation of clothing messages. In short, the code has no generative capacity. Its users enjoy no combinatorial freedom.

The clothing code, to use the terms of Jakobson's point discussed above, is almost fully constrained. It does not have a complete ascending scale of freedom. The code specified not only the components of the message, but also the messages themselves. These messages come, as it were, pre-fabricated. Because the wearer does not have this combinatorial freedom, the interpreter of clothing examines an outfit not for a new message but for an old one fixed by convention. Combinatorial freedom can be exercised by the wearer only with the effect of baffling the interpreter. Combinatorial freedom cannot be exercised in clothing without depriving this clothing of its combinatorial potential and effect.

This aspect of the clothing code was anticipated by Jakobson. In an article entitled "Language in Relation to Other Communication Systems" (1971), Jakobson argued that for certain nonlinguistic means of communication, the code is a collection of messages rather than a means for their creation. Unlike language, which establishes signs and the rules for their combination into messages, a system such as clothing gives no generative opportunity, and must therefore specify in advance of any act of communication the messages of which the code is capable (cf. Culler 1975: 3–54).

It is because of the absence of the principle of combination (and the generative freedom it allows) that informants decode clothing ensembles as they do. The decoding process consists in accurately identifying a clear message (already specified by the code) through the accurate identification of the highly redundant, mutually presupposing elements in which the message consists. Or it consists in struggling with an interpretation made difficult by a heterogeneous set of elements for which the code has made no provision. For the clothing code, novelty of the sort possessed by language is not an opportunity for communication but a barrier to it.

It should be noted that Neich attributes a syntagmatic aspect to clothing only with considerable misgiving. He acknowledges, first, that clothing does not appear to have the same combinatorial freedom that is evident in language; second, that clothing does not have the same linear, discursive quality as language; and, third, that there are among the Hageners fixed clothing syntagms—messages "that the individual no longer has to combine for himself" (1982: 221). But these are only cautions. Neich insists finally that self-decoration has sufficient linearity and combinatorial freedom to be grouped with language and treated according to the terms of a structural linguistic model. It is my contention that the model does not apply. The interpretive efforts of my informants suggest that clothing does not exhibit combinatorial freedom, and is therefore encoded and decoded in a way quite incompatible with the structural linguistic model. Indeed, I would go further and say, as I have done above, that when a clothing message exhibits the combinatorial aspect of language it renders itself imprecise. The model therefore does not only fail to bring to light aspects of clothing, it positively misleads us in our attempt to understand its expressive properties.

THE EXPRESSIVE PROPERTIES OF MATERIAL CULTURE RECONSIDERED

Students of material culture have resorted more than once to a model of language to aid them in their attempts to understand the expressive properties of their data. It is the burden of this chapter to suggest that this critical reflex is, perhaps, ill advised. Those of us who seek to take account of the expressive aspect of material culture in these terms are condemned to work in the failing light of an ill-chosen metaphor. There is no question that the metaphor once encouraged insight and research of a valuable kind. But as long as we continue to insist on the similarities between material culture and language, we will remain imperfectly aware of important differences.

This is not to suggest that the metaphor should be abandoned. It is to suggest that the terms of our analysis should perhaps be shifted to examine not the similarities but the differences between language and material culture. The metaphor will serve us just as well as a study in contrast as it once did as a study in comparison.

Let me propose four topics that come to light when one considers the differences between material culture and language as expressive media. For instance, we might consider whether the nonlinguistic codes of material culture communicate things that language proper cannot or, characteristically, does not. Do cultures charge material culture with the responsibility of carrying certain messages that they cannot or do not entrust to language? Forge, for one, argues (1970: 288) that this is indeed the case, and it is likely that a critical eye to the ethnographic literature will reveal other instances in which material culture undertakes expressive tasks that language does not or cannot perform.

When we contemplate the possibility that language and material culture differ in their communicative ends, it becomes particularly important to understand how they differ as communicative means. Take, for example, the apparent difference identified in this chapter between the codes of clothing and language. It has been suggested that clothing does not possess a combinatorial freedom and that it is therefore incapable of creating new messages. This account of clothing suggests that it is, in a sense, a "closed" code. It suggests a passing resemblance between clothing and the mythic thought and the activity of the bricoleur described by Lévi-Strauss (1966: 17). Like this thought and activity, clothing provides society with a fixed set of messages. It encourages the use of the code for the purpose of semiotic repetition rather than innovation. It allows for the representation of cultural categories, principles, and processes without at the same time encouraging their innovative manipulation. Language, on the other hand, is a much more "open" code and more closely resembles scientific thought and the activity of the engineer, which, as Lévi-Strauss notes (1966: 19–20), are constantly creating new messages and allowing events to have an innovative effect on structure. Clothing is constant in its semiotic responsibilities, language is changeable.

In short, clothing is a conservative code. Culture can therefore trust to this instance of material culture messages that language might abuse. It can encode in clothing and material culture information it wishes to make public but does not wish to see transformed. As Miles Richardson puts it, "material culture continues to have an existence, as it were, apart from the drift and flow of opinions, attitudes, and ideas" (1974: 4).

Second, we may ask whether material culture as a means of communication works in more understated, inapparent ways than language. Are its messages less overt and their interpretation less conscious than those of language? It is likely that future research will decide this question in the affirmative. The semiotic information of material culture appears typically to seep into consciousness around the edges of a central focus and more pressing concerns.

The inconspicuousness of material culture gives it several advantages as a means of communication. First of all, it makes material culture an unusually cunning and oblique device for the representation of fundamental cultural truths. It allows culture to insinuate its beliefs and assumptions into the very fabric of daily life, there to be appreciated but not observed. It has to this extent great propagandistic value in the creation of a world of meaning.

Furthermore, the inconspicuousness of the messages of material culture also permit them to carry meaning that could not be put more explicitly without the danger of controversy, protest, or refusal. Particularly when the message is a political one and encodes status difference, material culture can speak sotto voce. Political statement can therefore be undertaken with diminished risk of counter-statement (cf. Givens 1977; McCracken 1982: 82).

Third, it is possible that material culture and language differ in the relative universality of their codes. My research suggests that within a single speech community that shares a relatively uniform code for language, there can exist quite marked differences in the code for clothing. Different age-groups and classes will encode and decode clothing messages in a strikingly disparate manner and with a low degree of mutual intelligibility. The study of clothing and other instances of material culture may serve thus as an opportunity to study social and ideational diversity. Bernstein's pioneering work (1975) on the diversity of language codes in contemporary England may serve as a model for this study, but here again we must attend as much to the ways the codes of material culture differ from this model of language as we do to the ways they do conform to it.

Finally, it must be observed that material culture as a means of communication is severely limited in the number and range of the things it can communicate. And it cannot exercise the rhetorical powers which language possesses. No nonlinguistic code allows us to communicate the medical condition of an aunt in Winnipeg, our opinion of the Thatcher government, or our judgment of the latest South American novelist. Material culture allows the representation of only a very limited number of things in only a very limited number of ways. And it cannot be used to express irony, metaphor, skepticism, ambivalence, surprise, reverence, or heartfelt hope. Material culture allows very little expressive scope.

The study of the expressive properties of material culture must reckon with a paradox. Material culture is, as I have tried to demonstrate in this chapter, extremely limited in its expressive range. Deprived of combinatorial freedom and generative potential, it is a relatively impoverished means of communication. It stands as a kind of mystery, then, why culture should utilize it for any communicative purpose, when it has a code as subtle and sophisticated as language as an alternative. The answer to this paradox must be that material culture, for all its apparent limitations, has certain virtues not shared by language. It is apparently possessed of semiotic advantages that make it more appropriate than language for certain communicative purposes. I have sought to note three of these advantages above, and it seems to me that the study of material culture will be advanced by the discovery of others. The research strategy that seeks out the differences between material culture and language promises, I think, a more thoroughgoing understanding of the expressive nature of material culture. It promises to show us how and why it serves as a useful medium of communication.

9

DEFINITION AND CLASSIFICATION OF DRESS:
Implications for analysis of gender roles

Joanne B. Eicher and Mary Ellen Roach-Higgins

Dress is a powerful means of communication and makes statements about the gender role of a newborn child soon after birth. Although newborn childrens' first dress may be gender-neutral, their sex soon prompts kin or other caretakers to provide them with dress considered gender-appropriate within their particular society. Further, specific types of dress, or assemblages of types and their properties, communicate gender differentiations that have consequences for the behavior of females and males throughout their lives. This essay presents a sociocultural definition of dress and a classification system for types of dress that are compatible with this definition. We also discuss the relevance of the system in analyses of relationships between dress and gender roles.

Although in this paper we emphasize the use of the classification system to clarify and unify the content of anthropological and sociological study of dress and gender; the system is applicable to all work on the sociocultural aspects of dress. A major advantage of the system is that it brings together a number of related concepts, travelling under various names, within different theoretical and research contexts, under the rubrics "body modifications" and "body supplements."

PROBLEMS WITH CLASSIFICATION AND TERMINOLOGY

As we address the problems of classifying types of dress, we recognize that the dressed person is a *gestalt* that includes body, all direct modifications of the body itself, and all three-dimensional supplements added to it. Further, we acknowledge that only through mental manipulation can we separate body modifications and supplements from the body itself—and from each other—and extract that which we call dress. Despite these limitations, we choose to focus on the concrete reality of dress that has describable properties, such as color, shape, texture, surface design, or odor. We also take the position that the direct modifications of the body as well as the supplements added to it must be considered types of dress because they are equally effective means of human communication, and because similar meanings can be conveyed by some property, or combination of properties, of either modifications or supplements. For example, the design and color of a facial scar (a body modification) can be as accurate a means of conveying high social status as a supplemental robe of a particular shape and color. However, rarely do the stated or implied classifications of dress found in the literature take into account all possible categories of body modifications and supplements or their properties. Classification of dress as draped or tailored, for instance, presents a very limited view of dress. It concentrates attention only on variations in body enclosures that surround the body in cloth or other pliable materials, such as animal skins or plastic sheetings. Left out is a whole range of body modifications, from skin coloring to perfumes and hairdress. Likewise, those who opt for

Adapted from Joanne B. Eicher and Mary Ellen Roach-Higgins, "Definition and Classification of Dress: Implications for Analysis in Gender Roles," in *Dress and Gender: Making and Meaning,* edited by Ruth Barnes and Joanne Eicher (Oxford: Berg, 1992), pp. 8–28.

the use of the word clothing as a single category to encompass all types of dress run a similar risk, for the term clothing also restricts dress to the assemblage of items that happen to cover the body in some way. The omission of body modifications from the study of dress can be a serious loss, for it may lead to false conclusions regarding the social significance of dress. For example, modifications in hairdress may communicate information that has more influence on how human beings see and understand themselves and others than supplements such as robes, foot coverings, or jewelry.

The use of the term "appearance" as a category that subsumes various types of dress also has its limitations. In some ways appearance is more than dress and in other ways less. It is more than dress because it takes into account body features, movements, and positions, as well as the visible body modifications and supplements of dress. It is less than dress because it leaves out what may be some of the most intimately apprehended properties of dress, that is, touch, odor, taste, and sound.

Accompanying the problems of classification are vexing questions about the use of terminology. In designating types of dress, writers frequently use ethnocentric, value-charged terms such as mutilation, deformation, decoration, ornament, and adornment. When they use these terms, they are usually applying their own personally and culturally derived standards to distinguish the good from the bad, the right from the wrong, and the ugly from the beautiful, and thus inevitably reveal more about themselves than about what they are describing. They are also forgetting that dress considered beautiful in one society may be ugly in another, and that dress considered right in one social situation may be wrong in another.

When classifiers label a type of dress or some aspect of it as ornament, adornment, or decoration, they are clearly making a value judgment regarding its merits as an aesthetically pleasing creation. Similarly, their calling a type of dress a mutilation or deformation indicates they have judged it to be nonacceptable. What they omit is whose standard they are applying— and this is a critical omission, for the classifiers' application of these evaluative labels is no guarantee that the wearers, or other viewers, concur with their judgments. Terms thus far discussed as value-laden (mutilation, deformation, ornament, and adornment) are also ambiguous terms. They are ambiguous because they reveal relatively little about type of dress, but a great deal about functions. Like the term "cosmetic surgery," they involve and emphasize the dual functions of dress: as a means of communication between human beings and as an alterant of body processes.

Viewers who label types of dress as mutilations or deformations are registering conscious or unconscious disapproval of certain kinds of body modification, perhaps scarification, tooth filing, or head binding. Their negative reactions are based on what these types of dress communicate to them. Facial scars, for example, may communicate interference with body processes in a way that seems to threaten health and survival. They may also communicate ugliness within the value system of the viewer's own culture group, because their observable properties lie outside the cultural range of body modifications that can be accorded a degree of attractiveness. In other words, their usage is so sharply different, culturally speaking, that they simply are not eligible for consideration as marks of attractiveness or beauty by the viewer who comes from outside the culture. A displayer of scars within one culture and a person with a face lift in another may each undergo risk in order to achieve social approval. Thus scars and face lifts are more alike than different; a search for beauty and a general disregard for risks to health or body functioning is indicated by each.

An additional term that is popular in current literature, but difficult to interpret, is "physical appearance." Some writers use the term to indicate qualities of the natural body, others to identify characteristics of the body and any direct body modifications (as in skin color or hair shape and texture). Still others use the term to summarize a totality consisting of body and garments, jewelry, and other supplements, as well as any direct body modifications. Such fluctuation in usage introduces ambiguity in concept and limits the usefulness of the term physical appearance in discussions of dress, or, for that matter, in discussions of body characteristics.

Defining dress

In our discussion so far we have been intentionally supporting use of the word "dress" as a comprehensive term to identify both direct body changes and items added to the body, and have presented reasons for rejecting a number of overlapping, competing terms found in the literature related to dress. We have also stressed an important sociocultural aspect of dress: that it is imbued with meaning understood by wearer and viewer. Having taken this sociocultural stance, we define dress an assemblage of body modifications and/or supplements displayed by a person in communicating with other human beings. Defined in this general way, the word dress is gender-neutral. This general usage does not rule out that, in specific contexts or with specific inflections, the word may be used to convey socially constructed, gendered meanings. When specifically preceded by the article "a" or converted to the plural form, the word dress, according to current usage, designates feminine garments. Similarly, when used in the verb form to designate dressing the male genitals to the right or left in the custom tailoring of men's trousers, it takes on a masculine meaning. A further virtue of the term

dress is that its use avo[...] introduced by words lik[...] and the lack of clarity or [...] terms like physical appea[...] classification system we pr[...] follows from the general de[...] presented.

A classification system for types of dress

Three previous works moved terminology and classification systems away from the built-in contradictions of the long-used clothing-versus-ornament schema. Doob (1961) took a step toward isolating what we call dress by considering changes in the appearance of humans as changes of the body and changes on the body. What he left out were the properties of dress that evoke other than the visual sensory responses, that is, odor, taste, sound, and touch. Roach and Eicher (1973) and Eicher and Musa (1980) presented systems that went beyond the visibly observable aspects of dress to include these other categories. The classification system that follows in Table 1 is based on ideas set forth in these earlier works.

Table 1 Classification System for Types of Dress and Their Properties

Types of dress**	Properties							
	Color	Volume & proportion	Shape & structure	Surface design	Texture	Odor	Taste	Sound
Body modifications								
Transformations of								
a. Hair								
b. Skin								
c. Nails								
d. Muscular / skeletal system								
e. Teeth								
f. Breath								
Body supplements								
Enclosures								
a. Wrapped								
b. Suspended								
c. Pre-shaped								

...ontinued)

...s of dress**	Properties							
	Color	Volume & proportion	Shape & structure	Surface design	Texture	Odor	Taste	Sound
d. Combinations of ab, ac, bc, abc								
Attachments to body								
a. Inserted								
b. Clipped								
c. Adhered								
Attachments to body Enclosures								
a. Inserted								
b. Clipped								
c. Adhered								
Hand-held objects								
a. By self								
b. By other								

© Mary Ellen Roach-Higgins and Joanne B. Eicher

The range in types of dress, as shown in the classification system, allows us to provide a method for accurately identifying and describing types of dress that relate to gender roles and other social roles. It also allows us to appreciate the potential variety in dress. In the classification system, we focus on the first part of our definition of dress: an assemblage of body modifications and supplements. Listed in the left-hand column are the major categories of dress—modifications and supplements—and their subcategories. As the subcategories show, parts of the body that can be modified include hair, skin, nails, muscular-skeletal system, teeth, and breath. Body parts can be described in regard to specific properties of color, volume and proportion, shape and structure, surface design, texture, odor, sound, and taste. Supplements to the body—such as body enclosures, attachments to the body, attachments to body enclosures, and hand-held accessories—can be cross-classified with the same properties used to describe body modifications.

By manipulating properties of body modifications and supplements, people communicate their personal characteristics, including the important distinctions of gender. Even when forms of dress and Their properties are largely shared or similar for both sexes, gender distinctions can be clearly communicated by a minimum of manipulations of dress. For example, if the hair of males is expected to be cut short and that of females is expected to grow long in a particular society, the shape and volume of hair immediately communicate to observers the gender of the individual under scrutiny.

Relevance of the classification system in analysis of dress and gender roles

The definition of dress and the classification system we present unites two major human acts (modifying the body and supplementing the body) that invite sensory responses to and interpretations of the resulting outward similarities and differences of human beings. The preponderance of visually recorded properties in our classification system indicates that we can expect the visual stimuli of dress to outweigh the impact of other sensory stimuli, such as sound, touch, odor, and taste, in establishing gender identity. An additional reason why the visually observable properties may have more impact is that they do not require close proximity to be noticed by others. On the basis of this heavy weighting of visual impact and what we know about theories of communication, we can expect dress to precede verbal communication in establishing an individual's gendered identity as well as expectations for other types of behavior (social roles) based on this identity. The importance of dress in the structuring of behavior, as Polhemus (1989) points out, is that some of the information that is transmitted from person to person by dress is not easily translatable into words. Moreover, to give a detailed verbal report of all the information an individual's dress communicates (including gender) would be both time-consuming and socially clumsy.

At birth, when a child lacks verbal skills as well as the physical power and motor skills required to manipulate dress, adult caretakers (kin or surrogate kin who come to the aid of the child) act as purveyors of culture by providing gender-symbolic dress that encourages others to attribute masculine or feminine gender and to act on the basis of these attributions when interacting with the child. Because establishing gendered forms of dress for males and females provides a visually economical way to reinforce the fact that wearers have the sex organs that are the primary physical distinctions between the sexes, dress serves the macrobiological as well as the macrosocial system. Distinguishing sex by dress can encourage not only sexual overtures in socially approved ways, but also mating, which, in turn, as it leads to birth of children, guarantees the continuity of both the species and society. On a more micro level, members of the kin group who are likely to establish gendered dress for the newborn are also those who are most likely to have a stake in the mating that assures the continuity of the kin group. Only the name of an individual (where distinguished by gender) can compete with dress as an effective social means for communicating the sex of an infant (or a person of any age) to others who then know what gender expectations to apply in making their responses to the dressed individual.

Each society, or subgroup of a society, has its own rules regarding which body modifications or supplements should declare gender roles; to our knowledge, all make their declarations. A ribbon, but a tiny attachment tied to a wisp of a baby's hair, can announce a gendered identity as feminine. Similarly, within a specific cultural group a short haircut can be a body modification that invests a baby with a masculine identity. The examples given indicate that either a specific supplement or a specific body modification may be a significant symbol that elicits gender expectations and an anticipation that through time children will learn to direct their own acts of dress according to gender expectations. Age, therefore, is closely allied to gender in social expectations for type of dress. Furthermore, language is a strong ally in reinforcing social rules for dress of "a boy," "a girl," "a man," "a woman." As they grow older and develop increasing physical and social independence, children learn by trial and error to manipulate their own dress according to rules for age and gender. They usually acquire these rules via direct advice from adults or older siblings, or by following role models of the same sex, such as admired friends or publicly acclaimed individuals. For the most part, societies are lenient with young learners. Even when rules for gender-distinct dress are strict, children are likely to have more leeway in dress than adults. Thus a young boy may wear only a shirt when both shirt and preshaped trousers are *de rigueur* for a man, or a young girl may wear trousers when a skirt is proper for a woman.

Acquiring knowledge about gender-appropriate dress for various social situations extends to learning rights and responsibilities to act "as one looks." Accordingly, gendered dress encourages each individual to internalize as gendered roles a complex set of social expectations for behavior. These roles, when linked with roles others, represent part of social structure. Since each person's rendering of any social role is unique, this social structuring is constantly recreated (in its details) at the same time that its general configuration may appear to remain constant.

Prescriptions for dress according to gender and age may become increasingly complex as individuals progress through various life stages and participate in multiple societal systems, such as the religious, economic, and political. In each of these systems, differences in forms of dress for females and males can define, support, and reinforce the relative power and influence of the sexes. When specific differences in color, structure, surface design, volume, or texture distinguish dress of males and females, differences in social rank and power can be made obvious. Thus the differential in power and rank of males and females that determines who shall sit on the left and who shall sit on the right of the aisle in church can be made palpably visible by even slight differences in dress.

In the late twentieth century, in areas where technology is highly developed and the economic system is supported by a largely white-collar society, the male white-collar worker's biological presence has been diminished by the shape and volume of his business suit that masks his body contours. By comparison, shape and volume (in proportion to body size) of females' business dress reveals body contours more than the dress of males. This example of females' dress contrasts with dress in some less technologically advanced areas of the world where adult females, often to comply with religious codes, shroud their bodies in veils. It also raises questions regarding the relation of dress and the integration of females into positions of power equal to those of males within the respective economic systems. In some societies an interesting similarity exists between the body veil as a concealing gender-specific wrap for a female, and the Western business suit of a male as a somewhat rigid, preshaped body veil. However, the former is sanctioned by the religious system; the latter by the economic system.

As we have discussed ways in which gendered dress may be incorporated into religious and economic systems, we have touched on the relationship of dress to gender and power. We now turn specifically to this relationship within institutionalized political systems. The most important political information that the dress of people within a political system can convey is the right of the wearer to make decisions on behalf of people within a particular governmental unit. And the most important aspect of this dress, particularly for police and military personnel, is that it commands instant recognition of the right of the wearer not only to make decisions but to use force to maintain social order or wage war. A uniform based on a gendered-enclosing, preshaped, trousered outfit for males is at present a global standard for police and military dress. When females have entered this traditional realm of males, they have generally accommodated to wearing a preshaped uniform while maintaining feminine distinctions in modifications of hair or facial skin color. The uniforms, because they cover bodies, downplay the sexual characteristics of the wearer, as do requirements for identical color, texture, and general shape and structure. Another example of political dress is the voluminous enclosing robe of a judge. Although the robe can be unisex, shoes, modifications of hair, and any cosmetics that complete the judge's dress are usually not.

Some types of political dress are neither body-hiding enclosures nor uniforms. Instead, they are small attached, inserted, hand-held, suspended, or rigid preshaped objects. They include badges, buttons, ribbons, rings, medallions, crowns, and staffs. Often these smaller objects take on rich political meanings because of their "rarity." Four stars on a general's epaulets, an array of ribbons on a veteran's military uniform, a mayor's ribbon-suspended medallion, a pope's tiara, and an emperor's jewelled crown all communicate meanings relative to specific rank and temporal power of the wearer. They are available to women only if a society allows women to take the political positions these objects announce. In some cases, a queen's crown may only proclaim her husband's power, not her own.

CONCLUSIONS

In this paper we have developed a perspective for use in analysis of dress and gender roles. This perspective includes a definition of dress and a classification system for types of dress. We have also explored how the definition and system can free our discussions of dress and gender from some of the old assumptions, such as the necessity to classify all dress as either clothing or ornament. A few scholars have utilized perspectives closely allied to ours in analyzing the cultural significance of dress. As examples, we refer to studies by Kroeber (1919), Kroeber and Richardson (1940), and Robinson (1976). Their work involved developing methods for measuring properties of dress and searching for ways to link historical fluctuations in properties of dress to fluctuations in other cultural phenomena. Kroeber and Richardson measured aspects of dress that can be readily interpreted as volume and proportion, and also as shape and structure, as these properties were exhibited in a historical sequence of women's fashionable and largely preshaped garments. Several decades later Robinson showed that measurement techniques similar to those used by Kroeber and Richardson could also be applied in studying a type of body modification, that is, trimmed beards. These studies suggest that scholars can classify and make judgments about a variety of types of dress and their properties without resorting to biased, ambiguous terms or getting bogged down with the vast global accumulation of nomenclature for specific units of dress.

With our topic, dress, accurately identified, we can proceed to formulations of questions concerning what choices from a seemingly open-ended universe of body modifications and supplements—and their properties—individuals and social groups make. Within a given cultural group, we can explore whether dress tends to have a narrow range of types to identify gender roles and direct behavior of males and females in gender-specific ways versus an elaborately detailed system of distinctions with alternate choices. We can consider whether body supplements, versus body modifications, prevail in establishing gender distinctions or whether some balance is maintained. We can also compare the influence of variables such as age, sex, and technology, and types of kinship, religious, economic, and political systems on gender distinctions, as well as the points of variability in dress that support these distinctions.

Another topic relevant to the United States since the late 1960s is the types of dress that can support equality in economic roles of men and women. In a kind of natural experiment, women working in white-collar jobs began to choose tailored business suits with a jacket similar to a man's suit jacket, worn with either trousers or skirt. Such dress was adopted by women maintaining ideologies from relatively conservative feminist to radical feminist. Somehow this ensemble stood, in the ideology of the time, as a claim for equal opportunity for women and men, particularly in the economic arena. As time went by, masculine properties in colors, texture, garment shape, and even the suit itself, gave way to more feminine-distinct features in dress, such as bright colors and surface designs in fabric. As a result, radical feminists felt betrayed (Lind and Roach-Higgins 1985; Strega 1985). However, what had occurred was easily predicted by anyone who gave serious thought to Bohannan's study of the Tiv reported in 1956. The suit as a political statement had yielded to fashion, just as among the Tiv men and women the old fashion in design and texture of scarification gave way to the new. Those who felt betrayed failed to accept or recognize that fashion (often mistakenly considered characteristic only of societies with complex technology) is a pervasive social phenomenon that may prevail over ideology, taking over a once politically potent symbol and drawing it into the fold of fashion. This takeover in no way rules out that dress functions as a powerful though often underestimated system of visual communication that expresses gender role, which is usually intertwined with age, kinship, occupational, and other social roles throughout a person's life. From womb to tomb, the body is a dressed body, and caretakers typically introduce the young to gender-differentiated dress and often dress the dead in gendered garb. Thus each human being enters and exits life in dress appropriate, for the sociocultural system into which he or she is born and from which he or she departs.

10

THE ANTISOCIAL SKIN:
Structure, resistance, and "modern primitive" adornment in the United States

Daniel Rosenblatt

MODERN PRIMITIVES: An anthropological inquiry into a contemporary social enigma—the increasingly popular revival of ancient human decoration practices such as symbolic/deeply personal tattooing, multiple piercings, and ritual scarification. "Primitive" actions which rupture conventional confines of behavior and aesthetics are objectively scrutinized. In the context of the death of global frontiers this volume charts the territory of the last remaining underdeveloped source of first-hand experience: *the human body.*
— Back cover copy, [Vale and Juno,] *Re/Search #12: Modern Primitives* [emphasis in original]

The epigraph above is drawn from a book of photographs and interviews that came out in San Francisco in 1989. The book presents the practices and opinions of people engaged in the decoration or modification of the body. The practices discussed include large-scale, often abstract ("primitive") tattooing, piercing and wearing jewelry in various parts of the body, and ritual or decorative scarification. Many of the people photographed or interviewed in the book are involved in one or more of the "alternative communities" that flourish in San Francisco (e.g., gay, lesbian, punk, S/M, or New Age), although some deny any such associations with a larger collectivity, asserting instead that they do these things as an expression of their "individuality" (Vale and Juno 1989).

As an anthropologist whose more canonical work deals with the politics of "cultural revival" in the contemporary Pacific, I find this book and the practices it describes intriguing. Looking at the book, it seems as though the whole history of Western speculation about other cultures has been tossed into a blender with more than a little New Age mysticism and some contemporary sexual radicalism thrown in besides. Indeed, I cannot avoid the sense that this is some sort of fun-house mirror image of the mobilizations of "tradition" that are such a striking feature of the contemporary Pacific.

However, despite the obvious differences between appeals to a generalized notion of an exotic primitive by people living in the heart of the industrialized world, and appeals to particular local traditions by those for whom the West is the exotic "other," it seems to me that a comparison of modern primitivism with "invented traditions" and "revivals of traditional culture" could be more than an ironic or decentering device. Indeed, my hope is that a study of the discourse surrounding primitivism taking place in the shadow, as it were, of anthropological discussions of culture movements can illuminate the ways in which, in each case, creative political practice and perduring structures of meaning render each other intelligible.

Of necessity, but also by intent and design, the analysis I undertake in this article is of a different kind than the one I am in the process of conducting on the Maori Renaissance in New Zealand (Rosenblatt 1996). Most fundamentally this is because this article is based on a limited number of textual sources (mostly the interviews in *Modern Primitives* supplemented by some

Adapted from Daniel Rosenblatt, "The Antisocial Skin: Structure, Resistance, and "Modern Primitive" Adornment in the United States," *Cultural Anthropology* 12, no. 3 (1997): 287–334.

secondary materials) and a limited personal familiarity with the community, rather than on formal fieldwork. I lived in San Francisco during the early and mid-1980s, when modern primitivism began to emerge, and I was a part of one of the "alternative communities" that gave birth to it. I knew people who engaged in body modification and I found it intriguing, perhaps attractive, although I have not myself participated in it. While that familiarity with the community is probably a precondition for my being able to read the interview texts in the way that I have in what follows, and certainly is why I thought to try, I would definitely not want to claim that familiarity with a community is equivalent to, or a substitute for, research (see Gullestad 1990). Rather, the authority of the interpretations in this essay must rest not on the *mana* derived from an immersion in an exotic community (Clifford 1988a) but rather on the richness of the interviews in *Modern Primitives*, and on the suitability of those interviews as data for the kind of analysis I am attempting—which I should therefore try to specify.

My aims in this article are twofold: first, to illuminate the activities of US modern primitives by placing them in their cultural and historical context and, second, to use this example to make a general argument about resistance movements and their relation to existing social and cultural structures. In analyzing modern primitives I show how they mobilize both basic Western understandings of the world as embodied in cosmogonic mythology and classical economic theory (Sahlins 1996) and more immediate and historically particular American ideas about selves, society, and experience (Cannon 1989; Fox and Lears 1983; Lears 1983; McCracken 1988). In the process, I deploy a conception of cultural systems that understands them less as determinants of social activity and more as providing a framework for such activity—that is, as constituting the possibility of meaning. It is these "conditions of meaningfulness" that I seek to explore for the practices represented in *Modern Primitives*.

SKIN SHOWS: THE TATTOO RENAISSANCE

In the last 20 or 30 years, tattooing in the United States has undergone a renaissance that has transformed the activity. For a long time, tattoos were disreputable marks, stigmatized as something only marginal, lower-class people would acquire. They were the province of sailors, bikers, carnival freaks, and so on. Cliff Raven, a pioneer of the new style of tattooing, describes his clientele at the Chicago Tattoo Company during his early years in the business as "ordinary people—Mexican factory workers, Polish gas station attendants, 99.9% male" (quoted in A. Rubin 1988b: 237). Most of the work was "flash" off the walls of the tattoo shop: standardized designs printed on large sheets of paper, which were purchased by the artist and hung around the shop. From what was displayed, the client could choose a Walt Disney character, a representation of the Rock of Ages, a service insignia, or some other design. While some clients had a number of tattoos, rarely was there any sort of large-scale integrated design work.

The changes in tattooing began in the 1960s and accelerated during the 1980s and 1990s. They affected both the kinds of people who got tattooed and the kinds of designs that were being done. Most artists seem to agree that the impetus for these changes came from two places: the hippie movement and the growing awareness of Japanese-style full body tattoos among artists in the West (A. Rubin 1988b; Vale and Juno 1989: 114; Wroblewski 1989). My own experience would suggest that in the 1980s, the punk movement also drew different kinds of people to tattoos and influenced the designs that were prevalent.

Lyle Tuttle in San Francisco was the first tattoo artist to become a celebrity of sorts. During the 1960s, he tattooed Janis Joplin, Peter Fonda, and Joan Baez, triggering a minor fad in tattooing among the middle class (Vale and Juno 1989: 14). This was one of the first instances of tattoos becoming publicly acceptable in the United States outside a marginal milieu. At the same time, tattoo practitioners were coming to take their craft more seriously as an art, and drew upon its high status in other cultures, particularly Japan, to argue against the seedy image it had in the United States. It seems likely that tattoos' popularity among 1960s countercultural sorts helped to precipitate this turn to the "East" among tattoo artists.

Tattooing and the "other"

One of the first to bring Japanese designs to the United States was Sailor Jerry Collins, an artist working in Hawaii. His work and the Japanese style seem to have inspired a number of the most prominent artists working today. Vyvyn Lazonga, an artist who got her training in an old-fashioned street shop in Seattle, recalls the impact Japanese designs had on her:

I think my original, primal inspiration was this photograph of an Oriental woman with long black hair who had a dragon tattooed around her body, starting with her ankle and wrapping up around— it was the most gorgeous thing I had ever seen. Visually I was drawn to this tattoo because it wasn't a mishmash of little designs; it was large, graphic, unified, and done on a beautiful woman. This really inspired me and I began to think of all the beautiful things that could be done. (quoted in Vale and Juno 1989: 124)

Similarly, Don Ed Hardy, recognized as one of the foremost artists in the United States today, emphasizes the respect given to tattoos in Japan as part of what drew him to study Japanese work:

I kept studying Japanese art and practicing the Japanese style of tattooing which to me was like the pinnacle; it seemed to be the only viable form of high art tattooing in the world at that time. And through Jerry's introduction I began corresponding with a Japanese tattoo artist. (quoted in Vale and Juno 1989: 64)

Another source of new designs and inspiration for US tattooists was the "tribal" tattooing of Polynesia, Micronesia, Melanesia, and Borneo. In the 1960s, Lyle Tuttle went to Samoa to get a tattoo because "every Samoan I'd met—man, woman or child—was enthralled with tattooing." Tuttle has a "full body suit" (i.e., his entire body is covered with tattoos, except for his hands, feet, and face) and notes with pleasure that the Samoans "loved his tattoos" and "treated him like royalty." He was given a chief's name and a *kava* ceremony, which he admits he "didn't really understand"

(quoted in Vale and Juno 1989: 116–17). The experience of being in a place where tattoos are a respected part of the cultural mainstream rather than the mark of marginalized outsiders seems to be an emotionally moving one for US tattoo artists. That experience, or stories of it passed on through the tattoo community in the United States, may be part of why "primitives" have come to seem a source of succor and inspiration for alienated Westerners. Those who have, through tattoos, entered into relationships with supposed primitives find their experiences to be emblematic of the existence of a kind of transcendent humanity that is central to any valorization of the primitive as a source of alternatives to mainstream Western culture. Dan Thome, a former merchant seaman, settled for a time in Micronesia and learned to tattoo using traditional hand techniques. He now sees part of his mission as helping people preserve their techniques and designs. In addition to traveling around the islands tattooing people in exchange for fish, sleeping mats, lava-lavas, and fruit, he is attempting to record the remaining "authentic" tattoos on older people. Thome feels that it is very difficult for a foreigner in Micronesia—there are "a million 'little' mistakes you can make" (quoted in Vale and Juno 1989: 134). But through his tattooing practice and having tattoos, he feels he has found a way to connect with Micronesians:

What I like about tattooing is: it seems to really transcend those cultural and linguistic barriers, especially with the old folks. They see this work; they know it's not exactly the same as theirs, but they know what a person went through to get it. They know this person is not a dabbler. They know this person is not just coming in with a camera and a tape recorder to take something from them. And being tattooed—that's fine, but if you're tattooing, that's even more because suddenly you assume something like a traditional role in the community. And some of these Islands are in fact Stone Age cultures to this day—well, maybe they use a steel adz to chop out their canoes, but … (quoted in Vale and Juno 1989: 134)

It is worth noting that the marginal status of tattooing in the West in fact contributes to its ability to establish such connections between disaffected Westerners and the victims of colonial expansion. Because tattooing was frowned upon and suppressed by missionaries and colonial officials, someone like Thome was able to escape to some extent the categories of people and relations established by the colonial situation. The difference established in the eyes of Micronesians by Thome's tattoos in turn helps establish tattoo's potency as a symbol for Westerners of "something human" that resists a monolithic Western "system" that is seen as responsible for both colonialism abroad and cultural conformity at home.

The links that have been constructed between tattoo in the United States and elsewhere have contributed much more to American tattooing than novel designs and increased respectability. As a result of these links, tattoo (and body decoration in general) came to be seen as something with a long history: an ancient and thus essentially human practice.

The identification of Western tattooing with tattooing as practiced in other cultures is part of what allows US artists to see tattooing as a spiritual activity. In some cases, this is because they believe that the designs had sacred or hidden meanings in their original contexts, but more general associations of the exotic, the ancient, and the irrational come into play as well. For example, because tattooing is ancient and widespread it is seen as an expression of a basic human need for rituals that give life meaning. Therefore, when someone in the United States today gets a tattoo, the act "connects them to the rest of humanity" (Don Ed Hardy, quoted in Vale and Juno 1989: 53) because they are participating in a spiritual quest in common with people from all of the other cultures that practice tattooing.

It is a commonplace within the modern primitive community that the Judeo-Christian tradition frowns on tattoos. This contributes to the ability of tattoos to signify an identification with non-Western or at least alternative ways of thinking. For example, that one cannot be buried in an Orthodox Jewish cemetery with a tattoo is one of those emblematic snippets of information that everyone seems to know. That tattoos are seen in the Judeo-Christian tradition as a defilement of the body is, for Vale, itself a reason to be pleased at their current popularity:

> Tattooing and piercing are basically forbidden by the Bible in the book of Leviticus, and most of the world is ruled by Biblical religious beliefs—even Africa now. I want to encourage anything that's a statement against Christianity, because over the last 500 years Christian missionaries systematically destroyed virtually all of the world's diverse cultures, making the world a *much* less interesting place. (quoted in Vale and Juno 1989: 95, emphasis in original)

Yet the current interest in tattoos is not *just* based on their ability to represent and effect an act of identification with other cultures. The associations that tattoos have in the West with bikers, carnival sideshows, sailors, and working-class men remain part of their meaning for many people. This distinguishes body modification from other New Age valorizations of "primitive cultures" that are seen by many modern primitives as more "middle-class." Chris Wroblewski, a photographer who has published a number of books on tattoos, argues that tattoo has recently been accepted as an art form because of the Japanese and "primitive" influence, but that its shady background in the West gives it a kind of credibility that is lacking in other art. The previous disreputability of tattoo is what allows it to be an enactment of resistance to the cultural mainstream:

> Certainly the street legacy of tattooing lingers on in the public's imagination, but it could be argued, however, that it is precisely this background—the street—that has prevented tattooing from becoming consumed by the establishment, culturally dry-cleaned, and then regurgitated as effortlessly as canned drinks or washing powder. (Wroblewski 1989: 11)

Vale's comment that Western colonial expansion has left the world a "less interesting" place captures one theme running through common critiques of modernity: namely, that the net effect of modernization is to homogenize daily life. Here in the United States this is often connected to a nostalgia for such Americana as freak shows, sword swallowers, and all-night diners. These things become emblems of an earlier, less homogenized social order, and of an authentic folk culture at odds with conventional middle-class values and threatened with disappearance. While the tattoo renaissance—in part because of the way it draws on overseas sources—is a separate phenomenon from the fascination with a homegrown bizarre, that fascination is mobilized by the current interest in tattoos.

The theme of homogenization appears in the work of more academically-minded cultural critics as well, including Herbert Marcuse and the French Situationists. The same conception of society lies behind the academic distinction between "popular" and "mass" culture, in which the former is seen as a site of possible resistance to the homogeneity produced by the latter. Both the use of tattoos to resist incorporation into the mainstream and the popular and academic interest in the "folk" and the "bizarre" reflect compelling native (i.e., Western) conceptions of capitalism that model modern society on the factory: the end product of socialization is taken to be identical human beings and what differences exist are the result of resistance in the human material being worked. In this context, human and cultural oddities become signs that some sort of "escape" from the culture into a more "authentic" life is possible.

Tattooing and the self

Tattooing is both a public and a private act. When people talk about their tattoos, about getting tattoos, and about living with tattoos, they move back and forth between what it means to them and the reactions other people have to their being tattooed. Overwhelmingly, tattoos are seen as representing or expressing some aspect of the self. The duality in the way people understand and talk about tattoos reflects a similar duality in our notion of the self—on the one hand, it is something private, asocial, and individual, and on the other hand it is something public, a matter of other people's perceptions, and of a place in a collectivity. As expressed in the way people talk about their tattoos, these two aspects of the self are sometimes felt as contradictory, and at other times as complementary. Indeed, one of the things tattoos seem to be "about" is reconciling and expressing these different aspects of the self.

One of the biggest differences between the "new" tattooing associated with modern primitives and the more traditional tattooing of sailors and bikers is the current emphasis on one's tattoo being "personal." As I noted in discussing the origins of the tattoo renaissance, until the 1960s most tattooing in this country involved someone walking into a shop without an appointment, selecting something from what was displayed on the wall, and having it applied on the spot. While this still happens (Sanders 1988), many tattoos now arise out of a collaborative creative effort between the artist and the client. Don Ed Hardy (interviewed in Vale and Juno 1989: 50–67) emphasizes the need for a "fit" between the client and the tattoo. Ideally, for Hardy, the tattoo should represent something essential about the client, something that may have been repressed by society. While most tattoo artists still have books of preprinted designs, these designs are now seen as examples of what can be done, rather than as templates for particular tattoos, according to Hardy.

In contrasting traditional off-the-wall tattooing with modern primitive custom work, it would be a mistake to assume that only the latter is about expressing identity. The difference is rather that custom work invokes a different set of assumptions and ideas *about* identity. It is common, indeed characteristic, for people in our society to construct an identity by the selection of mass-produced goods (McCracken 1988); the Marine who gets a tattoo related to his branch of the service and the biker who gets a skull with wings are engaging in such an activity. By contrast, the emphasis on custom work and on the collaborative process between artist and recipient in modern primitive tattooing reflects a widely held notion that such an identity can only be an approximation of "the self," which is thought of as preexisting any standardized social identities. Vyvyn Lazonga, who now does custom work, got a skull with batwings from an artist of the "old school" as her first tattoo. She later had it covered, and explains:

At first I was really proud of it; I'd go places and show it to people, but ultimately the imagery was too intense—I couldn't live with it …. They didn't really have any choices back then. And I wasn't really a killer woman or a biker mama—I lived with the design for a little while, but I quickly discovered its limitations, and I didn't like being limited that way. (quoted in Vale and Juno 1989: 125)

Hence, while tattoos in general are about marking identity, the tattoo renaissance has fostered an emphasis on more private and subjective aspects of identity—on the use of tattoos to represent those aspects of the self that resist the categories of society.

For some, the exploration of self involved in getting a tattoo is combined with participation in New Age explorations of non-Western healing techniques and forms of knowledge. Vyvyn Lazonga reports giving one of her clients a tattoo consisting of stripes across her back and arms to represent a cat, the client's animal totem spirit (Vale and Juno 1989: 126). Before her untimely death in July of 1983, Jamie Summers, a student of Don Ed Hardy, was perhaps the foremost practitioner of this approach to tattooing. She saw her art as centered on the development of intuition in shamanistic terms. Working with Helen Palmer, a psychic from Berkeley, she developed designs through an extended series of consultations with her clients. The idea behind this process was that designs should emerge from "interior sources" in the client rather than from the artist or through a conscious intellectual decision (Don Ed Hardy, interviewed in Vale and Juno 1989: 61; A. Rubin 1988b: 256–58). Even when tattoos are not so explicitly linked to mysticism, they are more than mere decoration: they are a transformation of the body and therefore of the self.

In general then, tattoos are often used to represent and objectify some private, intuitive, and affective self, which is conceived of as being opposed to a public, rational self. While such a self is thought of as having an existence prior to the tattoo, the tattoo can be part of the process of getting in touch with that self, and the act of marking the skin seems to be an act of claiming or reclaiming the self. Don Ed Hardy speculates that tattoos are popular in prison because no one can take away your skin; tattoos, he says, are "one of the only expressions of freedom there" (quoted in Vale and Juno 1989: 51). Many people emphasize the power of such acts of reclamation.

In one sense, tattoos *are* very like "fashion," at least fashion in the subcultural, "street" sense of the term: they are an outward sign of who one is and a visual marking of difference from people at large. Yet tattoos differ from clothing in a number of respects. Being *on* the skin, not over it, they are closer to the "real person": one can play with fashion, adopt different identities at different times, but tattoos are always there. Because they are on the skin, there is an erotic element to tattoos: they remain when you have removed your clothes. This is an eroticism which contrasts with that of clothes. Clothes are about attraction, employing a play of revelation and concealment, whereas tattoos are about a self that transcends the moment of unveiling. And there is an inevitable individuality to the process: even if getting a tattoo becomes fashionable (as it certainly has recently), the choice of a design is always an act of self-definition.

The permanence of a tattoo, and its perceived connection to some inner self, lend a kind of authenticity to tattooing and give people a sense that in getting a tattoo they have done something real about their relationship to the world.

In sum, individuals seek to express and reclaim themselves through the act of getting a tattoo; the design of the tattoo should ideally reflect some aspect of the self that is otherwise without public expression or is repressed by our society. This can involve the appropriation of designs from other cultures that are seen as more in touch with certain aspects of human nature than our own; the tattoo in this context may be part of a larger exploration of ways of knowing and being in the world that our society has lost in its preoccupation with material goods, instrumental knowledge, and rational self-control. The ability of tattoos to carry such symbolic weight derives from the fact that they permanently alter the body, which is seen as the locus of a self that resists or precedes the individual as a member of society. Yet the growing popularity of tattoos as an index of dissatisfaction with society at large does not mean that there are not certain continuities between the way in which people employ tattoos and activities more accepted by the mainstream. On the one hand, people use tattoos to express and alleviate dissatisfaction with the sorts of roles offered them within the mainstream. They mark their bodies so as to claim for themselves a kind of final refuge against oppressive social conditioning. On the other hand, in seeking to improve their lives through development of their selves, they participate in a general cultural preoccupation that finds more conventional expression in things like assertiveness training and the self-improvement manuals of Dale Carnegie. In particular, the popularity of tattoos has paralleled a general cultural preoccupation with the body that has led to widespread obsessions with diet, exercise, and plastic surgery. Further, tattoos are able to carry the symbolic weight they do only because by modifying the skin they become a culturally recognized vehicle for talking about the self. It is because they are "ancient" and emblematically human rather than a peculiarity of our own culture and because they involve a permanent commitment that tattoos are able to be differentiated from these other phenomena.

PIERCING AND SCARIFICATION: DECORATION, S/M, AND ECSTATIC EXPERIENCES

Just as people who would once never have worn a tattoo are now doing so, so too parts of the body that would once never have sported jewelry are now bearing rings. Not only are multiple ear piercings commonplace for both sexes, but piercings of the nose, lips, tongue, eyebrow, and navel are no longer particularly strange on college campuses and in hip urban neighborhoods. Piercings of sexual organs—nipples and genitals—may not be as common (and, of course, their popularity is more difficult to gauge), but they are certainly not unheard of, which is itself a change from 20 years ago. Less widespread, but also not extraordinary, is the practice of cutting the skin in such a way as to leave a permanent scar. Cutting and piercing have roots in both the S/M and punk communities, but they have recently been linked in people's minds with tattooing under the general rubric of body modification and, like tattooing, are often seen as part of a revival of primitive, or non-Western, practices. According to Jim Ward, piercer, publisher of *Piercing Fans International Quarterly*, and founder of Gauntlet (a store that makes

and sells piercing jewelry), while piercing of publicly visible parts of the body is done for primarily for aesthetic reasons, nipple and genital piercing is usually done to enhance the experience of sex or for the sake of the experience of being pierced (interviewed in Vale and Juno 1989: 161). Similarly, scarification is about the act of being cut as well as about the resulting scar (Raelyn Gallina, quoted in Vale and Juno 1989: 104–05). Despite these differences, piercing and scarification, like tattooing, involve acting on the body as a way of presenting, constructing, and knowing the self. In addition, like tattooing, piercing and scarification are figured as practices with a long history that offer access to non-Western and premodern ways of living. In what follows, I want to both examine what people seek in the experience of being cut or pierced and explore the connections between the search for extreme experiences and the embrace of the primitive.

People I talked to made a distinction between "decorative piercings"—such as nose rings, multiple earrings, navel, eyebrow, lip, and tongue piercings—that are normally visible, and nipple and genital piercings, which are normally hidden. No one (as far as I know) has made the sorts of claims to being "beyond fashion" for decorative piercings that have been made for tattoos, nipple and genital piercing, and scarification. Yet in some respects, nose rings and the like clearly do belong in the same class of things as the other sorts of body modifications I have been discussing: their popularity has grown at the same time, people move easily in conversation from one to the other and refer in general to "piercings," and many people combine these practices.

Moreover, like the other practices, decorative piercing of the body is associated in people's minds with primitive or exotic peoples. When asked why he got pierced, Greg Kulz recalls having seen *National Geographic* when he was growing up and having read in a book on Papua New Guinea that people there wore cow bones and pieces of grass through their noses to keep away evil spirits. Not liking evil spirits "too much," he got a nose ring (quoted in Vale and Juno 1989: 155). Even when lacking such specific referents in another society, jewelry attached to the body in other than the usual places conveys some sort of impression of wildness or the exotic to both wearers and onlookers—indeed, several centuries of imagery focusing on lip plugs, neck rings, and other "oddities" reinforce the association and testify to the fascination that the West has had with what other people do to their bodies.

Most important, decorative piercings—along with tattooing, scarification, and other sorts of piercings—mark difference by acting on the body. Many tattoos are invisible on the street, as are (in most situations) nipple and genital piercings. Because they are associated with these other practices, decorative piercings can index the possibility of unseen body modifications or, more generally, a commitment to using the body as a tool for exploring the exotic.

The association between nipple and genital piercing and either "primitive peoples" or social criticism is less obvious, but seems almost as strong. Nipple and genital piercing in the United States originated in the (mostly gay male) leather or S/M community, and while nipple piercings have become fairly common among people with only peripheral connections to that community, genital piercing is probably confined to people who also practice hard-core S/M. According to Jim Ward, "Ninety percent of modern people do genital piercings to enhance their enjoyment of sex" (quoted in Vale and Juno 1989: 161). Genital piercing is only a small part of S/M, and much S/M makes no explicit claims to have anything to do with reviving particular "primitive" practices. Yet the oppositional claims made by proponents of piercing and its connection to the primitive, take place within a larger discourse about self, sexuality, and Western culture that is common to much of the S/M community. An identification of the essential self with a liberated sexuality informs much S/M practice and the meaning of piercing must be understood in this context, although it is not exhausted by it.

Many people interviewed in *Modern Primitives* see the non-Western world as a place where the sort of explorations they are engaging in would not lead to the kind of ostracism that occurs in our society. Genesis P-Orridge, a musician, performance artist, and devotee of piercing and primitivism, sees primitive societies as actually sophisticated in that they "integrate different aspects of life and psychology" and do not reject the

mentally ill but accept their differences as divine gifts. Similarly, P-Orridge sees primitives as more open to sexuality than are people in the West:

> I think that in tribal situations, even though they do ultimately develop sexual rules and regulations, they've also experimented with far more variety and are prepared to accept initiation rites, and what we would consider to be taboo activities. They see tattoos, markings, piercings as being a natural, on-going part of one's life. (quoted in Vale and Juno 1989: 178)

In general, practitioners of S/M interviewed in *Modern Primitives* and *Urban Aboriginals* (Mains 1984) feel they are exploring basic human urges, associated loosely with either our "animal" or "primitive" nature (Mains 1984: 81). Many people talk about S/M as a source of relief from the alienation they feel in their everyday lives. One of the leathermen interviewed by Mains gave up a well-paying executive position in Boston to move to the West Coast to be a full-time slave (1984: 70–71). Another, an executive at an insurance company, recalls his amusement at having flashbacks to whipping scenes during business meetings. He feels that his leather life is full of real human emotion and finds that recalling it helps him when he is "outnumbered by those people" (Mains 1984: 38).

For many leathermen, an immersion in sexuality is what makes the more conventional aspects of their lives bearable; for others, pursuing sexual pleasure is an opting out of "society"—understood as the world of work and competitive status-seeking. Sheree Rose suggests that society is not set up to accommodate this sort of activity "because it requires a lot of time and energy away from society." Rose continues, "It's not that you don't want to work, but: your career and getting ahead in the world is no longer your Number One concern" (quoted in Vale and Juno 1989: 113). Many speak of S/M or piercing as a way of knowing they are alive. Genesis P-Orridge takes the argument a step further: material possessions are compensation for lack of the sort of expression provided by traditional rituals and practices and by modern explorations of the primitive. We only find these things satisfying due to our "cultural conditioning" (Vale and Juno 1989: 178–80).

In sum, many participants in S/M see in it a possibility for the expression of individual human desire and thus the realization of individual potential. Yet although it is the self that is explicitly at issue for these people, its expression is marked by the construction of a difference from others: those who work, those who do not experience the real emotional contact achieved through administering and receiving pain, those who are satisfied by flashy cars and other signs of status and achievement—those, in short, whose inner selves correspond to society's expectations of normal behavior. At the base of this is a notion that "society" as an abstraction is antithetical to the fulfillment of individual desire.

It is ironic then that Christianity is the defining feature of "the West" for so many involved in modern primitive practices, since in its overall structure this conception of the oppositional relation between society and the individual is a fundamentally Christian one. For example, St. Augustine, whose writings shaped Christian doctrine, argued that the justification of earthly political institutions was the constraint they put on man's sinful desires (City of God [(1467) 1984]: 19.14–16). In the thinking of modern primitives, the conception of the relationship between individual and society is much the same, except that desire is not seen as sinful but rather as a route to salvation of some sort. As in Augustine, sexuality is the model for all human desire (City of God [(1467) 1984]: 14.15).

The association of sexuality and selfhood in the S/M community, and the common opposition to society, is at once an expression of deeply rooted cultural themes and the product of a particular historical situation. There are compelling reasons why this particular Western understanding of self and society should be meaningful to a community that grew in the wake of the gay liberation movement at the end of the 1960s. Modeling themselves on the civil rights movement earlier in the decade, lesbians and gays constructed sexual preference as a kind of ethnic identity: sexuality was not a series of actions so much as a primordial attribute of the person. The political aim of the movement was to gain recognition and acceptance of gayness as an acceptable form of sexual behavior and personal expression. This political construction

of sexuality as self-expression gained power from the fact that it is mirrored in the experience of individual people who, in the act of surrendering to forbidden desire, discover themselves as "gay." They acquire an important part of their identity by participating in sexual acts and in coming to accept those acts as part of their selves. The overwhelming presence of the gay community within most alternative communities in San Francisco has surely contributed to the centrality of sexuality to people's understandings of the relationship between society and the individual in that city, and beyond.

As I have noted, nipple and genital piercings are distinct from other aspects of S/M in that they not only evoke some generalized notion of primitive peoples as less sexually repressed and thus more fully able to express themselves, but they also index the primitive through what is seen as the appropriation of particular practices. Much is made of the fact that penis piercings are practiced in other places. Sheree Rose notes that the *ampallang* (a piercing horizontally through the head of the penis, with a small ball protruding on either side) is recommended in the *Kama Sutra* (Vale and Juno 1989: 109); Doug Malloy, an eccentric millionaire whom Fakir Musafar describes as "the father of modern piercing" (quoted in Vale and Juno 1989: 24), notes that the ampallang is common throughout the areas surrounding the Indian Ocean and claims that it is sometimes demanded by women in Borneo as a condition for having sex with a man (Vale and Juno 1989: 25). Thus piercing is able to represent not only a generalized knowledge of the self obtained through participation in ecstatic experiences, but particular esoteric bodies of knowledge about sexuality and human capacity that have been garnered over the course of thousands of years of experimentation by cultures with a more sophisticated knowledge of these areas of human existence than our own.

There is a process of projection involved in invoking the primitive as a model for sexual experimentation— these practices are being given a sexual content or at least a kind of sexual content that they do not have in their original contexts. This is clearly true in the assimilation of Native American rituals such as the ghost dance (which involves piercing the chest muscles) to S/M in the film *Bizarre Rituals: Dances Sacred and Profane*, in which Fakir Musafar and Jim Ward appear (Jury and Jury 1987). In that film, the assimilation does not involve specific comparison to practices current in the leather or S/M scene but does invoke a generalized notion that the aim of such practices is to transform pain into pleasure and that these practices reflect a broader understanding of what constitutes sexual activity than is current in this culture (Fakir Musafar, in Vale and Juno 1989: 13–15).

Much of what I have said about S/M in general and piercing in particular can be applied to scarification, or ritualized cutting. Cutting seems to be both decorative and sexualized. Robin Boutilier notes that having cut herself on the shoulder she noticed that the scar tissue had taken on a "pleasurable, sensual quality—I had acquired an unexpected new erogenous zone!" (quoted in Vale and Juno 1989: 182). Later, she added a series of raised welts on her right arm by cutting and then systematically removing the scabs to stimulate more regenerative tissue growth. Although she mentions the erotic quality the cut areas have taken on, Boutilier also speaks of them as adornment.

Cutting seems to be of particular appeal to women, and several practitioners report it to be most common among lesbians (Vale and Juno 1989: passim). Raelyn Gallina, a lesbian piercer and jeweler who works mainly with women, speaks of cutting as a reclaiming of the body. She generally does cuttings that are pictorial designs and often rubs ink into them to preserve the design. While this process resembles tattooing, Gallina emphasizes that the design derives its significance from serving as a reminder of the experience of being cut. Like other sorts of body modification, cutting is represented as an act of asserting the self:

A lot of times being cut—the act of being cut and surviving it—is a very strengthening and powerful experience for people. Especially for people who've been either in abusive situations or gone through a lot of "stuff" in their lives. To ask to be cut (not in a violent situation, but in a loving, supportive, trusting situation) and then bleed and then end up with something beautiful … and then it heals and you have it and you're proud of it—that can be very

empowering. It can be a *reclaiming* for a lot of people. (quoted in Vale and Juno 1989: 105, emphasis in original)

The act of reclaiming the body has a double meaning for women: it is seen as a response not only to the general Western denial of sexual pleasure as a spiritual activity, but to the particular denial of sexual pleasure as an appropriate activity for women to pursue and to the appropriation of women's bodies as objects of other people's desire by advertising media and the fashion industry. Although most of the people interviewed in *Modern Primitives* and most of the people I talked to emphasize that cutting and piercing are about a more inclusive definition of beauty, it seems highly likely that the popularity of scarring among women (especially lesbians) has *something* to do with its negative connotations within a more traditional view of what is appealing in a woman.

Cutting, as well as piercing, both permanent and "play," are spoken of as ritual activities. Often piercing takes place semipublicly. Sheree Rose had a nipple pierced in front of almost one hundred people one night at a meeting of the Society of Janus, an S/M club. "It felt," she says, "like a rite of passage. Like I'm brave enough to do this" (quoted in Vale and Juno 1989: 109). On another occasion she was invited to a meeting of the Pierced and Tattooed Club for gay men, through her friendship with Jim Ward:

Being the only woman in a room with 20 or 30 mostly nude, tattooed and pierced guys was quite an experience. They were really wonderful with me.

In the living room was a low table where Jim would do the piercing. Everyone would gather round and hold the subject's hand or foot, and when the piercing was over everyone smiled and laughed or clapped. I was scared to do it, but the feeling I got from being there with all these people around me was—I felt I was in some ancient ritual that had been reenacted many, many times. I got another nipple pierced. (quoted in Vale and Juno 1989: 109)

Noteworthy here is the characteristically individualistic understanding of the term *rite of passage*. Despite the fact that Rose is talking about a relatively formal event, she is not using the term to describe the passage from one socially recognized state to another by means of an accepted ritual act (or series of acts). Rather, in emphasizing the way she confronted and overcame her fear, she uses the term to link being pierced with acts such as climbing a mountain, or being in a war—other difficult or painful experiences that are commonly described by the term. In this usage (which we can think of as the Western folk meaning of the term), individuals confront themselves, learn about themselves, grow up, or something similar; whatever transformation they undergo is on the inside and may or may not be marked on the outside or recognized by others.

Indeed, the comparison of these practices to trials of endurance captures something essential about them. While the explicit emphasis in cutting, piercing, and S/M is on the exploration of the primitive and the surrender to sensuality and pleasure, there is a subtext of sacrifice and pain that I, at least, cannot ignore. While the spiritual content of these activities is based on invoking other traditions that supposedly do not deny the body in the way that our own do, they also index Western traditions in which enduring pain is a denial of the body in favor of the spirit. The primitive is commonly invoked in New Age movements that do not focus on modifying the body, and similarly, there are approaches to celebrating sexuality as self-discovery and subversion that involve neither pain nor the permanent modification of the body. Thus, the appeal of cutting and piercing must rest, at least in part, on their ability to combine a long-standing possibility of valorizing sexuality to oppose society with the mainstream notion that mortifying the flesh is a route to transcendence.

CONCLUSION

One of my goals in this article has been to explore the complexity of the relationships between the intentions of actors and systemically constructed meaning. The general argument takes the form of the claim that culturally salient notions of "the primitive," "society," and the "self" allow people to understand their actions on the body as forms of resistance to some totalizing entity often characterized as "the state," "the church," "the Judeo-Christian ethic," or "Western society." Within this general framework I have tried to (a) describe and explicate those notions, as manifested in the discourse of those who identify themselves as "modern primitives"; (b) suggest reasons why the "primitive" has been such a salient, fruitful, and perduring category for thinking about resistance since its origin; and (c) explore why particular features of this primitivism speak to people living in the United States today. The point has been not simply to show the ways in which people are at once enacting and resisting but to try to specify the system of meanings within which they do so: to engage, in other words, in cultural analysis. To that end, I have (a) argued that the possibility of using "the primitive" to criticize capitalism is built into a system in which "progress" is conceived as a consequence of the biblical fall from grace; (b) looked at the ways in which bodies come to be objectified tokens of the self which are amenable to ritual manipulation; (c) explored the ways in which Western notions of the self figure authentic selfhood as prior to and outside of society; and (d) suggested that the way these kinds of bodily manipulations become political acts can be understood in terms of the development of a therapeutic ethos based on the recovery of the self in response to the experience of consumer capitalism.

The effects of practices such as those employed by modern primitives are difficult to predict, or even to specify after the fact. The vehicles that seem to people to be appropriate as resistance because they are loci where power comes into consciousness as a regime are not necessarily places where an alteration will upset the balance of the larger system. Thus, while Foucault has shown us that the body is certainly a focus for the exercise of power that contributes to the maintenance of the status quo, it does not follow that resisting the exercise of such power will effect a broad change in existing social relations. A parallel can again be drawn with culture movements in the Pacific. While it is certainly the case that people's desire for Western goods made possible the cultural humiliation that presaged their entry into the world system, it is far from clear (indeed highly improbable) that their current valorization of their indigenous cultures can effect a substantial reduction in either their participation in a consumer economy or their dependence and embeddedness in the capitalist world system (see Keesing 1989; Sahlins [1988] 1994).

But culture movements may change their experience of living within that system (Buck 1993; Keesing 1992; Rosenblatt 1996). Similarly, movements like modern primitivism have the potential to alter the experience of living in our society for their participants. One possible effect is sociological: such movements create communities of opposition. In analyzing the particular practices associated with modern primitivism, I attempted to demonstrate that in spite of the individualistic ideology underlying the movement, its appeal rested in part on the ways in which the practices facilitated the creation of a community. And by constituting a community in terms different from those of the mainstream, resistance movements do change some aspects of the system. Furthermore, their ability to effect more fundamental changes may be as much a function of the ways in which they create community as of their specific content—after all, was not the essence of Marx's argument about the inherent contradiction in capitalism (stripped of any determinate view of historical progress) the claim that industrialization created a concentration of workers in the cities that offered the possibility of collective activity aimed at seizing control of the means of production from those responsible for such industrialization? But this may not be giving enough credit to the power of symbols.

Modern primitives seek to contest the meaning of desire; in doing so, they strike at something fundamental to modern society. The distinctive feature of modern capitalism (as a cultural system) is that it constitutes the basic human relationship to the material world as libidinous and offers temporary satiation in the form of the commodity. With the shift to consumer (as opposed to industrial) capitalism, desire becomes central to the functioning of the economy as well. If, for an earlier form of capitalism, it was necessary that people postpone the fulfillment of desire in order to engage in labor, and forgo consumption in favor of the accumulation of investment capital (Weber [1904–05] 1985), then

for today's economy they must instead surrender to the impulse to consume, preferably on credit and before they have actually achieved the means to do so (Baudrillard [1968] 1996; Lears 1983). Modern primitives posit a distinction between authentic and inauthentic forms of desire and enact that distinction in a culturally salient way by ritually invoking the idea of the primitive. The skin becomes a kind of battleground on which the self and society contest each other, and the decorated body becomes an indexical icon of the self's (possible) victory (Silverstein 1981; Tambiah 1985). By these practices, modern primitives may have found a way to recuperate the 1960s notion that desire is a force with the potential to undermine capitalism (e.g., Cohn-Bendit and Cohn-Bendit 1968). If so, they will have achieved this in the face of a widespread view of the failures of 1960s radical movements that argues that "the 'disruptive' element in desire … [is] not subversive of the capitalist economy but constitutive of its power" (Michaels 1987: 48, quoted in Jameson 1991: 202). In seeking to reconstitute desire as an antisocial, antimodern force, modern primitives attempt to harness for their own ends a force that the larger society encourages at every turn, and should they have any lasting effect on the larger society I suspect it will be because of this fact.

In closing, I must note an irony here: many "real primitives"—that is to say, people not of the West—who have had the (dubious?) privilege of participating in Western consumer society, may find our society alienating not because we stifle individual expression or suppress desire but because, not valuing our kith and kin, we are left *only* with individual expression. Certainly, for Maori (with whom I did my doctoral fieldwork), resistance to the "capitalist world system" is achieved not so much by manipulating the self as by building communities, and by finding roles for communal and tribal institutions in the modern world. When Maori get tattooed it generally expresses an identification with a group more than an exploration of the self; or if it is the latter, it is part of a more general "self-exploration" that involves gaining knowledge of genealogy, tribal stories, and sacred sites. But this is simply to reiterate one of the points of this article: namely, that primitivism is about "us," not "them."

11

STYLE AND ONTOLOGY

Daniel Miller

INTRODUCTION

The title of this paper is intended to offer a challenge to one of the most pervasive assumptions in contemporary cultural studies; that which is embedded in the term "superficial" and which implies that there is a relationship between surface and lack of importance. At the heart of Western philosophy lie a series of interrelated assumptions, embedded in metaphor, which greatly constrain our ability to comprehend major transformations in the modern world. The culprit is the pervasive ideology of what may be called "depth ontology" whereby we tend to assume that everything that is important for our sense of being lies in some deep interior and must be long-lasting and solid, as against the dangers of things we regard as ephemeral, shallow or lacking in content. These become highly problematic metaphors when we encounter a cosmology which may not share these assumptions, and rests upon a very different sense of ontology.

The importance of these metaphors lies not only in the narrow and sometimes parochial pursuit of philosophy but in the tendency of these ideas to be infused in more general, often moral, judgements on the world at large. Most recently we have seen a spate of criticisms of modern society as increasingly superficial, ephemeral and lacking in depth. Writers on post-modernism, in particular, talk of a loss of authenticity under the conditions of late-capitalism (e.g. Harvey 1989; Jameson 1991), which they identify with a new superficiality. Fashion is held up as a mechanism which accentuates all those elements of the modern condition, its fragmented, transient and superficial nature, which seem to result in almost a quantitative loss of being.

For the purposes of this paper, however, it is the particular application of these ideas to the world of clothing which is of concern. Fashion and style refer to a relatively ephemeral relationship with one's sartorial presentation and thereby invite the accusation that this relationship is also a trivial one. People who appear to devote considerable resources of time and money to this pursuit thereby demonstrate the triviality of their nature. This example of depth ontology is clearly bound up in ideologies of gender, since it is women, in particular, who are associated with such activities, and there are several well-known newspaper cartoon strips (e.g. Blondie, the Gambols) which have for decades used the image of the fashion conscious female to "illustrate" the superficiality of women more generally. In this paper I will, however, concentrate on an equally insidious form of prejudice which is directed again black people where an emphasis on style is again seen as a sign of lack of capacity for depth or seriousness.

It is not easy to confront assumptions which manage to unite abstract philosophy and mass circulation cartoon strips. An attempt to reverse both the assumptions and implications will be attempted in three stages. Firstly, a description will be given of the actual operation of style through ethnographic observations on the social relations of clothing in contemporary Trinidad. Secondly, I will discuss some

Adapted from Daniel Miller, "Style and Ontology," in *Consumption and Identity*, edited by Jonathan Friedman (Chur: Harwood Academic Publishers, 1994), pp. 71-96.

recent writings on the possible existence of a particular "black trope" which has been argued for in recent studies of language and literature, but which here is then re-applied to the case of clothing. Thirdly, it will be argued that underlying this perspective on style and the process of Signifyin(g) (Gates 1988), may lie an alternative approach to ontology which reverses the typical assumptions of the Western depth metaphor.

TRINIDAD

In Trinidad it is useful to distinguish between what might be called "style" and "fashion." One of the differences between these two is that style appears as a highly personalized and self-controlled expression of particular aesthetic ability, as opposed to fashion which is the dissolution of individual identity through appearance in a strictly conventional, if internally diverse, category of appearance. With style, however, there is the search for the particular combination of otherwise unassociated parts which can be combined to create the maximum effect. Here originality is a major criteria of success as is the fit to the wearer. Thus the bearing of the person, the way they move, walk, turn and act as though in natural unity with their clothes is vital to the success of the presentation. This distinction seems to be established in colloquial use, for example the fashion column of the *Trinidad and Tobago Review* (February 1991) states "Fashion is sameness. To be in fashion is to be wearing the similar designs, fabrics, colours, etc. that everyone is wearing. Style is an individual matter, it is one of personal choice, it is wearing what you look best in."

The distinctions are easier to view in men's clothing. In general men are much more resistant to the development of separate conventional clothing forms for major functions. At a wedding, the best man and closest relatives may appear in a suit though often with some flamboyant element such as an extravagant bow tie which distinguishes this from the merely conventional suit. Other men, however, wear clothing which is only slightly more formal than daily wear, appearing in well-creased, belted trousers and sports shirts (termed jerseys) and buttoned shirts. In general these would be similar to clothes worn for work. Some of these same men will however embrace a highly competitive sartorial display for occasions such as fêtes and house parties. Here the key elements are shoes such as designer trainers, jeans and a wide variety of hats. Out of this group a certain portion attempt to carry through such conspicuous dressing into their everyday appearance. Twenty years ago such males were termed *saga* boys, today there is no clear term but the word dude borrowed from the United States is perhaps the most common label. These males combine sartorial originality with ways of walking and talking that create a style which is generally regarded as never letting up from conspicuous display. The local term for such behaviour is "gallerying."

The notion of style as a personalized context for fashion items emerges more clearly through an examination of fashion shows. These shows are an ubiquitous feature of modern Trinidadian life, and are found at all income levels. The people of the Meadows might go to the show of a well known Port of Spain designer hosted by the Lions or Rotary club, or at a major hotel in the capital, but they also might meet people from St Pauls or Newtown at a fashion show hosted at one of the shopping malls, while fashion shows are also held for small fund raising ventures in Ford, and at many school or church bazaars. For wealthier audiences the models may perform as rather cold or austere mannequins, as such they are essentially vehicles for demonstrating expensive items for sale. This is however, the less common form of modelling and is reserved for the more exclusive designer shows. In most fashion shows and in all those held by low income groups, the clothes are displayed in a very different mode which emphasizes a unity between the form of dress and the physicality of the body which displays them. Movements are based on an exaggerated self-confidence and a strong eroticism, with striding, bouncy, or dance-like displays. In local parlance there should be something "hot" about the clothing and something "hot" about the performance. For fashion shows at bazaars, schools and in Ford or similar communities, the models are not professional but local people and the clothes are either purchases of, or made by, the wearer. At these local events there is no attempt to sell the clothing and the whole ethos of the show is outside the commercial arena. The origin of the clothing is often of no concern to the audience and nor is any intrinsic quality or monetary value. The clothing is really an adjunct to the performance itself, to the way the persons move on the stage, and the frame for the performance is established by the models being friends, relatives or schoolmates of the audience.

The concept of style which emerges from such shows comprises two main components; individualism and transience. The individualism emerges through a necessary fit between the clothes and the wearer. The person attempts to develop a sequence of sartorial forms which are seen as expressive of themselves and their character. The clothing is complemented here by a selection of belts, costume jewelry, shoes, a wide variety of hair forms and styles and skin tone. The aim is to construct a style which can be judged in the performance. Although they may refer to current general trends such as "ragamuffin" style or tie-dye, they are also idiosyncratic juxtapositions of elements in ways that make this wearer conspicuous and able as against the competition. The sartorial achievement is easily incorporated into a general sense of easy accomplishment at a variety of arts, ranging from music to witty speech.

The second element of style is its transience; the stylist may take from the major fashion shifts in Trinidad but only as the vanguard. Hand painted shirts are fine when they have yet to be acknowledged as the dominant fashion, but at that point the forms are given over to be incorporated into more conventional forms such as young teenage fashion while the stylist moves onto something new. Apart from the fête the key arena for such display is the workplace, especially for the female working in an office environment. Although the office party in particular is the occasion for tight fitting dresses with sequins and frills at the bottom and bare back and shoulders, the daily work-place is also an arena of intensive sartorial display and competition. Where there is a standard uniform as at a bank, small variations and alterations are still discernible that allow room for this element of transient display.

The link between clothing and transience is most forcefully expressed through Carnival for which, traditionally, individuals constructed elaborate and time consuming costumes which, even if identical forms were worn each year, had to be discarded and re-made annually. Seasonally relevant clothing may also be purchased for other events such as Christmas or commonly a new swimsuit for going to the beach during the long Easter weekend.

The source of the originality in a sense is irrelevant, it may be copied from the soap operas or the fashion shows which come on television, it may be sent from relatives abroad or purchased while abroad. The oil boom encouraged imported elements when "everybody and their tantie went to the big apple and returned with designer or imitation designer things," it may be simply recombinations of locally produced elements but it is, if possible, always new and vanguard and destined for a particular occasion. In practice only certain persons can achieve these ideals but others will attempt to follow as soon as possible and at any rate before their own peers.

Not every Trinidadian is stylish. Style exists simultaneously with a quite different orientation to clothing which expresses another side to Trinidadian life, one devoted to religion, to the family as a descent group and to the celebration of the home and the interior. Such clothing is closely associated with life-cycle events such as weddings or christenings and also religious events such as attendance at church or temple. Clothing for such occasions is marked by shiny surfaces (as opposed to the matt of informal attire); preferences may be for silver, gold, metallic greens, blues and reds, and shiny or slinky black, pearl and white. The covering-up aesthetic is continued into this arena with the considerable use of layering and ruching (gathering up in layered crescents) in dress and skirt patterns, always complemented by stockings and high-heeled shoes. Stockings appear to be one of the key emblems of a more formal dress, which carries over to work situations. Shoes also must be appropriate, the tendency being to wear closed-in forms for church and open toes for leisure. There are variants to this, for example, the dress code for elderly females and for young girls of East-Indian descent is based around white and pastel dresses with an abundance of frills, flounces, bows and lace effects. These forms are not shiny but equally are quite distinctive from the matt informal wear of most other groups. Young women would also vary the basic code by using similar fabrics but creating slinky low-cut or body-hugging dresses or striking combinations of, for example, black blouses and silver skirts complemented by highly conspicuous displays of elaborate costume jewellery.

Attendance at a few such life-cycle events reveals a striking degree of conventionality and repetition. It is as though nearly all the clothing is made from a few agreed elements of material and design. The use of shiny surfaces of ruching, slits and straps are simply recombined so that one works merely with the permutations of this highly restricted set. Indeed often the dresses themselves appear as patchworks of elements with a silver lozenge set within a pearly white layered bodice for example. Amongst the older generation, in particular, these are associated with wide-brimmed hats of similar shiny materials. The result may be new but not novel and is therefore still conventional. The players act competitively but within constrained and agreed parameters of display, such that again it seems reasonable to talk of a normative form.

The desire for new outfits may have very different consequences within the opposed frame of their appearance. Although the wedding epitomizes a normative sartorial style it is more accurate to broaden this into sections of the population who even at other events tend to wear clothes within the permutations of the selected range of elements, thus the newness of the event based item is countered by the ever-sameness of the collective apparel. The clothes do represent the individual wearer in competition, but only within highly restricted forms where to go beyond the convention would be to fail within the terms of the event. For the stylist, however, the appeal is precisely to the unprecedented (at least for them) nature of the event and the appearance. Fashions may be used but they are not sufficient for the purpose which must then be supplemented by the creative ability of the wearers. This should not be exaggerated, since most individuals also have particular items such as dresses which are especially comfortable for dancing or a hat by which they have become known and which establishes a more stable personalized repertoire.

For fashion, as opposed to style, the idea of newness is accepted as an expression of individual competition but in a manner which does not encourage genuine innovation. This is also reflected in the response to another kind of fashion, the new ideas for women's clothing which break like waves over the island's shores during the course of the year. Examples were exceptionally wide belts or belts with butterfly clasps, treated denim such as acid wash or individually painted T-shirts and dresses. Those who emphasize the normative are not vanguard in their acceptance of such fashions, but it seems that if the style reaches a kind of critical mass then virtually the entire community acknowledge it through purchasing at least one representative item, as indicated through a survey questionnaire. In a sense, by doing so, they suppress the threat of disconformity through the ubiquity of acceptance. They have turned the new into the conventional.

This is reflected in a dichotomy noticed by workers in market research. In their analysis of regional difference the central area and the south are seen by the major companies as areas of high brand loyalty, such that the name of a brand was usually synonymous with a product range, all toothpaste is.. etc. This was associated with general stability compared to the capital but when change came it came quickly and massively. The previous dominant brand was drastically reduced and a new brand emerges so that beer which was always brand A is now brand B, etc. The pattern seems closer to the cusp image of catastrophe theory than the more familiar lenticular curve of product diffusion.

There is a clear opposition between the stylist and the merely fashionable. As a means of characterizing traditional clothing norms in order to transcend them the two most common derogatory terms were *moksi* (pronounced mooksi) and *cosquel*. *Moksi* is a general term for things which look old fashioned and has related connotations of country based as against town or poverty based as against middle class. *Moksi* then is the unsophisticated backwoods look which has yet even to acknowledge its own demise or indicates the inability of the person to enter into competitive display. There is not surprisingly a resistance to such depreciation. Householders with a dominant maroon will affirm that maroon is bright in contrast to red. Bright, which is the term for modern, here refers back to the period when maroon did indeed replace red as the more up to date version of this color category.

The other pejorative term, *cosquel*, is a term for something overdone or juxtapositions which fail, it is a vulgarity that indicates an attempt to style but a failure of taste. The wrong colors have been placed against each other, or an effect has been overdone and thus its possibilities lost. There are also some more general taste parameters, for example, too exclusive a concern with matching colours shows wealth, in that this can be an expensive project but also a certain lack of taste, since as a retailers put it "some who would know better, will contrast." Terms of approval often use reverse slang, as the well dressed are flattered by being told that they are looking "sick," "bad" or "cork."

To conclude this description, the ethnography of clothing use suggests a clear tension or dualism, on one side of which lies that relationship with dress which we term style. Style is a transient aesthetic which favours individual originality in new combinations. It is orientated to the exterior and to display and is based around particular events. There is a considerable stress, not only on individualism but also competition and the refusal of normative order. There co-exists in Trinidad a relationship to clothing which by international and local canons tends to be denigrated as dowdy, vulgar and unappealing. Style is closely related to new forms of the arts and design, to Carnival and to steelband. Here, Trinidad is usually accredited with a highly developed aesthetic positively appraised by visitors and linked to the general articulation today between black diasporan populations and the sense of style, which is the larger context I now wish to address.

STYLE AS SIGNIFYIN(G)

The ethnographic evidence suggests that there is indeed a strong association between some Trinidadians and the sense of style, one which is as much accredited by those who practice style as by those outsiders who attest it. There are a number of ways we could attempt to account for this. One perspective would follow Fanon (1986) who was perhaps the most successful theorist in accounting for a wide range of attributes which were seen as essential qualities of "black" peoples during colonialism. Fanon tended to concentrate on the projection of attributes by whites which were then introjected by the black population as an expression of their relationship to the hegemonic group. For example, the attribute of sexuality as raw "nature" was objectified in this personification of otherness, but also introjected into an appropriated sexuality by black West-Indians, particularly in their sexual relationships with whites. It might be argued in an analogous fashion that style as superficiality was introduced as the "other" to the Western self-construction of itself as true Civilisation with roots in deep classical history. Thus black people could be seen as expressing something as immediate and close to the surface as style, because they lacked the historical and ontological depth, which made whites inept at style but profound. Fanon would probably have then argued that over time this situation would be transcended dialectically by a new self-conscious black identity which constructs style as critique.

A number of more recent studies have adopted an alternative view of the attributes ascribed to the black diasporan population and its subversive potential vis à vis colonial powers. In some cases the attribute is also credited with origins prior to slavery in West African traditions which were then refined or tempered by experiences in the diaspora. The most relevant version, in as much as it focuses on the question of a particular black style, is found in the book *The Signifying Monkey* by Gates (1988). Gates is mainly concerned with language, and the second half of his book is entirely devoted to black fiction in the United States. His concepts were, however, much influenced by a series of studies on the particular nature of black speech or black "talk," including the work of Labov and the ethnographic studies of Abrahams on black vernacular styles.

The core of Gates' argument is contained in chapters 2 and 3. Here he focuses on the concept of "to signify." In conventional semiotics this implies a symbolic relationship between a signifier and a signified, i.e. we signify about something. But for Gates there is a particular form, which he calls "Signifyin(g)," where it is more appropriate to think of Signifyin(g) upon something. Gates suggests that: "Signifyin(g) is a rhetorical practice that is not engaged in the game of information-giving, as Wittgenstein said of poetry. Signifyin(g) turns on the play and chain of signifyers, and not on some supposedly transcendent signified" (1988: 52). Gates argues that the relationship is an interpretive one which refers back to previous interpretations, rather than to any original signified. One of the best images comes from jazz. Music is an especially interesting media in as much as Langer (1942) pointed out that it does not usually symbolize in the conventional discursive sense, i.e. it does not generally signify something (although it can be made to do so). In jazz, music more clearly signifies upon, that is the musician not only takes up themes and develops them fugue-like but very often returns to pastiche or development of well known rhythms and tunes from previous compositions. In ordinary speech both musicians and others will refer to Signifyin(g) upon someone or something.

The primary concern is, however, with language. Here Gates follows the work of Abrahams on the ethnography of speaking

"'When a black person speaks of Signifyin(g), he or she means a style-focused message ... styling which is fore-grounded by the devices of making a point by indirection and wit' ... Signifyin(g), in other words, turns on the sheer play of the signifier. It does not refer primarily to the signified; rather it refers to the style of language, to that which transforms ordinary discourse into literature. Again, one does not 'Signify something; one Signifies in some way'" (Gates 1988: 78, quoting Abrahams 1976: 52).

The implication is quite similar to the observation overheard by the anthropologist Manning (1973: 62–63) during research in Bermuda, where the bartender at a club says "no conversation around here is boring until you stop and listen to it."

From chapter 3 onwards Gates concentrates on rhetorical forms such as parody and pastiche as used in literature in particular. The implication of this is to link the black trope with the advent of postmodernism since forms such as pastiche have been argued to be the key attributes of this era. For Gates, as in some accounts of postmodernism, there is a celebration of these forms as embodying resistance against hegemonic cultural dominance. Gates gives various examples of pastiche employed by black diasporan populations for subversive purposes. There is, however, a tension in this book between the more politicized aspects which tend to implicate a relationship between a manifest content and a hidden polemic, and the main argument which is directed precisely against any such relationship of depth and surface in order to develop the idea of Signifyin(g) working along a single plane.

The work of Gates is clearly an aid in the development of a model of style which directs attention to identity as constructed on the surface. But the problem with which this discussion commenced was the attitude which remains condemnatory of this cultivation of the surface, rather than spending time and money on what are usually regarded as proper values and deep concerns. To relate these two aspects of the problem we need not only to document the form of style but also to address the question as to why a particular population might be identified with it.

As a first step we can go back to Gates and the various arguments over the origins of this tendency. Gates provides one of the clearest arguments for a black diasporan trope with specific origins in West Africa. His first chapter is titled "A Myth of Origins: Esu-Elegbara and the Signifying Monkey." The origins of Signifyin(g) are traced to the position of certain Yoruba trickster figures within West African cosmological systems. I am unable to comment on the validity of this argument, but in so far as it is used to ground contemporary tendencies in postmodernism, in particular ethnic origins, there are clearly difficulties. Not the least of these would be the availability of alternative origin myths. For example, one would guess that twenty years ago when hermeneutics was more prominent in cultural studies, an argument could have been put forward that the Judaic tradition of textual interpretation and Talmudic discourse which was acknowledged as an influence in the emergence of the hermeneutic tradition was thereby the precursor to that element of circularity, that is the interpretations of interpretations, which are now used to link Signifyin(g) to postmodernism. Furthermore other interpretations of West African e.g. Yoruba art would stress quite different elements of "transmission" (e.g. Thompson 1983).

Gates does not, however, rely merely on the documentation of origins. There are, after all, many aspects of West African culture which clearly do not figure in the world of diasporan black populations. The second stage in any attempt to construct a linkage between these two would need to apply itself to the historical developments which took place during and after slavery. The most powerful argument of this form rests on the notion of surface as a defensive strategy against the condition of extreme degradation. Toni Morrison in her novel *Beloved* has a number of sections where she seems to implicate such a response: "so you protected yourself and loved small. Picked the tiniest stars out of the sky to own … Anything bigger wouldn't do. A woman, a child, a brother, a big love that would split you wide open in Alfred, Georgia" (1987: 162). The precarious existence given by the condition of slavery precluded any internalization of love, since there was no knowing when this love-object might be wrested from one. The result being a kind of adaptive tendency to keep things on the surface, to refuse any internalization and thus to minimize one's sense of loss.

Again I do not want to attempt to assess such an "explanation," but it may be useful to note again the limitations of too close an identification between ethnicity and any phenomena as general as style. Firstly the wider ethnography of Trinidad (Miller 1994) reveals that style is only an attribute of a section of even the ex-African element in the population. There are equally powerful and authentic expressions of the black community which eschew any such concerns and are devoted to quite different values orientated towards the project of internalization, creating a sense of stability, property, descent and religiosity. It would be quite wrong to, as it were, disenfranchise half the black community because they do not conform to an image of radical form which happens to appeal to a certain intellectual fraction. Their cultural orientation may be quite as authentic an expression of their historical experiences as style.

It may therefore be preferable to contextualize the arguments made about black style within the more general contention that within modernity is a struggle for the objectification of freedom within which this sense of transience and surface has a particular attraction. The contemporary relevance of style emerges then out of a continued relevance. It may be that there are precursors in particular regions, and it is certainly the case that the condition of slavery would have fostered an extreme concern with the expression of freedom, but it is the continued imperative to objectify forms of freedom which make this historical trajectory complete itself, as it were, within contemporary forms. For this reason, the authenticity of style derives not from whether one can claim descent from some particular origin, such as slavery (though for writers on postmodernism it is increasingly often "creolized" descent which is romanticized), but rather whether as consumers we appropriate the possibilities given by these histories for strategies of identity construction today. Certainly in contemporary Trinidad the sense of West Indian style may be as fully expressed by those of Chinese or East Indian origin as those of African origin.

ONTOLOGY

To account for the continued significance of style we can turn instead to the argument with which this paper started. I want to suggest that the metaphors used in colloquial discussions of "being," a reflection, in part, on philosophical discussions of ontology, are the context within which we formulate attitudes to style. It is not merely that ideas of depth and surface are applied in both cases but that they have consequences for each other. Indeed it is the taken for granted aspects of our language of being which make it so difficult for style to be properly appraised. We lack a relativist perspective on ontology, which would allow us to consider properly that construction of being which is radically different from the assumptions of Western philosophy and its associated colloquial discourses.

The concept of superficiality may well be responsible for the extreme difficulty writing about clothing as fashion with any profundity and overcoming the resistances established by our immediate sense of the trivial nature of this subject. Probably the most successful attempt to pronounce on some "core" to fashion was Simmel's (1957) essay on the subject which rests on the tension between individualism and sociality. In my ethnographic account of Trinidad this tension is clearly present but in a very different form. In Europe Simmel implies a simultaneity to these two imperatives, fashion operates to relate and reconcile them as well as to express this contradiction. In Trinidad, by contrast, the relationship to clothing splits into two. We have a highly normative form of fashion in which individuals are subsumed into convention, and we have opposed to that a highly individualistic and competitive sense of style.

Style, as a particular and separate mode, has its context in a wide range of other aspects of culture which again seem to take a feature identifiable as a tendency within Europe and extend it or clarify its logic as a form in Trinidad. If individualism is taken as an example of this difference, then its consequences in Trinidad may be explored. The form of individualism found in the Trinidadian stylist results in a cautious approach to the construction of relationships, avoiding the sense that they are maintained merely in order to fulfil normative obligations. Many of the features of "West Indian Kinship" may be understood as a desire to keep social relations within a voluntaristic framework, such that one chooses to have a close relationship with a sibling or cousin because one wants to and not merely because one is expected to do so by reason of birth. This provides much more fluidity and flexibility as to who actually performs the role of "mother," or "close" relative. This family is of tremendous consequence and just as "viable" as that form of bounded and constant family which local churches and educationalists have insisted Trinidadians ought to have adopted, but it is distinctly different.

Similarly the stylist may resist being defined by their type or place of work, or any similar institutionalised source of identity (Yelvington, forthcoming). Work is often relegated to a minor aspect of life, such that it is leisure which is considered to be the true and proper arena where real life takes place, while work is a mere interlude. This attitude does not prevent complex organizations being built up and sustained by people committed to these values. A steelband can form and persons put in many weeks of practice in order to give a performance of Bach, Wagner or calypso, but with a feeling that this is within their own control. It is a voluntary organization in competition with others and highly sensitive to any attempt to impose control or threaten the self-conscious voluntarism of the participants (see Mandle and Mandle 1988 for the comparable case of basketball in Trinidad).

Individualism then becomes part of the more general objectification of freedom, and the transience of style and its opposition to interiorization is found to be echoed in attitudes to social relations. One of the most common expressions heard in response to any misfortune, from a passing insult to the break up of a relationship, is "doh (don't) take it on." Littlewood (1985: 277–78) provides a clear instance of this in his analysis of a depressive condition known as *tabanca.* This is a kind of moping sickness, leading to solitary contemplation and even suicide, but as Littlewood notes it is also something of a standard joke. The reason for this is that *tabanca* represents a failing in the maintenance of those values which espouse transience. A man in his relationship with women is expected to retain his phlegmatic cool, relationships are something he can take or leave. If, however, he starts to become more deeply involved, if he allows this relationship to become internalized as something in which he has invested himself, then he stands in danger of considerable loss if the relationship should fail. When this woman leaves him or when she commits adultery his failure to keep the relationship on the surface becomes evident, and *tabanca* follows.

Perhaps the most popular leisure activity in Trinidad is the "lime" in which a group of people either hang around a street corner or travel in a group, for example, into the countryside to "make a cook." A feature of the lime is the genre of verbal insult which is known as "*picong*" or giving "*fatigue.*" One of the attributes of fatigue is to ensure full group participation in events. For example, on a river lime, the individual who did not strip down and bathe would leave themselves open to becoming the major recipient of the developing rounds of insults. The individual characteristics of the limer would then be picked upon, an older male might be asked "when you alive yet you could cook?" or about whether any remaining hair is really his. An inappropriate piece of clothing, an accident or mistake might be thrown back at the "guilty" party many times in a variety of forms with appellations such as "mother-cunt." Such *picong* almost always remains good-humoured, because the recipient knows that they are being judged by their ability not to take this on.

This often witty and always barbed invective between friends makes the lime a kind of training ground in which one is steeled against taking in the abuse which can be received in life. Most Trinidadians would certainly assert humour and wit as central to their self-definition and would see it as contributing to their sense of cool, and their ability not to take things on, as well as to their sense of style. The person without a sense of humour would be in danger of being seen as "ignorant" and prone to violence. Humour helps to keep things on the surface, it keeps conversations focused upon delivery and style rather than content and message, and in this sense is a good complement to clothing.

This context to style also effects the wider relations of consumption. These may be summarized by reference one of the most popular contemporary novels in Trinidad at *The Dragon Can't Dance* by Earl Lovelace (1981). This book focuses upon an impoverished community, but one closely associated with style and the creativity of steelband and Carnival. For the protagonists there are clear views as to the proper nature of consumption, and the value of transience over accumulation: "but nobody here look at things as if things is everything. If you had more money, you buy more food; and if is a holiday, you buy drinks for your friends, and everybody sit down and drink it out, and if tomorrow you ain't have none, you know everybody done had a good time" (1981: 103).

It is consumption, and most especially the purchase of clothing as reciprocity, which establishes relationships, especially across gender. Clothing is central to the project of externality but the novel stresses the complex relationship between person and surface evident in the metaphors of masking and masquerade. Clothing may become problematic as

when the calypsonian Philo embarrassed by success: "decorated himself in gaudy shirts and broad-brimmed hats with long colourful feathers stuck in them, as if he wanted to hide himself, to make himself appear so *cosquel* that any fool would know that he had to be found elsewhere, apart from the costume, within it" (1981: 155).

This concern with the relationship between the surface of the person and the mask is evoked by the title of the book (the Dragon is a form of masquerade) and by Carnival itself. This self is created by its displays "he wanted nothing but to live, to be, to be somebody for people to recognise, so when they see him they would say: 'that is Fisheye!' and give him his space" (1981: 59). The book ends in the tragic consequences of style as a medium for radical action, as the protagonist's political protest becomes a gesture of defiance but with no clear idea of how this should be followed up. Their failure implicates the contradictions of style as the construction of being:

> So many things we coulda do, and all we wanted was
> to attract attention! How come everything we do
> we have to be appealing to somebody else? Always
> somebody to tell us if this right or wrong, if it good or
> bad …. Is like we ain't have no self. I mean, we have
> a self but the self we have is for somebody else. Is like
> even when we acting we ain't the actor. (1981: 188)

Under such conditions the novel seems to argue a political revolt could be no more than playing masquerade as in Carnival. Indeed the history of radical politics in Trinidad from the 1970 Black Power revolts to the attempted coup by Black Muslims in 1990 seems to bear this out, in as much as both movements were closely articulated with the sense of style and both seemed to begin and end as political gestures.

This wider context to style provides for the bridge to questions of ontology. There is a consistency between this cultivation of the surface and the transient with the consistent refusal of interiorization or sedimentation or fixity derived from institutional or role given forms. This must have implication for identity and in turn for the sense of being. At first the concept of identity appear to be rendered quite empty. There is not social status or agreed position to give placement, or substance which is constant within. Instead being is created through a strategy of display and response. In going to a party or forming a relationship, the individual usually aims high, attempting the best style, the wittiest verbal agility and, if possible, the most prestigious partner. But one only finds out if this is the case from the response of the day, how people react to you and appraise you. It is each particular and assumed transient activity that tells one who one is. It is the event itself that gives judgement, that acts as a kind of reverse omen-taking which establishes also who one has been. However, this is only a specific event or relationship, there is no accretative value. Its implications hardly carry beyond the event itself, so that the position has to be recovered again on the next occasion. It is in this manner that an identity is constructed which is free, that is minimally subject to control. In this strategy style plays a vital role, since it is the ability to change which renders one specific to the event.

The concept of superficial is entirely inappropriate here. Certainly things are kept on the surface, and it is style rather than content which counts. This is because the surface is precisely where "being" is located. It is the European philosophical tradition and, in particular, the conservative philosophers such as Heidegger, for whom being and rootedness are effectively synonymous, that make it difficult to understand how the very possibilities of modernist speed and ephemera can become the vehicle for both viable and authentic existence.

The situation in Trinidad is complicated by the sheer force of those authorities within the island who would wish to retain the denigration of superficiality. The demands of style, the desire to keep things on the surface, and a preference for constant change may very easily become elided with a sense of the trivial and of mistaken prioritization in consumption. It should be noted that this critique comes not only from institutions of the establishment, such as the church and the education system, but is equally shared by the radical political movements who despair at the lack of commitment they associate with an orientation to style, an ambivalence evident in Lovelace's novel. There is then no single "Trinidadian," let alone "black diasporan," cultural form. I have attempted to abstract and normativize that approach associated with "style" but this is constantly opposed even within the communities associated with particular abilities or affinities with style.

By placing the desire for style and the uses of clothing in this comparative context the anthropological project of relativizing phenomena is re-established. The critique within this chapter is directed against an ideology which insidiously forces us to regard consumption as superficial and trivial, and which therefore insists that the increasing importances of consumption is symptomatic of a loss of depth in the world. This example of a universalizing attitude to modern mass consumption is clearly expressed in writings on postmodernism, which may be viewed as merely the most recent manifestation of aesthetic and philosophical ideologies which lie at the core of "Western" thought. From the perspective of Trinidad, where many of the supposed characteristics appear with unusual clarity, the deluge of recent writings on the assumed global condition of post modernity or some culture of "late-capitalism" appear parochial and sterile.

The study of consumption has been viewed as the end of anthropology, a symbol of increasing homogenization and the elimination of cultural difference as the anthropological object of study. The new ethnography of consumption points in the opposite direction, to consumption as pivotal to any future anthropology, since it is increasingly through modes of consumption that differences in culture, even at the level of differences in ontology, are constructed.

PART 3

MATERIAL CULTURE

PART INTRODUCTION

Dress doesn't just *mean* stuff. It *is* stuff: layers of fabric, leather, or beads, objects wrapped around, hung on, or embedded in the body. This part of the reader explores how the materiality of what we wear shapes and impacts its social importance.

It is no accident that the work of Daniel Miller ended the last section. It also creates an effective bridge to this one. Daniel Miller, working with his colleagues and graduate students at University College London, has been one of the most vocal and influential voices within what has come to be known as "material culture" studies.

Material culture scholars like Miller treat dress and fashion as material, in more than one sense of the word. They are material in that they are composed of matter—actual physical substance that occupies space and can be acted upon by humans and nonhumans alike. And they are material in that they *matter*, having real social and cultural consequence to the people who make, sell, exchange, and wear them. In the words of Kaori O'Connor, "material culture studies begin at the beginning. For clothing, that starting point is cloth, either woven or 'made', as with felt or *tapa*" (p. 93). In her contribution to this volume, the cloth in question is Lycra, a "man-made fibre" whose social and cultural meaning is inseparable from its origins in the techno-capitalist matrix of fiber science. Agency, she claims, is built in to Lycra. Every thread of a Lycra-made garment was wrought out of human intention and action. That agency, woven into the clothes we wear, shapes how we wear it, what we wear it for, and the meaning it holds in our lives.

Jane Schneider's article provides a useful synthesis of existing work in material culture studies with the larger body of thought in the nascent anthropology of dress and fashion. The utility of this piece lies in Schneider's unwillingness to simplify the work that has come before hers. "Cloth and clothing," she writes, "is always restless and multi-dimensional" (p. 99). It cannot be distilled down. It cannot be reduced to one thing. The capitalist, commercial purposes of cloth do not eliminate older meanings and purposes routed in tradition or local cultural practice. Clothing can serve the interests of the powerful and the weak simultaneously. It can reinforce the status quo while undermining it from the inside. Artisanal and industrial traditions of clothing production exist side by side and continue to inform one another. The hegemony of Western fashion is undermined through myriad acts of conscious consumption and repurposing. How cloth and clothing matter, that is, is always a partial, messy, and unfinished story, one that continues to unfold in complex and contradictory ways.

But cloth and clothing aren't just woven with contradictory meanings. They are also woven with intimacies and connections. Indeed, they serve to create and reinforce connections between people. Sophie Woodward's contribution to this volume describes the way jeans—that staple item of contemporary casual dress worldwide—are employed in the forging of social intimacies, whether between mother and daughter, boyfriend and girlfriend. A woman, for instance, might wear her significant other's pair of jeans as a way of holding them close, maintaining a link with them when they are not around. "The very appearance of cloth and clothing," she writes, "is one that lends itself to associations with connectedness, with rich metaphorical potential in terms of the weaving together of people, and the fabric of their relationships" (p. 109). It is not just types of clothing that hold meaning, then, but specific items of clothing, with their own unique histories and trajectories.

This is true in England just as it is in Mali. African wild silk, Laurence Douny explains in his article, is a critical component of bride wealth. It is the preferred material for wrapping the bodies of the dead, and it helps define, through continued ritual use, the collective Mande identity. But for Douny and the Mande people he describes, wild silk matters, not simply for its social or ritual meaning, but for its material properties, and specifically, its sheen. Wild silk is shiny. It draws the light, and in doing so, it draws attention. Its rich social meaning in everyday Mande life is not arbitrary but connected explicitly with this material property, along with its relative scarcity and cost.

Materiality, then, is an aspect of dress and fashion we ignore to the detriment of our work. The form and substance of clothing materials matter to our theorizing of dress and fashion. So does the labor that goes in to producing those materials. In Panama, where the *mola*, or female blouse, is a critical wardrobe item for Kuna women, along with an important item in marketing Kuna identity to tourists, production takes up an enormous amount of time. "Women," writes Margherita Margiotti in her article that concludes this section of the book, "are almost continually taken up with the relentless everyday sewing of *mola* blouses in the house, together with the acquisition of poplin and printed fabrics for their wardrobe" (p. 124). To understand the meaning of *mola* in everyday Kuna life, we have to understand the work that goes into weaving them, the physical presence that they occupy within Kuna households, and the way they circulate as goods and gifts. Like Woodward and Douny, Margiotti is interested in how *molakana* (the plural of *mola*) are used to forge relationships, construct intimacies, and establish the terms of contact between Kuna people and tourists. "Aspects of Kuna sociality," she argues, "become accessible through an analysis of *molakana* as relational garments, that is, as garments that are made out of, and in the context of, relations" (p. 124). There is, then, material culture scholars remind us, no separating the materiality of garments from the relationality of them. They are woven together with the same thread.

12

THE OTHER HALF:
The material culture of new fibres

Kaori O'Connor

THE MATERIAL CULTURE OF NEW FIBRES

Conventionally, material culture studies begin at the beginning. For clothing, that starting point is cloth, either woven or "made," as with felt or *tapa*. In the case of anthropology at home, focusing on fabric is a useful way of avoiding the confusion induced by concentrating on constantly changing fashion styles. Fabrics have long been seen as artefacts, transformed as Ingold (2000) puts it, out of brute matter, in this case out of "natural" fibres such as cotton, wool and silk, which are literally beaten into submission to culture. This is the nature-into-culture model, in which the physical and social processes of transformation are the objects of interest, not the materiality of fibres, which remains unexamined, and in which surfaces are deemed to be significant, not what lies beneath or within them. This model may work well enough in pre-industrial, artisanal and small-scale contexts, but is woefully inadequate for the society in which we live, where mass production is the rule and "meaning" does not spring from long established tradition, or through the physical processes of making by hand, as for example with hand-weaving or quilting.

The challenge this poses to established approaches to cloth is seen in the fact that in the seminal anthropological work on the subject, Weiner and Schneider's (1989) *Cloth and Human Experience*, the examples of capitalist societies dealt with were either pre-industrial or involved handwork, as with hand embroidery done for tourists. Tellingly, all of the societies studied employed cloth made of natural fibres.

At home today, the picture is very different. Regardless of consciously expressed preferences for natural fibres and fabrics, more than half of the fibres we wear today are man-made. Globally, 40 per cent of the world fibre production is cotton, 2.5 per cent is wool and 0.2 per cent is silk. Apart from statistically insignificant fibres such as ramie and jute, the rest is comprised of man-made fibres in two main groups—synthetics (such as polyester) and cellulosics (such as viscose rayon)—along with speciality fibres such as spandex, the best-known brand of which is Lycra. And yet, to date, there has been only one anthropological investigation of the social and cultural aspects of synthetic fibres in our society, Schneider's (1994) pioneering study of polyester. Like Mintz, whose 1986 work on sugar she cites, Schneider goes beyond social and technological history to throw light upon the workings of capitalism as a cultural system, demonstrating how changes in the production and consumption of synthetic fibres in America—peaking in 1969, then declining steadily through the 1970s and 1980s—were coincidental with broader cultural movements and the formation of new social groups in which the category "natural" took on highly charged symbolic meaning, and in which synthetic cloth and clothes came to carry negative moral values. Here, the very specificity and materiality of polyester—its feel; its mode of production, which raised environmental issues; its association in the public mind with science and modernity; the kinds of clothes for which it was used—illuminate wider issues and processes. In itself, this represents a substantial advance on understanding what cloth and clothing can tell us about our society as a whole, but it is possible to go further—to an even more

Adapted from Kaori O'Connor, "The Other Half: The Cultural Material of New Fibres," in *Clothing as Material Culture,* edited by Suzanne Küchler and Daniel Miller (Oxford: Berg, 2005), pp. 41–59.

basic form of materiality—the *fibre* of which cloth and clothes are made.

Man-made fibres fundamentally alter our understanding of the relationship between persons and things, because the difference between man-made and natural fibres is one of kind rather than of degree. While natural fibres such as silk are basically "as found" the unique feature of man-made fibres is that they can be created "to order." Instead of processing a natural fibre in hopes that it will fit requirements, requirements can be established in advance, and the fibre created specifically to fulfil them. Thus a fibre can be created to respond to changes in heat or light, to carry electronic information, to resist moisture or retain it, to destroy odour-causing bacteria or exude a perfumed aroma, to change surface colour and pattern under different conditions, and to stretch or contract. Easily characterized as "active" in contrast to "inert" natural fibres, these new techno-textiles have been described as "smart," "intelligent" and "sapient" (e.g. Küchler 2003). Because the fibres have been created from scratch, the distinction between inner and outer, surface and interior, becomes less relevant. It is no longer a clear case of "culture" being laid on the surface of "nature" and indeed synthetic fibres blur the boundaries between them. This effectively moves the goalposts of material culture to a more fundamental level. Schneider's study began with finished cloth, and focused on the competition between producers of synthetic and of natural fibre fabrics. By beginning even earlier, with the very invention of a fibre, one can trace the interplay of culture and commerce entailed in the creation of new forms of materiality, and better understand the various factors that account for a fibre's success or failure in a wider social context. With man-made fibres, it is even more the case that, as Pastoreau (2001: xiv) said of clothes, "there is nothing anecdotal or romantic, not to mention aesthetic, about clothing; it is a veritable social system."

Usefully for analysis generally, the specificities of man-made fibres introduce or tie together a number of factors, contexts and agendas that an evolving critical anthropology at home is now having to address. For example, the economics of new fibres, which carry extremely high development costs, are such that for a fibre to be successful it must go into mass production. This situates studies in a broad and inclusive sector of society, the mass market, in a trajectory that begins with invention and finishes not with purchase, but with end use. By following a fibre through its many forms and stages—not all of which are successful—we gain insight into how a complex mass market works, and the ways in which producers and consumers are interdependent. Man-made fibres take a long time to bring to market and, usually, a long time to establish. This introduces time and process to the analysis, allowing us to see the ethnographic present as just one episodic moment in a larger stream (Moore 1994). Indeed, the sheer scale of the fibre industry makes it virtually impossible to understand what is going on in the ethnographic present without reference to the archival past. Studies of man-made fibres also oblige us to engage with the paradigmatic form of capitalism, big business. Despite the romantic image of the lone inventor, epitomized today by the iconic garage in Palo Alto where the first home computer was devised by the founders of Hewlett Packard, in the world of chemical fibres it has always been the case that only big business has the resources to develop and commercialize entirely new products. In the past, this process has been seen by the social sciences in one of three ways. Histories of innovation tend to portray technological development as part of an inexorable and untroubled scientific progress in which human agents appear to play no part (see Noble 1977 for a critical account; and Handley 1999 for an example relating specifically to fibres). In cultural studies, as we have seen, it is individuals and images that are privileged and the material world largely ignored, although at the same time capitalist production is decried as manipulation by big business of the consumer. Third, social histories engage the larger context and longer view with varying degrees of success (see Strasser 2000 for an exemplary example), but like technological histories they tend to deal only with successes not failures, and as such present only a partial view. A further attraction of man-made fibres is that they allow us to move beyond these limitations by introducing a form of archival resource little used by anthropologists to date—commercial archives.

Once considered almost archaic, archives, as Showalter (2001) notes, have become highly fashionable. Wardrobes are spoken of as personal archives, and fashion designers giving collections of their past works to museums speak of them as "material archives." This renewed interest in records and material objects can be seen, I argue, as a reaction to the excesses of postmodernism. Businesses in our society, particularly family businesses and those with strong corporate identities, have often created and maintained commercial company archives. What begins as a record of daily work becomes a memorial over time, and it is the latter quality that has often accounted for their preservation. The documents kept in these collections are frequently diverse, and can consist of personal and business correspondence, production records, salesmen's receipts, laboratory records, internal memoranda, market research reports, press releases, transcripts of meetings, promotional materials, sales aids and retail ephemera, company magazines and newsletters, advertisements, newspaper cuttings, radio and television transcripts, examples of products and even expense receipts. That advertisements are but one element among many in these collections is significant. Miller (1997[a]). has argued that the importance of advertisements is overstated in studies arising in competing disciplines, which, using textual analysis as a primary tool, foreground the advertisement and its deconstruction, while ignoring the advertiser's intentions and other forms of commercial activity that present themselves to ethnographic and archival view. In these studies the producer-consumer relationship has been largely seen in terms of hierarchy, dominance and submission, framed by the discourses of capitalism (Miller 1997a: 153), and also of gender, in which the producer is cast as wholly dominant and exploitative of consumers. O'Barr (1994) has noted that there is very little in the advertising-centred literature about the producer's intentions that is more than assumption or speculation and he has criticized historians and analysts of advertising such as Marchand (1985, 1998) for failing to consider the objectives and motives of producers from the perspective of the producers' own experience. Easily accessible in the public domain, and even more easily taken out of context, advertisements (or, more accurately, interpretations of advertisements) provide a partial perspective at best. It is only with the greater array of sources contained in a full commercial archive—combined with ethnographic observation and information from other sources—that a more detailed and nuanced picture begins to emerge about how material things come into being in our society, and what happens to them, their producers and their consumers over time. Commercial archives relating specifically to man-made fibres are a particularly important resource for understanding this process because of the specific properties of fibres alluded to above. Because fibres can be created to order, knowledge of consumer preferences and desires regarding both cloth and clothing, and an awareness of social change and values, become highly important to fibre producers. Technological expertise alone is not enough. As commercial archives show, producers have to engage successfully with culture in order to attain commercial success, and in the case of fibres this engagement is a highly complex process. A knowledge of how this process has worked in the past is essential to understanding what is happening in the present, where the dynamics of culture and commerce, production and consumption, are central to our constantly expanding material world, and where new fibres shape the way we live, and are shaped by us in return. In addition, because they deal with the mass market, reading a producer's archive is a useful corrective for those accustomed to the micro-perspectives of diversity. To date, academics have shown some reluctance to examine commercial archives on the grounds they are "biased," but there can be no justification for ignoring the authoritative sources on production simply because they have been generated by the producer.

MAN-MADE FIBRES: THE EARLY YEARS AT DUPONT AND THE CASE OF WASH AND WEAR

Many of the man-made fibres in our wardrobes have been produced by a single firm, E.I. du Pont de Nemours and Company, commonly known as Dupont. This transnational American corporation, the oldest industrial company on the Fortune 500 list, was until recently, through its textile division, the world's largest integrated fibre business, operating in

50 countries and with an approximate annual revenue from fibres of $6.5 billion (US). As Charles O. Holliday Jr, the CEO of Dupont put it in 2002, "We're not just the leader in this industry. We, more than anybody, created this industry." Not just producers of man-made fibres, Dupont were also inventors, with an unrivalled programme of applied and fundamental research. It was in Dupont's laboratories that many of the products that made or make up our material world were created, including nylon, the wool-like acrylic fibre Orlon, the wash-and-wear polyester Dacron, fire-resistant Nomex, the synthetic rubber Neoprene, super-strong Kevlar, stain resistant Teflon and stretchy Lycra. The company maintains an extensive archive covering all their fibres, and the research I carried out there provided the material for the account that follows, and the background for a larger and ongoing project involving ethnography as well as archival investigation ([O'Connor] 2004a and in preparation, also 2004b).

Initially, Dupont entered the man-made fibre field at the end of the First World War by buying the American rights to a cellulose fibre—"artificial silk"—that had first been developed in France. Dupont's interest in the fibre had been aroused by the fact that it involved nitrocellulose technology in which the company was well versed since the first product it had manufactured was gunpowder, and it had also noted that imports of artificial silk from Europe had grown steadily throughout the war when natural silk from the Far East was not available. Dupont opened factories to produce the fibre, and expected it would be a relatively straightforward matter to sell it to the New England textile mills that dominated the American cloth-producing trade at the time. However, when Dupont salesmen went out on the road with the new product, which they called "Fibersilk," they encountered immediate opposition from the mill managers who declared synthetic fibres to be a "fly-by-night novelty," and castigated Dupont's salesmen for "wasting their precious time talking about something that was artificial and therefore ridiculous." Dupont soon found that the production of new man-made fibres also necessitated the production of meaning. Although imported artificial silk sold well and was widely used, mainly for underwear and hosiery, the company discovered that it was regarded by the public as a cheap and often shoddy substitute for natural silk, a "budget" choice without any cachet—associations that were not attractive to a company whose products had always been synonymous with quality. Having been attracted to man-made fibres by the simple synergy of compatibility with its other chemical products and potential profits, the company now found itself confronted by culture in the form of embedded ideas about the new materials on the part of the mills and of the public. More challenging still, this was a different kind of public.

Dupont's entry into man made fibres coincided with the emergence of a new group of consumers. As the official history of the firm put it:

> The decade of the 1920s was featured by the dramatic mass emergence of many interesting phenomena, including the radio, the motion picture and women. Most, including women, had been around for some time: only now did the scene suddenly swarm with them. (Dupont 1952: 91)

Or rather, only now had women become independent consumers in significant numbers. Women in the 1920s, Dupont noted, were increasingly entering the business world, even ousting male stenographers. Women gained the vote, drove automobiles, wore ever-shorter skirts that showed off their hosiery, replaced boned corsets with rubberized girdles, and abandoned heavy underwear for filmy lingerie. Movies set the fashions, generating a demand for cheaper, more modish clothing and accessories. In the home, women wanted new appliances such as refrigerators, which were changing food buying patterns and creating demands for new kinds of packaging. Not only were women beginning to earn their own money; they increasingly took on the role of purchasing agents for the whole family. In fact, Dupont concluded, "now that women had the asking power, there was almost no end to the good things women demanded of industry and especially its chemical branch" (Dupont 1952: 91).

Dupont soon found that the French fibre was extremely difficult to work with. Instead of continuing with a flawed product in the face of opposition from mills and the public, the company decided to find out what women wanted, and then use its laboratories and engineering technology to develop their own fibre to order. Turning to the fledging field of market research, Dupont funded a national study to poll 10,000 women on what they wanted from artificial silk. What women wanted, the survey revealed, was not another silk, but completely new kinds of outwear materials that were resistant to soiling, easy to clean and care for, that held their shape, were durable but also soft, were comfortable in warm weather, smart in appearance and reasonably priced. No single natural fibre had these qualities.

These expressed preferences reflected the emergent postwar lifestyle in which unparalleled leisure and mobility led to a demand for easy living, easy shopping and easy care. Yet despite these nascent social trends and expressed preferences, Dupont found that in practice the majority of manufacturers and consumers remained resistant to the idea of artificial fabrics and fibres generally. Acceptance was given a boost in 1924 when Dupont and other producers agreed to give artificial silk a new generic name—"rayon"—from "ray" for its sheen and "on" to suggest a fibre, as in cotton (Rutledge 1966). This enabled consumers to think of rayon as a fibre in its own right, and not as an inferior version of another, natural fibre, and it also helped to overcome the mills' opposition. As a Dupont salesman recalled "naturally the old time cotton mills thought anything 'artificial' was blasphemy in the textile trade, and it wasn't until the term 'rayon' was coined that we were able to make any dent on the market." Even a new name was not enough. The company discovered that in order to be successful it had to do more than make a new fibre and sell it to the mills. It had to promote a new way of living and of thinking about cloth to the consumers and the retailers who served them.

Dupont's artificial silk survey set the pattern for what became a fundamental part of their textile business. The company built up a textile marketing department unparalleled in the trade, embracing market research, advertising, promotion, publicity and retail services. Formal market research involved commissioning surveys "to tell us how we are doing, what people really want, and where we should put more effort." It differed from advertising in that it came from the consumers rather than being directed at them. Findings went to

the research and technical departments, to inform ongoing refinements of the fibres. For as long as they produced it, Dupont never "finished" with a fibre; the laboratories were constantly working on improvements and new applications in response to changing needs. New fibres were introduced to the manufacturers and the public in intensive promotional campaigns that promoted the idea of the fibres, their performance and the new modern lifestyle of which they were part, as well as actual garments made by particular manufacturers. The important point here is that although the type of garment was already familiar to consumers, garments made of the new fibres had entirely innovative properties: the fibre and fabric, rather than the style, influenced everyday life. There were pictures in magazines of women golfing in figure-hugging non-sagging knitted sweaters or getting out of cars in skirts with no wrinkles, and men bounding down the gangways of airplanes in uncreased suits. Salesmen threw themselves fully clothed into swimming pools to show how well suits made of the new fibres weathered the experience. There were in-store demonstrations, fashion shows, trade fair exhibitions, sponsorship of events, talks at women's clubs by Dupont representatives, and promotions on radio and in the new medium, television. Each time a new fibre was introduced, Dupont had to go through the same process. In the company's words,

> Back in the 1950s and 1960s, the sale of man-made fibres had to be built in part on describing the advantages of these new fibres not only to the industry but also to the consumer. Consider such common apparel as sweaters which can be washed without shrinkage, undergarments needing no ironing, skirts and trousers with permanent pleats and creases, and outwear staying fresh-looking despite high humidity … None of these had any meaning before the advent of nylon, Dacron and Orion.

Yet despite market research and extensive publicity, the success of new fibres was by no means instant or guaranteed. For example, ease of washing and after care were among the most important features of an ideal fabric as revealed by the artificial silk survey undertaken in the 1920s, yet in the 1950s, when Dupont finally introduced wash and wear Dacron, intensive promotion was still required. A stalwart of Dupont's wash and wear promotion initiative was the manager of the information services for the Textile Fibers department. His hobby was collecting old-time household equipment, especially antique flat-irons which, he said, symbolized the tedious task that traditionally had been women's most disliked household chore. He used his flat-irons as props in presentations he gave to women's groups across the country on the theme of "*Your Mothers and Grandmothers Never Had It So Good*," highlighting the way that Dupont had pioneered the development of man-made fibres that freed women from arduous ironing board drudgery. "There has been a complete transition from the once inflexible routine of wash on Monday, iron on Tuesday and maybe work furiously on Wednesday to finish the job" he would say, going on to extol the virtues of Dupont's easy care fibre that could be put through an automatic washer and dryer and emerge in less than an hour, ready to wear. At an appropriate point, he would step behind a screen that had been provided, change into a lounging robe, and then toss his wash and wear suit into the washer and dryer included among his props, continuing to talk while the suit was being laundered. Later, he changed back into the freshly washed suit and finished his lecture, the whole operation taking about forty minutes. The audience, he reported, found it "fascinating." The idea of educating the consumer was nothing new; most of the literature that surrounds the British Great Exhibition of 1851 and the foundation of London's Victoria and Albert Museum were prompted by such ambitions. But these were highly patrician images of didactic persuasion. The real innovation was the investment in a far more interactive relationship that was as much based upon being educated by consumers as educating them, and was one of many new attempts to engage in this kind of collaborative meaning making.

Also new were the intensity and speed of social change. As incomes rose, ever more people enjoyed better homes and cars, better living and, Dupont realised, a new culture. As a company representative observed, "Time to enjoy these possessions became an all-important commodity, free time over and above the job and the household chores, and that is what we

are selling. Our fibers in the last analysis mean more free time" (Keller 1955: 128). In order to promote their fibres, Dupont had to promote "modern living." By selling culture in order to sell cloth, the company was literally helping to create the fabric of a new society, and was being shaped by it in return. However, the process was, and is, far from straightforward.

CONCLUSION

The example of wash and wear illustrates a number of features of man-made fibres as material culture. First, there is the way they highlight the dynamic of history and illuminate social change. The long lead time, some thirty years in this case, between the first consumer survey and the launch of the product, means that consumer needs and values may have changed by the time the fibre appears. The newly enfranchised and independent American woman of the 1920s was very different to the conventional, domestically-orientated woman of the mid-1950s. It is difficult to imagine having to encourage women in the first group to give up the drudgery of ironing, in the way that was necessary three decades later. The initial conservatism with which wash and wear fibre was regarded in the 1950s is an indication of the way in which cloth, with its associations of "cleanliness," "order," and the performance of ritualistic labour, is linked to deep cultural values and ideas about social roles. These changed again in the 1970s when wash and wear, having gained acceptance, fell out of favour, a victim of a fundamental shift in social values, attitudes and practices that returned natural fibres to popularity. Now, in 2005, when fibre producers are trying to promote technically advanced textiles, it is wash and wear that has become the standard of conservatism. "New fibres?" the head of production of a leading British fashion chain aimed at women aged sixteen to twenty-five said to me, "It doesn't matter what these new fibres can do. 'Can I put it in the washing machine and will it come out the same as when it went in' is all our customers care about." This also points to the second thing that distinguishes man-made fibres, fabrics and clothing from the naturals—they are *performance* fibres, not fibres whose primary appeal depends on "style" or "look." Man-made fibres are not inert, they have been created to *do*. They are the materializations of expressed cultural values, the realizations of culturally approved action, but their success or failure is tied to a historically specific mutually constitutive process between producer and consumer, production and consumption in which neither producer nor consumer is dominant. As Sahlins (1976[a]: 185) put it, although it may appear to producers as a quest for profit and to the consumer as an acquisition of useful goods, it is basically a symbolic process:

> this view of production as the substantialization of a cultural logic should prohibit us from speaking naively of the generation of demand by supply, as though the social product were the conspiracy of a few decision makers able to impose an ideology of fashion through the deceits of advertising. Nor need one indulge in the converse mystification of capitalist product as a response to consumers wants. (Sahlins 1976[a]: 184)

Third, the use of commercial and marketing records presents a very different and more complex picture than that arising from advertisements. The difficulties encountered, and periodic failures of fibres give as much, if not more, insight into cultural dynamics as accounts of successes alone. The special qualities of man-made fibres give special insights into the workings of the complex, capitalist commodified world in which we live and, at the same time, present the opportunity for more philosophical reflections. Agency is built into man-made fibres, but this agency can only operate in specific cultural contexts—are "smart" fibres truly sapient in their own right? And is the agency they have greater than that which was put into them? More work in this field is needed to advance both kinds of understanding. Not merely of academic interest, the congruence of commerce and culture will determine whether these new fibres will successfully reach a mass market.

The material presented here has been largely historical, but this has been necessary in order to establish the way in which the industry works, something which is not immediately apparent if investigations are confined to the present. As Sahlins (1976[a]: 37) puts it, ethnography with time and transformation built into it

is a distinct way of knowing the anthropological object, with a possibility of changing the way in which culture is thought. I have concentrated on clothes and fibres, in order to restore cloth—the missing half—to the overall fashion equation, and to highlight the importance of man-made fibres generally. Indeed, after a long period when clothing and style dominated the field, the pendulum of interest is swinging the other way, with the most interesting developments coming from new fibres, both because of their technical capabilities (see Braddock and O'Mahoney 1999) and appearance. As a study commissioned by Dupont to mark the millennium notes, "The spheres of chemistry and high fashion are drawing ever closer together, redefining the boundaries of what is wearable" (Wolf and Schlachter 2000: 26). It has long been recognized in anthropology that the most illuminating studies, such as Bean's (1989) work on Gandhi and *khadi*, involve both cloth and clothing, and that interrelationship is the next area that studies at home must explore. Küchler and Were (2003: 5) discuss the ways in which "cloth and clothing are used in the Pacific as powerful surfaces that have contributed to new ways of thinking and being"; the same can be said of new fibres in our society, but here I would argue that the power is not limited to surfaces. The clothing aspect of new fibres greatly enriches the potential in the field. For example, the migration of fibres from one kind of garment to another, used in very different ways because of cultural impetuses, tells a much more complex story than simple changes of style. I am currently engaged in an ongoing study of the fibre Lycra, and the clothing and cultural uses to which it has been put. Perhaps no other single fibre illustrates the dynamics introduced here. Invented by E. I. du Pont de Nemours (Dupont) and launched in 1959 after some twenty years in development and an investment of $10 million (US), it is now recognized as the world's eighth top textile brand and continues to evolve along with its consumers. It is hoped that this forthcoming study and the work presented here will help to further develop the study of contemporary cloth and clothing as material culture, bringing to an end a period in which, whatever we as anthropologists do in other societies, we live at home in a material world that is largely unexamined.

13

CLOTH AND CLOTHING

Jane Schneider

Cloth and clothing constitute the widest imaginable category of material culture, covering a spatial domain that extends from the miles of textiles annually produced by hand or factory to the most intimate apparel of the human body, and a temporal domain whose earliest moments, lost to archaeology because of poor preservation, pre-date the neolithic. Encompassed within the category are the familiar dualities of Western social thought: production versus consumption; utility versus beauty; the gift versus the commodity; symbolic communication versus the materiality of colors, designs, shapes, and textures. Many accounts of the historical processes leading up to, and following from, the capitalist industrialization and marketing of cloth and clothing center around the duality most integral to the triumphalist narrative of European civilization: the West versus "the rest." This chapter attempts to transcend these oppositions.

As a political-economic and cultural system, capitalism historically overlaid and displaced, but did not eliminate, arrangements that privileged elite consumption, in which the opportunities for self-enhancement were intensely hierarchically distributed. Rather than label these earlier arrangements "pre-" or "non-capitalist"—appellations that imply, in the first instance, their eventual disappearance and in the second, an absence or lack—we will (experimentally) refer to them as "courtly," highlighting their elitism. Capitalist and courtly societies differ with regard to how cloth and clothing are produced and consumed, but the contrasts elude simple oppositions.

"Productivist" explanations for the emergence of capitalism center around technological innovation and the mobilization of wage labor in the textile sector. Emphasis is also placed on the capture of raw materials through colonial and imperial projects. Yet these foundations for capitalist development are more compelling when juxtaposed to the special genius of capitalism, which is its ongoing democratization of the possibility for self-enhancement through consumption. Because this democratization presupposes low-cost goods, the two aspects—heavy-handed interventions in production and the cultivation of desire—are integrally related.

"Self-enhancement" loosely refers to energizing the self and close others, perhaps organized in small groups, through life-affirming practices and rituals. Examples involving cloth and clothes include transforming the body and its surroundings in ways considered aesthetically or sexually attractive; dressing well to accrue prestige, the respect of others, a sense of worthiness or empowerment; generously distributing textiles to consolidate friendships and followings; and signalling through clothes an identification with particular values or constituencies. Cloth and clothing consumption is always restless and multidimensional. The point is that, in modern capitalist society, its enhancing qualities are, or can be, within the purview of virtually everyone.

Whereas, in the consumption sphere, capitalism corrodes courtly hierarchies, in the sphere of production, an opposite kind of rupture has occurred.

Adapted from Jane Schneider, "Cloth and Clothing," in *Handbook of Material Culture*, edited by Christopher Tilley, Webb Keane, Susanne Küchler, Michael Rowlands, and Patricia Spyer (London: Sage Publications, 2006), pp. 203–19.

Different from the proletarianizing and colonizing strategies alluded to above, the courtly production of cloth and clothing hinges on the ability of elites to acquire precious raw materials and finished goods through deputized trade or tributary exactions, and to patronize or attach to their courts beehives of artisanal activity—skilled, knowledgeable, artistically inclined, selflessly dedicated as the case may be. Under such arrangements, manufacturers enjoy a meaningful sphere of autonomy; they control product design and decisions and, to a considerable degree, the organization and rhythm of work. As a result, courtly systems of production are less dehumanizing and exploitative than the system of capitalist manufacturing. These distinctions between courtly and capitalist dynamics help frame the following discussion.

ELITE EXUBERANCE AND THE DYNAMICS OF FASHION

The elitism of courtly societies generated the fundamental elements of fashion. American social philosopher and friend of Franz Boas, Thorstein Veblen considered this proposition in his 1899 book, *Theory of the Leisure Class*. Conspicuous display marked high position, although the content of the display might vary. The aggressive, trophy-hungry "robber barons" of Veblen's day mimicked the pursuits of a leisured aristocracy, engaging in wastefully honorific expenditures such as hiring an excessive number of (well dressed) servants and ostentatiously abstaining from labor. Women, he proposed, consumed vicariously, beautifying their households and making themselves into ornaments for the sake of the household head. Uncomfortable, impractical, corseted garments advertised their idleness. By contrast, religious elites carried austerity to extremes, being cloaked in the ornate but severe garbs of exaggerated devotion.

Whatever the mode, Veblen argued, gratification depended at least in part on obtaining superior, beautifully crafted products, whose aesthetic qualities and obvious expense created a magnetic effect. Attraction is a critical element of fashion. So is being "in vogue," a condition that required excluding status inferiors from the scheme (except as the indebted recipients of hand-me-downs and gifts). As the potlatching ethnography suggests, when envious commoners acquire the means to emulate, there unfolds a race to stay out in front, rendering fashion inherently unstable.

This approach to fashion, in which elites build themselves up through conspicuous pursuits and do not like to be copied, found resonance in Georg Simmel's 1904 definition of the phenomenon as evolving through a dialectic of conformity and differentiation, imitation and individuality, adapting to society and challenging its demands [Simmel (1904a) 1971]. But it also encountered criticism for being too reductive, narrowly defining goods as signifiers of status and assuming that innovations come only from the top (Slater 1997). In Bourdieu's more subtle "practice theory," society's many groups are shown to articulate and deploy their own criteria for achieving distinction, their respective constituencies having grown up in a particular habitus, learned in an embodied way particular customs and dispositions, and acquired particular tastes. Arbiters of taste, armed with insiders' expertise, amplify the resulting differences, although not irrevocably. Under some conditions, the values accumulated in one hierarchy, say robber barons, can be converted into the values of another, say priests (Bourdieu [1979] 1984).

In fairness to Veblen, he did recognize several kinds of hierarchy—economic, religious, military. Moreover, his insights about the drive for invidious glory—the dynamics of "upward chase and flight"— are easily expanded to include other aspects of glory than merely communicating status. At the core of courtly sumptuosity is a complex of relations between persons and things in which persons make themselves, their surroundings and their close others, more vital through myriad ritual performances, through hospitality and generosity, through absorbing energy from the spiritual and aesthetic dimensions of objects, as well as through showing off. Overtly communicative displays are only one piece of the puzzle and perhaps not the most significant.

That courtly sumptuosity is a complex phenomenon of great historical significance is suggested by the widespread enactment of sumptuary laws following the late Middle Ages, when intensified commercial exchange between continents placed more wealth in circulation, in the service of developing polities. Minutely regulating items of dress in relation to social rank, the laws presumed to defend courtiers from the pretensions of newly rich merchant and trading groups. In Tokugawa, Japan, sumptuary legislation went so far as to specify the number and material composition of the thongs that commoners could have on their sandals (Roach and Eicher 1979: 13). In Europe, Protestant reformers, scandalized by the explosion of consumption going on around them, supported sumptuary legislation out of a kind of anti-materialism.

How effective were the regulations is another question, even when violators were threatened with capital punishment. Renaissance Italy saw merchant elites brazenly overtake the courtiers in the latest styles. These included particolored doublets and hose of silk and wool in which the sleeves were of contrasting colors, the pants legs also, and the body of another color still. Slashed with hundreds of cuts to reveal a different color underneath, such garments invited individuals to design their own color schemes, causing (male) court fashion to change "with a rapidity … unknown before" (Chamberlin 1967: 52–6).

A fascinating detail was the emergence, in this moment, of tailoring as an additional level of both cost and instability. In many of the early cloth traditions continuous weaving, sometimes yielding a tubular construction, was believed to harness a fabric's spiritual essence, or express the continuity of kinship and descent, so much so that cutting it was taboo. Fashioning lengths of cloth on the body was a matter of folding and draping. It was generally done, moreover, with all-purpose fabrics, suitable for covering a table or bed, swaddling an infant or shrouding a corpse, as well as adorning a living, adult body (Keane 2005). With tailoring, the line between cloth as clothing was fully crossed. Consisting of pre-cut pieces reassembled through sewing, tailored clothes opened up a whole new realm of crafting and variation, their architecture constituting an additional ingredient, over and above colors, motifs, and textures, for constructing an aesthetically attractive body, a vibrant and sexual

person, a glorious elite. And shapes, too, could change with the fashion swirl, camouflaging or exaggerating the body's contours.

Europeans were not the first to tailor their garments. The narrow, brocaded men's cloths of West Africa were traditionally assembled with an eye for shape—an example of widespread Islamic (and Jewish) craftwork with needle and thread. Limb-encasing pants and jackets protected many peoples from the rigors of climate and warfare. Yet these examples stopped short of the perpetual mutation—the high-velocity turnover—that appears to have taken hold in the courts of the precociously mercantile cities of Renaissance Italy. Here, in the early sixteenth century, Baldassare Castiglione published what is considered the founding text of fashion history, The Book of the Courtier ([1528] 1953), which argued for treating the "natural" body as a human creation, reflecting humans' ideas.

THE "RISE" OF INDUSTRIAL CAPITALISM

Renaissance Italy's exquisite dyed silk and woolen cloth, crafted by well regarded artisans, was a stimulus to manufacturers in England—cited by most social theory as the original capitalist land. An interesting textile-centric debate pits "productionist" accounts of English capitalism against analyses that take consumption into account. In the former, the emphasis is on factory mobilization of alienated and unskilled labor; technological innovations in spinning and weaving; and harnessing colonial sources of raw materials—above all, cotton. For some, the prime mover was a burst of creative energy dating to the mid-eighteenth century and yielding the flying shuttle, spinning jenny, water frame, and spinning "mule" (which combined the advances of the water frame and jenny). With the application of steam in 1790, spinners could accomplish in 300 hours what it had formerly taken 50,000 hours to produce (Wolf 1982: 273–4). Others highlight the putting-out system, through which merchants of the seventeenth and eighteenth centuries avoided the expensive labor of urban guild manufacturing, advancing raw materials, spinning wheels and looms to peasant households, organized for "piecework." More developed in Europe than in

Asia (see Kriedte[, Medick and Schlumbohm] 1981), in England, the putting-out system was an efficient source of household linens for colonial as well as home markets, and of the so-called "new draperies"—light, woolen broadcloths, made from the long-staple fiber of sheep well fed on improved pastures, and inexpensive enough to permit the wastage of tailoring. The cotton entrepreneurs devised another organizational breakthrough, modeled on plantations in the Caribbean and Ireland, these in turn a source of strategic raw materials: a strictly disciplined labor force was concentrated in a factory setting, lowering production costs by a staggering amount.

The consumerist approach to the "rise" of industrial capitalism is equally textile- and Anglocentric but directs attention to the "sumptuosity engine" of the Elizabethan court, which stimulated desires throughout society but left them unrequited. With the abandonment of sumptuary legislation at the turn of the seventeenth century (see Freudenberger 1973), and the vast increase of wealth owed to colonial expansion, challenges to courtly elitism became both feminized and general. In the words of Chandra Mukerji, whose 1983 book *From Graven Images: Patterns of Modern Materialism* is an exemplary "consumerist" text, fashion became, for the first time, an "open cultural system."

The democratization of what was once courtly fashion continued apace, the more so as capitalist institutions and practices took hold in continental Europe. Images of Paris after 1789 suggest a spreading euphoria in which classes formerly in the shadows of courtly sumptuosity appeared on the streets in bright colors and captivating shapes. Under the Second Empire, bourgeois women acquired the new identity of "shoppers," encouraged by an emergent institution: the department store. Offering luxurious-appearing goods at prices ordinary consumers could afford, this emporium also provided an exciting and beautiful space in which to look and dream (see Williams 1982).

CAPITALIST EXPANSION AND ARTISAN PRODUCTION: EUROPE AND BEYOND

The tension between productionist and consumptionist understandings of capitalism reappears in the vast literature on cloth and clothing as these manifestations of material culture have been affected by capitalism's spread. A rather pessimistic productionist bias is evident in characterizations of capitalism as a concatenation of forces that, rather like a juggernaut or steamroller, flattens everything in sight. Applied to cloth and clothing, this includes the idea that industrial manufactures are damaging to their hand-crafted equivalents and the artisans who make them.

Not that evidence for this hypothesis is lacking. Mission schools taught embroidery, sewing, and knitting to colonized women and children—textile arts that made extensive use of industrial materials while undermining the transmission of indigenous skills, above all patterned weaving (Schneider 1987: 434). Clever industrialists produced batiks expressly to compete with the Javanese craft, roller-printing copies so precise as to duplicate the hairline capillaries that occur in hand dyeing when the wax paste develops cracks (Matsuo 1970). They also made factory versions of *adinkra*, the terracotta mourning cloth of the Asante, simulating the *kente*-inspired embroidery that Asante artisans added for prestige (Polakoff 1982). Artisans who had been displaced from hand weaving and dyeing by the competition of machine-made goods often met an unhappy end, being forced into unemployment, migration, or the rather ironic situation of cultivating textile raw materials for manufactories in the metropole. Surely the most dramatic collapse of cloth traditions to occur in a context of fiber exports was that of plantation slaves in the Americas. Recruited in regions of Africa with important weaving and dyeing traditions, these laborers did not spin, weave or dye any of the cotton they grew, and were dressed in clothes made from factory yardgoods imported from Europe.

There are, however, a number of counter-indications to such a bleak picture. Far from always threatening a craft, industrially produced elements may stimulate it. Plain factory textiles contributed, like their commercial Indian forerunners, to the batik traditions of Java and Nigeria; their smooth surfaces meant that the wax or starch tracings of the designs could be applied with greater intricacy and precision, using finer instruments. Inexpensive and smooth factory cottons were attractive to the saturation indigo dyers of Kano in Nigeria, while embroiderers on every continent welcomed synthetically colored, machine-manufactured thread. Consider, too, the crafts that depend entirely on commercial and factory textiles for their execution—the appliquéd mola blouses of the Panamanian Cuna Indians, the cut and drawn "embroidery by subtraction" that Nigeria's Kalabari execute on commercial madras and gingham, and the quilted compositions of African-Americans in Surinam and the United States (Schneider 1987: 439–40).

Artisans' eagerness to acquire industrial yarn or cloth reflects not so much the steamroller effects of capitalism as the latent demands that are continually generated by the lively competitive processes of courtly sumptuosity, both within and across societies. As we have already emphasized, aesthetic competition placed a premium not only on skilled labor, constancy, and craft excellence, but also on access to raw and processed materials with good reputations. Because such characteristics as the range, saturation, and fastness of colors, the fineness and density of weaves, the tensile strength of warping threads, the intricacy of decoration, gave an edge in aesthetic rivalries, cloth and clothing makers characteristically pursued with interest newly available material possibilities, both before and during the expansion of European-generated capitalism. The response to newly available reds more than makes this case. Cloth artisans of colonial Africa and Native North America—areas on the margins of the Coccidae dyes—avidly unraveled cochineal and kermes-dyed commercial cloth so as to be able to add this color to their product (Schneider 1988).

Artisans in the path of capitalist expansion have also responded to emergent markets for hand-crafted cloth and clothing spawned by tourists, travelers, and others nostalgic for courtly styles, by concerned citizens attracted to "ethnic arts" as a gesture of solidarity with oppressed or exiled minorities, and by the many movements of "ethnogenesis" that have surfaced amidst independence struggles and in immigrant communities. But ethnographers accounts of craft revitalizations are often ambivalent as antidotes to the bleak, productionist picture of juggernaut capitalism. On the one hand, they point to opportunities for indigenous textile artisans to regain income and dignity from meaningful employment, and for indigenous women and men to become entrepreneurs and leaders of ethnic claims. On the other hand, however, they dramatize a series of compromises.

For example, rural households, beholden to native entrepreneurs who "put out" raw materials for piece-rated weaving, sewing, or embroidering during the slack season of the agricultural cycle may experience a degree of exploitation comparable to that of the European countryside on the eve of industrialization (Waterbury 1989). Often artisans lose artistic as well as economic control over the final product, modifying their wares in response to market pressures. Nor are consumers necessarily aware of this. Tourists purchasing "Thamelcloth" hats and tunics in Nepal, or in shops in New York City, believe them to be the products of the "righteous labor" of Tibetan refugees when in fact they are turned out in a Kathmandu factory (Hepburn 2000: 290–6).

In other examples, debasement and care coexist as producers apply high standards to the cloth they make for indigenous ritual and social purposes, for elite consumers of ethnic dress, and for discerning outsiders. Studying the "craft commercialization" of Zapotec weaving in Oaxaca, Lynn Stephen (1993) learned that US intermediaries attempted to get local weavers to incorporate "oriental" carpet motifs into their designs, just as they had given weavers in India Zapotec motifs to copy. The Oaxacan artisans resisted, worried that an "inauthentic" product would lose market share. In the end, the viability of a textile craft often depends on the mediation of "fair trade" and human rights organizations publicizing faith-fulness to an "authentic" ancestral tradition. Hendrickson's (1996[b]) analysis of Pueblo to People catalogs promoting Mayan *traje* or dress is fascinating in this regard. Producers of *huipils* are represented as living in small, rain-forest villages lacking in modern technology. Personalized relationships with them are invoked, as if to convert alienated commodities into animated possessions. Seeing the people behind the goods suggests that their spirit resides in them and buyers are led to feel engaged in a social relationship across cultures.

Finally, social movements of "sartorial" resistance have from time to time challenged juggernaut capitalism within the sphere of production. India, rich in its own cloth traditions, several of them quite commercialized, repulsed waves of Manchester cottons as part of its struggle for independence. Choosing a captivating symbol of both economic autonomy and spiritual worth—the spinning wheel—and defining women spinners as the core of the nation, Gandhi advocated the production and wearing of hand-spun and hand-woven white cotton *khadi* and the boycotting or burning of imported English textiles. Descriptions of his initiative (e.g. Bean 1989) point not only to the circumstances of cloth manufacturing but also to the consumption sphere, where, as we will see, the pessimistic outlook on Western capitalism has also been up-ended.

THE HEGEMONY OF "WESTERN FASHION"

The processes through which industrial textiles and clothing challenged and displaced, yet also stimulated, artisanal cloth production are paralleled in the consumption sphere by the hegemony, the contradictory meanings, and the limits of "Western fashion"—generally more tailored than other dress traditions, consisting of many more components and accessories, and strongly differentiated according to gender and function. Spanish and Portuguese colonists followed by northern Europeans set this process in motion, first and foremost by penetrating and disrupting existing courtly hierarchies, together with their ongoing practices regarding cloth and clothes.

Colonial histories draw attention to European colonizers' heavy-handed dumping of surplus merchandise, establishment of "company stores," and habit of dazzling untutored audiences with machine-made wonders never seen before. Marketing research, credit advances, image promotion, and advertising also spread in the wake of colonization (see Burke 1996). In an apparent contradiction, missionaries and colonial officials criticized indigenous peoples for adopting Western finery, mocking as ridiculous their presumed desire to participate in the new order; yet these same missionaries and officials imposed Westernized standards of appearance and behavior as a criterion for religious conversion or "civilizational" status

(e.g. Thomas 2003). For this reason, too, elements of Western dress spread vigorously around the world.

And yet, there is no clear story regarding the gravity of the damage wrought by this stylistic invasion. To the Rhodes-Livingstone ethnographers of the 1940s, Africans' love of dressing up and going to dance clubs was an index of urbanization—of the steps being taken by migrants to Copperbelt cities to distance themselves from their rural past and engage with a wider, more cosmopolitan world, of which their white oppressors were the reference group (Wilson 1941). As a kind of life force, the new elegance promised to bestow power, or at least the respect of others, by symbolic means. A less benign explanation was put forward by Bernard Magubane in 1971. For Magubane, as for Franz Fanon, adopting the oppressors' clothing styles showed the extent of Africans' suffering, and the depth of their pathological colonial psychology of self-hatred, The Société des Ambianceurs et des Personnes Élégantes (SAPE)—a tradition of Congolese urban youth competitively sporting Parisian finery—and *Oswenka*—a fashion competition for adult men working in South African mines and donning "swank" suits, ties, shoes, socks, and shirts during their leisure hours—have provoked similar arguments over interpretation (see Ferguson 2002; Friedman 1994[b]; Gondola 1999; Scheld 2003).

It is interesting and perhaps significant that Magubane wrote during the apogee of "productionist" theory in anthropology when the Marxist concept of the fetishism of commodities—their magical capacity to mask the labor processes embedded in them—relegated the analysis of consumption to second place, a distraction from the project of workers' liberation. Add to this the contemporary influence of Frankfurt School scholars who considered the entertainment and consumer industries of capitalist societies to be the source of a deadening, unfulfilling conformity and escapism. That working people—and by extension colonial subjects—desired "Western fashion" could only be because they were manipulated by images and promotions.

New and less pessimistic assessments of the diffusion of Western dress were unleashed by anthropology's turn toward cultural theory in the late 1970s. A preliminary move, accomplished by Mary Douglas and Baron Isherwood in *The World of Goods* (1979), was the legitimization of consumption as a respectable rather than trivial research topic. *The Social Life of Things,* edited by Arjun Appadurai in 1986, celebrated this shift, offering several case studies of "consumer revolutions" shaped by cultural particulars (see also Miller 1995[a]). There followed Marshall Sahlins's landmark essay "Cosmologies of Capitalism" ([1988] 1994), which explicitly rejected the idea that the West's industrial, capitalist manufactures victimized non-Western peoples and adulterated their cultures.

To the contrary, local concepts of status, means of labor control, and aesthetic preferences dictated a range of outlooks on Western goods. Sahlins relished recounting that in 1793, in a letter to George III, the Chinese emperor famously expressed disdain for European fashions, deemed inferior to Chinese cloth and clothing. A different, but equally ironic, outcome emerged in the Sandwich Islands, where chiefs defined their European visitors as mythic figures descending from the sky to re-enact their ancestral Kahiki. Already obsessed with marking rank through spiritually animated adornments, they coveted the newly available English broadcloths, allowing Sahlins to quip that "the capitalist mode of production is organized by *mana.*" Other instances of the courtly adoption of Western dress would seem to amplify his argument. The pre-1950s rulers of Nepal, a country that had not been colonized, classified Europeans, whom they knew from a distance, as "barbarians." Yet they avidly consumed European cloth and clothing, initially attracted to tailored garb for military purposes, and interdicted commoners' access to these exotic imports through sumptuary legislation (Hepburn 2000: 282).

Outside of anthropology, scholars attached to the Birmingham School of Cultural Studies interpreted the purchase and display of industrially produced goods by marginalized, working-class youth as acts of creativity and resistance. In 1979, Dick Hebdige, overturning Frankfurt school dismay over popular culture, declared that British Teddy Boys in their Edwardian jackets, mods in their Italian suits, and punks flaunting shirts held together with safety pins were engaged in a process of *bricolage,* expressing rebel identities through a re-articulation of what they bought. Hebdige did appreciate, however, the eagerness of capitalist fashion designers to reappropriate subcultural styles, newly configuring their edginess for wider markets. His work has been influential in recent analyses of Hip Hop culture showing clothing and music styles to intersect in an ongoing dialectic of rebellion and appropriation.

Rather than treat consumers as passive or manipulated subjects, and the non-Western consumers of Western clothing even more so, the developments in cultural theory of the last quarter of the twentieth century pointed in the opposite direction: consumers are active agents in the construction of their own histories, even when adopting the very fashions of those they seek to resist. Thus Jean and John Comaroff argue for the incubation of revolutionary potential in colonized Southern Africans' evolving Christian identity—an identity indexed by mission-prescribed Western clothes (Comaroff 1996; Comaroff and Comaroff 1997: see also Thomas 2003).

THE GLOBAL FACTORY

The democratization of shopping is integrally related to vast and growing inequalities in the sphere of production and in the "life chances" of people around the globe. Associated with disinvestment in the first industrial societies, since the mid-1970s, the industrial production of cloth and clothing has spread to every continent, incorporating volumes of new workers, and sucking up Asian, African and Latin American as well as European capital. Increasingly, China is the "workshop of the world." Yet cloth and clothing manufacture have remained remarkably resistant to technological change. Synthetic fibers, made by forcing petroleum products through "spinarettes" (resembling shower heads) render laborious spinning unnecessary, while their high tensile strength allows for accelerated weaving (Schneider 1994). Machine innovations have reduced wastage in cutting. Nevertheless, labor is, has always been, and probably always will be the largest cost factor in making cloth and clothing. Assembly and sewing in particular remain highly demanding of the human hand; most fabrics are simply too fluid to trust to machines alone. As of the late 1990s, 13 million people were formally employed in textile manufacture worldwide, 6 million in garment manufacture, and this is not counting the millions who work in the informal sector, at home or in clandestine workshops (Dicken 1998: 283–6).

Between 1970 and 1993, 420,000 jobs were lost in textiles in the United States, and 180,000 (mostly unionized) jobs in the garment sector, cutting and tailoring. In the same period, the "revolutionary retailers" launched an assault on labor, paying substandard wages to clerks and stock persons in their own outlets, explicitly discouraged in the case of Walmart from unionizing; and contracting for product from export processing zones, *maquilladoras* and sweatshops around the world. In such locations, employees tend to be young and female, often pressed into spinning or sewing by rural families suffering from crises of agricultural dislocation. The fragmented nature of the contracting arrangements constitutes a formidable obstacle to regulating what are often appalling working conditions: seven-day weeks with twelve to fourteen hours a day at times of peak demand; poor ventilation; accidents related to speed-up; and vulnerability to disemployment as the contractors relocate to zones where wages are lower still.

According to geographer Peter Dicken (1998: 294–5), the concentrated purchasing power of the great chains gives them "enormous leverage over textile and clothing manufacturers." In effect, they have combined state-of-the-art communications technology, design capability, and far-flung "parts producers" into a singular colossus—the extraordinarily unequal counter-part to the democratization of fashion. Ian Skoggard, an anthropologist who researched shoe production in Taiwan, notes that the images highlighted in Nike's New York shrine to athletes, with its Fifth Avenue address, Greek columns, and videos of sponsored players and teams, would be tarnished if a consumer campaign were to dwell on the working conditions of its Asian suppliers (Skoggard 1998[a]). Yet, even when they are aware of the circumstances of production, most consumers feel gratitude for capitalism's incredible gift: the possibility for sartorial self-enhancement under the almost affordable combination of credit and bargain

sales. What is more, the young women who work in the sweatshops desire, themselves, to partake of this gift.

THE PRESENT-DAY SARTORIAL ECUMENE

Given that, today, "commercial" cloth and clothing are produced in the "global factory," the old problematic of the hegemony of "Western fashion"—its relation to unequal power and resistance—seems quite beside the point. Paris, Milan, New York and London continue to be the pre-eminent centers of high-end design, but Tokyo, Hong Kong, and Shanghai are credible competitors (see Kondo 1992; Li 1998; Skov 2003). Most important, the high end is generally less relevant to the overall picture. As Karen Tranberg Hansen puts it, an increasingly vast proliferation of styles has definitively squelched emulation as a significant ingredient in clothing decisions, encouraging an unfettered individualism as it ushers in processes of "bricolage, hybridity, and creolization" (Hansen 2004[b]: 4–5). And yet, the "sartorial ecumene," to borrow Hansen's felicitous expression ([Hansen 2004b]: 10), is far from a level playing field, given the powerful engines of consumerism and the production relations that accompany it. Three broad developments suggesting, respectively, resistance, courtly revitalization, and full participation in consumer culture are sketched below.

Of immediate visual impact are the widening zones of morally "conservative" dress, for example the sari in India. As Mukulika Banerjee and Daniel Miller (2003) document in their beautifully illustrated book on the subject, this garment is now made of industrially manufactured cloth, more often polyester than silk or cotton, and worn in conjunction with tailored blouses. As well, it has undergone a process of homogenization, promoted by entertainment celebrities as well as political leaders, in which divergent regional methods of folding and draping are subsumed under a common national style, "the Nivi." Emblematic of pride in the nation, the sari has convinced all classes of women, from village field workers to employees in offices, to wealthy women of leisure, that it augments their "possibilities of aesthetic beauty, female mastery, sexuality and the cult of the maternal." Putting it on, women try to live up to "the kind and quality of person that the sari now requires and stands for" ([Banerjee and Miller] 2003: 235–6; see also Tarlo 1996).

Because the sari's potential to evoke sexuality has triggered the sort of anxiety that attaches to trendy, consumerist clothes, however, some Indian women prefer the Muslim-influenced *shalwar kamiz*, a garment of trousers and tunic that hides, rather than reveals, the body. (So do long skirts, the hallmark of female modesty in the Middle East, where, in contrast, the early twentieth-century introduction of trousers for women provoked censure and even riots. See Gillette 2000: 97.) Moral concerns are uppermost in veiling, a spreading practice in Muslim societies across the globe. Many of today's veiled Muslims are caught up in (male-led) political struggles addressing the Arab-Israeli conflict and US intervention in the Middle East. More broadly, veiling seems powerfully to symbolize women's subordination to men. At the same time, however, conservative Islamic dress is a reminder that, throughout history, unprecedented squandering associated with a suddenly yawning chasm between rich and poor has triggered moralistic responses focused on justice and fairness. Thus St Francis, the son of a prosperous leather merchant in a time of spreading opulence in Florence, held his rough, undyed robes together with a (pointedly not leather) rope belt. Several ethnographic studies point to the veil as similarly materializing a broad moral critique.

Following the 1970s emergence of an Islamic youth and student movement in Malaysia, for example, upwardly mobile, urban educated women adopted conservative dress, their apparent identification with "revivalist ideals of motherhood [and] male authority" occurring despite the fact that neither veiling nor female seclusion had characterized their society in the past. According to Aihwa Ong (1990[b]), the movement "railed against the decadent lifestyles of *nouveaux riches* Malays, considered too secular and materialistic." In adopting the *minitelekung*, a cloth that "tightly frames the face and covers the head, hair and chest," and the long black robes or *hijab*, women both experienced and expressed a sense of moral righteousness in relation to the sensuality of consumer culture, and the polarization of wealth and extreme poverty that its capitalist foundations had spawned.

Java is another place where veiling spread among university students in the late 1970s, in the context of a pan-Islamist movement, the practice having had no roots in local clothing traditions. Because in Java, unlike in the Middle East, veiling is an obstacle to secular employment, is criticized by public opinion for communicating sanctimoniousness and fanaticism, was for a while prohibited by government decree, and is even disapproved of by parents, persisting in the practice is disruptive of significant social ties and is a matter of soul-searching and determination. In the narratives of women who wore *jilbab*, or Muslim dress, Suzanne Brenner (1996) discovered that a moral crisis had been set in motion by an unchecked and "disgusting" consumerism on the part of moneyed elites, juxtaposed with the suffering of an increasingly destitute "underclass." For the morally anxious person, veiling bestows a sense of calm, self-mastery, and renewal (see also Abu-Lughod 1990; Göle 1996; Hoodfar 1991; Mernissi 1987).

Another set of images from today's sartorial ecumene presents "ethnic dress" as a counter-weight to consumer culture, but not in a very compelling way. For one thing, iconic elements of ethnicity are products of historical and continuing interactions with Western and commercial fashions. They are not themselves emblems of an authentic "cultural heritage." Second, adopting them in urban and modern contexts, although it elicits approval from some groups, invites stigma or opprobrium from others. Where governments of multi-ethnic states are seeking to create a national identity, overriding ethnic difference, government officials may propagate ethnically neutral models of dress or mandate uniforms for schools and other public arenas. Finally, to the extent that elements of an ethnic wardrobe are produced by artisanal labor, their cost may exceed by far the cost of commercial wear. This circumstance means that only ethnic leaders are able to acquire the full regalia demanded by life-cycle rituals and ceremonial events; others must borrow to enjoy the symbolically and materially transformative properties of "traditional" dress. It should be noted that, through dense relations of borrowing and lending, ethnic communities manifest the principles of generosity and clientelism that underpin social solidarity in courtly social forms.

Reviewing several decades of ethnographic research in Africa, James Ferguson (2002) proposes that non-Europeans' adoption of commercial dress codes has been an "embarrassment" to anthropology, whose stock in trade is the viability of local cultures. Hence anthropologists' tendency to celebrate local reworkings of the codes, finding assertions of opposition or autonomy in them. Meanwhile, however, their anthropological subjects are increasingly caught up in the kinds of modernizing and urbanizing processes that so impressed the ethnographers of the Copperbelt in the 1940s. Why not conclude, Ferguson argues, that, in getting swept up in contemporary fads and fashions, people are expressing their desire, and their *right*, to participate in modernity? Wearing commercial clothes is a way to cultivate a modern consciousness appropriate to the modern condition. Hansen's remarkable study of used clothing in Zambia (2000) is a case in point. A global commodity chain originating in the charities of the first industrialized countries delivers a vast array of barely worn, up-to-date clothing to the rest of the world. (The squandering United States ships out no less than 50 million tons per year, much of it manufactured or partly manufactured "off-shore.") Zambians enthusiastically rummage through used clothing markets and frequent resident tailors who fashion the necessary and wished-for alterations. The thrust of Hansen's analysis is to save their love of doing so from the charge that it is externally driven. "Cultural and subjective matters," rooted in a past of courtly arrangements in which elites' capacity for enhancement far exceeded that of commoners, is part of the motivation; the other part is the capacity of "modern clothes" to empower their wearers, imbuing them with the confidence of accruing respect.

And yet, Hansen's study also communicates a deeper truth about the sartorial ecumene, one that brings us back to this chapter's insistence on integrating the spheres of production and consumption. If it weren't for the secondhand markets many Zambians would be in rags, because over the 1980s and 1990s, decent work almost disappeared. Rummaged fashion narrows the gap in appearance between rich and poor, rural and urban, North and South. Evoking hoped-for opportunities and chances—what Keane (2005) poignantly calls "expectations of history"—it permits the well attired person to imagine a better future. Sadly, the author concludes, dreams of a better life can also be illusory—at best a transient and vicarious way to escape the economic powerlessness wrought by the downward spiral of current trends.

14

JEANEALOGIES:
Materiality and the (im)permanence of relationships and intimacy

Sophie Woodward

*I wear his jeans when I'm on my own in my flat … I don't know why …
I guess it makes me feel like I'm still close to him, kind of comforted …*

Georgia, a woman in her early twenties living in London, is wearing the jeans of a man she is in an ambiguous on-off relationship with when she utters these words to me. After spending the night with him at his flat, she borrowed them the next morning to keep warm on the journey home and continues to wear them when she is back in her own flat. Wearing the jeans, she feels he continues to be, in some part, present with her and makes her more able to deal with the ambiguity of her relationship to him. During ethnographic fieldwork that I conducted into women's wardrobes in the UK, several women I worked with wore their boyfriend's jeans, and "boyfriend" jeans themselves are currently a well established category of jeans in the UK. Georgia's example raises the ways in which clothing is used to negotiate women's relationships to others. The very appearance of cloth and clothing is one that lends itself to associations with connectedness, with rich metaphorical potential in terms of the weaving together of people, and the fabric of their relationships. The connectedness of woven cloth is extended both to metaphor and also to anthropological attempts to see the process of weaving and exchange of cloth as symbolizing kinship relationships (Weiner and Schneider 1989). The embeddedness of clothing in people's relationships is, however, not given the same attention by Weiner and Schneider (1989) for

clothing in the West and the wider context of fashion. Instead, clothing in the contemporary UK is subsumed under fashion, and concomitant associations of image, appearance and individualism. It is the contention of this chapter that, in the context of the UK, the relationships people have to clothing are not reducible to wider contexts and values of individualism. This chapter will focus upon the material acts of wearing, donating and borrowing denim jeans, as a means through which relationships to others are negotiated.

One of the predominant relationships in the provisioning and gifting of clothing in countries such as the UK and US is that between mother and daughter (Clarke 2000; Corrigan 1995; De Vault 1991) as particular taste patterns are inculcated, and as an act of love, although this relationship may become more contested as the daughter moves to adulthood (Miller 1997[c]). In my initial ethnography on women's wardrobes there was a clear contrast between the long-term gifting of clothing over time between mothers and daughters and the lending of clothing between relatives or long-term friendships and more short-term clothing exchanges (Woodward 2007). The type of clothing lent and the expectations of whether it will be returned immediately or not served to create and reinforce the relationship. In this chapter, I focus in

Adapted from Sophie Woodward, "Jeanneologies: Materiality and the (Im)permanence of Relationships and Intimacies," in *Global Denim*, edited by Daniel Miller and Sophie Woodward (London: Bloomsbury, 2011), pp. 145–58.

the main on a particular kind of relationship, between women and their boyfriends. In light of this focus, it may appear somewhat unexpected to use the trope of the genealogy, which seems to imply a structured family history. When this structured formalized set of relationships is mapped onto the passage of clothing, it would imply that clothing, or jeans, would be similarly rigidly structured as they are used to define relationships between generations. Alternatively, at the level of broader cultural histories, to talk of a genealogy of jeans, a "jean-ealogy," conjures up associations of the lineage of denim jeans as descending from Levi-Strauss in the late nineteenth century and the well established histories and stories of denim jeans. The jeanealogy suggested in this paper is somewhat different from either of these, as it forms part of my broader orientation to clothing in the context of the UK, which is to focus upon the everyday and ordinary practices of selection, wearing and choice of clothing. The meanings that arise from the jeans do not originate from the creativity and authorship of the designer but instead through the ways in which denim is worn and exchanged and as it comes to enable and materialize everyday relationships. Therefore, the jeanealogy is understood in a much more fluid, less formalized sense than conventional notions of the genealogy would allow for.

The notion of fluidity in personal relationships is emphasized by writers on intimacy within contemporary British society. Giddens (1991, 1992) suggests that the changes in the labour market amongst other social changes—for example sex is no longer wed to procreation—means that there is a shift in the structuring of relationships and a transformation of intimacy. In his account, this leads to a greater diversity in relationships, and the "pure relationship" that is "entered into for its own sake" (Giddens 1992: 58). At the core of Giddens' idea is what Jamieson has termed "disclosing intimacy" (Jamieson 1998: 1), where the relationship is negotiated and maintained through the verbalization of feelings and desires. Whilst there are many critiques of Giddens' ideas, in relation to the emphasis upon choice and ignoring persisting gendered inequalities, the primacy given to the verbal and spoken is of particular concern in this article. I opened this chapter with the spoken words

of a woman I worked with ethnographically; however, these words carry meaning when situated in the context of much wider observations of her practices. These words are not ones she would ever articulate to the man she is seeing. As material culture, the jeans do not reflect the relationship, but her wearing of his jeans are a medium through which she is able to articulate that which she is unable to verbalize to him. In her critique of Giddens, Jamieson (1998) discusses the multiple layers of intimacy, as verbalizing feelings are only one expression or aspect of intimacy. The jeans may therefore externalize contradictory aspects of a relationship, for example in terms of dependency and independency. A similar contradiction is exemplified in the pure relationship, expounded and idealized by Giddens, which is not bound by tradition and entered into freely, yet simultaneously carries within it the possibility for this union to breakdown. In this chapter, I will suggest that clothing effectively externalizes the fragility of a relationship, which dovetails with Weiner's claims, albeit in a very different context, where she suggests that the "softness and ultimate fragility of these materials capture the vulnerability of humans, whose every relationship is transient" (Weiner 1989: 2).

PERSONALIZATION THROUGH WEARING

The material upon which this paper is based comes from ethnography carried out in London and Nottingham over a fifteen-month period of women's wardrobes (see Woodward 2007 for full details of the methodology and research findings). There were twenty-seven women in total in the research sample, recruited through snowball sampling. Over half of the women were connected to each other through kinship, work, or friendship groups (three networks in total). To suggest that denim jeans offer the possibility of connections to others seems to pose something of a paradox, given that they are cited by many women I worked with as being an item of clothing to which they have a very personal relationship. There are pairs of jeans that women would not let anyone else wear—for example, when women have found the elusive "perfect jeans" or a pair that they have worn over such a long period of time because the intimate personal relationship that they have to the jeans would be disrupted by someone else wearing them. However, several of these same women also wore the jeans of their boyfriends or partners. In many cases this is due to the larger body size of their boyfriends, as women are easily able to fit them. By virtue of the denim carrying the former wearer, women are able to negotiate a relationship to someone else, and in some instances use it to expand upon their own personal aesthetic.

AUTHENTICITY AND MASCULINITY

Steph, the first case study, is a woman in her early twenties who is originally from Ireland and wears her boyfriend's jeans regularly. Although he is still living in Ireland, and as such is not present with her all the time, Steph is not wearing the jeans as a sentimental reminder of him but primarily to expand upon her own wardrobe. This is part of a wider tendency that emerged from the main ethnography, where women do not necessarily treat items gifted or passed on to them as cherished heirlooms or items that reify a particular person or relationship. Although the act of wearing serves to establish a connection to others, as the relationships to others are externalized in items of clothing, women are able to use these same relationships to expand the possibilities of who you can be through clothing (see previous discussions of this in Woodward 2007). Women may be able to expand their usually personal aesthetic through the taste of a friend or their mother. This strategy, at the micro level of the wardrobe, is mirrored in the wider practices of wearing vintage or second-hand clothing (see Clark and Palmer 2004; Gregson and Crewe 2003), where it is possible to imagine the narratives behind the garments. It is an affordable way to expand upon the possibilities of what can be worn and it allows a perceived stepping outside of mainstream fashion.

Wearing her boyfriend's jeans, for Steph, is part of her wider attitude to clothing as she states on numerous occasions that she loathes the high street (despite buying items such as her skinny jeans from there). Over two years, she gradually made her boyfriend's jeans a part of her wardrobe, first wearing them when he left them in her flat as he stayed over, and now, she owns two pairs that he has had to relinquish to her, it would seem, permanently. She wears her jeans almost every day alternating between wearing her boyfriend's jeans, and her other skinny drainpipe jeans (which were the fashion at the time when I was working with her), which she wears with trainers and her "rocker" t-shirts. Different types of jeans are the basis for her to create very different daily looks. Steph's boyfriend is around four inches taller than her; he is narrow hipped, but wears the jeans loose on him. On her they are low slung, and she has to hold them up by wearing a chunky belt. They are straight-legged jeans, and are so loose fitting that they do not cling to any part of her body; the legs are too long that she has to turn them up on the outside. She wears the oversized jeans with fitted pink or cream silk camisole tops, and soft silk-mix, angora or cashmere cardigans. Although the jeans are unmistakably men's jeans, as the crotch starts half way down her thighs, the combination with the pink camisole, and the soft angora cardigan in pale colours means that the overall look is far from masculinized. In many other cases, jeans are valued through the personalized way in which a pair of jeans adapt to the wearer's body. For Steph, these particular jeans, through their voluminousness, serve to emphasize the smallness of her body. The only place that the denim has started to wear down and soften is at the base, where she trips over the edges of the turn-ups. In adopting a masculinized style of jeans, and rejecting a conventional femininity that jeans might allow, she serves to emphasize her vulnerability and delicateness as she constructs an alternative mode of femininity (such as in Holland 2004). The femininity that is articulated through the jeans serves as a repudiation of the hypersexualized, semi-clad masquerade of femininity that is present in many mainstream representations of young women (Levy 2006).

Steph exemplifies a core contradiction many young women embody between the desire to be fashionable through participating in fast fashion and simultaneously wanting to reject and repudiate the fashion mainstream and the femininity it embodies. Her verbalized dislike of high-street fashion becomes practice through shopping in charity shops, and also in wearing her boyfriend's jeans. She is able to thus deal with the potentially alienating features of mass fashion in terms of both the rapidly changing temporal cycles and its perceived inauthenticity. Although authenticity is a highly contested term, it was used by many women I worked with in discussing their relationships to clothing. It is a term through which they articulated their own practices; the authentic is often perceived as being in opposition to commercially produced styles. This opposition is problematic when seen in the light of the ways in which commerce appropriates and represents everyday consumption patterns. In the case of denim jeans, this happens through processes such as distressing, where the abrasion of the fabric through wearing is replicated through commercial design processes. It also happens through the selling of "boyfriend jeans" in various high street stores, as they tap into the borrowing practices that women partake in. Boyfriend jeans are both a commercially produced style, and are also, in Steph's case, based upon borrowing her actual boyfriend's jeans, as she tells me they are the "real thing," as they come to seem more authentic by virtue of once being worn by her boyfriend. In wearing men's jeans she is also drawing upon the original narratives of denim jeans, which, in its origins, is a masculinized trajectory. The jeans she borrows are pure cotton (with no elastane fibres, as is the practice with the majority of current women's jeans), which serves to accentuate the authentic connotations of the masculinized, pure cotton, blue denim. She has worn the jeans on and off for two years now, and the jeans have become more personalized through both her boyfriend and Steph wearing them. This process over time allows her to step outside of the constantly changing temporal cycles of fast fashion. They can be seen to form a rejection of the alleged speed of fast fashion, as they acquire their meaning through a slow process of abrading and being worn down. The jeans become personalized not by directly taking on her body shape (as is the case when women wear more fitted jeans over a period of time). Instead as the jeans are worn down at the base as they drag on the floor and so the relationship between her body and the jeans is different to that which her boyfriend

had (as the worn-down area of the knees falls below her actual knee).

MULTIPLE WEARERS

In the preceding example, the jeans are seen as authentic because they were not bought by Steph as the commercial women's wear category of "boyfriend jeans" but belonged to her boyfriend. In other examples in my fieldwork, authenticity is evidenced in the histories of wear that are apparent in the fabric. It derives from the patina of age, which is present in denim where the fabric has abraded and become softened as the soft white cotton fibres show through. This wearing can be either a personalized process, as they are worn habitually over a long period of time, or, in the example to be discussed here, of someone who not only wears the jeans of a former partner but jeans that have been worn by several members of her extended family. Vivienne, a former political campaigner and researcher in her fifties living in north London, has one pair of jeans that used to be black denim but are now worn down to a faded grey colour, with soft white patches, where the soft cotton fibres have worn through. These jeans are fourth hand and were given to her by her daughter's boyfriend (formerly worn by her daughter, and her boyfriend's father). In the previous example of Steph the jeans externalize the relationship between two individuals and in a broader sense this is what boyfriend jeans encapsulate. This example serves to highlight the ways in which multiple relationships, and also forms of intimacy, may be present within one item of clothing. Jamieson (1998) has argued that the intimate relationship between two people, as exemplified by Giddens' pure relationship (1992), has been idealized in contemporary society. This idealization has served to obscure, in Jamieson's account, the multiple forms of intimacy—such as practical caring, dependency, sharing—within any one relationship and within many different forms of relationships.

So too here, the journey of the jeans does not reify one relationship, but has incorporated several family members. The jeans do not carry any one person's body, but are gradually altered by each wearer in turn.

The jeans have passed between more than one family, making a connection between both.

Although, in the previous example, Steph is not treating the jeans as something to be preserved as they are—she still refers to them as her boyfriend's jeans (even though they have been longer in her possession). They are strongly associated with the former wearer and, as they are loose and baggy, they have not taken on Steph's body even through repeated acts of wearing. In the case of Vivienne's jeans, they are not used to remember a specific person, but rather by being worn by a series of people, each person leaves their traces on the garment as it materializes the network of connections between them. The vestigial traces of the wearers are present within the worn down nature of the jeans, yet as the jeans have been passed between people, these traces overlap and it is hard to identify any individual pattern of wear. The jeans come to materialize the passage of time and the construction of the family. The connections between people that are being discussed here are very different from formalized notions of a genealogy. Weiner and Schneider (1989) cite Gitting's research into funerals and the transition in the seventeenth century to people having to provide their own black drapes for funerals. They discuss this as a point of transition for clothing in the context of the West as it "no longer expressed the continuity of the groups with ancestral authority and their reproduction through time" (Weiner and Schneider 1989: 11). What this does not account for is the informal passing on of clothing or gifting of items, which establishes a connection between generations or between family members. Even in a climate with dominant values of individualism, this always exists in relationship to wider social relations in which it is embedded from which it arises. The individual is always constituted relationally, seen through clothing practices in the wearing of borrowed and gifted clothing. As these relationships develop and change throughout the life course, Stanley (1992) has questioned and challenged the conventional way that biography is understood as the story of an isolated individual. Instead she argues that significant others cannot be reduced to the position of "shadowing figures" as the biographical self is constructing through relationships to others. This is

seen as much within the wardrobe a woman owns, as women draw in their relationships to others in their clothing choices. This is reflected within an individual item like Vivienne's jeans, which carry many different wearers. Each individual personalizes the item and the one pair of jeans interconnects many different people.

In both the cases of Vivienne and Steph, the wearing of the jeans of others allows a stepping outside of fashion, borrowing clothes from others is an alternative sourcing strategy to the high street. This is part of Vivienne's wider strategies towards clothing, as she owns very few new items of clothing, with many being so old and worn that they are falling apart, as her daughters often pass items up to her. Although this distancing of themselves from fashion can be linked to buying and sourcing from second-hand shops there is a point of difference as bought second hand involve an imagined, anonymous narrative. For Steph, she is wearing jeans that connect her to one other person, and for Vivienne, the jeans allow her to become part of a woven network of the narratives of a series of people. It allows her to define herself through her connectedness to others; it is jeans that allow her to do this most effectively as it carries the personalized traces of the wearers, yet the jeans have now softened so much in places that they are threatening to disintegrate all together.

THE IMPERMANENCE AND FRAGILITY OF RELATIONSHIPS

Vivienne's jeans have lasted long enough to carry the imprint of several wearers, but they will not last forever. The simultaneous durability and fragility of denim will be explored through this final example of Georgia, a woman in her early twenties. The jeans in questions cannot be called her "boyfriend" jeans, as she has an ambiguous relationship with a man whom she has been "seeing" for over six months. He refuses to use the word "boyfriend" and she is unsure whether he is seeing other girls; they meet up regularly, yet the lack of definition of their relationship means she feels uncertain as to when he will come and see her next.

This example highlights the problems with Giddens' (1992) pure relationship, which is based upon the freedom of choice of two individuals, who are self-reflexive over their feelings and desires, which leads to a relationship between equals. Numerous critiques of Giddens, such as Jackson (1996), suggest that this fails to account for the persistence of inequalities. As Duncombe and Marsden (1999: 103) note, what contemporary relationships characterize more widely is not the equality that Giddens so optimistically touts, but that sexual differences persist. Georgia exemplifies this, as she confides on occasion that she wishes he was her boyfriend. Although she harbours this wish at the moment, while he thwarts her desire for a steady relationship, this situation may well change were he to capitulate. For Georgia, a key part of her social relationships are friendships with other women, a key topic being the hopelessness of men. This highlights a problematic and complex relationship between public narratives, personal narratives and everyday practice.

There are public stories about gendered expectations of relationships—for instance that "all women want commitment" and "men want to sleep around" (Hollway 1984), another one being "all men are bastards," which Georgia at times highlights. The narrative she adopts does not negate the fact that she simultaneously expresses a desire to be connected to this particular man, and how these public narratives of "wanting a good boyfriend" seep into her own expectations. This also highlights a paradox between a possible desire for independence, being single and bonding with her female friends, and also the desire for connection. Dependency and connection to others start to raise questions about the "pure relationship." This example also problematizes an understanding of relationships based merely upon the verbal, as is assumed in notions of "disclosure" taking a central place in a relationship, which does not allow for contradiction. This is similarly true for the notion of reflexivity: wearing his jeans may also signify an absence of reflexivity and a desire, on occasion, to allow a material connection to this man, without verbalizing her contradictory experiences and feelings. These may be too complex to articulate. This reflexivity is also not gender neutral; Hochschild (cited in Heaphy 2007: 142) develops the idea of emotional labour in particular workplaces that some women have to master as part of their jobs. Heaphy (2007) has argued

that this is as true at the level of relationships, where the expectation is for women to be more reflexive.

Even when Georgia's man is not in her flat, he is still present by virtue of the items he has left there. Some are left deliberately, such as a toothbrush and a warm winter jumper, and others are items she has bought back to her flat when she goes to see him. If they go out one evening, and she goes back to his house, so as not to look like a "dirty stop out" (her words) the next day, she borrows a pair of jeans or a shirt. For days after, she may carry on wearing the jeans, but only around the house, until he reclaims them on his next visit. He is over six inches taller than her, and so, as in the first case study, when the jeans are worn they hang loose from her hip bones, and drag over her feet unless she rolls them over at the top. When she first puts them on, they still carry his scent, and are softened by him wearing them. The jeans are still animated by the last time he wore them as they have loosened around his knees, carrying the smell of his sweat and aftershave, as if they are a living garment making him seem present in her flat still. The size and looseness of the jeans emphasize her vulnerability as the jeans carry her absent lover's ghostly presence. She is able to feel comforted by wearing the jeans in the face of the uncertainly of whether she will see him again. She wears them when she feels her most vulnerable, and as she can still remember the feel of his body and arms around her, the jeans wrap around her body too as they mediate his presence and his absence.

When she feels her most vulnerable, she is only able to partially verbalize this, as instead it is materialized: her simultaneous vulnerability and connectedness to him, as the jeans act as a form of security and stability that the relationship itself may not offer. The jeans have taken on his body shape and his scent and in wearing them it is as if she is able to inhabit the second skin of his jeans.

She only wears the jeans in the house and, even then, it is only on occasion and as such wearing his jeans is in many ways very different to her usual relationship with her clothing. Wearing the jeans helps her to negotiate the uncertainty of this particular relationship. There is a strong assumption that clothing in the contemporary UK is about "expressing yourself," or is linked to individuality (see Woodward 2005 for a critique of this). In this instance,

Georgia is adopting a completely opposite strategy: she is relinquishing her claims to be an individual in this moment, and instead wants to attach herself to her absent lover. When she is alone, after he has left her—this is when she feels vulnerable. Wearing clothing owned by others (or in other occasions gifted) enmeshes the individual back into social relationships: in this case her relationship to him when they are apart. As I have already discussed, the self is always constituted through multiple relationships, yet on this occasion it is only one relationship that she can conceive of herself through, and the clothing allows her to continue the connections to him. Wearing his jeans allows a simultaneous acknowledgment that she feels comforted and also her sense of vulnerability.

She is also implicitly acknowledging that the relationship itself is not permanent. The connections between clothing, social relations and permanence have been explored, albeit in very different contexts, by Weiner (1989). In two examples, in the Trobriand Islands and Western Samoa, she explores how cloth is used to symbolize kinship relationships and groups and how these same kinship identities are "translated into political authority" through clothing, (Weiner 1989: 33). Her discussion is useful in highlighting how the properties of cloth are such that, in each case, they effectively manage to materialize kinship relationships and their connections to authority. The cloths she refers to in the Trobriand Islands are bundles of banana leaves (which involve extensive labour) and women's fibrous skirts (which are distributed after someone's death). Women's cloth wealth "serves as the anchoring matrilineal force, demonstrating the success of regeneration in the face of death" (Weiner 1989: 40). In the case of Western Samoa, where chiefs' rankings are also associated with certain descent groups yet are not given by birth, the cloths she refers to are fine mats made from pandanus fibres, which are delicately plaited and soft as fine linen (and are more demanding to make than Trobriand bundles). The question Weiner (1989: 62) addresses through both of these examples is why cloth, which she terms "soft wealth" is utilized as a symbol of authority and kinship identities, and not "hard wealth," which would serve as a more permanent record. Weiner argues that it is precisely the impermanence of cloth that makes it effective as it captures the vulnerability of power. The cloths utilized

in each case have some permanence, when they outlast an individual life-span, yet the characteristics of cloth are such that "as it rots and disintegrates, bring to the histories of persons and lineages the reality of life's ultimate incompleteness" (Weiner 1989: 63).

Although this is a very different context from the one I outlined earlier in this chapter, the ideas about how cloth effectively materializes permanence and impermanence can be applied to the issue of the way in which denim mediates relationships to others. Denim carries the former wearer on numerous different levels; the most fleeting way being the traces of the living body directly after wearing, as the fabric is still warm from the body and carries its scents, which disappear as the jeans are washed. The fabric itself also carries the wearer in a more permanent way through continued wearing, the moving body leads to body- and usage-specific patterns of wearing and the fabric wears down. The more fleeting traces of the living body and the slightly more permanent traces of bodily movements co-exist. In Georgia's case she wears the jeans to feel connected to her absent lover, yet at the same time, as his living traces do not remain, and she has to give back the jeans, she simultaneously recognizes that the relationship itself is fleeting. Denim very effectively mediates this ambivalence, due to the ambivalences that inhere to the fabric—it is both rigid and it softens; it lasts but it does not last forever. This sense of the impermanent traces of others is present in all of the examples discussed, as the wearing of the jeans of others allows for informality in the connections between people. For example, Vivienne's jeans have taken on several wearers and are able to incorporate different branches and members of the family. Weiner's primary focus is upon the making and the exchange of cloths, yet in my ethnography, although items are passed on, the emphasis is upon the wearing and the relationship between body and garment. Through this dynamic relationship, the form and texture of denim changes, as it is mutable and shifting in its interplay between toughness and relative durability, with a process of change and ageing as the fragile soft threads are revealed.

CONCLUSION

This chapter has used the idea of a "jeanealogy" as a tool to think about how denim externalizes and helps negotiate a particular kind of relationship. A genealogy in its most widely applied incarnation involves tracing a family tree right back to the original ancestors. This is understood in an evolutionary sense, or even in the popular meanings as tracing a family's previous generations in an attempt to plot the family's ancestors. The jeanealogy proposed in this article is somewhat different. Weiner and Schneider can be seen to embody the classic anthropological sense of a genealogy when they note that in the West clothing does not express a groups continuity "ancestral authority and their reproduction through time" (Weiner and Schneider 1989: 11). However, the relationships that I am considering here are more fluid and informal.

Taking the example of Vivienne as a case in point, the daughter has now separated from the boyfriend from whom she received the jeans, and the jeans have disintegrated. In many instances there is not such a convenient correlation between the biography of the clothing and that of the relationship, as a desire to remember someone might outlive the clothing that disintegrates and dies too soon. This example does, however, highlight the impermanence of relationships that are absented from a formal genealogy. The jeanealogies I have traced here are informal, intransient, and partial as they may include fragments of incomplete relationships. This is particularly apt in the case of boyfriend jeans, given that these are predominantly worn by younger women and such relationships are particularly vulnerable to terminating.

The three examples all show different ways in which women may negotiate their relationships through clothing. For Steph this is about a relationship to a specific individual, her boyfriend, yet the jeans are a means through which she can expand upon the possibilities of her own wardrobe. Relationships are instead a means through which to expand upon the possibilities of the self (Osteen 2002), as clothing is a material means through which this can be negotiated. The individual and relationships to others are not mutually exclusive but relations to others may be the medium through which women may construct a personal aesthetic. What Steph's example has in common with that of Vivienne is that both use jeans that were originally someone else's in order to step outside of mainstream fashion and use the slower life cycle of a pair of jeans in order to do this. Even if commerce attempts to appropriate the slow process of ageing of a pair of jeans through processes such as distressing, for many women I worked with this carries connotations of inauthenticity, as fast fashion attempts to pick up the personalization and the gradual changes of a pair of jeans.

In Miller and Woodward (2007) we discussed how the generic-ness of a pair of jeans is something that people could use to reattach them to the world when they feel the most vulnerable and separated from social relations. This was discussed in relation to an ethnographic example of someone who was paralysed with indecisions over what to wear to a party and ended up wearing a pair of new jeans. In this chapter, I have instead discussed how denim jeans are used to reconnect the individual to a very specific relationship; by drawing upon denim's capacity to carry the former wearer. Whilst on some occasions the wearing of jeans may be about the creation of an individual look, at other times it is very clearly about mitigating against the problems of feeling adrift from connections to others, as jeans are able to articulate this feeling of vulnerability and reconnect the individual. In a wider sense, it has been argued by many that there are fewer norms, traditions and guidelines for relationships, seen in the decline in traditional institutions like marriage, and also in the shifting meanings of these institutions. At the same time, I would contend that alongside a decline in such clearly defined traditions, there are also persistent normative expectations, in some of the examples discussed here, of how a relationship should be. There is paradoxically less security as many traditional expectations have been eroded, yet normative ideas persist alongside inequalities. Despite shifts in intimacy and ways of relating, the relationship is far from the freedom of choice that Giddens supposes. In the examples discussed here, jeans are able to mediate multiple contradictions between dependency and independence, the burden of love and the comfort of support (as expounded by Beck and Beck-Gernsheim 1995) and vulnerability and connectedness.

15

WILD SILK TEXTILES OF THE DOGON OF MALI:
The production, material efficacy, and cultural significance of sheen

Laurence Douny

INTRODUCTION

African wild silk is perceived as a material of prestige and it has been used for centuries in regional textile industries. This "unexpected luxury" (McKinney and Eicher 2009) that is used in textiles that are associated with wealth and social status very often strikes one as being cotton. Examples of wild silk are found in embroidered works displayed on Hausa *babban riga* gowns (Douny 2011; Perani and Wolff 1992), but also in woven textiles such as the Yoruba *Sanyan/AsoOke* cloth (Perani and Wolff 1999) or Malgasy *Lamba* (Peigler 2004). Because of its coarse and lumpy texture wild silk appears far less lustrous than the well-known Mulberry silk produced by the *Bombyx mori* silkworm. The Dogon of the *Tommo* and *Tengu-kan* areas of Mali produce a wrapper that contains wild silk strips called *tombe toun*. This fabric is composed of grades of white or light blue and indigo narrow woven strips that display horizontally and that are made of dyed indigo hand-spun cotton and white silk yarn. The wrapper is an original Marka-Dafing textile that would have been produced for the past 200 years by the Dogon, according to oral tradition. In addition to being an essential component of bride wealth, this prestigious cloth that is worn and praised by women for its "sheen," and therefore strength, is used as a shroud to honor the dead. These wrappers also retain prestige for local and regional ceremonies as they materialize both Dogon and collective Mande identity (Douny 2013). Due to its "sheen," *tombe toun* as a "must-have" traditional garment is a means by which women can successfully display their prosperous social status at local public events. In other words, *tombe toun*, which is seen as an affair of women from its production to wearing it, presents a fashion opportunity through which Dogon women in rural areas enhance their well-being and personal worth. Moreover, wild silk wrappers bear Malinke aphorisms, which remind people of social codes and moral values as well as prescribing social behavior. The price of the wrapper is based upon the amount of wild silk that the fabric contains and that is treated as a rare and unique material. Nevertheless, the wrapper's production involves multiple costly stages operated by craft specialists who are mostly Dogon women and men, ranging from processing of raw materials to indigo dyeing. Yet, it should be noted that while wild silk is processed by Dogon women and woven by Dogon men weavers, the dye work of Dogon wrappers is carried out either by Guara women, who are Dogon of the dyer specialist caste, or by Marka-Dafing men of the Sokura area in Mali. Hence, the production of these wrappers involves complex gendered economic networks established amongst the Dogon themselves and with the Marka-Dafing of Mali, who also provide Dogon women with cocoons.

Adapted from Laurence Douny, "Wild Silk Textiles of the Dogon of Mali: The Production, Material Efficacy, and Cultural Significance of Sheen," *Textile: The Journal of Cloth and Culture* 11, no. 1 (March 2013): 58–77.

Grounded in an ethnography of materials (Küchler 2010), this article looks at the production and social usages of Dogon wild silk textiles by focusing on the material properties of wild silk and more specifically on its "sheen," that is conceptualized by Dogon people as *daoula* and that refers to a living force that resides in all people, things, and animals. In this respect, I show that Dogon perception and appraisal of wild silk as a material of power not only rests on its aesthetic and economic values but overall on its medicinal, magic, and material property of durability, that all fall into the definition of *daoula*. Here, I shall place particular emphasis upon the transformative processing of cocoons into yarns that enables drawing the "sheen" out of raw materials. As a result, I am concerned with the social significance of wild silk materials in contemporary Dogon society, which I envisage in terms of their material efficacy. Within efficacy, I consider the material properties and qualities inherent to wild silk that constitute its *daoula* and therefore the wrappers' capacity to produce a particular effect on people (the wearer and the viewer). In addition, the sheen of wild silk as a characteristic of brilliance constitutes a visual manifestation of its inherent material properties and values that signify social status and through which Dogon women perform their individuality by wearing wild silk wrappers that stand as a popular yet unique visual mode of self-display (Rowlands 2011). I discuss the production and materiality of wild silk as "sheen" or *daoula* through the lens of the anthropology of techniques (Lemonnier 1992), which considers efficacious actions upon matter as a way of seeking implicit forms of knowledge about producing and using these wrappers. In other words, this paradigm and method underline modes of production that are described through detailed sequences of ethnographic observations (operational sequences) about the matter "in-the-making" (Ingold 2007). Yet, I see the "making" or production of the *tombe toun* wrappers as well as their daily and ceremonial uses or "doing" as standing in the same continuity (Naji and Douny 2009). In other words, I propose that wild silk is acted upon in the same way as the cloth made of this material acts visually upon individuals through its particular striped design made of wild silk that objectifies cultural

meanings as they bear one or several aphorisms. These woven syntax remind Dogon people of social order, values, and behavior.

DAOULA: THE MATERIALITY AND VISUALITY OF SHEEN

Sheen creates visibility and defines modes of visuality (seeing and being seen) that are culturally coded. In West Africa, sheen remains a dominant visual characteristic that defines cultural aesthetics and local expressions of material identity, personal worth, and power. Sheen is a visual property that certain surfaces possess and that is magnified by virtue of reflecting light. It attracts the "eye" and triggers a reaction or emotion in the viewer. The triad sheen, light, and color is embedded into cultural and multi-sensorial experiences of the social, natural, and spiritual worlds that materialize in what Saunders calls an "aesthetics of brilliance" (Saunders 2002: 209). Boesen (2008) describes Wodaabe cattle herders and traders of Central Niger with their aesthetics of luminosity and luster as a criterion of cultural self-achievement and so of high value. Luster is expressed in many respects, in the preservation of shiny material elements of a Western origin in their home, the whitening of calabashes used as domestic vessels, or men dancers' "grimaces" that enable them to display the whites of their eyeballs and their impeccable white teeth that are enhanced by face painting and sunset light (Boesen 2008: 595). In many places, sheen is sought after and when it cannot be obtained through natural substances and materials, industrial alternatives are developed and used, such as Lurex yarns and rayon that are woven with cotton (Picton 1995). In West Africa, "brilliance" is certainly an effective means by which people make themselves stand out in a crowd, successfully displaying their wealth and social status. Rowlands notes that in Cameroon: "Aesthetically the emphasis is on sheen and luminosity rather than on a particular color … the preference for textures and colors that shine" (Rowlands 1994: 115–16). Rowlands continues, noting that the visual impact of bright colors associated to sheen that connote maturity and reserve are social markers of personal achievement as well as physical beauty and thus personal worth (Rowlands 1994: 116). Furthermore, the "brilliance" of textiles is tantamount to the "gleam" of precious metals and minerals used in beaded, gold, or silver jewelry that is always kept highly polished. Other well-known techniques of producing "sheen" are found by beating cotton damask using heavy wooden mallets that confer rigidity to surfaces, a special glazed or metallic sheen. These various examples show that many techniques can be used to transform, reveal, maintain, or intensify the brilliance of materials while acquiring values and meanings throughout the making processes.

In many West African cultures, sheen represents social visibility, prestige, wealth, and position in a hierarchy. Ben-Amos suggests that, in Benin, shining brass magnifies the power of monarchs by conveying a sense of beauty mixed with fear (Ben-Amos 1980: 15). In many ways, colors, light, and sheen can dazzle and at the same time repel. One last aspect of the significance of sheen that can be underlined lies in the relationships between sheen and the sacred. Shining created by light and colors can also be imbued with spirituality (Pinney 2001). As Bourdier has shown, Tokolor mosques in the Sudano-Sahelian style are bathed by a beam of natural light that strikes the name of God inscribed on the opposite wall so as to materialize divine truth "Allah is light" (Bourdier 1991: 67).

In Dogon culture, wild silk is one means by which visual sheen is achieved; other examples can be found in masks and tunic decorations that include metallic elements such as coins that also create a particular acoustic environment around the body in motion. However, in Dogon culture the concept of sheen is not restricted to the notion of visual "brilliance." In fact, it also has to be understood as the inherent values and thus material properties of wild silk, such as its durability, strength, medicinal and magic properties, all described as *daoula*. By definition, the term refers to an active and living force that resides in all people, animals, and objects and which makes them "appreciated or liked by everyone" as an informant puts it. Their *daoula* has an emotional impact on the viewer, triggering respect, esteem, or admiration. To clarify, the notion of *daoula* is expressed as "sheen" in the sense of first the intrinsic, positive, and permanent values of wild silk and second the efficacy or potency of its materiality, which manifests visually as brilliance through shades of white or light blue that are obtained through various processes. In other words, Dogon explain that what they actually see in the wrapper and what matters to them profoundly is the white (*pii*) lines of silk that objectify and reveal "sheen" or *daoula* and that Dogon more generally define as *kongonron* so, that is "something (wild silk) that shines like the sun," which they say is the brightest existing light. Therefore, in Western terms I presume that the "sheen" or *daoula* of wild silk can be understood as the "aura" of the textile, without any reference to religion or spirituality, but that appears more as a positive value that lies in the properties of wild silk and that emanates or shines out of the fiber and makes people like the wrapper more than any other textile. The visual aspect of sheen or *daoula* of the wrapper is said to increase and so to improve over time through wearing the wrapper as well as through repeated washing. In fact, as the cotton element of the wrapper wears out, silk becomes visually brighter. The durability and strength expressed as *tawanso* (or *see balla*) of the yarns stands the test of time when compared to cotton. As Dogon women say, cotton dies but wild silk will always remain. One last point to note is that wild silk wrappers are highly valued because of their aesthetics and price, certainly due to the rarity of the material and their costly manufacturing, but overall because of Dogon knowledge and techniques of production surrounding wild silk. In fact making wild silk wrappers requires particular knowledge about the nature and materiality of this mystic and dangerous insect product (*djina diie odjo* or *kaba ko*), as well as the technical process/production of textile (*Dogon toun*) forming an indigenous science of wild silk. Hard work, savoir faire, and the mastering of wild silk's *daoula* through various techniques constitute other forms of values that Dogon people recognize when they look at the wrapper, as these techniques serve to create a visual dimension by drawing out what resides in materials and objects through material and symbolic transformations (Warnier 2006). Consequently, the "sheen" of wild silk, and therefore its visibility or visuality, endows various forms of social, moral and material values that add to the aesthetics and worth of the wrapper.

THE MATERIAL EFFICACY OF WILD SILK

The material properties of wild silk that women define as its tensile strength, durability, and brilliance as well as its medicinal and magic properties are identified as unrivaled values or *daoula*. In fact, Dogon women observe that while cotton stripes wear out, wild silk weaving stands the test of time. Wild silk challenges time and the aging human body that once wore the wrapper. In colonial times, domestication of moths found in Nigeria—later dropped because of production costs—had been considered to manufacture parachutes because of the remarkable tensile strength of the material (Golding 1942). Beyond interpretations relating women's investment in durable cloth to their precarious living conditions, locally produced fabrics prevail over imported cloth and clothing because of its outstanding quality but also because traditional cloth made of local raw materials stands as a local science and embodied practice that is inscribed in the long term and therefore forms a heritage they call *atem/atiembe* and that Dogon are proud of. Brilliance that is obtained through complex transformative process involving cooking, beating, carding, spinning, and washing the threads is said to improve through time. I also gathered from Dogon women that the material confers medicinal and magic properties. In fact, living larvae found in the cocoons are often consumed to cure diabetes (*cikoro nouran*), tetanus ("*min*" called "the incurable wound"), as well as to reduce high blood pressure. In addition, a decoction of twigs or wood on which wild silk cocoons are spun is used to purge children who suffer from a chronic form of malaria that is diagnosed as *kono*, a term that refers to the owl that casts the disease on small children by stealing their souls. The same wood in contact with the cocoons can be smoked to heal migraines caused by malevolent spirits. Finally, as explained by a Dogon marabout (Muslim holy man who possesses mystic powers), wild silk yarns may be used to seal amulets as well as to sew the magic leather pouches on hunters' shirts. He continued that the efficacy of silk in this particular garment lies in the mystic properties of the insect-secreted substance that is found in bush or forest areas perceived as dangerous because they host multiple forms of spirits or djinns. In West African Islamic magic, silk threads are also dipped into the inky rinse of Koranic boards, impregnated with Koranic verses written for recitation, and then folded into a leather charm. In both cases, wild silk yarn's mystic and powerful materiality is reinforced through magic. Consequently, the transformation processes about producing wild silk are also means of bringing out the *daouala* or remarkable values of the matter, as well as ways of mastering this "natural force."

WILD SILK WRAPPERS AS MODES OF VISUAL COMMUNICATION

The white/blue and indigo stripe design of *tombe toun* wrappers bears one or several aphorisms that remind people of society's moral values and express critiques to particular individuals. The nonverbal communication function of African wrappers such as the East African *kanga* or *Kalabari* dresses of Nigeria has been unwrapped elsewhere (Beck 2000; Michelman and Eicher 1995). In a similar way, the woven bands of wild silk wrappers act as a meta-language of which visual expression is created and enhanced through the sheen of white silk contrasting with indigo stripes. Here, wild silk as a material of power enables expressing and legitimizing messages that cannot be verbalized otherwise. In other words, proverbs that are expressed in both Malinke and Dogon languages reach their targets because of the efficacy of wild silk that lies in its materiality. In this case, wild silk wrappers are means of communication by which social inadequacy is contained, for instance, by preventing women from confronting verbally and therefore subverting the authority of their husbands or of the elders, yet allowing them to express their points of view and critiques. In other words, *tombe toun* wrappers materialize power relationships that are negotiated through visual and material display, providing that people share the same cultural codes. The proverb "*Sinan reme dabe*," meaning "the co-wife walks by the front door without looking up," expresses the settling of scores between two co-wives. In plain terms, this visual aphorism is way of expelling the co-wife from the compound. Fatou explains the social mechanism of these aphorisms as follow: "you look for weakness of your enemy and that is what you put in the wrapper." In the same way, "*Den wolo kadi,*" meaning "it is good to have children," indicates rivalry between a woman who has children and her co-wife who does not have any. *Tombe toun* wrappers also enable one to address serious issues by enabling avoidance of fatal conflicts. For instance, the design called: "*Dabali zou bo ya yere kalla*" meaning "witchcraft goes back to the one who does it" enables one to react to witchcraft with impunity. Finally, these proverbs can express an axiom of wisdom that is commonly accepted as a form of truth, for instance: "*sanaa ke lon e dabe ake lon e ke wali fe,*" which means "action is better than words." In sum, wild silk wrappers as expensive items of power constitute a notable form of meta-language as well as an effective marker of social visibility that enables Dogon women to express messages that could not be spoken otherwise, because of the devastating social consequences these critiques would instantly and inevitably bring with words.

WILD SILK WRAPPERS AS A MARKER OF SOCIOCULTURAL VISIBILITY

Wild silk indigo striped wrappers have always been considered by Dogon women as their most precious item of clothing. In fact, this new fashion was introduced in Dogon rural areas some 200 years ago by Marka-Dafing people and through trade but also inter-ethnic marriages. At that time in the Dogon region, clothing was restricted to plain white cotton and plain indigo dyed cloth. Salimata explains that *tombe toun* rapidly became highly coveted because of its sheen or *daoula* that attracts the eye and makes women socially visible, often expressed as "making oneself feel important." As one can observe during national festivals such as *Gina Dogon* and *Women's Day* (March 8), Dogon wild silk wrappers express regional identities. At *Gina Dogon* in February 2011, dozens of performers were line dancing and proudly representing their *Tengu or Tomo-kan* community and their ancestors that the wrapper represents through its particular design and thus visuality. As Jeanne explains, the wrapper also acts as a reminder of Dogon women's worth: "when I wear it (the wrapper), I feel beautiful and I pay tribute to my community." Wild silk makes women visible, as opposed to cotton cloth that makes women "unseen," expressed by Dogon as: "*tombe toun kouni banga kouwa pere kouni toun banga ire,*" meaning "A woman who wears *tombe toun* is ten times more visible and 'expressive' than a woman who wear cotton."

WILD SILK WRAPPERS AS VISUAL MARKERS OF SOCIAL PRESTIGE AND STATUS

Overcrowded places like markets are social spaces where Dogon women very often enjoy outshining their rivals by dressing up conspicuously: a situation that inevitably generates gossip and criticisms from jealous women. In this sense, wild silk wrappers are visually compelling because of their sheen that imparts visibility to the wearer, who can stand out among people dressed in wax print, or plain indigo garments and Western clothes. As Lere explains:

> Tombe toun is a very visual thing because of its sheen. If you want to be looked at, but also want to be heard, then you just have to wrap it (tombe toun) around to become straight away the target of griots who eagerly and loudly compliment you. So, they don't stop raving about your outfit, your beauty and elegance through songs and by declaiming your family's history. You are glorified, it shores you up because it makes you visible.

Here, Lere's quote reveals that the wrapper brings fame and therefore social recognition by revealing the social status of wearer as well as bestowing beauty and honor on women. Although *tombe toun* wrappers made of wild silk alternatives such as kapok are worn by a lot of women because they are more affordable, they are immediately spotted by other women as "counterfeit." As I observed, many old Dogon women often possess several wild silk wrappers that they have accumulated over time, through making and buying. These personal collections represent their personal worth and pride in being able to afford wild silk and being highly knowledgeable about making these fabrics. In the same way, the striped design of wild silk textiles reinforces ideas of personal worth as its colors materialize significant events in women's life cycle, such as her marriage, birth of children, and funeral. These events are expressed by *tombe toun*'s indigo and white/light blue color. In fact, the color white called *pii* is generally associated with marriage, baptism, or funerals and it signifies an event that stands out from everyday life, as it brings about a new state of things. On the other hand, indigo or dark blue, perceived as a different tone of black, symbolizes moistness and fertility (Brett-Smith 1990–91: 164–5) and it is worn in everyday life as a means to symbolize "quotidian life." Thus, the combination of both colors materializes the complementarities of happy or sad events in a woman's life, signifying completeness.

CONCLUSION

In this article, I have focused on the cultural significance of wild silk as a costly and rare material that endows the materiality of sheen which in Dogon society is expressed as *daoula*, an active force that lies in wild silk and that concerns first its inherent value in terms of material properties of durability, strength, and brilliance that improves over time, as the material is perpetually "evolving." Second, it encompasses the medicinal and magic properties of wild silk in curing illness and protecting against malevolent entities. Finally, with regard to its aesthetic and economic values, the making process of these *tombe toun* wrappers and the transformation of wild silk, in particular, allow drawing forth the sheen or *daoula* from the raw material. Through the transformative process of wild silk that requires knowledge and skills, Dogon women act upon matter and thus master the vital force of wild silk. Finally, the prestigious wrapper stands as a marker of social visibility, a celebration of women that in the meantime materializes Dogon and Mande identities as well as legitimizing social codes and moral values. Therefore, in a Dogon view, the sheen of wild silk is not only a visual quality but it overall describes a series of material properties that constitute the efficacy of wild silk and thus its materiality.

16

CLOTHING SOCIALITY:
Materiality and the everyday among the Kuna of Panama

Margherita Margiotti

Mola (pl. *molakana*), the female blouse made by Kuna women of Panama, has long captivated the imagination of Western tourists and art collectors (Howe 1998; Tice 1995). Stephen (1991) suggested that *mola* has to be considered an art form and an economic resource rather than only as a form of clothing (Sherzer and Sherzer 1976). *Molakana* no longer deemed suitable for wearing by women are discarded from the Kuna women's pile of desirable garments and sold to tourists, or they are directly produced especially for this market. In both cases, female blouses are divested as garments and circulate as commodified indigenous artefacts. In spite of a few notable exceptions (Salvador 1976, 1978, 1997; Sherzer and Sherzer 1976), studies of *molakana* have tended to prioritize symbolic and market values at the expense of the key dimension of *mola* as clothing, with its materiality and life cycle connected to the life of its makers and the contexts of its manufacture. This article seeks to elucidate this overlooked dimension of Kuna clothing by focusing ethnographically on the multifaceted and everyday aspects of *molakana*. It is argued that clothes occupy a prominent place in the making of Kuna sociality, and by focusing on the making, gifting and divesting of *molakana* as clothing, key aspects of Kuna social life are explored.

The mundane aspects of the *mola* in connection to sociality and to the experience of its individual producers became apparent to me on a quiet morning in Okopsukkun, one of the inshore atolls of the archipelago of San Blas (Panama) where I conducted fieldwork. As I sat with my host Nixia Pérez on the narrow space in front of the house, she took from a bucket a *mola* she was sewing and began cutting out small filling motifs on the contours of a design she had already realized. These are small triangles, dots, lines or other shapes of different colours that are used to fill any empty space within the *mola* designs. Fascinated by the visual density she was minutely crafting, I asked her whether or not she liked a *mola* blouse without the filling motifs, a naïve question that led her to burst out laughing. Obviously, she replied, that a *mola* without filling motifs is just unfinished. A few moments later she added that in a similar way people build houses one near to the other to live with each other in one dense and compact community. She thus commented on how inconceivable a life seemed without kinspersons around her, like that of some mainland Darién indigenous people who live in scattered houses near the Colombian border, so remarkably different from the nucleated and crowded villages of San Blas. After suggesting that the dense nature of the motives on the *mola* blouses were linked to their way of living together, Nixia kept sewing her *mola* with small filling motifs.

By living in the village, it quickly became obvious to me that women are almost continually taken up with the relentless everyday sewing of *mola* blouses in the house, together with the acquisition of poplin

Margherita Margiotti, "Clothing sociality: Materiality and the everyday among the Kuna of Panama," *Journal of Material Culture* 18 (December 2013): 389–407.

and printed fabrics for their wardrobe. As part of the female attire, the sewed front-and-back designed *mola* blouse wraps tightly on the upper part of the body, and is combined with geometrically designed bead arm and leg bands, a printed head-covering and a printed fabric wrapping the hips and legs as a skirt. Removed from the female blouse, *molakana* are displayed in the major ethnographic museums of the world. This article focuses on everyday aspects of Kuna female clothes and on the life cycle of these crafted garments. By considering clothing in its materiality (Küchler and Miller 2005), I will discuss how aspects of Kuna sociality become accessible through an analysis of *molakana* as relational garments, that is, as garments that are made out of, and in the context of, relations. In his seminal essay on gift exchange, Marcel Mauss (1966) was concerned with the binding force of the gift, by means of which personhood and agency act as mediatory forces connecting people. Condensing social relations in themselves as indexes (Gell 1998), objects create binding relations between people through exchange. Here, I call attention to the material and everyday lived qualities of clothes as objects that both mediate the relationships between people and similarly condense values and styles of sociality in themselves. While key aspects of sociality are elucidated in considering clothes as relational garments, I will also discuss how the life cycles of clothes and persons inform one another. The life cycle may well be considered a key entry point to this analysis of clothes in two ways: on the one hand, individual experiences of making and using objects take place within the time—space frame of human life and, conversely, objects in themselves possess a life cycle expressed in the various stages of production, use and disposal.

PERSPECTIVES ON CLOTHING

According to 19th-century historical sources, *molakana* were initially long tunics with a narrow band of cut and sewn designs decorating the lower edge (see Salvador 1997). With time, the decorated band expanded and the tunic shortened, eventually reaching the current shape, where the blouse covers only the torso and the cut and sewn decorated panels cover the whole front and back of the blouse. Despite the lack of more specific historical data, it is, however, not completely speculative to suggest that *molakana* might have developed from body painting, made using the black and red dye obtained, respectively, from *genipa* and *bixa orellana*. Body painting is practised nowadays in the form of a black line painted along women's, and sometimes men's, noses; and by reddening women's cheeks and those of medicine men about to go to the mainland forest to gather plant medicines. Moreover, some authors suggest that earlier, more elaborate forms of body paintings transformed into today's labour-intensive activity of making clothes with imported fabrics (Hirschfeld 1977; Salvador 1978, 1997). With increasing trading and commercial relations, developed by Kuna men over the last two centuries (Howe 1998), fabric became an article purchased from non-Kuna outsiders, along with haberdashery items such as "scissors, thread and needles" (Salvador 1997).

Sewing a *mola* involves superimposing two or more layers of fabrics of different and highly contrasting colours. Designed patterns and figures are realized through a reverse-appliqué technique, by cutting them on the top panel and sewing it onto the one below. This process can be repeated as many times as the number of layers used to make a *mola*, thus increasing the variety of colours of the composition and its visual complexity without losing the clarity and impact of the designs. Kuna adult women are constantly engaged in making *mola* in their time off from daily chores and often visit the local shops in the village to buy new poplin fabric, which is regularly shipped from Panama City through a system of trade organized with wholesalers and with the help of Kuna intermediaries. Fabric is a costly good and thus every bit of it is used, each woman keeping a multicoloured stockpile of fabric oddments, used to fill the little spaces within designs and to make decorative motifs.

The vast literature on *mola* has mainly considered its production, visual aesthetic and use (Hirschfeld 1977; Parker and Neal 1977; Salvador 1978; Sherzer and Sherzer 1976), the value of *molakana* as artefacts for sale (Tice 1995) and related gender issues and changes. In what follows, I begin with some information on *mola* making to then stress how *molakana*, as materializations of designs and of the capacity of making designs, hold such a compelling place in the creation of everyday sociality.

MAKING DESIGNED CLOTHES

To set the scene for my discussion, it is worth noting that for a girl in Okopsukkun, the village where I conducted the bulk of my fieldwork, the opportunities for learning to make *mola* are constant, since *mola* making is an ordinary activity of adult women, sitting together on the house's patio and sewing.

A girl begins to practise with a small panel of fabric, previously cut by an older kinswoman, with one large geometric pattern. There is no formal teaching, and when a girl finds it difficult to sew the angles of the design, she passes the panel to a kinswoman who does it for her, while the girl watches. Sewing around the angles and curves of a designed pattern is initially difficult to master. Through practice and sitting for long afternoon hours in the patio with her kinswomen, a girl learns and refines her sewing technique. The second difficulty is mastering the cutting out of designs from the fabric on which the sewing operations depend.

According to my informants, the most difficult operation to master is the design itself, drawn on the fabric with a pencil. The panels of fabric are designed first and later cut and sewn. Designing the fabric is the most important aspect of creating a beautiful *mola*. Designing a *mola* is difficult for two reasons: firstly, a design is reproduced from an image or, more rarely, an object and adapted to the material. Secondly, and connected to this, designing a *mola* implies the visual control of the rectangular space of the fabric cloth in relation to the cutting and sewing which follow. Therefore, making a *mola* always implies the recollection of an image (cf. Fortis 2010) which is designed and adapted to the sewing techniques to realize a blouse.

Not all the women are capable of successfully designing a *mola*, and they may ask other experienced women to design the *mola* panels for them. There is a repertoire of *mola* designs still sewn on *mola* blouses that is called "old," "ancient" (*serkan mola*) and attributed to the designs that former generations of women made on their blouses, hammocks and beadwork. The current inventory of *mola* designs is almost infinite, and also reproduces images from Western magazines, writing, everyday objects or *mola* patterns recollected from published books. The possibility of realizing a variety of different designs is based on superimposing and cutting out several layers of fabric, as described above, to realize potentially infinite designs according to the maker's desire. It is hardly surprising that it takes a long time before a girl is capable of autonomously making her own wardrobe composed of numerous *mola* blouses for daily use. As an element of the female attire, *molakana* become "lived garments" (Banerjee and Miller 2003) on the body of their users, sharing intimacy as a crafted and designed surface on the skin and manifesting the embodied skills of their makers.

The association between bodies and clothing has been noted in Amazonian literature in relation, amongst other aspects, to the phenomenal and symbolic qualities of designs covering outer, containing surfaces in relation to inner, contained substances. Gow (1999) argues that the capacity of painting with designs among Piro women rests on women's control of the flow of fluids, such as blood and manioc beer. My own research among the Kuna was initially motivated to understand notions about body fluids and their transmissions, and how this articulates within a larger system of exchanges to make and unmake persons and to forge desired or undesired consubstantial relations. As I found out, the Kuna make no direct reference to body fluids such as blood, beer or reproductive substances when they talk about *mola* making and its usage. Nevertheless, I wish to suggest that there are aspects of the bodily experience of making *mola* that point to a variety of associations between fertility, the human life cycle and the phenomenal qualities of the everyday experiences of making designs.

Chapin (1983), in his ethnography of Kuna notions and practices of healing, emphasizes the overriding importance of the Kuna idea of an invisible, immaterial reality (*ney purpalet*), underlying and intimately linked to the visible, material world (*ney sanalet*) (cf. also Nordenskiöld 1938; Severi 1993). He suggests that to understand Kuna worldview and everyday practices we need first to grasp this dichotomy. What is visible and material in this world has an invisible and immaterial counterpart in another world, or another dimension of this world. This relates also to ideas about conception, pregnancy and birth. The foetus, while being contained and formed within the mother's womb, resides also in the House of the Grandmother (*Muu Neka*), a celestial figure in charge of forming the body of human and animal foetuses, and of providing them with their first clothing, the amniotic sac (Chapin 1983: 404; Nordenskiöld 1938: 367). Fortis (2010) has explored the Kuna category of design through the case of amniotic designs, i.e. the designs that Kuna people say cover the amniotic sac and which are made by Grandmother during the period of gestation. He argues that designs are essential to understanding Kuna notions of body and personhood and that amniotic designs, by mediating the relation between human beings and animal entities, are a key component for the formation of human bodies. He further suggests (Fortis 2014) that the layered nature of *mola* panels is similar to Kuna midwives' descriptions of the amniotic sac and that both share the characteristic of being covered with designs.

Building on these insights, in what follows I explore the analogies between the embodied everyday aspects of *mola* making, women's fertility, the uses of different female attires and their divestment as clothing according to particular phases of the female life cycle. I wish to argue that the human reproductive cycle and that of *mola* making present fascinating analogies. *Mola* making is a female activity intimately connected with the making of babies, and making designs, along with other artefactual activities (cf. Fortis 2014) is a manifestation of women's capacity to give birth. Furthermore, I suggest that, by exploring aspects of *mola* making and their usage within the framework of everyday relationships between kinswomen and of their relations across generations, we gain key insights into Kuna forms of sociality. We thus become able to look in greater detail at the aesthetics that inform Kuna daily practices of relatedness, underlie their ideas of kinship and organize the characteristic spatial layout of crowded Kuna island villages (Margiotti 2009).

BODY MOBILITY, FERTILITY AND CLOTH-MAKING

In spite of the relative availability of purchased T-shirts, jeans and shop-bought skirts that Kuna girls wear during the course of their childhood and adolescence, young girls agree that *mola* blouses are "beautiful" (*yer dayleke*) and they wear them during public gatherings at the village house and at school as part of the Panamanian school uniform. Store-bought clothes are usually dismissed after marriage when a woman transforms what was once the attire used during village gatherings and for particular occasions into an everyday clothing style. Her husband and her in-laws might be explicit in saying that they want the woman to be dressed as "a real woman" (*ome sunnati*). This change presupposing enough clothes in the wardrobe for daily use presupposes also consistent economic resources for purchasing fabric and haberdasheries, in addition to the equally consistent resources for finding time needed to make *molakana*. Semi-permanent beadworks are coiled tightly around legs and arms and changed every three or four months with new and differently coloured ones, worn together with *mola* blouses and matched with the skirt (*sapurret*) and headscarf on a daily basis.

Occasionally, large T-shirts or just a bra are worn, especially in the morning at home. T-shirts are considered comfortable for breastfeeding and for activities in the house, and women would also wear them in the morning for a quick walk to the nearby grocery shop to buy rice in exchange for coconuts, or for a quick walk to the house of a close female kin for gossiping or borrowing something. In the flow of morning activities, a T-shirt paired with an old *sapurret* is the preferred attire, with women engaging in constant micro-gestures of adjusting their *sapurret*, fastening and refastening it when getting up after sitting or when they walk, or adjusting leg and arm beadworks when they slip down during work.

In the afternoon, when more formal visits take place between houses, women wear their newest clothes to visit their in-laws, together with their husbands who have returned from the sea or the gardens. They would feel "ashamed" (*pinke*) if they did not wear a *mola* blouse, a bright coloured *sapurret* and a red head covering fastened or just pulled over the head. Men are explicit in their comments about the beauty of Kuna women dressed in *mola* blouses. After marriage the expression of sexual desire between husband and wife is part of the everyday exchanges that characterize the conjugal pair.

The generation of offspring is considered an outcome of these conjugal exchanges in the form of mixing and solidifying different sexual substances in the women's womb. With the child "housed" in its "Grandmother's House"—as people metaphorically call the womb during pregnancy—a woman progressively discards most of her ordinary clothes as they become too tight, especially in late pregnancy. Women will choose large T-shirts instead of *mola* blouses and not wear their beadworks which might cause their legs to swell up, thus going through a process that might recall shedding their skin (see Fortis 2014). Although my informants never used the metaphor of skin, *mola* blouses and beadworks seem to fit well within the image of a "second skin" (Allerton 2007) for their properties of wrapping and adorning the body of their wearer with designs.

Late in pregnancy, with the beadworks removed, a woman would lie down in a hammock with an old *sapurret* pulled over her legs, or fastened under her now prominent body, chatting and surrounded by close female kin and children. If a visitor came to the house, she would remain in the hammock ignoring all the social interactions taking place, but making sure to pull the *sapurret* well down to cover her legs and arms. Only during the night, with a large towel pulled over her shoulder and under the cover of darkness, would she feel confident to visit her kin and in-laws. In this flow of life and with this close material connection between fertility and clothing, the corporeal experience of pregnancy among the Kuna is one of distinctive reduced mobility. According to Kuna notions of reproduction and gestation, a woman controls the processes of clotting and solidifying of sexual fluids into a baby by means of following special restrictions, involving her reduced mobility and activities, and the avoidance of particular foodstuffs. Both women and men must keep apart from activities deemed dangerous in pregnancy and engage in others positively associated to foetal containment and formation.

From the domestic space where a woman tends to remain secluded in a state of reduced mobility, she engages in intensified activities of clothes making, lying down on the hammock or sitting. *Mola* making might in itself be described as an activity of transformation, concerning the realization of sewed designs on layered fabrics, analogical to the transformation and hardening of sexual substances that is taking place in the womb during pregnancy. If this analogy seems far-fetched, it is nonetheless clear that, in addition to reduced body mobility, pregnancy and *mola* making share a series of clothing metaphors used to describe the making of babies and the amniotic sac, which, as noted above, Kuna people describe as intrinsically designed.

Sitting and sewing, a woman enjoys the company of her kinswomen engaged in similar activities of *mola* making, while children run in and out of the house and are scolded when they touch sewing threads and fabrics. When in turn children grow up, and a woman ages, there occurs a change in the type and temporal pattern of her activities. In contrast to younger women, who tend to work and carry out activities in groups, elderly women are more solitary and the time they spend on the production of clothes decreases substantially. This is reflected in the less elaborate style of their designed blouses. Nonetheless, they make and gift *mola* blouses to their granddaughters, and, importantly, they prepare and serve food to younger family members, an activity that defines elderly women's position in the kinship cycle as the givers of nourishment (Margiotti 2009). This introduces the dimension of intergenerational relations, which is integral to the way in which notions of self and relations are firmly anchored in the gifting and receiving of clothes.

GIFTING CLOTHES

My mother made lots of *molakana* for my daughters
How much she made *molakana*!
She made lots of *molakana* for my daughters
When they got married, she gave *molakana* presents to them.

This is a drunken woman singing about her dead mother during a puberty festival.

The literature on craft making based on Marxist analytical frameworks has tended to highlight the development of labour and the economic potential of crafted items for market selling (Goody 1982). During my fieldwork, I realized that Kuna people were particularly concerned with the relational aspects of both selling and gifting clothes. In particular, the stress tended to be on creating intimate relations among persons, either in the sense of re-investing the currency obtained from *mola* selling by purchasing consumable and school items for children, or in the sense of gifting *mola* blouses to young girls as a way of creating kinship relations with them.

In both cases, the selling and gifting of clothes was used to express idioms of kinship relations, gender identities and differences, in which adults' work contributes to the raising of children. The Kuna draw a sharp contrast between young boys and girls in relation to clothes. Boys and girls are often carefully dressed up in store-bought clothing. However, I often heard that boys manifest a spontaneous disinterest in clothes by refusing to remain properly dressed for longer stretches of time. In contrast, girls start taking an interest in their clothes early on and entertain themselves by playing with old garments discarded by their older kinswomen. The gift of clothes to baby girls or young girls constitutes an example of this mode of constituting intimate caring relations between generations of kinswomen. The close relation that a woman has with her kinspersons is explained with reference to the care she received during childhood through the gift of clothes. Sons, less demanding in terms of clothes and other material needs, tend to leave their house of birth to find a woman and get married.

It is usually claimed, in cases of arguments between mothers and daughters, that clothes have been continuously gifted to stress the close relation between the giver and the recipient. For instance, one woman lamented that her married daughter moved out of the house along with her husband and children, leaving her alone, "despite me bringing her up and buying her clothes since she was a little girl." Here, I argue that *mola* blouses are considered essential to the creation

of enduring affective relations between kinspersons. Below, I also suggest that the beautification of bodies through clothing is a manifestation of moral and social values.

Before a woman becomes able to make clothes, she receives them as a gift instantiating the love and affection of her adult kinswomen. When a baby girl is born, she receives blankets with *mola* appliqué from her mother's sisters, or her grandmother, and she is soon adorned with golden necklaces and bracelets, gifted by her father, older brother or grandfather. Furthermore, her kinswomen make *mola* appliqué to sew onto sundresses, tiny dresses and skirts, and later onto shop-bought little tops and T-shirts. There is no immediate return gift in these forms of giving, yet the implicit expectations created by cloth giving is the creation of enduring relations among kinswomen, which are reflected in their co-habitation after marriage. In the literature on Amerindian social organization and residence modes, uxorilocality has been described as a form of post-marital residence based on the control of young men through women (Turner 1979[a]). During my fieldwork, I noticed that great stress was put on the gifting of clothes, seen as generating enduring ties between kinswomen who thus want to live with each other, while men, attracted by women, want to live with their wives. Clothes giving, instead of an idiom of control, was viewed, and consciously commented on, as driving women to live together and reciprocate the care received from their close kinspersons in the form of body adornments and embellishments.

At another level, the gifting of clothes also occurs when a woman gets married, involving this time a novel set of relations established through marriage. I have heard that newly married women in Okopsukkun are gifted *sapurret*, printed fabrics and headscarves from their parents-in-law as signs of care. One woman said that her father-in-law gave her all the beads and fabric to make clothes and body decoration so that she could change her usual shop-bought and ready-to-wear clothes into the proper Kuna female attire. Therefore, if the clothes and jewels gifted to a young girl point to the creation of close kinship ties, dressing in the proper Kuna female attire points to a new set of positive relations, created this time through marriage and conjugality and manifesting the expression of moral and social values of well-being and conviviality.

THE LIFE CYCLE AND THE DECAY OF CLOTHES

In many respects, garments that are discarded as clothes still occupy an important role in the everyday visual and sensorial experiences of people in their houses. Clothes become re-usable materials that do not necessarily cover the body as garments, though they maintain a mediatory role in connecting people. They remain central in what people do and in what they gift to others, even when the impermanence and fragility of clothes render their disposal as garments inevitable. Here, I want to argue for the significance of the impermanence of clothes within the transformational stages of the sociality in domestic relations. Elements of female attire are still used in everyday life when they stop being used as clothes. In spite of the decay and impermanency of fabric, discarded garments occupy a mediatory position in the sensorial experiences of people bound together in the flow of everyday domestic life. In the following, I want to describe the somatic experience of being dressed in specific elements of female attire and what happens to them when they are considered too old to wear.

Almost every day, women wear the *sapurret*, the skirt made from imported fabric, wrapped and twisted around the waist, and they are constantly engaged in adjusting and re-wrapping it. Mastering this gesture without the help of strings or cords takes time, and concerns about the *sapurret* slipping down emerge often in the form of same-sex jokes between women. A similar re-adjusting of the leg and arm beadwork bands is displayed when they slip in the course of domestic activities. Working by the mainland river, for example collecting pebbles, women wear an old *sapurret* or remain in a petticoat, using the *sapurret* to carry materials to the canoe. When an infant takes a nap, the mother takes a *sapurret* from her pile and pulls it over the infant as a blanket. When a *sapurret* becomes too old and faded, it is worn for bathing, fastened around the bust, or it may be worn over the shoulders in the chilly morning and evening air. When

a baby can sit autonomously or crawl, an old *sapurret* is used as a blanket on the ground. When a *sapurret* has become too old even for such uses, it is cut into strips for making basket handles or used as an apron when chopping and preparing meat or vegetables.

Like the *sapurret*, the headscarf, *muswe*, is pulled over the hammock underneath a sleeping infant as "bed linen," and young girls may play with their kinswomen's old *sapurret* and *muswe*. As an element of female attire, *muswe* is alternatively worn loosely or rolled and wrapped around the head. It may be momentarily slung over one shoulder and later re-adjusted and rolled up on the head. If a woman is travelling by motorboat to another village or sitting in a sunny place, she may shade herself and a child using her *muswe*. As Salvador (1997: 161) notes, the style of wearing a headscarf accentuates or hides a woman's face in particular settings. For instance, an old woman may cover her mouth with a *muswe* to hide missing teeth. A *muswe* hides a woman's face when she weeps and mourns her deceased relatives during mortuary ceremonies. During puberty festivals, when women perform autobiographical songs about their deceased relatives, they similarly hide their faces with *muswe.*.

Old *mola* blouses are worn in the house. During my fieldwork in Okopsukkun, I noticed on many occasions that when *mola* blouses become too old and faded even for such use, the designed panels are unstitched from the blouse and sewn together, forming larger blankets. These are then used to cover the white cane walls of the house, for the practical purpose of concealing the interior of the house from the sight of curious villagers walking through the pathways during the night. I suggest that in this movement from covering the body surface to covering the house walls, *molakana*'s characteristics linked with fertility are expressed across different levels. My Kuna informants drew an analogy between *mola*, the body and the house with its internal walls covered with old and faded *mola* panels. In their words, the house is a regenerating body, its internal structure described as its bones and its rounded shape as a pregnant belly. As a gestating woman, the house's internal surfaces would therefore appear to be covered with *mola* curtains, and therefore designed as the amniotic sac. This image fits with people's descriptions, presented above, of the womb as a moulding organ, itself understood as a designed cloth enveloping the foetus. Old midwives pay attention to the placenta and the remnants of the amniotic sac on a newborn, which sometimes they describe as layered and designed like a *mola*. In sum, *mola*, as the designed clothing covering female bodies, also covers the womb, which is itself an organ related to designs and to the capacity of moulding the body of babies (cf. Fortis 2014). The house, covered with *mola* panels, recalls the imagery of a womb transposed to another level, while at the same time it is the place where women make their *mola* blouses.

MOLAKANA IN THE MOTION OF KUNA SOCIALITY

In the late morning, when clothes have been washed and the house's patio cleaned, before preparing food and cooking, with children around after school, women gather together with their co-resident sisters or with their sisters-in-law to make *mola* blouses. Making *mola* partakes in the reproduction of the everyday continuity of Kuna life, centring upon "tranquillity" (*pokwa*) as a specific tone of sociality and the etiquette of specific relations. With relation to Kuna sociality, I argue that this tranquillity has moral, aesthetic and social connotations, and in the following I try and describe how tranquillity, sociality and *mola* making are all linked together. In the wide range of its applications, it is interesting to note that the noun *po* connotes the personal quality or attitude of self-control and observance of etiquette in contrast to the "lack of social rules" (*ioysar taet*, literally "to behave chaotically") that is often accorded to non-Kuna people. A person should act quietly with his or her in-laws, and also with shyness (*pinke*) and respect (*pinsaet*) through the performance of everyday activities instead of wandering around in the village or lying down on the hammock. The flow of everyday activities is described as a manifestation of tranquillity. For instance, in the early morning the village is described as quiet, with the dawn mist enveloping the island and people sleeping or sitting by the cooking fire to warm up. Morning is the time for carrying out

gendered productive activities at home, in the forest or the sea, where men produce food for their families. In the morning, when men leave their houses, the village is silent and still, and everything seems almost motionless. Women are at home, and the village paths are almost deserted, with children at school or babies taking naps between feeds.

Practically and conceptually, quietness reminds one that everyday activities are taking place and that nothing disrupts their flow. Men, as generators of food abundance, are active outside the village space as well as in the house. Their activities take place alongside the female tasks of preparing home-made drinks and meals, doing the laundry and *mola* making. For adult women, tranquillity is linked to the creation of *mola* and to the corporeal behaviour related to such activity. On a practical level, tranquillity, as a distinctive feature of *mola* making, has curiously received little ethnographic attention, but it is the essential pre-condition for the minute tactile and visual activity that is key to the realization of *mola*.

As described above, making *mola* blouses is governed by an elaborate set of procedures related to reduced mobility. These procedures imply the strong control of movements, with women sitting and bending their heads and shoulders slightly to cut, fold and sew layers of coloured fabric, progressively revealing a graphic form, among the layers. The fine work of *mola* making is an intense labour activity (Hirschfeld 1977), done at home and alternating with other everyday activities.

In short, quietness or tranquillity designate highly desirable states of sociability, connected to the ideal of conducting a peaceful social existence that is not disrupted by problems, conflicts or illness (*poni*), that nonetheless were an all too frequent occurrence in Okopsukkun during my fieldwork. This ideal of tranquillity is characterized by the monotonous and relentless repetition of daily activities that people carry out according to the values of kinship (Gow and Margiotti 2012). In this sense, tranquillity indicates the degree of emotional bonds that certain relations require in order to continue. Tranquillity implies a kind of reciprocity between a husband working in the forest and a woman at home acting in a self-controlled way by means of realizing beautiful clothes. Women working together to make *mola* are implicitly manifesting their respect and thoughtful consideration (*pinsaet*) for matrimonial relations by means of not wandering around in search of sexual partners. On the other hand, the relation between women is described as connoted by a kind of propensity for jokes and unrestrained behaviour, mornings of quiet *mola* making are interspersed with outbursts of laughter. Lowland South American ethnographies have analysed sociality as something to be continuously created rather than as a state of existence already achieved and taken for granted (McCallum 2001; Overing and Passes 2000). The stress has been on practices aimed at achieving particular affective states conducive to desirable relations among co-residents. As I have shown in this article, among the Kuna, clothes play a crucial role in the production of the values that people strive to continuously generate in order to live well within their communities.

CONCLUSION

In this article, I have shown how everyday Kuna sociality becomes visible through an analysis of *molakana*. I have argued that Kuna female clothes mediate the relations between women and their infants, siblings and in-laws, and that their making contributes to the creation of quietness in everyday life. I have shown the salience of *molakana* in the sensual and material world of Kuna women and how they materialize kinship relations and a particular aesthetic of social life that values tranquillity. The ethos of Kuna life unfolds before our eyes when we look at the specific practices and social relations through which *molakana* are created.

Answering my naïve question, Nixia Pérez pointed at the intrinsic similarity between Kuna aesthetics of sociality and *mola* making, between living with each other in the comfort of kinship relations, sewing *mola* in company with one's kin and creating patterns of visual density by minutely adding small filling elements around larger designs. The technology of making and wearing clothes recalls the technology of forging relatedness and fostering intimate ties, between sisters engaged in similar activities, and between mothers and infants. Women exchange knowledge of clothes making, and they experience analogous dimensions of temporality in the making and wearing of *mola*.

When I arrived in the village of Okopsukkun, one man told me of a conversation he had had with an anthropologist, who suggested that since textiles, scissors, needles and thread are all acquired from non-Kuna people, *mola* are not authentically Kuna. His reply to that anthropologist was that it is Kuna women who make *mola* and transform fabrics into beautiful clothes that are distinctively Kuna. As I later realized during my fieldwork, there is reticence regarding teaching non-Kuna women how to sew *mola* blouses. Panamanian women often wear dresses, shirts, T-shirts and skirts with *mola* appliqués made by Kuna women and purchased in markets and shops in the capital. Kuna women comment positively when a *wakome* (foreigner woman) wears clothes with *mola* motifs, but they intentionally keep their sewing techniques for themselves. In these ways, women's making and using *molakana* provides a fascinating angle through which to understand how the life cycle of people and clothes are dynamically related to one another. A sewn *mola* recalls and acknowledges these nuances of Kuna sociality and relationality, materializing them onto the outer surfaces of the living person who wears it.

PART 4

DRESSING THE BODY IN CULTURE

PART INTRODUCTION

Even when stripped of our clothes, claims Katherine Frank, we remain dressed in culture. From our gait and posture to the way we groom and style our hair, there is no escaping the visual imprint of our regional and historical identities. Culture leaves its mark on our bodies. It reveals itself in how we hold our eyes, our lips, our hands. It gives away something of who we are, even when we attempt to hide it. And for this reason, we can never be truly naked.

The chapters in this part of the reader speak to the active and dynamic ways that dress works to shape our cultural identities, with or without our clothes on. Tonye Erekosima and Joanne Eicher write about processes of cultural authentication among the Kalabari people in Nigeria. They discuss how imported gingham and madras cloth is taken up locally and made to serve a variety of purposes, from enhancing a woman's femininity to establishing lineage. Wrapping oneself in cloth, their work demonstrates, is an act that establishes (and reestablishes) boundaries between people, marks one's place in a particular group, and defines one's place in the world.

Elisha Renne continues this theme in her chapter on cloth among the Bùnú Yorùbá people of central Nigeria. For Renne, as Erekosima and Eicher, cloth is less about its material properties than what it *does*. It expresses social connections, ties of family and intimacy. It marks changes in social status, demarcates ritual and ceremonial space. "Using cloth," writes Renne, "Bùnú villagers concretely construct and reproduce ideas about their social world" (p. 140).

This is another of the key anthropological insights on dress and clothing. Dress and clothing do not passively reflect meaning. They help produce it. Or rather, people produce meaning through dress and clothing. Jonathan Friedman's contribution, for instance, discusses the sartorial trends of young men in the Congo of the 1950s. Dressed in stark black and red styles that connoted to them the sophistication of French existentialists, *sapeurs*, or largely unmarried, unemployed youth with a penchant for dressing sharp, used their style to remake their place in Congolese society. For them, dress did not just reflect status. It helped establish it in the first place. "Clothing," writes Friedman, "is more than property or the expression of one's already existent self, or the fulfillment of an imagined self. It is the constitution of self, a self that is entirely social" (p. 152).

This does not mean, however, that the social self is stable, singular, or consistent. Deborah Durham's contribution to this volume emphasizes the fluid and contradictory nature of the selves produced through dress. Using Herero women in Mahalapye, Botswana, in the late 1980s and early 1990s as her example, Durham argues that the meanings of dress, forged through continuous practice, are always multiple. "Instead of reducing its meaning," she says, "I hope to retain the color of the dress, the sense of wearing it, the uncertainty and the ironic sensibility it provoked" (p. 155). Through the daily practice of dressing, she claims, Herero women enact the dynamic "heteroglossia" of everyday cultural life.

The same goes with undressing. Katherine Frank, in the chapter that concludes this section, shows that there is nothing bare or essential about nude women's bodies. The ways we perceive them, relate to them, or desire them are always culturally mediated. Her chapter on dancers in American strip clubs emphasizes that "nudity is not just a state of being, but is, rather, a social *process*" (p. 166, emphasis in the original). We cannot avoid culture by choosing not to play the games of fashion. We cannot even strip ourselves of it when we take our clothes off. It continues to act on and through us. We are shaped by it, marked by it. But through our personal comportment, the way we stylize our acts of dress and undress, we help forge those very social processes that shape us.

17

KALABARI CUT-THREAD AND PULLED-THREAD CLOTH

Tonye Victor Erekosima and
Joanne B. Eicher

Buguma is the cultural center of the Kalabari people inhabiting the delta at the southern tip of Nigeria. The Kalabari are spread out over a number of other urban as well as rural settlements, including Abonnema, Bakana, Sangama, Teinma, Tombia, Soku, and Degema. This paper will describe a particular imported cloth with openwork designs worn by the Kalabari people, analyze its use, and expand on the concept of cultural authentication as it applies to this openwork textile.

Imported lightweight gingham and madras cotton cloths, commonly called "George" in many parts of southern Nigeria and *injiri* by the Kalabari, are highly esteemed and worn by both Kalabari men and women as wrappers. The cloths of interest here are a variety of gingham and multicolored madras, often with subdued backgrounds of indigo, black, violet, brown, and sometimes red or orange, on which local craftswomen have imposed another design by cutting threads and removing them. Wrappers made from such cloth are generally worn during ceremonial occasions, and women also wear them as fashionable attire.

Women artisans create the new designs by two painstaking processes. The first involves lifting threads singly or in groups with a needle and snipping them off with a razor or penknife. The result is called *pelete-bite*, or "cut thread" cloth. The second method requires the artisan to lift certain weft threads with the needle and then pull them out completely. This process results in *fimate-bite*, or a "pulled-thread" design.

Both *pelete-bite* and *fimate-bite* openwork patterns are superimposed on checked, striped, or plaid cloth. Given the limits of the warp and weft structure of woven textiles, an amazing number of geometric patterns result, and daring intimations of the curve have been attempted. The artisans produce two basic types of patterns: regularly repeated ones that are the same in both directions of the cloth, such as variations of checks on checks to break up the patterns, and asymmetrical designs, which may include such motifs as letters of the alphabet. A refinement of abstraction and balance is achieved despite the simple techniques used to execute the designs. One example of their artistry is executed on the cloth called *Kieni*. *Kieni* cloth was named after King Charlie "Cane" Amakiri (Amachree), who was Amanyanabo from 1900 to 1918. He had initial importation rights over it.

Apparently, before the Europeans arrived, a type of sturdy waterproof cloth (*okuru*) made from fine, raffia-leaf strands, was worn by women as a wrapper when they harvested marine delicacies from the river beds. At this time, we have little written documentation about earlier cloth worn for festive and ceremonial occasions. By the 1870s, however, that the imported

Adapted from Tonye Victor Erekosima and Joanne B. Eicher, "Kalabari Cut-Thread and Pulled-Thread Cloth," *African Arts* 14, no. 2 (February 1981): 48–51, 87. Published by UCLA James S. Coleman African Studies Center.

injiri was available as the basis for *pelete-bite* and *fimate-bite* is shown by a few photographs from this period still extant in some Kalabari households. They picture women with bodies decorated with paint, a variety of coral beads, silk scarves, and other materials, among them *injiri*.

We propose that *pelete-bite* and *fimate-bite* enhanced the importance of the special occasions at which they were worn, and that these occasions, in turn, provided the opportunity for the cloth to communicate and reinforce the community values it represents. Some aspects of the value system that underlay the use of *pelete-bite* and *fimate-bite* must be considered in order to demonstrate the concept of cultural authentication. We suggest that the social etiquette of Kalabari women, the overall context of cultural resources (including artifacts and design inspiration), male-female role expectations, and kinship affiliation coalesce in *pelete-bite* and *fimate-bite*.

In social etiquette, the Kalabari woman projects a sense of style through a unique preoccupation with *iria-bo ti* or "feminine elegance." This aesthetic quality is quite staid and refined, and is the converse of the *asa-ti* or "dashing, sporty living" of the menfolk. Disciplined manners, taste in speech, body control, and meticulous dress are reflected in the subtle patterns of *pelete-bite* and *fimate-bite*.

The material resources available to the Kalabari for creating such cloths involve a number of imported products, such as woven gingham and madras cloths, needles, penknives, and razor blades. There exists, in addition, a heritage of traditional designs for inspiration. One possible source for the design patterns was decorative shapes and forms that Kalabari women had been cutting and painting long before any foreign cloths became available. The hair and bodies of young maidens were the media for these traditional design patterns; their hair was shaved to form patterns on the scalp, and their bodies were beautified with designs painted with camwood and other dyes by older women. Animal-motif symbols developed in relation to ritualized representation of the water spirits and also a variety of geometrical forms depicting lizard or crocodile skins, turtle shells, and python markings appearing on palm-frond screens for mounting

ancestral or deistic icons (Horton 1965) are possible additional sources of design inspiration.

Male-female role expectations are a third significant factor in the creation of this cutwork. Among the Kalabari, women seem to be the creators while men represent the producers. For example, only women are presumed to have ever seen the "Water People" at their dances or to have learned from them the choreography that is introduced into the Ekine society. But only men may perform the dances or don the masquerades. The dances and masquerades are regarded by the Kalabari as eminently in the domain of personal and group achievement. In deference to the female realm of inspiration and creativity, however, members of the exclusively male Ekine society have Ekine-ba, a goddess and patroness who is believed to be the originator of aesthetic skills. Real-life males and females fit into the differential social roles of man and woman. Women guard the culture's creative impulse, and men translate its adaptive strength in pragmatic activities. The vitality of both creativity and production can be maintained only as long as various ceremonial occasions and representational forms are employed to reinforce awareness and commitment to these equally essential and complementary societal missions. Women are kept from switching sides; they are excluded from donning the *owu* masquerades because this is "a culture where such store is set by virtuosity in the masquerade, and where a man's prowess with a particular *owu* is one of his most important attributes" (Horton 1960[a]: 32). Nevertheless, such dance festivals involve the participation of the women as spectators and "hostesses accompanying the gods." With shuffled steps and hand-clapping, women turn out for the occasion in *pelete-bite*, reaffirming their status as creators.

An additional aspect of social identification is that *pelete-bite* and *fimate-bite* symbolize lineage. A special madras cloth called *epe injiri*, which is ordinarily worn with cut patterns, serves this function for the Ombo family, one of the major Kalabari House groups (Jones 1963). An outsider who dons it during ceremonial occasions invites public stripping. Nevertheless, cloth that identifies family or House membership is not always exclusively used by that family or House. Often a wealthy merchant exclusively imported cloth of a specific pattern from overseas, and it became named after him, as was the case with the *Kieni, Anabraba,* and *Membere.* The textile, either with or without cut patterns, was reserved by him or his family only for ceremonial occasions. Anybody, however, could buy it and wear it on general occasions, and anybody could pay to get patterns cut on it.

The successful trade and enterprise of Kalabari men with the outside world is necessary to obtain the cloth that will be transformed into *pelete-bite* and *fimate-bite.* However, the acquisition of *injiri,* although a valuable input into the culture, does not sufficiently explain the concept of cultural authentication. Creativity of the women is mandatory. Therefore, we propose that cultural authentication requires not merely the acquisition and borrowing of artifacts but their transformation (at differing levels of adaptation) to make them a part of the receiving culture.

Using the example of imported cloth as utilized by the Kalabari, we offer the following levels of cultural authentication: (1) *selection,* the borrowing and using of cloth as it exists; (2) *characterization,* the "naming" of a cloth to make it more easily "visible"; (3) *incorporation,* the exclusive owning of a specific cloth by a particular group (family or House); (4) *transformation,* the creating of a modified cloth that has an additional design cut on it. Cloth at this level of creative adaptation is most valued and prized.

An illustration of these levels involving the use of imported cloth by the Kalabari to satisfy the needs of social identification follows: (1) The individual chooses and wears a commercial cloth of modern trade for self-enhancement and for making a statement about positive self-acceptance. To do so is to "dress up." The "dressed-up" person is valued at a level different from that of the same person attired for work and production. (2) The person wears a cloth with a "name," heightening the sense of positive self-presentation. This cloth may be more expensive than others, but it is not necessarily so, and the cloth's higher price may not reflect higher quality but only greater exclusiveness. (3) The person wears a restricted cloth for ceremonial occasions, which shows that he or she belongs to a specific lineage, for example, that of the royal family or an important House. (4) The person wears a cloth indicating that he or she belongs not just to a restricted group but also to a distinctive culture. When a Kalabari person wears *pelete-bite* and *fimate-bite,* with their cut-thread and pulled-thread designs, he or she exemplifies cultural authentication at this level.

This openwork may be said to represent preeminently for all Kalabari the women's creative imposition of a refined aesthetic symbolism—as a link to the sublime experience—upon one material prize from the men's commercial exploits. The cloth serves to communicate the harmony of the Kalabari world by linking cultural ethos, women, men, and artifacts. Thus, the sophistication of the patterns the Kalabari women design, despite the simple techniques employed, derives from the traditional cultural values as a whole, not idiosyncratic fancy or the prestige of foreign example.

Kalabari commitment to such authentication has led to such cynical sayings as "What the people have decided, the gods accept" (Horton 1960b: 274). This last sentiment was applied to justify Kalabari adoption of the motor-driven boat to speed far away the "year-old-bundle-of-sins-and-troubles" that they had extracted from the town through traditional New Year cleansing rites. And it could apply, just as easily, to any other artifact of foreign make—such as the textile import that is the base of the prestige Kalabari cloth—and ritualize it into a transformed object that belongs in their own world. This process of ritualization is carried out largely by the activity of women.

The extended significance of this analysis of an imported and reworked cloth in Kalabari culture is the suggestion that cultural authentication exists in other African encounters with cultural artifacts. Therefore, we present a brief note on African aesthetics. We propose that the degree of involvement in aesthetics varies for any artifact of African culture, whether indigenous or foreign. Adoption of artifacts may be appraised at these levels: selection, as in acquiring some specific cloth or other artifact to wear or use; characterization, as in distinguishing particular cloth or other artifacts by special naming; incorporation, as in placing such cloth or other artifacts into particular social categories or making them part of an ensemble;

and transformation, illustrated by the infinite variety of *pelete-bite* and *fimate-bite* designs.

Other artifacts can be used as examples. The Nigerian adoption of the truck has involved the concept of naming as a form of characterization (the second level of cultural authentication) in terms of various proverbs and sayings written on the "forehead" of the truck, such as "No Telephone to Heaven." The building of a truck base into a mammy wagon for rural to urban transportation with its ramifications for a readapted social existence is an example of transformation (the fourth level of cultural authentication). The Yoruba *adire eleko* provides still another textile example from West Africa. The artist uses imported printed cloth as a base and transforms it by overlaying a starch resist stencil design.

The progression of levels meshes together sentiment and symbolism as well as social roles and artifacts. The depth of man's aesthetic response to objects in his environment increases as sentiment, symbolism, social roles, and artifacts become more integrated with the special uses of the objects. In a sense, then, art is the world to the African. Conversely, in a successive ascent from artifacts to affect, all the world is art.

We propose that the concept of cultural authentication may be useful for analyzing still other examples of borrowing and transformation in technology, aesthetics, institutions, values, and practices. The implication is that to make modernization an African experience, the needs of Africans can be served by acknowledging and encouraging the creative process of cultural authentication.

18

CLOTH THAT DOES NOT DIE:
The meaning of cloth in Bùnú social life

Elisha P. Renne

When you have money,
some people will be angry;
When you have cloth,
some people will be angry;
When you have children,
some people will be angry;
Cloth has many uses.

Bùnú Yorùbá song

The Bùnú Yorùbá people of central Nigeria mark every critical juncture in an individual's life, from birthing ceremonies to funeral celebrations, with handwoven cloth. In rituals such as that for installing a chief or for traditional marriage, cloth is used to express changes in the status of individuals as well as in the social connections of kin, affines, and other supporters. As dress, it ranks chiefs and distinguishes them from commoners. In tailored and untailored forms, it may be used to demarcate gender as well as educational status. Further, handwoven cloth is worn to distinguish ritual events from everyday affairs where commercial, industrially woven cloth prevails. Using cloth, Bùnú villagers concretely construct and reproduce ideas about their social world.

Until recently, cloth weaving and dyeing were also a major facet of Bùnú economic life, as they were for many other Yorùbá-speaking groups in southwestern Nigeria (Boser-Sarivaxévanis 1975; Lamb and Holmes 1980; Picton and Mack 1979). Women processed, spun, dyed, and wove cotton that was grown by men. Many of these cloths were sold by women in large local markets, and profits from cloth sales were a primary source of income. As in Incan, Indian, and medieval Mediterranean societies, where cloth production and consumption were major factors in local economies, handwoven cloth in Bùnú had important social, political, and religious implications for both ritual and everyday affairs.

This industry no longer exists. Yet handwoven cloths are being kept for ritual use and a few older women still weave them. *Why, if cloth is rarely woven today, does it continue to play such a vital role in Bùnú social life?* In attempting to answer this question, I consider cloth use and production in Bùnú society from approximately 1900 to the present.

The many distinctive cloths used in Bùnú reflect various aspects of village society. In a way, then,

Adapted from Elisha P. Renne, *Cloth That Does Not Die: The Meaning of Cloth in Bunu Social Life* (Seattle: University of Washington Press, 1995).

this book is as much about a small group of people associated with a particular past and place in central Nigeria as it is about cloth. Indeed, I argue that focusing on things such as cloth may be as rewarding a way to understand the changing complexity of social life as organizing material according to more abstract categories such as family or political organization. The study of such everyday objects can often provide special insights since "the aspects of things that are most important to us are hidden because of their simplicity and familiarity" (Wittgenstein 1978: 129). An analysis centering on a concrete object may, ironically, be one of the best ways to approach the fleeting quality of social relations in "the everyday world of lived experience" (Jackson 1989: 13).

Furthermore, cloth has specific characteristics appropriate to the analysis of certain aspects of social life, particularly the relationship between the individual and society. Because of its skinlike proximity to the human body, cloth is intimately associated with the individual. By absorbing bodily substances such as saliva, mucus, and sweat, it may be thought to assimilate attributes, such as saintliness, of a particular wearer. Yet cloth is also the product of social life; its construction reflects contemporary technologies and tastes that are based on knowledge accumulated from past generations. In this sense, wearing cloth links the individual with others, past and present, situating the person in society. The dual position of the individual in society, who is "contained in sociation and, at the same time, finds himself confronted by it" (Simmel [1904] 1971[b]: 17), may be emphasized by playing upon the two-sided quality of cloth. A wearer's sociality may be publicly expressed by the side of cloth facing outward, while an individual's private concerns and intentions are associated with its other side, facing inward.

This Janus-faced quality of cloth, which suggests the opposition inherent in group and individual interests, nonetheless underscores the fact that both sides are of a piece. A person is distinct from society despite personal effacement, as when masquerade costumes and uniforms are used to disguise or minimize individual identity and project a generalized social role. Cloth may also be used to hide individual deformity and disease, representing the kind of socially duplicitous

but judicious behavior praised in this Yorùbá *oríkì* poem (Barber 1991: 140):

Bí ò sí aṣọ	If there were no cloth
Mo ní à bá ṣiṣe	We would surely be at fault
Bí ò sí aṣọ	If there were no cloth
À bá ṣiwà hù	Our blemishes would be exposed
Bíi kókó, bí oówo	Like lumps, like boils
Bí íkù	Like swollen hips
Bí àgbáàrín	Like grape-sized swellings ...

Alternatively, an individual may wear diaphanous silk or fine linen which simultaneously covers and reveals, suggesting the good intentions of a wearer who has nothing to hide.

It is this oscillation between group and individual identities and interests, in part, that propels social life. Individuals seek a sense of community while striving to achieve personal goals, which, for many reasons, they may only partially realize. These conflicting aims do not reflect different phases of structural order and disorder ending in a communal harmony (Turner 1969). Rather, they reflect the ways in which social and individual aspirations provide a continuous counterpoint for each other, resulting in a tension that is never ultimately resolved. This tension is illuminated by a further consideration of the conjunction of ideas and particular qualities of cloth.

IDEAS, THINGS, AND THE QUALITIES OF CLOTH

Emile Durkheim, who stressed the benefits of society for the individual, observed the importance of material things in conveying specific ideas and sentiments. Things exhibit a certain dialectical quality in that they are invested with meaning but may themselves be integral to the reproduction of ideas that contribute to group unity in time and space. For example, old cloths kept and handed down from ancestors are associated with past beliefs and practices. Their value is derived from this connection with the past and with the number of individuals previously associated with these cloths. Such accrued value is referred to as "inalienable wealth" by Weiner (1985) who discusses how "ancestral" objects legitimate present-day claims to authority in ways which newly made objects, no matter how costly or prestigious, are unable to do. One of the central problems in societies where "ancestral" things such as cloth are retained is the necessity of "keeping-while-giving" ([Weiner] 1992), whereby the need to maintain sociability through exchange must be countered by the keeping or replacing of cloths on which individual and group identities rest.

Further, in many societies cloth is often used in ceremonies of birth and rebirth to represent the beginning of social and spiritual identity for individuals. Moments after birth, infants may be swaddled, covered, and carried with special cloth that provides both a womblike security and a social identity. Corpses may be wrapped with an abundance of cloths that, it is believed, will support them in the next world (Darish 1989: 135) while reinforcing the status of kinspeople who remain in this one.

Cloth may also be used to support the moral and ideological assertions of religious groups. In West Africa, Muslims wear tailored garments associated with Allah (Perani 1989) rather than untailored cloths. These cut and tailored garments contrast with uncut cloths woven on looms with a revolving warp, implying circular continuity (Schneider and Weiner 1986: 180). This circularity is suggestive of reincarnation, associated with indigenous religious beliefs about rebirth. In another West African context, literate Christian converts who were freed slaves chose to wear costly European dress, enhancing their new position as political elites in southern Nigerian (Mann 1986) and Sierra Leonean (Spitzer 1974) societies. Furthermore, cloths associated with the past and reproduced exactly through an intentional "conspicuous archaism" (Cort 1989) may be employed by a modern, educated elite to adapt to economic, political, and religious change and simultaneously to maintain a sense of continuity and timelessness. Thus cloth is used in asserting competing group claims, in reconstructing traditions, and in constructing new beliefs.

Cloth not only covers human bodies and is passed on through time, it is also wrapped around trees and rocks (Feeley-Harnik 1989; Mack 1989) and draped over houses (Blier 1987; Smith 1982). Used in these ways, it suggests a common connection and compatibility of scale among natural, domestic, and personal domains (Jackson 1989). These connections are also reinforced by the metaphors based on cloth and by a weaving imagery common in many languages. As a symbol of interconnectedness, one speaks of cloth that "ties people together," of the "interweaving of the social fabric," and of the "warp and weft of social life" (Weiner and Schneider 1989: 2).

Yet cloth has contradictory and ambiguous associations as well as beneficial ones. As the Bùnú song that begins this chapter suggests, the good fortune—money, cloth, and children—of some is cause for the resentment and anger of others. The song expresses what Simmel ([1904] 1971[c]: 91) called an "awareness of dissonance" in social life, an appreciation of the contradictory side of interpersonal and group relations in which conflict coexists with general social ideals. The ambiguous position of the individual who must continually juggle self- and group interests is reflected in the suggestively sinister overtone of the song's final line, "Cloth has many uses." These uses may be for good or ill. Like the gift that should project selfless generosity but also entails competitive challenge, cloth used to represent social unity and harmony may also be used to defeat rivals and to express conflict. Thus, while cloth may be socially beneficial—as a source of economic power, as a symbol of family and group unity, as a marker of political ranks, and as a link between the living and the dead—it has other, more subversive, sides. Cloth may conceal malevolent intentions (Schneider and Weiner 1986: 179) and be used to threaten (Brett-Smith 1989), as well as represent more positive ideals. The multiple and contradictory ideas associated with "the many uses of cloth" make it a particularly appropriate vehicle for examining the complicated ambiguity of human intentions and social life.

"CLOTH ONLY WEARS, IT DOES NOT DIE"

The fact that cloth is impermanent, that it shreds and frays, expresses ambiguity as well. An awareness that material things such as cloth may be lost, wear out, or decay may be used to express the difficulty of maintaining social continuity in the face of disruptive change and the finiteness of death. Unless specially preserved, cloths—like human bodies—eventually disintegrate and disappear. Yet despite their propensity to wear and decay, objects such as cloth may be kept because of their ability to "confound time" (Küchler 1988: 629) in other ways. Indeed, the actual quality of durability or hardness is not necessarily the basis of this immortality, for as Küchler (1988) has observed in the case of Malangan wood and fiber sculpture, memories associated with a particular object that has rotted or burnt may equally serve this purpose. In some cases, the ability of cloth to absorb and emit odors makes it a particularly evocative source of memories—as was Ṣóyínká's mother's handwoven aṣọ òkè cloth: "Wild Christian's bedroom ... was a riot of smells, a permanent redolence of births, illnesses, cakes, biscuits and petty merchandise. This varied from the rich earth-smell of aṣọ òkè [handwoven cloth], to camphor balls and hundreds of unguents" (Ṣóyínká 1988: 77–78).

Bùnú villagers use cloth to evoke memories by representing ancestors as masquerades and recreating the political claims of particular kin groups in chieftaincy rituals. Cloth may also be employed medicinally to confound time—its use is believed to prolong an individual's life by countering disease—reflected in the Bùnú Yorùbá incantation *Gbígbó káṣọ í gbó, éè kú*—"Cloth only wears, it does not die." This incantation may be intoned when particular medicinal substances are given to patients. Its imagery suggests that while individuals and cloths may wear out, children and new cloths will replace them. The incantation relates cloth to ideas about individual mortality, social continuity, and the circularity of time and of space—represented by the regeneration of ancestral spirits in individual bodies and by connections between earthly and spirit worlds. Using cloth, Bùnú villagers address the problem of how to maintain continuity in social life, despite the disruption of conflict, disease, and death.

The ideas of individual human bodies "wearing" into dust, of undying souls returning to the spirit world, and of worn but undying cloth appear to be conflated. In order for the recycling of souls and cloth to continue, old bodies and cloth must wear out and be reproduced. Thus the impermanence of cloth and human bodies is the very quality by which undying social continuity is achieved. This paradox is the key to understanding the continued importance of handwoven cloth in Bùnú social life through which individuals and groups extend identities and claims through time.

CLOTH IN WEST AFRICA AND NIGERIA

As early as the eleventh century, cloth was used to distinguish political and social ranks among members of West African royal courts: "Among the people [of the Kingdom of Ghana] who follow the king's religion only he and his heir apparent (who is the son of his sister) may wear sewn clothes. All other people wear robes of cloth, silk, or brocade, according to their means" (al-Bakri, cited in Levtzion and Hopkins 1981: 80).

Cloth production and trade were important economic factors for many precolonial West African kingdoms and groups (Gilfoy 1987; Sundstrom 1974). At the end of the fifteenth century, Portuguese merchants traded European cloth along the coast of West Africa. By the early sixteenth century, a yard of cloth had become a principal unit of exchange.

Along the southern Nigeria coast, the cloth trade continued to expand with important ramifications for indigenous weavers. Dutch and English merchants began purchasing huge quantities of locally produced cloth from trading stations in the Kingdom of Benin. Consisting of three or four joined pieces, these cloths were known as *mouponoqua* by Nigerian traders and as "Benin cloth" by Europeans. However, they were most likely the products of women weavers from other coastal groups and from the Nigerian interior rather than from Benin itself (Landolphe 1823; Ryder 1965). These plain indigo blue or blue and white striped cloths were bartered for gold, ivory, and slaves in Ghana, Gabon, and Angola (Ryder 1969: 94). Cloth continued to be used as a primary measure of value, but the indigenous cloth "piece," or *pagne*, replaced European cloths as the standard measure (Fourneau and Kravetz 1954; Ryder 1969: 208).

In southern Nigeria, even after the beginning of the eighteenth century when trade in indigenous cloth had declined, further European trade on the coast and exploration of the interior, along with missionary endeavors, ensured the continued use of cloth in African-European encounters. In the eighteenth and nineteenth centuries, it headed the lists of items essential for maintaining good relations with Nigerians.

While a number of European merchants recorded information about cloth trade on the Nigerian coast from the sixteenth century on, less is known about cloth production and trade for the comparable period in central and northern Nigeria. Yet nineteenth-century explorers, such as Clapperton, Barth, and the Lander brothers, suggest that cloth production and trade played a prominent role in the economic life of the kingdoms of northern Nigeria. This prominence is evidenced by Barth's enthusiastic description of the cloth trade of Kano and its environs:

> There is really something grand in this kind of industry, which spreads to the north as far as Murzuk, Ghat, and even Tripoli; to the west, not only to Timbuktu, but in some degree even as far as the shores of the Atlantic, the very inhabitants of Arguim dressing in the cloth woven and dyed in Kano; to the east, all over Bornu, although there it comes in contact with the native industry of the country; and to the south it maintains a rivalry with the native industry of the Igbira and Igbo, while toward the southeast it invades the whole of Adamawa. (1857, 1: 511)

Barth's mention of the "rivalry with the native industry of the Igbira [Ebira]" is relevant here as it probably refers to the cloth production of their immediate neighbors, the Bùnú and Owé Yorùbá of Kàbbà, as well. Unfortunately, there is little documentation of the cloth trade around Kàbbà during this period. Yet Frobenius, who visited the large market at Bida in 1912, observed that the production of cloths that came from Bùnú and Kàbbà was "enormous," exceeding Nupe women's cloth production in volume.

The economic vitality of the West African cloth trade generally was also evidenced by the presence of European representatives of textile firms who collected samples of West African cloths to be manufactured in Europe and then exported to specific African markets (Steiner 1985). An important part of British colonial policy centered on promoting the production of raw materials such as cotton and exporting British manufactured textiles back to the colonies (Johnson 1974). These cotton-growing and cloth-selling schemes failed in southern Nigeria, initially because of the low prices offered by British cotton firms and because of the competition for raw cotton by Nigerian weavers whose products continued to be in demand because of their lower price and durability. Later, economic disruption caused by the 1929 world depression and the world war, along with competition from Japanese and Indian textiles, undercut British textile imports during the colonial period.

At present, Nigerian textile manufacturing firms produce large amounts of commercial cloth. While the number of weavers has declined, handweaving continues in Nigeria, particularly by men weavers in Ìlọrin and Ìséyìn and by women weavers of Okene and Akwete. The use of handwoven cloth as prestige dress (Boyer 1983; Lloyd 1953) was bolstered by a 1978 ban on textile imports, which was formulated in part to encourage industrial and handwoven textile production in Nigeria. Further, governmental agencies and the press have promoted the wearing of handwoven cloth as both patriotic and fashionable, thus extending its economic, political, and cultural importance in Nigerian social life.

The diversity of West African and Nigerian textile traditions has been treated in several general surveys on cloth types and looms. While the cultural importance of cloth in West African societies—in funerals, in chieftaincy installation, in spirit possession, as bride-wealth payments, and as currency—has been noted, the social significance of cloth and its production has received relatively little attention in West African textile literature.

This study focuses on the social relationships formed and maintained through the use and production of cloth in one central Nigerian society. However, it also includes information about specific cloth types, their production and marketing, thus complementing studies of women's handweaving production elsewhere in southwestern Nigeria where similar loom terminology was used and long-distance cloth trading was also common. This study of Bùnú cloth contributes to our general knowledge of handweaving in the Yorùbá-speaking areas of southwestern Nigeria as well as to the particularities of Bùnú history, geography, and society.

BÙNÚ YORÙBÁ SOCIETY

The Bùnú Yorùbá people are one of several small ethnic groups living near the confluence of the Niger and Benue rivers in central Nigeria. The Bùnú and three neighboring groups (the Owé, Ìjùmú, and Yàgbà), who speak a dialect of the Yorùbá language, are collectively known as the Northeast or O-kun Yorùbá, the term *o-kun* referring to a common greeting used in the area (Krapf-Askari 1965: 9). These groups are sometimes called "fringe Yorùbá" because of their location on the periphery of the Yorùbá-speaking heartland to the southwest. They are also "fringe" in the sense that while they share some characteristics with southwestern Yorùbá groups, they are distinct from them in several ways.

Situated in savannah country to the north of the tropical rainforests associated with the south, the area gets a shorter rainy season as well as smaller quantities of rain, which limits agricultural options and, hence, economic surplus available to northeast Yorùbá farmers. Furthermore, their inland position limited them to overland trade as opposed to the riverine or intercreek trade that favored the economic positions of groups such as the Ìjèbu Yorùbá to the south. These geographical limitations on the accumulation of wealth and on mobility are reflected in the less hierarchical forms of political organization and traditional religious cosmology in Bùnú compared with southwestern Yorùbá groups. There are no specific royal clans or lineages, for example, because appointment to royal office is based on rotation among three clan groupings. Nor is there the elaborate pantheon of gods and goddesses associated with southwestern Yorùbá groups. Nonetheless, the Bùnú and other northeast groups speak a similar language and share common cultural practices such as Ifá divination, and some claim a common origin.

Bùnú District consists of hilly savannah, interspersed with heavily timbered forests. While colonial officials were interested in tapping Bùnú's natural resources, other developments such as the building of roads and schools came later to Bùnú than Kàbbà (in Kàbbà District), which was the divisional capital, and the more centrally located Yàgbà and Ìjùmú (Gbẹ̀dẹ̀) districts. Bùnú with its sparse population and poor roads is relatively undeveloped compared to other northeast Yorùbá districts. Because of their isolated location and particular history, the residents of Bunu District have tended to maintain certain traditional practices including handweaving.

History

In precolonial times, Bùnú consisted of several small kingdoms, each with a large town or village ruled by a head chief or king (*olú*) and council of chiefs. Individual settlements were said to be founded by individual hunters whose descendants formed large villages and, at times, walled towns (Krapf-Askari 1966; Ọbáyẹmí 1978b). Their small size does not imply that these settlements were static, for both trade and warfare linked these groups with large kingdoms to the south, east, and north—at Benin, Idah, and Bida, respectively.

During the mid-nineteenth century, horsemen from the powerful Nupe kingdom centered at Bida to the north invaded the entire area. Shortly thereafter the Nupe established a tribute system in Bùnú whereby people, agricultural produce, and cloth were given in return for protection from further raiding (Mason 1970: 205; Ọbáyẹmí 1978a). One of the results of Nupe raids in Bùnú in the nineteenth century was migration, particularly in the southern part of the district where villagers moved to more defensible positions near Ebiraland. These forced and voluntary migrations had important cultural ramifications for the Bùnú Yorùbá, who have incorporated certain Nupe and Ebira cultural practices.

In 1897, a constabulary force of a British firm, the Royal Niger Company, routed the Nupe from northeast Yorùbá areas. In 1900, Bùnú District, rather arbitrarily organized, came under the political control of the British colonial Protectorate of Northern Nigeria. Since independence in 1960, Bùnú District has become one of two districts that make up the Kàbbà-Bùnú Local Government Area, a countylike administrative unit in Kogí State, Nigeria.

Social and economic organization

Currently, most Bùnú towns and villages are located next to the two main roads that bisect the district. Affiliation with a particular Bùnú village and associated rights to farmland and chieftaincy titles are ideally based on descent reckoned patrilineally from an ancestral male village founder. In reality, historical, political, and economic exigencies have led individuals to make bilateral claims in these matters. However, patrilineal identity is reinforced by virilocal residence after marriage since most children are born among their father's people. Married women, nonetheless, retain rights within their own patrilineal homes, which are often in nearby villages where they frequently visit. In general, individuals maintain ties with both patrilineal and matrilateral kin.

During the 1920s when British colonial officials assessed the district, Bùnú village economy consisted of subsistence agriculture, cloth production, and trade, with a distinct sexual division of labor. Women wove and traded cloth, while men farmed and hunted. This situation gradually changed during the colonial period as better roads and transport made alternative economic opportunities available. At the end of the twentieth century, Bùnú village women and men are principally engaged in cash-crop production along with subsistence agriculture, growing yams, cassava, sorghum, and maize on separate farm plots. Agricultural products are usually sold by women who take produce to major urban markets. Women have continued their role as traders although many have ceased weaving as an economic pursuit, partly because of the difficulties of acquiring materials and labor.

While farmland continues to be plentiful in Bùnú District, labor was also the factor mentioned by farmers as the primary constraint on production. Since farm labor and financial support are often supplied by one's children and other family members (see Caldwell 1976; Peel 1983: 120), older Bùnú villagers face the problem of how to establish and maintain the loyalty of kin. This is difficult in light of migratory pressures, such as employment, which lure young people to urban centers. However, Bùnú villagers who have migrated to cities often return during holiday periods when masquerade performances, chieftaincy installations, and marriages take place. Generational connections are maintained, in part, through the use of material things handed down, which include marriage cloths and chieftaincy regalia.

Local political organization

In Bùnú, village projects and dispute settlements are generally addressed locally, often by a group of older men who, through payments, village philanthropy, and common consent, acquire the title of chief. These men are responsible for organizing village-wide ritual performances and deciding whether strangers may reside in a village. They also serve as an interface between Nigerian federal and state government officials and Bùnú villagers.

Acquiring a chieftaincy title offers individual Bùnú men leadership opportunities in local political affairs. There are three grades (or levels) of chieftaincy positions that require successively larger amounts of cash, as well as family and community support, to acquire. Most adult men living in Bùnú villages have taken first-level titles; those with the second level are fewer, and the highest political office in Bùnú—the third-level title known as *olú* or king—is rare nowadays.

Presently, in all but a few Bùnú villages, chiefs are exclusively male. This monopoly of chieftaincy by men was not always the case. In the past, a woman could also take a chieftaincy title, which gave her authority to officiate in women's affairs and participate in decisions made by male chiefs. Now there are few women chiefs and Bùnú women acquire status through the performance of the traditional marriage ritual, *gbé obitan*.

Religious practice

Chieftaincy ritual in the past was closely related to belief in nature spirits (*ẹbọra*). Chiefs were responsible for the well-being of groups and communities through sacrifice to these spirits (Krapf-Askari 1966: 4), conceptualized as both amorphous and invisible. *Ẹbọra* spirits are believed to reside "under the water," in stones, or in other natural sites such as trees, rocks, hills, or termite mounds. Specific spirits are frequently associated with particular patrilineages, patriclans, or villages. While today most Bùnú Yorùbá are practicing Christians, many continue to acknowledge the existence of these spirits, thus reaffirming group identity and continuity. Patrilineal identity has also been maintained through sacrifices and prayers made to ancestral spirits at the graves of deceased patrilineal members. Also, generalized ancestral figures are represented by *egúngún* masqueraders, who may perform during funeral celebrations and at other annual events.

The living may communicate with ancestral or nature spirits through the efforts of an Ifá diviner, known as a *babaláwo*, "father of the secret." These men are consulted in everyday and ritual affairs for advice on a wide range of concerns. Many Bùnú residents continue to believe in the ability of diviners to communicate with spirits and in the efficacy of their predictions. Except

for the most strict of Christian practitioners, these beliefs are not viewed as a contradiction but rather as additional and complementary means of addressing the difficult problems of living.

Bùnú villagers have modified past practices—including chieftaincy organization, traditional marriage, farming, and religious ritual—to the conditions of living in modern Nigeria.

Similarly, handwoven cloth, now infrequently produced, has not been abandoned but rather its use has been adapted. For despite economic, religious, and political changes in Bùnú society that militate against the pervasive use of handwoven cloth as in the past, the desire to prevent illness and death, to avoid the enmity of others, to be generous while preserving one's own resources, these problems still persist. Cloth, perceived as protecting individuals and connecting groups with the past, continues to be used in attempts to solve these problems.

19

THE POLITICAL ECONOMY OF ELEGANCE:
An African cult of beauty

Jonathan Friedman

EXISTENTIALISME A LA MODE

In the Congo of the 1950s there appeared a number of youth clubs whose identity was tied to the French institutions introduced in the colonial capital of Brazzaville. The cinema had been introduced and was frequented by *les évolués* on a regular basis. Images of modern life a la Parisien were diffused via the new media and the cafäs, themselves associated with the new life style. The new groups which developed primarily but not exclusively in the quarter of Bacongo came to be known as existentialistes or *existos*. This was not due to any explicit adoption of Sartre's philosophy but to the fact that it was associated with a dominant mood and mode in Paris after the war.

The Congolese clubs adopted the colors black and red, among others, which they imagined to be the colors of their Parisian peers. In fact this was no more than the construction of an image at a distance of what was conceived as the Parisian Existentialiste since here was no correlation between the latter and black and red clothes.

These youth clubs, in which the average age was eighteen, were also mutual aid associations in which members contributed to each other's expenses and to the furthering of the goals of the group. Identification with a Parisian life style was part of a strategy of hierarchical distinctions in which different clubs competed with one another for status expressed entirely in the realm of clothing. Clubs had their own couturiers who were key figures in the fashioning of status.

> Bacongo was both feared and admired for its clothing. There was a kind of reverence for this quarter. (informant in Gandoulou 1984: 34)

In spite of the lack of interest in existential problems, the *existo's* entire existence was predicated on such problems and fashion as a project was a self-evident solution to personal survival in a colonized population where selfhood was identical to the appropriation of otherness.

The strategy of dress in the 1950s might also be contextualized in terms of the general transformation of Congolese society. Rapid urbanization, the increase in the wage based sector and the monetarization of the economy, the formation and spread of new forms of sociality—numerous associations for mutual aid, common projects and the maintenance of emergent ethnic identity. All of these transformations did not, however, succeed in dissolving the kinship networks that linked urban and rural areas and which absorbed a large part of the new urban income as well as providing food for hard pressed urban dwellers. The opposition between the developed south dominated by the Congo and the undeveloped north, represented increasingly by the Mbochi, came increasingly to the fore. The concentric hierarchy as represented by the Congo is one in which Paris>Congo>Mbochi>Pygmies>nature.

Adapted from Jonathan Friedman, "The Political Economy of Elegance: An African Cult of Beauty," in *Consumption and Identity* (Chur: Harwood Academic Publishers, 1994), pp. 167–87.

Another group, the Teke, are tricksters in the system, straddling north and south and making alliances with both. The Teke are often considered traitors (also tricksters) insofar as it is they who made the original treaty with De Brazza that surrendered the region to the French. Thus the strategy of dress partakes and even demarcates a set of "tribal" or ethnic distinctions that animate the political history of the Congo.

LA SAPE

If the *existos* were into clothes, they were also family men with jobs, well integrated into the developing urban culture of the country. The decade of the 1950s was one of economic expansion in which salaries rose faster than prices. This decade also led to the independence movement and the establishment of a national state all within the framework of a growing socialist ideology. During the 1960s these clubs declined, along with religious cult activity. Numerous spokesmen for the socialist movements attacked the clothing cults as offensive to African identity and the new social revolution. Instead, political engagement in the future and the simultaneous revival of traditional culture as nationalist spectacle became dominant. The former *existos* disappeared and from 1964–68 there were only a scatter of youth organizations, called *Clubs des Jeunes Premiers* who carried on the tradition of dress which had become a sign of Congo identity in the new multiethnic struggle for political power.

The new Congolese state like other African states had emerged as a class structure where instead of white colonials, local politicians now occupied the same hierarchy, imbued with the same values. In a system where consumption defines identity and where the trappings of modernity not only represent but are the very essence of social power, the social structure tends to take on the attributes of a perfect scalogrom of conspicuous consumption.

> If the Occidental meaning of the adjective "rich" qualifies individuals in terms of their possession of large properties, means of production, or having high paying positions, in the Congo … the idea of wealth is measured in terms of consumption power whose only value comes from the degree to which it is identified with Western consumption. (Gandoulou 1984: 41)

In 1968 the Congo were displaced by the Mbochi as the result of a military coup. From the point of view of Congo ideology this represented a barbarian invasion. At the same time the economy began to stagnate in a way that, in spite of the oil boom of the late 1970s and early 1980s left a permanently crippling mark on the prospects of future growth. In this period a second and more intensive wave of fashionable consumption made its appearance, located again primarily among the southern groups from Bacongo who had now been successively deprived of their political and bureaucratic positions as well as their leading ideological role in the country.

La Sape, from the word *se saper,* meaning to dress elegantly, connoting the flíneur of our own society, takes on an especially powerful meaning as it emerges among the youth clubs of Bacongo. As an institution it refers to *La Société des Ambianceurs et Personnes Elégantes.* While the earlier *existos* were employed family heads who had their own group tailors and competed as groups or teams, the *sapeurs* are largely unemployed, unmarried youth who rank local couturiers on the bottom of a scale that progresses upwards from imported ready-to-wears to the ranks of *haute couture,* and who compete individually in their strivings to attain the position of a *grand. La Sape* is a network of individuals that form ranked hierarchies by building reputation and clientäles in the larger arena of the urban night spots. Yet the ranked hierarchies that are the clubs themselves are a perfect mirror of clan organization.

> It is not unusual for Sapeurs to use the word "family" when referring to the club, they have a tendency to perceive the other members as real kin. (Gandoulou 1989: 90)

Each club generally has a name, a territory, a set of ranked sub-groups, specialized appellations and a division of labor. There are special rules and regulations for how members are to address one another, special linguistic usages and rituals that are symbolic of group identity.

THE PRACTICE OF ELEGANCE AND THE PRODUCTION OF STRUCTURE

The *sape* is a ritual program for the transformation of ordinary unranked youth into great men. It begins and ends in Bacongo, with a "liminal" phase in Paris. It consists in the continual build up of a wardrobe and ritual display at organized parties and dance bars. In Brazzaville one can begin to accumulate lower ranked clothing, *non-griffés,* copies and ordinary ready-to-wear. The move to Paris, *l'aventure,* is the beginning of the real transformation of the ordinary *sapeur* into a person of higher status. Paris is, as in the liminal phase of many rituals, a time and space of ordeals, where life consists of scrounging, by hook and crook, to obtain the cash and credit needed to accumulate a real *haute couture* wardrobe, called *la gamme,* i.e. the scale of great names in clothing. In one sense, Paris, as the center of *La Sape* is a kind of heaven, but in terms of hardship it is closer to hell. This contradiction is understood as the result of the low rank of blacks in the sacred abode of white power. The rank order of dress greatly elaborates on the earlier home based range of the *existos.* From highest to lowest, clothing is ranked as follows:

The same kind of hierarchy exists in all domains of body ornamentation. Labels play a crucial role. Westin shoes, for example, are ranked among the highest. There are other less well known English and French names and even copies, etc. all the way down to local sandals. Rank is essential and, therefore, no substitution is possible. This is the fundamental principle of *La Sape.* An excellent example of the strength of this constraint is the case of a factory producing imitation Capo Bianco crocodile shoes that in 1984 cost 5,200FF. The copies, quite excellent, cost only 900FF which enticed some *Parisiens* to buy them. When the word got around the reaction was positively deadly.

> *ah non, za fua zé* … you have buy real shoes. Even if the article is high quality, the moment it becomes known to be an imitation all is lost, *affaires zi fuidi.* The cheapest pair of croco(dile)s cost 2,000FF (Gandoulou 1984: 75). *za fua zé*—"that's it, its finished" *affaires zi fuidi*—idem. That won't do, *affaires zi fuidi.* The cheapest pair of crocos cost 2,000FF (Gandoulou 1984: 75).

The accumulation of *la gamme* is not merely about appearance as we understand it. It is not enough to have a certain look, for the look must be authentic and the only sure sign of authenticity is the label. Copies are not inacceptable but they have a lower rank in the system. Elegance is not, then, merely about looking elegant, about appearing in clothes that *look* like haute couture. It is about wearing the real thing and in this sense of being the real thing.

Another domain related to the transformation of the body is the practice of *maquillage a outrance,* the use of a mixture of strong chemicals, including bleach, to lighten the skin. The expression, *se jaunir,* refers to such widespread practices, but also means to become wealthy and powerful, i.e. to become more white. While this is one of the least expensive activities of the adventurer, the products used are variable and also ranked on the scale of elegance, according to their efficiency. The Lari (a Congo dialect) *kilongo* which has a strong connotation of "medicine" is the general term for this "makeup." While we do not have the space to discuss this very elaborate domain, it is noteworthy that its logic is identical to that found in other domains, i.e. the use of "medicine" in the accumulation of life force, expressed in the true beauty of light skin as much as in the elegance of clothing.

The *Parisien* maintains a continual contact with *sapeurs* at home, telling them of his adventures and most importantly of his acquisitions. At some point in this process he makes a *descente,* a return to Brazzaville to display his status rank. *La descente* is usually performed several times, and with constantly renewed ensembles, before the final return and attempted reintegration into Congolese society. This process is the making of a great man or *un grand,* a true *Parisien,* the highest category in the rank order. It is accomplished by means of the ritual gala, an expensive affair in which contributions are made from the entire club for hiring a dance restaurant, a band, food and drink. Invitations are made, and the night of the trial is a veritable potlatch of elegance in which the candidates must, as is said, *se saper a mort.* An official panegyrist introduces the star or hero, carefully listing his qualities and the entire gamut of his ensemble, clothing, shoes and makeup. His girlfriend, also dressed to the teeth, publicly embraces him and offers a gift after which others come forward with similar offerings. This is followed by a signal from the eulogist to the orchestra—several bars of intensively rhythmic music during which the *sapeur* displays himself for the public. The next *sapeur* is introduced, and this pattern continues until all the presentations are made. The function of this phase is the *initial frime* or pretense, here in the sense of ostentation. After the presentation begins the dance itself and the festivities are formally opened. What is referred to as *la danse des griffes* consists in the meticulous display of the entire array of labels on one's person during the dancing. This difficult task must also be accomplished with the utmost refinement. As there are several great *sapeurs* present at any one celebration, there are bound to be status conflicts. These are expressed in the exchange of elaborate gestures of disdain, superiority and studied indifference. A particular act of humiliation has been described by Gandoulou (1989: 115) in which a man steps on the toes of his adversary's Westin shoe, signifying *"ngé za fua zé"* meaning "you (familiar)! That won't do" interpreted as "you've got no place here." A *sapeur* must be very sure of his superiority before engaging in such acts. It is, furthermore, not uncommon that his adversary will slip out, change his clothes and/or shoes and return to defy his opponent (Gandoulou: [1989: 115]). Such celebrations of beauty generate an entire mythology of great men and are the intergroup condition of intragroup hierarchy in the clubs.

The structure of relations produced by these activities is one where a set of leaders or great men function as the equivalent of lineage chiefs in a vast network of clientship and exchange. A great man attracts dependents, who are eager to work as his slaves in order to gain access, however temporary, to his prestige goods, the lower orders of which are quite sufficient to build up junior hierarchies. The organization of the clubs becomes a hierarchy of great men, seniors, and juniors. A *sapeur* may often have what is referred to as a *mazarin,* named after the well known minister of Louis XIV, who functions as a personal servant and messenger. A network of clients emerges out of the prestige accumulated through the adventure of the *sape*. Clients, novices with great aspirations,

are able to gain access to social connections as well as borrowing the great man's apparel for use in their own exploits. There is also exchange and borrowing of apparel among great men themselves, a veritable circulation of prestige goods reminiscent of traditional Congolese politics.

This structure can only be maintained by the constant circulation of people from Brazzaville to Paris and back, with the continual accumulation of *haute couture* that defines the rank order of elegance. The objective limits of this process are determined by the economic conditions of the Parisian adventure. And the end point of this process reveals the precarious fate of *sapeurs* when they make the final return to Brazzaville. For the ultimate paradox of the entire project is that it begins and ends in consumption, yet generates no steady income. This question is more complicated than it might appear from a simple economic point of view. For insofar as the accumulation of labels gives rise to patron/client networks, there is often a means of converting such networks into income generating operations in the intricate informal sector characterized by long chains combining the sale and rental of just about everything. While many former *sapeurs* fall into oblivion, others manage to transform their elegance into real economic advantage. There are even extreme examples where the refinement of *La Sape* has been recognized internationally, enabling some to ascend the sacred heights of fashion's French Olympus, where they have become true gods of the movement. A recent sacred priest descended to Brazzaville in March, 1990, where he threw a real *bal des sapeurs* at the Hotel Mbamou Palace. The latter is frequented only by the really wealthy elite of the state-class and their European guests. This event, then, marked in no uncertain terms the capacity to convert image into reality. While only the "real" elite could afford to be present, the act itself legitimizes the entire project of prestige accumulation in its modern context.

PERSONHOOD AND THE SOCIAL SELF: ELEGANCE AS POLITICS

We have argued, thus far, for a certain unity in Congolese strategies of selfhood. Clothing is more than property or the expression of one's already existent self, or the fulfillment of an imagined self. It is the constitution of self, a self that is entirely social. There is no "real me" under the surface and no roles are being played that might contrast with an underlying true subject. One of the continuities in the nature of Congolese consumption, whether it be of people, the power of god, or clothing is the effect of fulfilment that it produces in the individual. *Sapeurs* often describe their state as drugged or enchanted. They participate in an all encompassing project that absorbs them completely.

> I am the happiest man in the world. I am driven by a superiority complex. You can walk right in front of me, but I don't see you. I ignore you no matter what your social rank except if you are my kin, of course. (Gandoulou 1989: 162)

The experience of the *sapeur* is not equivalent to that of the flâneur, as we suggested at the start of this discussion, for the simple reason that it is entirely authentic. No tricks are played on reality. The strategy is not to fool the audience, to use appearance as a means to status that is not rightfully attained. In a world where appearance tends to fuse with essence rather than merely representing it, dressing up is not a means but an end in itself. And yet there is a certain overlap in the very experience itself. On the one hand, we know from our experience, the way in which consumption can be used to overcome depression, how the visitor to the solarium, may account for his or her activity in terms of the feeling of wellbeing attained. If white is beautiful for them, tan may be beautiful for us and for some in a way that appears similar on the surface. Some studies of working class youth culture in England have also often stressed what would appear to be the stronger sense of identification with consumed products.

> The mod saw commodities as extensions of himself, rather than things totally independent of their maker or user and shrouded in a set of rules for their use. (Herman 1971: 51)

The fact remains that the Western consumer, no matter what his class, seems primarily engaged in the construction of an identity space that is by and large his own product, his own project. But it might be argued that there is a correlation between the weakening of the self, increasing narcissism and the increasing dependence on other directed consumption.

The *sapeur*, in confronting the social reality of state power that considers his very activity a threat to the social order, i.e. a threat to the identity of power and appearance, may begin to realize a difference between himself as a subject and his elegant image. Conversely, the cynical flâneur may become so absorbed in his own image that he loses all contact with the reality of himself as subject. The union of these two spheres, one characterized by the modern individual, the other by the holistic self, occurs in the realm of a more fundamental narcissistic condition. In our discussion of Congolese selfhood we have suggested that a specific kind of socialization in which individual initiative is everywhere thwarted and where the child is imbued with a cosmology in which he is represented as a set of elements connected to a larger kinship structure of life force, tends to generate an experience of self as totally dependent on the larger group. This is a social situation that reinforces the narcissistic state of childhood with a secure cosmological identity that functions in lieu of what in modern capitalist society are designated as ego functions. The modern individual socialized to experience himself as a self-directed organism, controlled by the projects of his own ego, can only regress to a narcissistic state when his ego projects totally fail. But this is not the secure narcissism of an interpreted universe. It is a state of total insecurity, the anguish of non-existence, that can only be solved by capturing the gaze of the other who can affirm one's own being. By contrast it might be said that for the holistic subject, the "gaze of the other" is always upon one, God is always watching.

The Western narcissist who dresses in order desperately to confirm his own being and value through others, is, in such terms, the abnormal extreme of the normally more self-conscious flâneur, who has lost his ego and become dependent on the other. The behavior of the *sapeur*, on the other hand, is an extreme variant of the normal other-directed self-adornment of the Congolese, a behavior that may inadvertently engender a sense of autonomous selfhood even if it begins as an attempt to accumulate the life force embodied in elegance. This tendency, however partial, is present in the self-understanding, even cynicism of the *sapeurs,* as expressed in the texts of their invitations to parties.

> … from the moment when, in the field of physical appearance, its esthetic, in other words, in the realm of the "social masque," one attains a perfect adjustment, almost too perfect, an absolute match with the *grand monsieur,* a rupture occurs: exaggeration, excess, "hyperconformism" ends by subverting the very norm that it strives to attain. (Gandoulou 1989: 170)

IMAGINARY POWER AND THE SUBVERSION OF THE REAL

The parody of elegance turns the *sapeur* into a delinquent, an intolerable sociopath, a danger to the very foundations of society. The amount of propaganda directed at destroying a group of youth who merely dress elegantly is indicative of the real threat that they pose to the state-class.

INVITATIONS TO PARTIES

The following texts indicate the degree of cynical self-knowledge expressed in *La Sape:* "Gaul was a Roman province for more than 400 years. The Gauls imitated the Romans—they dressed and lived like them—learned their language, Latin—gradually one could no longer distinguish the Gauls from the *Romans, all the inhabitants of Gaul were known as Gallo-Romans.*"

Les Azuriens

(people of the Riviera, Rivierians)

In Extasy

P. D. G. Pamphil Yamamoto Mwana Mode na Motätä na yä V. P. D. G. Ostinct Yarota P. D. H. Jeff Sayre de Vespucci who sows the *sape* and harvests success.

For their first appearance in the booming crackery (a great scintillating party) *the 3 Sicilians of the Riviera invite Mr. or Miss … to the super Boom that they are organizing on the 19th of March at Cottage (Hut) CI modern Bacongo at 14: 30.*

> Note: Indigenous people shall not be permitted entry, because the Society of ambianceurs and elegant persons (SAPE) detests indigenes. Come and see the beautiful labels of the finest *haute couture (Zibélé).*

The dangerous success of their project consists in the demonstration that one can reach the "top" without passing through the accepted channels of education and "work." This is the great crime against the identity of prestige and power. But it is by no means easily dealt with by the authorities. They cannot simply ignore this illegitimate elegance any more than they can give it up themselves, on the implicit understanding that clothes, after all, do not make the man. There is, then, an even more deadly logic at work in this subversion of symbolic hierarchy.

One of the most popular singers among Congolese youth is Boundzeki Rapha, known for two songs, the first "le parisien refoulä" and a year later, "le parisien retenu." The first deals with the failed Parisian adventure of the hero, who ends up in jail and is sent home where he decides to dedicate himself to the ways of his ancestors, i.e. to "work in the fields." This song ends with a clearly religious tone emphasized in the music. The second song takes up the question of the return to the old ways. It begins religiously again with the wise man instructing his child in the proper ways of life. The hero follows his directives but does not believe in them. This is followed by a set of old Lari proverbs.. "you search for your child, but he has been thrown away," "you search for grass (a field that can be sown), but it is gone …" a series of allegories expressing the desperate impossibility of survival. Then suddenly the main chorus bursts forth. "But I am beautiful, and people love me because of it, and if I am beautiful it is because I use *bilongo*" (i.e. I bleach my skin) … Refrain "*kilongo* c'est bon, *kilongo* c'est bon."

The cult of elegance, as cargo cults elsewhere, simultaneously rehabilitates the self and inverts the structure of power. It totally absorbs the subject into the project of the group, yet tends to produce an image of the unbound individual.

Throughout our discussion we have assumed that the practice of *La Sape* was somehow an attempt to capture power via the accumulation of the symbols of power. We did indeed argue that these symbols, *la haute couture,* were not expressions of but definitions of power, of the life force whose form is wealth, health, whiteness and status, all encompassed in an image of beauty. But, in understanding the world in modern terms, we failed to trace the logic through to its conclusion. The very discourse of symbolism legitimizes the materiality of power and wealth. Yet the logic of the political economy of elegance implies the converse, by undermining the significance of such realia. The state-class became great men of elegance by means of political violence and maintain that elegance by means of the theft of the state treasury, and even this can only be ultimately understood in terms of witchcraft and the magic of evil. As the accumulation of life force is the principle of the system, there is no essential difference between *La Sape* and other techniques of accumulation. In this logic, the *sapeur's* reply to the accusation of delinquency is simply, "we are no different than you even if our methods are less violent." Thus, in some deeper sense *La Sape* is all there is.

20

THE PREDICAMENT OF DRESS:
Polyvalency and the ironies of cultural identity

Deborah Durham

Tswana with whom I spoke in Botswana often "exposed" the sweeping and cumbrous Herero long dresses as a fraud. These dresses are of Western origin, they would tell me; they were copied from the white missionaries. Like anthropologists, these interpreters of cultural practice also tried to pinpoint a "true meaning" for the dress. In doing so, they effectively strip Herero women of colorful but superficial investitures to disclose the real people—universal humanity—underneath. In Botswana, only Herero women routinely wear "traditional ethnic" clothing. Divesting them of any implied ethnic purity, these Tswana comments assimilated Herero into the broader population of citizens of Botswana, who wear more contemporary Western-style dress. When I asked government officials about the ethnic composition of the broader population, they would always answer, "We are all Batswana here." By this, they meant that ethnic identity does not differentiate citizenship, that they are all citizens of the Botswana state. But they used the Tswana language term *Batswana* (Tswana people) instead of the more neutral *batho ba Botswana* (people of Botswana). Herero, too, recognized Tswana hegemony over the terms of everyday life and citizenship in their own term for unmarked, Western-style dress (*ozombanda otjitjawana*, Tswana-style clothing).

Following the lead of my Tswana interlocutors, in this article I, too, look critically at the Herero dress—not to uncover the universal and naked humanity underneath, but to examine the multiple layers of underskirts that support the outfit. Instead of reducing its meaning, I hope to retain the color of the dress, the sense of wearing it, the uncertainty and the ironic sensibility it provoked in Herero women in Mahalapye, Botswana, in the late 1980s and early 1990s, the period of my fieldwork. Herero often use the dress as an unambiguous, straightforward icon of Herero identity—for example, a woman in the dress figured centrally in all logos debated over the years for the Herero Youth Association (see Durham 1995a). Similarly, the ethnic label "Herero" was rarely, if ever, questioned for its validity. But the full meaning of both the dress and the label was much less assured. The very women who proposed the logo—women who wore the dress frequently to public and ceremonial events (although not in their daily lives)—tittered and murmured cynically, and the Association men exchanged glances, when a respected elder, invited to speak to them on New Year's Day 1989, admonished the women to dress Herero. In the Mahalapye Herero community, there is ongoing ambivalence, uncertainty, and debate over the dress and, through the dress, over the meaning of being Herero in the liberal, democratic, and Tswana state. But the dress is more than an abstract object framed by Herero and Tswana, just as people are more than just Herero and Tswana people. For those who wear the dress daily, as well as

Adapted from Deborah Durham, "The Predicament of Dress: Polyvalency and the Ironies of Cultural Identity," *American Ethnologist* 26, no. 2 (2008): 389–411.

for those who don it only occasionally, the dress is also a form of practice. Its lived sensibility and the practical projects it engages destabilize other frameworks of understanding. For "beings who stand inside and outside of it [society] at the same time" (Simmel [1904] 1971[a]: 14–15), the dress forms part of an ongoing dynamic between objective social forms and subjective experience. The dress is simultaneously a static icon of cultural identity and also a dynamic enactment of so-called transnational cultural flows. It is a physical impediment and restricts social movement; it is also a practical medium through which mobility and social connectedness are experienced; it is representative of dirtiness and backwardness and also of strength and growth. The dress is a burdensome constraint and also a sensible source of agentive autonomy.

In this article, I examine the specific situations and contents of Herero "dress-consciousness." I also explore the various ways in which items like the dress are endowed with meaning by their users. The sparkling polyvalency of objects and practices derives from the fact that their meanings are constituted in different and sometimes discordant ways. Meanings can—and do—undermine each other, reproducing "culture" as an unstable and fluid field of meaningfulness, pushing beyond Simmel's dichotomizing continua. As cultural practice, the dress is a logic of the concrete and a poetics of contrast, intellectualized reflection, inarticulate embodiment and subjective experience; its meaning bears the imprint of colonial and postcolonial relations of domination and struggles with foreign hegemonies. A conversation at a community gathering, a formal presentation at a civic celebration, idle chat during housework, the act of dressing itself—each of these moments may cast the dress in a certain light, but the meaning remains open-ended. Other forms of meaning may intrude and ambiguity surface at any moment. Dress is a shifty signifier for Herero, illuminating the slipperiness of ethnic identities and the nature of "culture" itself.

A MULTIMODAL "SPARKLE"

Undoubtedly much of the dense and slippery polyvalency of the Herero women's dress derives from these social contests and the shifting positionality of persons caught in "the web of group-affiliations" (Simmel 1955). As long as these multilayered social contests are not reduced to one contest between dominant Tswana and subordinate Herero, or to one between hegemonic Western transnationalism and a resistant indigenous localism, much of the "sparkle" (Bakhtin 1981: 276) of the Herero dress can indeed be traced out in the heteroglossic engagement of multiple social positions (cf. Abu-Lughod 1990; Ortner 1995). Gender informs ethnicity, and the history of the dress informs visions of current Herero transethnicity; age contradicts gender; rural and urban differences crosscut age-grades. Each attempt to define the dress engages dialogically with a myriad of other possible perspectives. These perspectives are not simply to be associated with social groupings: as people interact in different settings, they themselves come to recognize various perspectives. Heteroglossia is not, then, simply a condition of society at large. It is also a condition of individual consciousness; even "inner thought" enters into discourse with different potential meanings. The skeptical responses of female members of the Herero Youth Association to the old man's exhortation to wear the dress, mentioned above, take form as the young women recognize suggestions of a masculine, rural, gerontocratic, nonwage-earner image of an object that they themselves cast in a different light. And the old man's exhortation was itself prompted by his recognition that their vision of the dress was different. As Bakhtin notes, "forcing [meaning] to submit to one's own ... accents is a difficult and complicated process" (1981: 294); instead one often finds, as in the charged atmosphere of the Herero Youth Association that New Year's Day, a vivid Bakhtinian sparkle.

But the polyvalent engagement of group-based interpretations is in itself insufficient to account for the slippery overabundance of meaning bound up in the dress. The dress also is meaningful as embodied practice and sensibility. To explain its meanings exclusively in terms of socio-ideological forms reduces the dress's meaning, much as my Tswana interlocutors did when they claimed to unveil its cultural inauthenticity. To do so would suggest that uncertainty over the place of the dress in contemporary Botswana derives exclusively from struggles between status groups. But such an explanation is, while important, insufficient. Furthermore, to suggest that heteroglossia, uncertainty, and ambiguity are products of social fragmentation implies the romantic possibility of a comfortable premodern security in less "divided" societies. Uncertainty, ambiguity, and ambivalence are universal features of human living, as much a condition of so-called simple worlds as of any allegedly more complex modernity (see Levine 1985: ch. 3; Rosaldo 1989). In order to appreciate the fullness of the Herero dress's sparkle, its persistent evasiveness for even its most self-conscious wearers, and how it eludes stable ideological appropriation, I look at different modalities through which meaning is constituted.

SHIFTING MEANINGS

As I noted at the outset, when the Herero Youth Association debated logos for their organization over the years, the image of a seated woman in the long dress was always a central component. In 1990, as a member of the association and a participant in the debates, I asked why the logo should feature a woman, why one segment of the population should be iconic of Herero people. My question was met first with blank incomprehension and eventually dismissed. The dress was so obvious an ethnic signifier to the members of the association that my question, once recognized, seemed unimportant.

And yet several studies of southern African women's dress suggest that the fact that women bear the burden of ethnic representation is not innocuous. The dress and manner of rural, married Zulu women was subject to the careful controls of *hlonipa* (prescriptions of respect and avoidance) in which dress was a central symbol. In the 1980s, that men would insist that Zulu women wear traditional dress to Inkatha meetings was a direct continuation of the older domestic practice whereby women's "dress [is] concrete, visible evidence of the control their husbands have over them" (Klopper 1987: 16; Marks 1989; cf. Kuper 1973: 352 on Swazi). James (1996) discusses Sotho women's "traditional" dress as a form of empowerment. But James also finds that women and their dress styles are central to both local cultural and domestic reproduction, especially as men are drawn into Western-dominated arenas that undermine the political potential of the domestic sphere (James 1996; cf. Comaroff 1985, 1994; Mafela 1994 on Tswana).

For Herero women, too, wearing the long dress on a regular basis should be seen in reference to domesticity and the reproduction of a narrow social group (cf. Hendrickson 1994). In Mahalapye, women who don the dress as a daily practice do so either upon marriage or as they attain an unmarried domestic maturity. Although many of those who wear the dress are unmarried, widowed, or divorced, the married women who always wear Herero dresses often claim that their husbands require it of them and that they otherwise would wear Western dress styles. Even if it does not fully explain why married women wear the dress, this is a claim that is widely recognized and repeated. It is a claim that must be taken into account as a counterpoint to the embodied sense of the dress. Some women wear Herero dress at home, but Western styles at work. Women in Mahalapye who continue to wear the Herero dress in wage employment inevitably work in domestic pursuits, either as laundresses, seamstresses, or, in the past, as maids in white households. For those women who do not wear the dress on a daily basis, the occasions on which they put it on are (as already noted) largely those of social reproduction: to weddings, to funerals. (The Herero Youth Association is a formidable exception, as the members frequently don the dress to represent Herero in civic and other festivities; cf. Durham n.d.) Wearing the dress, younger women are praised for their reproductive potential: *atatatatata, wa pu, o muari* (Well, well, well, you have become beautiful, you are a young maiden). The word *omuari* also refers to a postpartum woman and signals sexuality, ripeness for marriage, and fertility. In a practical sense, as well, the dress is a nexus for confirming social (especially kin) relationships. The dress is very expensive. Younger women who want to wear one to a funeral borrow it from a female relative—specifically invoking the kinship relationship (a hierarchical form) as they do so. Younger women will also pester male relatives (or men they are attempting to convert into relatives) to purchase fabric for a dress for them, a request always phrased in terms of relationship, indebtedness for domestic services, or female dependence on men's resources. Seen through the lens of gender relations, the dress congeals a sense of women's dependence and even subordination; the domesticity of the dress refracts tellingly the non-ethnic space of citizenship I turn to in the next section.

But the Herero Youth Association chose the dress as the central feature of their logo for its other connotations: knowledge and strength. Both men and women often commented on how difficult the dress was to wear. People routinely wanted to assist me in assembling the layers, cinching tightly the high belt that held petticoats in place, buttoning the complex bodice closing that ran across the left shoulder and around and under the arm. "You dressed yourself?" they would ask, surprised and entertained, for young women did sometimes call for help or advice as they dressed. Only regular wearers in their 30s or older women admitted openly to knowing how to tie the headdress; most part-time wearers and younger women had someone else tie it for them. Overall, wearing the dress is difficult and requires skill.

More subtly, perhaps, bodily consciousness undermines stable interpretation of women's subordination, confinement to domestic reproduction, and dependence in the dress. Herero women enjoyed contrasting their freedom of movement and demeanor in the dress with what they perceived as constricted and obsequious behavior among Tswana women. They often pointed out to me the way in which women sat. In Botswana, a woman's thighs are a highly sexually charged part of her anatomy; while breasts may be bared, the thighs should never be uncovered. Tswana women and others in Western dress sit on the ground (men take the chairs) with their legs stretched out before them, or occasionally folded to the side, their knee-length skirts tucked tightly around their legs. Hisses, angry whispers, and fierce frowns are directed by both men and women at those women who have been careless in seating themselves. Herero women wearing the long dress have much greater freedom in sitting, and indeed their characteristic posture is cross-legged, with the knees slightly raised, their skirts flowing around or tucked at the ankles. This basic contrast of freedom of movement served as part of a fuller comparison between Herero and Tswana women made by two older women, with whom I chatted over tea as we watched neighborhood goings-on. Tswana women, they observed, almost sneak into a compound when they visit; they come up quietly from the side, deferentially. Herero women just walk straight (osemba, also morally upright). Furthermore, they said, Tswana women, when talking to men—and to women in authority—bow and hold their hands clasped before them. One of the women got up and pantomimed Tswana obsequiousness. Herero women would never do that, they assured me.

RESTRICTIVE MOBILITY

But the dress shifts easily from medium of skill, freedom of movement, and mastery of self and space to a restrictive and burdensome imposition. The dress experientially participates in a self-controlled and expansive *motility*, perhaps, but it also connotes through a practical logic a restricted *mobility*, one that is quickly picked up to inform a contrastive poetics of Herero and Tswana, Herero and Europeans, and to reflect upon the fate of minority ethnicity within the particular configuration of Botswana's liberal democracy. Women and men often told me that wearing the dress was *ouzeu*, a term that means both heavy, in the sense of weight, and difficult to do. As noted above, this difficulty can attest to Herero knowledge and skill; but people are also able to see a less sanguine, more constraining side to the difficulty of the dress.

The Herero dress *is* heavy: 10 or more yards of fabric go into the dress itself, then there are the *ozondoroko* (the petticoats), a shawl, and the headdress. Some elderly women abandon some or all of the petticoats as they age. Herero men, like the Ghanzi groom, often told me that the dress was too hot and too heavy to wear. Women, however, rarely spoke of the weight of the dress. Although they would readily agree with my suggestion that the dress was heavy, women who wore the dress certainly were aware that it did not prevent them from running after errant cattle or misbehaving children, hurrying from hearth to house and back again, and laboring long in the midday sun harvesting sorghum or weeding corn. Men emphasized the physical weight (*ouzeu*) of the dress, but women, perhaps responding in a subtle way to the sense of domesticity that clings to the dress, instead stressed the difficulty (*ouzeu*) of caring for the dress. Mahalapye Herero are meticulous about cleanliness, usually bathing twice a day and washing clothes often. Washing a Herero dress, scrubbing inch by inch the dirt caught up as the hem sweeps the dust, wringing the yards of water-heavy fabric, doing the petticoats and the headdress, and then ironing each of the pieces with a coal iron is a tiresome task that women most often do themselves (instead of handing them to children). But these domestic burdens also bring us back to the sense of skill as well as strength exemplified through the dress. Herero often contrasted their own competence in washing and ironing with the ineffectiveness of washing machines and with the laziness or ineptitude of Europeans or Peace Corps volunteers. I heard one story about a Peace Corps volunteer who stirred clothes around a bucket with a long stick!

It is significant that men's complaints about the dress make it out to be a physical impediment, as being too hot and heavy to wear. In part, of course, such statements implicitly contrast their own muscular strength with women's. But men's suspicion of the dress in relation to labor also picks up a general concern (shared, for example, by the young woman who desired a more urban situation) that being Herero is a disadvantage in Botswana's national society. Wearing the dress, as with other forms of advertisement of ethnic identity, is an impediment to mixing and participating in the national economy. Men may feel the pressures to find jobs and achieve position in society more acutely than women, who have other accepted means of survival, advancement, and prestige; therefore, men may be more anxiously concerned about the dress's relation to the wider national society. And, very importantly, men have no experience of wearing the dress. They have never enjoyed the sense of self-mastery embodied for women as they wear the dress. But both men and women do participate in the national economy. Herero women from Mahalapye had jobs as petrol attendants, bank clerks, nurses, teachers, shop assistants, office

workers in various district and national agencies, technical advisers, consultants and professionals in Gaborone, and one as a radio personality: none of these women wore the Herero dress except in Mahalapye and then only to funerals and weddings.

Concern with discrimination, and with the place of ethnic performances in Botswana, is intricately intertwined with ongoing national debate about the contours of Botswana's liberal democracy. Since Independence in 1966, Botswana has had a multiparty democracy. Although the success of its political system is often attributed to national ethnic homogeneity, such an attribution attests more to the success of Tswana hegemony than to actual homogeneity; censuses taken under British colonial rule show considerable diversity (cf. Schapera 1952). In the interests of radically nondiscriminatory liberalism, no census has gathered data on the ethnic background of the citizenry since Independence. Since 1986, when I began asking about the numbers of Bushmen and Herero in the country, representatives at the President's Office have consistently told me that "we are all Batswana here," and this exact phrase is echoed throughout government. Although the bureaucrats mean that they are all equally citizens of the state and that officially the government is staunchly antitribalist, it is also true that citizenship and the state itself are significantly setswana (Tswana language and culture). Setswana is the national language, the only medium of education until students are introduced to English (the official language) in advanced primary school; it is also the only African language on the national—and only— radio station (Janson and Tsonope 1991). Setswana *mekgwa le melao* (customs and law) pervade the legal and governmental system.

And yet, in spite of the clearly Tswana hegemonic discourses within the nation, Mahalapye Herero often embrace the official line of ethnic nondiscrimination. To my persistent questions about ethnic discrimination in banking, for example, people always blamed individuals (or themselves) and not group affiliation. They similarly attributed educational problems, dismissals from jobs, and failed political campaigns by Herero to the laziness, dishonesty, or poor performances by individuals—and usually pointed out other Herero with advanced master's degrees and good jobs or those who had been elected to District Council. Such examples and counterexamples are in line with official government policy and rhetoric, which privilege individual initiative and achievement over group attributes or communitarian ideals (ministers and bureaucratic officials pronounce on an almost weekly basis that "Batswana must work hard to develop themselves," and indeed most development schemes rely heavily upon individual initiative and execution).

The emphasis on individual initiative and responsibility and the claims that "we are all Batswana here" (not Kalanga, Lozwi, Yei, Subiya, Mbukushu, Ngologa, Xhosa, Herero, and so forth) are enacted and transacted primarily in those public spaces to which citizenship is tied by residents of Mahalapye: rights of access to land, educational opportunities, and jobs.

Although the issue is regularly raised by Kalanga and Yei people, the government steadfastly refuses to permit non-setswana languages in even early education, purportedly in the interest of economy and maintaining national community and communication. "Fired for Ikalanga?" (Ikalanga is the Kalanga language) screamed the private press headlines one week (Matumo 1989: 1). Whether or not the two women were actually fired for other faults (as the shop manageress claimed), the newspapers and their readers readily recognized the possibility and even likelihood that non-setswana languages (apart from English) were out of place in the public space of access and interaction of jobs. The story implied that non-setswana languages are acceptable in homes and neighborhood and community centers, but they impede equal access and equal opportunity to national resources.

Setswana, as the national language, is the medium through which a person transcends locality and moves from region to region. The citizens of Botswana are highly mobile: people cross the country to find scarce spaces in secondary schools; they are posted by jobs to distant sites and are required to move. Even agricultural patterns keep them moving between widely dispersed cattleposts, towns, and cultivable lands. Much of that movement depends upon the substitutability of individuals within positions as students, civil servants, and employees (as Anderson describes for the nascent

national bureaucracies, 1991: 55–56, 121–22; cf. Weber 1978: 983). Ethnic dress, like ethnic language, disrupts the image of an undifferentiated citizenry. Layered together—like the underskirts that support the dress—images of domesticity and ethnicity, and of wives' constraint by husbands' desires, sustain a perception that the heavy skirts of the Herero women's dress are restrictive, a drag on both physical activity and the socioeconomic mobility desired in the context of Botswana's liberal democratic society.

TRANSNATIONAL FLOWS

If, on the one hand, the Herero dress seems to speak of confinement and constraint in the dynamics of Botswana's national political economy, it also represents a kind of agentive and historical transnationalism to its wearers. In a spectacular reversal of our Western expectations, perhaps, the Herero dress exemplifies to its wearers their own self-aware participation in transnational dialogues. In this mode, it contrasts specifically with the more local constraint of what we would call modern Western-style clothing. This inversion of common Western assumptions of "tradition" and "modernity" serves as a salutary warning to those who, seeing modern Western forms around the world, automatically read them as evidence of a compulsory Western dynamic, mobilizing non-Western peoples under the spell of a drearily domineering West-centered aesthetic. Herero women's reflections on their dress are a counter-example to a widely held notion that tradition (especially outside the West) is necessarily represented as timeless, ineffably local, and autogenetic. Hobsbawm (1983), for example, defines "invented tradition"—which the Herero dress undoubtedly is—as a representation of invariance (in the context of change). Lipovetsky makes his provocative argument about the role of fashion in constituting the individualism that underpins modern democracy through a rather trite and unsustainable contrast with "human beings [who] are not recognized as the authors of their own social universe, when customs and principles for conducting one's life, social requirements and taboos, are held to result from a moment of origin that has to be perpetuated, changeless and immobile" (Lipovetsky 1994: 18; see also the more pessimistic version of Ewen 1988: 22–23).

Herero occasionally pass time by discussing the transnational aspects of their dress, even when not pestered by anthropologists. Sitting in a compound in mourning one day, a group of women discussed the German missionaries as the importers of the long dress (in what became German South West Africa, and much later Namibia, where Herero lived at the time). To this, one woman added a speculation on the possibility of Dutch influence on the headdress (had she seen the folkloric flying-nun contraption?). At a sweltering New Year's party in the Herero chief's homestead in 1990, a middle-aged primary schoolteacher called me into the shade. She wanted me to confirm what she had just told one of the oldest men in the community, that Herero had adopted the long dress to give respect to Queen Victoria. I also heard speculations that the style had been borrowed from Afrikaner dress. In all of these reflections, Herero actively chose and borrowed from other nationalities—and sometimes from several.

Today, Herero are a transnational people: most Herero live in Namibia, but there are significant and interacting communities across Botswana and in South Africa. Mahalapye Herero were very interested in the ways in which Herero practice varied as Herero interacted with and borrowed from their neighbors. By and large, they did not regard these variations as a form of degradation or corruption; they perceived degradation more in decreasing use of and literacy in otjiherero in any form. When they could receive Namibian Herero radio broadcasts, people listened to them, laughing over dialectical differences, idioms, and passages they could not at all understand (some of which they attributed to borrowings from German instead of English, some of which they attributed to drift). In addition to the radio, visiting between communities produced both awareness of difference and convergences, as young people picked up trendy Namibian phrases from refugees in Botswana or visits to Namibia, or South African Herero were tutored in the pan-Herero burial society Otjiserandu. Furthermore, the Germans, English, and Afrikaners who contributed to Herero differentiation were said to have taken on Herero practices. I was often told that

white women in Namibia wore the long dress at Herero events as a sign of respect. Within Mahalapye, several non-Herero wore the dress: myself; a Kalanga woman married to a Herero man; and a few young girls who, although they had Herero mothers, were considered partly Tswana. Although historical documents talk about a Herero capitulation to European dress in the heavily oppressive conditions following the German-Herero War of 1904, the histories related by Herero women in modern Botswana tell of dynamic exchange and positive action, with choice and independent agency as central features, both in the past and in the present.

Nowhere is this more marked than in the schoolteacher's suggestion that Herero copied Queen Victoria's dress. Herero women not infrequently wear (relatively) identical dresses. This might be the outcome of a practical, economic venture as they jointly purchase a bolt of fabric. Or the dresses might be uniforms, which populate the southern African scene as people are members of a church, an occupational group, a school, a choir, a burial society, or a cultural society like the Herero Youth (cf. Comaroff 1985: 205, 220–21; Durham n.d.). In each case dressing alike both expresses and constitutes mutual venture, interrelatedness of interests, investments, and activities, as well as sympathies and tastes. For Herero, these examples represent forums and forms for projects and personal development. Saying that Herero actively adopted Queen Victoria's dress, the teacher did not imply a perverse, ironic, and subordinate Herero mimesis of fetishized European power (cf. Taussig 1993). Instead she drew on cultural images of a decisive mutuality, a centripetal move in Bakhtin's term, one motivated by persons not distant powers. That she should depict the dress's history in this way is not surprising, for in attempting to impose a historical image on the dress, she drew upon its experiential gestalt of self-determination, her sense of individual agency as a mode of social interaction in Botswana today, and upon a subtle but powerful contrastive poetics.

For to a large extent the ultimate salience of Herero agentive historical internationalism is formed in a poetics of contrast (Comaroff and Comaroff 1987) played out against the more obviously transnational style that dominates Botswana's sartorial scenery. Everyone recognized that blouses, skirts, dresses, cardigans, blazers, and pantyhose were Western forms of dress. But when I spoke with Herero women and girls about these "modern" dress styles, they consistently refused to connect them overtly with contemporary Euro-American styles, and in fact often went to some trouble to distinguish southern African dress from European, African American, and West African clothing. Most Herero in Mahalapye disapproved of markedly European clothing, both for Europeans and Botswana's cosmopolitan urbanites (whose sense of style is different than the one I depict here): skirts were too short, or too long, the styles said to be not flattering to the African body. Europeans were noted for their disheveled clothing; people commented that the European women did not wear slips. My Herero interlocutors were relentlessly uninterested, when I broached the topic, in what was being worn in Paris, London, or even my hometown Chicago, because clothing in these places was irrelevant to what one wore in Mahalapye, in the capital Gaborone, in Namibia or South Africa. *Ghanaian* was a term of indulgent dismissal for West African styles; *Afro-American* was applied with amused disapproval to people whose hair was too long. Furthermore, people never invoked ideas of a deep history or of contemporary change in reference to the dominant local style. Perhaps because few people had the financial means to constantly adapt to changing fashion, fashion—in the sense of rapid change of and an interest in new styles—was not an issue when choosing or evaluating clothes. Although undoubtedly styles changed, they did so unremarked. The Herero residents of Mahalapye noted personal quirks (extra long ties worn by one youth, for example), and registered an urban-rural dichotomy based more on wealth than knowledge, but they did not comment on transient historicity, in terms either of ephemeral fashion or evolution of modern style. Woven in and out of the conversations I had with Herero, as much in the unspoken as in the spoken, ran the image of contemporary dress styles—what we wear, they said—as both fixed and local.

For Herero, that local style was called setswana, Tswana-manner (or in otjiherero, otjitjawana). People would ask, "Are you dressing herero or tswana for the funeral?" (*mo zara otjiherero poo otjitjawana kombakiro?*). The term *setswana* for modern styles of clothing, styles that are at least partially represented as invariant and localized, reflects back on the Tswana hegemony in everyday public life. It also, however, captures a sense of powerlessness within the regional markets on the part of consumers: that these two experiences correspond in clothing is also significant.

In terms of style, the range of clothing available was not as wide as is currently the case in the United States. There was a fairly uniform selection of clothing available through outlets dominated by South African retailing chains (Pep Store, Cash Bazaar, and the more pricey Guys & Gals) that dominate the downtown areas of urban villages like Mahalapye. South Africa is the immediate source for a considerable proportion of consumer goods available (78 percent in 1985), either as manufacturer or as importer. Young women received and circulated among themselves a number of mail-order catalogs that featured South African addresses (by looking through these with women, I learned about attitudes toward local and international styles). Clothes purchased from Botswana merchants or catalogs were simply assumed to originate in South Africa, apart from a few items made by local seamstresses and tailors, most of whom copied commercial clothing or specialized in school uniforms. Like the South African state, these goods were experienced as simply available and were not thought to respond to Botswana consumers' desires (or agency).

Both Herero and setswana styles do change over time in response to people's decisions. And there was certainly room for choice and distinction within setswana styles; the women of the Herero Youth Association who designed its setswana uniform argued for years between sky blue and navy blue and between a six- or four-gore skirt. With respect to current Herero dress, one could also easily say, as Liza Dalby does for kimono in Japan, that the "terrain has narrowed … to the detriment of free-wheeling variation" (1993: 112). Stylistic choices are actually reduced by contrast with Western clothing. Nonetheless, a consistent inverted interpretation emerged across situations and conversations. People emphasized active aspects of imitation, adoption, and choice when they reflected on Herero past styles, but they stressed passivity, lack of choice, and lack of self-determination in relation to setswana style. The poetics of contrast articulated within this register speak directly to the ambivalences and ambiguities of the individual within the regional economy and the Tswana-dominated state. A Herero past filled with choices, international interactions and exchange, and prospects for self-definition is contrasted with selected images of the fate of modern members of the Tswana state, where choice and personal desire often seem disregarded. Children are assigned to distant schools, young graduates are placed in remote areas far from any relative, husbands and wives are posted to jobs on opposite sides of the country, jobs are hard to come by and (some think) hardly worth searching for. Most public services are run as monopolistic parastatals or direct organs of the state. Although a sense of nondifferentiation of style contributes to the hope for an undifferentiated citizenship in the liberal democratic society, it also suggests the powerlessness of citizens—and, in particular, citizens who find the long dress a medium of self-expression—to alter the basic circumstances of their lives through choice. Within this particular contrastive scope, the Herero dress itself represents choice—not an imposition compelled by domineering husbands, but a masterful act of self-definition in the present.

THE PREDICAMENT OF CONSCIOUSNESS

In the event that the preceding section seems to suggest that Herero in east-central Botswana are lost in a double-conscious limbo (simultaneously Herero and citizens of Botswana), I will stress—as I have throughout this article—that consciousness of being Herero involves multiple registers. These registers are not finally integrated as one patterned gestalt. Rather they sustain a profound sense of uncertainty. Even outside the experience of wearing of the dress, various possibilities contend. For example, when the Herero chief's election (by the village) to Mahalapye's customary court was threatened by the sitting (Tswana)

chief's politicking, Herero were uncertain whether to blame party politics or ethnic politics—most blamed the competition between multiethnic political parties. If the local economy seems at time restrictive, with high unemployment rates, insufficient schools, and arbitrary postings by public and private employers, Botswana is also a country filled with choices to which people willingly address themselves. Elections and voting are frequent occasions, whether in national or district affairs or in the numerous churches and societies to which people belong. Mahalapye people choose between living at cattle posts, on cultivated lands, in the urban village, or in one of Botswana's cities. By the mid-1990s, Herero choirs singing Herero songs (in addition to their better-known Tswana repertory) were regularly appearing in civic performances and in larger urban contexts. A Tswana man, marrying a Herero woman, insisted on a Herero wedding ceremony. Within this society of choices, in which individuals and their agency are repeatedly confirmed, being Herero itself becomes something of an optative performance, a membership enacted much as other church, school, job, and associational memberships, a simple uniform over the universal citizen's body—and not a form of resistance to setswana hegemony.

Vibrating within the sparkle of a multiple consciousness, Herero readily see their dress, like their lives, through the multiple lenses available to them, sometimes uncertainly, sometimes ironically. During one informal discussion, a group of Herero women laughed over non-Herero visions of the dress: South African Afrikaners were said to call the headdress "pillows," Tswana to think that the horns were supported inside the scarves with sticks—sending the group into gales of laughter, a laughter directed both at their own costume and at the ignorant perplexity of outsiders. As Clifford writes of the "predicament of culture" encountered by cultural critics and anthropologists in the condition of modernity, Herero live in "a pervasive condition of off-centeredness in a world of distinct meaning systems, a state of being in culture while looking at culture" (Clifford 1988[c]: 9; cf. also Simmel [1904] 1971[a]). It is commonplace to see this predicament of consciousness as a condition of modernity and social complexity or, as Young does, a deplorable predicament of "double vision"—of being in and looking at—for "the woman [who] lives her body as object as well as subject" (Young 1980: 153; cf. more sanguinely Csordas 1994). The privileging of coherence, and of the disambiguated control of categories, and the idea that incoherence or ambiguity stems exclusively from the nature of society, find their source in Enlightenment-period epistemology and social theory. Subcultures, then, as well as superstitious women, are a source of anxiety. I suggest here that multiple meanings are not tragic; instead, embodiment and sociality form a sparkle around objects. Meaningful objects and experience like the Herero dress seem to me rather like quantum particles: shimmering in indeterminacy, alive with a perhaps endless range of possibility, when captured in a technology of representation—words—reduced to one, or only several, of their states.

The dress is for Herero much more than a "uniform" of culture. It is culture. It is more than an icon of cultural difference, or gender, or a style; it is more than a tradition, or ethnic condition, among many. "Culture" is a predicament beyond modernity's conjunctures and beyond a semiotics of structure and difference. Under the impact of the "culturalisms" (Appadurai 1996: 15) of the present, anthropologists are coming increasingly to think of culture in terms of "identities," forms of representation within dynamics of difference and exclusions (Appadurai 1996: 12–14, 44; cf. also Clifford 1988[c]). Certainly the Herero dress appears in the representational context of memberships, exclusions, and identifications—as the logo of the Herero Youth Association, the admonitions of the old man to the association's members, and the use of the dress to contrast Tswana and Herero women attest. Nonetheless, as anthropologists also know, cultural practices are not coterminous with social divisions; there is both heterogeneity within groups and commonality across them. "Cultures" may not exist in any classic sense. As Herero confronting the predicament of their Victorian-Wilhelminian-Dutch-Herero dress make clear, culture is a process of group definition, but it is also a process of forming commonalities in spite of distinctions between an "us" and a "them." Mahalapye Herero reflect on adopting the dress as an act of mutuality, of sharing some sentiment and appreciating some disposition; hence, it made sense to them that I, or a Kalanga, or unknown whites in Namibia would wear the long dress. The deliberate walk of a Tswana chief, the typical tardiness of a politician's wife to meetings, these, too, were examples of the motility condensed in a Herero dress. It may be that embodied meaning forms a more durable ground for the extending of mutual understanding, formed as it is in the inarticulate (cf. Bloch 1991). The embodied subjectivity of the dress, its experiential sensibility of autonomy and competence, is not finally thought by Herero as exclusively Herero, even if it may be momentarily mobilized into an ethnic politics. For if "culture" divides people, is it not also the means of bridging self and other?

21

BODY TALK:
Revelations of self and body in contemporary strip clubs

Katherine Frank

I spend a lot of time preparing before I go onstage at a strip club, which seems almost counterintuitive—spending all day getting ready to take off your clothes. Preparation is ongoing, of course—most dancers have regular salon appointments for manicures, pedicures, facials, body scrubs, waxing, highlights or coloring, or hair extensions. Many dancers also spend a lot of time in the gym. But a work day has its own routine, at least for me. Early in the day, I go running, usually only two miles since I'll get lots of exercise later on. I eat one large meal mid-day (so that I won't be too full later but also won't get too hungry), and start drinking my eight glasses of water. I go to a tanning booth for a short session, and then do my floor exercises—450 stomach crunches, push-ups, and stretches. When it gets closer to my shift I wash and condition my hair and exfoliate my skin in the shower. I don't have to shave because I always wax instead—that way you don't grow any nasty stubble or razor bumps around your bikini area. After showering I apply self-tanner, let it soak in for fifteen minutes, and then apply scented body lotion and let that dry as well while I check for chips in my nail or toenail polish. I check for stray hairs along my pubic line, ankles, eyebrows. I dry my hair and set it in large rollers. Then, still undressed, I apply stage make-up to my body—covering bruises, blemishes, ingrown hairs, or discolorations. I follow this with an all-over bronzer—it would be easier and less messy if I could just bake in the tanning bed for longer, but I'm trying to minimize the skin damage from years of dancing. While the body make-up sets, I apply perfume on my pulse points and then begin putting on my facial make-up. A bit of concealer, M.A.C. stage powder, eyebrow pencil, eyeshadow in several colors, white eyeliner, dark eyeliner, mascara, tinted powder on my cheeks, lip liner, lipstick. I wait to apply glitter to my body until after I do my face—it is nearly impossible to get off your hands. I don't always use glitter, but on nights that I do I apply it to my chest, stomach, and butt, and lightly on my arms and legs. I usually use glitter with a gold tone, which looks warm under the black lights. After the glitter, I wash my hands and take out the rollers (it's okay if the remaining glitter gets in my hair). Using a hand-held mirror and the full-length one, I do a 360-degree check of my body, looking for anything I might have missed.

Then I drive to the club, where I'll have time for a touch-up before having to take the stage for my shift—a bit more lotion, perfume, or vanilla-scented body oil, lipstick—and another 360-degree body check. The lights, of course, will perfect the work that I've already done. I select a costume from the choices in my locker—long gowns, two-piece bikinis, a schoolgirl outfit with a ridiculously short skirt, cocktail dresses in black, white, and red. The dress, of course, I'll be taking off. But the accessories I choose will remain, as they are an important part of being nude, part of the costume. Our removable g-strings come in a variety of glow-in-

---

Adapted from Katherine Frank, "Body Talk: Revelations of Self and Body in Contemporary Strip Clubs" In *Dirt, Undress, and Difference: Critical Perspectives on the Body's Surface*, edited by Adeline Masquelier (Bloomington: Indiana University Press, 2005): 96–121.

the-dark colors, some with beading or glitter. Jewelry, including belly chains and ankle bracelets, always looks good under the lights. High heels, sexy leather boots, elbow-length gloves, boas, thigh-highs, garters… And, of course, a nice, small purse that matches my outfit for storing the cash. Over the course of the night, I return every so often to the dressing room to make touch-ups and change outfits. Dressing, undressing, dressing, undressing—for an eight-hour shift.

At the end of the shift, I change once more—into sweatpants—and head home to count my money, shower, and climb into bed … naked.

Nudity, it has been argued, lies in the eye of the beholder and not simply in the exposure of the body's surface, and what constitutes nakedness is generally seen by anthropologists as varying by context and culture. The implication of this variation, and in the need for a "witness," real or imagined, is that nudity is not just a state of being, but is, rather, a social *process*. Strip clubs, as venues in which nudity is commodified, standardized, and regulated and where bodily revelations are sought and purchased, provide a dynamic illustration of the production of nudity and its meanings. Drawing on ethnographic research in U.S. strip clubs, this chapter explores the ways that nudity is produced, controlled, and made profitable by the state, the clubs, and the dancers. The focus here is on strip clubs that feature female dancers and cater to primarily heterosexual male audiences, though these are not the only kind of clubs in existence. In addition, I examine some of the dynamics of concealment and revelation in interactions between exotic dancers and their customers, especially as these are shaped by gender and social class.

CONTEXTUALIZING NUDITY IN STRIP CLUBS

It is a focus on bodily exposure that distinguishes strip clubs from other kinds of bars and nightclubs (though this boundary may be disappearing with some of the increasingly risqué fashions for women) and the focus on sexualized looking in a *public* atmosphere that differentiates the strip club from many other forms of adult entertainment such as pornography, prostitution,

and oral or manual release in a massage parlor. Yet the desire to visit strip clubs is more than just a desire to passively see women's bodies, even for the most voyeuristic of customers. There are many ways to potentially "see" naked women—peeping, viewing pornography, reading medical texts, or developing intimate relationships with them, for example. These visits, then, must also be seen as expressing a desire to have a particular kind of *experience* rooted in the complex network of relationships between "home," "work," and "away," an experience that I have elsewhere analyzed as "touristic" (Frank 2002a). Touristic practices, according to sociologist John Urry, "involve the notion of 'departure,' of a limited breaking with established routines and practices of everyday life and allowing one's senses to engage with a set of stimuli that contrasts with the everyday and the mundane" (1990: 2). The sights that are gazed upon are chosen because they offer "distinctive contrasts" with work and home and also because "there is an anticipation, especially through daydreaming and fantasy, of intense pleasures, either on a different scale or involving different senses from those customarily encountered" (1990: 3). The behavioral structures of everyday life are indeed inverted for many customers inside the clubs; for example, women do the approaching rather than the men and thus face the possibility of rejection; women "ask" to be looked at naked ("Would you like to buy a table dance?"); and usually private performances of sexual desire or sexualized display of the nude body are suddenly made public. Further, while intimate relationships between individuals may be covertly facilitated with money in everyday realms, inside the clubs this facilitation is blatant, immediate, and far less apologetic (though no less complicated in its various enactments). Nudity serves as a visual reminder of these social inversions—a sign of the difference of the setting from work and home as well as the difference of the women and the behavioral codes that govern the exchanges.

Though a strip club may be touristic for the male customers, and even for the regulars in particular patterned ways, it is, first and foremost, a workplace for the dancers. Granted, stripping may be a means of rebellion for young women in addition to being a lucrative job, especially for those in the middle classes (Frank 2002b; Johnson 1999). On the other hand, the fact remains that the parties to the transactions are coming to the encounters with different purposes—the men for leisure, the women for labor. These different purposes and meanings are not rooted in essential gender differences; rather, they are informed by labor relations as well as social positions (including, but not limited to, gender). Certainly these categories of worker and leisure seeker are not absolute: customers may conduct business activities at strip clubs, for example, and most customers are also workers in other arenas. Likewise, there may be some dancers for whom stripping feels more like leisure than work, at least on certain days, and a large component of the job involves engaging in practices associated with leisure—drinking alcohol, dining, conversing, flirting, having fun (or at least appearing to), and, especially, being undressed. Yet in the immediacy of the encounter, the money nearly always flows in one direction only—from the customer to the dancer (until later, when the dancer is asked to pay the establishment a cut of her earnings). Further, even though a man may be conducting a form of business on the premises, it is usually precisely because this space is inherently "not work" for him that it has been chosen. Thus, while one or both of the participants to any transaction may be "playing" at any given time, this play is firmly situated within a larger framework of cultural and economic relations.

It is within this framework that the dancers' bodily revelations become meaningful, and hence profitable, for themselves and for the clubs. Nudity, of course, has an assortment of sometimes conflicting meanings in the contemporary U.S. and can at different times (and to different observers) signify a variety of things, including but not limited to innocence, naturalness, authenticity, vulnerability, sexual power, truth, revelation of one's inner self, humiliation, degradation, a lack of self-respect, immorality, sexual accessibility, and a prelude to sexual activity. To see someone without clothes, especially in a public setting, can thus be confusing (even if expected) and requires interpretation by the participants involved. Anne Hollander argues that humans have invented both the notion of the "naturalness of nudity" and that of the "wickedness of nudity" (1975), and these kinds

of interpretations reemerge in many elements of strip club exchanges and in the debates that erupt about their existence. Similarly, art historian Mario Perniola points out that a paradox emerges in opposition between clothing and nudity due to the fact that Western culture has both Hellenistic and Hebraic roots. As Dennis Hall quotes Perniola to explain,

> In Western thought's Hellenistic roots, on the one hand, we have a reverence for nudity based upon the ability to see the "naked truth," "the metaphysical ability to see beyond all robes, veils, and coverings to the thing itself in its exact particulars." ... Getting to "the naked truth" is a process of getting undressed, getting free of clothing. From this perspective, being clothed is a privation. In Western thought's Hebraic roots, on the other hand, we also have a reverence for the condition of being clothed as a mark of humanity. "Clothing prevails as an absolute," Perniola suggests, "whenever or wherever the human figure is assumed to be essentially dressed, when there is the belief that human beings are human, that is distinct from animals, by virtue of the fact that they wear clothes." ... Getting to the truth is a process of getting dressed, putting on clothing. From this perspective, being naked is a privation. (Hall 2001: 70)

Public nudity is embedded in a host of additional symbolic and emotional meanings, again often ambivalent and frequently revolving around issues of power and control. Stripping an individual of his or her clothes as a form of military action, a punitive measure, or a means of humiliation is widely understood as a means of exercising power. At the same time, people who willingly or purposefully shed their clothes in public are often criminalized or stigmatized and seen as dangerous (powerful?) or pathological—"trenchcoaters," streakers, nudists, strippers. Prohibitions on nudity have long been seen as part of society's repression of natural sexuality and the body, both in academic theories and in folk understandings; thus, nudity can appear as transgressive, even dangerous to the civilized order. Patrons, being subjects to and of the same discourses as other individuals, also bring ideas about nudity as transgressive, dangerous, and liberating to their visits to strip clubs and their encounters with dancers. The notion that strip clubs were somehow an expression of a transcultural, transhistorical, "natural" male sexuality that was repressed in everyday life was important to many of the customers (despite the fact that there are many men who do not find the clubs appealing). Similarly, the idea that strip clubs were places in which one was at risk for physical or moral contamination was also motivating and eroticized for the regular customers. Men who disliked strip clubs, on the other hand, often claimed to see them as boring, commercialized, or contrived. Customers sometimes described themselves as "adventurers," dancers as "brave" and "wild," and strip clubs themselves as places "outside of the law" (Frank 2002a).

In strip clubs, customers also bring their own sexual histories to the transactions, as well as their beliefs about gender, sexuality, and consumption. Despite many individual differences, I did find patterns among the regular customers, those men for whom visits to strip clubs were a significant sexualized practice. Though few of the men claimed to be religious, and they overwhelmingly expressed support for the dancers' right to disrobe and the "naturalness" of such an act, their enthusiasm usually quickly waned when I asked about how they would feel if it was a wife or daughter onstage. Many of the regular customers claimed to be married to very conservative women who had more extreme views about nudity and sexuality than they did. There were some customers, for example, who stated that they were never allowed to look at the bodies of their wives or partners, even during sex—in these cases, nudity might be fascinating, awe-inspiring, or even upsetting. Even for those men who did have access to private revelations of the female body, the fact that they were paying for live, public performances meant that there were additional emotional layers enwrapping their interpretations of their encounters— mixtures of shame, anxiety, excitement, and desire. If it is true that "there is no apprehension of the body of the other without a corresponding (re)vision of one's own" (Phelan 1993: 171), some of the pleasure in these commodified encounters arises from complicated, and concurrent, fantasies of security (rooted in the

ritualized performances of sexual difference that unfold in the clubs) and fantasies of rupture or transgression (rooted in the feelings of degradation, vulnerability, and freedom that many of the customers felt would accompany their own public nudity) (see Frank 2002a).

The relationship of nudity to forms of power and control has long been bolstered by the regulation of bodily exposure by state and local governments in the U.S., as well as by the ways that those regulations are proposed, implemented, and debated in public forums. Though I do not have space here to detail the development of modern exotic dance out of other entertainment forms such as vaudeville, burlesque, and cabaret shows, it is important to realize that the history of striptease is thoroughly shaped by the history of regulation and the conflicts that surround sexualized displays and behaviors in American public culture. The distinctions made between art and obscenity, lewd or acceptable behavior, and moral or immoral forms or representations of sexuality can be seen as ongoing arguments that are carried out in legal forums, academic treatises, public culture and the media, and living rooms around the country. Frequently what is indecent in one decade is commonplace in the next (think of the scandal over the bodily exposure of famous burlesque star Lydia Thompson in the late nineteenth century—she wore *tights* and made them visible to an audience) (Allen 1991), yet that does not mean that the transgressions of the day are perceived any less seriously by their participants or treated less harshly.

Regulations against striptease have often been justified in the name of social control and public safety. Anti-burlesque campaigns, for example, surfaced almost immediately after the entertainment form arrived in America from Europe during the late 1800s, and continued to escalate throughout the 1930s. While early protests against sexualized entertainment often focused on the sexual depravity or suspected prostitution of the female performers, later campaigns against burlesque, according to historian Andrea Friedman, began to focus on the supposedly dangerous and aggressive sexuality of working-class males, especially when exposed to female nudity or immorality. Such campaigns, she argues, "offered an opportunity to articulate deep-seated concerns about male sexual orderliness in a profoundly disorderly world," and such fears of the out-of-control or aggressively sexual male would surface again in the 1950s and 1970s anti-pornography movements (1996: 237), and, arguably, have gained force in current debates about striptease. Such campaigns can also be seen as reflecting a class bias, with working-class or lower-tier forms of entertainment being penalized more harshly than those designated "art" and enjoyed by relatively privileged audiences (Foley 2002; Hanna 1999).

Despite attempts in every era to regulate theaters that featured different forms of striptease, however, it has continued to thrive and evolve as an entertainment form. This process of upscaling in strip clubs escalated in the 1980s, and upper-tier "gentleman's clubs" now exist in addition to neighborhood bars and run-down, red-light-district venues. The number of strip clubs in the United States has been growing rapidly; there were around 3,000 venues across the nation in 1998 (Hanna 1998). This growth has not occurred without the eruption of either national or local conflicts, however, and efforts to distance strip clubs from their illicit associations have become increasingly important to the club owners given the opposition that has arisen in a number of communities. Striptease is seen as dangerous and socially disruptive by conservative segments of the population and thousands of taxpayer and private dollars are spent in attempts to eradicate strip clubs in communities across the nation. Because of their lingering working-class associations, and the persistent, often erroneous belief that they are indelibly linked to prostitution, crime, and other "negative secondary effects," strip clubs have already been subject to more severe regulations than other kinds of entertainment, and some municipalities have attempted to use restrictive regulations to close down adult businesses altogether: requiring extremely bright lighting, prohibiting tipping, requiring bikinis or cocktail dresses at all times, stipulating that excessive distance be maintained between the entertainers and the customers, etc. (Hanna 1999). In 2000, despite a lack of sound evidence that strip clubs cause negative secondary effects, the Supreme Court upheld legislation regulating exotic dance in the city of Erie, Pennsylvania, ruling that "nude public dancing itself is immoral" (Foley 2002: 3). Immediately after the ruling, clips from a video taken at a nude club played repeatedly on the evening news, with only small digitized blurs over the dancers' breasts and pubic area—symbolic of the pasties and g-strings that the dancers would now be wearing. Instead of being something that individuals would need to consciously seek out, such images were broadcast into living rooms across the country as a sign of the "dangerous," but ever fascinating, exposed female body. In Laurelton, the combination of full nudity and alcohol was regularly under fire from this kind of restrictive regulation, and there have been numerous legal challenges to the clubs there.

The intricacies of the many battles that were fought in locales across the country throughout the twentieth century would be impossible to detail here, as would the complexities of the justifications that continue to be given for regulating, harassing, shutting down, or allowing venues that offer the display of sexualized female bodies to their patrons. Instead, it is important to realize that regulation and scandal does not just repress unruly "natural" desires in the name of civilization and order, but actually helps to create and shape those desires (Foucault [1978] 1990).

MANIPULATING REVELATION: NUDITY AS COSTUME

The naked body, as should be evident from my field notes at the beginning of the chapter, can be conceptualized as a kind of palette and was so conceptualized, consciously or not, by the dancers. As Paul Ableman writes, true nakedness is rare if we mean "the nakedness of people whose body surface is both unadorned (with clothing or ornamentation) and unmodified (by tattooing, painting, or scarification)" (1982: 15). Similarly, Terence Turner discusses the Kayapo of the Amazon, who exhibit an elaborate code of bodily adornment despite the fact that they do not wear clothing (lip plugs, penis sheaths, beads, body painting, plucked eyebrows, head shaving, etc.) and writes, "the apparently naked savage is as fully covered in a fabric of cultural meaning as the most elaborately draped Victorian lady or gentleman" (1979: 115). Dancers, in the sense that Turner is referring to, are probably less naked than the rest of us under our clothes.

One of the first things that a new dancer learns is how to adorn, present, and move her body in ways that are legal, profitable, and comfortable. Dancers continually modified their skin through grooming (cleansing, hair removal, texturizing of the skin), make-up, scents, and tanning. Some dancers sported an all-over tan (leading customers to continually ask where they sunbathed), others wore bathing suits even in tanning beds in order to have a distinct line between white and brown skin; some created tan lines with makeup or chose not to tan at all. Body make-up could be used in different ways in addition to creating the highly desirable tan—to highlight and contour the breasts or to cover blemishes or tattoos, for example. Skin was the absolute boundary in Laurelton and thus a particular object of fascination. Though a customer might have contact with a dancer's clothing (she could wrap a boa or a dress around his neck, for example), he was officially not allowed to touch her skin during a dance. Though contact might surreptitiously be made by the dancer (holding the customer's hands, brushing his skin with her hair, etc.) or customer (welcome or unwelcome), bouncers patrolled the clubs and such unsanctioned behavior was rare.

Hair has deeply symbolic meanings in many cultural systems (see, for instance, Obeyesekere 1981; Rooks 1996) and may become meaningful in different times and places through color, length, style, and so forth. The hair on the head, as well as the hair elsewhere on the body, is connected to gender systems in the U.S.: women are expected to remove hair on their legs, armpits, bikini line, and face, for example, yet long hair on the head is generally associated with femininity. Dancers almost always conformed to this expectation of hair removal on their-own, were asked to by the management, or were penalized for not doing so by the customers. In addition to the hair on their legs and under their arms, in the nude clubs many dancers also removed all of the pubic hair from the labia, leaving only a small strip in the very front (sometimes now called a "Brazilian" wax

by salons as the popularity of the style grows among the general public). Most women in the clubs, though certainly not all, wear their hair relatively long to meet customer and management expectations of a feminine style. Hair extensions are increasingly common and are replacing wigs because they look more natural and will not become dislodged during a dance. Longer hair has the advantage of being able to highlight particular body parts—it can be pulled in front to hide and then reveal the breasts; in a rear-view pose it can brush the top of the buttocks; it can conceal or emphasize the eyes. Hair color may also be used to send signals to customers and be associated with particular looks and personalities—the bubbly or sexy blonde, the exotic brunette, the feisty redhead. Though wilder styles and colors were found at the lower-tier clubs, particularly among younger dancers, the upper-tier clubs tended to be more standardized.

Accessorizing the body did not stop at the skin or the hair, of course, and numerous kinds of plastic surgeries are undergone by dancers perfecting their look: breast implants, breast lifts or reductions, lip injections, nose jobs, liposuction, tummy tucks, labia standardization, etc. Other kinds of body modifications included tattoos and piercings, especially tongue and clitoral piercings, and were increasingly common in the younger dancers (something that many of the older male customers commented on as marking a difference from their generation). While breast augmentations and other kinds of standardizing surgeries usually served to enhance a woman's value in the industry, tattoos and piercings did not necessarily do so. Dancers also modified their bodies for the job through dieting and physical training such as working out and body-building.

Though nudity itself has been referred to as the "primal costume" (Lewin 1984), there are few, if any, dancers who do not continue to fashion their nude bodies through accessories like high heels, boots, boas, jewelry, make-up, or other specialized or theme costuming options. Performance theorist Katherine Liepe-Levinson writes that, for strippers, "[c]ostumes are environments for bodies, and like the interior design of theatres, they not only frame those bodies, but also engage the wearers and viewers in environmental reciprocities with cultural symbols of gender and desire" (1998: 37). Costumes help shape customer perceptions of dancers as they mingle with the audience, and thus sometimes influence which customers a dancer will interact with on a given night. Further, even as a dancer undresses, her body may retain traces of her outfit and garner complex valuations of classy or "trashy" associated with particular kinds of adornment and the way that she wears them.

Dancers often appropriated standard cultural fantasies in their self-presentations and often self-consciously mixed behavioral patterns with symbolic fashion choices. Some women based their approach to customers on the "bimbo" stereotype—bubbly, giggly, and light-hearted—and might wear bikinis, brightly colored clingy gowns, or theme costumes, depending on the rules of the club. Similarly, some dancers presented themselves as the "girl next door"—as students, friends, or even possible lovers (though only in fantasy), and might wear cut-off shorts and tank tops, sundresses, or "tasteful" gowns. Others took up the position of "bad girl"—dressing in black and leather, talking dirty, promising dominance or adventure. Still others, like myself, switched approaches depending on mood, type of customer, and what the other dancers were doing that evening. One would rarely find a whole club of dominatrixes because the customer base usually would not support it; on the other hand, one might find any number of plaid-skirted schoolgirls circulating amongst the audience. Sometimes costumes were chosen to fit body types—a small-breasted woman, for example, might have a more difficult time pulling off the "sexy secretary" than one who was literally spilling out of her business suit. Although the schoolgirl look was profitable for dancers with a wide range of body types for different reasons, a very flat-chested or young-looking dancer might be advised to try out the look. Many dancers also avoided particular looks that they found physically or morally uncomfortable. Some did not like little-girl looks, for example, while others would not wear items associated with S&M.

An aesthetics of feminine excess (Waggoner 1997) works well in the sex industry, as everything can be overdone as a means of generating attention: necklines can plunge, skirt lengths can rise. Make-up can be exaggerated. Fetish boots might have platform heels and rise eight inches from the floor. Again, valuations may be associated with particular kinds of costuming. Dancers may employ signs of wealth and glamour, and costumes can be extravagantly accessorized in a manner far too opulent (or trashy) for the average middle-class woman. How these signs are read by the customers varies, but is often patterned by the setting. In everyday life, of course, attracting too much attention can be risky or annoying for women and the clubs could thus offer a safe place in which to try out forbidden looks or movements (Frank 2002b; Johnson 1999). Many of the costumes worn in the clubs would be completely inappropriate in other spheres and at other times (which is part of the fun of being a dancer and part of the reason that at Halloween so many women suddenly become strippers, prostitutes, "sexy teachers," or cats in skintight catsuits).

Perniola writes that in the figurative arts, "eroticism appears as a relationship between clothing and nudity." That is, eroticism is "conditional on the possibility of movement—transit—from one state to the other" (1989: 237). This is so in a strip club as well—though perhaps a few customers would still be titillated if the dancers took the stage already nude—but with an added, *gendered* transit as dancers also move between categories and potentialities, performing as "fantasy girls" who may be simultaneously, or alternately, virgins and whores (Egan 2003). Though costumes are variable, there are certainly two themes that continue to reappear in dancers' self-presentations and adornments: sexual availability/knowledge and innocence/untouchability. These themes emerge in a paradoxical relationship to each other—no dancer is actually sexually available within the confines of the club (or we are no longer talking about stripping) and no dancer is innocent in all social circles when her transgressions (disrobing in public and for money) become known.

***

Nudity is produced, controlled, and made profitable by the state, the clubs, and the dancers in strip clubs.

Through multiple social processes, bodily exposure comes to be meaningful and revelatory. While dancers exercise agency in their everyday lives (as all of us do) and in their interactions in strip clubs, we must be cautious in analyzing these venues as celebratory sites, at least for now. As a dancer, I often found myself prohibited from expressing myself in the way that I wanted—by the laws prohibiting me from touching particular parts of my body, by the managers who regulated my outfits and interactions, and even by the customers, who wanted particular kinds of moves, poses, and looks. Working in a lower-tier club may mean that one sacrifices some income for more flexibility—this is a choice made by more privileged dancers, however. Those dancers who worked in the lower-tier clubs by necessity often expressed a desire to move up to the flashier, more upscale clubs because the money and the working conditions were better. Customer, dancer, and community beliefs about gender and social class influence the meanings that underlie the transactions negotiated in strip clubs and mean that the dynamics of concealment and revelation are part of wider social processes. To see nudity as essentially liberating or transgressive is to miss the many ways that the meanings of nudity, and the effects of nudity, are produced within existing social relations.

PART 5

DRESSING THE COLONY, FASHIONING THE NATION

PART INTRODUCTION

The Indian tradition of taking off one's shoes when entering a home, notes Helen Callaway in her chapter in this part of the reader, is a legacy of colonial rule. The British were uncomfortable with "natives" wearing shoes in their presence. They considered it as a display of equality. So Indians had to take theirs off when entering the homes or workplaces of colonial officials. The same courtesy did not extend in the opposite direction. When entering the homes or temples of Indians, the British kept their shoes on.

Dress, since the earliest days of empire, has played an important role in maintaining the wide gulf in power between colonizer and colonized, just as it served, since the formation of the earliest states, as a means of distinguishing between elite and commoner. "The practice of imperial rule," writes Callaway, "developed into a total cultural mode including not only these special ceremonies, but patterns of order and discipline regulating minute details of everyday existence for the rulers, and extending with far-reaching effects into the lives of their subjects" (p. 180). Shoes were one of those minute details. Within the structured system of the colonial regime, they were elevated to the status of a symbol.

Over the course of the Twentieth Century, as colonies achieved independence, and new nation-states were born, dress played an important role in defining citizenship and establishing one's relationship towards systems of power. Uniforms solidified rank and order. Traditional ethnic dress became national dress, and national dress took on a new symbolic importance, representing the shared identity of a nation's people and the way they represent themselves to the outside world. But nation-states are not a given. These distinctly historical social formations are always tenuous at best. People need to be continually reminded of their shared identity, made to embody the attributes of proper national citizenship. What better way to do that than with what we put on our bodies?

The chapters in this section explore the role of dress and fashion in reinforcing colonial regimes and national interests. We begin this section with Callaway and her review of British colonial literature on dress. For British colonists in sub-Saharan Africa, India, and elsewhere, she argues, dress was a discipline. It reinforced a moral order. It established proper parameters of interaction between local peoples and colonists, solidified their respective roles. Dress was a tool of colonialism, which the British used to discipline colonists and colonized alike. Hence the obsession with uniforms. Hence the rigid, heavy formality of colonial dress, even in the face of intense heat and humidity.

Jean Comaroff and John Comaroff continue this theme through their nuanced analysis of colonial dress practices and policies in early twentieth-century South Africa. Dress, they argue, was implicated in a larger strategy of "conquest by consumption" (p. 186). "The struggles over the way in which Tswana bodies were to be clothed and presented," they write, "—struggles at once political, moral, aesthetic—were not just metonymic of colonialism. They were a crucial site in the battle of wills and deeds, the dialectic of means and ends, that shaped the encounter between Europeans and Africans" (p. 187). The Comaroffs do not read dress practice as simple impositions upon African subjects. Dress was employed in ways unpredictable to the colonists, ways that may even resist or undermine the intended ends. "Western dress, in short, opened up a host of imaginative possibilities for the Africans. It made available an expansive, expressive, experimental language with which to conjure new social identities and senses of self, a language with which also to speak back to the whites" (p. 188). It is important, their works reminds us, not to oversimplify the functionality of dress. It never *only* does one thing. It is rife with contradictions. When we dress we embody those contradictions, both adopting and manipulating those ideologies imposed on us from on high.

Ann Marie Leshkowich demonstrates a similar capacity for embodied contradiction in her discussion of the *ao dai*, the supposed "national costume" of Vietnam. The *ao dai*, she claims, has become an important national symbol since Vietnam became independent in the 1970s. It is worn for beauty pageants and featured in films, ads, and tourism brochures. For many Vietnamese, both at home and abroad, the *ao dai* has an ability to conjure up a national sentiment unlike any other garment. And yet the *ao dai* took on such a meaning, not because it is some time-honored traditional garment. In fact, it has a relatively brief history, with a decisive influence from China and Western fashion. It is "both traditional and stylish," writes Leshkowich, Its hybrid character lends it its potency, representing both what Vietnam has been and what it is becoming. It is distinctly Vietnamese, and yet a Vietnamese that is at home in the "modern" world, a Vietnamese announcing itself on the world stage.

Modernity, Carla Jones's chapter demonstrates, is a continuing preoccupation underlying practices of dress in the postcolonial world. But it has to be the *right kind* of modernity. In the Indonesia of the late 1990s, where Jones did her fieldwork, the right kind of modernity is a highly gendered and class-based one. The right kind of modernity is one that is compatible with the Indonesian government's goals of national development and which liberates itself from the "backwards" tendencies and attitudes of the rural peasantry. But it shouldn't stray too far from those cultural characteristics identified as "Indonesian." It must retain something of the visual attributes of long-standing gender norms. It should retain its distinctiveness, its recognizibility. One should strive towards a modernity that is cosmopolitan and forward thinking, but not too corrupted by Western cultural excess, in other words, an *Indonesian* modernity. In this chapter, Jones describes a personal development seminar in Yogyakarta, Central Java, where middle-class women learn to dress and present themselves in ways in that conform to such a conception of modernity. In so doing, they are participating in a larger process of Indonesian nation building, cultivating in themselves the characteristics necessary to move Indonesia forward.

National character, then, is not something that is so much *revealed* through dress as produced by it. That is no doubt one reason the Danish government has been so interested in promoting fashion. Fashion, notes Marie Riegels Melchior in her contribution to this volume, has become synonymous with a particular type of postindustrial modernity, a creative cosmopolitanism with real economic potential. Denmark, in its efforts to become the "fifth global fashion center," is thus re-fashioning itself as a major player in transnational creative economy. Melchior's chapter uses Actor-Network Theory to better understand "the relationship between issues of national identity, fashion design, and the fashion industry" (p. 219). Her goal here is not to reduce fashion to national identity, but to demonstrate its complex entanglement within it. Fashion has an important role to play in national development today, just as dress did in the colonial regimes and states of the past.

22

DRESSING FOR DINNER IN THE BUSH:
Rituals of self-definition and British imperial authority

Helen Callaway

In *Return to Laughter*, the novel written by American anthropologist Laura Bohannan (under the pseudonym of Elenore Smith Bowen) about fieldwork among the Tiv of Nigeria in the late 1940s, the narrator recounted her first night in the bush. After her bath, she found that her British-trained servants had set out her clothes for dinner—her mosquito boots and her most backless evening dress. Surprised, she decided that her first evening as an anthropologist in the field deserved a celebration, and she donned formal dress for the occasion. While eating her dinner in what she thought was lone splendor, she spotted a slit in the thatch and realized that, in the lamp light, she was fully displayed to the curious local inhabitants. She reflected, "Impervious to the stares of natives, generations of Empire-building Englishmen have sat on boxes in jungles eating their custard and tinned gooseberries in full evening dress. An American like myself can only feel that somehow she's been tricked into going on a picnic in high heels" (Bowen 1954: 15).

She did not repeat the ritual of dressing for dinner until months later. This came on Thanksgiving, a specifically American holiday, following a distressing experience of the death in childbirth of her Tiv friend after the elders had refused the anthropologist's plea to get medical help and instead hurled fierce accusations of witchcraft at each other. Feeling deeply confused and depressed, she resolved never again to forget her identity. She had changed her mind: "The English were quite right. One had to dress for dinner. One needed a symbol, some external sign, to assist daily remembrance of what one was" (1954: 207). By putting on formal evening dress for a special dinner, she intended to seal herself off from the Tiv community. Yet this passage, with its ironic undertones, cannot be taken in an unambiguous way. She realized that such artificial means of regaining her identity were alien to her, a sign that she was no longer herself.

DISCIPLINE AND DOMINANCE

Since the Second World War, at least, the British colonial officer dressing for dinner in the middle of the jungle has been a familiar butt of cartoonists and comedians. This image of stiff formality and aloofness remains one of the pervasive stereotypes of the British Empire. Why would a district officer after a long, hot day "dealing with the natives" have his bath, and then, particularly if dining alone, endure the tropical heat in a dinner jacket and tie? Who was his audience? What was the purpose of this ritual?

This seemingly incongruous image serves as the starting point for an investigation of the symbolism of dress in the exercise of imperial domination. At the height of its expansion, around the turn of the twentieth century, the British Empire ruled a quarter

Adapted from Helen Callaway, "Dressing for Dinner in the Bush: Rituals of Self-Definition and British Imperial Authority," in *Dress and Gender: Making and Meaning*, edited by Ruth Barnes and Joanne B. Eicher (Oxford: Berg, 1992), pp. 232–47.

of the world's land surface and nearly a quarter of its inhabitants. The individual officer dressing for dinner alone can be seen as one end of a spectrum culminating in the elaborate attire worn for the grand ceremonies of empire, which represented power and authority in a bravura of color and style. Dress became a visual marker for distinctions of race, gender, and social rank.

Records show that dressing for dinner was standard among the ruling elites throughout the era of the British Empire, in its most isolated outposts as well as its social centers, for parties or when dining alone. A *sahib* tells about this custom: "If you dined out pre-1914 anywhere in India privately, it was a tailcoat, a boiled shirt and a white waistcoat, with a stiff collar and a white tie. Long after they gave this up in England we continued to do it in India" (Allen 1976: 112). Even a lone tea planter in upper Assam followed this social rule, putting on a dinner jacket as a way of retaining his self-respect. He told his servants, "Now this is a dinner party and every night is a dinner party and you will serve my dinner as though there are other people at the dinner table" (Allen 1976: 99).

The wife of a colonial officer in Nigeria during the first decade of this century wrote in her memoirs, "If for some reason our dogcart was out of action, bath-towels were flung over saddles and we rode to dinner parties, I in a long low-necked dress, my husband in white mess jacket and the French-grey cummerbund of Northern Nigeria" (Leith-Ross 1983: 48). A woman education officer sent forty years later to a remote area of Nigeria recounted that "in an evening in the bush I always wore a long dress to keep up my morale" (Dinnick-Parr as quoted in Allen 1980: 155). She remembered occasions when the development officer would join her for dinner—"he in a dinner suit and I in an evening dress"—and afterward they would walk along the bush path talking. The local inhabitants gathered to see them, wondering "why we were all dressed up and covered ourselves when it was so frightfully hot."

Depending on the position of the observer within the colonial hierarchy, the ritual of dressing for dinner held different values. Opposing views of this social convention were presented by two British wives in Northern Nigeria during the early years before the First World War. The first commentary comes from Sylvia Leith-Ross, a remarkable woman who arrived in 1907 as the bride of a colonial officer. A year later her husband died of blackwater fever, and in her shipboard journal returning to England she noted that, of their original party of five who had gone out thirteen months earlier, she was the only one left. Over the next sixty years, Leith-Ross returned many times to Nigeria—as an education officer, anthropologist, and (during the Second World War) as a member of the intelligence service.

Her memoirs tell of an episode in 1913 when she was being poled up the Benue River in a steel canoe, accompanied on the first part of the journey by a colonial officer in his own canoe. A problem had arisen:

> We had always dressed for dinner. This was a rule that could not be broken, either at home or abroad, at sea or on shore, in the Arctic Circle or on the Equator. But alas, there was very little space indeed in our steel canoes. A compromise was necessary … One evening Armar would change his bush shirt and I would change my khaki skirt; the next, I would change my white blouse and Armar would change his khaki breeches. Between the two of us, we had obeyed our code and had upheld our own and our country's dignity. (Leith-Ross 1983: 69)

She explained, "When you are alone, among thousands of unknown, unpredictable people, dazed by unaccustomed sights and sounds, bemused by strange ways of life and thought, you need to remember who you are, where you come from, what your standards are. A material discipline represents—and aids—a moral discipline" (1983: 69). In the system of ideas of this society, the discipline of dress was linked directly to the discipline of a moral code. She noted details of dress in a photograph taken in 1907: "The men wear helmets and are coated and trousered, collared and tied … The four women present sit in a group apart, in summery but long-skirted, high-necked, long-sleeved dresses, elaborate hats tilted at a becoming angle" (1983: 55–56). Correctness of attire characterizes this portrait from the high noon of empire.

As a staunch supporter of British rule, Leith-Ross connected attention to proper dress with the courage and fortitude required for the task of governing alien peoples: "Ridiculous as it may seem to find moral significance in a casual group photograph, one begins to understand how it was that such a handful of men could dominate the land" (1983: 56). In this single image of what was considered to be appropriate dress, she condensed various levels of the colonial vision: personal and national dignity, self-discipline linked with an altruistic moral code, the fortitude required for imperial rule, and a few British men dominating a vast territory.

Despite the sharpness of her observations, Leith-Ross did not discern the hidden assumptions behind this social convention. The lone officer dressing for dinner in the jungle could identify himself with his countrymen, but also, as Wilkinson pointed out (1970: 134), the individual's self-assurance was even more bolstered when the etiquette represented that of a traditionally superior class—in this case, the gentry. Many of those who entered the British Colonial Service were not of the upper social strata, but from the middling ranks—the sons of clergymen and schoolmasters. By joining the Service and taking part in its rituals, they could fulfill their aspirations for higher social status, some of them eventually being awarded knighthoods. Interpreted in this wider context, "dressing for dinner" becomes the visible sign of "innate superiority" in the elite social tradition transmitted through the public schools, the military academies, and the ancient universities. Even those officers who had not experienced this privileged background quickly assimilated its unwritten rules and conformed to its code.

The second view comes from outside the Colonial Service during: the same period. Mrs. Horace Tremlett related her experience in Northern Nigeria in 1914 as the wife of an engineer for a tin-mining company, a social position deemed inferior. The title of her book, *With the Tin Gods*, appears innocent, an apparent reference to the tin explorers, but it turns out to be a highly charged anti-imperialist pun. She told of the antagonism existing in government circles toward the mining enterprise. While acknowledging that some uneducated miners ignorant of native customs stirred up a great deal of trouble, she added with gentle sarcasm

that government officials feared that the prestige of the white man was in danger of being lowered by the arrival of common poeple who did not own dress suits. She commented, "For they are very punctilious in Nigeria on the question of dress clothes" (1915: 264). The officer, she explained, "clings so desperately in Nigeria to his dress suit, not because he wishes to look nice, but because he knows he is expected to live up to certain traditions, and because he likes to feel that he is a gentleman—especially if he has any doubt on the subject" (1915: 165). In her view, colonial officers in Nigeria were not exactly examples of high moral standards; she hinted at their affairs with African women. Her conclusion was trenchant: "The white man there is king as he is nowhere else in the world; and a most diverting spectacle he is, playing little tin god to his black subjects" (1915: 238). In the range of colonial literature, this view is unusually subversive.

SUPERIOR PERSONS

Even as late as 1940, Lord Lloyd, then Secretary of State for the Colonies, told a group of young officers about to take up their first appointments:

> You are not going to have a soft job. You will indeed have plenty of hard work and not too many of the comforts of life, and quite possibly no lack of danger, but I know you would not have it otherwise. … In what other task can you have so much power so early? You can at the age of twenty-five be the father of your people: you can drive the road, bridge the river, and water the desert; you can be the arm of justice and the hand of mercy to millions. (Jeffries 1949: 19)

These echoes of Kipling were, of course, main themes in the ideology of power, paternalism, and service (service to the British Crown).

Known in India as the "heaven born," officers of the Colonial Service were specially selected for their leadership qualities, ideally developed (though not always in practice) through education in favored public schools, such as Eton, Rugby, or Harrow. This was followed by training in a military academy or by university education in Oxford and Cambridge. This male ruling group saw itself and was seen by the British establishment to have "natural" or innate superiority. In this system of ideas, social hierarchy was legitimated by various "scientific" theories. The anthropology of the late nineteenth century, for example, set out the range of racial groups on an evolutionary scale, at the top of which stood Victorian British society. Again, upper-class men were considered superior by birth to working-class ones, according to arguments based on inherited genetic qualities. In relation to women, men were defined as superior on physiological and medical grounds, which, in turn, provided reasons for limiting women's intellectual and social development. (The sisters of these men gained their education at home until well into the twentieth century.)

The concept of the "gentleman" was pervasive, encapsulating a cluster of meanings: social superiority in the right to bear arms and in the identification with the landed gentry, and moral superiority derived from the code of chivalry. By the late Victorian period, public schools had incorporated this concept into every aspect of school life, from organized games as the means for creating team spirit, to the custom of fagging (older boys ordering younger boys to do menial chores) as a way of training leaders and loyal followers within a hierarchical system. In his biography of Dr. Arnold of Rugby, Lytton Strachey stated that teachers and prophets have strange histories after their lifetimes:

> The earnest enthusiast who strove to make his pupils Christian gentlemen … has proved to be the founder of the worship of athletics and the worship of good form. Upon those two poles our public schools have turned for so long that we have almost come to believe that such is their essential nature, and that an English public school-boy who wears the wrong clothes and takes no interest in football is a contradiction in terms. ([1918] 1948: 187–88)

The schoolboy retained the heightened values of correctness of dress far longer than his declensions of Latin verbs. His education included both compulsory uniforms and compulsory games, encouraging military virtues and the obligations of empire. From the uniforms of schools and military academies, young men graduated to those glorifying imperial rule.

UNIFORMS AND THE MAN

In her essay, *Three Guineas*, first published in 1938 and written against the threat of growing fascism in Europe, Virginia Woolf took up the subject of what women can do to prevent war. Writing with controlled anger and charged sensibility, Woolf presented a glittering satire on the world of male institutions. As a key symbol in her portrait of male competitiveness and hierarchy, she described the splendor of the clothes worn by professional men in their public capacity:

> Now you dress in violet; a jewelled crucifix swings on your breast; now your shoulders are covered with lace; now furred with ermine; now slung with many linked chains set with precious stones. Now you wear wigs on your heads; rows of graduated curls descend to your necks. … Sometimes gowns cover your legs; sometimes gaiters. Tabards embroidered with lions and unicorns swing from your shoulders; metal objects cut in star shapes or in circles glitter and twinkle upon your breasts. Ribbons of all colors—blue, purple, crimson—cross from shoulder to shoulder. After the comparative simplicity of your dress at home, the splendour of your public attire is dazzling. ([1938] 1986: 23)

She noted that not only are whole groups of men dressed alike summer and winter, but every button, rosette, and stripe has its symbolic meaning and its specific rules regulating its use. Even stranger than these clothes, she went on, are the ceremonies men perform together, always in step, always in the uniform proper to the man and the occasion. The explanation for such decorative garments she found in their advertisement of the social, professional, or intellectual standing of the wearer. These costumes with their symbolic traditions draped the male in mantles of social prestige.

Yet men seemed blind to the remarkable nature of these clothes. In a revealing footnote, she quoted the words of a male judge summing up a case: "Women cannot be expected to renounce an essential feature of femininity or to abandon one of nature's solaces for a constant and insuperable physical handicap. Dress, after all, is one of the chief methods of women's self-expression. … In matters of dress women often remain children to the end" (1986: 170). Woolf added that the judge himself was wearing a scarlet robe, an ermine cape, and a vast wig of artificial curls, but he seemed unaware of his own elaborate attire. To point up her theme of the absurdity of such venerable traditions, the book's illustrations show unflattering photographs of male decrepitude in professional dress: an ancient general bedecked in medals and ribbons, an elderly archbishop with a richly embroidered cassock, a rotund judge in elegant robes and wig, and gowned male academics in pompous ceremonial procession.

How does this disquisition on professional dress relate to her theme, the prevention of war? For her, the connection was obvious: the finest clothes are those worn by soldiers. These uniforms impress the beholder with the majesty of military office and induce young men to join the service. How a military uniform strengthens a man's image of masculinity has been analyzed: "It gives him a head-dress which exaggerates his height; it puts a stripe on his trousers to exaggerate his apparent length of leg; it gives him epaulettes to exaggerate the width of his shoulders" (Laver 1969: 73).

Woolf's vivid analysis of male institutions with their decorations, public honors, patriotic rhetoric, uniforms, and war-making provides an excellent foundation for exploring the symbolism of dress in the exercise of British imperial power. The colorful and ostentatious costumes served to constitute and maintain hierarchies of race, gender, and social rank. While men gained their splendor and glory through their impressive uniforms and professional dress, women were forbidden to wear such clothes, as Woolf pointed out (1986: 25). Yet, as shown later, some enterprising women manipulated modes of dress to exercise power in their own ways.

THE THEATER OF EMPIRE

Imperial domination has been seen mainly in terms of standing armies, superior military technology and organization, economic exploitation, and cunning political strategies of divide and rule. In recent years, however, another dimension of the exercise of power has come into focus—that of spectacles, rituals, and mass ceremonies—not only displaying the authority of British rule but subtly incorporating the indigenous princes, emirs, or chiefs as subordinates into a descending hierarchy that brought all the people into the encircling embrace of the British Empire (Cohn 1983; Ranger 1983).

Anthropological analysis reveals how the practice of imperial rule developed into a total cultural mode including not only these special ceremonies, but patterns of order and discipline regulating minute details of everyday existence for the rulers, and extending with far-reaching effects into the lives of their subjects (Callaway 1987: 55–82). Power and rank were rendered visible in material forms and social processes. Townships were laid out with majestic government buildings, splendid ceremonial thoroughfares named after British sovereigns, and exclusive residential areas insuring social separation of the rulers from the ruled, as well as hierarchy within the ruling group. The Warrant of Precedence governed precise details of formal behavior both in the official interaction of administrators with native rulers and in the everyday social life of the dominant group itself. In this choreography of empire, the display of dress in all its forms carried a heavy weight of symbolic meanings.

Certain rules were deliberately demeaning. Because the wearing of shoes by Indians in the presence of the British was seen as an attempt to establish relations of equality, Indians were required to remove their shoes or sandals when entering into what the British defined as their space—their offices or homes. At the same time, the British always wore shoes in Indian spaces, including mosques and temples. As an exception, those Indians who habitually wore European clothes in public were allowed to wear shoes for such occasions as receptions and balls (Cohn 1983: 176–77).

Elaborate dress became a significant means of asserting authority. Before the young Curzon set out on his exploration of the India's northwest frontier, he prepared for his visit to the Amir of Afghanistan by calling at a supplier of theatrical costumes in London where, for a modest sum, he hired "a cluster of gorgeous stars of foreign orders, mostly from the smaller States of Eastern Europe. To these he added an enormous pair of gold epaulettes in a case the size of a hat-box" (Rose 1969: 268). On his journey he gathered a "glittering pair of patent leather Wellington top boots" and "a gigantic curved sword with ivory hilt and engraved scabbard," plus a cocked hat and a handsome pair of spurs. In this spuriously acquired uniform, he considered himself appropriately dressed for his audience with the Amir. Later, as Viceroy of India, Lord Curzon proved himself gifted in producing imperial spectacle of a scale and grandeur never before reached.

Interestingly, these great ceremonies developed in Victorian India to establish and maintain British authority were justified on the basis of the assumption that Indians had a special susceptibility for parades and show (Cohn 1983: 188). This theater of empire reached its culmination during Lord Curzon's rule with the series of special events in January 1903 to celebrate King Edward VII's coronation. British India soon dubbed it "the Curzonation," knowing who would be in the durbar's center spotlight (Fowler 1987: 280). The Viceroy planned this series of ceremonies and festivities in great detail—some seventy-seven pages in print. Lady Curzon, meanwhile, designed her own range of exquisite gowns to represent the feminine side of this confident masculine authority.

The first event on December 29, 1902 was the State Entry into Delhi with a procession of gaily painted elephants, drugged to keep them docile in the crowds. On the biggest elephant of all, an ancient slow-moving giant, was the silver-gilt howdah of the Viceroy and Lady Curzon. The next great ceremony came on January 1, the durbar itself, with a multitude of twenty-six thousand people gathered in the middle of the day for the proclamation declaring King Edward VII King of England and Emperor of India. Five days later, after numerous festivities—sports matches, receptions, garden parties, special dinners, balls, fireworks—came the climax of the Delhi durbar. The State Ball was held in the Moghul Palace, where the Viceroy and the Vicereine made their grand entrance to the strains of the national anthem, he in white satin knee breeches, she in her famous peacock dress, with four thousand guests parting to line their route through the length of the ballroom to the marble podium. Lady Curzon's gown was "made of cloth-of-gold, embroidered by Delhi's superb craftsmen, with metal threads and real emeralds

in a pattern of peacock feathers so that the cloth beneath had virtually disappeared" (Fowler 1987: 290). Her own resplendent creation, she posed in it for photographs and a large oil portrait, which became, after her premature death attributed to over-exertion carrying out imperial duties, the identifying image of this American heiress who played her star role as Vicereine of India.

For these gala events, some eighty distinguished British guests arrived on the SS *Arabia*, among them the Duke and Duchess of Marlborough, the Duke and Duchess of Portland, Lord and Lady Derby, Lord and Lady Crewe, and other members of Curzon's set. They brought with them no less than forty-seven tons of dresses and uniforms (Fowler 1987: 283).

It should be noted that in mobilizing the Indian nationalist movement, Gandhi subverted this symbolic authority by calling for Indians not only to return all honors and emblems granted to them by the imperial government, but also to dress in simple homespun peasant dress instead of the Western clothes or "native" costumes decreed by the imperial rulers (Cohn 1983: 209). The paradox of dress symbolism was exposed in the drama of nationalism: if the British dressed up in splendid uniforms to establish and maintain authority over the Indians, the nationalists dressed down to grasp back the power that had been wrested from them.

These imperial ceremonies, reaching their height in scale and magnificence in Curzon's India, were transferred complete with dazzling military parades and brilliant uniforms to the far reaches of the empire in Africa and the Pacific. The governor of a colony held unique power, combining the roles of personal representative of the Crown, prime minister, head of the civil service, and leader of the colony's social life. His dress uniform was suitably impressive: "He was entitled to wear either a white uniform with white and red plumes in his colonial helmet or, in cooler climates, a dark blue uniform with a cocked hat and white plumes. Gold and silver gorgets, epaulettes, buttons, and frogging and an elaborately decorated sword completed the uniform" (Kirk-Greene 1978: 228–29).

Special ceremonies marked the arrivals and departures of governors to and from their colonies. The triumphant entry of Sir Bernard Bourdillon to the Nigerian scene in 1935 has been described:

On the morning of his arrival we all went down to the Customs wharf, the men in white uniforms and the ladies superb in their best. … The Regiment mounted one of its immaculate guards of honour and the band played on a flank. The invited guests sat uncomfortably in their finery on hard chairs, carefully arranged in the order in which they had to be presented. The guns (brought specially from Zaria) fired their slow salute from across the water. … Then the tall figure of Sir Bernard came down the companion way in his blue uniform and plumes, with his dazzling wife. (Niven 1982: 148)

There were numerous lesser ceremonies as well, requiring uniforms which defined position and rank. Sir Rex Niven recounted the occasion of a Governor's return from leave:

This was quite a show, with guards of honour, and booming guns and waving bunting. … It was the first time I wore the very undistinguished khaki uniform prescribed for us juniors, complete with our war medals; we did not qualify for the full white civil service uniform, with its obliterating 'Wolseley' helmet, until we had completed seven years service. (1982: 14)

It should be noted that the full dress uniform also included a sword—if obsolete as a weapon, a potent symbol of masculinity.

In a colony the official residence of the Governor, known as "Government House," was the center of imperial display, as shown in this glimpse of Lagos in 1921: "When Clifford gave parties or balls at Government House, all the men had to wear full evening dress, with starched shirts and collars, white waistcoats and tails. … I remember one ball at which the staircase was lined on each hand by soldiers wearing scarlet and gold zouaves and fezzes while the Governor received at the top" (Niven 1982: 21).

If the prescribed dress of the male colonial officers was characterized by pomp and plumage enhancing masculinity, that of their wives was marked by propriety and femininity. The gender division in dress was strongly marked: men wore designated uniforms and robes (even the dinner jacket might be considered such), while women were able to exercise more choice

in colors, textiles, and design, as long as they kept to models appropriate for the occasion. The biographer of Lady Curzon noted that she took immense pains preparing her magnificent wardrobe for India with the guiding thought, "She must be ultra-feminine when the men were ultra-masculine" (Nicolson 1977: 138). In an unusual case, Lieutenant Governor Palmer of Northern Nigeria sympathized with the sensibilities of Muslim rulers by ordering European women to wear veils for public occasions (Heussler 1968: 134).

WARDROBES FOR THE TROPICS

In Delhi and Bombay, Lagos and Nairobi, the servants of empire gave even greater attention to dress than their social equivalents back at home. Not only did they self-consciously maintain their identity and prestige, as has been shown in their daily routines of dressing for dinner and their grand ceremonies, but even in small outposts they turned everyday social life into a competitive whirl. London and Paris dictated women's fashions, despite the contrasts in climate, with only a few modifications to meet the threat of the sun and the onslaught of mosquitoes. All too often the assigned quarters in an isolated post seemed a mismatch of social expectations and setting. Airing clothing during the rainy season in Nigeria, Elinor Russell commented, "It always looked incongruous seeing a dinner jacket or evening dresses hanging outside a mud hut in the middle of Africa" (1978: 90).

In most cases, a personal wardrobe sufficient for the entire tour had to be acquired. In 1902, Lady Lugard took with her to Northern Nigeria forty-six trunks and cases besides her trousseau, including household items for the new Government House at Zungeru (Perham 1960: 75). Women embarking for the tropics gained advice on their wardrobes from relatives and friends or from books such as Mrs. Lyttleton's *How to Pack, How to Dress, How to Keep Well on a Winter Tour of India (for Ladies)* (1892) and Constance Larymore's chapter on "What to Wear" in *A Resident's Wife in Nigeria* ([1908] 1911).

A photograph of Larymore in Nigeria shows her in an Edwardian floor-length gown of a heavy material, with long sleeves and high neck. It is daunting to think of wearing this in tropical heat with the necessary petticoats and underclothes. Admonishing that leaving off corsets for the sake of coolness was a huge mistake, Larymore allowed no compromise on the necessity of taking at least six pairs: "*Always* wear corsets, even for a *tête-à-tête* home dinner on the warmest evenings; there is something about their absence almost as demoralizing as hair in curling-pins" ([1908] 1911: 288).

In West Africa, mosquito boots were essential. Larymore suggested for ordinary use a pair of black canvas gaiters, buttoned and reaching to the knee: under a long evening dress, these gave protection against the ravaging bites of mosquitoes. Even such a utilitarian item was subject to changing fashions and local customs. Hats for protection from the sun were considered a necessity for both women and men, with stern warnings on the danger of even a few rays of sunlight touching a bare head. While trekking in Northern Nigeria in 1924, Violet Cragg noted, "Our present hut is large, but not sunproof, so that we have to wear hats all the time, even in the bath!" (Cragg n.d.: 9). While women, as well as men, were required at all times to protect their heads from the perceived harmful rays of the sun, they were not, however, expected to wear the spine pads essential to men's outfits before the First World War (Kirk-Greene 1955: 108–11).

Two types of hats, the double *terai* and the sun helmet, were described by Berry. The first was "side brimmed, of heavy felt and literally one hat over another" (1941: 135). In the early morning when the sun was low, she pulled them apart and wore the inside hat, but in the midday sun, even the double *terai* was not adequate. This required the pith sun helmet, with the ventilation holes in the crown carefully covered. Women found ways to make these attractive, as Berry noted, "I frankly lifted an idea from the chic wife of a tin-mine manager; several lengths of chiffon in bright colours; I pinned on over the crown the one best suited to the costume of the day; tan, white, stop-red, or kelly green, leaving a yard or two to float, Lady of Shalott fashion, out behind" (1941: 136).

Although few women chalked up the three thousand miles that Constance Larymore rode on horseback during her first tour in Northern Nigeria in 1902, riding habits were essential for most parts of the empire. The question of the "astride" position arose in the early years of this century, for which Larymore advised an ordinary bicycling skirt or else "full bloomers worn with shooting boots and puttees and a rather long-skirted coat" ([1908] 1911: 283).

UNCONVENTIONAL WOMEN AND THE MESSAGES OF DRESS

As a visual code, modes of dress carried multivalent meanings within the wider cultural system of imperial authority and privilege. Most women conformed to appropriate feminine dress, but some donned unconventional attire to travel in areas otherwise inaccessible to them, or, in a few instances, to protest against imperial rule itself. Although independent Victorian women travelers took on daring adventures and identified with male achievements, they usually dressed in the prescribed manner.

Mary Kingsley, for example, made her way through the tropical forests of Central Africa in the same long, heavy black skirt and long-sleeved, high-necked blouse that she wore in London and Cambridge. She denied ever wearing trousers, although a shipboard friend divulged that she had brought with her a pair belonging to her brother and changed into them for wading across a river or crossing a swamp (Frank 1986: 62). While guarding her feminine appearance, disclaiming any male prerogatives, Kingsley was able to free herself from gender restrictions during her travels in Africa.

Gertrude Bell, during her extensive travels in the Middle East as a historian and archeologist before the First World War, always dressed in clothes appropriate for an Englishwoman. Riding out from Jerusalem into the desert in 1900, she was introduced for the first time to a "masculine" saddle; she reassured her father, "You mustn't think that I haven't got a most elegant and decent divided skirt" (Winstone 1978: 63). After she and her brother had attended the Delhi durbar in 1903, they travelled around India, she in a sun helmet, a cotton gown, and a fur coat—a combination she found suitable for the variations in the Indian climate (Winstone 1978: 85).

Reporting on the empire as colonial editor for the *The Times* of London during the 1890s, Flora Shaw dressed in dark Victorian gowns, whether touring the mining district in Queensland, Australia, where she "went down three mines, crawled duly on hands and knees down unfinished shafts, looked on while the width of reefs was measured" (Bell 1947: 133) or making midnight visits to the gambling saloons of Dawson City to assess the miners' lives in the Canadian Klondike (1947: 209). When she married Sir Frederick (later Lord) Lugard, however, she discarded the dark clothes she had considered appropriate for her professional work to wear white gowns in her new identity as the wife of a leading administrator in Africa (1947: 250).

Supporting the empire in their various ways, these women claimed the privileges accorded to Europeans on their travels in foreign lands. Because of imperial constructions of racial difference, they were able to gain the status assumed by white males (Birkett 1989). Yet at the same time, they endorsed conventional Victorian gender roles and actively resisted women's suffrage, Gertrude Bell becoming a founding member of the Anti-Suffrage League (Winstone 1978: 110) and Lady Lugard joining later. Perceiving themselves as exceptional women, they were able in this way to live the contradiction between their attention to feminine appearance and their pursuit of masculine achievements.

On occasion, women dressed in "native garb" for particular objectives. Adela Nicolson, who published poetry under the name of "Laurence Hope," disguised herself in 1890 as a Pathan boy in order to follow her husband on an expedition through the rugged, lawless country on the frontier between India and Afghanistan (MacMillan 1988: 206–07). Alexandra David-Neel similarly transformed her appearance to that of an oriental woman in order to make the pilgrimage to the holy city of Lhasa, closed to foreigners (Birkett 1989: 119).

Of greater significance, because they were perceived as dangerous by the rulers, were those who dressed in local clothing out of sympathy with the people. Amy Carmichael, who worked as a missionary in South India for over fifty years, was criticized for damaging British prestige when she began wearing Indian dress (MacMillan 1988: 212). Just before the turn of the century, Sister Nivedita (née Margaret Noble) came to Calcutta, where she studied Bengali and was initiated into a Hindu religious order. Becoming friends with many leading nationalists, she sided with those advocating the most radical measures of protest and was called by her own countrymen a traitor (MacMillan 1988: 118). The admiral's daughter, Madeleine Slade, rejected the Raj to become a devoted disciple of Gandhi; on her voyage to India, she dramatically burned all her fashionable Paris clothes to dress in Indian outfits (MacMillan 1988: 117).

But these protests were isolated individual cases. In the history of the British Empire, the symbolism of dress served simultaneously to heighten masculinity by contrast with feminine modes, thereby reinforcing the asymmetry of gender roles, and to maintain social exclusiveness by indicating distinctions of position and rank. The uniforms and prescribed clothing brilliantly enhanced the imperial spectacle and the dominant power this represented.

23

FASHIONING THE COLONIAL SUBJECT

Jean Comaroff and John Comaroff

THE EMPIRE'S OLD CLOTHES
Christianity does not seem to be looked on [by the Bechuana] as
a life to be lived, but rather as a garment to be worn, which may be
put on or taken off as the occasion requires.

LMS, *South Africa Reports*, 1914

In seeking to reconstruct the agrarian economies of Bechuanaland, the colonial evangelists might have conjoined cultivation to Christianity, the Bible to the plough. But they did not privilege production above all else. As we have stressed throughout, they set their sights on *total* transformation: on altering modes of exchange and consumption at the same time; on making subjects by means of objects; on "increasing artificial wants" in order to persuade Tswana of the benefits to be had by cultivating themselves and their land in a Christian manner (*RRI*: 270). In this respect, the grand tautology of the Protestant Ethic gave an elegant circularity to their vision. Proper, propertied, prosperous agriculture and self-possessed labor might seed the Christian spirit. But prosperity was itself the reward of a pious heart and a disciplined body. Both—prosperity and piety—were therefore to be enjoyed, and to be measured, in sober, not too conspicuous consumption.

We move on, then, to the efforts of the London Missionary Society (LMS) and Wesleyan Methodist Missionary Society (WMMS) to recast Tswana patterns of consumption. This the clerics took to be a task at once lofty and mundane. Their divine duty, as they saw it, was to elevate the soul by overdetermining the ordinary, to nurture the spiritual by addressing the physicality of everyday life.

It is hardly necessary to point out that consumption, as an idea and a species of activity, has to be understood here in its nineteenth-century British sense. There was a widespread faith in the positive attributes of the market, especially in its capacity to convert differences among objects and abilities, wants and needs, into a single order of negotiable values. This integrative function lay, of course, in the exchange of consumer goods and services through the standardizing medium of money. By its graces the social order was animated and shaped: an ethos of enterprise was induced in right-minded people; persons of energy and discipline were rewarded; the well-off were separated from the poor, and the various classes and estates found their proper level in the world. No wonder, in this light, that the civilizing mission was founded on the conviction that commodities and commerce might shape new desires, new exertions, new forms of wealth, even a new society (see Philip 1828,1: 241f.); that civilization was to be promoted by the encouragement of discerning consumption, through which Africans would learn

Adapted from Jean Comaroff and John Comaroff, "Fashioning the Colonial Subject," in *Of Revolution and Revelation, Volume Two* (Chicago: University of Chicago Press, 1997), pp. 218–3 to want and use objects of European provenance in a refined Christian manner; that, by being drawn into the workings of the market, would-be converts might develop a healthily competitive urge to fashion novel identities.

In this respect, the evangelists in South Africa shared one thing with some other early European colonizers: an impulse not merely to make non-Western peoples want Western objects (Sahlins 1989), but to have them use those objects in specific ways. In many places across the expanding eighteenth- and nineteenth-century world, imperialists and their mercantile associates tried to conquer by implanting new *cultures* of consumption. Over the short and medium terms at least, they often focused less on extracting labor, raw materials, or exotic goods than on promoting trade that might instill needs which only they could satisfy, desires to which only they could cater, signs and values over whose flow they exercised control. The idea that cultures are (re)constructed through consumption is no mere figment of the postmodern or postindustrial imagination, as some have said (Baudrillard [1973] 1975; cf. Appadurai 1993). It is as old, as global, as capitalism itself.

A general point here: it may be argued that, over the longer run as well, early modern European empires were as much fashioned as forged or fought for (cf. E. Wilson 1985: 14). As worlds both imagined and realized, they were built not merely on the violence of extraction, not just by brute force, bureaucratic fiat, or bodily exploitation. They also relied heavily on the circulation of stylized objects, on disseminating desire, on manufacturing demand, on conjuring up dependencies. All of which conduced to a form of bondage, of conquest by consumption, that tied peripheries to centers by potent, if barely visible, threads and passions. Indeed, the banality of imperialism, the mundanities that made it so ineffably real, ought not to be underestimated. Cultural revolutions, not least those set in train by European colonization, usually root(ed) themselves on modest terrain, in simple acts of fabrication, use, exchange. Even the most elaborate social formations arise from such quotidian acts. Weber and Marx understood this well, to be sure. That is why the latter vested his mature account of capitalism

in the unobtrusive career of the commodity, that "very queer thing" (1967,1: 71) whose workaday production, distribution, and consumption built the contours of an epoch, a whole world.

But not all objects, nor all exchanges, are born equal in history; nor are they borne equally across the globe. For the colonial evangelists in South Africa, the most crucial realm of enlightened consumption hinged on the human form. It was on the body that the commodity came into physical contact with, and enclosed, the self. To a nineteenth-century religious sensibility—keenly attuned as it was to the moral, theological, even cosmogonic significance of cloaking the revealed anatomy—the treatment of the domesticated physique was an everyday sacrament. In cleaning it, housing it, curing it, and clothing it lay the very essence of civility. In this chapter we examine these processes and their place in the colonial encounter. We begin, now, with the effort of the Protestant mission to cover African "nakedness": to re-dress the savagery of Tswana by dressing them in European fashions, by making them receptive to the ethics and aesthetics of refined attire, and by insinuating in them a newly embodied sense of self-worth, taste, and personhood.

Like consumption, "fashion" also had a wide fan of resonances in the contemporary European imagination. Not only did it epitomize the capacity of the commodity to envelop the self, to insert a culturally legible screen between human beings and the world. It insisted, too, on "pure contemporaneity" (Faurschou 1990: 235; Simmel [1904] 1971[a]: 296) *and* constant movement (E. Wilson 1985: 3), situating those who kept up with the styles of the moment in the cosmopolitan here and now; those who did not, by contrast, were rendered "out of date," provincial, parochial. What is more, the very idea of fashion affirmed the modernist assumption that identity was something apart from one's person; something to be produced, purchased, possessed; something that had continually to be "put on" and "shown off" (Bowlby 1985: 27–28; see J. Williamson 1992: 106). This rendered clothing the manufactured good *par excellence*. Hence its centrality in colonial evangelism: it made the "native" body a terrain on which the battle for selfhood was to be fought, on which personal identity was to be re-formed, re-placed, re-inhabited. At the same time, the Nonconformists in South Africa would be caught in a bind: on one hand, they were to appeal to the modernist potential of fashion to alter Tswana sensibilities, to individuate them; on the other, their stress on unaltering verities drew them to the "traditional" (unfashionable?) value of sober sameness and uniformity.

The sartorial adventures of the mission did not occur *in vacuo.* They were caught up in the more general British effort to incorporate African communities into a global economy of goods and signs; this itself being a critical dimension of the rise of capitalism—which, Macfarlane (1987: 173–74, after Weber) reminds us, had long been intimately tied to "the massive growth of the English cloth industry" (cf. Schneider 1989: 180f.). The evangelists themselves, as we know, sometimes invoked the commercial interests of Great Britain in speaking of their own objectives. Livingstone (1857: 720), for example, once said: "I have a twofold object in view, and believe that, by guiding our missionary labors so as to benefit our own country, we shall therefore more effectively and permanently benefit the heathen."

This "twofold object" was to be sustained for much of the century. McCracken (1977: 31) cites an anonymous letter to the *Church of Scotland Missionary Record* which, in 1876, argued that colonial evangelism was "a grand outlying business investment." In making "savage men … realize their wants and needs, and thus awaken[ing] in them *healthful tastes,*" asserted the writer, the missions were a palpably positive, profitable force "in our markets." One historian of religion has recently gone so far as to argue that there was a "clear parallel," perhaps even a symbiosis, between the great missionary societies and the magnates of Manchester, the former wishing to convert the world, the latter to clothe it (Helmstadter 1992: 9).

But the Nonconformists were not simply seeking to dress up British mercantile interests in pious clichés. Their campaign to clothe Tswana in European manufactures—like all their interventions into colonial commerce—were intended to effect, as John Philip said, a "revolution in the habits" of the Africans. Historically speaking, these exertions were no less significant for the fact that they focused on fashion

and the aesthetics of embodiment rather than on the brute materialities of political economy; in any case, as we just said, cloth and capitalism were deeply imbricated in one another. Nor were they merely a representation, an outward expression, of a more "real" history being made by others elsewhere. The cultural exchanges that took place between Southern Tswana and the missionaries began, on their own account, to generate a new economy; an economy at once material and moral, social and symbolic, stylistic and sensuous. Both the Europeans and the Africans—and the traders, adventurers, and brokers of various backgrounds who plied the spaces between—invested a great deal in the objects fabricated by, and passed among, them. They encoded, in compact form, the structure of a world-in-the-making.

They were also to tell a story full of surprises, of mischievousness and misapprehension and misgiving. This chapter of the story recalls how many Tswana refused at first to "buy in" to the dictates and dress codes of the mission; how the evangelists themselves began to don garments not unlike those they denounced; how the fashioning of the South African frontier was implicated both in the "improvement" of the uncouth at home and in the development of the British idea of charity; how, in Bechuanaland, the import of Western styles gradually gave rise to parodic experiments in synthetic design; how, in time, these styles played into the making and marking of new social classes, new patterns of distinction, which ruptured existing communities of signs; how, despite their faith in the Gospels of Jesus and Adam Smith, the Christians were to learn that commerce and civility did not always go hand in glove; how commodities rarely produced converts, although they converted people to the global order of goods; how, over the longer run, Tswana self-presentation was altered in a colonial order that fashioned men into migrant laborers and led women to adopt the ethnicized "folk" costume of the countryside. All of which conduces to one conclusion: that the struggles over the way in which Tswana bodies were to be clothed and presented—struggles at once political, moral, aesthetic—were not just metonymic of colonialism. They were a crucial site in the battle of wills and deeds, the dialectic of means and ends, that shaped the encounter between Europeans and Africans. And transformed both in the process.

CIVILITY, CLOTH, AND CONSUMPTION

[I]n this day the angel of Democracy [has] arisen, enshadowing the classes with leathern wings, and proclaiming, "All men are equal—all men, that is to say, who possess umbrellas."

E. M. Forster ([1910] 1992: 58)

The campaign to introduce European fashions into Bechuanaland might have appeared "trifling," explained Robert Moffat (1842: 507; echoing Wesley 1986: 248) to his British readers. But decent clothes were "elements of a system … destined to sweep away the filth and customs of former generations." As this implies, some of the Nonconformists set great store on the need to force African bodies into the straitjackets of Protestant personhood. More than just demand "civilized" garb of those who would enter the church, they sought to scramble the indigenous code of body management in its entirety—and then to reform it inside out. For their part, Tswana were not slow to grasp the potent role of Western apparel in the colonization of their world. When, for example, Chief Montshiwa began to perceive a challenge to his legitimacy from the Christians in his realm (*RRI*: 262f.), he ordered his daughter "to doff her European clothing, … to return to heathen attire," and to leave the Methodist congregation (Mackenzie 1871: 231). His royal counterparts in other chiefdoms did similarly, sparking several bitter style wars and struggles over freedom of dress.

From the first, Southern Tswana appear to have treated Western adornments as signs of exotic forces: as quintessential *sekgoa* (things white; Burchell 1824, 2:432, 559; cf. Somerville [1802] 1979: 109). Some European clothes had, like beads and buttons, preceded the mission into the interior, where they are said to have been regarded as "a badge of the highest status" (Burchell 1824, 2:432). An early report from Kuruman tells how the Tlhaping chief addressed his warriors prior to battle in a "white linen garment," his heir wearing an "officer's coat" (R. Moffat 1825: 29). In a published account of the incident, Moffat (1842: 348) says that the garment was a chemise of unknown origin, and included a picture of the ruler "cutting capers" in it before the "Bechuana Parliament," this as evidence of the "absurd" use made by heathens of civilized attire. Such items of dress might have derived their potency from their alien provenance, but they resonated with vernacular symbols as well. White, for instance, the color of the baptismal gown—itself much like a chemise—was also the color of the concoctions and fibers placed on the body in indigenous rites of passage (J. Comaroff 1985: 98). Likewise the military uniforms borne inland from the Cape Colony by Khoi soldiers: their mystique was probably heightened by their association with a mobile frontier people regarded by Tswana with a mix of awe and fear. Yet the interest they evoked seems to have been fed by long-standing local concerns with the magical properties of battle dress. Observers were to remark the unusual, even parodic, deployment of Western attire, most notably petticoats and hats, by Khoi (e.g., Campbell 1822, 2:64f.). This, too, must have communicated itself to Tswana, who, as we know, had their own proclivities for playing with the power of embodied objects—and who, according to Burchell (1824, 2:432), accorded these "Hottentots" the highest prestige precisely because of "their Colonial dress." In the upshot, as elsewhere in southern Africa, European garb took on great value, value inseparably material and metaphorical. And it increased dramatically, in the 1820s and 1830s, with the coming of the evangelists (Baillie 1832: 447; Hughes 1841: 523; see below).

Western dress, in short, opened up a host of imaginative possibilities for the Africans. It made available an expansive, expressive, experimental language with which to conjure new social identities and senses of self, a language with which also to speak back to the whites. In the early days, before missionaries had been very long in permanent residence—and before they began to present a palpable threat to chiefly authority—royals tried to monopolize the garments that traveled inland from the Colony. These were often worn in an iconoclastic fashion, most notably for ceremonial audiences with visiting Europeans. Thus John Philip (1828, 2:126–27):

Having erected our tents, we paid our respects to the family of Mateebè … Mateebè was dressed in a pair of pantaloons, a shirt and waist coat, with a cat-skin caross over his shoulders … [The queen] wore a printed cotton gown, which had not been much used, a large and rather handsome shawl, and her head was covered by a handkerchief, neatly tied behind. The young women were dressed in gowns … and above these, each of them wore a jackall-skin caross, which served as a covering by day, and a blanket by night. They were covered with a profusion of ornaments.

Already visible here are the signs of a synthetic style that was to be much in evidence later on; among them, the overlay of European garments with skin cloaks. This was an aesthetic fusion abhorred by the evangelists, who tended to describe it as if it were a particularly disgusting form of sartorial miscegenation. They never managed to eradicate it.

From the time they arrived to find Tswana "naked," or wearing an indecent mix of garments, the missionaries expended a remarkable amount of effort and cost on altering the appearance of their would-be converts. The task was made difficult, at the outset, by the distance of colonial markets and by the infrequency with which traders passed through the country. But the Nonconformists were determined, as Robert Moffat (1842: 505) put it, that the Africans should "be clothed and in their right mind." The phrase itself—which crops up in evangelical narratives from other parts of South Africa (Seif 1995) and the world (e.g., Langmore 1989: 168)—is from Luke 8.35. Tellingly, it refers to a man who had been possessed by demons, like Tswana allegedly afflicted by the devil, and who had long gone about naked. Healed by Jesus, he is said to have dressed and regained his reason at the same time. The irony here, however, is that, as Western apparel became more closely associated with Christian control, it became more equivocally regarded—to the extent that, in some quarters, sartorial experimentation ceased entirely. Most senior royals turned their backs on *sekgoa* garb and identified assertively with *setswana*. At least for the time being. In due course, they would don European dress once more. Meanwhile, though, the few who persisted in wearing trousers and the

like were "ridiculed and even abused for adopting the white men's customs and laying aside those of [their] forefathers" (A. Smith 1939, 1:337; cf. Campbell 1822, 2:64). One was prevented from joining in a communal rite until he took off the offending attire.

As we have noted, the campaign to clothe the Africans was inseparable from other aspects and axes of the civilizing mission. In order to dress Tswana—or, rather, to teach them to dress themselves—the Nonconformists had to persuade women to trade the hoe for the needle, the outdoors for the indoor life (Gaitskell 1990). This intention was visible in some of the earliest episodes of the mission encounter. Thus Broadbent wrote, in 1823: "Two women came into my hut, one of them belonged to the King … I let them taste my tea and presented each of them with a needle, thread and thimble."

In this domain, however, the Nonconformists, creatures of their own culture, relied largely on the "domesticating" genius of the "gentler sex" (cf. Hunt 1990); most of their wives and daughters started sewing schools at once (Mears n.d.: 46; R. Moffat 1842: 505). These, in turn, provided a felicitous object for female philanthropists back home. They sent the pincushions and needles with which to stitch together the seams of an expanding imperial fabric (cf. Gaitskell 1990; R. Moffat 1834: 124). Because the production of leather clothing had previously been a male preserve, the schools had limited appeal at the outset. In the early years, too, they lacked a regular supply of materials, despite British charity. But by the late 1830s some Tswana women were already taking in sewing for payment (M. Moffat 1967: 17); this being another area in which the Christians stimulated commerce well before the arrival of colonial markets in goods or labor. As important, however, the industry of these women marked them, and those who consumed their wares, as church people—thus producing a means of signifying difference in communities with a Protestant presence.

Even if the evangelists had succeeded immediately in persuading large numbers of Tswana to outfit themselves in European garb, local manufacture would have been unable to meet the demand. Hence the mission societies made further appeal to the generosity of the Great British Public. The growth of the factory and fashion systems, each encouraging obsolescence, had by now provided a copious supply of used apparel for the poor and unclad at home and abroad (cf. Genovese 1974: 556, on the American south). And so, when the Moffats returned to Cape Town from a visit to the United Kingdom in 1843, they sailed with fifty tons of "old clothes" for the Kuruman station (Northcott 1961: 172). These garments, it seems, were not exactly cut out for the social and physical conditions of Bechuanaland: Livingstone commented scathingly about the cast-off ballgowns and starched collars given by the "good people" of England to those "who had no shirts" (Northcott 1961: 173). But a letter from Mary Moffat (1967: 17–18), written in 1841 to a woman well-wisher in London, shows that she had thought carefully about the adaptation of Western cloth and clothing to just these conditions. Charity was mediated by culture:

> The materials may be coarse, and strong, the stronger the better. Dark blue Prints, or Ginghams … or in fact, any kind of dark Cottons, which will wash well—Nothing light-colored should be worn outside … All the heathen population besmear themselves with red ochre and grease, and as the Christians must necessarily come in contact, with their friends among the heathen, they soon look miserable enough, if clothed in light-colored things … If women's Gowns will not be too heavy work for you, they may be made with bodies to fit very stout women … *I* like them best as Gowns were made 20 or 30 years ago, or rather I should say *as the fashion is now*, except the tight sleeve, which would be a great misery in a warm climate. … For little Girls, Frocks made exactly as you would for the Children of the poor of this country, will be the best. (Original emphasis)

While any European clothes, even diaphanous ballgowns, were better than none, more somber, serviceable garb was ideal. Dark blue attire, especially, resisted the stains of a red-handed heathenism that might "rub off" on the convert. Black Christians, Mrs. Moffat suggested, were like the British poor: neither had the ability yet to produce the wealth or wherewithal to gain entry into the world of fashion—and, hence, were marked by the drear, dismal uniformity of their

dress. Not that these Tswana were as undeserving as the underclasses at home. Added Mrs. Moffat approvingly (1967: 18–19): they "wisely condemn any gay thing, if *flimsy* … [and] are economical in their clothing, taking all possible care of it … as long as it can be made to hold together" (original emphasis). Taken to excess, of course, such frugality also offended the Protestant ethic: "Whereas it is the duty of poor women to be shy of ostentation in dress," declared the *Evangelical Magazine* of 1815, "it is most certainly not the business of wealthy women so to behave" (Tudur Jones 1962: 194; cf. Wesley 1986: 249f.). By extension, neophyte Christians, in pursuit of material and spiritual self-improvement, ought to be stirred by a desire for modestly fashionable, refined apparel. To this end, it was important that they be moved to participate in the civilizing exchanges of the colonial marketplace.

The fact that Mary Moffat's letter was addressed to a woman was itself predictable. Ready-made garments, as well as haberdashery, were moral tender in a rising domestic economy that was thoroughly feminized. Recall that, in England, middle- and upper-class Christian wives, largely excluded from the workplace, had become mistresses of consumption (Davidoff and Hall 1987); they were also the primary purveyors of charity and noblesse toward the poor. By sending their cast-offs to Africa, these gentlewomen sought to dress and domesticate the bare bodies of the benighted abroad, making this their special contribution to colonialism. Their munificence was intended to display virtue and, presumably, to elicit gratitude (cf. Genovese 1974: 555). It was also meant to draw peoples like the Tswana into the global order of British Christendom. But largesse carried its own dangers: it could inhibit ambition. Due care, therefore, had to be taken not to promote indolence. Here the missionaries and their benefactors trusted to the sheer charm of commodities. Clothes from the center of civilization, they hoped, would awaken a desire for self-enhancement, for a life of righteous earning and careful spending. Mary Moffat (1967: 19) concluded:

> Those who have property, are inclined to lay it out very sparingly, sometimes more so than we could wish, but by our sometimes being able to supply

in a *measure* the necessities of the poor, they are stimulated to make larger purchases, least [*sic*] the poor of the people should look better than themselves! I have often been pleased to see this effect produced, as they by such means make more rapid advances in civilization. (Original emphasis)

Thus it was, mainly through the exertions of mission wives, that the germ of the European fashion system arrived on the African veld. With it would come the peculiar conjuncture, in the culture of capitalism, of competitive accumulation, symbolic innovation, and social distinction (Bell 1949). But its export to this edge of empire also underscored a deep-seated ambiguity in the Protestant ethic. Among Tswana, where Christians lived cheek by jowl with heathens, the industrious were encouraged to procure commodities in order to set themselves off from the "indigent." Yet, given their strong puritanism, the evangelists could not but worry that the drive toward sartorial civility and consumption might degenerate into vain acquisitiveness. As late as 1877, for example, the Rev. Hepburn's joy at baptizing six "servants" in "decent" clothes at Shoshong was vitiated by his fear that the men would become "puffed up with self-importance."

Ascetic angst focused most sharply on female frailness, however. For, insofar as women were the prime subjects and objects of fashion, femininity was associated with things of the flesh. Willoughby was not alone in grumbling, toward the end of the century, that many Tswana matrons were in thrall to ridiculous hats and costly garments; much earlier, one of his colleagues expressed relief that "our native ladies have not yet adopted the crinoline, that social abomination of which they have been shown bright exemplars." It was a matter of time, he thought, until they would—all of which made it imperative to keep tight bounds on the sartorial self-expression of those who joined the church. Again, while the Nonconformists sought to produce an elite driven by virtuous wants, they were also heirs to a creed that accommodated the lower classes at home; theirs was a doctrine that sanctified poverty and contained physical pleasure in the cause of eternal grace. The early evangelists resolved the dilemma by portraying their mostly humble adherents,

in contrast to the "carnal" heathen, as sober, deserving recipients of Christian charity. And they clothed them in the cotton prints whose color and texture would become a hallmark of the mission—and, later, of a rural "folk" style that typified the status of Tswana peasant-proletarians. It was a style that some literati of empire found profoundly ugly, blaming it for the erasure of "native" beauty.

As the years wore on, the LMS and WMMS directed their energies increasingly toward the creation of a black petite bourgeoisie. But, throughout the century, they advocated improvement and self-reliance as an ideal for all: hence their efforts to bring traders and, with them, the goods needed to make civilized subjects. The Nonconformist clothing campaign played a large role in stimulating that demand, not just for garments but for all the elements of the European sartorial economy (Hattersley 1952: 87). Much, for instance, was made of the fact that, unlike "filthy skins," garments of refined manufacture needed to be washed and maintained, binding wives and mothers to an unrelenting regime of "cleanliness"—a regime epitomized, to this day, by the starched uniforms of black women's Prayer Unions (Gaitskell 1990). It was a form of discipline that the missions monitored closely, ensuring brisk sales of soap and other cleansing agents both personal and domestic (cf. Burke 1996). Thus Wookey, in 1888:

> One has to preach to the people about things which would sound strange to English ears. For example, … one has to take up the subject of cleanliness, and give them a sermon on washing themselves and their clothes. The consequence has been a sudden run on the soap at the stores.

Moffat (1842: 507), alive to the interests of his bourgeois audience, claimed that such activities opened up "numberless channels for British commerce," especially in personal requisites, "which but for the Gospel might have remained forever closed."

This claim was echoed by others. From 1830 onward, mission narratives speak, with pleasure, of the "decent raiments" worn by loyal members of the church. They also note, as we did above, that more and more Tswana evinced a desire to possess European apparel—and that the garment trade was flourishing

(Baillie 1832: 447; R. Moffat 1842: 219; Read 1850: 446). By 1835, in fact, one merchant reported that Tlhaping were "particularly anxious for ready made clothes," where before "nothing was desired [by them] but beads." In just two months he had sold more than a hundred shirts. "They even purchase with avidity waistcoats," he added, obviously surprised (A. Smith 1939, 1:250). The clothing of the heathen had begun in earnest.

The fact that people were buying Western attire did not mean that they would necessarily wear it in the manner favored by the mission. Anything but, as the Nonconformists were to report, with regret, for many decades to come; we shall return to this in a moment. Nonetheless, they found much to cheer them: the sedate style of an Anglophile Christian elite was taking shape—and becoming visible (e.g., Hughes 1841: 523). Read (1850: 446), who had accompanied Campbell into the interior in 1813, returned in 1849 to find

> Many of them … [are] not only well, but respectably clad in English manufactured clothing: the men, many of them with surtouts or coats, waistcoats, trousers, Wellington boots, polished, starched collars &c to their shirts, beaver hats, and here and there watches: almost, if not every man with a wagon. The women in gowns, shoes, stockings, and good shawls; mostly with caps and bonnets. … Surely this also is not a failure.

While modesty forbade mention of underwear among the faithful, we might assume that the Christians sought to lay the outfits of their followers over a decent foundation; one James Liebmann (1901: 163) referred to the "dear, good ladies [of Exeter Hall] who spen[t] their time in making, and embellishing with beautiful embroidery, flannel nether garments for the poor, benighted blacks" of South Africa. "Bloomers"—female drawers here—became a staple of needlework classes in South African schools for all races in the early twentieth century; they must have had their antecedents in mission sewing circles. Further, they are listed in Schapera's (1947: 230) Bechuanaland merchant inventories for the 1930s as "an old line, but increasingly in favour"; these lists also show men's

cotton undervests and short underpants to have been "popular" (pp. 229, 231). Because they were invisible to the eye, it is impossible to know for sure how and by whom such intimate apparel was actually used. Not so in the early nineteenth century, however. The "unmentionables" worn then by Tswana often intruded upon the gaze of white observers. The idea that such finely wrought items of clothing should be hidden from view might have expressed mission notions of concealed virtue. But it conflicted with the Tswana sense that beauty was for display. Such garments, clearly, were not being put on in ways intended by their European makers.

SELF-FASHIONING ON THE FRONTIER: THE MAN IN THE TIGER SUIT

Western dress had an effect on Southern Tswana quite different from that intended, or envisaged, by the evangelists. Some turned their backs on it entirely until they could do so no longer. Others put it on enthusiastically, and in a manner recognizably orthodox. But the most immediate and visible response—and, for many decades, that of the great majority—was somewhere in between: a synthetic, syncretic style which, to European eyes, appeared absurd. And, when not actually promiscuous, faintly comical (R. Moffat 1842: 506):

> A man might be seen in a jacket with but one sleeve, because the other was not finished, or he lacked material to complete it. Another in a leathern or duffel jacket, with the sleeves of different colours, or of fine printed cotton. Gowns were seen like Joseph's coat of many colours, and dresses of such fantastic shapes, as were calculated to excite a smile in the gravest of us.

Some years later, as Willoughby's notes indicate, a similarly fantastic array of styles were no less in evidence—and regarded as no less absurd:

> Boboyan in celluloid collar and very heavy boots. Sometimes trousers big enough to contain all the furniture in the wearer's house, as well as the limbs that are thrust through them. And sometimes hardly

reaching the ankles. Coat that Abel wore with patches of nearly every material in my wife's wardrobe. Hats that look as if they might have covered the heads of several generations … generally soft felt, but occasionally bell-topper. Very common to see boys wearing nothing but a shirt, which they have bought at a local store for a shilling. Occasionally a second-hand ulster that has got too shabby for its European owner. But the women's hats are most amusing—such hats! Silks and satins are not rare among the wealthy. Many women spend as much on clothes in a year as would keep my wife well-clad for ten years; and when they have bought their expensive garments, their last state is worse than their first. Intermixed with all this, the suffocating fur-robes which are the sign of wealth among them, and the absurd straw bonnets, that are almost like bee-hives. [Willoughby 1899]

Several things emerge clearly from this fragment: first, and most obvious, that the Tswana penchant for unconventional styling increased over the years, especially among those who could afford it; second, that the wealthy were spending considerable sums of money on fancy clothes; third, that their less affluent, younger compatriots also wore store-bought items—if, on occasion, little else; fourth, that some had to make do with shabby hand-me-downs, often obtained from Europeans. Elsewhere in his notes, Willoughby adds that a few older, poor Tswana had "nothing" to cover them, intimating that they continued to wear only the sparse garments of *setswana*. His own reaction to all this? That those who put on these clothes looked much the worse for their wear. This was not purely an aesthetic judgment. It expressed, beneath the amusement, a sense of disgust at the expense, extravagance, and insobriety of Tswana fashions—and at their non-Christian spirit.

Like Moffat (1842: 506), Willoughby wished for a congregation of "well-dressed believers." But both discovered that this was not an easy objective, given the self-willed cultural reaction of Tswana to their outreach. What is more, as both also found out, the sartorial contrast between convert and heathen was not always as clear-cut as some of the earlier accounts (e.g., Hughes 1841: 523) might have suggested. True, those who repudiated *sekgoa* were easily distinguished from those who donned modest Christian garb. In the spaces separating these extremes, however, there developed a good deal of convergence and overlap. Take, for example, a ceremony that occurred in January 1868. John Mackenzie (1871: 461; 1883: 268), who orchestrated this event—the opening of a new church at Shoshong—and who sought to ensure that it would be attended by Christian and non-Christian alike, described their dress in detail:

> Heathen men with hoary heads … came, leaning on their staffs. Full-grown men—the haughty, the cunning, the fierce—came with those younger in years. … As to their clothing, the heathen dress admits of little variety. But many appeared dressed partly or wholly in European attire, and here there was variety enough. We had the usual members of the congregation, some of whom were neatly dressed. But sticklers for "the proprieties" would have been shocked to see a man moving in the crowd who considered himself well dressed, although wearing a shirt only; another with trousers only; a third with a black "swallow-tail," closely buttoned to the chin—the only piece of European clothing which the man wore; another with a soldier's red coat, overshadowed by an immense wide-awake hat, the rest of the dress being articles of heathen wear, etc. etc.

To the evangelists, such dramatic moments offered a disconcerting reflection of the process, the dialectic of style and self-fashioning, they had set in motion. But the "eccentric" attire adopted by the Africans—redolent, as it was, of anomaly, anarchy, impropriety—was not only visible on the ceremonial stage. As the century wore on, it became an ever more quotidian feature of Tswana life. And it caused the Christians more than just passing anxiety. As Douglas (1966) would have predicted, these hybrid outfits came to be seen as dirty and contagious, a concern later echoed by state health authorities, who blamed the partial adoption by "natives" of "our style of dress" for their susceptibility to disease (Packard 1989: 690; see chapter 7). For another, by flouting British dress codes, they called into question the normative authority of the LMS and WMMS. Where mission "uniforms" were introduced to mark the compliance of those who entered church schools and associations (see volume 3), the colorful, home-made creations of others cried out in obvious counterpoint: the former signaled an acceptance of the Protestant ethic and its aesthetic, the latter parodied both.

In not conforming to Nonconformism, the riotous *couture* contrived by so many non-Christians implied a riposte to the symbolic imperialism of the mission *tout court*. It spoke of a desire to harness the power of *sekgoa*, yet evade its control. A similar tendency manifested itself in respect to domestic architecture. In both domains, the bricoleur contrasted, on one hand, with those who rejected everything European, and, on the other, with those who identified with the church and its values. In broad terms, this tripartite division corresponded, as Bourdieu ([1979] 1984) and Vološinov ([1929] 1973a) might have anticipated, to the embryonic lines of class formation encountered in the previous chapter: the nascent petite bourgeoisie stuck closest to the polite norms of Christian fashion, the poorest tended to adhere most strictly to *setswana*, and those between were most likely to experiment with fusions of the two. This, as we shall see, does not exhaust the grammar of colonial aesthetics. But it does make the point that style was deeply implicated in the active construction—not the passive reflection—of radically new social distinctions; distinctions that, over the long run, eluded the schemes and dreams of the civilizing mission.

From the midcentury onward, as Southern Tswana were drawn more tightly into the regional political economy, the means for making those distinctions were increasingly provided through commercial channels—and affected by market forces—beyond the control of the evangelists. As a result, the fashioning of the frontier took a series of new turns. Apart from all else, the sheer volume of goods pumped into Bechuanaland rose markedly. On a visit to Mafikeng in 1875, Holub (1881, 2:14) noted that, aside from the small elite and from youths dressed in *setswana* outfits, the population persisted in its patchwork of styles. But the makeup of the mixture had subtly altered. Items fabricated from "skins, either of the goat, the wild cat, the grey fox, or the duyker gazelle" were worn with "garments chiefly

of European manufacture" acquired from traders—without, it seems, the moderating intervention of the mission and its stress on things plain, blue, and uniform (cf. Willoughby 1899: 84). Mafikeng might then have been a nominally Christian Tshidi-Rolong town, lacking any white presence. Yet store-bought commodities comprised a growing proportion of its cultural mélange.

What is more, British aesthetic conventions themselves were being used in ever more complex ways. Both in the honor and in the breach they marked widening social and economic differences. Sometimes they did so in unexpected ways. This was evident, for example, in the changing garb of "traditional" rulers and royals. As we noted above, they had responded earlier to the missionary challenge by reverting, assertively, to *setswana* costume—and by insisting that their Christian subjects do likewise. Nor was this reaction confined to Southern Tswana communities. In his effort to win the chiefship of the Ngwato in 1885, one pretender, Khamane, sought the backing of "the old heathen men" by pledging to resume circumcision and rainmaking. To underscore his point, he "gave orders to the young regiment to strip off all European clothing [and] to meet naked in the chief's court." Adult males, including converts, were then commanded to prepare the "warcap," which had been part of the ritual paraphernalia of battle. When the Christians refused—arguing that this spelled a resurgence of "charms, circumcision, idolatry, and a whole army of attendant evils"—Khamane accused them of political disloyalty. Did not English soldiers also wear uniforms?

By the late nineteenth century, however, with the colonial state closing in, few but the most far-flung Tswana sovereigns (H. Williams 1887: 111) harbored any illusions about the habits of power. Some tried to make the best of a difficult situation by seeking, ambitiously, to encompass all sides of a fragmentary world. John Mackenzie (1871: 105) records the fascinating case of Sechele, who, in 1860, had a suit tailored from "tiger"—that is, leopard skin, all "in European fashion." According to the missionary, many Kwena thought that their ruler wished "to make himself a white man." But the matter was surely more complex. In refashioning the skin, itself a symbol of his office, he seems to have been signifying an intention to transform and extend his authority: to legitimize it simultaneously in *setswana* and *sekgoa*, in terms of both European *and* Tswana political cultures, thus to contrive a power base greater than the sum of its parts. Mackenzie (1871: 106) added: "His position … [was] that Christianity might be engrafted upon heathen customs, and that the two could go together." Although he might not always have succeeded, Sechele was adept at playing games of parallel politics, and at navigating cultural borderlands. Other rulers, most notably the Tshidi and Ngwaketse sovereigns (Holub 1881, 1:291), took another tack. They dressed, for a time, in ostentatiously fashionable European garb, whose opulence set them off not merely from non-Christian commoners, but also from their less extravagant Christian subjects. Among the latter, it appears, they counted the evangelists. Seeing that the trappings of "tradition" could not secure their privilege or position, these men, like other Tswana royals, set out to acquire the signs of the order that engulfed them. This form of royal dandyism involved only male dress (cf. J. Comaroff 1985: 219; J. Mackenzie 1975: 42). Later, though, the Christian bourgeoisie would display its status as did its European counterparts: through the attire of its women.

CLOTHES, COLONIALISM, AND CULTURAL ASSERTION

This sartorial history reveals some of the complex cultural dynamics at play in the colonial encounter. The exposure to Western commodities and modes of consumption encouraged peoples like the Tswana to deploy new objects in diverse ways. But these objects were embedded in practices and forms of relationship destined to transform their world. Clothes, and the domestic regimes they implied—being both signs and instruments of incorporation into the subcontinental economy—indexed the manner in which wider political and material forces came to rest on individuals. European norms of dress and comportment pervaded the public sector, laying out an aesthetics of civility and an order of values that positioned whole populations in a hierarchical socioscape. Indeed, the effort to fix black

identity, to inscribe it in backward "ethnic" cultures, was central to the very construction of colonial society; of a society in which class divisions were fragmented and realigned along racial lines, with a concomitant curtailment of the scope for African political self-expression.

And yet, far from being a simple narrative of colonial domination, the story of Tswana "folk" *couture*—like all the other stories of cultural encounter we have told—has a paradoxical, ambivalent, even contradictory character. At two levels. First, to the extent that it took on the dated, dark shapes and colors and textures preferred by Mary Moffat and her ilk, this "traditional," ethnicized costume owed much to Nonconformist influence. But, insofar as it did, it turned its back on the other side of mission ideology: the injunction to aspire to newly individuated identities through (ever more refined) consumption and sartorial self-fashioning. Second, as a reaction to colonial evangelism, female folk dress seems to have spoken, simultaneously, in opposing registers. On the one hand, it appears, outwardly, to have accommodated to the ideology and moral regulation of the mission. On the other, it gave voice to a form of symbolic self-assertion, albeit modest and muted. For, even as they put on Christian garments, most Tswana women insisted on retaining distinctively non-European—distinctly *setswana*—elements of style in their dress. And this in the face of active discouragement on the part of the church.

Let us explore this last practice further, since it underscores some of the symbolic complexities of the colonial encounter. It also illustrates quite how subtle may be indigenous responses to the European outreach. And quite how much by way of African self-assertion may be missed by inattention to the silent practices of the everyday lives of ordinary people.

It is clear, from both merchant records and Victorian photographs, that store-bought cotton and woolen blankets became an integral part of Tswana costume during the second half of the nineteenth century. These objects were called *dikobò*, Setswana for the skin cloaks that had once been so important in marking social identity (by contrast to coats and jackets, which were known by their Dutch term, *baatje* or *baki*). Here, as elsewhere in South Africa, they were a key ingredient, among the motley mix of African and European elements, in the creation of a specifically "ethnic" garb (Tyrrell 1968: 93). Nguni women in the eastern Cape, for instance, dyed them with ocher and made them into skirts, breastcloths, and capes, the stuff of a refurbished "native" style; it distinguished those who wore it, as "red" or "blanket" people, from members of the church (cf. Shaw 1974: 102; see above). This defiantly self-conscious use of the blanket as a sign of so-called "tribalism" was quite unlike that found in Sotho-Tswana communities. There it was put on as an outer mantle over European garments, by Christians and non-Christians alike, completing the everyday peasant wardrobe—and enclosing all its wearers in an outer layer of *setswana*. The difference between the two usages seems to have echoed fundamental dissimilarities in the way in which these populations were drawn into the regional political economy (J. Comaroff 1985: 30).

For many Tswana, the mode of fastening store-bought blankets replicated earlier, gendered practices. As with karosses, men's were secured at the shoulder, women's across the breast—albeit with the all-purpose safety pin (cf. Tyrrell 1968: 93). While there is little information on the colors favored by Tswana in the late nineteenth century, later records show that they preferred fancy patterns, especially those incorporating white and red. These contrasted with the sober blues and blacks that still dominated the rest of their attire (Schapera 1947: 228, 230). Comparative evidence, most notably from among Southern So-tho, suggests that blankets disclose much about aesthetic volatilities. Some time back, Tyrrell (1968: 93) noted that, while their basic function had varied little over the previous century, "fashions" in shade and design had shifted a good deal. Balinese imports, introduced by a German trader, were popular early on, only to be eclipsed by the "Victoria" line, which depicted the "beloved" British queen. It is ironic, in light of this history, that Moshweshwe, the heroic Sotho king, once declared his people to be as close to the English sovereign "as the lice in her blanket" (Tyrrell 1968: 91). Manufacturers have often used historical images in their efforts to shape local taste: airplanes and bombs commemorated World War II; the crown and scepter marked a royal

visit to Basutoland in 1947; more recently, "Freedom," "Lesotho," and "Independence" have been included in various motifs. How precisely these signs were, and are, interpreted remains uncertain; although it has been said that, in the past, African consumers have read them differently from the way their producers anticipated, paying more heed to color and overall effect than to imagistic detail (Tyrrell 1968: 91).

Among Southern Tswana, factory-produced blankets had all but replaced skin cloaks by 1900. And they continued to be worn late into the twentieth century in both ritual and everyday contexts. This in spite of the opprobrium of the evangelists, who objected to the blanket just as they had done to the kaross; as Wookey noted in the 1880s, they occasionally tried to proscribe its use entirely: "We have had to make a rule that no man shall be allowed to the ordinances who comes in a dirty blanket instead of a clean jacket or shirt. The latter, except for laziness, are as easily procured as the former." If cleanliness was next to Godliness, what was clean was European! Aesthetic ethnocentrism masqueraded, here, as moral virtue.

The battle over the blanket was, truly, a cultural struggle. Blankets shared one attribute, above all others, with skin karosses: their versatility. That is why they offended the missionaries, for whom the refinement, civility, and aesthetics of dress depended on the functional specificity of particular garments: on their being put on in a particular manner, at particular times, by particular people, over particular parts of the body, for particular activities. That is also why the Christians were so amused and irritated when Africans wore articles of clothing—indefinite rather than definite articles, that is—in ways for which they were not designed. And why *dikobò*, coverings of assertively undifferentiated form and function, could not but appear primitive in their eyes. For the Tswana, by contrast, it was their very capacity to serve as an all-purpose, enveloping mantle that commended these objects. Notwithstanding earlier evangelical efforts, ordinary people had neither the desire nor the means for a wide range of highly specialized manufactures. They purchased a limited number of commodities, *dikobò* among them, with which to craft ensembles that had to serve many ends; ensembles that varied little with season or occasion. Blankets, having the virtue of flexibility, could be worn as warm, yet easily removable, apparel—a second might be pinned around the waist in cold weather—and could also be wrapped about the upper body to cradle babies. In addition, they provided bedding on the road and ground sheets on which to sit, and were sometimes tied to poles or leafless trees for shade. So they were regarded as indispensable by labor migrants, of whose predicament they were iconic: *dikobò* were put to one set of uses en route to town, another while in the city, and yet another on return to the rural reserve. Not surprisingly, vehicles of mass transport were popular motifs.

Here, then, the topography of contrast. On one side, a European sensibility according to which, broadly speaking, the more specific the use to which something was put, the more refined the object, the more cultured the practice, the more civilized the person. On the other, the old Tswana penchant for multi-functionality, which associated versatility and plasticity with use-value, social worth, and, often, beauty. These two poles—both tendencies, of course, neither of them simple lived realities—charted the terrain of everyday practice. All Tswana, according to their means, abilities, backgrounds, and tastes, found themselves navigating that terrain, ever more so as the colonial world hemmed them in. Nor was this confined to the domain of cloth and clothing, fabric and fashion. It expressed itself as forcibly in the realm of architecture and domestic life.

In sum, while Tswana elites followed the dictates of European fashion, seeking to master *sekgoa* in the cause of *embourgeoisement*, the dress of ordinary people was a product of cultural patchwork. Cultivated against missionary opposition, their bricolage was wrought in increasingly confined spaces, with mass-produced materials garnered through an imperial market that pervaded their lives. As the early African creations, so bizarre to the foreign eye (cf. H. Kuper 1973: 335), gave way to a more lasting colonial "native" style, Tswana men put on their khaki clothes, took up their blankets, and moved between country and city in growing numbers. A few youngbloods, home after contracts, sported flashy wardrobes bought at urban stores. But most migrants lacked the means for such purchases, even if they had wanted to make them. For the majority, only blankets domesticated the prescribed uniform of the workplace, distinguishing the garb of African peasant-proletarians as fringe citizens of the modern world order.

Their womenfolk, on the other hand, refashioned the dress of *setswana*, wearing a costume that fixed them on palpably "ethnic" ground. Some of its features would endure for decades. This style bore the imprint of Christian moral discipline, yet it retained, in its blanketed elegance, a sense of distinct origins, even an aura of independence and reserve. While Tswana females had internalized many of the signs and dispositions *sekgoa*, they drew on them to give voice to their own condition. They had been absorbed into a nation-state in which they were not citizens; into a city-centered world that refused them a permanent urban home; into a universal "civilization" that depicted them as tribal, parochial, different in kind. Although they had to work with materials bequeathed them by the colonial political economy, they did not just buy into the ready-made persona offered to them. In this, their attire was symbolic of their general situation. And through it they represented themselves volubly: fabricated largely from foreign materials, it nonetheless expressed a locally tooled identity that elaborated on the vicissitudes of their history. The apparent conservatism of their costume echoed the fact that they had, in many respects, been made hostage to a newly politicized "tradition." But it also spoke of the effort to conserve a particular mode of life. And, like the continuing Tswana attachment to cattle, it implied an unwillingness to be seduced by the restless dream of social advancement through endless consumption.

Just after the turn of this century, at a time when more and more Tswana were donning their new uniforms of class and color and gendered ethnicity, Georg Simmel ([1904] 1971[a]: 305) observed: "It is peculiarly characteristic of fashion that it renders possible a social obedience, which at the same time is a form of individual differentiation." In a single sentence, Simmel captured the original intent, and the ideological imperative, behind the mission effort to redress Tswana. His genius was to see how intricately connected were style and stratification, individualism and social interdependence—and how the delicate balance between self-expression and collective constraint was mediated, in everyday life, by such things as the cut of one's coat. What he could not have grasped in full, however, is just what happens when these connections and processes cross cultural frontiers, there to become the object of other kinds of politics and social assertion. In Simmel's own cosmopolitan milieu, the lines of class and distinction were well-grooved; the fashion system ran along familiar contours, even if it sometimes moved in mysterious ways. In colonial South Africa—where cultural exchanges and struggles were part of a society under construction—style did not *reflect* existing realities. It was part of their very making, part of the fabrication of a world divided along newly sharpened axes of discrimination and difference. And, today, of ethnic pride. Which is why its significance endures, if in altered form, in the current world of positively valued identities.

24

THE AO DAI GOES GLOBAL:
How international influences and female entrepreneurs have shaped Vietnam's "national costume"

Ann Marie Leshkowich

On 10 September 1995, the Miss International Pageant in Tokyo awarded the prize for "Best National Costume" to Miss Vietnam, Truong Quynh Mai. The Vietnam Airlines flight attendant wore a blue and white silk brocade *ao dai* (pronounced "ow-zai") consisting of three elements: (1) a long, close-fitting tunic with mandarin collar and high slits up the side seams, (2) loose pants, and (3) a donut-shaped coiled hat. The outfit is often referred to as Vietnam's traditional or national costume. Today, a formal ao dai like Miss Vietnam's is typically worn by brides, performers, and models, and on special occasions. Worn without the hat and fashioned from less sumptuous fabric, the ao dai is a common uniform for civil servants, tour guides, hotel and restaurant workers, and high school students.

Within Vietnam, Miss Vietnam's victory was heralded as more than simply a prize for a beautiful outfit. An article in Vietnam's fashion press described the ao dai as symbolizing Vietnam's "national soul" that had "once again been honored in front of thousands of international spectators" in Tokyo (*Thoi Trang Tre* October 1995: 43). By affirming the ao dai as the embodiment of Vietnam's traditions and signifying the country's incorporation into the modern global community, Truong Quynh Mai's award represented a victory for her entire homeland.

International recognition boosted the ao dai's domestic appeal. While Miss Vietnam was accepting her award in Tokyo, I was living in Ho Chi Minh City in order to study female traders in the cloth and clothing industry (Leshkowich 2000). Within days of Miss Vietnam's victory, many of the market stalls and tailor shops where I conducted my research had posted pictures and signs promising customers custom-made ao dai "just like Miss Vietnam's." While these signs testify to many entrepreneurs' speed in capitalizing on a potentially lucrative news event, the Miss Vietnam advertisements and increased interest in ao dai are in fact part of a larger effort by Vietnamese designers and sellers to market the garment as a domestic product that has earned the approval of foreign fashion experts, thus making it both traditional and stylish, or what Vietnamese tellingly call *"mo-den"* a term taken from the English word "modern."

While global circumstances have prompted nations around the world to develop and promote a "traditional costume," understanding Vietnam's ao dai craze requires attention to a second question: why has this particular garment been selected to portray Vietnam on the international stage? The answer lies in the garment's history. Although the ao dai has become synonymous with traditional Vietnamese culture and feminine virtues, the garment in fact has a relatively brief history marked throughout by significant foreign influence—first Chinese, then French and American. I suggest that the ao dai can best be viewed as

Adapted from Ann Marie Leshkowich, "How International Influences and Female Entrepreneurs Have Shaped Vietnam's "National Costume," in *Re-Orienting Fashion: The Globalization of Asian Dress.* Sandra Niessen, Ann Marie Leshkowich, and Carla Jones (London: Bloomsbury, 2003), pp. 79–116.

possessing a hybrid character. In today's environment of globalization that demands and structures standardized displays of cultural distinctiveness into a kind of homogenized heterogeneity, the ao dai's hybridity makes it particularly well suited to convey comprehensible and compelling messages about Vietnam's national character to both domestic and foreign audiences. In this capacity, it also serves as a vehicle for debating the positive and negative effects of globalization on Vietnamese cultural identities.

NATIONAL COSTUMES AND THE GLOBAL CIRCULATION OF DIFFERENCE

One of the most striking features of globalization is the frequency, speed, and ease with which people and things from different parts of the world come into contact with each other. Given that this contact has largely been prompted by capitalist forces originating from Europe and North America, most early observers of globalization found cause to be concerned that the encounter between different things and people would be a homogenizing one in which non-Western cultures would be transformed in the West's image. Something about this contact, however, led not to the erasure of difference, but to its validation. In today's global economy of mass-produced goods, the new and the unique have come to be prized as such, and possessing such items or knowledge about them marks one's status as a facile navigator of global cultural "scapes" (Appadurai 1990, 1996).

This development is a double-edged sword. On the one hand, an appreciative global audience for such things as African art, Chinese acupuncture, and Indonesian textiles leads to the continued use and production of those items or practices. On the other hand, what may seem a practical feature of globalization—the ability to encounter and appreciate difference—has in fact become an ideological technique for maintaining power. As with colonialism and Orientalism in past centuries, globalization has been a vehicle for serving up elements of the world so that these features can be assessed and appreciated by cognoscenti. The effect is what Jones and I refer to as "homogenized heterogeneity" or what Richard Wilk (1995) has called

"structures of common difference": certain types of diversity are picked up and placed into categories so that they can be understood and controlled. We might think of this as a kind of patchwork quilt of cultural diversity. The color and pattern of each square may be individually or locally produced, but the way they are stitched together, the overall structure of the quilt, the commissioning and placement of each square, and even the very idea that a quilt should be constructed at all—these decisions are all controlled by globalization's powerful centers, typically located in North America and Western Europe.

Homogenized heterogeneity is perhaps most evident in the idea of a "national costume." It has become standard practice at international events such as the Olympics, beauty contests, world's fairs, visits by foreign dignitaries, and even international policy meetings for different groups to display their identities through the donning of traditional dress, usually by women. Participation in the global community in fact seems to require as a price of admission that each member develop and be prepared to display a costume that visually signals its history and distinctiveness so that it can be remembered and understood as it circulates through staged displays of global culture. Although the national costume's status as an unspoken requirement might seem oppressive, peoples distant from global power centers more often seem to interpret it as a chance to capture the attention and respect of a global audience, however stereotypically or fleetingly. To have one's cultural identity validated, even when one does not control and may be ambivalent about the process of display, can nonetheless be a desirable achievement.

While the presentation of a national costume on a global stage is an interesting site for exploring the commodification and circulation of cultural diversity, I am even more fascinated by the impact of such displays on the home audience. What happens when the traditional costume, now bearing the stamp of global approval, returns to its purportedly original context? How do the supposed owners of the traditional costume respond to it? Addressing these questions requires attention to another site for the circulation of difference: a domestic context in which national identity, images of traditional femininity, the lure of international power, and the simultaneous desire for "local" authenticity and modern cosmopolitanism mingle to shape perceptions of the so-called national costume. For the ao dai, these conditions have combined to make the national costume a trendy fashion, as processes of "self-exoticizing" (Kondo 1997; Savigliano 1995; Tarlo 1996) lead young, urban Vietnamese women and the media to see and newly appreciate the ao dai as outsiders might. It is in this way that people, particularly women, become globalized consumers of externally produced versions of the traditions that appear to be uniquely theirs.

Attention to the international and domestic circulation of national costumes thus challenges the image of tradition as localized, timeless, authentic, or uniquely the product of the group with which it is associated. We come to see that people wear or appreciate these outfits, not because they are performing some kind of essentialized identity, but because they have acquired global cultural criteria for discerning the value of specific visions of their own traditions. In addition, by showing women in places such as Vietnam participating in the globalized consumption of fashion, such a project challenges another cherished notion: that Third World women are involved in globalization exclusively as oppressed, localized producers.

USING CIRCULATION TO CHALLENGE PRODUCER/CONSUMER BINARIES

One of the most popular ideologies of globalization is that it has fostered an increasingly stark dichotomy between First World citizens as consumers and Third World citizens as producers of the items consumed in the First World.

According to this account, the rise of consumption in the European and North American societies of the so-called First World (or what Wallerstein (1974) calls the "center") has been accomplished through the expansion of global systems of capitalist production that exploit workers in the Third World ("the periphery"). As feminist scholars have pointed out, this gap between First World consumer and Third World producer is often gendered, so that a contrast emerges between the housewife as the prototypical First World consumer and the Third World factory worker as a young woman with "nimble fingers, slow wit" (Ong 1987: 151) whose disempowered status as a woman makes her particularly vulnerable to exploitation in the workplace.

With respect to clothing, this logic of globalization has become so prevalent that just about any consumer of clothing in the United States expects items bearing a "Made in X" (i.e., not "the USA") label to have been created by oppressed Third World women working under harsh conditions. It is for this reason that students of mine are often surprised by my pictures of a Ho Chi Minh City marketplace that show female vendors proudly displaying their stock of Levi's jeans, both genuine and fake. The conventional wisdom about the global circulation of Levi's does not include the possibility that Third World persons can be active agents of consumption, let alone a part of global culture partaking of and reinterpreting fashion knowledge generated in the First World.

The image of those same young Vietnamese women wearing ao dai sits more comfortably. Wearing ao dai "fits" Vietnamese women, for they are consuming the clothing that has rightfully been bequeathed to them through history. Such a conclusion is deceptive, for the ao dai's history and contemporary examples of its manufacture and use, as I describe below, demonstrate that the decision to wear an ao dai is just as influenced by global fashion trends as is the decision to buy Levi's.

Whether Third World women wear ao dai or Levi's, recognizing that they are not just producers of fashion but globally aware consumers whose choices fuel fashion trends does not necessarily simplify our interpretation of their actions. When they are doing so with respect to a supposedly traditional item of clothing, understanding their intentions and the effects of their actions becomes even more complicated. Consider a young female Vietnamese garment worker who uses part of her earnings to buy an ao dai to wear to a special event. Is she expressing her identity as a traditional Vietnamese woman, an identity that has remained largely unchanged, despite the transformations wrought by colonialism, war, socialism, and globalization? Or, is she responding to the international recognition of the ao dai as a beautiful Vietnamese national costume that has made "ethnic chic" trendy? Is the ao dai an expression of her personal taste? Or, is she buying one because she's been told (by elders, by peers, by the media) that she must have one because it is appropriate for a certain occasion?

Faced with such an act of consumption, I find myself asking why we should be forced to choose between these divergent interpretations. The consumption of fashion is not simply a system ordained by some invisible panel of experts, nor is it an unconstrained process of individual selection or identity construction. Answering these questions requires looking beyond the act of consumption to try to understand the forces and processes that enable that consumption. What is needed is attention to contexts in which production and consumption, global symbolic meanings, and local interpretations appear simultaneously and are mediated through the agency of individuals.

Circulation is one such arena. Through the circulation of clothing items in marketplaces, shopping malls, and curbside venues, consumers confront products, form and realize consumption preferences, and provide retailers with valuable cues about fashion trends. By documenting how small-scale traders and tailors in Ho Chi Minh City design and market Vietnam's national costume to their customers, I wish to demonstrate the utility of a focus on the circulation of fashion. Located between various sets of extremes—the local and the global, the traditional and the modern, production and consumption—the traders I studied serve as cross-cultural translators and fashion mediators. These processes of mediation depend in large part upon and are facilitated by exchanges of information, money, and fashion materials among traders, tailors, and their overseas kin. A major theme emerges from this account: contrary to images of petty traders as mere drones in the retail network, the successful Ho Chi Minh City stallholders and boutique owners I met participate in global networks of circulation and have capitalized on them in order to fashion themselves as what Ulf Hannerz (1990) has described as savvy cosmopolitans: skillful cross-cultural translators of style positioned at the heart of

the formation of consumer tastes. What is perhaps most surprising about this example is not just that female stallholders and their middle-class customers in Vietnam are embracing cosmopolitan orientations toward fashion, but that they are doing so with respect to a garment supposed to be the quintessential emblem of Vietnam's enduring cultural distinctiveness. While this is obviously a feature of contemporary globalization, the history of the ao dai reveals that the garment has long played this same role of helping Vietnamese both fit into and distinguish themselves from powerful foreign cultures.

THE AO DAI ON THE WORLD STAGE

While growing wealth has certainly enabled Vietnamese consumers to increase their consumption of clothing and other consumer goods, the hyperbolic nationalistic rhetoric surrounding discussion of the ao dai suggests that this particular commodity carries a significant cultural load. The ao dai is a polyvalent symbol that both embodies Vietnamese identity and represents it to others. To the domestic Vietnamese audience, Miss Vietnam's award in Tokyo signaled that the ao dai has become part of the international language of fashion. This in turn has created two pressures, each of which presents drawbacks and opportunities.

The first pressure centers on the desire and injunction for cross-cultural communication. On the positive side, economic openness in the form of trade and foreign investment draws Vietnamese into systems of relationships that afford the opportunity to display Vietnamese culture to foreigners in a sort of free marketplace that places a premium on authenticity and distinctiveness. Miss Vietnam was one of forty-nine equal contestants—a metaphor for Vietnam being one of many countries whose traditions and history deserve outsiders' respect and appreciation.

The drawback is that something gets lost in the process of representation and translation. Communication of culture involves modification, and this can lead to static images in which the rich heritage being represented becomes flattened or caricaturish. The ao dai becomes a kind of free-floating symbol available to non-Vietnamese to be picked up and reinterpreted. This was already evident in the early 1990s, when the movie *Indochine* inspired an Asian-themed fashion trend known as Indo-chic. Taking the ao dai and the more common peasant outfit of brown or black pajamas as cues, design houses such as Chanel and Richard Tyler released their own variations. A *New York Times Magazine* fashion spread made the cycle complete by taking these clothes to Vietnam, where they were modeled by regular Vietnamese women. From the perspective of Vietnamese observers, the problem with such acts of translation and reinterpretation is that the clothing code associated with the garments' Vietnamese origins becomes garbled. A photograph taken in Ho Chi Minh City's colonial post office paired a lavish ao dai with a peasant conical hat—a combination that would be incongruous in daily Vietnamese life. The mandarin collar and frog closures originally celebrated as the height of modesty by a conservative Confucian dynasty were now described for Western eyes as "like erotic flash points" (Shenon 1993).

With cross-cultural communication, therefore, comes a loss of control over the meaning of the items being displayed and the risk that their integrity will be compromised or degraded. While the ao dai's history suggests that such integrity is in fact chimerical, for there has never been a single, pure form of the garment, the outfit's current availability as one style among many on the international market raises the stakes involved in the myth of authenticity, even as it makes that myth harder to maintain.

The second pressure comes from the opportunity that allowing foreign goods into Vietnam affords for borrowing and adapting ideas, developing exciting new clothes, and marketing items that the public will view as raising its quality of life. One man who has taken advantage of the opportunities offered by Vietnam's open markets is an artist named Si Hoang, who by the mid-1990s had become one of Saigon's top ao dai designers. Si Hoang's ao dai designs first appeared at the Miss Ao Dai competition in 1989. Credited as the first designer to paint, rather than embroider, the ao dai, he has liberally borrowed from non-Vietnamese artistic movements. From the West, he has adopted features of abstract art, such as in a recent collection of ao dai inspired by Picasso and Matisse. Closer to home,

Si Hoang has turned to the ethnic minority groups living in Vietnam's highlands. In 1996 he released a collection of painted velvet ao dai that employed motifs from these groups' weavings. When I spoke to him at the time, he was working on a show that would feature ao dai inspired by each of Vietnam's fifty-four ethnic groups.

Just as foreign embracing of the ao dai sparks a fear that outsiders will misinterpret the garment's meaning, experiments with foreign influences by designers such as Si Hoang lead to the parallel fear that Vietnamese themselves might forget which version of the ao dai is "authentic" and thus lose this cherished form. Si Hoang himself seems acutely sensitive to such concerns. He repeatedly emphasized in our conversation that his designs consist exclusively of decorative innovations, such as painting or buttons. He has not tampered with what he refers to as the traditional design of the ao dai: "I think that the ao dai we have had up to now, its design has already reached perfection. If I changed the way of tailoring or designing it, then it wouldn't be an ao dai anymore, but something like the cheongsam of China or a dress worn by Westerners." To Si Hoang, then, the ao dai's form is what makes it quintessentially Vietnamese.

While Si Hoang asserts that the authenticity of the ao dai lies in its form, the history that I recounted above—one which is well-documented by Vietnamese and French historians—suggests that the ao dai's shape evolved in foreign influence throughout its history, now becomes celebrated as the pinnacle of a Vietnamese tradition that must be carefully protected against undue outside influence, even as it simultaneously serves as a vehicle for encountering and mediating that influence by representing Vietnam in the global organization of cultural diversity.

In the rhetoric of contemporary cultural politics, the ao dai's protean identity as partly foreign and yet uniquely Vietnamese makes it a contingent and contested symbol susceptible to hyperbolic assertions of its "true" nature. Precisely because the meaning of the ao dai seems to originate from so many sources, it facilitates a discourse in which diverse people can participate. With its flowing lines and mandarin collar, it seems exotic to foreign fashion cognoscenti, but the

French colonial influences on its cut and design mute this effect. Unlike other Vietnamese customs, such as teeth lacquering or betel-nut chewing, the ao dai is exotic enough to be enchanting, but not so Other as to be inaccessible or unpalatable.

The garment has a similar effect on domestic audiences. The ao dai is uniquely Vietnamese in that no other culture wears the costume on a regular basis, but part of its attraction lies in the fact that it is not an ordinary garment made banal by its prevalence in daily life. It occupies a middle ground between the foreign and the domestic that makes it well suited to represent Vietnamese resilience and the ingenuity required to incorporate outside ideas without losing one's identity. This hybrid character, rather than the ao dai's purported indigenousness, makes it the quintessential symbol of Vietnamese identity. That such a Vietnamese cultural icon is now celebrated by international audiences rather than demeaned as inferior, as was the case for other elements of Vietnamese society during the centuries of Chinese and French occupation, adds to its domestic appeal. The ao dai, like Vietnam, has arrived on the international stage.

TO MARKET, TO MARKET: HOW TRADERS MARKET AND CONSUMERS SELECT AO DAI

The average Vietnamese consumer purchases an ao dai in one of two ways: either she goes to a tailor, chooses a fabric from her inventory, and has her sew it, or she goes to a market, picks out the fabric herself, and then takes it to a tailor. The former offers convenience, while the latter offers greater selection and cheaper prices. As part of my dissertation research, I spent a year observing daily life in both these settings. My research focused on Ben Thanh market, a large and famous structure located in the center of Ho Chi Minh City. Offering just about everything the average Saigon consumer might need, Ben Thanh contains over 150 stalls selling fabric and 350 specializing in clothing. Women own and run approximately 85 per cent of these stalls. On the higher end of the retail spectrum are Saigon's downtown tailor shops. Also largely run by women, these shops cater to both foreign tourists and wealthier locals. In both settings, I spoke at length with

merchants about how they selected and marketed their goods. I also observed hundreds of transactions with customers in order to get a sense of what features they sought and the strategies sellers employed to clinch the purchase.

As Saigon consumers become more fashion-conscious, the sellers of cloth and clothing in Ben Thanh market make a concerted effort to persuade a customer that a given item is the newest, most "mo-den," and best suited for her particular coloring and figure. To do this, they often copy the designs of famous makers such as Si Hoang or use props such as catalogs and fashion magazines to convince the buyer of the popularity of a particular item. One day while I was speaking to a stall owner who specialized in ao dai fabrics, two customers, a mother and daughter, approached. They were looking for ao dai fabric for the daughter, a woman in her early thirties. The initial stages of the transaction focused on what color and styles would be appropriate for the daughter's coloring, with green emerging as the consensus choice. The seller held up each of the panels being considered and wrapped them tightly around her chest in order to show the customers how the hand-painted design would look on the bosom and flowing toward the ground. She also showed the buyers "catalogs," which consisted of photo albums she had assembled herself from a variety of snapshots and Vietnamese fashion magazines. She mentioned that the panel in which the buyers seemed most interested was copied from a design by Si Hoang. Throughout the exchange, the potential customers maintained a rather cynical stance toward such claims, but they finally selected precisely the panel that the seller had identified as based on a mo-den Si Hoang design.

Like most other sellers in Ben Thanh market, this stallholder had carefully selected the panels displayed in her stall in accordance with her reading of local consumer tastes. She then marketed her designs as cheaper versions of these prestigious mo-den items. As the shopping encounter described above illustrates however, the trader was not simply supplying items to meet pre-formulated consumer demands. Rather, she was an active shaper of ideas about what constitutes the mo-den and fashionable. Like most customers

I met, the mother-daughter pair in this transaction came to the stall with vague preferences as to ao dai color and design. They actively solicited the trader's advice about how to concretize these desires, although they carefully cloaked their need for information in an air of indifference that would strengthen their bargaining position as the transaction moved toward a conclusion. Despite their skepticism, the consumers seemed swayed by the trader's performative display of fashion knowledge, particularly her familiarity with Si Hoang's designs and ability to produce evidence in the form of homemade catalogs to substantiate her claims. This marketplace encounter thus entailed a transformative process of negotiation and exchange in which a certain knowledge about the desirability of a Si Hoang design was produced. Two consumers who may previously have had only vague ideas about Si Hoang and his designs left the stall obviously pleased with their decision to partake of this fashion trend, while the trader subsequently decided to devote even more of her stall to knock-offs of designer creations.

In addition to copying famous local designers, many Ben Thanh market traders pay close attention to the tastes of overseas Vietnamese who comprise a significant portion of their customer base. In the year 2000, over 300,000 overseas Vietnamese visited Vietnam (*The Saigon Times Daily*, 10 January 2001). Most of these visitors stayed in the South, as this region had previously been their home and many of their relatives remain there today. As Saigon's most famous market, Ben Thanh is a popular stop for visitors, and most make sure to buy ao dai fabric for themselves, their relatives, and their friends abroad. At the end of December 1996, one fabric seller told me that the vast majority of her customers during the past few weeks had been returning Vietnamese. Climatic and cultural differences between Vietnam and the temperate regions where most overseas Vietnamese now live have prompted ao dai fabric sellers in Ben Thanh to stock a greater array of fabrics, particularly heavier ones such as velvet and thick brocade. They also offer more daring styles, such as flocked velvet, in which bits of pulverized material create a pattern against a sheer, see-through background. Designs have likewise become bolder, with velvet panels decorated with lavishly sequined dragons or phoenixes becoming increasingly popular. Finally, because many overseas Vietnamese prefer ao dai with the tunic and pants sewn from matching fabric rather than the customary white or black, many stalls now stock a wide array of undecorated ao dai fabric.

Overseas Vietnamese also have a direct influence on Saigon tailors' ao dai designs. During the late 1970s and early 1980s, when the ao dai had fallen out of favor in Vietnam, overseas Vietnamese in the United States continued to experiment with style innovations. A student of mine who grew up near Little Saigon in southern California recalls the 1980s as a time when Vietnamese-Americans wanted to make the ao dai look more "Western." Fashion shows featured puffy sleeves and sweetheart necklines, or even more daring variations, such as sleeveless and one-sleeved tunics. While most Vietnamese returning to have ao dai made in Vietnam request the more "authentic" traditional form, some do voice a preference for a different neckline, a certain cut, or a particular length. The resulting styles transform the ao dai into something closer to an evening gown, as befits the special occasions for which most overseas Vietnamese will wear the garment. The tailors with whom I spoke in downtown Ho Chi Minh City told me that while some of these designs might not be appropriate for domestic tastes, others could be adapted. Some described overseas Vietnamese ao dai as more luxurious (*sang trong*)—a fitting symbol of Vietnam's prosperity and the aspirations of many middle-class Vietnamese to the kind of lifestyles they imagine their kinfolk enjoying abroad.

CIRCULATING FASHION KNOWLEDGE WITHIN THE DIASPORA

While overseas Vietnamese customers play a role in traders' and tailors' selection of ao dai merchandise, the overseas Vietnamese population with whom these businesswomen have the most frequent and prolonged contact are their relatives. By the late 1990s, remittance flows between the nearly three million Vietnamese émigrés and their kin in Vietnam were widely estimated to exceed one billion US dollars annually. More than 80 per cent of this money was sent directly to individuals, rather than being invested in official development projects. While much of this money is used to cover day-to-day living expenses or one-time expenditures, such as a new television or motorbike, many of the tailors and traders I know use remittances as investment capital for their businesses. Perhaps even more significantly, the packages relatives mail back to Vietnam contain more than money. In addition to letters, Vietnamese resettled abroad regularly send foreign videos, CDs, fashion catalogs, magazines, and snapshots of daily life or special occasions in their adopted countries. For small-scale fashion entrepreneurs, these materials provide a valuable source of information about international clothing styles and trends, and they waste no time in capitalizing on this knowledge. Tuyet, Mai, and Tien provide three typical examples of the ways in which capital and information from overseas Vietnamese can facilitate the development of small businesses.

On one of my first shopping excursions when I arrived in Saigon in 1994, I visited nearly every store located on the main strip of tailor shops along Dong Khoi Street. After seeing about a dozen nearly identical displays of merchandise, I entered a large boutique featuring more colorful and innovative styles. Fashioned from the same materials—raw silk, brocade, and light silk—as the clothes in neighboring shops, the items in this store blended Western clothing forms and colors with Vietnamese accents. Thinking that this store featured the most chic and up-to-date styles, I asked the owner, Tuyet, about the origins of the designs; she replied that they were all her own creations. A woman in her late thirties, Tuyet had worked as a secretary for a state firm until about five years before. Noticing the rapid increase in tourists and explosion of domestic consumerism, she opened her tailoring and clothing store with capital pooled from immediate and extended family living both within and outside Vietnam. Tuyet's sister, who lives in Seattle, has encouraged her to expand her business and regularly sends her newspaper columns and magazine spreads about fashion trends. Tuyet prides herself on providing superior-quality silks and designing styles that appeal equally to Vietnamese and foreigners for wear in business and professional settings. While she also offers standard tourist articles, she sees her future success as lying in cross-cultural styles that transcend kitsch. Right before my return to the United States, she told me that her sister had offered to help her open a boutique in Seattle.

Mai and Tuan are a married couple in their forties who own a large clothing stall in Ben Thanh market that specializes in a variety of women's clothes, including dresses, suits, tops, and leggings. Mai designs all of the clothes herself. Her three younger sisters help with the sewing and patterns. Mai has been selling clothing for over twenty years. A college student when the North Vietnamese army captured Saigon in 1975, Mai was forced to leave school when her father, a colonel in the South Vietnamese army, was sent to a reeducation camp and her mother was forcibly relocated to the Mekong Delta. To support her siblings, she started selling clothing on the black market. At that time, most of Mai's goods were smuggled items sent into the country by Vietnamese who had escaped abroad. Mai slowly developed her business and acquired a stall in Ben Thanh market in the mid-1980s. After several unsuccessful attempts to flee Vietnam, Tuan eventually joined Mai full-time in running the stall. Their business has grown steadily since the advent of economic reforms in 1989.

Both Mai and Tuan pay close attention to new styles, particularly to catalogs that friends and relatives in the United States send them. Mai often adapts drawings from Vogue, Butterick, or Simplicity catalogs, which she then promotes to her customers as "sewn from a catalog just sent from America." With an average turnaround time of less than a week, Mai can quickly translate the newest foreign styles into items that she knows will appeal to her loyal customer base of small shop owners and other traders. Tuan's sister lives in North Carolina and occasionally sends them some money, but the amounts are small and typically intended to help support Tuan's elderly parents. Nevertheless, Mai and Tuan dream of expanding their business, and their overseas relatives and friends form a key part of the plan. Tuan explains:

> I would like to open a factory, but I don't have the facility yet. In the future, I think that the piece of land

Mai and I have bought could serve as the production plant. We'll buy machines and then have some other workers work from their homes. We could have about thirty people working for us, that would be good. Most of our customers would be domestic, but we also have so many friends and relatives [overseas] who can help us with the American market. They know fashion, they know what styles are popular there with the *Viet Kieu* [overseas Vietnamese], who like goods produced in their homeland. They'd help us be able to sell and develop, and we would also make clothes cheaply following catalogs. The clothing would be popular and the price would be right, not too expensive.

Like Mai and Tuan, Tien, who owns a stall in one of Ho Chi Minh City's wholesale markets, sees his overseas relatives as a key resource helping him to expand the women's clothing and pajama business that he owns with his wife. Tien's mother-in-law has lived in the United States for ten years and recently sent the family a computer, complete with graphics programs to help Tien design clothing. She regularly mails Tien fashion catalogs such as McCall's, which he credits as the primary source of inspiration for his designs. Although a computer and occasional catalogs may seem like a relatively small contribution to Tien's business, Tien describes these kinds of exchanges as essential to maintaining his competitive edge: "In this way, *Viet Kieu* send back some of their gray matter [i.e., their knowledge and skills] to help us out in Vietnam."

While Tuyet, Mai, and Tien sell mostly Western-style clothing, information and goods received from overseas Vietnamese can also help traders reinvent supposedly traditional merchandise. The Ben Thanh ao dai trader described above freely admitted to copying a Si Hoang design; indeed the resemblance of her and other traders' items to Si Hoang creations makes them considerably more attractive to their customers and likely results in higher profits. I have also documented trends in ao dai styles and fabrics that I believe originated with overseas Vietnamese customers' preferences. Occasionally, I would hear a Ben Thanh trader tell a domestic customer that a type of fabric she seemed interested in was "very *mo-den*.

The *Viet Kieu* who come back to visit home buy this type of fabric a lot." Downtown tailor shops stock many types of ao dai panels, and I have also heard boutique owners tell prospective customers that an overseas Vietnamese had just bought a large quantity of a certain style. The implication is that the style is somehow trendier or more fashionable because a Vietnamese living overseas, who presumably has more cosmopolitan tastes, selected it.

Unlike Mai's touting of her fashions as inspired by American catalogs, traders' statements about the ao dai's appeal to overseas Vietnamese stop short of suggesting that the ao dai designs themselves have anything but a local origin. One explanation may be that their statements are accurate; the ao dai is simply a homegrown product that is little affected by input from outside sources. My research, however, suggests a different interpretation. Given the variety and importance of traders' contacts with overseas Vietnamese in other aspects of their fashion businesses, it would be naive to assume that these relations have no bearing on their ao dai designs. Indeed, occasional offhand comments and my observations in the marketplace suggest that these interactions do have an impact on the ao dai. Unlike other articles of clothing, such as dresses, skirts, pants, and suits, however, the ao dai is a symbolically charged item whose appeal rests largely on its associations with Vietnam's national history and character. Just as Si Hoang downplays Chinese, French, or American fashion sensibilities in asserting that the ao dai evolved directly from the Vietnamese *ao tu than,* small-scale ao dai sellers are reluctant to admit that they have been influenced by overseas Vietnamese tastes or by ao dai-inspired styles from the foreign designers who have promoted Indo-chic. So much of the ao dai's cultural currency stems from its aura of supposed indigenous authenticity that too much discussion of the impact of foreign ideas, or even overseas Vietnamese tastes, might contaminate the article and threaten tailors' and stallholders' positions as its purveyors.

In representing an ao dai style as popular among overseas Vietnamese or in using information about the ao dai supplied by emigrated relatives to rework their own versions of the original item, traders must walk a fine line between concealing this interaction and reaping the benefits that such foreign prestige imparts to their products. When a panel of judges in Tokyo proclaims the ao dai to be the best national costume, they put an international seal of approval on the garment. This acclaim can be freely celebrated within Vietnam for it does not call into question the garment's sacred status as a marker of authentic Vietnamese identity. Similarly, Si Hoang can use cubist images or ethnic weaving motifs to decorate his ao dai, so long as he is careful to point out that he preserves and respects the garment's time-honored form. When, however, foreigners or quasi-foreign Vietnamese participate even marginally in transforming the ao dai sold to domestic consumers, they challenge perceptions of the garment's authenticity. The traders and tailors I know must balance the attraction of disclosing the sources of their stylistic innovation with this need to preserve the ao dai's sacred orthodoxy.

CONCLUSION: COSMOPOLITAN WOMEN, TRADITIONAL FASHIONS

In this chapter, I have documented the historical emergence of the ao dai as an ambivalent but potent symbol of Vietnamese identity. Its hybridity makes it particularly appealing to contemporary domestic consumers, who see in the garment the opportunity both to assert national tradition and to embrace an international vision of cosmopolitan chic. They are supported in this project by ao dai producers and sellers, who use a combination of overt displays of local taste and covert acquisition of international knowledge from diasporic kin to fashion themselves and their goods as authoritative representatives of style.

In spite of impassioned cultural rhetoric touting the ao dai's indigenous authenticity, attention to the circulation of the ao dai domestically and globally in both the past and the present reveals that its enduring popularity stems from its multi-national, hybrid origins that make it a garment amenable to interpretation by both Vietnamese and non-Vietnamese in standardized displays of cultural distinctiveness, or homogenized heterogeneity. Whereas earlier versions of the ao dai were crafted by cross-cultural elites, such as a Confucianized emperor or a French-educated artist, today's ao dai is being shaped by thousands of independent tailors, mostly women, who draw on a varied cross-cultural array of resources. Through its history of incorporating foreign influences in uniquely Vietnamese ways, the ao dai is not just a fitting symbol of Vietnam's past, but of a globalized present in which innovative women engage in transnational, multi-faceted personal relations and transform them into productive, profitable resources.

25

DRESS FOR SUKSES:
Fashioning femininity and nationality in urban Indonesia

Carla Jones

On a hot afternoon in Jakarta in June of 2000, I listened carefully to one of Indonesia's foremost "experts" on professional dress and lifestyle explain her reasons for worrying about Indonesian middle-class women. Eileen Rachman, owner of a nationally renowned self-improvement course for women, writer of a syndicated magazine column, and expert in a traveling workshop series on dress and manners, explained her reason for the need for these programs thus,

> Carla, I must confess that sometimes I am embarrassed by Indonesian women's lack of appreciation of 'lifestyle.' I see Indonesian women, especially when I am traveling abroad, who make me feel ashamed because they don't know how to interact with others, they dress awkwardly, and they just don't seem world class. They just don't have a lifestyle. I feel it is a kind of responsibility for me to help them become more developed.

Her comment was telling for its frankness, but also as an indication of how seriously the appearance and manners of Indonesian women were understood to be to a larger national debate on the future of Indonesian national culture.

In this chapter I suggest that a significant site for the contest over the terms of modernity in contemporary Indonesia is women's bodies, particularly through their dress and manners. I describe how middle-class women in the central Javanese city of Yogyakarta strove during the late 1990s, through a private course of personal development, to educate themselves and others on the appropriate ways of personal appearance and presentation. The course instructors and students were involved in cultural production, by distinguishing themselves from and with other class and status groups both within and without Indonesia, through consumption.

I situate my discussion of how Indonesian women citizens learned to value and consume fashion in a larger history of national development strategy in Indonesia. I make two separate but related points in my argument. First, I analyze how new forms of expertise, manifested most explicitly in private personal-development courses, educated women citizens into consumers of Indonesian *fesyen*, through knowledge about both the "traditional" uniform for women, the sarong and lace blouse ensemble called the *kain kebaya*, and the more apparently Western-styled professional skirt-suits and other outfits. The effect of these new discursive forms of expertise was that women instructors and students in the courses I studied learned to perform femininity in ways that created new gender and class identities. Following the work of Judith Butler (1990), and by extension Michel Foucault ([1977] 1995;[1978] 1990), I suggest that such performances disciplined women into normative femininity but also allowed women consumers to see

Adapted from Carla Jones, "Dress for *Sukses*: Fashioning Femininity and Nationality in Urban Indonesia." *Re-Orienting Fashion: The Globalization of Asian Dress.*, Sandra Niessen, Ann Marie Leshkowich, and Carla Jones (Oxford: Berg, 2003), pp. 185–214.

their performances as providing important cultural and material effects. Second, I argue that the women I knew considered their consumer work to be just that, cultural work essential to personal progress in the public sphere, rather than merely pleasure located in the private sphere of the home. The argument that women's consumer activity is often undervalued or made invisible, by imagining it as self-indulgent pleasure, has been an important contribution in American feminist research (see, e.g., Conroy 1998; di Leonardo 1987; Hochschild 1989a, b). However, there is still little research on the ways in which new class and gender formations outside the United States interpret women's consumer activity.

CLASS-IFYING WOMEN IN YOGYAKARTA

In the late 1990s, women in Yogyakarta who could afford to do so chose to find information on how to achieve a modern feminine lifestyle through private personal-development courses. I base my argument in my fieldwork on one such course on personal development, where women strove to educate themselves and others in the appropriate techniques of personal appearance and presentation. Ubiquitous attention to personal grooming and fashion choices was evidence of how the feminine self was increasingly under siege in the later years of the Suharto New Order regime, which began in 1965 and ended in the Asian Economic Crisis in 1998. Women were not to appear too rich, too backward, too poor, or too un-Islamic. Women therefore used their surfaces or "social skin" (Turner 1979[b]) as a communicative palette through which to negotiate their social worlds. Terence Turner argues that decoration (or lack thereof) of the body is a universally "symbolic stage upon which the drama of socialization is enacted" (112). However, I show that it is within particular histories and relations of power that dress and decoration can become a dominant element of the moral self. This is particularly interesting when there are forces actively trying to sell commoditized elements of this self to a target population, as was the case during the intensive advertising and marketing period of the heady last years of the Suharto regime. Indeed, a shared value

of the importance of appearances, which the course I studied exploited, was in fact not new to Indonesian men or women. However, what the course did was to emphasize this value in new ways that were related to the history of the preceding thirty years.

Theoretical approaches to the study of consumption have often focused on the domestic sphere, because consumption seems to occur in private and for apparently personal reasons. Yet in making these assumptions, such approaches have also often dismissed consumer choices as either personal expression or imitative, strategic gestures designed to manipulate a viewing audience. For example, Thorstein Veblen's analysis of consumption argued that clothing choices were attempts of particular class members to emulate the styles of the classes just above them ([1899] 1994). In part because of the emphasis theorists of Marx have placed on the role of production in forming class positions, until recently consumption has been understudied as a significant site for cultural work. Yet consumption can be a site for collective negotiation, as in the case of national debates on culture, while still offering a limited but material space for creating individual identities. This is particularly stimulating to consider in the context of women's uses of fashion. Veblen's critique of consumption interpreted the consumption of fashion as a uniquely feminine foible and plight. According to Veblen, women are trapped in a larger social system that forces them into meaningless attention to tasteful display. Fashions are particularly rich sites for such display, then, for it is through the clothing on women's bodies, and the fact that women seem to be so magically enamored of the allure of that clothing, that women can come to be seen as victims of a system that prevents them from producing. The display of status, often through clothing, ultimately serves to enhance the image of the man who produces the income supporting that consumption. Women in Veblen's analysis are thus limited by an economic and gendered system that turns them into consuming servants for men. In short, a man only looks as good as his wife's "look."

By contrast, more recent work on consumption suggests that Veblen's approach ignored the important cultural and personal meaning generated through consumption, particularly in the face of changing social conditions. This new attention to consumption has emphasized the possibility for a variety of alternative functions of consumption, including political resistance, kinship work, and identity formation, even as those changing social conditions create new class inequalities. Indeed, women in the course I studied did acquire techniques of display that equipped them to perform their femininity competitively, sometimes even above their material class positions, but such performances could, on occasion, also reveal the borders of gender and class identities. As a result, women's consumer choices in general, and fashion choices in particular, were not simply secondary manifestations of urban public culture in 1990s Indonesia. Rather, women's appearance choices were culturally productive acts central to creating that culture.

An important element of how this cultural work was made and circulated was the role of local and national elites. The global/local gap that globalization theories have cast as abstract was a much more complicated dichotomy for local elites in Yogyakarta, one which they mediated by offering fashion information to their fellow women citizens. For example, although foreign styles were visible on imported television programs, the personal development course I studied offered locally esteemed women a forum to inform students on how to adjust and correct such styles for the Indonesian context. In so doing, local elite women transformed their prestige into a form of noblesse oblige, securing their own positions, while introducing qualities they valued, such as national or religious identity.

The parallel use of the idea of development as both personal and national is not surprising to those who are familiar with the Suharto New Order state. Development was the explicit goal of the Suharto regime, which Suharto called the New Order to contrast with the perceived chaos of the previous regime of President Sukarno. In the context of gender in contemporary Indonesia, this is especially interesting. Indonesian citizens were constantly exhorted to focus their energies on the goal of development. Yet the kinds of people into which Indonesians were to become transformed were gendered. While to Americans this may seem natural, given anthropological discussions of gender roles in the region it is surprising. This is a region where women have enjoyed financial power, and access to divorce and property and inheritance rights; a region where conceptions of gender difference emphasize complementarity over hierarchy (e.g., Errington 1990).

National rhetoric about development did not emerge in a vacuum, however. The language of development and enforced order was shaped in part by international discourses about development, through which the Suharto regime benefited directly. By ensuring stability through political repression and endorsing the story of Indonesia's development as the creation of an emerging market, the last fifteen years of the regime saw considerable economic growth, averaging annual growth rates of over 7 percent. In addition, while the elite grew fantastically wealthy, urban areas also saw the growth of a class of working poor and a growing middle class. As a result, the 1990s in particular in urban Indonesia were marked by considerable foreign and local investment dedicated to increasing Indonesian consumption, evidenced by the construction of large air-conditioned malls, traffic jams on city streets due to increasing car ownership, and generally conspicuous consumption. Yet while consumption was increasingly located in private homes, homes that were gated and locked from contact with neighbors, it was simultaneously one of the central symbols of public life in this period. Increased consumption was the sign that Indonesia had arrived on the world stage. As a result, consumption was not simply a secondary part of social life. Rather, it was generally acknowledged that consumption was one of the important sites for negotiating meanings and identities. From its foundations, then, this new middle class was marked by anxieties and struggles over the role of gender in the formation of a uniquely Indonesian form of modernity. Being middle class meant more than just access to financial resources, but was a symbolic position as well, requiring self-surveillance and display, much as Pierre Bourdieu has argued ([1979] 1984: 254–56). Being middle-class was more than access to the means of production, it meant access to the means of consumption.

One characteristic of both men and women in the new bourgeoisie was the sense that the future of Indonesian national social life would be shaped through the efforts of self-cultivation and self-fashioning. The sense that the individual should be a personal project, almost a career, was linked to broader goals of social transformation. Although the specific visions of the future varied, depending on the particular group, most shared the opinion that self-discipline, manifested in confident, responsible citizens, would be the building blocks for Indonesia's collective future. Unfortunately, the reverse logic was difficult to bear when the economic crisis hit, because then the enormous social devastation was experienced by almost everyone I knew as both a national disaster, but most acutely as personal failure and shame.

However, the rhetoric of self-sacrifice for the common good was directed much more clearly at women citizens than at men. Indeed, the sort of disciplinary practices that the women I knew enthusiastically sought out were significant because they were in most instances the sort of practices that are almost invisible in Western society. The tools for achieving a successfully disciplined and gendered body were not only available for purchase for those who chose to attend the course, but collectively and consciously valued by both the instructors and students. This contrasts with the sort of class-exclusive hoarding of expertise that Bourdieu describes as one way that privilege is reproduced (1984). Because the privileged classes make the rules of social interaction appear natural, while not revealing those rules, members outside the class group are often prevented from full participation. In contrast, instructors of the femininity course I studied considered it their obligation to share this knowledge with women who aspired to be like them.

NEW CULTURES OF EXPERTISE: THE PRIVATE FEMININITY COURSE INDUSTRY IN 1990S INDONESIA

In the decade prior to the economic crisis a small industry of instructional femininity courses flourished in many Javanese cities, as well as on Sumatra and Bali.

The national expert quoted at the beginning of this chapter is one of the best-known femininity instructors, whose particular expertise is focused on white-collar career fashions and manners. However, the course I studied was offered by a small private business college run by a modernist Islamic institute (Achmadiyah) in a prestigious part of Yogyakarta. Like many such colleges, it offers short courses on business presentations, public relations techniques and public speaking, in addition to a course called "Personal Development" (*Pengembangan Pribadi*). I use the term femininity course to describe these courses because, although it is not based on the Indonesian term for the course, it conveys the gender-specific content of the course. However, the Indonesian course title is instructive. The course uses a different term to refer to development than the more ubiquitous term "*pembangunan*." In part because *pembangunan* referred to state-sponsored national development projects, such as large concrete edifices and the national car and airplane projects, it seemed ill suited to describe personal change. Rather, the private course in Yogyakarta used *pengembangan*, based on the verb *kembang* meaning to bloom or flower, as a more poetic and appropriate term to describe self-realization, and because it felt a step removed from the term that had been colonized by official definitions.

Based directly on the early twentieth-century American finishing program John Robert Powers, the course title suggested that the class concerned general self-improvement, and therefore might be helpful to both male and female students. However, closer reading of the course themes revealed that the information conveyed was oriented to women. For 350,000 rupiah each (approximately $175.00 (US) or about one month's income for many students) approximately twenty students would meet two evenings a week for six weeks. Students came from a variety of backgrounds, but often were the daughters of low- to mid-ranking civil servants or teachers. They were instructed on subjects such as personal grooming and how to select and apply makeup, put together day and evening outfits, engage in polite conversation and eat Western-style meals. In general, two concerns seemed to motivate both the instructors and the students of the course: (1) the need to not be "left behind the times" (*ketinggalan jaman*) in an era of globalization and (2) to distinguish class and status differences, in particular to not appear "*kampungan*" or literally "village-like" or backward.

Goals for most students included career and social advancement, which they couched in terms of desire for increased self-esteem, the sort of self-mastery and sense of identity that was appealing at a time of social flux (*percaya diri* or literally "belief in oneself"). Instructors in the course measured student self-esteem through vocal and carriage skills. Particular emphasis was placed on appropriating fashions and personal skills from expert sources (such as local and foreign magazines, television, and motivational philosophies such as Stephen Covey's) in ways consistent with what was considered Indonesian and feminine. The course I studied had been open for five years, although similar courses had been successfully operating in the capital city Jakarta since 1982.

The Jakarta courses featured nationally respected designers and fashion consultants, both male and female, some of whom traveled to offer weekend one-day intensive seminars in smaller cities. Local variations on the course, including the Yogyakarta course I studied, incorporated the expertise of these same designers and experts through magazines. Eventually the Jakarta courses expanded to cover a wide variety of lifestyle and consumer subjects beyond fashion, including one-day seminars on interior decorating, cooking, and etiquette. Full courses had appeared in Solo, Surabaya, Denpasar, Medan, and Yogyakarta by the early and mid-1990s. During the first few years of the course's operation in Yogyakarta, the students were primarily middle-aged wives of advancing civil servants. The skills taught at such courses were thought to be useful to women in their forties and older, helpful in finding ways to keep their husbands faithful, especially as their husbands advanced professionally and their careers required increased public socializing. By the time I conducted my fieldwork from 1996 to 1998, the majority of students in the course I studied were young women, aged 25 to 35, who were preparing to graduate from various levels of post-high school education and were seeking employment. The same skills taught earlier to keep husbands faithful were

then deemed useful for young potential employees in getting work or keeping a boss content. In general, the economic advantages for students in taking the course appeared clear. Graduates of the class were successful in getting jobs at the various offices, banks, and retail outlets in Yogyakarta. Indeed, the Matahari department store, anchor store of the main Yogyakarta mall, sent all its new retail assistants through a version of the course before formally hiring them. The most high-profile success stories from the programs were cases of graduates who had gone on to careers as presenters on local television programs.

Yogyakarta as an urban site is in a unique position. As a secondary city, it is thought to be not as exposed as Jakarta is to the cultural influences of globalization, but neither is it insulated, in large part because of increasing international tourism to the city and some multinational companies producing there. In addition, the women who ran the course often saw themselves as the first line of education for women arriving from rural settings just outside the city. The instructors therefore imagined themselves negotiating among good and bad taste. Good taste came from international influences acquired from personal travel to Australia, Singapore, or Europe and America, foreign magazines acquired through friends and family abroad, and Jakarta-based mass media. These sources were used to counteract the influences that students were perceived to bring to the classroom, such as rural backwardness and nouveau riche enthusiasm for displaying new wealth through flamboyant fashion choices, such as wearing brands or logos visibly on one's clothing. As a result, the instructors served as intermediaries in the often theoretically abstract global–local dichotomy. As mid-level elites and as women of considerable local respect, some with family or other personal ties among the *priyayi* or aristocratic class of the Yogyakarta sultanate, they served as vehicles of expertise on self-cultivation. Rather than simply reinforcing the model of Javanese power relations in which junior-status citizens seek the advice and blessings of royalty, the instructors' appeal and cachet was a hybrid of appeals to both their Javanese prestige and their reputations as people who move around the world. Travel and access to international standards of good taste was just as important in determining their prestige as ties to the Yogyakarta royal court.

The instructors therefore felt a responsibility to the students, and their own developmentalist agendas, and were consequently highly attuned to global trends. Although they clearly profited from the course, all the instructors insisted that they were involved in the course because they did not want Yogyakarta to lose out in an era of globalization. Consistent with this, instructors intentionally kept the fees at the same price throughout the economic crisis (thereby, because of the drop in the value of the rupiah and dramatic inflation, effectively cutting the cost of the course by two-thirds) in order to keep it available to precisely those students who "needed" most what the course had to offer—i.e., tools for social mobility. In other words, if lower-middle-class women could most benefit from the content of the course, then the fees should be kept within range of that clientele. This decision also prevented the course from closing altogether, as its many local competitors did during the economic crisis.

The course's explicit goal was to transform women's tastes and manners and as a result, transform their personalities (*kepribadian*) and their social status. At base, both students and instructors shared the opinion that personal development was the result of recruiting information, such as what styles are current or on the way out, in the service of change in social position. The goal of self-transformation was to be achieved through self-discipline. The basic assumption was that one's inner life is shaped if not determined by surface performances. Disciplining one's appearance would therefore result in alteration of the self. In fact, every student learned that the only way to fully know herself was to see herself in the eyes of others. Instructors frequently exhorted students to internalize the instructions from the course, stating after explaining various rules on dress or makeup, "you should really just make these rules your '*common sense*,'" using the English phrase that communicated global cachet. Instructors also reminded students that the transformation might not be immediate, but students should be patient for the benefits to accrue.

The primary contrast to a polished, up-to-date woman was the "*kampungan*" woman, a negative identity associated with both rural backwardness and nouveau riche tackiness. One of the reasons why the label "*kampungan*" was so threatening was that, increasingly, young village women were earning income through wage factory and domestic work. Economically, national development was to be achieved through neoliberal policies aimed at producing a successful export-oriented economy, based in large part in producing garments for sale in developed economies. The production of textiles and clothing, which are among the most labor-intensive industries in modern economies (Dicken 1998: 296), have been increasingly moved offshore to low-wage countries, including Indonesia. Textile-production factories have been key sites for entry-level work for rural women migrating to cities. Indeed, development rhetoric outside Indonesia, particularly in response to the anti-sweatshop movement in the United States, has argued that garment-factory jobs are a first step on a ladder of economic development. Throughout the late 1990s, Indonesia's textile and clothing exports were third behind oil/gas and wood exports, comprising roughly 12 percent of GDP, and 28 percent of total foreign exchange exports (approximately $12.6 (US) million) (*Europa World Year Book* 1999: 1772–78). Textile production was therefore central to the economy. However, in public rhetoric on development, the New Order state did not focus on the material importance of textile production in the national progress narrative, instead promoting the accomplishments of heavy industry and high technology projects. In contrast, factory women were frequently symbols for a national struggle over what would be Indonesia's national culture.

As Aihwa Ong has described for Malaysia (1990[a]: 385–422), young women leaving parental surveillance to work in factories often face public criticism for their consumer behavior. Islamic groups in particular expressed concern that young women earning income away from parental control become negative elements in the wider culture. Similar rhetoric circulated in Yogyakarta. A frequent example of this was cited by young men whom I knew in Islamic student groups in Yogyakarta who complained of extravagant consumer behavior among factory women and domestic helpers returning from overseas. These women were accused of returning to their villages wearing jeans or Nike tennis shoes, signs that were interpreted as proof of inadequate control over their appetites or lack of moderation. As a result, women who dressed in a *kampungan* way were not simply revealing their bad taste, but also revealing their failure to exercise self-control in general, including the sexual arena. As one young male academic confidently assured me, "Factory workers and domestic maids returning from abroad wearing those expensive tennis shoes, you know, they are usually having free sex." Understanding the link between appearance and sexual propriety better explains the mandate of the femininity course to create "good women." Frugality and sexual modesty as attributes of Islamic identity were key elements of such a woman. As a result, the stakes were high for women to give evidence of their grasp of middle-class propriety and good taste.

One of the other key distinctions between fashions recommended to students was based on a temporal scale, i.e., that left to their own designs, students might select "looks" that were out-of-date but about which they did not know they should feel embarrassment. As a result, the instructors felt their role was to explain the many choices available to women in selecting clothing that was attractive, current, yet proper. A strong sense of timelag shaped this assumption, a gap of both development and time between global cities, such as Paris or New York, from which good taste emanated, and its arrival in Indonesia. In this way, consumer goods such as fashion and makeup told a story about oneself to oneself and to others. Goods communicated one's position in a world of either more or less developed people (cf. Wilk 1990). Staying on top of trends required vigilance, and failing to inform oneself of what was "in" or "out" would reveal one's proximity to or distance from centers of power. Although access to communication from such perceived centers had increased through mass media and the internet, the women I knew still perceived themselves to be in a system in which Yogyakarta was a marginal site, second to Jakarta and global cities.

Similarly, students might be inclined to choose fashions that were direct imitations of Western fashions. But with instruction, students could learn what was wrong with Western fashions (that they are too sexy), while acknowledging the fact that Western fashions are clearly the international standard. As one celebrity explained in a magazine interview:

> If an Indonesian woman is seen walking in the mall in a miniskirt, … or dressed without even a bra! Even if this esthetic [*esthetik*] is beautiful and sexy, she is undoubtedly immediately going to be thought of as a "naughty woman." If an Indonesian woman is so unfortunate as to acquire that label, there are many consequences that follow … [E]ven for special parties one must think a thousand times first [before selecting an outfit]. (Asokawati 1998)

This concern with appearances seems to confirm broad Western stereotypes of Asian cultures in general, and Asian women in particular, as obsessed with "face," or outward appearances as linked to prestige or shame (cf. Hevia 1995). Dorinne Kondo argues that the perpetuation of this stereotype ignores the fact that the stakes involved in personal appearance can be high, not only for some imaginary group of Asians, however, but for most humans (1997). In fact, students' motivations should not be misunderstood as evidence of women who were either vain or gullible, but rather of women who fully grasped the importance of bringing into line all elements of their lives in order to achieve "*sukses.*" After all, real jobs were gained or lost and husbands really did threaten to or did leave wives for younger women. Moreover, the question of whether or not to take such a course was always couched in terms that the information was just too important to risk ignoring.

COURSE INSTRUCTORS' GOALS

Although the course material appeared to focus on the manipulation of the surfaces of women's bodies, through fashion, hair styling, or etiquette, teachers insisted that the course was really one part of a whole transformation of students' personalities. The most explicit theme of the course was self-confidence. Teachers repeatedly mentioned that this was the most challenging part of instruction also, because they were working against what they perceived to be thousands of years of "tradition" in which Javanese women were valued for being demure and shy (*malu*). The force of generations felt to the instructors as though they were struggling against an impenetrable wall of backwardness. The section of the course on public speaking in particular was important in this regard. Instructors struggled to get students to speak up and enunciate clearly, based on a model of speech designed to train television anchors.

Yet if the goal of the course was to change women on a personal, even psychological, level, why the focus on dress and appearance? The notion that the changes one made could be life-altering was central to understanding the popularity of the course. Students described the course as a way of altering one's *sikap* or character. The acquisition of knowledge and taste necessary for pulling off a look involved a change in one's mode of thinking, and such change could not come without focus and dedication. The director for the John Robert Powers franchises in Asia, during a visit to Jakarta in 1997, emphasized the importance of self-discipline in achieving the goals of the course, saying, "The most important thing is the desire to change." Several women in the class explained to me that one could not expect to become an attractive and modern woman without cultivation. As one student explained, "It isn't just going to happen … " ("*Tidak akan terjadi saja*"). Transforming oneself into a woman whose image is current and attractive and conceals any backward roots, requires learning. Another student explained, "This course gives me the theory, but if I am going to be successful, I have to apply this theory in practice. I will have to constantly remind myself throughout the day how to stand and how to smile. It's hard these first few weeks, but hopefully it will become a habit."

Instructors also encouraged students to see themselves as being observed and assessed, aware constantly that they were being watched by others. The goal was for students to internalize the feedback they received from all of their encounters with others, until they learned to see themselves as others saw them. As one expert was quoted as saying in *Femina*:

In Eastern culture, including that of Indonesia, the value of what is appropriate or not appropriate is highly connected with a woman's "image" (*imaj*) in the eyes of society … "Fashion" is a form of nonverbal communication. If a woman chooses to appear or wear clothes of a certain style, it is a way for her to indirectly say that she wants to state who she is and her point of view on life, what her personality is, her character, and much more. … (Asokawati 1998)

The course therefore offered not only the tools for learning how to construct one's appearance but also for learning how to look at each other. In this regard, students were taught to focus the gaze they were learning to apply to themselves on others as well. Instructions on how to assess someone in social interactions were part of the rules, such as "If a person wears glasses, they are probably in the category 'intellectual'" or "If you want see if someone is neat, look at her shoes. If her shoes aren't clean or appropriate, it doesn't matter what else she is wearing." However, this strategy gave students the impression that they should in fact be able to achieve the "looks" exemplified by the instructors, even though they did not have financial or local access to the cosmetic products used in teaching. Consistently, the name-brand consumer goods used for teaching aids were not available for sale in Yogyakarta. To purchase those products, the prices for which were far beyond what most students could afford, students would also have had to travel to either Jakarta or Singapore.

Nonetheless, students were regularly asked to identify themselves by work type and personality type from a predetermined list of choices when selecting hair, makeup and wardrobe styles. Women who saw themselves as being a "librarian" selected a certain style, while women who selected "swimmer" or "artist" were given different style advice. Interestingly, rarely did students work as artists or librarians. The desirable jobs the students sought were in banks, hotels or administration. But the students were not just expected to find an identity and then enact its style. While this may appear as a simple transfer of expertise on various looks from the instructors to the students, I suggest there was more agency involved. Instructors offered these identity choices as explicitly universal, arriving from America but true generally for any woman. The language in both the courses and the fashion magazines that were consulted were peppered with English-language-derived fashion terms. Tips on "*gaya jaket*" ("jacket style"), "*memilih vest*" (picking a vest) or "*kesempatan memakai jins*" (occasions for wearing jeans) might indicate that Indonesian fashion and language are relying on global references for what were local creations.

However, instructors in the course told the students that these labels were to be applied loosely, and suited to the lives of Indonesian women. Instructors sought to point out that "looks" do not have naturally fixed meanings. "Modernization does not just mean techniques, but an adaptation of modes of thinking," said one instructor. "It is hard to separate the technology of the clothing from the meaning that can come with it. We have to fill these fashions from the West with our own interior meaning" (*batin*). Instructors reminded students that Western fashions had particular meanings appropriate to their original contexts. An example of this was the Western value of wearing comfortable footwear which was unattractive to the instructors, but which they interpreted as an effect of Western practicality. Likewise the Western power suit, with large shoulder pads, was too aggressive for Indonesian women but was appropriate for American women who are in positions of power. To make an outfit appropriate to the Indonesian setting meant not just a shift in the outfit itself, but an understanding of why this was necessary. For example, fabric colors were to be adjusted to maximize the Indonesian ideal of fairer skin. White fabric was explicitly forbidden, as it contrasted with dark skin, making one look even darker. Off-white fabrics were recommended instead to maximize the local value for fair skin. Matching shoe color to handbag color was of particular importance. In addition, one instructor stated that even though "power suits" were to be the global trend for 1998, it did not mean they could be worn in Indonesia, or Yogyakarta especially, without at least some modification, usually meaning longer skirts or higher necklines in keeping with the fact that "we are Muslim women." Students were told that their greatest concern should therefore be with changes in trends. Careful attention to styles should precede any fabric purchase or garment design. Women were encouraged

to exercise a critical eye in assessing fabrics, avoiding the temptation to purchase just because something was on sale. Instructors encouraged students to select natural-fiber textiles (often imported) over abundant and inexpensive synthetics (usually locally made). Fabric for outfits should be sewn into garments within two months of purchase, or the fabric would be out of style. One instructor enjoyed making this point by showing a piece of fabric that was a year and a half old, calling it "antique."

DISCIPLINED STUDENTS, GENDERED STUDENTS

Dress, therefore, as a method for forming one's personality, was also an indication of one's success as a gendered person. This position confirms claims by theorists such as Judith Butler (1990) and Dorinne Kondo (1997) who argue that appearance and clothing are more than simple attributes of gender subjectivity but are in fact constitutive of it. Butler in particular claims that performing gender *is* gender, that there is no natural, authentic performer behind the act. A similar value on performance seemed to guide much of the advice in the femininity course. Although instructors frequently referred to various "laws of nature" (*hukum alam*) that dictate women's lives, such as "all women want to be beautiful," or "women like to shop," simply being born as a genetic female by no means guaranteed a successful woman. Rather, to fully realize one's potential as a woman required effort, and could perhaps be achieved through taking a personal-development course. One instructor described the success the course could have by pointing out a recent graduate. "When she arrived here for the course, she was a guy (*cowok*). Really a guy. The way she stood, the way she dressed. The change has been amazing. Since she took the course, she has become a woman." In contrast, women who refused to take their personal appearance seriously as a feature of their social position were not fully female. One woman friend who had married a doctor but continued to go around her house in a housedress, rarely leaving the house or dressing up, was described by her husband's family and friends as "not a woman." "Just because she has given birth doesn't make her a woman," one acquaintance said, proposing that she should take a personal-development course. Indeed, her mother-in-law, who felt her son was being shamed by his wife's behavior, offered to pay for enrollment, but she refused. The fact that her son eventually no longer chose to live with his wife and children was therefore understandable considering that his wife's personal appearance was inconsistent with her gender and class status.

It was in the context of New Order gender ideology that the importance of class distinctions, in particular the contrast to being *kampungan*, was most clear. In the context of late New Order Indonesia, an environment saturated with selling the joys of being modern, any sign of less-than-modern taste was what students were paying to erase. While most students knew that they would probably never use the same brands of skin cleanser or hire the same tailors as the instructors, because of their different access to financial resources, the instructors nonetheless insisted that creative and attentive students could achieve similar results at a lower cost. A theme of the college was "looking good doesn't mean doing more shopping." Techniques emphasized savvy shopping instead. Students understood that they could appear to be more professional or wealthy than they might in fact be by striving for a complete "look." For example, the wardrobe rules in the course included ways to assess a tailor, evaluate fabrics and choose styles appropriate to one's body type. The final exam for the course required the students to model day- and evening-wear outfits that they had commissioned. The instructors, in order to assess whether the students had in fact selected good tailors, inspected the inside seams and hem stitching of the garments in deciding if the student had paid too much for the outfit. So prevalent was this value of succeeding at the appearance game at as little cost as possible that I knew several women

who could have enrolled in the course but chose not to, not because of lack of interest or funds, but because they felt that they could acquire the same knowledge through careful attention to women's magazines and soap operas on television.

Consumption of fashion, as appearance work, was therefore a way of performing and thereby producing gendered social difference in the late 1990s Indonesia. Although the importance of appearances was a shared value among both instructors and students of the course I studied, the details of what styles said about the self, and more importantly, what styles constituted the self, required instruction. As a result, middle-class women in urban Indonesia were not simply consumers limited to the private sphere, but producers engaged in contests over meanings and identities in late New Order Indonesia. While claiming that the search for self-improvement was purely for personal success and happiness, and indeed in many cases in fact acquiring a degree of the self-confidence and identity they sought, these women endorsed development ideology in ways that often had unintended personal and social consequences. Many of the women I knew perceived of their self-cultivation as a conscientious attempt at reconfiguring the dominant relations of power they felt the state was inscribing on them. They imagined themselves to be rejecting an official model of femininity for a more appealing and liberatory version that embraced attractiveness and women's professional work. In conceiving of themselves as needy of personal development, as continual works-in-progress, the instructors and students in femininity courses such as the one I studied engaged in practices that both produced new individual subjects and reinscribed them into a larger community of citizens nonetheless participating in the persuasive project of a nation in development.

26

"DOING" DANISH FASHION:
On national identity and design practices of a small Danish fashion company

Marie Riegels Melchior

INTRODUCTION TO THE DANISH FASHION INDUSTRY

Looking at a world map of the fashion industry, Denmark is rarely what comes to mind as a key destination, except to those who are somewhat knowledgeable about the fashion industry. Such a person would perhaps know of Denmark as the home country of Helena Christensen, former "supermodel" in the 1990s and today living in New York; as the home country of the former Balmain couturier Erik Mortensen (1926–98); or perhaps as the world leader since 1979 in exporting mink and fox fur for the high-end fashion industry. Approximately 12 million mink fur skins are exported annually, according to the Danish fur breeders' organization *Kopenhagen Fur*. However, in the eyes of the Danish fashion industry and the Danish government, Denmark is currently considered a "fashion nation" with the future potential to become what is rhetorically called "the fifth global fashion center," following in the footsteps of Paris, London, Milan, and New York. But what is Danish fashion and how is it done? What is the specificity of Danish fashion? How is it practiced and by whom?

This is the main concern of this article; at the same time, actor-network theory (ANT) will be introduced as an appropriate materiality-invoked research approach to studies of fashion. The article is concerned with understanding the relationship between issues of national identity, fashion design, and the fashion industry from a practice-based perspective, and hereby continues related discussions particularly present in dress research of the relationship of folk costumes and national identity (e.g. Leilund 2007). First, however, I will give a short introduction to the concept and phenomenon of Danish fashion.

DANISH FASHION: A BRIEF HISTORY

Today the term "Danish fashion" is often treated by the industry as synonymous with the "Danish fashion industry." In statistical terms, this means that Danish fashion is estimated to consist of approximately 620 companies registered by *Statistics Denmark* as "wholesalers of clothing" (Deloitte 2008). Furthermore it is recognized that the industry employs approximately 11,328 people and in 2008 had an annual turnover of 23.6 billion DKK, of which about 90% was gained on export (21.4 billion DKK). The three main export markets of the industry are Germany, Sweden, and Norway (DTB 2008: 2–3). On the basis of these numbers, the industry is often described as the fourth biggest export industry of the Danish manufacturing industries. This is based on the combination of the export profits of Danish wholesale companies of clothing, textiles, and leather goods. In addition, what characterizes the industry

Adapted from Marie Riegels Melchior, "Doing" Danish Fashion: On National Identity and Design Practices of a Small Danish Fashion Company," *Fashion Practice* 2, no. 1 (2010): 13–40.

is that it is dominated by three major companies that account for an estimated 75% of the industry's total export profits. These are Bestseller A/S, BTX Group A/S, and IC Companies A/S. The remaining industry is composed primarily of small-sized companies of approximately four to nine full-time employees, mostly owner-managed. The companies are customarily defined as either price-driven or design-driven. Some companies compete mainly on prices, and rely heavily on minimizing manufacturing and distribution costs. Other companies base their market position mainly on design and the branding of their goods.

However, to speak of a particular Danish fashion is a fairly new phenomenon dating back to the early 1960s, when a general transition of the perception of fashion occurred internationally as well as in Denmark due to changing lifestyles, the growth of youth culture, and the general social and economic development in countries of the Western world. A transition from class-based fashion to consumer-based fashion production occurred, as framed by the American sociologist and fashion researcher Diane Crane (2000: 132). From a Danish perspective, these developments were perceived to be led primarily by changes within the American clothing industry, introducing the concept of "teenage fashion," which reached Denmark in the latter part of the 1950s, and by the youth designer fashion coming out of London during the 1960s. Together they contributed to new initiatives for Danish clothing manufacturers to start collaborating with local and professionally trained fashion designers and the rise of independent boutiques selling Danish as well as internationally produced youth fashions. Previously the manufacturers had been accustomed to basing their clothing production on anonymous design following international fashion trends set by Parisian *haute couture* fashion houses. By integrating professionally trained fashion designers in the production of Danish ready-to-wear, the clothes turned into branded goods, labeled with the name of the fashion designer in addition to the manufacturer's company name. These labels were often written in English, indicating the rising contemporary export focus of the industry; market expansion was necessary for the Danish fashion industry to stay in business, as the import of foreign fashion made the home market increasingly competitive. The new fashion designers of the time were, among others, Søs Drasbæk (1937–2007), Margit Brandt (b. 1945), Mugge Kølpin, Lise-Lotte Wiingaard, Bent Visti, Sysser Ginsborg, Lars Hillingsø, Lennart Råholt, and Kirsten Teisner. They worked both with their own labels, often in their own name, as well as on a freelance basis for Danish clothing manufacturers.

In the 1960s, as today, the emergence of a Danish fashion industry was followed by an identity debate. The qualities deemed to be significant to fashionable clothing designed and produced by the Danish fashion industry were its characterizations as functional, wearable, and fashionable. Danish fashion was perceived as being highly modern, young, and priced at a level accessible to a wider group of people compared to the clothes from international fashion houses. However, interestingly enough, in the perception of Danish fashion there were no direct references to any Danish dress traditions or the use of any specific Danish crafting techniques. Connecting Danish fashion to Danish history or the image of Denmark was not an integral part of the design, although now and then the styling of Danish fashion for photo shoots would utilize historic Danish buildings or iconic landscapes as settings.

During the 1970s, this interest in pointing out the specific significance of Danish fashion changed, as the Danish clothing industry was met by economic struggles due to new trade regulations and increasing competition from low-wage manufacturing countries in Europe and Asia. Still, it was the general opinion of the industry's trade organizations that independent fashion design could make strong branded goods for export, but many manufacturers did not want to take the risk of selling clothes based on independent design when their profit margins were limited. Instead they preferred to stay faithful to a business model selling international trend-following clothes at the lowest price possible. This gradually changed the perception of a particular Danish fashion. During the 1980s it was not uncommon in Denmark to speak of Danish fashion as "copy fashion." To change this perception of Danish fashion, initiatives to mark Danish-made clothes with a hang tag stating "Made in Denmark" next to a drawing of the Danish flag were taken. The intention was first of all to make Danish fashion consumers aware of buying Danish and thereby support the industry. But the outcome did not change the situation. The production of clothes was outsourced and the industry transformed.

In the early 1990s the headlines in Danish newspapers even forecast the demise of the Danish fashion industry. Due to further increased competition from abroad with the opening towards manufacturing and trade from Eastern European countries, many Danish clothing manufacturing companies had to close down if they had not managed to move their production facilities abroad or convert their companies into so-called "concept houses" (meaning becoming wholesalers of clothing focusing on design, distribution, marketing, and retail, rather than manufacturing). Nevertheless, the Danish fashion industry survived, but it was in the shape of concept houses that a renewed interest emerged in identifying Danish fashion as something unique and worthy for export. Young fashion designers of the 1990s began at first to materialize a new Danish fashion. With the possibilities of producing at low cost in India and other Asian countries, they developed a fashion design image inspired by a bohemian look based on Indian embroidery techniques and the frequent use of glittering sequins for decoration, which would become an iconic symbol of Danish fashion at the time. For the subsequent ten years, fashion designers and fashion brands such as Susanne Rützou, Munthe plus Simonsen, Bruuns Bazaar, and Day Birger et Mikkelsen dominated the Danish fashion scene.

These developments gave rise to a growing Danish fashion scene and a stronger belief in the potential of the Danish fashion industry for international success. The economic boom of the late 1990s and early 2000s further strengthened investment in the industry, along with the Danish government's interest in the Danish fashion industry as a model of how to transform local industries from production-based to knowledge-based due to globalization. And in addition, the government saw the potential through promoting its local fashion industry to upgrade Denmark's image

abroad from being a country of agriculture to being a modern, forward-looking nation attractive for foreign investment, tourism, and fashion shoppers, as well as a place to live for cosmopolitan and young workers. In 2005 this government interest was further stated through a report on the Danish fashion industry and its potential, published by the Ministry of Economics and Business Affairs. In the report it was declared that institutionalization and knowledge sharing were needed in the industry, but it also acknowledged that the industry had the potential to make Denmark/Copenhagen what was termed "the fifth global fashion center" after fashion cities such as Paris, London, New York, and Milan. One outcome of the report was the establishment of the network organization Danish Fashion Institute in Fall 2005 based on shared government and industry funding. The objective of the institute was, first of all, to coordinate the biannual Copenhagen Fashion Week (February/August) and secondly to initiate coordinated branding of Danish fashion locally as well as in immediate export markets.

Within this new situation and the work to follow by the Danish Fashion Institute in branding Danish fashion and seeking to understand and describe what the institute called "the DNA of Danish Fashion," I found it relevant to ask more in-depth: what is Danish fashion and how is Danish fashion done? For theoretical inspiration I chose to turn to poststructuralist ANT in order to be able to investigate the complex practices of national identity constructions in contemporary fashion design. To allow the in-depth analysis required by ANT, I further chose to base my research on a single case study of the small Danish fashion company named Mads Nørgaard-Copenhagen. Selecting this fashion company as my case study was due to its smaller size, characteristic of the majority of Danish fashion companies, being owner-managed, its ties to Danish fashion history, being a well-known fashion brand in Denmark due to its range of iconic fashion statements mainly within menswear fashion, and the company being very deliberate and outspoken of its brand identity.

The case study ended up, in order to follow one of the methodological slogans of ANT: "Follow the actors" (Latour 2005: 12), being based on interviews and ethnographic research conducted during the time period 2005–7. In my fieldwork I decided, in order to understand how Danish fashion is done, to observe first of all the design process of the Mads Nørgaard-Copenhagen Summer 2006 collections for menswear and womenswear, by participating in the meetings of the company's design team. This further led me to observe the production of the company's first fashion show during Copenhagen Fashion Week in August 2005. Additionally I decided to participate in the sales meeting and later on the promotion of the Spring 2008 menswear collection at the French fashion fair *Tranoi Homme* in Paris.

My focus in the case study has been on the making of fashion within the production and distribution phases of a fashion company and not in relation to consumption. The research techniques used during my fieldwork have been taking notes and doing photo documentation while at the different sites of observation. This way of generating research material has been followed up by semi-structured interviews with key people in the company to gain clarification as well as in-depth explanation. Together this research material forms the basis of my analysis.

Before turning to the case study, I shall elaborate on the chosen research approach of ANT.

ANT AND THE STUDY OF FASHION

To put it briefly, ANT can be described as a poststructuralist research method rather than an applied theory (Latour 2005; Law 2004). Rather than outlining grand theories, it is the aim of ANT to be a non-deductive way of understanding how the world is performed, and how it is complex, diffuse, and messy, based on methodologically ethnographic fieldwork. As such, ANT has a strong pragmatic sensibility. As an agnostic research method, it does not seek to evaluate what is right and what is wrong, but to describe and analyze the world in all its complexity and heterogeneity as it is performed in practice (Latour 2005; Law 2004; Law and Mol 2002). Furthermore, a main characteristic of ANT is its principle of general symmetry and its abandonment of a priori distinctions between the common oppositions within modern

thinking such as nature vs. society, material vs. social, actor vs. structure, etc. Instead ANT promotes the understanding of the modern world through concepts of the hybrid, assemblage, and multiplicity (Latour 2005).

The history of ANT dates back to the late 1970s and the laboratory study of the construction of scientific facts by the French philosopher Bruno Latour and the British sociologist Steven Woolgar (Latour and Woolgar [1979] 1986). Their studies introduced a perceptual mode where hard facts are seen as momentarily stabilized networks of human as well as non-human actors (e.g. machinery and results documented in scientific papers). An actor is in this respect not only a person, but something (a kind of entity) having an effect on something else. What is studied through ANT is how networks are stabilized or destabilized through what is termed translation processes, by which the configuration of actor-networks is changed (Callon 1986).

With ANT one can imagine that "all solid melts into air" in the sense that what is studied is all that is involved in the formation of a stabilized actor-network. To some extent this is the case, and the challenge of ANT is therefore when and where to start or stop one's analysis, as the actor-network description in principle is endless. However, the point is not to make a complete description of actor-networks but, based on an ANT analysis, to nuance the understanding of the world and its complex nature by continuously asking new questions to one's research object through the study of how the world is "done" in practice.

For my study of Danish fashion based on an ANT research approach, how Danish fashion is "done" is the main point to achieve and unfold, which I shall do in what follows through the case study of the small Danish fashion company Mads Nørgaard-Copenhagen.

MADS NØRGAARD-COPENHAGEN

The company Mads Nørgaard-Copenhagen is a well-known fashion company in Denmark largely because of its ties to Danish fashion history through the family relations of the founder and owner, Mads Nørgaard, and for its range of nationally known iconic fashion statements, predominantly within menswear fashion. Furthermore, the frequent quoting of Mads Nørgaard in local newspapers and fashion magazines has made him and his fashion brand recognized by most Danes.

Mads Nørgaard (born 1961) has no formal training within the fashion industry. His knowledge about fashion, fashion design, and the fashion industry is obtained through his upbringing as the oldest son of the founder of one of Copenhagen's first youth fashion boutiques, *Nørgaard paa Strøget* (in 1958) and through his own experience within fashion retailing since 1986, when he opened his first menswear fashion shop next to Nørgaard paa Strøget on the main shopping street of Copenhagen.

Mads Nørgaard-Copenhagen started as a retail company, but slowly moved into wholesale. In 1996 the company began designing their own menswear collection, which was followed by a womenswear and a children's wear collection. These collections were first sold on the national market, but entered export markets in Scandinavia and northern Europe in 2001. In 2005 to 2007 the company invested in further export to the USA, as did other Danish fashion companies. The turnover of the company was in 2007 just below 10 million DKK, and it employed nineteen full-time employees; Mads Nørgaard and two of these employees formed the company's design team. At the time of the fieldwork the company was selling to approximately 100 stores in Denmark as well as abroad. The company had one main concept store in Copenhagen, shop-in-shops at the Danish department store *Magasin du Nord*, and one franchise store in Oslo, Norway.

Characteristic to the Mads Nørgaard-Copenhagen brand and its design is to keep a simple silhouette at the same time as having a cool attitude. In that sense the company's design is very different from what has been considered the identity of Danish fashion during the late 1990s and the beginning of the twenty-first century, as described above.

Significant designs to the Mads Nørgaard-Copenhagen menswear collection are the long-sleeved cotton T-shirts, both in single color and two-color stripes, as well as a woolen knitted sailor sweater designed after a heritage pattern dating back to the late nineteenth century according to the company.

The cotton T-shirts are still manufactured in Denmark and the company demonstrates their pride in the fact that the T-shirts are "Made in Denmark." Both Danish references have become key to establishing the brand profile, as Mads Nørgaard often stresses that the Mads Nørgaard-Copenhagen fashion design in his opinion has its roots in the modern Danish design tradition of the 1930s, and pays a particular tribute to what has become a Danish design classic, the PH-lamp, designed by the architect Poul Henningsen (1894–1967). Even though contemporary Danish fashion is referred to as bohemian, Mads Nørgaard also finds it appropriate to apply this tribute to Danish fashion in general, though he sees his design most deliberately expressive of the values and aesthetics of the PH-lamps.

I think the PH-lamp is the best picture of Danish fashion. It is solid and honest. Designed to be used. And it succeeded in that respect. The lamp is used in almost all Danish homes. It is the same with all these Danish fashion brands. Everybody can afford them. You don't need a lot of money in order to buy Danish fashion. Perhaps not buying the fashion of Munthe plus Simonsen. But affordability is a precious Danish value. However, when you look at the Danish design tradition (in furniture, ed.) in the twentieth century, there is a significant distance from fashion brands such as DAY Birger et Mikkelsen, Bruuns Bazar etc. The distance is much shorter to what we do. And if you look at this design tradition in relation to the dressing habits of the Danish consumer, then young Danes have historically been interested in second-hand clothing—wearing classics. For example our sailor's sweater or the T-shirt my father produces. In that respect we are more an outcome of Danish design traditions than the fashion design highly decorated and embroidered with sequins etc!

Additionally, in the brand-bible of the company published in 2007, the mission of the company is stated: "Our goal is to contribute to the continuous development of fashion through relevant and accessible contribution for the benefit of the individual user." The core business idea is that "in a world of constant change we are in love with fashion and innovation. At the same time we feel that change is often happening too quickly in the Western world. That is why we build our collections around a core of classics that stay year after year—as long as they are still in fashion." These statements are further summarized in the quotes selected for the brand-bible, such as "People have the power," by the American singer-songwriter Patti Smith, and "What you wear should support you in your ways and beliefs," by Mads Nørgaard himself.

ASSEMBLING DANISH FASHION AT THE SALES MEETING

A two-day sales meeting takes place in late June 2007 for the upcoming Spring 2008 collection, which will go into fashion fairs and be presented in showrooms for the next few months before being put into production. All of the in-house sales people of the company are gathered at the meeting, as well as the external agents, each representing their international market. There are agents representing Japan, the USA, Austria, Germany, Switzerland, the Netherlands, Belgium, France, Sweden, and Norway.

The sales meeting takes place in an old factory building recently transformed into a restaurant and beach club at the entrance to Copenhagen harbor. In the room, tables are set with white tablecloths and silver chandeliers that soften the otherwise rough and edgy atmosphere of the old factory building. Along the walls are placed racks of samples of the new collection divided into menswear and womenswear.

At the meeting, the design team and Mads Nørgaard are only present at the beginning. Mads Nørgaard briefly introduces the collection, which is named "Mash-up," the music industry term where different genres are mixed up for the purpose of creating something new. For the design team, part of the concept of the collection as "mash-up" is that each style can be mixed with other styles according to the wish of the wearer, supporting the fashion statement of Mads Nørgaard cited in the company's brand bible: "What you wear should support you in your ways and beliefs." Mads Nørgaard explains that the beginning of the collection was an inspirational trip to London, back to "where street fashion started," as he declares.

Walking around the city the design team got a feeling of the contrasts between the different areas, and the clothing and design traditions of Savile Row, the street famous for men's tailoring, and Camden Market, known since the early 1970s as the marketplace for everyday fashionable clothes and arts and crafts. The design team got a feeling of the tension between high-street fashion and street wear, between what is elegant and what is young, urban, and hip. In the collection these tensions have been transformed into silhouettes that are defined as "lean" as opposed to "tight." Lastly, Mads Nørgaard explains that the color scheme of the collection is based on the modernist painter Yves Klein (1928–62) and his significant color "International Klein blue."

After this introduction, the sales meeting begins with the head of sales introducing the collection, presented on live in-house models or hangers. The head of sales introduces each style by commenting on the planned wholesale price and describing any known problems regarding the design, needed volume for production, etc. Now and then the agents want to touch and study the styles regarding the quality of material, sewing details, and design, while they give their feedback to the design team for further adjustments. When it comes to the presentation of a green V-neck, cotton-knitted sweater from the menswear collection, a discussion starts among the agents on whether the design team are right to introduce a reverse visual labeling on the left breast panel with a stitched square indicating the square woven label of Mads Nørgaard-Copenhagen normally sewn inside the clothes. The agents' responses are very different. The Scandinavian agents find the suggestion tedious. The Danish menswear sales person proclaims: "The label is not convincing. For the price of the sweater my Danish customers want a plain non-branded sweater." In Denmark, Mads Nørgaard-Copenhagen is known for its basic designs and quality at what is considered a good price. Being non-branded is part of the company's brand identity. However, according to the American agent, this detail on the sweater has to be further developed and in her opinion introduced to all other knitwear styles of the collection. It adds value to the style, as she argues. It makes what she considers Mads Nørgaard-Copenhagen's simple design have character and distinguishes it from other street wear brands similar to Mads Nørgaard-Copenhagen. As she expresses it: "This will help me tell the story of Mads Nørgaard-Copenhagen's anti-fashion attitude." The Dutch agent agrees with her. He also needs some marks of differentiation in order to convince the Dutch and Belgian buyers that they are getting something particular when they buy Mads Nørgaard-Copenhagen, even though much of the collection in his opinion resembles what local Dutch fashion companies are designing and is not particularly an example of Danish fashion.

After the sales meeting, the design team's response to the discussion is to withdraw the idea of the white stitched square in the collection's knitwear. When I ask the head of sales why the decision was made, he explains that the design team did not feel ready to implement the detail-ing yet and found it complicated to get the stitching right in production so it would not look cheap or like a design error, but rather as an added value to the clothes through design.

The incident demonstrates first of all how different markets ask for different actor-network assemblages of the collection, and secondly it indicates the complexity of doing Danish fashion and wanting to identify the DNA of Danish fashion, the objective of the Danish Fashion Institute as mentioned in the beginning of this article.

Being a representative of Danish fashion, Mads Nørgaard-Copenhagen needs no special material marketing to extend the existing neck-labeling informing the buyer and consumer of the brand identity on the Danish market. Mads Nørgaard-Copenhagen is a Danish household name, known to many Danes partly due to the public profile of Mads Nørgaard, who is often mentioned in local newspapers and fashion magazines, and partly because of his family ties to the fashion boutique Nørgaard paa Strøget, as previously mentioned. On the contrary, the white stitched square will, according to the Danish sales person, inter-fere with the existing image of Mads Nørgaard-Copenhagen by making its design as even more visually branded goods. The white stitched square is, so to speak, an unwelcome actor that the sales person wants to keep outside the actor-network of Mads

Nørgaard-Copenhagen's collections. If included it will, in his opinion, destabilize the actor-network and, in other words, harm the brand identity of the company on its home market.

The situation seems to be the direct reverse of the viewpoint of both the American and the Dutch agents. If the white stitched square is included in the actor-network it will in their opinion strengthen it—strengthen the stabilization of the actor-network of Mads Nørgaard-Copenhagen on the American, the Dutch, and Belgian markets, at least. This material specificity is to the foreign agents regarded as important for transforming Mads Nørgaard-Copenhagen into an internationally recognizable fashion brand among other fashion brands of apparently similar design, as the company does not have the same resonance abroad. In the agents opinion, outside Denmark and Scandinavia, Mads Nørgaard is not a well-known fashion designer or fashion commentator, if at all known to the general fashion consumers. His story and the story of the company need to be told, and according to the agents it is not enough to do it verbally or through advertising campaigns. In the agents' opinion, it has also to be materially supported, as an integrated part of the design of the clothes.

The occurrence of this discussion at the sales meeting can when perceived through the ANT approach teach us more about the complexity of "doing" Danish fashion and getting the message of a national fashion identity, in all its complexity, across national borders in a market as international as the fashion market. As seen in this case, qualifying national identity to fashion design appears to be dependent on various practices due to specific contexts. In that sense, and drawing on the work of the Dutch ANT scholar Annemarie Mol, the understanding of national identity in fashion multiplies (Mol 2002). National identity in fashion has, to use the terminology of Mol, "multiple ontological forms" depending on where it is supposed to be situated, at least when the design of the fashionable clothes is not based on already internationally recognized iconic national design traditions, as in the case of Mads Nørgaard-Copenhagen according to the Dutch and American agents. One stable actor-network cannot be transported from one contextual setting to another without being transformed as it is said in ANT (Latour 2005). Even though Mads Nørgaard finds his brand tied into Danish design traditions and values, and is recognized for this locally, it is challenging for fashion companies such as Mads Nørgaard-Copenhagen to be recognized as Danish fashion in a concise way, delivering a clear message of the values of the Danishness of Danish fashion when selling on a market outside Denmark. Outside Denmark, his T-shirts, simple cuts, and use of classic silhouettes become generic of their kind. It has a Western and European atmosphere to it, but is difficult, if at all possible, to differentiate as something particularly Danish. To that extent, a Danish fashion identity is not yet constructed strongly enough as a stabilized actor-network in itself to be communicated as such outside Denmark. Particular cuts, styles, colors or crafting techniques are not present and widely known as Danish, as in, for example, the Scottish tartans, German lederhosen, dirndl dresses, embroidered felt jackets, Japanese kimonos, Indian saris and colors (orange, pink, red), Norwegian knitwear patterns, etc. And without such stabilized actor-network of Danish dress traditions it is not an option to exoticize a stereotypical version of Danish dress traditions with the aim of constructing a Danish fashion identity.

The situation at the sales meeting do further point at the challenges of wanting to identify the DNA of Danish fashion and coordinating its branding as it is the case of the recently established Danish Fashion Institute. Wanting to identify a common denominator of fashion design made in Denmark is difficult not only due to the practices of fashion design crossing national borders, as demonstrated in the first situation presented from my fieldwork, but also due to the fact that different market asks for different marks of differentiation. For a small company like Mads Nørgaard-Copenhagen, and the majority of companies of the Danish fashion industry, it seems a challenge to build a strong brand identity outside their home market. Consequently, it further makes it challenging to brand Danish fashion representing the whole fashion industry in Denmark. The case study at Mads Nørgaard-Copenhagen shows that the current interest in fashion's national identity is rather a national issue of governmental and institutional interest, than a directly integrated part of the practices of fashion design.

SAME, SAME BUT DIFFERENT

Returning to the hype of fashion's national identity, as highlighted in the beginning of this article, Teunissen has stated in the book *Global Fashion Local Tradition* (2005), that this tendency could be understood as a reaction to the globalization of the fashion industry which has intensified over the last ten to twenty years. It has challenged the industry to find ways of being competitive, where the promotion of national specificity to fashion design is one strategy among others. Teunissen further says that there is a tendency within parts of the international fashion industry to operate in a global industry but with "a local accent," meaning using local dress traditions and craftsmanship to make their fashion contribution distinct or incorporating a "search for authenticity" in fashion design, reversing the common relationship between the exotic product and the current Western fashion tastes. The tendency today is not that the exotic product has to adapt to Western fashion tastes, but that it "remain at the centre of attention and, with a few details, acquire a fashionable look so as to satisfy international tastes" (Teunissen 2005: 11).

Using the approach of ANT to understand this tendency in the fashion industry in this article has opened an insight into how working with national identity in the fashion industry is done. In particular, ANT has the strength to unfold the relationships among actors and their formation into actor-networks, and to understand how actor-networks are assembled through different practices, as illustrated through the case study of Mads Nørgaard-Copenhagen. ANT, so to speak, stimulates the micro-empirical perspective and is not aimed at making a grand theory of fashion design and national identity. ANT has its focus on complexity; how the world is a mess, and has the ambition to describe it as such in order to be more nuanced in its understanding of it.

Through the looking glass of ANT, the extracted parts of my fieldwork at Mads Nørgaard-Copenhagen presented here demonstrate precisely the complex field of fashion design and national identity. ANT is neither able nor willing to put forward singular answers; instead through the nuanced description of the fashion design process and how Danish fashion is "done," it has made it possible to see how, in the case of Mads Nørgaard-Copenhagen, issues of national identity are not directly a focus in the design process as otherwise stated by Teunissen. The lack of an awareness of local dress traditions in Denmark could be one reason for the different situation. Another reason is that the focus of fashion's national identity is first of all an issue of governmental and institutional interest, often supported by the representation of fashion by fashion media, which seems to be the situation in the Danish case. With the research approach of ANT and hereby following the many different actors forming the actor-network of Danish fashion this has become clear and leads us to ask additional questions in order to further, and in even more depth, understand the complexity of "doing" Danish fashion.

In the case study of Mads Nørgaard-Copenhagen it has led me to consider further questions, among others: to what extend shall national identity of fashion design determine the building of a fashion brand and materialize in its collection? How shall a Danish fashion company as Mads Nørgaard-Copenhagen react to the ambitions and industry policies of the government regarding the identification and promotion of a Danish fashion brand? Why are Danish dress traditions nonexistent as reproduced by the Mads Nørgaard-Copenhagen design team and in general by Danish fashion designers? And further with the Danish government's ambition of making Denmark/Copenhagen "the fifth global fashion center" and promoting Danish fashion, is there a need to be more ambitious and revise the curriculum of Danish fashion design education by introducing teaching elements of cultural heritage, local craftsmanship regarding the making of clothes, and the history of previous acknowledged local dress traditions?

These questions I will not answer here, as the purpose of the article is to point at a more nuanced understanding of the role national identity plays in relation to the fashion design and the fashion industry and to introduce ANT as a research approach to fashion studies. Instead in what follows I will summarize my main points.

CONCLUDING REMARKS

Understanding the current attraction of the interrelationship of global fashion and local tradition through the case of the Danish fashion industry and more specifically the single case study of the fashion company Mads Nørgaard-Copenhagen, this article has introduced a poststructuralist research approach to the subject matter. Informed by ANT and based on the empirical case study of the small Danish fashion company, Mads Nørgaard-Copenhagen, the complexity of the social-material practices of national identity has been unfolded in relation to the practices of fashion design. It has been demonstrated that there is still a gap between industry policy, government agendas, and the hands-on practices of fashion designers and fashion companies such as Mads Nørgaard-Copenhagen, making it currently challenging to fulfill the ambitions of building a strong collective Danish fashion brand and securing its international recognition among fashion buyers as well as consumers.

Introducing ANT as a research approach to studies in fashion demonstrates a way of studying that includes the materiality of fashion design much more literally, and overcomes the often reductionist results of *reading* fashion. However, as is pointed out, the approach will not lead to grand theories of fashion, but will rather provide detailed description on a micro-empirical level leading to qualifying further research questions.

Depending what one's research goal is, this can be seen as either a weakness or a strength of the research approach. Acknowledging the complexity of fashion and our still-limited knowledge of it, I do however see ANT as one way forward for future fashion studies that will further open our understanding of fashion and its many dimensions. Let us follow the actors, as Latour dictates!

PART 6

CLOTHING, CLASS, AND COMPETING COSMOPOLITANISMS

PART INTRODUCTION

Dress, the previous two parts of the reader effectively demonstrate, often serves the interests of colonial regimes and national governments, visually distinguishing one society from another and reinforcing the boundaries between them. But dress can also serve to differentiate distinct, often hierarchically positioned groups within a single society. It has, to use the American social critic Thorstein Veblen's terminology, an "invidious character" (Veblen [1899] 1994: 3). Veblen was particularly interested in the class dynamics of late nineteenth-century American cities and the status games members of the middle and upper classes played to demonstrate their superiority to those who occupied a lower rung in the social hierarchy. Veblen referred to the practices by which the relatively rich distinguish themselves from everyone else as "conspicuous consumption." Dress took its place among a number of class-based practices, from going to the "right" golf courses to eating at the "right" restaurants, that serve to reinforce the social status quo. The rich stay rich, at least in part, because they know how to tastefully dress like the rich.

Veblen's work drew attention to the class functionality of dress, and it went on to influence many prominent class theorists, including, most famously, the sociologist Pierre Bourdieu. Though Bourdieu himself did not specifically write about dress, preferring instead to focus his attention on matters of taste in music, art, and household decoration, he has nonetheless become an important theoretical resource for anthropologists attempting to theorize the invidious character of dress. Unlike Veblen and Bourdieu, however, anthropologists of dress and fashion have tended to emphasize the contradictory character of class-based practices. People around the world use dress to navigate a complex path through a messy cultural terrain. The chapters in this part of the reader explore the myriad status games that people throughout the world play and how individuals, locked into playing those games whether they want to or not, bend the rules, cheat, or simply learn to navigate them as best they can.

Deborah Heath's article on the dress practices taking place in Kaolack, a multiethnic, predominantly Wolof city in Senegal, starts us out with an important reminder that status games are not just a matter of powerful groups acting on the less powerful. The social practices of dress, she argues, "embody a dialogue between dominant and alternative or oppositional voices" (p. 232). Borrowing the concept of "heteroglossia" from the Russian literary theorist Mikhail Bakhtin, she calls for attention to how dress is a dynamic process of meaning production, in which meanings intersect, overlap, and overtake one another in a continual dialogic exchange. It is not enough, then, for anthropologists to assume that the dress practices of a group reflect their social status. We have to see these practices as operating within a larger cultural field, full of "social and ideological complexity and contradiction" (p. 241). Class formation and reproduction are never unidirectional. They are produced through continual struggle between differently positioned social actors.

Schoss presents another rich example of the kinds of heteroglossic dress practices Heath describes. Focusing on the sartorial style of tour guides in Malindi, a coastal city in Kenya, Schoss shows how these "cultural brokers" use clothes, demeanor, language, and other communicational tools to construct bridges between their world and the tourists' worlds. They embody a cosmopolitan identity, she claims, built in part, through the clothes they wear and the way they wear them. Yet this cosmopolitan identity does not make Malindi tour guides the same as the tourists they host, nor is it taken up in precisely the same way by each tour guide who assumes it. There is not one single cosmopolitanism spreading across the globe, homogenizing the world's populations. Rather, Schoss argues, the Malindi case shows that processes of globalization are producing a "multiplicity of cosmopolitanisms" (p. 250) forged by differently situated local actors adapting to uniquely configured circumstances.

These intersections produce dynamic new syncretisms, new, hybridized cultural formations with their own distinctive patterns of dress. They also often exist in dynamic, sometimes unresolvable tension. Such is the case in San'a, the capital of the Yemen Arab Republic, where Annelies Moors did her fieldwork. Islam and fashion, she explains, are often seen as ideological opposites in San'a. And yet many women find ways to embrace both. Even covered from head to toe in loose black garments, women are able, in small, sometimes barely perceptible ways, to attend to the vicissitudes of fashion. As such, women's garments have undergone visible changes over time. Many women adopt a sophisticated, cosmopolitan sensibility, even while presenting themselves modestly. "Fashionable Muslim," then, is not a contradiction in terms. It is a distinctly contemporary stance, a way of situating oneself in multiple global discourses at once.

Emma Tarlo, in her contribution to this reader, furthers this argument by focusing on the role of dress in forming "cosmopolitan Pan-Islamic Muslim identities" among Londoners of South Asian descent. Tarlo is interested in the practice of being "visibly Muslim," i.e., of marking oneself through clothing choice as a member of the Muslim faith in a diverse society where Muslims remain a minority. To be visibly Muslim is to make a series of choices, Tarlo explains, about how "Western" or "cultural" one wants to appear, and how willing one is to draw the ire or suspicion of white Londoners and the older generation of South Asians, who often accuse the younger generation of looking "too Islamic." By pushing against the constraints and expectations of both the dominant culture and their parents' culture, such young Muslim women are helping forge a new set of parameters for being young and Muslim in England today.

Adeline Masquelier, in her chapter, looks at the dress practices of young Muslim men in Niger. Though they are subject to less restrictive expectations by parents and peers—Masquelier claims that they often resist the very notion that what they wear should reflect their Muslim identity—they are no less preoccupied by what they wear. Name brand T-shirts, sneakers, and jeans are a must. Keeping abreast of the latest streetwear trends on the global scene is critical. Dress and fashion, she argues, are two of the primary tools at young men's disposal for advancing in the class hierarchy, proving their status to their peers, or laying claim on their place in a transnational youth culture they feel destined to view from afar. Young men in Niger never forget their peripheral status. It informs their attitudes, their preoccupation with style. But at least through wearing the right clothes they can feel more a part of the global scene. They can remake themselves as modern cosmopolitans.

This emphasis on being, or becoming, cosmopolitan runs through the chapters in this part of the reader. But not everyone see this as an admirable goal. Eric Silverman's chapter chronicles the conservative "anti-fashion" dress practices of Orthodox Jews, living in societies that don't necessarily share their concern with modesty. How women in particular dress, explains Silverman, is of dire concern to orthodox rabbis, as it is to the women themselves. Dressing modestly, on the one hand, can be seen as a gift. It frees women from the mandates of fashion. Plus, it protects them from the male gaze. On the other hand, modesty is a burden women bear on behalf of men. It is not the responsibility of men to avert their own gaze or manage their own lust. That falls on women, who are continually scrutinized and judged by patriarchal standards. Nonetheless, orthodox women remain enmeshed in the currents of fashion, whether they choose to follow them or not. They are not above consumerism, nor do they refrain from all forms of vanity. To be orthodox today, Silverman concludes, is to be engaged in an unresolvable set of contradictions: to be at once modern and traditional, involved in the larger society yet devoted to one's own group. The same could probably be said about each of groups discussed in this section. Cosmopolitanism isn't something that is adopted or rejected once then forgotten about. In order to be maintained, cosmopolitanism must be continually managed, reaffirmed, and negotiated.

27

FASHION, ANTI-FASHION, AND HETEROGLOSSIA IN URBAN SENEGAL

Deborah Heath

In the regional capital of Kaolack, a multiethnic, predominantly Wolof city in Senegal, the social practices of dress and the production and decoration of textiles embody a dialogue between dominant and alternative or oppositional voices. This dialogic process is what Bakhtin (1982) calls heteroglossia. Communicative practice in a given society, as Bakhtin conceives of it, entails both a centripetal, unifying aspect tending toward a single cohesive ideological system and a centrifugal aspect marked by stratification and diversity. This perspective sheds light on the dynamics of hegemony that shape the practice of *sañse*.

The concept of hegemony, as formulated by Gramsci (1971), refers to the control that the dominant groups in a society exercise through ideology, by winning the consent of the dominated. Recent writers (among them Scott [1985] and Sider [1986]) have followed Raymond Williams (1977) in conceiving of hegemony as a dialectical process, grounded in social practice, that necessarily includes challenges to dominant ideological structures. It entails a dynamic much like that which Bakhtin refers to as heteroglossia. Seen from this perspective, variability and contradiction are intrinsic, not incidental, to hegemony.

In the following passage, Williams suggests that what Bakhtin would call centrifugal forces are inherent in hegemony:

> A lived hegemony is always a process. It is not, except analytically, a system or a structure. It is a realized complex of experiences, relationships, and activities, with specific and changing pressures and limits.
>
> In practice, hegemony can never be singular .... It has continually to be renewed, recreated, defended, and modified. It is also continually resisted, limited, altered, challenged by pressures not at all its own. (1977:112)

It is because of this, Williams says, that our understanding of hegemony must include the concepts of counterhegemony and alternative hegemony, "as indicative features of what the hegemonic process has in practice had to work to control" (1977:113).

Sañse and the social practices that surround it constitute a complex dialogue in which there are, on the one hand, counterhegemonic impulses and, on the other, tensions and alliances between alternative hegemonic interests, which include the hegemony of Western fashion, the dominance of the Senegambian urban elite, and male control of resources. This is, in the words of Bakhtin's colleague Vološinov, "an intersecting of differently oriented interests within one and the same sign community ... [in which] differently oriented accents intersect in every ideological sign" ([1929] 1973[b]: 23). As a code, a context of performance, a set of social relations, *sañse*, along with the various social accents with which it is inflected, is a focal point for the construction of social identity and difference.

Adapted from Deborah Heath, "Fashion, Anti-Fashion, and Heteroglossia in urban Senegal," *American Ethnologist* 19, no. 1 (1992): 19–33.

IDENTITY AND DIFFERENCE IN SENEGAMBIAN FASHION

Sañse is highly valued in the cities of Senegal and The Gambia, particularly among women. The elegant sartorial style of Senegalese women—the well-starched, copious folds of their colorful garments, accompanied by matching headdresses and abundant quantities of gold jewelry—draws praise, when well executed, from women and men alike. Achieving such a style is, however, expensive. In order to make a statement about the social position occupied or sought by the person so adorned, *sañse* deploys luxury commodities, costly fabrics as well as precious metals.

Sañse forges a link between having and being, displaying both wealth and social identity. As such, it is an indexical communicative act (cf. Silverstein 1976); that is, it derives its meaning from its context of use, pointing to the larger social hierarchy within which an actor is situated. At the same time, *sañse* is part of the broader discourse of Senegambian urban culture, in which diverse and often contradictory codes intersect.

Certain public ritual occasions are the principal settings for *sañse*: life-cycle rituals such as baptisms and weddings; religious events such as Muslim feast days or meetings of Islamic associations; and electoral events such as political rallies. These are performance events at which social identities are constructed and maintained; this is the "front stage" on which the politics of reputation is played out.

Identity construction necessarily entails the marking of difference. *Sañse* and the social practices that surround it are inflected by accents of identity and difference on a number of levels: tradition and modernity, "Western" and "African" style, religious devotion and heterodoxy, autonomy and dependence. These may be seen in terms of heteroglossia, which, with its dialogic perspective on the process of meaning production, "refers to the constant interaction between meanings, all of which have the potential of conditioning others" (Layne 1989:25). This complex intersection of meanings figures in the continuous generation of new styles that constitutes fashion in urban Senegambia.

In cities like Kaolack, urban tailors, invariably male, meet and help to create the demands of their customers with an impressive, rapidly changing array of styles, those for younger women often incorporating design elements of apparent Western origin, such as flounces, lace, and fitted, zippered bodices. Roland Barthes (1985), in *The Fashion System*, identifies the continual proliferation of "new" or "novel" goods and the concomitant creation of new "needs" that we associate with fashion as intrinsic features of capitalist commodity production. Weiner and Schneider relate this to a discussion of historical changes in the social uses of cloth:

> Capitalist production and its associated values reordered the symbolic potential of cloth …. [B]y encouraging the growth of fashion—a consumption system of high-velocity turnover and endless, ever-changing variation—capitalist entrepreneurs vastly inflated dress and adornment as a domain for expression through cloth. (1989: 4)

This process has been under way in Senegal and The Gambia for some time, as Gamble, writing in the 1960s, attests:

> Although Wolof dress is unmistakable, a study of old photographs shows many changes in dress and hair style. … In Dakar elegant Wolof have been chosen as mannequins, and are provided with free dresses, in order to stimulate interest in new styles. The result is that fashions are said to change every six months instead of every two years. (1967:80)

Sañse, as fashion, certainly appears to reflect the hegemony of capitalist consumerism, a global system in which commodities produced in central places carry a high symbolic value. Gamble's informants in The Gambia (c. 1960) offer an image of the political economy of the Wolof fashion system, in which news of the latest trends in urban women's apparel is dispersed through a hierarchy of central places: "Gambians say that St. Louis copies Paris fashions, Dakar copies St. Louis, while Bathurst [Banjul, capital of The Gambia] copies Dakar" (1967: 79–80).

Still, fashion is not monologic. Although Senegambian fashion is clearly implicated in the dynamics of hegemony, it is important to bear in mind that hegemony, in Bakhtin's terms, has a centrifugal as well as a centripetal dimension. What Gamble describes is not a unilinear process of diffusion, in which dominant cultural forms are passively received and accepted. While *sañse*, or high fashion Senegambian-style, often incorporates elements derived from the centers of commoditized fashion production in Europe or the United States, the process is a selective one, and one, moreover, in which the end products explicitly express their "Africanness," along with what appear to be imported stylistic details. Moving beyond Barthes's ([1967] 1983) structuralist account, we see that there is motion in the fashion system (cf. Trouillot 1982), not all of which originates in the system's central places.

Tailors in Kaolack or Banjul may peruse Western fashion magazines, looking for elements of metropolitan haute couture, such as novel necklines or sleeve styles, in order to enhance their customers' costumes. Still, as Gamble says, "the final result is unmistakably African" (1967: 80). We might say, pace Hobsbawm and Ranger (1983), that both tradition and modernity are invented, or represented, through *sañse*, at the same time that structures of inequality are reproduced through the public display of material resources.

Although some younger women wear stylish jeans or "Western" dresses as everyday garments, on the important public occasions at which *sañse* is performed the preferred costume for adult women is the *mbubb*, or *grand boubou*, a voluminous unfitted garment that is less tailored—more "African," according to my informants in Kaolack—than the costumes women wore 30 years ago to social events in the coastal cities of Senegal and The Gambia. This garb is consistent with the development of a nationalist ideology before and after Senegalese independence in 1960, and with the articulation of that ideology by an urban elite for whom the sartorial expression of tradition has become part of a Senegambian urban style.

Two types of cloth figure among the most highly prized in the execution of *sañse*, one imported, the other a traditional handwoven fabric. The first is imported machine-made damask, or *basang*. Prospective buyers are keenly aware of differences in quality; top-grade damask is called *basang ris* (French, *basin riche*). Some *basang ris* receives, as it were, an overlay of tradition

after it arrives in Africa. Overdyed (*cuub*) with indigo in tie-dye or embroidery-resist designs, it brings an even higher price.

The second type of fabric is the luxurious strip cloth with its brightly colored designs standing in relief against a white or black background, woven by Manjak weavers from southern Senegal and Guinea-Bissau. The designs and technology of Manjak cloth originated in the highly valued cloth currency produced by African slaves for the Portuguese on the Cape Verde Islands, beginning in the mid-1500s (Carreira 1968: 163–64). As with other types of strip cloth, the lengths of Manjak cloth are normally sewn together to form a wrap cloth. Because of its high price, however, Manjak cloth is often sewn in horizontal bands on a less expensive piece of fabric the same color as the background behind the embroidered designs on the strips.

The ensemble conventionally worn by women on ceremonial occasions consists of an ankle-length wrap cloth (*sér*) and a capacious overgarment (*mbubb*, or *grand boubou*) with matching headscarf (*musóór*, from the French *mouchoire*). Quality damask (*basang ris*) is the cloth of preference for a fancy *mbubb*, and often for the whole ensemble. Since Manjak strip cloth is quite heavy, it is used for the wrap cloth alone. About five meters of cloth are needed to make a *sér*, *mbubb*, and *musóór*; in 1982 an ensemble made from high-quality damask cost 13,500 cfa, about $67, more than a month's income for a great many households in Kaolack. Elaborate machine embroidery is *de rigueur* for a fancy item of apparel. Normally done by male tailors, it augments the price of the finished garment; a sumptuous, heavily embroidered ensemble can cost 50,000 cfa ($250) or more.

Women confront the discrepancy between economic constraints and the expense of *sañse*'s luxury commodities in a number of ways, with some women having more options than others. Poorer women content themselves with outfits made from the inexpensive, machine-printed cotton called *legos*, named after Lagos, Nigeria, though now produced by Senegal's state-supported textile industry, SOTIBA-SIMPAFRIC. Widely available in Kaolack's central market, which is known in Wolof as *marse bu mag*, the Big Market, its colorful patterns often imitate those of the more costly textiles—strip cloth, embroidery-resist, batik. Here we see centripetal and centrifugal impulses simultaneously at work.

In one sense, these simulations reproduce a hierarchy of prestige through a process that seems calculated both to mitigate and to yield profit from the desires of women of lesser means. In this case, the mass-production of simulated luxury commodities not only serves the financial interests of the state (SOTIBA-SIMPAFRIC) but also reinforces the perceived value of the cloth that is imitated. In another sense, the cheaper imitations—which are never confused with the luxury fabrics that they imitate—signal social difference, reinforcing both the distance between women of greater and those of lesser means and a sense of identity, through exclusion, among lower-class women. At the same time, the dominant cultural prescription to *sañse*, or dress well, using the best possible materials, is compelling. As I will illustrate, women use a variety of strategies to achieve this end, drawing on different sets of social relations.

CLOTH, RECIPROCITY, AND THE POLITICS OF REPUTATION

Using the circuits of reciprocal exchange that reproduce ties of kinship, friendship, and patron-clientage, many women are able, in spite of limited income, to acquire the luxury textiles that well-executed *sañse* requires. Such gift-giving, like the performance of *sañse* that it may facilitate, is important to a woman's reputation for largesse. Thus, while these exchanges reinforce the solidarity of ongoing relationships, they also reproduce social asymmetry.

Women may assist one another with ceremonial expenses, including the purchase of appropriate finery, through *tontines*, revolving credit associations, in which members contribute a fixed amount on a regular basis, with each member in turn receiving the total amount. Children learn the principles of this form of mutual assistance through membership in a *mbotaay* (association) called *ndey dikke*. At the meetings of one such group in Kaolack, each child contributed 100 cfa per week, with the total of 2000–2500 cfa, the price of two meters of cloth, going to a different child

each time. Supervised by a young married woman known by the fictive kin title of mother, *mère*, of the group, the children, mostly young girls, would gather together in the afternoon on a weekly basis. Using upside-down bowls as percussion instruments, they would spend most of the time singing songs, with the *mère* overseeing the collection of money and the distribution of the cloth.

Women also give one another cloth at baptisms and wedding ceremonies, thus helping to create and reproduce the bonds that constitute women's social networks. At such events, a careful count is kept of the type and amount of cloth or the amount of cash that each guest gives, and the recipient is expected to reciprocate when attending future ceremonies held for the gift-givers, ideally bringing gifts of greater value than those received. Older informants told me that people used to expect that gifts would be reciprocated with prestations of equal value; they likened the recent heightening of expectations to contemporary monetary inflation.

The social practices of gift-giving and display that surround *sañse* encode both hierarchy and reciprocity. As an index of social identity *sañse* is linked to Wolof notions of honor (*kersa*), discretion (*sutra*), and service, which situate individuals in society in terms of their relations to, and behavior toward, others. In Wolof culture, the possession and display of material goods are intimately tied to notions of generosity and hospitality (*teranga*). Related to this is the notion that wealth (*alàl*) is an aspect of honor and respectability. One's reputation is based on possessions, not merely for their own sake but as an index of one's capacity and willingness to bestow gifts on those of lesser means, especially those who perform services of various sorts.

Following long-established tradition, a prospective groom may offer cloth as part of the brideprice he gives to the family of the bride-to-be and later to the bride herself when the marriage is consummated (Ames 1955). A woman may also receive a damask ensemble from her husband or suitor on the occasion of a life-cycle ceremony such as a baptism. Such prestations, along with other visible ceremonial expenditures, make a public statement about what the woman's suitor or husband has and who he is, a message that will be reiterated each time the beneficiary wears her new attire. He will, therefore, discreetly make every effort to use his own ties to patrons, friends, and kin to meet these costs. The element of discretion (*sutra*) is important to the politics of reputation in terms of concealing the gift-giver's own social and material indebtedness, thus maintaining his reputation as a person of means, honor, and restraint.

Sañse, as a public display of someone else's generosity, may be seen as a service, as a communicative act in which a woman conveys a message on someone else's behalf. This is called *jottali*, a subordinate's transmission of goods or verbal services for a superior (*kilifë*) (Irvine 1974: 327). Thus, a woman may properly be expected to carry out this task for her husband, who is considered her *kilifë*, or master. This set of cultural norms extends, as I indicate below, beyond the domestic sphere.

Whereas wealth and generosity are seen as markers of high status, physical and verbal activity connote low status. The restraint ideally associated with high status poses a dilemma in the politics of reputation, since acquiring and maintaining both wealth and a good reputation often involve a level of activity inconsistent with high status, *Jottali* helps to resolve the contradiction. By physically moving through space, or conveying a message in a public setting, those in service to a superior protect and enhance the latter's reputation for the *kersa*, or sense of honor manifested through restraint, that is appropriate to those of high status. The following section depicts the way that *sañse* figures in this dynamic within the context of patron-client politics.

SAÑSE AND ELECTORAL POLITICS

During the 1982 regional political campaign, there was an advertisement broadcast on Radio Kaolack for an event organized by one of the factions of the ruling party, the Parti Socialiste. In the course of this announcement, the praise singer transmitting the message on behalf of his patrons made a special plea to young women: "*Xale yi! Nangeen ñów di sañse seen sañse bu rafet*" ("Young ladies! Please come dressed up in your [most] beautiful finery"). The well- dressed

women who attend a public function like a political rally are considered an important part of the ambiance.

Insofar as *sañse* is a public presentation of wealth (*alàl*), it enters into the politics of reputation. To have wealth and to dispense it generously are important elements of high social standing. To display it too ostentatiously, however, would run counter to the Wolof notion of *kersa*. So it is that women, through *sañse*, may transmit (*jottali*) the message that their male *kilifë* are men of means, at the same time allowing the latter to behave with appropriate reserve. In this, *sañse* resembles the wearing of livery by nobles' servants in Europe during the Middle Ages:

> Dressing established vertical links in the society, articulated ties of dependency as the ligaments of the social order. A noble's servant … embodied and displayed his power. Display thus became one of the principal political obligations of service. The point was to demonstrate not merely that you belonged to someone else … but that he was powerful. … Fashion in this sense also demonstrated the political and personal advantages of being in some man's service. (Fox-Genovese 1987: 12)

In the setting of the political rally, I would argue, women's *sañse* makes a general statement about the worth or social standing of the *kilifë* (usually male, sometimes female) of a particular party faction. In the competition for clients, the presence of well-dressed women is evidence of faction leaders' success in attracting high-status followers.

At the same time, it should be noted that some women, such as well-placed politicians or traders of independent means, control their own material resources and are in a position both to finance their own sartorial purchases and to maintain their own clients. The Wolof proverb "*Xarum waay, gaynde waay*" ("The sheep of one person, the lion of another") refers to the fact that nearly everyone in the Wolof social hierarchy occupies, at various times and in various contexts, the roles of both server and served, patron and client. So it is that *sañse*, as a public display of wealth, carries a double message. It indicates two possibilities that are in no sense mutually exclusive: first, that the well-dressed woman has been well provided for, generally by her husband or suitor; and second, that she is a person of independent means, herself in a position to grant largesse to others.

Two factors reinforce the link between these two connotations of *sañse*. First, both cloth and gold, though often procured as gifts, are considered a woman's inalienable possessions, which she has the right to convert to other uses and to take with her in the event, for example, of divorce. Second, while a woman's husband is expected to support her and their children, any income she makes through her own labors is hers to dispense as she chooses. *Sañse*, then, is a multivalent index of both autonomy and dependence in relations between women and men.

SAÑSE AND THE POLITICS OF RELIGIOUS RITUAL

Islamic religious meetings in Kaolack, occasions for the members of women's *dahira*, or associations, to *sañse*, offer an illustration of how women's sartorial practice in this regional capital reproduces both bonds of friendship among women and social stratification. A meeting of the Murid Islamic order that I attended in Kaolack was held at night under a large tent, well illuminated inside and out with electric lights. Here and there, large, hand-painted portraits of Murid religious leaders provided spots of bright color. Inside, the disciples, both women and men, walked in a large circle, swaying rhythmically in a slow two-step and sometimes clapping in time with religious verses chanted in Arabic or Wolof by a male singer holding a microphone. The measured cadence of the singing and of the disciples' movements went on until dawn, with some individuals periodically leaving the circle to join the audience seated in the rows of surrounding chairs. Others spontaneously relinquished their seats to enter the circular procession.

The event was an occasion for members of the urban bourgeoisie to demonstrate not only spiritual devotion but also wealth and largesse. In a broader sense, it demonstrated the centripetal impulse in the construction of hegemony, with the voices of the two primary factions of the regional ruling class, the

Muslim clergy and the urban bourgeoisie, intersecting in the practices of *sañse* and public prestation. At the same time, the collective actions of some of the women attending the meeting demonstrated their partial autonomy.

Before the meeting, members of one women's *dahira* had pooled their resources so that all the group's members could appear in identical ensembles, made of white *basang ris*, high-quality damask. In ritual contexts white is the color of spiritual purity: it is the color of the cloth used to swaddle a newborn infant on its naming day, to cover a bride's head when she is delivered to her husband's household, and to shroud the dead before burial. In the context of the religious meeting, the women's matching white ensembles underscored their shared identities as devout Muslims and their potential for autonomous action as adepts with the means to make generous prestations to their spiritual leader.

The members of the *dahira* displayed their matching finery as they entered the promenade in a bloc, following one another in single file. Like others in the circle, they made cash prestations to their religious leader, the *sëriñ*, with the amounts announced over the loudspeaker to the assembled congregation. Through their collective performance of *sañse* and their publicly acknowledged tithing, the women accomplished two things. First, they paid homage to their religious guide, their *kilifë*, for which they could expect *barke* (spiritual grace) in return. Second, they made a statement about their position in society. Their collective strategy, the pooling and equal distribution of resources within the group, allowed them to enhance the prestige of each member. This is, as was mentioned earlier, a route to increased autonomy that women routinely use in other spheres as well, pooling individual resources and acting in concert to acquire goods for sale at a better price or to meet the ceremonial expenses of life-cycle rituals, for example.

Yet not all of the women attending the meeting had the means to *sañse* as elegantly as the members of the *dahira*. And many who joined the circuit of adepts would give only a few coins, unlike the bills in large denominations held aloft by those striving to maintain a reputation for generosity. On the edges of the circle, women, observing the discretion (*sutra*) that the politics of reputation demands, would covertly pass money to their impecunious friends so that they too might participate by making a modest contribution.

The tent's interior defined a social space that established both inclusive bonds of identity and internal stratification. Outside, near the tent's entrances, were women excluded entirely from the main stage of this performance event and from participation in the prestations and the sartorial display. Dressed in the inexpensive cotton prints called *legos*, these vendors of snacks and souvenirs were collecting money rather than giving it away with fanfare. The material needs of the vendors restricted them to the periphery of the event, far from the center of activity where reputations were enhanced through public display and the dispersal of wealth. Their position as marginalized actors in this ritual event bespoke their position as subordinates in the larger system of stratification.

Sañse, then, marked both identity and difference among the various participants in the religious meeting. From the public display of the *dahira* members to the trading activities of the women outside the tent, the social practices that constituted the event as a whole reproduced both the solidary bonds of friendship between women, enhancing their autonomy, and social asymmetry, setting some participants apart from others.

ANTI-FASHION AND MUSLIM HETERODOXY

There is another group of Muslim adepts who use their attire to make an active, oppositional statement about both fashion commodities and their own relationship to the wider society. At the edges of the dominant system of sartorial expression in urban Senegal, a process of recuperation and symbolic reappropriation is at work. Members of an unorthodox Muslim sect called the Baay Fàl use scraps of brightly colored *legos* to fashion their distinctive voluminous patchwork pantaloons (*caya*). These form part of a counterhegemonic style and ideology.

The Baay Fàl are a subsect of the Senegalese Islamic order, the Muridiyya. The most visible Baay Fàl members are mendicants who renounce their worldly possessions when they enter a life of service to the Murid clergy. They claim to pattern their actions after those of their founder, Sééx Ibrahima Fàl, devoted disciple and companion of Murid founder Sééx Amadu Bamba. Like Ibrahima Fàl, the Baay Fàl adepts let their hair grow, reportedly in order to carry heavier loads for their *kilifë*, religious masters. Another element of their costume is the large studded clubs that they carry, used for self-flagellation in ceremonies meant to demonstrate the depths of their religious devotion, as well as to symbolize their role as enforcers for the clergy.

The Baay Fàl style may be likened to what Halliday (1976) calls anti-languages, codes such as prison argot or underworld slang, used by members of subordinated groups in part as an expression of resistance. Anti-languages express the ideology of what Halliday (1976) terms "anti-groups," groups who frame their collective identities in opposition to the dominant sectors of society. Using the cast-off remnants of fashion's commodities, the Baay Fàl have created their own anti-fashion, a counterhegemonic style grounded in part in an ideological critique of consumerism.

Along with their patchwork costumes, other everyday practices of Baay Fàl disciples exemplify their rejection of what some of them characterize as worldly materialism. Their diet consists primarily of leftovers that they gather house-to-house by supplication. Many refuse to drink imported tea or instant Nescafé, the beverages of preference for most city dwellers. Instead, they favor hot, sweetened milk or infusions made from local plants, a choice that adepts say is a way of respecting their own traditions and rejecting foreign influences. The Baay Fàl also have a reputation, it should be added, for consuming alcoholic beverages, in violation of the tenets of orthodox Islam that are supported by the Murid clergy. This, among other practices, reflects a strong sense of an autonomous Baay Fàl identity, which one adept described this way: *"Duñu jullit, duñu murid, baay fàl lëñu"* ("We're not Muslims, we're not Murids, we're Baay Fàl").

Younger Baay Fàl frequently proclaim an identification with the Jamaican Rastafarians, whom they imitate by twisting their uncut hair into dreadlocks. The Baay Fàl anti-language thus enters into the transnational traffic in counterhegemonic styles, mediated in this case by the discourse of pan-Africanism and the commodification and worldwide distribution of reggae music. At the same time, Baay Fàl anti-fashion, with its implicit critique of worldly materialism, has been appropriated and reconverted to fashion commodity: the state-supported SOTIBA-SIMPAFRIC produces a *legos* print simulating Baay Fàl patchwork.

Oppositional styles, then, are subject to appropriation and commodification, just as elements of dominant styles may be taken over and redefined in oppositional terms (cf. Hebdige 1979). As Kress and Hodge (1979: 76) point out, anti-languages are both parasitic, drawing on the rules of the hegemonic code, and oppositional, inverting certain elements of that system of rules. In Bakhtin's terms, anti-languages, seen in relation to the dominant discourses to which they are linked, have both centripetal and centrifugal dimensions.

EMBROIDERY: RECUPERATION AND THE SIMULATION OF LUXURY TEXTILES

Manufactured obsolescence, as Barthes (1985) points out, is integral to the "fashion system," the result of a continual displacement of yesterday's fashions with those that are even more novel. As a result, "a disproportionate volume of cloth ends up in the ragbag or as hand-me-downs when compared to non-capitalist circulation" (Weiner and Schneider 1989: 11). At the same time, when fashion and its consequences are seen as part of a global system, we are confronted with the local responses of those in peripheralized regions, including their active efforts to recuperate and redefine the cast-off fashions of the more fully industrialized and commoditized core.

Senegal participates in the worldwide circulation of used clothes from core to periphery, for enormous bales of such clothing are collected in Europe and the United States, shipped to Senegal, and subsequently parceled out to vendors, usually ending up in urban marketplaces. In the Big Market in Kaolack, these secondhand clothes are sold in a separate section in one corner of the market. I should hasten to add that,

far from being regarded as highly sought-after items of high fashion, these clothes are known in Wolof by the tongue-in-cheek term *fëggë-jaay*, which means "shake-and-sell." Though elements of style may be diffused from the central places of the fashion system, Western provenance does not guarantee prestige in the indigenous codes of Senegambian fashion. Purchased and worn by those of lesser means, these imported used clothes are clearly not held in high esteem. Still, as I will reveal in more detail below, women put this clothing to their own creative uses, some of which can be seen, I will argue, as modes of resistance.

Women in Kaolack who do not have the means to acquire the expensive, high-status Manjak strip cloth may use their leisure time to make embroidered facsimiles of it. The women use inexpensive materials, most often unbleached muslin and yarn recuperated by unravelling secondhand sweaters, which may be purchased in Kaolack's Big Market. (The sweaters may be found in the corner of the market that is devoted to the sale of the "shake-and-sell" clothing mentioned above.) Using pencil and ruler, women trace their designs on the muslin before beginning their needlework, some of which attempts to replicate the geometric patterns of Manjak strip cloth. Like its model, this handiwork is frequently done in narrow strips and then sewn onto a large piece of cloth to make a wrap cloth (*sér*) or its shortened version, the *becó*, which is worn as an underskirt. Doing embroidery is often a social activity, with friends working on their needlework as they visit one another. While women frequently embroider wrap cloths and underskirts for their own use, such handiwork also changes hands in gift-giving between women at weddings and baby-naming ceremonies, or to honor a special guest. Thus, women's needlework contributes to the household economy, providing the means to meet obligations with a minimal cash outlay.

According to Jane Schneider (1980), the embroidered needlework done for the trousseaux of women belonging to the 19th-century rural elite in Sicily served a similar function. Her analysis provides interesting parallels and contrasts with the traditions of women in Kaolack. A form of convertible wealth, the yard goods that a woman of the Sicilian landed gentry embroidered for her trousseau had not only use value but also potential exchange value. "Their content was at once ornamental and, when stored for emergency conversion, essential" (Schneider 1980: 351). Like the Senegalese embroidery that imitates the prestigious Manjak textiles, the sheets, linens, and lingerie embellished with the needlework of Italian women originally imitated highly prized drawloom brocades (Schneider 1980: 347). In both the Sicilian and the Senegalese case, the high-status fabric serving as the symbolic reference point for embroidery requires the technology and skills of a tradition of weaving controlled by artisans, generally male, supported by wealthier patrons. The embroidered facsimiles, on the other hand, represent patient, repetitive women's work, domestic labor requiring neither a long apprenticeship nor expensive materials. In each instance, furthermore, this gender-based distinction between productive activities, as well as the differential prestige of the final products, needs to be understood in terms of class divisions and political economic factors.

In the Sicilian case, Schneider sees women's embroidery figuring in the process of class formation and in center-periphery relations. Embroidery was originally confined to the women of the aristocracy, spreading in the late 19th century to the rural bourgeoisie, according to Schneider (1980: 329), through a process of "status emulation," a concept drawn from Veblen's theory of the leisure class. Following economic transformations near the turn of the century, the landed gentry, part of the elite of the peripheral region of Sicily, assumed a position as intermediary between the rural Sicilian population and the dominant groups in the centers of power. Their change in status was reflected in what Schneider refers to as their emulation of the lifestyle of the aristocracy, or "modeling behavior" (1980: 332).

Recasting Schneider's analysis in terms of the concept of heteroglossia, I would like to suggest that status emulation becomes one moment in the dialectic between centripetal and centrifugal impulses. Thus, on the one hand, imitation of the material accoutrements of hegemonic groups, such as drawloom brocades or Manjak strip cloth, is an aspect of the centralizing process by which dominant symbol systems incorporate

the practices of subordinate groups. At the same time, in producing such objects subordinates borrow from a hegemonic idiom but express themselves, to use Voloshinov's term, in their own accents. Such symbolic production may be seen not merely as emulation of a high-status code but also as what Michel de Certeau (1984) calls "poaching," a kind of counterhegemonic appropriation that reaffirms the distinctiveness and partial autonomy of the diverse voices within a stratified system. This becomes most clear in cases such as the one described below, in which the same women who make embroidered imitations of expensive strip cloth use their needlework as an oppositional genre.

CONCLUSION

In contrast to those who propound Saussurean structuralism, which he criticizes ([1929] 1973: 58–61), Vološinov sees contradiction and conflict as the norm in both language and social relations, with primacy given not to the abstract language system but to concrete contexts of meaning production. The concept of multiaccentuality—like Bakhtin's concept, heteroglossia—assumes that alternation, variability, and contestation are intrinsic to communicative practice. As these concepts indicate, use of the "same" code by members of different groups within a society does not normally indicate ideological consensus or uniform interpretation and experience. It is through the interplay of alternative forms and meanings that the politics of identity and difference unfolds.

Anti-languages, such as the Baay Fàl style of dress, are intended to exclude (dominant) outsiders while expressing the oppositional identity of marginalized groups. Hodge and Kress (1988: 87) note that certain high-status codes, of which *sañse* is an example, may, in a similar way, be inaccessible to (dominated) others. These two cases might be seen as illustrative of diglossia (Ferguson 1959), in which a "high code" and a "low code" are associated with a dominant and a subordinate group respectively. This, however, gives an incomplete picture of communicative practice, except in those extreme cases in which segregation or coercion limits dialogue between the dominant and the dominated.

Insofar as there are ongoing social relations between different social strata, most communicative practice is better described in terms of heteroglossia, in which the accents of various groups intersect. Though *sañse* is the dominant sartorial code in Senegal and The Gambia, it is not univocal. It is not practiced exclusively by the very wealthy nor is it accomplished by the same means by all women.

Variations in the execution of *sañse*, in the means of performance, give rise to its variable meanings. Investigating the social uses of cloth and clothing in urban Senegal, I have shown how hegemony is constructed from the dialogue of centripetal and centrifugal voices, with cloth subject to the same processes of signification and domination as other forms of communicative practice. The production of meaning—in this case as in others—draws on the full range of material and symbolic resources.

Identifying heteroglossia as an intrinsic feature of each and every expressive act, of communication itself, is consistent with a relational and dialectical view of both signification and culture. The intersection of interests in the shared signs of a society drives the productive character of communicative practice, the function of communicative practice being not simply to mirror social relations but to produce them and to play out social and ideological complexity and contradiction.

28

DRESSED TO "SHINE":
Work, leisure, and style in Malindi, Kenya

Johanna Schoss

It's lunch time. A group of four young men enter the small eating establishment, loudly greeting the men already gathered there at several long tables. The restaurant is filled with men, all of whom seem to know one another. Conversation and good-natured joking flow between the groups of diners. The men entering together are dressed in similar fashion: slacks in solid colors—either blue or red, sharply pressed button-down shirts, expensive watches, leather loafers. A few moments later another group arrives. They are dressed in a more varied fashion; one wearing jeans, a T-shirt emblazoned with the Hugo Boss insignia, and sneakers; another in brightly colored windsurfing shorts, tank top, and plastic flip-flops. They enter with a commotion, calling out loudly: *Ciao! Ciao belli neri!*" Animated conversation, now in Italian, ensues back and forth across the room.

This could be an unremarkable scene in a trattoria somewhere in Italy, possibly near the ocean. But the scene is Malindi, a mid-sized town on the Kenyan coast. The eating establishment is a small, wooden, thatch-roofed kiosk located along a dusty footpath, in the back regions of the open-air marketplace. And all of the men present are Kenyan, largely Swahili. What, then can explain this behavior—the range of Western clothing, the inclusive conversation in Italian?

To an observer leaving the restaurant, passing through the marketplace crowded with retailers of varied ethnic identity, Malindi would appear a rather typical East African coastal town. In one direction, the dusty roads of the town center are lined with two-story, white-plastered, balconied shops in an architectural style found throughout Kenya and other parts of the former British empire. Behind the market, moving away from the town center, is the densely-populated neighborhood of Shela, with its single-story, thatch-roofed houses, built of coral stone blocks. It is only as you walk east from the town center, toward the Indian Ocean, that a second and seemingly discontinuous Malindi appears. Here the road, popularly called "Tourist Road," is lined with luxury hotels whose verandas face the bright sand beaches and glistening Indian Ocean. The picturesque dhows of local fishermen dot the horizon, and tourists, in various European styles of street- and beachwear, can be seen on the beaches and roadways.

Over the past twenty years, tourism has transformed Malindi from a fishing and agricultural village into a multiethnic urban center that annually hosts thousands of tourists, largely Italians and Germans. Malindi has a long history as one of the earliest mercantile towns of the East African coast, towns that have been involved in trade across the Indian Ocean for nearly one thousand years. The Swahili people who historically have populated these coastal cities are the descendants of Arabs who settled in the region and intermarried with Bantu-speaking Africans living along the coast. Traditionally, Swahili people, who were urban-based, distinguished themselves from their non-Muslim, rural-dwelling African neighbors, though the rigidity

Adapted from Johanna Schoss, "Dressed to 'Shine': Work, Leisure, and Style in Malindi, Kenya," in *Clothing and Difference*, edited by Hildi Hendrickson (Durham: Duke University Press, 1996) pp. 157–188.

with which these two populations identify themselves as distinct ethnic groups appears to have increased over time under the influence of the British colonial administration (Willis 1993). Currently, the vast majority of the rural population surrounding Malindi are Giriama, an ethnic group that is among eight closely related groups collectively called the Mijikenda. Malindi today is highly ethnically heterogeneous, with both Swahili and Giriama living in town, along with numerous relatively recent arrivals from other parts of Kenya. Tourism has served as a major impetus for in-migration to the area.

The restaurant of our opening scene, which offers home-style Swahili food, is a favorite lunch spot for men working in the tourist industry. Given their structurally central position, such people act to some degree as mediators, or "culture brokers" (see Cohen and Comaroff 1976). While tourism infiltrates all arenas of the Malindi community—as a force of social, cultural, economic, and political change—the critical encounter between locals and foreigners takes place through the intermediation of specific members of the host community. That is to say, certain individuals, most often through their employment activities, either formally or informally, have intensive and ongoing contact with European tourists. Thus, they serve to mediate between tourists and other members of the local community, many of whom have little regularized contact with the foreign tourists. Evans (1976: 192) captures several key characteristics of the culture broker when she describes such individuals as "often bilingual, innovative, analytical about their culture, and active in introducing change and mediating between the local group and outside agencies."

While there are many kinds of culture brokers in Malindi's tourism economy, in this essay I focus on one category—tour guides. Within this category I include men who work specifically as tour guides as well as the vehicle drivers who escort tourists on safaris or daily outings and the people employed in tour and car rental agencies. Individuals engaged in tour guiding are found in both the formal and the informal sectors of the tourism economy. Those working in the formal sector are employed directly by tourism enterprises such as hotels and tour agencies;

others are self-employed, independently offering tourists their services as guides. The men working in these two domains exhibit significantly different sets of practices, while at the same time they all share one critical characteristic. Unlike others working in the tourist industry, who earn a living by providing a particular service—such as waiters who work in hotel restaurants and who mediate tourists' experience of Kenya in the process—tour guides earn their income exclusively through their abilities to act as cultural mediators. In practice, tourists have much more intense and sustained interactions with tour guides than they do with other members of the Malindi (or any host) community. Several studies (e.g., Almagor 1985, de Kadt 1979, Smith 1989, Towner 1985) have focused on the role of such mediators in structuring tourists' experiences of foreign locales. Erik Cohen (1985), lending an historical perspective to the inquiry, notes that the role of tour guide has undergone several transformations but ultimately derives from two roles—those of "pathfinder" and "mentor." The contemporary tour guide incorporates the qualities and functions of both of these earlier roles. In the pathfinder mode, the tour guide leads visitors not through uncharted territory, as in times gone by, but through the tourist landscape, in particular "providing [tourists with] privileged access to otherwise non-public territory" (Cohen 1985: 10). In the mentor mode, the tour guide is likened to the tutor who accompanied the pupil/traveler on his European Grand Tour, providing the pupil/traveler with the insights with which to interpret his experiences. In this respect, the tour guide serves as a mediator and educator, responsible for translating and interpreting local culture to the tourists. The tour guide also becomes a mediator between tourists and local residents; by providing tourists access to the local culture and community, the guide also becomes responsible for both buffering tourists' experience of the unknown and protecting the community from the European "Others."

Perhaps the most important role played by these culture brokers is that of interpreter. Cohen (1985: 14–16) refers to this aspect of the guide's role as the "communicative function." The tour guide acts as an interpreter in multiple ways. First, he literally acts as a language translator because he is competent in the languages of both the tourists and the local community. Further, rather than simply showing tourists what is there to be seen, the tour guide essentially creates the landscape (both physical and cultural) that tourists view by his selection of "attractions." With these "attractions" he directs the tourists' gaze (see Urry 1990), both by revealing to them the local life and landscape and by concealing other possible scenes and objects from the tourists' view. This process of structuring the tourist gaze is one way in which tour guides engage in cultural brokerage, but it is also an act of interpretation, in that the guides provide a context for the tourists' reading of and consumption of the local scene. And finally, tour guides are translators in that they provide tourists with a "translation of the strangeness of a foreign culture [that of Malindi, of Kenya, and of Africa more generally] into a cultural idiom familiar to [them]" (Cohen 1985: 15).

The tour guides' ability to translate from one cultural idiom to another stems from their possession of what Hannerz (1990) calls "the cosmopolitan perspective." The "cosmopolitan," as opposed to the "local," is someone who is exposed to a multiplicity of cultures, but more than this, Hannerz (1990: 239) suggests that the cosmopolitan perspective is:

> a stance toward diversity itself, toward the co-existence of cultures in the individual experience, … a state of readiness, a personal ability to make one's way into other cultures through listening, looking, intuiting, and reflecting.

Malindi's tour guides are characterized both by this intellectual and aesthetic orientation toward "the Other," and by possessing the requisite competence to maneuver their way through alternative cultural systems.

The cosmopolitan identity of Malindi's tour guides is based upon their understanding of, control over, and successful deployment of Western goods, practices, and cultural knowledge. Through their sustained interaction with Europeans, tour guides have become very adept at understanding how tourists of different nationalities behave in terms of dress, speech, and action, as well as learning to anticipate what tourists expect and even—as many tourism entrepreneurs would say—how tourists think. These locals have also learned to embody European styles of dress and behavior. It is not enough to *know what clothes to wear*, as do the suit-wearing bureaucrats. Rather, one must also *understand how to wear the clothes*—the bodily comportment, the cultural competence that makes the act of wearing believable. These "upcountry" bureaucrats control the overt forms of Western culture, but somehow fail to grasp its substance. For dress, it seems clear, is synecdochic for Western material forms and cultural understanding in general. Thus, it is not surprising that Malindi's tourism professionals present and represent their involvement in the global tourist economy and their relations with European tourists through their selection of particular styles of Western dress and comportment. The choice of styles varies quite markedly between the group of men who work in the formal economic sector—employed by largely foreign-owned tourism enterprises—and those men who are self-employed in the informal economic sector.

COSMOPOLITAN STYLES IN MALINDI'S TOURISM ECONOMY

As the opening description of tourism employees suggests, both formal- and informal-sector tour guides wear Western clothing. Certainly it is true that many Malindi residents (both men and women), regardless of their occupations, wear Western clothing routinely. In addition, more traditional items of clothing and styles of dress are still very often worn throughout the community. The most commonly worn local items of dress include the *kikoi,* the *sarong,* and the *kanga.* The *kikoi* (Swahili; plural *vikoi*) is a male item of dress, very often worn by fishermen. It consists of a colored length of sturdy cotton fabric (five feet long by three-and-a-half feet wide), fringed at the short ends, with a decorative band running lengthwise at each edge. It is worn tied lengthwise around the waist and held in place by rolling down the top edge, as if to form a waistband. A somewhat different version of the locally produced *kikoi* originates in South India. It is also called *kikoi* or, more commonly, *sarong,* and is constructed of softer, more intricately decorated cotton. This fabric is purchased already sewn into a circular column. It is worn in the same way as the locally produced *vikoi*— wrapped tight at the waist and rolled down at the top to secure it. Such items of clothing are "traditional" in that they have a long history of use on the Kenyan Coast among both Swahili and Giriama men.

Another quite similar item of clothing is the *kanga* (plural *kanga*), also called *leso* in Coastal areas. Like the *kikoi,* it consists of a rectangular length of cotton, with an elaborately decorated border and complementary field design. In most cases, there is a proverb written in Swahili at the bottom of the central field. These items are produced in Kenya, as well as in other countries (China, India, the Arab countries), and are worn throughout Kenya. Among Swahili people, they are considered strictly women's apparel and worn in matched sets of two pieces, one wrapped at the chest, or at the waist if worn with a shirt, and the other wrapped over the shoulders. Among Giriama, however, men will also wear *kanga,* tied at the waist as are *vikoi.*

As detailed below, Malindi's tourism culture brokers wear these traditional items of clothing in some settings, but they more typically wear Western clothing. In wearing this garb, they stand out from the local community, even those dressed in Western-style clothing, in quite overt ways. Both beachboys and tour leaders dress so as, it is said in a local idiom, "to shine." Their appearance draws attention to itself, marking their access to expensive goods and a comfortable lifestyle. Minou Fuglesang (1994) has discussed this notion in Swahili society, looking at the *kupamba*— the ritual during which a bride is publicly presented to the women of the community for the first time. For this ceremony the bride's hair, skin, and body are carefully prepared through beautifying treatments. If the preparation is successful, the bride will "shine," meaning that her inner beauty has been brought out, but also that she has properly chosen and worn fine clothing, makeup, jewelry, and other accessories. Thus, Fuglesang further notes that "to 'shine' is associated with new commodities and the 'trendy'" (128). And indeed tour guides "shine" because their garments stand out for their notable newness, quality

of manufacture, and European origin (as opposed to Western-style clothing produced in Kenya or elsewhere in Africa). Beyond the particularities of the items worn, tour guides' dress is marked by a high degree of self-consciousness about the act of wearing these garments. Unlike the often haphazard ways in which other locals may mix and match Western clothing, tourism employees conscientiously combine items of clothing into a consistent and identifiable style; a style that is intentionally cosmopolitan. But, formal-sector tour leaders and beachboys assemble Western clothing into two different, very distinctive cosmopolitan styles.

These styles encompass not only dress, but also bodily comportment and consumption practices. Thus *style,* as I use it here, refers not merely to a way of dressing, but more importantly to the way in which people present and represent themselves to others in a manner that implies an underlying ideological vision (see Hebdige 1979). Style, in effect, is a way of being in the world; one that demonstrates conscious choices and speaks to differentiated sociocultural systems of value and meaning. Indeed, these two cosmopolitan styles are readily distinguishable through distinctions that, to the outside observer—be it the anthropologist or the tourist—seemingly lie "on the surface," in the visual forms and appearances of the garb and in the observable behavior patterns. And yet, the crucial distinction between the two styles lies beyond the realm of the visible, embedded in differing ideological orientations. These styles become the tangible markers of two very different strategies through which formal-sector and informal-sector tourism employees engage with the tourist economy. I will return to this point after a detailed discussion of each style.

THE FORMAL SECTOR: TOUR LEADERS, SAFARI DRIVERS, CAR RENTAL AND TOUR AGENCY PERSONNEL

Tour leaders (including the range of men working in formal-sector tour enterprises) deploy a constellation of Western goods and practices in what I have called the *professionalized* style. Typically, these men wear slacks, button-down dress shirts or polo-type sport shirts—always clean and carefully pressed—and shoes imported from Europe. They may also wear jeans or logo-embossed T-shirts, but these items are always very crisply pressed and new-looking. They may also wear khaki safari suits; this is particularly common among safari drivers. On occasion, they opt for traditional clothing in the form of a *kanzu*, a long gown often worn for prayer at the Mosque and ritual events. Most often, however, these men wear slacks in solid and somewhat subdued colors. In fact, most tour agencies have some kind of uniform, which consists of solid color pants of one or two designated colors (such as red or blue) and white shirts—short-sleeved and buttoned-down, with buttoned front pockets and epaulets. Nevertheless, employees have a good deal of liberty in adopting such uniforms, liberty that they fully exercise in their daily choice of clothing—for example, by pairing the appropriate solid-colored slacks with a striped or patterned shirt. Overall, their style is what would be described locally as "smart" (in Swahili, *smarti*)—that is, polished, sharp-looking, and well put together.

Malindi's professionalized tour guides similarly endeavor to effect a Europeanized look that even the Europeans cannot quite match. What one notices about their dress, without being able to immediately point to it, is their uncanny ability to look at the end of a ten-hour work day in the equatorial sun, precisely as they looked when they first got dressed—gleaming shirts, still pressed razor-sharp and unsoiled by the day's heat; never appearing less than absolutely neat, contained, and "smart."

These formal-sector employees maintain this professional appearance most of the time, both at work and in their free time—at discos in the evening with friends, for example. In a few limited contexts tour leaders allow themselves to "dress down," wearing shorts or *vikoi*, casual T-shirts, sneakers, sandals, or even bare feet. Such contexts include occasions when they escort clients on beach outings, in their own homes, or on Friday afternoons or Sundays when relaxing with friends at their *maskani* (meeting place). Only the first of these contexts is work-related, and in this case casual attire is appropriate. Tour leaders would consider dressing in slacks and shoes for a beach or fishing outing to be as ludicrous as bureaucrats who arrive for

a tour of the Marine Park wearing suits and ties. The other two settings that are exceptions to this strict code of "professional" appearance are settings completely outside of tourist domains. Private homes and local *maskani* are places where tourism professionals can truly relax, because these places are, for the most part, inaccessible to tourists. While beachboys may bring tourists into their neighborhoods, and even to their own homes, they would rarely bring them to a neighborhood *maskani*. Friday afternoons or Sundays are significant because, during the peak tourist seasons, these are virtually the only times tourism professionals can escape the demands of their jobs. Even when not officially working, tour leaders consider themselves to be in the public eye in professional terms whenever they are in public spaces that are accessible to tourists. Thus, they maintain their professional appearance and demeanor when relaxing in the evening with friends at restaurants or night clubs, even if they are not accompanying clients.

For the most part, these men purchase much of their clothing directly from Europe. Other items they have custom-made for themselves by local tailors. Apart from items like *vikoi*, they rarely buy clothing produced and mass-marketed in Kenya. Professionalized tour guides explained this antipathy for locally produced clothing in two ways. First, they complained that Kenyan-made clothing intended for local consumption was poor in quality and shabbily constructed. Second, other items intended for the tourist trade were considered to be rather absurd. One tour leader, wryly commented on such mementos by saying, "What kind of clothes would I buy here in Kenya? A 'JAMBO KENYA' T-Shirt with elephants on it?" Such attitudes toward clothing highlight the activities of guides as culture brokers. They are able to convincingly direct the tourist gaze toward the stereotypical commodity representations of "Africa," at the same time rejecting those images as characterizing or encompassing themselves.

INDEPENDENT TOUR GUIDES: THE BEACHBOYS

The beachboys have a much more flamboyant and unpredictable style, which consists of often outlandish and wild combinations of colors and patterns of European clothing and accessories. They commonly wear shorts; bright colored windsurfing pants are among the more popular, but long and baggy, or shorter running-style shorts are also common. Jeans are another common clothing item; in 1989–91 many beachboys were wearing the stylishly torn variety. These items are paired with brightly colored and variously patterned shirts or T-shirts, sneakers or bare feet. In terms of "traditional" dress, beachboys will wear *vikoi,* though only one beachboy in Malindi routinely wears *kanzu* and most of the others rarely do. Another typical feature of beachboys' attire is the fanny pack—called *kipauchi* in Swahili, an item that is apparently very popular in Europe. Such packs are ubiquitous in Malindi now and are used by formal-sector tourism employees as well, though among beachboys they are practically de rigueur. Locals get these packs either by trading with tourists, or by gaining access to those given to tourists by local tour agencies. As with other clothing items, beachboys prefer the brightly colored fanny packs. Among the goods that make up the beachboy style are items of clothing that I call "indigenous chic." These are clothing items made from some transformation of a local item—one example is *kikoi* or, more typically, *sarong* material tailored into a pair of loose-fitting, drawstring trousers. These pants, and other similar items, have an interesting history in that they were initially transformed into pants by local tailors on demand from tourists. Tailors and shopkeepers began stocking them as a part of their regular stock; beachboys eventually took up wearing them, and now tourists buy them, thinking that they are adopting something of the local style (though within the local community, *only* beachboys wear such items). Another "indigenous chic" style is clothing made from three-inch squares of many different fabrics. Local tailoring shops use their scrap materials to make pants, vests, and hats that have a dazzling, multi-colored, quilted appearance. In general, beachboy style draws upon both the more avant-garde and funky elements, and more casual trends in popular Euro-American fashion.

The "indigenous chic" items of the beachboy style are purchased locally in tailoring shops that also make clothing for tourists. Most other items are European in origin, but unlike their formal-sector counterparts, beachboys are less likely to purchase these items directly. Rather, they get a lot of their clothing by trading with tourists—as, for example, in exchange for wood carvings. They receive other items as gifts or as payment for tour guiding services they have provided. And in some cases, they may purchase items directly from Europe, or receive them through the mail as gifts from clients. Unlike the dressing style of formal-sector tour guides, that of beachboys is highly marked within the Malindi community. In local slang it is sometimes referred to as "*kichizi*," a word that has the sense of funny, comical, or unconventional. One adolescent boy described beachboy dressing habits to me in the following way:

> They wear very short shorts. They wear the same clothes for months at a time, without washing them, until you can not even tell what color they are supposed to be—they are the color of mud.

While the description is not empirically accurate, it does reflect the ambivalence with which beachboys' dress and overall comportment is sometimes viewed by the community at large. Of course, there is a good deal of variation among beachboys with regard to both clothing and comportment, and some beachboys dress in a more conventional style, similar to their formal-sector counterparts. For the most part, however, their self-presentation is unconventional, as indeed is their insistence on creating their own niche in the tourist economy rather than simply choosing among the opportunities offered by the formally structured industry. By dressing in the "beachboy style," these men both practically and symbolically preclude their formal-sector employability (see Ewen 1988: 64–77ff).

OTHER ELEMENTS OF STYLE

Items of dress are not the only Western goods consumed by local tour guides in Malindi's tourism economy. Commodities that are less tangible, those that may be best thought of as commoditized practices, also enter into the equation of cosmopolitan styles.

Among these practices, perhaps the most apparent one is leisure. Both beachboys and professionalized tour guides, particularly the younger men, participate fully in the cycle of leisure activities that are intended for the consumption of tourists. For example, the discos held nightly in various hotels are, without fail, packed with these men, whose presence in number sometimes overshadows the tourists themselves. This is so despite, and in conscious opposition to, various past and present efforts to limit locals' presence in such places. Peake (1984) details how in the early 1980s hotel managers and local police authorities made efforts to restrict local access to tourist areas; efforts that angered many locals, particularly beachboys. While most of the hotels sponsor a disco featuring a popular deejay one night of the week, in 1984 there was only one enterprise that operated strictly as a disco every night. The management of this disco, Club 28, held a dance contest every Saturday night, with prizes for the winners. Although this marketing ploy was geared toward tourists, beachboys and prostitutes, with the tacit assistance of the disc jockeys, soon began to dominate, consistently winning nearly every contest. The management responded by opening a new and more impressive disco, the Stardust, with entrance fees double those of Club 28. Peake (1984: 120) notes that "the 'capture' of Club 28 was hailed as a great victory by the beachboys." Between 1989 and 1991, Club 28 continued to be a favorite nightspot for beachboys and other local cosmopolitans, as did the Stardust, despite its high entrance fee.

Local cosmopolitans consume tourist-designated leisure activities throughout the year, but do so particularly during the days between Christmas and New Year's Eve (the peak of tourist high season). At this time of year, even locals who never routinely attend the discos will go as part of the holiday festivities, and tour guides will be present every night. During this time, the hotel managements raise the disco entrance prices to often astronomical levels (sometimes equivalent to the price of nightclubs in Manhattan), but nevertheless the dance floor is always dominated by an overwhelming proportion of locals. By New Year's Eve, the disco is so crowded and the beachboys so rambunctious in their dancing that tourists rarely brave the dance floor.

Indeed it is an essential aspect of the cosmopolitan style of tour guides that they dine in tourist hotels and restaurants, frequent discos, drink expensive liquor, travel by taxi or private car, and so forth. Unlike many other members of the local community, they have incomes that allow such expenditures, but more importantly, their legitimacy as cosmopolitans depends upon it. As with their choice of clothing, beachboys and professionalized tour guides consume leisure in markedly different ways. They make use of similar leisure settings and practices, but in doing so they comport themselves in strikingly distinct ways. Similarly, they represent their participation in and consumption of such activities in significantly different ways.

Tour leaders, in such settings, (and this is true of their practice overall) present themselves with an extraordinary degree of reserve; they must, as they say, remain "cool." They drink alcohol, but not to excess. They avoid loud, obtrusive, or unruly behavior. In part, tour leaders' decorous behavior is linked to their rationale for being in tourist settings at all. They often justify spending time in nightclubs because it is part of their work. Indeed, they often serve as host to their agency's clients, escorting them to Malindi's various leisure settings. Even when they are not with a group of clients, however, they maintain this demeanor, because they are always, in effect, "on the job." They see themselves as always in view of tourists, tourism investors, and managers. Thus they carefully guard their "professional" appearance both within the tourist economy and in front of the local community. At the same time, tour guides behave with this remarkable reserve because it is this quality that they hope to put forward, both to the local community and to the participants of the tourist economy, as their defining personal and professional characteristic. In short, their "reputation" (in the sense of the Swahili notion of *heshima*) rests upon representing themselves as confident, dependable, highly qualified, and always in control.

Beachboys, on the other hand, engage in such leisure activities with an abandon that is often not matched even by the tourists themselves. They have a fairly earned reputation for making a public display of drinking heavily, fighting in public places, and generally causing scenes. On occasion, some beachboys' behavior results in their being thrown out of these leisure settings. At such times they can begin to frequent the disco or bar again only after long negotiation with the establishment's management. Their behavior during these evening outings frequently becomes a topic of disapproving conversation in the local community the following day. In their tendency toward excess, they seem to consume leisure in its most marked, most "tourist-like" form.

There is one important issue that needs to be clarified at this point. The practice that the culture-brokers consume, the "leisure" in which they engage, is explicitly leisure as conceived and constituted by Western cultural understanding. It is leisure as Urry describes it: "leisure activity which presupposes its opposite, namely regulated and organized work" (1990: 2). Leisure, in this sense is very much an historical development, linked closely to the emerging industrial economies of nineteenth-century Europe. Detailing the legislative and organizational changes surrounding nineteenth-century industrial work forces in Britain, Urry points out that along with increased routinization and control over industrial labor forces, formalized recreational events and structured holidays increasingly came into effect. Such policies followed on the theory that structured breaks from work helped to increase labor-force efficiency and workplace discipline (Urry 1990: 17ff; also see Cummingham 1980). These institutionalized holidays, in turn, were directly linked to the rise of the British seaside resorts, one of the early sites of contemporary mass tourism.

This form of leisure, as structured nonwork, stands in marked opposition to local practices in Malindi, where social interaction, "relaxing," and labor are continuous and undistinguished activities. Thus, for example, beachboys spend much of their time while on the streets looking for clients, sitting casually and talking with groups of friends. To a foreign eye this looks like a form of leisure, but by local consideration it is merely an unmarked aspect of daily life and an aspect that is integrally interwoven with labor activities (cf. E. P. Thompson 1967). In fact, it is an essential part of their daily work, in that beachboys exchange important information and keep each other updated as to the current tourism situation in Malindi through

such informal conversational settings. While tour guides are often furthering their business interests while "at leisure" in such tourist facilities as hotels and nightclubs (seeking clients, etc.), they are also *explicitly* consuming structured leisure for its own sake, as do the tourists. Urry, in his discussion of the rise of tourism and its linkages to the rise of structured participation in "leisure," suggests that "acting as a tourist is one of the defining characteristics of being 'modern'" (1990: 2). Indeed beachboys are explicitly trying to appropriate the practices of tourists—including leisure styles and practices, in effect making themselves members of an international tourist class. And yet they consume leisure practices in a manner that sets them outside of this international tourist class, because—unlike the tourists who return to the routine of work when the vacation ends—beachboys act like tourists throughout the year. Just as the formal-sector tour leaders surpass Western tourists in the manner of wearing of Western fashions, beachboys exceed the tourists in their continual and conspicuous pursuit of fun-seeking.

Indeed overt displays of conspicuous consumption are the most striking feature of beachboys' participation in tourism-linked leisure activities. For example, beachboys often will celebrate a successful day of work by spending all their earnings in a lavish public display, buying all their friends drinks and demonstrating their control over large amounts of cash. Some beachboys even express the philosophy that if they do not spend their often substantial income readily, they will not earn more money the next day, but if they do spend their earnings freely, they can feel confident that they will earn more the next day. From many beachboys' point of view, it would appear that the whole point of earning good incomes working as tour guides is to enable themselves to spend that income publicly. At the same time, many beachboys use their earnings on private forms of consumption, such as household expenses or remittances to their extended families. When among their fellow beachboys, however, they generally downplay or in some cases completely hide these private expenditures. Other beachboys, however, redistribute very little of their often substantial earnings to their immediate or extended families and/or to other members of the community.

The professionalized tour guides also earn relatively large incomes, and their professionalized style and identity indeed depends upon having this financial security. They also spend money on leisure activities, but they do not make their spending publicly known through conspicuous displays in leisure settings, as do many of the beachboys. On the contrary, they spend a good portion of their incomes on the support of their own families as well as assisting extensive networks of kith and kin, a practice that is widely recognized within the local community. In doing this, the professionalized guides reinvest their earnings in traditional Swahili values of social reproduction as economic providers, and in doing so they index their own status as social adults (cf. Fuglesang 1994: 193). In fact, such men are quite willing to severely limit their consumption of leisure activities during the low season, but even at this time of year they would find it difficult to refuse a request for assistance. In part this is because the obligation toward family and community assistance is so integral to their "professional" reputation and style, and in part because they are loath to admit publicly to financial hardship themselves.

CONCLUSION

The styles inhabited by Malindi tour guides make claims for the guides' membership in a supralocal cultural identity, that of cosmopolitan participants in "world culture." Numerous authors have noted the role of tourism, global mass media, and increasing mobility of and dislocation among the world's population in creating new arenas of cross-cultural visibility and dialogue. Many suggest that such forces are contributing to the development of a "global ecumene" (Hannerz 1989, 1992) or a transnational "public culture" (Appadurai and Breckenridge 1988), arenas of economic exchange in which new cultural forms and identities are being formulated and debated. Deena Weinstein (1989) suggests that it is "cosmopolitanism" or "transnationalism" itself that is the major commodity being exchanged in this arena. As an exchangeable commodity, "cosmopolitanism" (or "transnationalism") takes various forms, such as highly celebrated world events, style, consumerism, and perhaps most importantly, the knowledge of these forms and events. Further, the transnational event or form becomes a sort of symbol that both stands for itself and offers a coherent meaning—it offers its audience, the consumers, "membership in a world community transcending national, ethnic, or class communities; a community in which only the human as consumer and the consumer as human are relevant" (Weinstein 1989: 65). Although this process has accelerated during the last half of this century, Stuart Ewen notes that global consumer culture has its origins beginning with nineteenth-century factory production. He suggests that a "new *consumer democracy*, which was propelled by the mass production and marketing of stylish goods, was founded on the idea that symbols and prerogatives of elites could now be made available on a mass scale" (1988: 32). Membership in this global community of consumers, then, implies a state of cross-cultural equality. It is this theoretical equality to which one young Malindi man was referring to when he answered my queries about his newly adopted beachboy style of dress. "What do you mean?" he responded. "They're only clothes, aren't they? Anyone can wear them." I would suggest that the styles of Malindi tour guides are indeed cosmopolitan, or transnational, forms of this sort. And as such, tour guides (and other local culture brokers) consciously draw upon this symbolic value of "equal membership in world culture" in their ongoing effort to reconfigure the terms of tourist interactions.

Yet, the emerging "global cultural economy" (Appadurai 1990), to which mass tourism acts as a major contributor, is not giving rise to *one* newly forming modernity, *one* homogenized cosmopolitan identity. Rather, transnational contact lays the ground for the emergence of a *multiplicity of cosmopolitanisms*. Equally, "Westernization" is not a process that presents itself whole cloth—or perhaps I should say, fully clothed. The distinct styles through which local cosmopolitans incorporate and deploy Western goods and practices encode conscious attitudes and coherent strategies for addressing the globalizing tourism economy, and the encounter with the West in general. Style, consequently, articulates both alternative cosmopolitanisms and alternative means of managing social, cultural, and economic transformation.

29

FASHIONABLE MUSLIMS: Notions of self, religion, and society in San'a

Annelies Moors

Islam and fashion are often seen as standing in a tense relation. For Islam as the realm of the spiritual and the sacred, that of eternal values and virtues does not sit easy with fashion, which belongs to the field of surface and form, and is characterized by rapid change and great fluidity. This is the more so in San'a, the capital of the Yemen Arab Republic, often described as a traditionalist city, where the influence of conservative strands of Islam is clearly present and where access to public space is strongly gendered. It is true that some authors, such as Yamani (1997), who discusses shifts in dressing styles amongst the leading families of the Hejaz (Saudi Arabia), acknowledge the presence of fashion in such societies. But they tend to see wearing fashionable dress as restricted to family circles or all-female settings where women do not need to cover. They underline the strong contrast between fashionable styles of indoor dress and the uniformity and sobriety of outdoor dress.

Since most San'ani women appear in public covered from head to toe in black garments, and also often wear a face-veil, San'a seems indeed an unlikely site for the emergence of fashionable styles of outerwear. In spite of these considerations, this contribution argues that fashion is part and parcel of women's outdoor dressing styles in San'a. As it turns out, the ways in which women appear in public has been subject to considerable public debate for over forty years. In the 1960s one of Yemen's best-known poets,

Muhammad al-Sharafi, took a strong stance against women's complete covering in one of his collections of poetry, a stance that evoked sharp responses in the Yemeni press. In the decades to come women's dress remained a topic of discussion. *Salafi* booklets, often written by authors from Saudi Arabia and published there, yet widely available in San'a when fieldwork for this research project was conducted (between 1997 and 2002), not only called for women to stick to the strictest forms of Islamic dress, including a face-veil, but were also highly suspicious of fashion as an institution. In their rejection of fashion, the notion of an intrusion from abroad was never far away, as is evident in their stance against "global brand names" that come to us "from here and there" (Ahl al-Shaykh 2000: 12), and against the images presented on television screens and in fashion magazines, such as the *Burda* (or in Arabic, *al-burdayyat*) (Usra 2001: 4). Yet it is their strong rejection of fashion that points to the importance of fashion in women's everyday sartorial practices.

This article focuses on the shifts in the styles of women's outerwear in San'a and the ways in which they themselves link their dressing styles to authentic San'ani traditions, to ideological and religious convictions, and to matters of style and aesthetics. In contrast to widely held assumptions, not only modernist women critical of a *salafi* stance are engaged in wearing fashionable outerwear, but also women protagonists of an Islamist or *salafi* position, who may be critical of fashion as an

Adapted from Annelies Moors, (2007) "Fashionable Muslims: Notions of Self, Religion, and Society in Sana," *Fashion Theory* 11, nos. 2–3 (2007): 319–346.

institution, find it hard to avoid fashion altogether. Perhaps even more striking is the importance younger women who do not take such an explicit religious or political stance attach to being fashionable.

SHIFTING STYLES IN DRESS AND FASHION

The large majority of women in San'a wear long black loose outer garments, virtually all cover their hair, and many also cover their faces. Yet, the styles of dress in the streets of San'a are far from uniform. Especially in the popular quarters, women's outdoor dress is more colorful. Women there sometimes cover themselves with the *sitara*, a mainly red and blue dyed large rectangular cotton sheet that for over a century has been produced in India for the Yemeni market. While on short errands in the neighborhood, they often quickly throw the *sitara* over their indoor dresses. For more formal visits another style of dress is worn, the all-black two-piece *sharshaf*, consisting of a cape, worn on the shoulders, and a long overskirt. Younger women, in contrast, especially the more educated ones but also some older women from higher-status families, can be seen wearing a one-piece, loose-falling, full-length overcoat, the *balto*. At the turn of the twenty-first century wearing an *abaya*, which is similar to the *balto*, but made of thinner material, giving it a more elegant, dress-like appearance, had become the fashion of the day amongst university students and other young educated women.

HIERARCHIES OF AUTHENTICITY

The above hints already at some differences that matter in San'ani women's sartorial practices, that is age, education, status, occasion, and location. Both the *sitara* and the *sharshaf* are considered traditional San'ani styles of dress, in spite of the fact that the former is imported from India and the latter was introduced to Yemen by the Ottoman Turks. While the *sitara* in its present colors (blue with red) was prevalent in San'a from the 1920s on (Mundy 1983: 535), it is the higher-status *sharshaf* that women nowadays usually have in mind when they refer to the "typically San'ani style

of dress." Whereas up till the 1962 revolution, which turned the northern part of Yemen from an Imamate into a republic, the *sharshaf* had only been worn by a very small number of women closely related to the Imam (Mundy 1983: 539), in the course of the 1960s it rapidly gained popularity amongst the middle strata as the more formal style of dress; nowadays, it is also increasingly worn by poorer women and women in rural areas.

It is also the *sharshaf* that was the target of Muhammad al-Sharafi's attacks on covered dress in the 1960s; the title of one of his collections of poetry that aroused much debate was *The Tears of the Sharshafs*. Yet, as it turns out, the *sharshaf* was a quite flexible style of dress. In the 1960s and early 1970s it was worn by the first generation of young women who went to or stayed longer in school, the category most interested in wearing fashion. While the skirt of the *sharshaf* had always been amenable to a variety of styles—with pleats sometimes smaller and at other times larger and folded in different ways, and with the skirt itself wider or more narrowly cut—in the revolutionary days of the 1960s some young women started to experiment with a shorter *sharshaf*, worn either with modern stockings or with fashionable wide-legged trousers underneath, rather than with the traditional Yemeni pants, the *sirwal*, that fitted tightly around the ankles. By the early 1970s the *sharshaf maxi*, with a skirt similar to the then fashionable maxi skirts, also appeared on the streets of San'a; elite families returning from Beirut were amongst those introducing it to Yemen. Whereas the color was always black, the material could differ; shiny satins were particularly popular. Although in the decades to follow the *sharshaf* was slowly replaced by more fashionable styles of dress, amongst well-educated and publicly active women in their late thirties and forties a few still purposely wear the *sharshaf*. Framing their arguments in terms of authenticity, they point out that they do so to hold on to a real San'ani tradition. In a rather different vein, Amal al-Shami (1956–2001), a critical writer from a conservative family of religious judges, donned a *velvet sharshaf* (without a face-veil) as a way of rebelling against social and family pressures (al-Mutawakil 2001: 20).

MODERNIST AND ISLAMIST CONVICTIONS

At about the same period, by the early 1970s, young San'ani women interested in wearing fashionable dress introduced a new style of outerwear, the *balto*, a long overcoat, sometimes with cuffs and a belt. The first to introduce this style of dress were those from high-status families that had been abroad; they either brought such coats with them, or had them made to order. Wearing a *balto* on the streets of San'a did, as some of the pioneers still remember, draw many comments from bystanders. Showing the shoulders and with set-in sleeves, it was seen as more similar to male than to female styles of dress and women were taunted with terms such as "*dejle, dejle*" (the term for a male coat) or "*naqsa sitara*" (the *sitara* is missing). As the 1970s were also the heyday of labor migration of Yemeni men to the Gulf States, especially to Saudi Arabia, the amounts of cash entering the economy rapidly increased, which strongly stimulated the commodification of consumer goods, such as dress.

The *balto* was, however, not only a sign of fashionable modernity. If full-length and loosely cut, it also was an acceptable style of dress in the eyes of the conservative Islamists, who, in the course of the 1970s, started to gain influence in North Yemen and were supported by the regime against the more left-wing nationalists. In fact, the *balto* was quite similar to the styles of dress that women who were close to the Islamists had started to wear in Egypt and later in Syria (where it was called by the Koranic term *jilbab*). The *balto* then was not only brought to San'a by modernist Yemenis who considered this a modern yet suitably modest style of dress, it was also brought to San'a by the many women teachers from the Middle East, some of whom were ideologically close to the Islamists, such as for instance the Syrian teachers who took refuge in Yemen after the Hama massacre in 1982.

The main difference between those wearing a *balto* as a fashionable style of dress, on the one hand, and those affiliated to the Islamists or *salafis*, on the other hand, became visible in how they covered their hair. The former often wore a *maqrama*, a long thin rectangular scarf draped over the hair or a large, often colored, square headscarf as common elsewhere in the Middle

East. The latter, in contrast, would cover their heads with a *khimar*, that is, a larger and thicker black piece of material that is tied in the back of the neck (over a small underscarf, that also covers the forehead) with the material then drawn to the front to completely cover the upper part of the body, similar to the headgear worn with the *sharshaf*. Often extending to the waist, it would hide the shape of the shoulders, an issue the *salafi* authors were much concerned about. In Yemen in the early 1980s, wearing such a long *khimar* was strongly associated with Islamist sympathies. Another sign of distinction was the black socks and gloves some *salafis* would add to their outfits in order to avoid showing any skin. Islamist and *salafi* women prefer the *balto* over the *sharshaf*, which in their words, "covers better." For, in contrast to the one-piece *balto*, the upper part of the two-piece *sharshaf* may easily reveal the garments worn underneath. In a similar vein, practicality is also an issue that some professionally employed *salafi* women brought to the fore when presenting the advantages of wearing the *khimar*. In the words of Malika, an employee holding a high position at an Islamic charitable organization, "Once you have tied the *khimar*, it is easy, it stays in its place, while a *maqrama* you continuously need to pay attention to; it may slip so you need to make sure that it stays in place. With a *khimar* you can even run." The strong determination with which Malika moved around, aided no doubt by her sports shoes, clearly expressed the position of authority she held over subordinate *salafi* men at work.

By the 1990s, the *balto* had become the most commonly worn style of outdoor dress amongst students and young women professionals, often but not always black. Fadwa, who had grown up in Kuwait where she had not worn covered dress, not even a headscarf, usually wore a light grayish blue *balto* after returning to San'a when she went to study at the university. But at her work—where she was a teacher at a girl's high school—she did not do so, because, as she said, "The girls take their teacher as their role model and would want to imitate me." Fadwa was concerned that the girls would put pressure on their families to buy them similar, in their eyes, fashionable *baltos*. Other women who wore colored *baltos* stated that the public often assumed that they were not Yemeni, but part of the Syrian, Jordanian or Palestinian migrant communities. Whilst the majority wore black, none of them argued that Islam prescribed women to wear black. Some young women did so because it was customary in their social circles, where it was often seen as a San'ani tradition, others argued that they considered black more elegant and sophisticated, or simply more beautiful.

A MOVE TO ELEGANCE

Around the mid-1990s, younger women from the more traditionalist households also replaced the *sharshaf* with the *balto*. By the beginning of the twenty-first century, however, women started to turn to another lighter style of outdoor dress, the *abaya*. Although quite similar to the *balto*, it was made of thinner material, often two layers of material to make sure that it would not be transparent. Because of this thinness of the material, the *abaya* had a more distinctively elegant and feminine look. Such an *abaya* is designed more similar to a wide, full-length gown than to the all-covering *abayas* commonly worn in Saudi Arabia, that are thrown over the head and do not show the shape of the body at all. It is this new style of *abaya* that is heavily criticized in the *salafi* booklets. A prominent Saudi religious functionary, for instance, issues a warning, stating that:

A dangerous phenomenon is spreading amongst Muslim women and that is that some women wear the *'abaya* on the shoulders and cover their heads with a headcloth that in itself is an embellishment. Such an *'abaya* follows the body and shows the chest and the shape of the body. This dress is worn as fashion. (Ahl al-Shaykh 2000: 13)

Or, in the words of another author:

O daughter of mine. Beware of the revealing *hijab* that is spreading amongst the women these days and that is characterized by:

1 The tightly cut *'abaya* following the body, that shows the attractiveness of the woman. Such an *'abaya* needs another *'abaya* to cover it.

2 Wearing the *'abaya* on the shoulders, as the original way of wearing it is on the head in order that it covers the body completely. Showing the head of the woman and her shoulders attracts the gaze towards her. (Al-'Umran 2001: 10–11)

Although using a different tone, some women would employ similar arguments to explain why they would not wear such an *abaya*. Khadidja, who works as a secretary for a Yemeni non-governmental organization argued that she preferred to wear a *balto*, because an *abaya* was more similar to a dress than to an outdoor cover or coat. As it did not conceal the body very well, she did not feel comfortable wearing this while going around in San'a.

It is evident that fashion has become thoroughly globalized and that the centers of fashion have multiplied. Yet, the speed of change in styles of dress does not only differ considerably from one setting to another, it also depends on the specific item of dress discussed. While replacing one garment with another, such as the *sharshaf* with the *balto*, is a relatively slow process of change, changes in one particular item of dress, such as the material and color of the *maqrama*, or the cut of the *balto* can be far more speedy. Yet, whatever the nature of the outer garments involved, multiple forms of distinction have always existed. There were differences in the design such as the width of the shoulders that could make last year's *balto* decisively out of fashion. Depending on the material used and the attention paid to the cut of the garment, *baltos*—as was the case with *sharshafs*—could vary from cheap, coarse, plain, mass-produced coverings to individually tailored, expensive pieces of high-quality material. Other forms of distinction, such as the type of the material and styles of decoration (such as small colored velvet or lace rims, and designs in the material) are all part of rapidly changing fashions. *Maqramas* and large square headscarves were particularly prone to a host of varieties. They could be made of a wide variety of materials, colors, and designs, could have pieces of strass, small beads, and other small embellishments attached, and could be draped and pinned in different styles, which for those in the know function as a measure of whether the wearer was up to date with fashion. And, of course, one can also, through accessories such as shoes and handbags, distinguish oneself as being classy and fashionable. However, it is changes in one particular item of dress, the face-veil, which have been at the center of debates about women's dress in San'a.

COVERING AND UNCOVERING THE FACE

The most striking change in San'ani women's dress took place in the early 1970s when a small number of young women started to go to high school or university without their faces covered. Whereas different styles of face coverings pertain to the field of fashion, the question of whether or not to wear a face-veil relates to both ethics and aesthetics.

The *salafi* booklets call for women to stick to the strictest forms of Islamic dress. In contrast to the majority view amongst Islamic scholars that holds it permissible for a woman to show her face and hands, they stick to a minority point of view that considers face-veiling obligatory. As Al-'Umran points out:

> There are those who argue that the *lawful hijab* consists of covering the head, the neck, the chest, the feet, the legs, and the arms, and they allow women to go with her face and hands visible. This is most remarkable, because it is known that desire and attraction are located in the face … This means that the face is the first thing that needs to be covered. (Al-'Umran 2001: 7–8)

Often such arguments are developed further to argue for the need to cover the eyes, for are not the eyes, in turn, the most attractive part of the face? Whereas in everyday life, most San'ani women find it too unpractical to cover their eyes, the various styles of face coverings they wear usually include a layer of thin material that enables them to cover the eyes if need be.

The authors of these booklets are not the first to hold strong opinions on San'ani women's dress styles. In fact, as mentioned before, in the late 1960s women's dress became a major topic of debate in the Yemeni press, when Mohammad al-Sharafi published a number of poems in the *Al-Thawra* newspaper to call for an end to wearing the *sharshaf*. The Islamists strongly condemned him, while secular literary critics came to his defense. Women did not express much support for al-Sharafi's stance, accusing him of only wanting women to show their beauty rather than to strive for greater participation in society (Moors 2004). In the following decades the struggle between conservative Islamists and *salafis*, on the one hand, and those taking a stance against their attempts to Islamize society and the state—be it Arab nationalists or socialists—continued at varying intensities. Yet, while in debates about women's dress the parties concerned were strongly antagonistic, in everyday life, changes in dressing styles were often gradual. Moreover, there were not only differences in the sartorial styles of those holding different ideological positions, but also interesting overlaps and convergences.

HIJAB ISLAMI: ISLAMIC MODERNISM AND WOMEN'S ACCOUNTABILITY

A major new trend emerged in the 1970s when a few San'ani high school girls did not put on face-veils. Whilst wearing a *balto* was still uncommon in those days, not covering the face was even rarer. Yet their actions were to be the beginning of a slow-growing trend. As Aisha, in her early forties, who had not been part of this group, explained:

> This move to leave the face uncovered started in the schools. Up to that time, girls had been looking forward to starting to wear the *sharshaf* and the *lithma*. Imitating their mothers it was for them an indication that they were grown up. That is what the girls of my generation did and we loved it. The first ones who did not cover their faces were girls from the South, the San'ani girls held on to the *sharshaf*. But when a new generation of San'ani girls entered the schools a few of them also no longer put on the face veil.

Amongst the first to do this, were girls from the more progressive families amongst the religious elite. Two sisters, the eldest slightly senior to Aisha, yet apparently moving in different social circles, were amongst the pioneers. Whereas their mother wore the *sharshaf* and a face-veil, the dressing style common to women of her background, the girls did not start to cover their faces. As Nabila, the elder of the two, now in her early forties said, "It was my father who encouraged us not to start covering our face. He would not even have minded if we did not cover our hair, but we did not want to do that." After her engagement at age eighteen, she went to study at the university. Although her husband tried to convince her to cover her face, she refused to do so and completed her studies without wearing a face-veil. The emphasis on *not starting* to cover the face was and still is important. As Fawziyya, a teacher at the university who had worn a face-veil and then gave it up, explained, "It is not a problem to walk around without covering the face, there are other women here who do that also. But my colleagues criticize me because first I was wearing the *niqab* and then I took it off. Because I took that step, they say that I no longer am the person I was before."

In contrast to al-Sharafi's poetic lines about love and beauty, these girls and their families used the arguments of Islamic scholars that covering the face is not obligatory in Islam, an argument similar to that made by modernists such as Qasim Amin in Egypt at the turn of the twentieth century. A new discourse gradually took ground that centered on the notion of *hijab islami*, Islamic covered dress, to argue for a style of dress that allows for showing the face and the hands. Whereas elsewhere, in countries such as Egypt, starting to wear *hijab islami* in the 1970s meant that women would wear more covering styles of dress, such as long-sleeved blouses, full-length skirts, and a headscarf that covered all of the hair, in San'a, *hijab islami* referred to just the opposite, to wearing a more revealing style of dress, as it implied uncovering the face. This resonates with how women described their sartorial experiences when going abroad. As Nabila who traveled to Egypt to work on her PhD said, "There we wore short skirts, that is mid-calf length. In those days that was very conservative dress in Egypt, at the time many women there were wearing shorter skirts, but for Yemeni standards that was very, very daring. Also we did not wear black, because we discovered that in Egypt only poor women wear black."

In uncovering the face there is, however, more at stake than taking a religious stance. It also transforms the meaning of being in public. Covering completely provides a measure of anonymity to the wearer. Although those who know a woman well may recognize her clothing, and especially her shoes, her comportment and her body language, there is always some element of doubt (also Makhlouf 1979). Wearing covered dress then makes it possible to escape some of the strict social control prevalent in San'a. People are well aware of this. In his poetry Muhammad al-Sharafi, for instance, not only addresses the issue that wearing covered dress is no guarantee of a woman's virtuousness, but also that such style of dress makes it, in fact, easier for women to transgress the boundaries of morality. On this particular issue, *salafi* women would agree. For whereas they argue for covering the face, they simultaneously emphasize that this in itself is not enough to make a virtuous woman; women need to cover for the right reasons. No longer covering the face then burdens young women with a new accountability. As Samira explained, the main concern of her father, who had encouraged her not to cover her face and for that reason received angry letters from some of his relatives, was whether she understood the consequences. "If you go outside," he said, "remember that everyone will know who you are and you will be held accountable for all your actions in the world at large." And indeed, as Samira told me, "We always let him know where we went, so he would not be caught by surprise when people told him they had seen us here and there."

While being a "personality" rather than an anonymous woman in public is what many educated and professional women strive for, they do not necessarily do so all the time and under all circumstances. Whether women do or do not cover their faces is also situational. It was and is quite common for young women who consider themselves as "unveiled" (that is, who wear *hijab islami*) to cover their faces in specific settings or under particular circumstances. Women who only wear a large light-colored headscarf when going to the university to teach, like Samira, may well cover completely in black when visiting the market, as they feel much freer then to go around and bargain with the shopkeepers. In a similar vein, when using public transport these young women often cover their faces to avoid being stared at; uncovering the face is far easier for those who are privileged to have their own car or have the financial means to take private taxis than for those who are dependent on crowded public transport. And it is particularly when dressed up to go to parties (wearing makeup and jewelry) that women choose to cover their faces. It is true that older rules, still prevalent in the early 1980s, that prevented unmarried high-status women from wearing makeup at all times (that is, also in all-female settings, see Vom Bruck 1997a) are no longer strictly followed. But the association between beautifying oneself and sexualizing the body is still sufficiently strong that most women avoid appearing in public wearing facial makeup. In other words, young women who most of the time are publicly present wearing *hijab islami*, easily switch over to covering the face when they feel it more convenient to do so.

COVERING THE FACE: CUSTOM OR CONVICTION

Most San'ani women did and still do cover their faces in public, but not necessarily because they consider it a religious obligation. Quite a number of them do so, as they themselves say, in order to stay within San'ani customs and traditions ('*adat wa taqalid*). They are well aware of the fact that there are interpretations in Islam that allow for showing the face. Still, they do not wish to go against the styles of dress commonly adhered to in their social circles; and if they themselves would like to go without face covers, they do not want to burden or confront family members and neighbors who may disapprove of this.

The importance of location becomes very visible when San'ani women who cover completely in San'a travel abroad. Photographs in family albums from the 1960s include those of San'ani women abroad publicly wearing short-sleeved blouses, short dresses and skirts, and minimal or no headscarves. For them covering was a manner of staying within the San'ani tradition that it was necessary to adhere to in San'a, but not abroad. Many women still follow such patterns, adapting their styles of dress when traveling.

When Samira's father went to the USA to study for his MA, she, her mother, and her cousin accompanied him. It was her mother who changed her style of dress most dramatically, moving from completely covered dress to outfits such as trousers with a blouse; she did not even cover her hair. Her cousin who had joined them to be able to study in the USA, had been one of the first San'ani girls to wear a *balto*, combined with a face-veil. She removed her face-veil and sometimes also her headscarf. Samira, in contrast, one of the pioneers of wearing *hijab islami*, continued to wear a headscarf and did so in a recognizably Islamic way, not showing any hair. Her father's attempts to discourage her from doing so, as this was at the time of the Iranian revolution and the hostage crisis, which had led to many anti-Muslim incidents in the USA, were to no avail.

In San'a itself there is a growing number of women who generally cover their faces in public, but who in particular settings, such as the university, at cultural clubs or at other sites where intellectuals gather, take their face-veils off, as it is precisely in such settings that they want to highlight their personality (a term they prefer over individuality). Some women also take off their face-veils when amongst their classmates or colleagues, putting them on either as soon as they enter the more public university grounds or when leaving the university and entering the streets of San'a. This was an arrangement followed by Fawziyya, a divorced woman in her late twenties with a young son, who lived with her mother in a conservative neighborhood. Not only working as an assistant teacher at the university, but also trying to build a career as a poet, she engaged in a long-lasting struggle with her family about uncovering her face. She first removed her face-veil during a trip to a writer's meeting in Baghdad to which she was invited. However, her family did not accept her moving around San'a without a face-veil. It was through the intervention of her mother's brother, who, in Fawziyya's terms was "less conservative and more open," that they agreed that she could wear *hijab islami* when in a work environment, but on the condition that she would cover her face in the neighborhood. Still, Fawziyya became increasingly dissatisfied with this solution, as she found choosing when to uncover and cover her face difficult and felt very hypocritical about acting in this way. In the end, after a newspaper published her picture without a face-veil with an article about her poetry, her brother agreed that as a writer it would be all right for her to uncover. He then managed to convince her mother of this.

Whereas most women cover their faces because this is common practice in their social circle, there is one category of women, close to the Islamist or *salafi* trend and using similar lines of argumentation as the *salafi* authors, who do so based on religious conviction. When traveling abroad these women either stick to wearing a face-veil or use Islamic arguments not to do so, that is, they argue that since the principle of covering is not to attract attention, it is better to uncover the face in countries where face-veils are uncommon. At the same time, there is an interesting contrast in their style of argumentation and that of the authors of the *salafi* booklets from Saudi Arabia. Compared to the latter, they are far less concerned with putting pressure on women to cover their faces. Whereas they may attempt to convince them of the virtues of adhering to the strictest forms of veiling, they also recognize that it only makes sense if women do so out of conviction rather than because of external pressure, for only then is it a sign of obedience to God. Furthermore, since religious scholars hold different opinions on this issue, women may themselves choose which opinion to follow. Implicitly, and sometimes explicitly, *salafi* women in San'a underline the contrast between Yemen and Saudi Arabia. Whereas in Saudi Arabia wearing covered dress is an issue of state policy, in Yemen women are free from state interference in their styles of dress.

FACE-VEILS AND THEIR MULTIPLE AESTHETICS

A different set of reasons for women to cover their faces, related neither to religion nor to custom, and even going against one of the principles behind covering the face—not to attract attention, particularly the male gaze—relates to the field of aesthetics. Various actors in the field highlight the fact that wearing a face-veil may actually enhance one's beauty rather than hide it. Some women themselves hint at this, when they acknowledge that they wear a face-veil in order to "hide their weaker

points" or, in a different vein, because "it protects your skin from the sun."

Such styles of covering the face are visible on the billboards above the doors of shops selling women's outdoor dress. While these billboards often show women without a face-veil, in those cases where they wear a face-veil it is one that does not cover much and highlights heavily made-up eyes, visualizing, even if in an exaggerated way, what Ahl al-Shaykh (2000: 11) draws attention to when he points to the increased popularity of a particular style of wearing the *niqab*:

> … In the beginning nothing was visible of the face, only the eyes. Then the *niqab* gradually started to become wider. Then part of the face became visible in addition to the eyes and this brought on temptation. Especially since many women put *qahl* [eye-blackener] when they wear it … (Ahl al-Shaykh 2000: 11)

Both *salafi* women and those who wear *hijab islami* acknowledge that some women who cover their face only do so to be more attractive; putting *qahl* around their eyes is seen as strong evidence of such intent.

Yet opting for particular styles in covering the face is not simply about trying to be more (or less) beautiful and seductive. There are also major changes in veiling styles, which have a particular aesthetic effect that intertwines with and build on notions of authenticity, modernity, and mobility. Aesthetics here does not refer to beauty, but rather to a particular sensibility and taste, a perception by feeling (Pinney 2006). Without going into too much detail about the various types of veils worn and running the risk of simplifying what is far more complex, three major styles of covering the face can be distinguished: the *lithma*, the *niqab*, and the *burqu*, each of which has a different aesthetic effect.

The *lithma* and the *niqab* have a very different look to them. For while the *lithma* consists of a long piece of black cloth tightly wrapped around both the upper and lower part of the face, the *niqab*, in contrast, is a free-flowing piece of black cloth of various lengths that covers the lower part of the face. The *lithma*, which is the very style of face covering that was worn together with the *sharshaf*, is seen as the embodiment of an authentic San'ani tradition, it stands for a strongly *localized* authenticity. Just as some women would continue to wear the *sharshaf*, also some—often older women—still wear the *lithma*; in fact, newer varieties have come onto the market, which consist of two pieces of round-knitted stretch material, which are easier and less time-consuming to put on and off. The *niqab*, in contrast, is not considered a specifically Yemeni way of covering the face but a style imported from elsewhere in the Gulf, where it is widely worn, and its referent is a far more cosmopolitan Islamic identity. It made its presence felt in San'a more or less parallel with the growing popularity of the *balto*.

Whereas a *niqab* is generally seen as a more modern style of covering the face than the *lithma*, wearing a very long *niqab* in combination with a *khimar* was the hallmark of Islamist women in the 1980s.

Weighting the desirability of wearing the *lithma* versus the *niqab* also brings in another issue, which is how these styles work differently on the body in terms of feelings of comfort and mobility. For each style enables certain movements, while disabling others. *Lithmas* are most convenient when flexibility in covering or uncovering the face is important. This is particularly so indoors. As also inside the house women may be confronted with men for whom they need to cover their faces, the lines between covering and uncovering only partially overlap with being outdoors and indoors (Vom Bruck 1997b). In such cases the *lithma* is especially expedient, as one can very easily and quickly pull it up and down the lower part of the face. The *niqab* in contrast, tied to the back of the head, is either on or off, which means that women need to be more on their guard; if they take it off they need to be sure that their privacy cannot be intruded upon. Yet, the *niqab* also has particular advantages. Many point out that it is more pleasant to wear, it is less hot and stuffy, and breathing is easier. Moreover, the *niqab* enables women to eat and drink in a more or less public environment, as it can easily be lifted a bit without showing the face. Although comfort and practicality are not necessarily decisive factors when choices are made about what to wear, an argument can be made that the flexible *lithma* is particularly suitable for those spending most time in the house, while the *niqab* has advantages for women

employees or students who are for longer stretches of time away from private space.

In the 1990s, "being fashionable" became more central in how women were speaking about covering the face. As amongst the younger, better-educated women the *lithma* is rarely worn, while the number of women who wear *hijab islami* is only increasing slowly, most San'ani women wear the *niqab*. But the ways in which they do so has quite substantially changed, for since the early 1990s a particular form of *niqab*, that is the *burqu*, has become increasingly popular. The *burqu* is a one-piece face cover attached to the back of the head with push buttons or a strap, that consists of two layers of material, a lower layer of opaque material that has a slit for the eyes, and a top layer of more transparent material that either can be used to cover completely (that is, also the eyes) or that can be thrown back over the head (allowing for the eyes to be seen). This new *burqu* was introduced in San'a by the migrants who were forced to leave Saudi Arabia and to return to Yemen after 1991. Whereas in Saudi Arabia the *burqu* would often be worn with a full *abaya*, an all-enveloping full-length cover, in San'a it is worn over a *maqrama* (the large, thin rectangular headscarf) and an *abaya* made of thin layers of material, which has sleeves and is worn on the shoulders. Such an outfit produces a body silhouette that is far more elegant than that of the heavier *balto*. It is this style of dress that the *salafis* fulminate against. These are the women who wear a face cover that would make them more rather than less attractive.

The above description does not start from certain categories of women wearing particular styles of dress, but traces actual changes in sartorial practices. Still, it needs to be highlighted that while it is true that there are differences in styles of covering the face, the boundaries between them are blurred and flexible. Whatever style of face-veil women wear, whether it is a *lithma*, a *niqab* or a *burqu*, "playing with the veil," be it through showing more or less of the skin around the eyes, concealing or revealing the eyebrows, letting it slip a bit and pulling it back up, and using eye-blackening is always possible. Moreover, individual women may change their styles of covering depending on the activities they are engaging in. Whereas Malika, for instance, wears a *khimar* when she is at work in the morning, in the afternoon when she goes on social visits, she sometimes changes to the *burqu*.

ISLAMIC FASHION OR FASHIONABLE MUSLIMS?

The development of such fashionable styles of women's outerwear in San'a invites an engagement with the rapidly growing literature on the emergence of Islamic fashion elsewhere in the Middle East, such as in Turkey and Egypt. Investigating whether *Islamic* fashion would also be a useful concept to analyze changing dressing styles in San'a, asks first for a brief investigation of the genealogy of this term.

ISLAMIC FASHION

From the early twentieth century on, wearing Western styles of dress, which included discarding first the face-veil and later also the headscarf, had gradually spread amongst the populations in the central states of the Middle East. However, starting in the 1970s an increasing number of women began to wear a style of covered dress that has been called the "new veiling" (MacLeod 1991). Such practices were labeled as new, because it was a new style of dress, visibly different from the covered dressing styles of poorer urban and rural women, and because it was first of all worn by young, well-educated, urban women, who would have been expected to wear Western fashions yet who consciously choose to turn to Islamic styles of covered dress (El-Guindi 1981; Göle 1996). This "veiling movement" was a grass roots, oppositional movement. Some of the women who started to wear this style of dress were part of the piety movement that had emerged in response to the increased secularization of everyday life (Deeb 2006; Mahmood 2005). For others wearing such a style of Islamic dress was a means to express their affinity to the cultural politics of Islamist movements, which entailed not only a form of resistance to Western dominance but also a critical stance *vis-à-vis* local authoritarian regimes, imported identities and an increasingly materialist culture (El-Guindi 1981, 1999[b]; Göle 1996). As part of such

movements, a uniform and sober style of covered dress emerged. Many involved expressed the desire that the new veiling would do away with fashion and, in particular, with sartorial distinctions between the wealthy and the poor (Navaro-Yashin 2002; Sandıkcı and Ger 2002, this volume).

However, it did not take long for Islamic *fashion* to emerge out of such simple, austere, and distinctively non-fashionable forms of Islamic dress. In the later 1980s and the 1990s, the Islamist trend itself became more heterogeneous, as it partly transformed itself from an anti-consumerist radical movement to a more individualized reformist movement with identities increasingly expressed through consumption (Navaro-Yashin 2002). The emergence of an Islamic consumer-culture led to a greater heterogeneity of Islamic dressing styles and an increased fashion consciousness among young higher-class Islamist women (Abaza this volume; Kiliçbay and Binark 2002; Sandıkcı and Ger 2002, this volume). Aesthetic judgments, taste dispositions, and cultural and financial capital assumed a greater significance in the ways in which Islamist women went about wearing Islamic dress and turning it into fashion (Sandıkcı and Ger 2005). In many settings, the greater heterogeneity in Islamic styles of dress has led to a greater presence of an *Islamic* aesthetic in the public sphere (Navaro-Yashin 2002).

Comparing changes in styles of dress in San'a with the developments briefly sketched above points to major differences. In San'a, new styles of dress did not develop in opposition to revealing, Western styles of dress, as Western styles of outerwear were and are virtually non-existent. More relevant is the contrast between those who wear covered dress because it is customary to do so and those who do so out of religious or political conviction. Yet the situation is far more complex than the simple opposition between "custom" and "conviction" allows. For there are two very different sartorial practices women who discursively refer to their knowledge of Islam (their "convictions") engage in. On the one hand, the small number of women who do not cover their faces use the notion of *hijab islami* to legitimize their sartorial practices. On the other hand, the women who argue for very strict forms of covering also refer to Islam, but they follow lines of argumentation that are similar to those of the *salafi* booklets, although they place a stronger emphasis on individual choice. As it turns out, an emphasis on conviction and choice that is grounded in Islamic concepts can induce divergent sartorial practices.

Labeling fashionable dress in San'a as *Islamic* fashion misses the point. For while *hijab islami* in Yemen is a style of dress that looks similar to what Islamist women wear in the central states of the Middle East, and which has increasingly turned from Islamic dress to Islamic fashion, those wearing *hijab islami* in Yemen are *modernists*, not Islamists. This is a strong example of the "undecidedness" of dress with the very same styles of dress having divergent meanings in different settings. Perhaps rather than defining San'ani dress as Islamic fashion, one could simply argue that far more women are nowadays wearing fashionable styles of covered dress.

FASHIONABLE MUSLIMS: SELF AND SOCIETY

According to Wilson (1985) the key feature of fashion is rapid and continual changes of styles. In her words, "Fashion, in a sense *is* change, and in modern Western societies no clothes are outside fashion; fashion sets the terms of *all* sartorial behavior … Even the determinedly unfashionable wear clothes that manifestly represent a reaction against what is in fashion" (Wilson 1985: 3–4). Although Wilson refers to modern Western societies, the very same argument can be made for San'a at the turn of the twenty-first century. It is true that the fact that the large majority of San'ani women are completely covered in black, often including a face-veil, may easily be seen as evidence that the world of fashion has bypassed San'a. Yet, as the above has indicated, even in the case of San'ani women's outerwear, fashion matters.

The many young women in San'a who cover their faces not out of conviction but because it is customary to do so, wear covered dress while simultaneously actively engaging with fashion. The incorporation of Yemen within the world of globalized consumption, has made ready-made fashionable styles of dress—continuously changing even if only in details—widely available in the market. The choices these women make about what to wear and what not to wear are not driven by considerations of piety. Rather, while staying within the boundaries of what is acceptable in their own social circles, many of them go for the newest and most cosmopolitan models in the market. In their case, the dialectics that Simmel (1957) pointed to as central to the development of fashion, that is the need to belong to a community and to aspire to some sense of individuality, are obviously at play.

Well-educated "convinced" women who wear either *hijab islami* or *salafi* styles of dress have a somewhat different relation to fashion. The former have no problem with "being fashionable," yet they frame this within a wider discourse of modernity, which includes the modernist notion of *hijab islami*. The *salafi* women, in contrast, use religious arguments not only to argue for the obligation to wear strictly covering dress but also to warn against wearing fashion. However, this does not tally with their everyday practices, for they also have joined the world of fashion by moving from *sharshaf* and *lithma* to *balto, khimar,* and *niqab.* Yet they link their preferences for such styles of dress to women's increased public presence. These newer styles facilitate women's mobility and participation in the public while they also "cover better."

Wearing certain styles of dress and fashion functions as a means of communication with others and, at the same time, also has an effect on the physical body and the spiritual self. As a non-discursive embodied way of being and acting, sartorial practices pertain to the field of the senses and feelings. Bourdieu ([1979] 1984) has developed the twin concepts of distinction and habitus to point to how such practices link social positionings and habitual actions and dispositions. As Tilley (2006: 9) has argued, things have their effects on persons through the ways in which they reproduce routinized and embodied ways of acting.

Yet, it is also important to realize that discursive practices, such as public debates, private admonitions, and prescriptive booklets may turn habitual actions into conscious, intentional ways of being. As indicated above, both modernists and *salafis* actively employ arguments grounded in particular Islamic traditions to argue for and against specific styles of dress.

Both those who either focus on sartorial practices in terms of identity politics (Ahmed 1992; MacLeod 1991) or those who underline the effects of particular styles of dress on the self (Mahmood 2005), reduce the multiple meanings of sartorial practices to one particular set of effects, impacting either at the level of society or at that of the self. Yet San'ani women's narratives about wearing particular styles of dress and fashion point to the multiple positions they may take up. *Salafi* women, for instance, consider wearing strict forms of veiling as a religious practice and as a technique of the self that helps them to become more modest and hence better Muslim women. Yet, they simultaneously take into consideration how their embodied presence affects others, and through wearing fully covered dress they highlight their sense of responsibility in removing all references to sexuality from the public. Furthermore, in doing so they also show to the world at large that they are good Muslims of a particular conviction.

Still, these *salafis* also recognize that there is always the possibility of a gap between styles of dress and personal convictions. Hence, wearing strictly covered dress in itself is not enough, as it may, after all, be worn for the wrong reasons. This does not only refer to being more attractive and attracting the gaze or to being anonymous and, hence, less the object of social control. At stake is the right intention of the wearer of covered dress. Such an emphasis on intent interfaces with women wearing *hijab islami*, who also air the same emphasis on intentionality. Such scrutinizing of the intentions of fully veiled women points to a different mode of being religious. Habitual action is no longer sufficient, religious conviction is what is asked for. Yet, whereas in matters of substance, those wearing *hijab islami* and very strict forms of covering stand in opposition to each other, the lines between either of these communities of conviction and those wearing fashionable styles of covered dress are not rigid. Individual women also mix convictions and fashion, depending on the settings they find themselves in, both inside San'a (in universities, markets or neighborhoods) and abroad. While dress impacts on women's bodies and souls, women also do things with dress.

30

LANDSCAPES OF ATTRACTION AND REJECTION:
South Asian aesthetics in Islamic fashion in London

Emma Tarlo

My contribution to this volume begins with a puzzle. Patterns, textiles and styles from the Indian subcontinent have a strong visual and material presence in British cities. Bustling shopping centres in areas with a large South Asian diasporic population offer sumptuous and varied displays of cloth and clothes of Indian provenance or resonance, often highly coloured and patterned or ornamented with embroidery, appliqué and sequins. These distinctive markets are the products of the collective imagination and labour of people from different parts of the Indian subcontinent and cater to their collective needs and desires (Bhachu 2004; Dwyer 2010). But the taste for things South Asian in Britain also stretches well beyond the confines of these ethnically charged neighbourhoods and has a complex history, caught up in long-distance relations of trade and imperialism (Breward, Crang and Crill 2010; Tarlo 1996). Whether in the form of a pashmina shawl, silk scarf or printed summer top, textiles of South Asian resonance or provenance have a well-established place in British wardrobes and feature both explicitly and implicitly in global fashions. The puzzle then, is this: why, when South Asian patterns, fabrics, colours and styles are so popular in Britain do they feature so little in the clothing designs produced and marketed by a new generation of emerging British Islamic fashion designers from South Asian backgrounds? How might one account for the apparent lack of interest or ambivalence to their rich South Asian textile heritage? And on what alternative sartorial heritage, real or imagined, do they draw?

It is sometimes argued that migrants and their descendants develop particularly intimate forms of attachment to the material culture and artefacts associated with their homelands. Such artefacts, it is suggested, are subject to high levels of emotional investment and sensorial engagement, sometimes acting as ritual tools or transitional objects in diasporic contexts. Whilst at first sight appearing to contradict this view, visibly Muslim fashions in Britain problematize these assertions in interesting ways. While British Asian Muslims often take distance from their South Asian textile heritage, it could be argued that is less about lack of intimacy with it than about the ambivalent feelings that intimacy with it engenders. Secondly, it is not that they are unconcerned about maintaining diasporic connections but that the material and emotional links they seek to forge through visibly Muslim fashions are about asserting an alternative diasporic identity and heritage, through which they trace associations not to South Asia but to the first generation of Muslims on the Arabian peninsula—the original Muslim ummah. This contribution explores how different aspects of this double diasporic identity are played out through the dress practice of British Asian Muslims, drawing attention to spatial and temporal elements of the diasporic imagination which revolves not only around remembered or imagined pasts and places but also projected futures. It argues that through dress people not only negotiate the tensions of this double diasporic heritage but also bring into being a new material

Emma Tarlo, "Landscapes of attraction and rejection: South Asian aesthetics in Islamic fashion London," in *Islamic Fashion and Anti-Fashion*, edited by Emma Tarlo and Annelies Moors (London: Bloomsbury, 2015), pp. 73–92.

heritage which makes future identities possible and brings them into being. In this sense, a cosmopolitan pan-Islamic Muslim identity is as much anticipatory as retrospective and fashion is one of the means by which it becomes attainable. How and why dress is such an apt medium for negotiating and concretizing ideas of identity and belonging is explored through a discussion of the intimate relationship between dress, body and place.

DRESS, BODY AND PLACE—AN AWKWARD INTIMACY

The most obvious feature of dress is its proximity to the body and the intimacy of our relationship to it. Whilst sociologists of the wardrobe rightly remind us that some clothing remains forever unworn or may be kept only for special occasions, it is nonetheless true that it is through being worn that dress springs into life and attains its primary purpose. This intimate relationship between our bodies and our clothes is not, however, without potential conflict. Bodies animate clothes, but they sometimes let them down, defying their intentions through inappropriate combination and usage. Similarly, clothes animate bodies, but they also constrain and frame them, modifying the actions of their wearers and inviting particular perceptions and responses from viewers. In fact, clothes and their wearers are often so tightly fused in the perceptions of others that their boundaries become confused and clothes become read not as additional adjuncts to the body but as physical extensions of it—a point beautifully captured by Magritte in his famous painting of a pair of boots with toes and toe nails—a painting which seems to ask, is it bodies that shape clothes or clothes that shape bodies, and how can we distinguish the boundary between the two?

In reality, clothing is of course detachable, and when people refer to it as a "second skin" they remind us of its difference from our "first skin," which would require a trained surgeon to remove it and without which we would not survive. Yet, in practice peeling off one set of clothes in favour of another is not as simple as the physical act of undressing might imply. Precisely because of the intimate association between people and what they wear, the removal or replacement of a particular type of dress by another is often perceived as problematic both by the wearer who may feel uncomfortable, conspicuous, unnatural or overexposed without his or her habitual dress and by those connected to the wearer, whether family member, friends or members of smaller or larger group formations such as nations or religious communities who may perceive a person's change of dress as an act of distancing or desertion, on the one hand, or proximity and affiliation, on the other.

At first sight, such observations sit uncomfortably with the suggestion that in a postmodern world people are free to dress as they please and to construct their identities and looks at will from the plethora of sartorial options on offer. Yet anthropological studies of dress practices in Britain show that despite the power of the fashion industry and the postmodern embrace of ideas of individualism and freedom of choice, people often remain relatively conformist in their actual dress practices, partly owing to the relationship and contexts in which these are embedded. In an ethnographic study of the dress practices of women in London and Nottingham, for example, Sophie Woodward suggests that wardrobes can in fact be read as archives of social relationships and contexts (2007). The expectations and tastes of mothers, daughters, siblings, husbands and friends all find sartorial expression in women's wardrobes as do memories of the circumstances and contexts in which clothes were worn—the home, the workplace, the club, the ritual event. In other words, clothes become saturated with personal and social life.

If clothing choices are fraught with the sartorial expectations of others, so too are they fraught with the sartorial expectations linked to place. In an evocative artwork entitled *House near Green Street, E 7*, the artist Helen Scalway explores the complexity of the relationship between people, textiles and place. By projecting and superimposing a richly embroidered, patterned cloth purchased in the popular South Asian shopping centre of Green Street onto the form of a local suburban brick house, she reminds us of how the South Asian presence in certain area of London has transformed the texture of the urban landscape and how patterns and material preferences migrate, mutate and take on different meanings in new contexts. At the same time, her artwork seems to suggest that the strong South Asian presence in areas such as Green Street creates a particular type of backdrop or frame which, like the relationship between dress and the body, is fraught with ambiguity. "The distinction between frames and their contents is less stable than may at first appear," writes Scalway, "they challenge each other, transforming themselves into new entities with new meanings" (2010: 177). So just as we might analyse the complex relationships of attachment and detachment between people and dress, so we might analyse the relationships of attachment and detachment between dress and place. In this sense, it becomes pertinent to explore how the sartorial expectations of place might enable or constrain the clothing choices and perception of people and how a South Asian wearing South Asian dress in one part of the city might look "in place," but the same person in the same clothes might look "out of place" in other locations (see also Jones and Leshkowich 2003). We can also think about how place of origin might attach so strongly to people that it becomes difficult to shake off.

DIASPORAS OF SOUTH ASIAN PEOPLE AND THINGS

How then do these relationships between people, dress and place play out in the context of the South Asian diaspora in London, and how do South Asian Muslims position themselves within this context? To answer this, it is useful to begin by making a distinction between the migration experiences of South Asian textiles and those of South Asian people. When one uncouples these two things, what becomes apparent is that detached from South Asian bodies, South Asian textiles and designs have long been welcomed into Britain and have circulated with relative ease. For example, in the sixteenth century, well before South Asian arrived in Britain in large numbers, Indian textiles were greatly admired for their superior technological brilliance, complexity of pattern and vibrancy of colour (Crill 2010). Indeed, throughout history we find repeated example of different segments of the British population incorporating and adapting Indian textiles to their own aesthetic and identity-building projects, whether used to add a sumptuous and bohemian flavour to the image of the British literati in the 1920s and 1930s or to convey ideas of nonconformism, sensuality and exoticism when used extensively by those asserting a hippy identity in the 1960s and 1970s (Ashmore 2010). Once detached from its original referent (the South Asian body), such clothing offered freedoms and the possibility of creativity and experimentation.

However, when South Asian dress and textiles arrived in Britain on the bodies of large numbers of South Asian migrants in the 1950s and 1960s, the clothes acquired very different associations. Instead of being perceived by people in Britain as creative tools for experimentation, they were read as permanent frames which fixed and defined the identity of their wearers as different, foreign, ill adapted to the Britain environment, "out of place." Here clothing seemed to be perceived not as a second skin but as the skin itself an indelible marker and visible proof of permanent difference, provoking not only curiosity but also ridicule, racism and suspicion (Bhachu 2004; Puwar 2002). In the interests of seeking accommodation and jobs and minimizing racist reactions, many first-generation migrants of South Asian origin found themselves downplaying the more conspicuous South Asian elements of their dress, modifying their appearances in this new environment. It is, I argue, the way in which dress and textiles of South Asian resonance have been used to essentialize people of South Asian origin that in part explains the ambivalence that many second- and third-generation South Asians feel towards wearing conspicuously South Asian patterns and styles in diasporic contexts.

There are a number of studies of South Asian diaspora dress practices that would seem to corroborate this view. Bakirathi Mani, for example, suggests that the juxtaposing of Western and Indian clothing styles popular amongst students of South Asian origin in the United States represents a deliberate attempt to disrupt biologically inscribed racial categories and to challenge the often assumed connection between skin colour and ethnic identity (Mani 2003). In Britain, some South Asian women speak of having hated being obliged to wear the salwar kameez for special occasions in their childhoods. Growing up in the 1960s and 1970s, girls wearing the garment looked and felt alien, foreign, old-fashioned and, above all, at odds with the surrounding fashion and culture to which they wished to assert their belonging (Tarlo 2010a). Others express feelings of warmth and attachment to the South Asian clothes in their wardrobes but do not necessarily feel comfortable wearing them except in domestic, ritual or social contexts which are predominately Asian. For example, in her study of the clothing preferences of British Asians, Shivani Derrington found people commenting, "I've never felt right wearing saris to work"; "I wouldn't say I'm the sort of person who needs to fit in but at the same time I don't necessarily want to stand out either"; and "I tend to make sure I've got something South Asian on me, like an accessory, but I tend not to wear an entire outfit" (Derrington 2010: 71–6). From other studies we learn how people up- and downplay Indianness in different contexts through the way they compose different elements of their outfit (Woodward 2007). Taken together, such examples seem to suggest a self-conscious play with elements of South Asian dress which demands both processes of engagement and detachment, suggesting that many seek to make reference to their South Asian roots without being defined by them. For some, this may involve a split between personal feelings of attachment and strategic practices of detachment—a split apparent in Nirmal Puwar's description of the contrast between the tactile and emotive intimacy many South Asians feel towards the colourful silky landscape of cloth and clothes they imbibed from mothers and aunts when children and the painful memories of experiences of racism and exclusion many had experienced wearing such clothes in British contexts (Puwar 2002) where they were considered "out of place."

How then do these experiences of intimacy and distance towards South Asian textiles play out in the milieu I have identified elsewhere as "visibly Muslim" (Tarlo 2010b)? By "visibly Muslim," I refer to the growing numbers of people whose affiliation to Islamic values, identity and faith are marked out through everyday dress practices and who have become a visible presence in the sartorial landscape of cosmopolitan cities in Britain, Europe and elsewhere. Here again, it becomes helpful to distinguish how people from different backgrounds respond to South Asian textiles, enabling us to recognize why some British Muslims appreciate South Asian styles and patterns more than others.

COSMOPOLITANISM AND ETHNICITY IN TENSION

While Muslims from South Asian backgrounds in Britain often assert attachment to Islam in part through a rejection of South Asian textiles and styles, this is not the case with Muslims from other backgrounds. In fact, whether white British, Afro Caribbean or Egyptian, Muslims from other backgrounds often develop positive associations with South Asian textiles and enjoy building fashionable Muslim outfits by incorporating elements of South Asian dress. Some talk with enthusiasm about the wonderful array of cloth and clothes cheaply available in the shops and markets in South Asian shopping areas such as Green Street, Southall, Whitechapel and Wembley. They also describe experimenting with bangles, scarves and jangly Indian skirts or tunics that they purchase in such locations. It is not that they are less concerned than South Asian Muslims with the idea of expressing a cosmopolitan Islamic identity but for them South Asian textiles, if worn to conform with Islamic ideas of modesty, provide a means of asserting such cosmopolitanism. This points to the significance of the interactions and exchanges that take place between different diasporic populations in cities such as London which are characterized by super diversity (Shukla 2001; Vertovec 2007). However, for Muslims from South Asian backgrounds, this same textile heritage seemed not so much inspiring as restricting. The clothes on offer in areas such as Green Street and Wembley seemed too saturated with ethnic associations to function as suitable Islamic dress, and to shop in such places seemed only to reaffirm one's ethnic identification rather than provide the means to constructing new cosmopolitan Muslim looks. What was desired by some was distance from the provincialism and intimacy of such areas where one's South Asianness became reinforced through the interpenetration of dress, body and place.

However, Muslims from South Asian backgrounds have been far from inactive in the development of new forms of Islamic fashion in Britain. This is hardly surprising given that over two-thirds of British Muslims are of South Asian origin even if this is not the heritage some of them most want to emphasize. As already suggested, when South Asian Muslims in Britain develop and wear new forms of Islamic fashion, they rely less on the perpetuation of South Asian patterns, prints, colours and styles than on their rejection. Significantly, this also involves differentiating themselves from their mothers whose clothing they increasingly consider insufficiently Islamic. When intergenerational conflict over dress emerges in British Asian Muslim families, mothers tend to accuse their daughters of looking simultaneously "too Western" (in their jeans or skirts) and "too Islamic" (in hijab and especially if wearing niqab) to which visibly Muslims daughters retort that their mothers' outfits composed of the salwar kameez or sari are "cultural" rather than "Islamic." Such outfits carry with them the connotations of their parents' places of origin in India, Pakistan or Bangladesh, which make them seem culturally tainted. They tell their mothers that they are ignorant of proper religious dress requirements owing to their insufficient Islamic education. Such arguments offer British Muslim youth a new form of teenage sartorial rebellion in which they claim the moral upper hand over their parents by asserting superior Islamic knowledge. Such iconic intergenerational conflicts have become the stuff of ethnic jokes, but they provide further insight into why stepping away from South Asian styles in favour of Islamic ones may feel emancipating to many young Muslims.

Objections to the many brightly coloured saris, salwar kameezes and *legha-choli* (skirts and shorts tops) readily available in British Asian shopping centres such as Green Street, Wembley and Southall are voiced in both aesthetic and moral terms. It is said that such clothes are too flashy in colour, flimsy in texture, body hugging in style, too exposing of the neck and arms, too eye-catching and glaring, too Bollywood and Barbie-dollish, too ethnic, too Asian and, for some,

too Hindu. Such clothes are increasingly defined as "Islamically inauthentic" by this new generation of young British Asian Muslims attracted to notion of a pan-Islamic identity. The failure of such clothes to place sufficient emphasis on the covering of the flash and concealment of the contours of the female body makes them seem immodest as does the preponderance of bright colours and abundant decorative elements, which are perceived as inappropriately eye-catching or flashy. Invoking classic feminist arguments about the objectification of the female body in combination with Islamic arguments about the importance of detracting male attention and protecting female privacy through covering, many visibly Muslim youth from Asian backgrounds now attribute superficial values to South Asian textiles and fashions which seem to objectify, sexualize and glamorize the female body in inappropriate ways.

This rejection of the vibrant and thriving British Asian dress and textile scene by those keen to emphasize their Muslim identify and faith involves not just a negative recoding of certain Asian styles and fabrics but also a positive engagement with a growing Islamic fashionscape which offers new alternative modest possibilities and invites membership of an expanding cosmopolitan Islamic milieu. Whilst critics of religious dress practices tend to perceive Islamic dress as retrograde and restrictive, young women who embrace new forms of Islamic fashion experience not only its disciplining effects (which they see as both challenging and rewarding) but also the opportunity it offers for transcending the local and engaging with a new landscape of material, moral and aesthetic possibilities associated both with the early Islamic community of the past and with an aspirational post-ethnic global Islamic community of the future. Nowhere is this cosmopolitan aspiration more apparent than in the hijabi fashion blogs, YouTube demonstrations and discussion fora, which have emerged on the Internet in recent years. Here, young Muslims located in different parts of the world, but many of them living in Muslim minority contexts, pick up on fashion trends from around the world (including North Africa, Arab countries and Turkey as well as London, New York, Paris and Milan) and represent these for discussion and potential adaptation by visibly Muslims consumers. Also featured on these Web sites are links to Islamic fashion stores and Muslim lifestyle magazines, which offer Muslim customers new ways of looking Muslim and feeling part of a global Islamic community with its emancipating potential to transcend the limitations of ethnicity and locality. Meanwhile, communication between Muslim women of different ethnic backgrounds takes place both through Internet discussion fora and chat rooms as well as in physical locations such as schools and colleges, where young people discuss and exchange clothing ideas and express feelings of solidarity and recognition with Muslims from different backgrounds. The fact that visibly Muslims dress is often treated with suspicion and hostility by outsiders in British, European, American and other Muslim minority contexts serves to reinforce the levels of solidarity and emotional attachment young women feel for such dress.

VISIBLY MUSLIM FASHIONS AS COSMOPOLITAN SOLUTIONS

Unlike in Turkey, where there is a well-established Islamic fashion industry targeted at Muslim women who cover (Navaro-Yashin 2002; Sandıkcı and Ger 2007; Gökariksel and Secor 2013), visibly Muslim fashions in Britain have grown up in a more piecemeal way through the personal clothing experiments of young Muslims in search of clothes which might fulfil their desire to put Islamic ideals of modesty into practice whilst at the same time looking fashionable, Muslims and modern. In this final section, I outline some of the solutions they have devised, placing particular emphasis on the cosmopolitan aspirations attached to fashions developed by Muslims from South Asian backgrounds.

Perhaps the most popular solution to the problem of what to wear developed by young Muslims in Britain and Europe has been the wearing of mainstream fashion garments adapted to what are considered "Islamic requirements of modesty" through processes of bricolage (Moors 2009; Tarlo 2010b). How "Islamic requirements" are understood varies according to

different interpretations of Islamic texts, but for many this is understood to include the covering of the head and skin, leaving only the hands and face exposed. By these criteria, jeans, skirts, blouse and dresses are all suitable candidates for visibly Muslim outfits when worn with headscarf. So, too, in theory is the popular North Indian and Pakistani outfit of salwar kameez worn with a *dupatta* (loose warp over the head and upper body). However, as already suggested, for many British Asian Muslims this outfit is too saturated with associations of ethnicity. Its efficacy as a suitable modern Muslim garment is further diminished by its wearing by Hindus and Sikhs as well as by its wearing by some South Asian Muslims who are less concerned with looking and behaving Islamically.

For these reasons, many young British Asian Muslims reject the salwar kameez and choose to build up composite outfits through selecting garments from mainstream fashion stores and adapting them to suit their criteria of suitable covering. Skirts are sometimes lengthened, tight jeans covered by loose tops, and short-sleeved or strappy dresses made acceptable by the insertion of long-sleeved polo necked blouses or jumpers underneath. In practice, many of these outfits are often highly tailored, and there is scope for a detailed and nuanced following of high street trends. In this way, a modern visibly Muslim aesthetic has developed in which emphasis is placed on the covering of the body surface through judicious practices of selecting, layering and coordinating garments which may have been designed with other looks in mind and through a skilful array of techniques of tying, layering and pinning the headscarf which has become a new form of personal art and is often the most conspicuous element of a young visibly Muslim women's outfit (Tarlo 2010b). Ironically, then, at a time when the salwar has made its way into mainstream fashion to some extent and finds popularity amongst British women from a variety of backgrounds (Bhachu 2004), it tends to be rejected by a new generation of visible Muslims from South Asian backgrounds who prefer to wear clothes less saturated with associations of ethnicity and place.

These outfits described are cosmopolitan through their alignment with global fashion trends which cut across regional and ethnic distinctions to some extent whilst creating a unifying identifiably Muslim point of reference through the headscarf, which can be worn to signify both fashion savvy and religious conviction. Variations of this fashionable Muslim look are found in many European contexts (see, for example, Bendixsen 2013, Christiansen 2013, and Salim 2013, for examples in Germany, Denmark and Sweden, respectively) and are further popularized in hijabi fashion blogs, but they also come under criticism from some sections of the Muslim population who criticize certain outfits for being too body-hugging, too sexually provocative, too aligned to consumerist values and insufficiently modest. Some British Muslims who seek to develop a more modest and less conspicuous appearance as part of their endeavour to improve the self take distance from consumerist values and cultivate a more pious way of being turned instead to full-length, long-sleeved outer garments available for purchase in Islamic shops. Such shops are often located in shopping centres specialized in South Asian fashions, but they stand in stark contrast to the latter owing to their more sombre and overtly religious feel. The generally specialize in religious literature, tapes, artefacts and perfumes as well as clothes and usually have recordings of religious lectures or music playing in the background. The garments they sell are mostly imported from North Africa or the Middle East and are usually dark or dull in colour. They include jalabiyas from Egypt and jilbabs and abayas from countries such as Syria and Dubai. Some of these represent forms of regional dress from different parts of the world which have in recent years become recorded as Islamic. For young Muslims with austere interpretations of what constitutes modest dress, such outer garments offer suitable covering worn with headscarves and, in some cases, face covers (niqabs) which are also available in such shops. However, for many young British Asian Muslims who want to dress Islamically, such garments are unappealing owing to their wide voluminous shapes, their thin and dark synthetic fabrics and the perception of them as "Saudi dress" which gives them a regional rather than cosmopolitan look which some feel is incompatible with British lifestyles and tastes.

A common theme which featured in my interviews with young British Islamic fashion designers from South Asian backgrounds was the extent to which the black jilbabs and abayas available in Islamic shops felt alienating and foreign. Some, like Sophia Kara of Imaan Collections, had tried purchasing and wearing an abaya but found herself feeling alienated and ill at ease and above all embarrassed to face work colleagues in such an outfit which she felt would be viewed as "old-fashioned" and "intimidating and off-putting." Similarly, Junayd Miah, one of the founders of the company Silk Route spoke of "all this stuff coming in from Dubai, Syria, Asia et cetera" being "so full of cultural baggage" and therefore inappropriate for British Muslims who wanted to maintain their sense of fashion and style. His comment pointed to the inadequacy of both Asian and Middle Eastern clothing options for British Muslim lifestyles. Not only did these options fail to meet the tastes of many young British Asian Muslims on aesthetic grounds, but they were also saturated with the connotations of foreign places and were therefore perceived as inhibiting and inappropriate for the contexts of their daily interactions with others in British cities. How, then, have young designers from British Asian backgrounds responded to these dilemmas by developing styles of dress which might be considered both fashionable and Islamic and which simultaneously have a cosmopolitan rather than ethnic feel?

The companies wish to discuss are based in London, Leicester and Nottingham—all cities with a substantial Asian presence and the entrepreneurs responsible for developing them are from second-generation Indian, Pakistani and Bangladeshi backgrounds. Whilst the designs they have developed are not intended specifically for Muslims from South Asian backgrounds, they are informed by their own experiences of growing up in British Asian families and contexts. In each case, they have tried to develop forms of Islamic dress which have a contemporary feel, blend to some extent with what they perceive as "Western fashion" but transcend the ethnic associations of Asian dress. In some cases, they place strong emphasis on the significance of the cosmopolitan nature of their designs through reference to the global Muslim community or ummah.

Massoomah is a company based in Nottingham and founded by Sadia Nosheen, who is from a British

Pakistani background and was raised in Stoke on Trent. Her designs are an attempt to take the jilbab which she considers "correct Muslim according to the Shariah" and to modernize it to suit contemporary British tastes and lifestyles. Her designs involve careful negotiations with what she calls "Western fashions." On one hand, she wants them to "still look like jilbabs" and "not be slave to fashion." On the other hand, she incorporates fabrics and design features which show a strong engagement with fashion. Hence, she brings in colours and fabrics that are "in season" but sticks to a relatively muted palette, referring to her preference for what she refers to as "safe and murky colours." Her designs grow firmly out of her own experiences and those of the young women around her. At university in her twenties, she faced what she called "the biggest dilemma of her life" when she wanted to dress Islamically but could not face wearing the black Arabic options available locally. Her solution was to make her own jilbabs using contemporary fabrics such as denim and corduroy and adding features like hoods and Kangaroo pockets. The popularity of her outfits in young Muslim circles in Stoke on Trent led her to expand to develop her own company. Speaking of some of her younger clients, she comments,

> They are going to have that Western taste. What they like is a product that looks like it's been bought in shop, is not cheaply made, looks like they've been to H&M, top Shop or Principles in terms of the workmanship and having labels with washing instructions. We want to be Islamic and dress Islamically but that does not mean we should compromise our standards.

It was clear when talking to Sadia Osheen that even if she wished to take distance from the fashion industry, she had imbibed some of its norms and follows certain of its trends. For example, she purchases roll ends of popular cotton and linen fabrics from wholesale suppliers in the Midlands so that some of the jilbabs she sells are from the exact same materials and are the same colours as clothes found in high street shops that season.

While Massomah jilbabs are on the whole rather plain and classical in design, the modern jilbabs

developed by the company Silk Route have a more trendy urban feel, incorporating features of sport and street wear such as stretchy fabrics, hoods, piping, combat pockets and rip effects. Alienated by both the Asian and Islamic clothes available, the young people behind the company had approached designers at the London School of Fashion and commissioned them to study urban street fashions and find ways of Islamicizing them, by which they meant making them conform to Islamic ideas about covering. Targeted at Muslims youth, the designs they came up with exuded a cool and sporty urban feel on which they have subsequently expanded. In 2012, the company's web site introduced the products with the following message: "The Silk Route shared the modest approach to clothing found in the Islamic-Faith and culture with the trendy sporty urban looks, vibrant colours and high grade materials used by many contemporary brands. The end product has had much praise, support and encouragement from the Muslim community especially the many fans and customers we have around the world." Placing emphasis on the global theme, Junayd Miah told me in 2010, "we live in a globalized world. Everyone is connected. We want to attract conscious Muslims all over the world and this is the identity we are hoping to create." He was keen to point out that his jilbabs played a role in catering for and connecting like-minded youth as far afield as Britain, Egypt and Nigeria who were all part of the expanding global ummah.

What is striking about the jilbabs produced and sold online and on the high street by Masoomah and Silk Route is the extent to which they have taken distance from fabrics, styles, patterns, colours and designs which have a South Asian resonance. This is less extreme in the case of fashions marketed by Arabian Nites and Imaan Collections, which are also global in orientations but which draw inspiration from design sources and techniques around the world, including South Asia. The designers behind both companies are British-born women of Indian Gujarati origin.

Arabian Nites is situated in the London Muslim centre just a few doors from the East London Mosque in Whitechapel, an area known as Little Bengal for its large population of Muslims from Bangladesh. Fashion designer Yasmin Safri opened the boutique in 2005, having previously worked in Selfridges and obtained a degree in product development from the London School of Fashion. Working in Selfridges, she had been stuck by the glamour and elegance of some of the wealthy customers from the Gulf and by their capacity to look both stylish and Islamic. Travelling to Dubai, she was struck by the contrast between the glamorous covered outfits worn by women there and comparatively dowdy, conservative "polyester and parachute" type jilbabs worn by Muslim women who covered in East London. Recognizing a commercial and aesthetic niche, she began to design forms of covered dress that might "bring a taste of the East to East London." Whilst the boutique's name emphasizes the Arabic connection, the clothes inside are eclectic, blending what she calls "Middle-Eastern and Indo-Continental tradition" with features from "Western fashion." Safri's intention is to show Muslim women who demonstrate that covered dress can be beautiful, stylish, glamorous, elegant and a pleasure to see and wear rather than simply being considered an "Islamic necessity." Whilst she does sell quite a number of black abayas to satisfy the conservative tastes of some of her customers, she also makes use of sumptuous colours and fabrics, incorporating embroidered fringes and elegant ruffs. And while she looks to Morocco, Egypt, Syria, India, Pakistan and Dubai for inspiration and employs craftsmen from India and Dubai, the garment she produces are not so much replicas of different styles and fabrics from around the world as reconfigurations of them. Whilst at one level her designs conform to the sartorial expectations of place in this conservative Muslim hub in East London, at another level they subtly subvert them by suggestion the glamorous potential of covered dress, leading some local women to perceive the boutique as an inspiration whilst other criticize it for the glamour and cost of some of the items on sale there. Nonetheless, the boutique attracts a steady flow of women with a preference for long, covered style, many of whom also wear niqab, as do some of the members of staff who work there.

An alternative way of looking fashionable, Muslim and cosmopolitan has been developed by Sophia Kara of Imaan Collections which is based in Leicester, a city in the British Midlands with a large population of people with South Asian roots. Significantly, in 2010 Kara began replacing the phrase "Islamic fashion" with advertising slogans such as "designer modest wear" and "faith friendly couture." Like Sadia Nosheen of Masoomah, she was initially motivated to enter the fashion industry partly through her aversion to the jilbabs available, but unlike Nosheen she is more eclectic and experimental in the styles of covered dress she creates. She cites her inspirations as "architecture, nature, even trees" and confesses a love of "buttons, feathers and vintage." She is keen to make covered dress less intimidating and off-putting as well as less submissive. She also likes to reach out to non-Muslims—hence the reference to "faith friendly couture." Whilst steering away from conspicuously Asian style, she makes ample use of luxury fabrics popularly used in saris and Asian glamour wear such as silk, georgette and metal-wire embroidery, especially in her bridal collection in which she does not hesitate to incorporate bright colours. The daywear she advertises is generally more subdued in colour and made from fabrics such as cotton, linen, felt and suede. Whilst she does not follow fashion trends too rigorously, she is aware of colour forecasts and the need to sell clothes that will go with the costume jewellery, bags and shoes that her customers are buying in high street shops. The global inspiration of her designs is evident from some of the names of the outfits advertised on the Imaan web site: Egyptian Queen, Arabesque, Kimono Wrap, Bohemian Princess, Silver Roman Empress and Grecian Dame. Whilst South Asian tailors and embroiderers are often employed to make these garments, the ethos and aesthetic is self-consciously cosmopolitan.

CONCLUSION

Through fabricating new type of visibly Muslim dress, a number of British Muslims from South Asian backgrounds are moving away from what they perceive as the constraints and limitations of a South Asian identity and aesthetic and fabricating outfits they consider modern, cosmopolitan and Muslim. Drawing on what they perceive as an older and wider geographic Islamic heritage as well as on contemporary global fashion trends, they contribute to the forging of new forms of contemporary cosmopolitan Islamic fashion with the aspiration intent of transcending the limitation of ethnicity and location. How far they perceive their designs as contributing to the forging of a global Islamic community or ummah varies. For some, such as Silk Route, this seems to be an explicit aim; for other, it is perhaps more a possible consequence than an intention. Part of this process of developing new forms of Islamic dress has involved moving away from a thriving British Asian fashion scene. But it is worth asking whether this rejection of South Asian aesthetics is as total as it seems. Returning to the artist Helen Scalway's point about how colour, pattern and ornament might travel, split and fuse in unexpected places, I suggest that elements of engagement with South Asian aesthetics remain visible in subtle ways in visibly Muslim dress practices in Britain. A certain love of colour, fine fabric and handcrafted ornament persists in many of the garments designed by Yasmin Safri and Sophia Kara. It is also apparent in the outfits of many young Muslims, particularly in the elaborate hijab-tying techniques they are developing which require skill and competence in the layering and manipulation of cloth and the appreciation of colour and texture. Is this perhaps a case of South Asian aesthetics re-emerging in new contexts?

31

FORGING CONNECTIONS, PERFORMING DISTINCTIONS: Youth, dress, and consumption in Niger

Adeline Masquelier

In Niger, young men often declared to me that dress was a matter of personal choice, not something that should be dictated by religion, politics, or parental expectations. Despite being largely unemployed and having limited resources, they take great care to cultivate a fashionable appearance. "You dress a certain way because that's who you are," twenty-year-old Habibou told me. His friend Moussa elaborated:

> Wearing an outfit is about desire. It's a personal thing. I may want to wear a certain type of dress that isn't going to please everyone. Let's say I enter the mosque with my T-shirt and I pray … My prayer will be accepted. What's unacceptable are T-shirts with designs that attract your neighbor's attention. Instead of concentrating on his prayer, he'll focus on the picture on your shirt.

Although the overwhelming majority of young men in Niger identify as Muslim, many of them—regardless of whether they are religiously observant—eschew locally tailored "Islamic" attire to adopt mass produced Western T-shirts (or tailored shirts) and pants. In contrast to the previous generation for whom dress signaled a specific Muslim affiliation, they often dismiss the notion that dress is an index of religious identity. Wearing Islamic dress doesn't make one a Muslim, they claim when feeling the need to defend themselves against accusations of religious laxity.

Dress, young men claim, is about self-expression, not conformity to religious or cultural norms. A young man known to his friends as Ronaldo often wore a green jersey advertising his fondness for the Brazilian national soccer team. "I took the name Ronaldo after my favorite player in my favorite team—Brazil," he told me. "My friends and I watch a lot of soccer. So I wear the team's jersey, it's who I am." Yet even as male youth claim that dress communicates "who [rather than what] they are," they also long to be transformed via some act of consumption into desirable others. By providing access to foreign media and commodities, the liberalization of the country's economy in the 1990s has facilitated the emergence of a local consumer culture. Many young people have embraced this burgeoning consumerism. Acutely aware that their expectations of social mobility are imperiled by the country's continued economic decline, they draw on the world of fashion as a resource for enhancing themselves and distinguishing themselves from their supposedly poorer, less cosmopolitan counterparts.

Previously young men achieved adulthood by seeking employment, marrying, and starting families. Since economic shifts produced by structural adjustment programs and liberalization policies have derailed Niger from a developmental trajectory, those who attended school on the assumption that education led to economic stability and social empowerment have experienced that they cannot find

Adapted from Adeline Masquelier, "Forging Connections, Performing Distinctions: Youth, Dress, and Consumption in Niger," in *African Dress: Fashion, Agency, Performance,* edited by Karen Tranberg Hansen and D. Soyini Madison (London: Bloomsbury, 2013), pp. 138–52.

secure employment. Unable to move out of their natal homes and set up households of their own, they are "stuck in the compound" (Hansen 2005). Regardless of their chronological age, they remain *samari*—youth (Masquelier 2005). Yet the very conditions that impede their becoming *cikaku mutane* (full persons) enable them to push boundaries and experiment with a range of identities before settling into mature social roles. These processes of experimentation and creativity are particularly visible in the domain of dress and fashion. Young men invoke their status as *petits* (juniors) to justify their adoption of trendy looks and their reluctance to dress like their parents. Dress therefore provides a lens through which to explore their practices of identity fashioning as they struggle to achieve social mobility while also capitalizing on their youth.

British cultural studies have emphasized the role consumption practices play in the formation of youth cultures resisting parental values and capitalist culture (Hall and Jefferson 1976; Hebdidge 1979). More recently, scholars have examined consumer culture as a site of gendered participation, enjoyment, and constraint through which young people remake themselves as youth, citizens, and social actors (Fadzillah 2005; Gandoulou 1989; Gondola 1999; Hansen 2008; Ivaska 2004; Lukose 2005). Meanwhile, Fernandes (2006) and Cole (2008) have demonstrated how the emergence of class is materially and discursively tied to economic liberalization and globalization. In his account of middle-class culture in Nepal, Liechty defines class as "not a thing, or a set of characteristics to be defined and measured, but as practice and process" (2006: 27). As a performative, contested identity, middle-class emerges out of the constitutive interplay of consumption, fashion, media, and youth. Building on these various studies, I consider how Nigérien youth, and young men in particular, harness fashion to claim distinction and cope with social exclusion. I examine how they draw on the semiotic power of dress to carve a place for themselves in the world at a time when Niger's media-saturated, globally inflected cultural economy encourages people to imagine alternative ways of being and belonging (Appadurai 1996). Drawing on Liechty's notion that class should be understood as a "constantly renegotiated cultural space—a space of ideas, values, goods, practices, and embodied behaviors in which the terms of inclusion and exclusion are endlessly tested, negotiated, and affirmed" (2003: 15–16), I highlight the shifty, intersecting, and occasionally unwitting ways that young men produce socioeconomic distinctions. The settings for my ethnographic study are Dogondoutchi, a provincial town of some forty thousand heterogeneous Hausa-speakers, and Niamey, the country's multilingual capital.

WE ARE *BRANCHÉS*: FASHION, CONNECTEDNESS, AND CONTEMPORANEITY

Dress has long been a vehicle through which people on the periphery constitute themselves as modern cosmopolitans. Even more so now that consumption has become the most visible means of asserting one's participation in global modernity. Far from being frivolous or sinful (as conservative Muslims claim), young Nigérien men's pursuit of "the latest" is motivated by a genuine desire to develop themselves by acquiring competitive skills and the material accoutrements that bespeak middle-class prosperity. Because dressing fashionably presupposes one has financial resources and access to information about the latest trends, youth who through sartorial investments distance themselves from so-called tradition can claim to be *branchés* (plugged in). One conventionally speaks of *brancher* an electric appliance by connecting it to a power source. By the same token, se *brancher* is to connect oneself to circuits of information via technology. In slang, to be *branché* is to be at once connected, oriented, and informed while *brancher* someone is to connect this person to someone else or arouse his or her interest.

According to twenty-five-year-old Issoufou, "un branché is someone who eats well, dresses well, attends parties, then returns home to do nothing." Issoufou's definition of branché captures the experience of educated youth who, like him, remain unemployed rather than engage in low-paying work. Elders may see the branché youth returning home to "do nothing" as lazy and unproductive, but to his peers, he embodies, through dress, consumption, and leisure, the very essence of success. Being branché, then, is not about enjoying financial stability so much as it is about projecting a stylistic savoir-faire enabled by one's consumerist engagements and grasp of current fashions. When socioeconomic conditions have simultaneously excluded youth from the labor market and targeted them as consumers, the branché's strategy is to resort to "virtual consumption." Convinced that social mobility implies participating in the drama of Western progress, young men obtain consumer goods in an effort to display standards of living they cannot afford (Jeffrey 2010). Lacking economic capital, they strive to acquire other forms of capital in their determined efforts to embody success.

Despite his limited income, Issoufou thus spent comparatively vast sums of money to acquire fashionable clothes and equip his girlfriend with similarly modish outfits. He kept up with trends by buying secondhand clothes when he couldn't afford new ones, borrowing items from friends, and even swapping goods for clothes from tourists. He once showed me a pair of fancy shoes and an expensive cell phone he claimed to have bought with the cash earned working for a shop owner for a few months. Keeping abreast of fashion, he intimated, was a constant struggle. In contrast, his friend Salissou largely expected his parents to finance his appetite for fashionable things. The privileges he enjoyed (while his lifestyle was subsidized) gave him a sense of entitlement and a savoir-faire that his less fortunate peers could not claim. It is through the possession of this kind of social capital that class distinctions emerge, Bourdieu ([1979] 1984) argued. Far from enmeshing them in a new "consumerist middle-class," as Liechty (2003) claims is the case for Nepalese youth, the diverse strategies young Nigerien men employ to access commodities often mobilize oppositions that reinstate social divides.

Scholars have recently examined the complex linkages between globalization and youth culture, arguing that processes of globalization cannot be adequately understood without a consideration of the pivotal role of youth (Cole and Durham 2008; Maira and Soep 2005; Nilan and Feixa 2006). This perspective highlights ways in which the notion of development informs both analyses of youth culture (through a focus on "maturation") and the study of globalization (through a focus on "progress"). Yet neither maturation nor progress can be framed as temporal stages along a forward-moving continuum, Maira and Soep (2005: xxiii) note. Far from homogenizing the world, the movement of people, goods, and images across national borders is predicated upon and has further produced deep inequalities. These inequalities, in turn, have upset the "neat chronologies of the modernist life cycle" (Cole and Durham, eds 2008: 11), making it impossible for many youth to successfully mature into social adults. Despite these failures, the dream of development is alive and well in Niger. There, technologies of self-fashioning such as dress are an important modality through which youth attempt to secure prospects in what Castells (1996) calls the "network society."

Young men choose from a variety of vestmental styles, but none of these are complete without a *salula* (cellular phone). As both a technology for forging connections and the ultimate symbol of connectivity, the salula is an indispensable accessory of the branché's accouterment. As part of one's *zamani* (modern) look, it must be prominently displayed: young men clip their cell phones on their belts or hang them around their necks. Those who cannot afford the real thing purchase the plastic toy version at local markets, wearing them prominently on their chests and going as far as borrowing them from each other when posing for photographs. The blue and pink toy phones hanging from the necks of jobless youth do not deliver actual calls but call attention to their wearers, highlighting the struggles these youth face as they aspire to be included in the ever-expanding universe of mobile telephony.

Although few youth can afford to call each other (when they do, conversations are remarkably short), ownership of a salula nonetheless signals membership in the privileged society of branchés individuals. It sets one apart from those lacking these means of communication. Urbanites and educated individuals are anxious to distinguish themselves from the supposedly backward *ruraux* (country folks). Abdou, a university graduate sent to teach primary school in a distant village, spoke of the terrible isolation he endured in a place where there was no network: "The worst is that I can't use my cell phone to call my girlfriend or receive news from my parents."

"Owning a cell phone is an obsession for [Nigérien] youth. They go to great extremes to procure one. When they succeed they make sure everyone sees it" (Baba 2003: 13). Not all cell phones are created equal, however. The price of available devices varies greatly. Top-of-the-line cell phones can cost as much as US$1,000. Those wishing to distinguish themselves from the average salula owner purchase phones with the latest features (special text messaging formats, glow in the dark, and so on). The value of cell phones does not reside solely in their capacity to impress: they are also used as a money reserve. When strapped for cash, owners sell their expensive phone and buy a cheaper model, which they'll trade in for a nicer one in flush times. It is not uncommon for young men to possess as many as three or four cell phones. Ironically, while this strategy enhances the illusion of connectivity, it often hinders communication: networks are overburdened, callers forget on which phone they saved a callee's number, and so on.

Cell phones, even if they have restricted connective capacities, bespeak young people's desire to hook up with the world. They are an essential tool of romance: one cannot hope to attract a girl's attention without displaying a cell phone clipped to one's belt. A local youth was rumored to have borrowed a substantial sum to purchase a cell phone that would impress his girlfriend. According to a high school student, "Some people don't even have a goat but they get indebted to buy a salula and seduce girls." The cell phone, twenty-two-year-old Moussa explains,

> is a symbol. To show off. If a girl sees you with a 50 000FCFA [$500US] cell phone and nice clothes, she'll think, "Oh, an *alhaji*[4] [wealthy trader]" or "Great! A *boss, je vais croquer* [I'm going to eat]."

Young women require a cell phone from their boyfriends both as a measure of the young men's attachment to them and a means of evading parental control when setting up romantic rendezvous. According to Moussa, "Girls use their phone to ask for things. They send you a text message: 'Hey, you, I need this. Please send me 2000 CFA francs.'" Lest young women be reduced to the status of gold diggers, it is

worth pointing out that while young men complain that romantic relationships are often mediated by money, their female counterparts describe them as unfaithful partners who like to sample other women. In the end, both young men and women are ambivalent about love and marriage. Lovers, they say, frequently betray each other, and it is difficult not to let material concerns overshadow sentiments.

Recall that those who are branchés "dress well." For many young men, this means adopting the chic ghetto look of rappers they see in the media or during live performances. In Niger as elsewhere, hip-hop fashions are synonymous with "modernity, cosmopolitanism, and a certain degree of savvy" (Moyer 2003: 101). Note that the Hausa term *zamani* (period) translates as *modernity* but also refers to fashion and trendiness. *Shina cikin zamani* (he is in the times) means *he is fashionable*. "We like novelty, it's in our nature to be attracted to new clothes," a young man told me. The up-to-date-ness evoked by zamani reinforces for Hausa speakers the sense that fashion is about connectedness and contemporaneity—that is, about situating oneself in time and space so as to catch up with the world. For Nigérien youth who routinely speak of the shame of being last (Niger ranks at the bottom of the UN scale of human development), fashion strategically bridges the disconnect between the world of poverty and underdevelopment they live in and the world "out there" filled with tantalizing, yet distant possibilities. As in Dakar where youth classify people on the basis of their shoes' provenance (Scheld 2003), foreign clothes or footwear signal the consumer's connections to other places around the world: Timberland boots or All-Star high tops "speak" of the U.S., whereas a Lacoste polo shirt or a soccer jersey bearing the colors of FC Barcelona suggests one buys "European."

SOCIAL TIES AND SARTORIAL INVESTMENTS

To appreciate young men's intense concerns with fashion, let's widen the lens momentarily and consider the role of clothing among the wider population. In Niger, men and women share an intense preoccupation with clothes, have an elaborate conception of what it means to be dressed stylishly, and spend comparatively vast sums of money to acquire fashionable outfits. Clothes are not mere adornment, however; they are centrally implicated in the creation and maintenance of social bonds. Men are responsible for providing clothing for their dependents. Wives and children eagerly await Babbar Salla (commemoration of Abraham's sacrifice) when they receive new clothes.

Cloth symbolically and literally binds people together. Once the marriage has been "tied," a bride waits to receive a *valise* (suitcase filled with clothes) from the groom before entering her new marital home. One might say that a man's gift of clothing to his bride tightens the marital knot. In the past, adoption was concretized through a gift of clothing from father to child. Destroying or getting rid of clothes, on the other hand, actualizes the severance of these relationships (Masquelier 1996).

Clothing communicates information about the wearer's identity: wealth, education, adherence to Muslim values, and so on. By wearing certain sets of clothes, people signal that they are (or aspire to be) members of a particular constituency such as the *umma* or the civil service. Conversely, clothing can set people apart (Bourdieu [1979] 1984). The distinctions that operate are not uniformly recognized, however. Those who go for the *alhaji* (pilgrim) look by wearing a *babban riga* are not necessarily practicing Muslims. By the same token, a young man's new sneakers and fancy watch may suggest that he has resources when in reality he is jobless. The deceptive potential of clothing enables people to create an appearance of wealth that contradicts their actual economic status. Dress, people say, is not always a good indicator of who a person really is. The recent adoption of *hijabi* (veil) in some Muslim households has spurred lively debates about "fake" veils, impious women, and hidden prostitution (Masquelier 2008). Deceptive or not, appearances "speak" (Barthes 1983). Youth are proficient in the language of fashion; they scrutinize each other's outfits to evaluate how much money was spent. A young man enumerated for me the value of the clothes his friend wore to visit his girlfriend: the khaki fatigues cost 6,000 CFA francs, his long-sleeved polo shirt could be had

for 3,500 CFA francs, and his imitation Gucci glasses sold for 2,500 CFA francs at a local market.

By putting on a recognizable brand (a Fila T-shirt or Adidas shoes), a young man exposes himself to his peers' discriminating gaze. Friends will "read" his outfit to determine his sartorial worth and whether he deserves respect. To successfully compete, young men pester their parents for cash to keep themselves in fashion. Any money they earn through sporadic employment goes to replenish their wardrobe (or their girlfriends'). Some sell drugs to satisfy their yearnings for consumer goods. Others steal or engage in illegal commerce. In 2004, a reputedly "good-for-nothing" youth stole most of the content of a bag of rice from his mother before disappearing from sight. A few days later, he returned wearing brand-new sneakers. There was no doubt in anyone's mind that he had bought the shoes with money obtained from the stolen rice.

Reading the value of clothing off of someone's body is a skill young women develop as they look for suitable boyfriends who will keep them fashionably attired. Lavishing gifts of cloth on a young woman demonstrate not only the genuineness of a suitor's intentions but that he can provide for a wife (Masquelier 2009). Despite widespread claims that romance is independent from finance, young people admit that the strength of a man's attachment to his girlfriend can be measured by the quantity and quality of her outfits. One day, an altercation occurred between a taxi driver and the young woman he courted over a large bill sent to the young man by a cloth saleswoman. Unbeknownst to him, the object of his affection had ordered large quantities of costly fabric from the saleswoman and sent them to a tailor. She wished to appear at the next round of wedding and naming ceremonies in brand-new outfits befitting her future rank as a middle-class housewife. Her suitor would pay for everything, she told the *commerçante* and the tailor. Their relationship had been tested by her extravagant spending. The young man knew he would have to contribute to his fiancée's wardrobe, yet the price he ultimately paid to secure her commitment was higher than anticipated.

Because it is a husband's duty to clothe his wife, a woman feeling inadequately provided for may ask for a divorce—or she may pressure her husband to buy her additional clothes. Women are sometimes accused of ruining their husbands to satisfy their lust for cloth and compete with their peers. Because, as the Hausa adage goes, a wife reflects the glory of her husband, men may have no recourse but to satisfy their wives' demands if they want to remain married. Upon leaving her husband of two years, Bibata told me that her dissatisfaction with the marriage stemmed primarily from his failure to equip her with new outfits. She could not bear the shame of attending social events dressed in drab, washed-out clothes when her friends wore brand-new, crisp attire. Besides reminding us that clothing indexes wealth, Bibata's story exemplifies how worn-out clothes speak of the quality of a marriage. Since clothing actively mediates husband-wife relations, women wearing tattered outfits in public visibly display their husbands' lack of marital commitment or their state of impoverishment.

The same logic dictates that a woman who remains married without receiving new clothes be perceived as strongly (and perhaps excessively) attached to her husband. Upon noticing that her niece Bassira, who previously received generous gifts of cloth and money from suitors, had been wearing the same worn outfits for some time, a friend exclaimed, "She must be truly in love!" Only genuine love, my friend implied, would keep Bassira in a relationship with a man who could not afford to substantially reward her for the favors he presumably enjoyed. Cloth and clothing, these cases remind us, "anticipate, acknowledge, constitute, recall and memorialize relationships" (Miller 2005: 17). They also highlight the gendered dimension of consumption and the tensions emerging when young women's visions of middle-class prosperity do not mesh with their suitors' social aspirations.

KEEPING UP WITH FASHION IS HARD WORK

At dance parties, young men and women dress with utmost care and invest a great deal of time and money in the creation of the total look: the "rapper" look for most young men, the "sexy" look for young women. These gender-mixed gatherings are widely condemned by conservative Muslims as sites of immorality and decadent consumption. In this overwhelmingly Muslim country, many believe that veiling, seclusion, and other practices aimed at limiting women's mobility and protecting their integrity should be more strictly enforced and that dancing and music should be altogether banned. To escape opprobrium and avoid having to tell their parents where they go (and what they wear) on Saturday night, young girls attending dance parties engage in clever subterfuges. Dressed in conservative outfits covering much of their bodies, they walk to a girlfriend's house after informing their parents that that is where they'll spend the evening. There they change into the racy outfit they brought with them: a *mini-jupe* (knee-length pencil skirt) and *baya* (tight tank top) or a pair of curve-hugging *pantalons pattes* (bell-bottom jeans) over a T-shirt with a low-cut neckline—and for the really adventurous, a clingy, sleeveless dress with a thigh-high slit, a hooded jacket, and high-heel mules.

Young men face less pressure to conform to local norms of modesty and rarely hide their sartorial acquisitions and whereabouts from elders. They may nonetheless encounter disapproving stares as they leave the house in full hip-hop gear to attend a social event: in the eyes of conservative Muslims, young men wearing modern clothes (*tuffafin zamani*) of Western inspiration act in disregard of Qur'anic teachings. True, all young men own at least one Islamic article of clothing: usually a simple *jaba*, more rarely the more expensive *babban riga*—the lingua franca of male Hausa dress. Yet the large majority rarely wears this item outside of wedding receptions and prescribed Muslim festivals where everyone in town visibly affirms their membership in the Muslim community through dress and diet. Because the *alhaji* look (achieved by wearing a babban riga) connotes piety, wealth, and respectability, young men adopt it whenever they wish to put the accent on their Muslimhood. Thus, youth do not stick to one performative script but instead shift from among several available performances ("urbanite," "rapper," "Muslim," or "relaxed") depending on the occasion. Each performance strategically situates them within a distinct social field, mobilizing class oppositions through the display of stylistic difference (rural/urban, alhaji/nonpracticing Muslim, educated/uneducated, etc.).

Dance parties are opportunities to impress but also compete with one's peers, and this is why one wears trendy and preferably new clothes. Twenty-three-year-old Aliʾou explains: "For celebrations, wedding receptions, and dances, we like to *sapper* [dress fashionably]. Me, I wear baggy pants and Paladium tennis shoes." For many young men, the de rigueur dress at dance parties includes baggy jeans (or khaki pants), oversized T-shirts adorned with the name of a widely popular rap artist (such as Eminem or 50 Cent) or the face of President Obama, a baseball cap, and high tops (or Timberland boots). Accessories (silver chains, bandanas, earrings) are part of the look many aim for. Other young men go instead for the *coupé-décalé* style, a controversial fashion (associated with a dance music and hedonistic culture of the same name) from Côte d'Ivoire that has earned a substantial following among youth striving to channel meager resources into self-enhancement. Wearing sleeveless jackets worn over clingy T-shirts or tight shirts and close-fitting bell-bottom jeans, they emulate coupé-décalé performers who "carve out spaces of *jouissance* in the face of diminished opportunities and real precarity" (McGovern 2010: 90). The world of easy money, decadence, and hipness conjured by coupeurs-décaleurs has been denounced by critics as "all style no substance." Not only does it lack the authenticity of hip-hop, some argue, but it has fostered an immodesty many find troubling. Those who reject hip-hop and coupé-décalé fashions and opt for the classic look (long-sleeved shirts, pleated pants, and dress shoes) associated with educated urbanites take no less care to polish their appearance: Shirts are impeccably clean, pants are neatly pressed, and shoes shine.

As elsewhere in Africa (Ferguson 2002; Newell 2005; Scheld 2007), young Nigériens employ creative strategies to "appropriate, gatecrash, cushion, subvert or resist the effects of their exclusion" (Nyamnjoh 2004: 39) from the world of wages and entitlements. Demonstrating one is a *dan zamani* (modern person) by keeping up with the latest sartorial styles takes skill and dedication. Buying new clothes is best. Some youths obtain clothes from suppliers in Niamey or buy them directly from traders returning from Tripoli or Dubai. Those who cannot afford new clothes (referred to as *qualité*) purchase secondhand *bosho* clothes (from *Boston*). Local *fripperies* (secondhand stores) sell a range of bosho, from ski jackets to baggy jeans and gangsta-style shorts to dress shirts as well as stuffed animals. Originally, bosho clothes were known as *kaya matatu* (dead people's things). Like hair extensions thought to be dead people's hair, they were spurned by local consumers. With the loosening of restrictions on used clothes imports and the continued impact of the economic crisis, bosho gained popularity among youth: "You can find nice pants for 750 CFA francs at the *fripperie* but the same ones will cost you 3,000 CFA francs if you buy qualité," a young man explained. In contrast to bosho items hanging from racks and trees or piled on the ground, qualité clothes come folded in crisp plastic bags. Bosho is thought to come ("on a boat") from the United States whereas qualité products are supposedly manufactured in China. The latter are judged to be of lesser quality than their vintage counterparts although their design follows changing trends more closely.

Young men complain about the shoddy quality of locally available consumer goods, highlighting the perceived contrast between life in Niger and life in wealthier countries, where everything from school bags to cell phones is allegedly of better quality. Hamissou explained,

> The stuff you buy here doesn't last. Our *salula* stop working after a few months. The shoes and shirts you buy fall apart quickly. Whereas your products are good quality. Even the soap we use is inferior. It's called SoKlean but isn't like the real Omo. You can tell by the lather, when you wash your clothes, it doesn't foam right.

Hamissou's description of how soap "doesn't foam right" because the local version is a pale imitation of the real thing provides a measure of the gap young Nigériens feel between the world they live in and the elsewheres they fantasize about. As [Brad] Weiss notes in his ethnography of marginality in urban Tanzania, this poignantly illustrates how "the dynamism and force of the global world constructed by these ... actors are clearly felt to lie elsewhere" (2009: 127).

Regardless of its quality, one must keep one's wardrobe clean and fresh looking: sneakers should remain in pristine condition (a problem with "cheap" knockoffs is that soles quickly come unglued), and clothes shouldn't lose their sheen after two washes. Aside from being able to select items from a vast array of stuff of differing origin, quality, and value, "clothing competence" (Hansen 2004[a]: 174) involves learning how to preserve the crisp and clean appearance of one's clothes. To that end, young men (and young women) avoid wearing their best clothes on a daily basis, especially if they are engaged in potentially sullying activities. One wears one's good clothes when it is important to be elegant. Before visiting their girlfriends, young men wash and iron their nicest clothes—borrowing items from a friend if necessary. Although none of them ever put it to me that way, young Nigériens would probably agree with their Zambian counterparts that dressing for self-enhancement is "hard work" (Hansen 2009: 118).

THE FUN OF DRESSING

Lest my discussion of fashion be construed solely as work, let me say in conclusion that Nigérien youth also perceive dressing up as a fun, pleasurable, and occasionally irreverent endeavor driven by the desire to challenge the status quo as well as the perception that all things, including having fun, are ephemeral. Thus, "fun" provides a useful lens through which to explore young people's relationship to global consumer spaces. Lukose notes, however, that "it is difficult to formulate precisely how one can rescue the 'fun' of fashion from its simultaneous demonization by the protectors of 'tradition' and by critics of capitalism who locate 'fun' as a mere diversion, a market-driven, consumer, middle-class subterfuge" (2005: 930–31). Recuperating the playful in young men's fashion practice implies recognizing that play is both experimentation and escape from the world of labor, adulthood, and social responsibilities. Firmly located in the here and now and unburdened by a sense of the past, "fun" is a mode of self-fashioning that privileges newness. It is marked by the tension between a desire to belong and a desire to "distinguish [one]self before others" (Simmel 1950[a]:

338). In the way that it channels their middle-class aspirations, it is a means of contradicting the rhetoric of failure that has come to define young men in this era of job scarcity.

Given the condemnation that youth's fashion exuberance draws from elders (for whom youth practices are often synonymous with triviality and immodesty), those seeking to affirm their maturity take pains not to dress like rappers or coupé-décalé fans. A young policeman in training explained, "When I was younger I dressed as an MC with baggy jeans, chains, and earrings. Now that I am a gendarme, a monsieur, I cannot dress like that. When I go out, I wear a three-piece suit. I must look respectable." Dress here was an inescapable dimension of the middle-class values the young man felt he typified now that he was gainfully employed. When I offered to buy a friend a pair of jeans as a goodbye present, he refused saying that he wanted his students to respect him. He too was well aware that youthful performances were scripted by a "politics of fun" (Bayat 2007: 433) that contradicted the kind of responsible personhood he wished to embody. Although he could barely sustain his wife and daughter on his meager salary as a temp high-school teacher, he strove to project through dress and deportment an appearance of maturity in keeping with his new status as a "full" adult.

Much of the value of being fashionable, Finkelstein (1991: 143) notes, rests upon successfully eliciting respect, approbation, and envy from others. Nigérien young men who, through their deliberate choice of fashion, articulate desirable social identities would probably concur. As they wait for adulthood and its attendant rights and responsibilities, they use dress as a personalized mode of conveying who they are or aspire to be, mapping out desired itineraries from unemployed citizens of the world's poorest country to fashion-savvy, branchés consumers. Focusing on their sartorial experimentations thus provides a window into the workings of social class. At a time when traditional mechanisms of social mobility are threatened and consumption is the most visible means of self-enhancement, understanding how socioeconomic identity and difference are staged and performed through fashion-centered practices is more relevant than ever.

32

FASHIONABLY MODEST OR MODESTLY UNFASHIONABLE?

Eric Silverman

In November 2006, thousands of ultra-Orthodox men convened in Jerusalem to address a religious crisis: spandex. "One of our generation's biggest obstacles," stated one rabbi, "is tight clothing … each and every one of us must stand guard and make sure his wife and daughters' clothing are modest." Although the symposium focused on women's attire, only men attended.

Traditional conventions of Jewish decorum, or tzniut, apply to all devout Jews, irrespective of gender. But in regard to clothing, tzniut generally pertains to women. In this chapter, I survey the canons and implications of modesty for understanding Jewish women's attire. These matters, reminiscent of earlier concerns about the Ghetto Girl, raise questions about gender and empowerment. The rules of tzniut, too, like contemporary debates over Muslim headscarves, highlight the still uncertain relationship between citizenship and pluralism in a modern liberal democracy.

THE MALE GAZE AND THE FEMALE BODY

Proper clothing, said the rabbis, like a Jew's personality, should stress restraint and humility. But the consequences of immodesty, to repeat, differ greatly with respect to gender. Men who violate tzniut insult God and erode the boundary between Jew and Gentile. By contrast, immodest women endanger men.

The rabbis, we also saw earlier, expanded the biblical concept of "nakedness" to refer to any public baring of female skin or hair beyond a hand-breadth. Indeed, a man who glances at a woman's little finger acts "as if he gazes at her private parts." As a result, ultra-Orthodox or Haredi men are prohibited from praying within sight of female "nakedness" or, by the same logic, within earshot of women's voices. In the rabbinic worldview, in other words, men are possessed by innate and uncontrollable desires dangerously unleashed by the merest sight and sound of a woman. But the rabbis did not seek to constrain men by censoring the masculine gaze—a gaze that essentially transforms, as per the Talmud, the entirety of womanhood into pudenda. Rather, the rabbis over-dressed women. A "partially revealed shoulder," wrote Rabbi Falk recently in his 600-page compendium on female etiquette:

> presents a stumbling block to a man who happens to see the woman or girl. It is essential that women and girls realize that it is their responsibility to ensure that men do not transgress … even inadvertently. (1998: 275)

Men's failings are thus made women's burden. The solution to male sexuality is for women to conceal their bodies.

To be sure, many Orthodox women applaud tzniut as a radical, liberating alternative to the sexualized and sexist objectification of female bodies that pervades

Adapted from Eric Silverman, "Fashionably Modest or Modestly Unfashionable?" in *A Cultural History of Jewish Dress* (London: Bloomsbury, 2013), pp. 86–111.

contemporary culture. Religious modesty highlights inner beauty and moral substance, not superficial appearances (see Schreiber 2003). Muslim men and women often advance the same claim for veiling (e.g., Alvi, Hoodfar, and McDonough 2003). Modesty, in this view, empowers women. But this modern interpretation finds little support from traditional rabbinic sources, wherein women must cover so men can pray. From this angle, tzniut amounts to little more than male power dressed as female honor.

MODESTY AND MORALITY

Today, a serious commitment to tzniut, pronounced *tznius* by Ashkenazi Jews, occurs only among the Orthodox. Yet devout Jews speak with no singular voice on this or any matter. Thus Modern Orthodox Jews dress in contemporary albeit conservative fashions. Men may pull on jeans, short sleeves, and sneakers; they often shave. More traditional women in the Modern Orthodox movement dress in long sleeves, high collars, nice shoes, and low hems. But others prefer sleeveless shirts, low necklines, denim, sneakers, and feminine-styled pants. They may also expose their hair.

By contrast, Hasidic and other Haredi Jews adhere to a far more stringent, often antimodern dress code. Men favor black suits, black hats, and white shirts. Haredi women, writes one traditionalist website, should:

> cover their elbows; wear skirts which reach a few inches below the knee, often mid-calf; generally avoid skirts with slits, preferring instead kick-pleats; cover their collarbones; wear stockings [thick and opaque, nothing sheer] and closed-toe shoes; avoid certain colors, especially bright red.

In his study of Hasidim in New York City, Mintz writes about a husband scolded by his in-laws for lax oversight of their daughter (1992: 176–78). He failed to insist on heavy stockings. When viewed through a secular lens, tzniut may seem excessive, even medieval and misogynistic. But to strictly observant Jews, tzniut honors women as the nurturers of the community.

Each Haredi sect advocates a particular approach to modest garb. Dark or flesh-toned stockings? Wigs or scarves? Can women don the latest secular styles? Should men avoid shorts and sandals? Some groups yield to the individual's moral conscience; others defer to their rabbi. All Orthodox communities, however, permit some variation to reflect differences in devotion as well as, perhaps ironically, more secular distinctions such as taste and wealth. All haredim, too, agree that women's clothing requires ongoing vigilance.

Take sleeves, for example. According to a contemporary Orthodox authority on Jewish law, generations of rabbis consistently censured as immodest the exposure of a woman's upper arms (Henkin 2003a). The limbs themselves are not licentious. Rather, a shirt or blouse that reveals the upper arms might also unintentionally expose a woman's breasts. For the same reason, rabbinic authorities ban loose short sleeves. Some authorities permit tight short sleeves, provided the garment covers most of the upper arm. Other rabbis permit loose sleeves that extend halfway to the elbows—but only to accommodate local custom or women with impeccable reputations. Short sleeves, in sum, warrant raised eyebrows and close scrutiny. To avert any possible impropriety, ruled Rabbi Henkin, the minimum length for a woman's sleeve is within a handbreadth of the elbows. The recommended length is for the sleeves to reach the elbows or, better yet, below them. Best of all, a woman's sleeves should extend to her wrists.

In general, writes Rabbi Falk, a properly modest woman dresses in unassuming yet cheerful and tidy outfits that please, moreover, her husband (1998; see also Ellinson 1992). Collars should fit snugly to prevent any accidental uncovering of taboo skin. For the same reason, Rabbi Falk recommends that women sew elastic bands inside their necklines and affix clasps or snaps between their blouse buttons. Garments must never cling to the body, reveal the contours of undergarments, or expose knees. A modest woman also avoids trousers, regardless of cut or style, since these garments hint at the shape of her legs and violate the ban on cross-dressing. Many Orthodox authorities similarly assail flashy belts, close-fitting maternity wear, bold perfumes, large earrings, eyeliner, long nails, artificial tans, and garments with slogans or patterns that draw attention to the breasts or backside. "Pretty dress," summarizes Rabbi Falk, "camouflages the real body rather than shows it off" (1998: 334).

Rabbi Falk casts considerable vitriol at slitted skirts: "the Jewish population deserves to be safeguarded from this public hazard" (1998: 320–24). The former head of the Rabbinical Court of Jerusalem, Rabbi Yitzchak Yaacov Weiss, agreed. "Lately," he said, "Heaven has been shocking us with dreadful accidents and illnesses" (Falk 1998: 323). Why? Because slits in women's skirts cause "many to sin and it is they [women] who thereby invite serious retribution on the community." Women's clothing is thus made responsible not merely for male behavior but also for the ethical standing of the entire community before a wrathful God.

The rules of modesty also apply to girls' athletics, sometimes with an ironic twist. In 2007, *The New Haven Register* reported on an unusual advantage for the girls' basketball team of Beth Chana Academy, a Jewish day school in Connecticut. Team apparel includes long skirts and sleeves. The uniform of the BCA skirts inhibits certain skills. But the team believes it possesses a distinct advantage: rivals look at the skirts and underestimate the team's talent. These young women manipulate traditional dress codes to challenge athletic opponents. Other Jewish women, I now show, use the very same rules to challenge the rabbis.

COVERED HAIR: SUBVERTING OR SUSTAINING PATRIARCHY?

The prevalence of veiling in ancient Israel remains subject to ongoing debate. Some forms of veiling, both rhetorical and real, persisted into early Christianity and the second century (e.g., 1 Corinthians 11:5; Edwards 1994: 154–55). Yet canonical Jewish texts rarely mention the practice (Marmorstein 1954). The classic rabbis directed much more attention to women's hair.

Upon marriage, the rabbis reclassified a bride's hair as "nakedness." Henceforth, any glimpse of her locks, like most of her body, remained the intimate privilege of her husband alone. Jewish religious law, in fact, requires married women, as well as divorcees and widows, to cover their hair in public. The rabbis

justified this decree on the basis of the biblical *sotah* ordeal whereby an Israelite priest uncovered the tresses of a suspected adulteress. Today, most devout women continue to conceal their natural hair. Even unmarried girls should, at the very least, contain their locks in braids and ponytails.

The medieval mystics saw unrestrained female hair as an invitation to demons. A woman guilty of such impropriety, declared Rabbi Chizkia in the Zohar, the central kabbalistic text, "causes poverty to descend on her home, her children not to reach the prominence they could have achieved, and an impure spirit to dwell in her home" (Falk 1998: 239). Hair itself was not the issue. Rather, I maintain, hair and clothing symbolized the rabbis' efforts to govern female agency, fertility, and sexuality.

The status of women's hair in Orthodox Judaism is far from simple. Most authorities construe a married woman's locks as intrinsically erotic and categorically immodest. They may disagree on precisely how much hair should be covered (Broyde 1991; Henkin 2003b). But they overwhelmingly agree that married women must do so. Yet some traditionalists, attributing no inherent status to female hair, permit married women to uncover their tresses in accordance with local customs (see Shapiro 1990: 150–54). In this view, Jewish law should reasonably accommodate societal standards (see Bronner 1993: 468; [S.] Weiss 2009). Of course, these Orthodox rabbis are no ethical relativists. They would never taste pork, for example, or allow men to pray "facing a woman's uncovered breasts even in islands or among tribes where women go topless" (Henkin 2003b: 134). Some rules might yield to social custom. But moral absolutes remain.

Yet even moral absolutes offer multiple interpretations. Some Modern Orthodox women now reconfigure their *hair* coverings as *head* coverings that serve, like men's yarmulkes, as a reminder of God (Berkovic 1999: 55; Landau 2008). Still, this quasi-feminist revision frames normative Judaism as masculine since women adopt a male garment, but men offer no comparable gesture. In response, many such Jewish women affirm that they actually seek to reclaim a commandment originally given to all Jews, at least in their view, but unjustly appropriated by the early rabbis exclusively for men. Head coverings thus sustain and subvert patriarchal authority. Wigs evidence a similar tension.

Jewish women in the Mishnaic and Talmudic eras, suggested Krauss, satisfied the modesty mandate in regard to hair by arranging "sumptuous" coiffures (1970) (e.g., M. Shabbath 6:1 [in Krauss 1970]). Only later did Jewish women put on head coverings, largely as a result of papal and royal edicts, but also, possibly, to differentiate themselves from bareheaded Christian women. Women's hair thus formed, along with clothing, another plank in the protective "fence" surrounding Judaism. Wigs, however, posed a unique dilemma.

Jewish women first took up wigs in the sixteenth century (Bronner 1993). Most rabbis initially opposed this innovation for its similarity to natural hair. Perhaps, too, as Bronner suggests, the rabbis also recognized that wigs allowed women simultaneously to uphold and contest male religious authority—to breach, but not shatter, the "fence" of orthodoxy. But any transgressive intent soon faded as the rabbis, likely seeking to reestablish control over women, quickly accepted wigs. Today, many Modern Orthodox wigs appear indistinguishable from natural hair, and even emulate the latest, sometimes seductive styles. These wigs appear to mock the very modesty they are intended to uphold (Carrel 1999: 176). Thus adorned, devout women join the wider, non-Jewish world even as they announce, however slight to behold, fidelity to tradition.

We can discern a similar tension in regard to Hasidic hair. Upon marriage, Hasidic women receive a life-changing haircut, which they renew monthly. Some communities trim the bride's tresses after the ceremony; others do so the following morning (Rubin 1972: 119). Each Hasidic group or "court" specifies the proper length for married women's hair. A few courts shave the head entirely. Hungarian Hasidim, such as Satmars, trim close to the scalp; Lubavitchers prefer longer hair, even a short bob (Carrel 1999: 167; Mintz 1992: 65). After shearing, women in the Reb Arelach court often save a single braid as a memento (Heilman 1992: 323). A Bobover groom's family weighs the bride's locks, and then pays her an equivalent sum

(Shapero 1987: 68 n. 125). Differences aside, these matrimonial haircuts symbolize a woman's doubled rite of passage from youth to adulthood as well as from parental control to a husband's authority. The bride's snipped locks also represent the loss of her virginity since Haredi Jews typically experience their first sexual encounter on their wedding night, or shortly thereafter (Heilman 1992: 322–32). Never again, for all these reasons, will a woman display uncovered locks, now understood as her "nakedness," to any other man but her spouse. Hasidic marriage thus requires women to relinquish autonomy over their hair, clothing, and bodies, which henceforth become the property and moral concern of their husbands and community.

After marriage, Hasidic women must always cover their hair or scalp with wigs, hats, snoods, scarves, and kerchiefs. Beneath these coverings they may also wear a mesh or fabric headband, called a *shpitzel*, which sometimes includes artificial bangs. In preparation for marriage, Hasidic women often go wig or *sheitel* shopping. Family and friends may host a *tichel* (scarf) party, an Orthodox version of a bridal shower. Religious head coverings, it is important to note, mainly signal denominational affiliation and politico-religious sentiment rather than, as in secular culture, individualism. A "fringe dangling out of a stylish beret" signals approval of modernity and Zionism (Berkovic 1999: 47). To reject these ideologies, another woman "girds a kerchief tightly around her head." In some Hasidic groups, a woman places a small cap atop her wig "lest, God forbid, anyone should think she has not covered her hair." Ideally, a Hasidic bride adopts her mother-in-law's approach to head covering (Carrel 1999: 174). Each court prefers a particular style: uncovered wigs, black scarves over closely shorn hair, kerchiefs or hats atop their wigs, and so forth. Hair, again like clothing, signifies communal boundaries. But all Haredi wigs must look like wigs, never natural hair. Some perceptible sign—a headband, scarf, or hat, the cut or overall appearance—must clearly indicate that the wig is, in fact, a wig.

Appropriate wigs, stipulates Rabbi Falk, should be short, neat, and symmetrical—no wild tresses, long locks, or irregular cuts (1998). Valid wigs and hats, too, must avoid any non-Jewish innuendo. At Wigs.

com, one can purchase styles named Sorcery, Beyonce, Bad Girl, Knockout, and Beijing. These will not do. Nor would any wig in the Raquel Welch Collection. Needless to say, ultra-Orthodox hats and wigs should never appear intended to draw attention or elicit erotic admiration.

Since Hasidic hair, writes Carrel, represents female sexuality, a woman who exposes no hair in public laudably displays total self-control over her libidinous desires (1999). Less meritorious women show varying degrees of hair. Indeed, Carrel identified in Brooklyn a three-tiered hierarchy of Hasidic women's head coverings, from most to least observant or *frum* (1999: 171–72):

I Scarf (*tichel*)
   entirely covers a woman's natural hair
   with headband (*shpitzel*) displaying pleated
   material but no simulated hair
   with headband displaying synthetic hair

II Covered wig (*sheitel*)
   100 percent synthetic hair, and scarf
   100 percent synthetic hair, and hat
   50 percent synthetic hair, 50 percent human hair, and scarf
   50 percent synthetic hair, 50 percent human hair, and hat
   100 percent human hair, and scarf
   100 percent human hair, and hat

III Uncovered wig (*sheitel*)
   100 percent synthetic hair
   50 percent synthetic hair, 50 percent human hair
   100 percent human hair

Hasidim see hair as the most public and crucial sign of a woman's religious convictions. Indeed, Hasidic hair reflects themes including a concern with boundaries, the assertion of masculine authority over women's bodies, the legalistic attention to everyday details, and the communal encompassment of individuality.

Despite the symbolic importance of female hair in Orthodox Judaism, some Haredi women seek to resist conventions while remaining true to tradition. For example, an online conversation about hair coverings appeared in June 2003 on "The Premier Frum Jewish Forum." The dialogue touched on ever finer nuances of hair coverings, including the moral gradation between narrow and wide headbands. To this, one interlocutor posted "LOL," the texting locution for "laughing out loud." This chuckle hinted at muted criticism of the entire matter and, in consequence, at much of the authoritative rabbinic outlook.

Other critical voices are more direct. One unhappy Hasidic wife, reported Mintz, wished to eschew head coverings entirely but nonetheless consented to wigs in deference to her husband (1992: 178). Yet even this concession proved inadequate for her father, who abhorred wigs as unseemly. He preferred a kerchief over a shaved scalp. If his daughter must insist on a wig, the father continued, she should at least have the decency to cover this travesty with a hat. But the daughter, who already yielded to male authority, did neither, refusing both the scarf and the hat. For this offense, said her father, she would bear full responsibility for any tragedy that might befall her husband or children. This woman yielded to patriarchy but also resisted a puritanical conservatism, thus upholding and undermining ultra-Orthodoxy.

Many Haredi women voice deep emotional attachments to their wigs, scarves, snoods, and hats (Schreiber 2003). Wigs often become central to an Orthodox woman's sense of self, the topic of endless conversations, styled again and again for important religious holidays. Head coverings visualize personal feelings of piety, pride, and holiness—in a word, individualism. Wigs, too, say many devout women, represent a degree of control over their own bodies and identities. The wig signals not phallocentric tyranny but feminine agency and empowerment.

Yet other religious women renounce head coverings. Traditionalists lambaste these women for vanity and ignorance. But devout women who reveal their hair arrive at this anguishing decision, which may even result in rejection by family, through serious contemplation of biblical and rabbinic sources. For them, what's in your head is more important that what's atop it (Brown 2003: 194). Still, I have shown that outward appearances are often deceiving—that wigs may pose a challenge to the very male authority that head coverings otherwise sustain.

TRADITIONAL HEAD COVERINGS AND MODERN CONSUMERISM

In the nineteenth century, Reform Judaism abandoned head coverings as part of a wider rejection of traditional authority, collective morality, and religious separatism. Understandably, Orthodox rabbis fumed (Kaplan 1991: 80). Conservative Judaism similarly rejected mandatory women's head coverings—with one exception. Most Conservative congregations now require head coverings on any congregant, male or female, who leads prayer or receives a ritual honor. In the pews, however, only men are obligated to cover their heads. In this sense, Conservative Judaism officially balances modern individualism with premodern gender.

Today, Reform and Conservative synagogues stock inexpensive ritual garments for congregants and guests, specifically yarmulkes, prayer shawls, and women's doilies or "chapel caps." In May 2008, a gross of mass-produced black and white, lace or taffeta doilies fetched about $45.00 from online vendors. Devout Jews require no such convenience. They come prepared for prayer as a matter of everyday attire. But acculturated Jews often need to fetch these items from bins and racks located just outside the sanctuary doors. No gesture or prayer attends to doilies and yarmulkes. You simply place the article atop your head and, after services, unceremoniously return it.

Inevitably, though, synagogue attendees in the United States occasionally arrive home with temple doilies or yarmulkes still perched on their heads or stuffed in their purses and pockets. Head coverings have no sacred status. They can even be tossed in the trash. But Jews generally prefer to stuff these errant items in closets, bureaus, kitchen drawers, and automobile glove compartments. This casualness introduces a brief, unintentional element of religion or ethnicity into the secular spaces of everyday life.

Many women prefer to wear personalized "chapel caps," not the cheaper coverings provided by synagogues, to match their tastes and outfits. Hello Doily sells "couture quality lace" and "special trims that are frosted with different combinations of pearls, sequins and delicate beads" (www.hellodoily.com).

This retailer "provide[s] beautiful head coverings that fulfill a women's religious and traditional obligations, while satisfying her fashion needs." A century earlier, of course, readers of *The American Jewess* pursued the very same elusive goal of blending style with ethnicity.

Glam Doily offers "classic," "seasonal," and "junior" collections that retail for about $30.00 to $40.00 (www.glamdoily.com). These doilies incorporate European lace, designer fabrics, and "the finest Swarovski crystals." Glam Doily styles—Venice, Black Sapphire, Paris Pink, Uptown Girl, Bermuda Sky, Versailles, and so forth—evoke worldly success, fun, and upscale elegance. They "will make any woman feel proud to be wearing a head covering." Here, again, we see a fusion of religion and secular culture that allows Jewish women to express their identity as good Jews and as good consumers.

LAW AND THE LIMITS OF MODESTY

Unlawful clothing is typically a matter of too little fabric. But even modesty has its legal limits. The desire to dress in religious attire, especially for women, sometimes violates the authorized appearance of citizenship. For example, British and American passport photos may include religious headgear but never veils or any obstruction of the face. The same criteria apply to British driving licenses. In the United States, the states regulate drivers' licenses, not the federal government, and thus policies regarding hats and veils vary. Some states issue photo-free licenses in deference to religious sensibilities. (These exemptions were initially granted to Christian communities, such as the Amish and Mennonites, who object to "graven images.") Most states permit applicants to wear religious head coverings for license photos, sometimes after signing an avadavat of belief. Legislative bills in other states, however, such as Minnesota and Oklahoma, seek to ban all head coverings and veils from driver's license photos. The Florida Department of Highway Safety and Motor Vehicles, in fact, revoked the license of a Muslim woman who refused an unveiled portrait (*Freeman v State*). After litigation, the state emended the law. The issue ensnares more than Muslim sensibilities. When

Missouri in 2007 started issuing photographic driver licenses, many Mennonites left the state.

Legal matters occasionally entangle Jewish head coverings. In 2006, the harassment of an Orthodox woman by a license branch prompted the Illinois secretary of state to affirm the right of Jewish women to wear hats for official identification photographs. A similar case occurred in 2008 when police in New York state required a Hasidic woman, arrested for welfare fraud, to remove her hat for the booking photograph. This demand, a normal protocol of law enforcement, outraged the local Hasidic community.

Outside of the occasional mug shot, however, devout Jewish women today generally encounter little opposition in Western democracies when dressing Jewish. Not so for American Muslim women. They often report employment discrimination after demands by leading companies—such as McDonalds, USAir, J.C. Penny, Abercrombie & Fitch, Disney, Alamo Rent-a-Car, and Quality Inn hotels—to remove headscarves in the workplace (e.g., McCloud 1995–96; [K. M.] Moore 2007). In most cases, the company emends relevant policies, issues an apology, and extends a job offer. Still, the face of female citizenship in the West is far more accepting of hats and wigs than headscarves and veils.

But not all organizations refuse to accommodate Muslim sentiment. A Fitness USA health club in Lincoln Park, Michigan, agreed to erect a partition between the female and mixed-gender sections of the gym. Some public pools and colleges, including Rutgers University, Massachusetts Institute of Technology, and Harvard University, now offer female-only swims, sometimes banning male lifeguards. In Jerusalem, Orthodox Jews can exercise at a "kosher gym" lacking music, televisions, and co-ed workout areas (www. koshergym.com). In Montreal, a YMCA agreed to install semi-opaque windows to protect the male pupils of a nearby Hasidic school from the sight of exercising women. Earlier, the school frosted its own windows—but the otherwise studious boys simply opened them or strolled outside during recess for a breath of fresh air. That the school reimbursed the YMCA did little to warm the frosty reception by some members, who saw the windows as blocking sight of Quebec's secular roots. The very same issue, rather more famously, surfaced recently in France.

Two centuries ago hats in France symbolized the tension between Jewishness and secular citizenship. France continues to wrestle with the legality of public displays of religious identity and clothing, only now in regard to Muslim headscarves. In 2003, President Jacques Chirac appointed a commission, chaired by long-time politician Bernard Stasi, to issue recommendations for the enforcement of *laïcité*, the official French doctrine of secularism. The concept of *laïcité* arose from a long history of strife over the role of the Catholic Church in society and governance. The doctrine permits private religious practices but mandates assimilation to ensure that "the cultural practices and ways of life of the minorities … converge with those of the majority" (McGoldrick 2006: 44). *Laïcité* legislates monoculture, not multiculturalism, and so allows the state to bar public expressions of ethnic and religious identity deemed antithetical to secular republicanism.

In 2004, Chirac accepted the Stasi Report and signed into law a ban on "conspicuous" religious displays in public schools. The act broadly targeted all religious symbols, including Jewish yarmulkes, large crosses worn by members of the Syro-Chaldean Church, and Sikh men's turbans. But the intent of the legislation was to curb the rise of separatist Islam by assimilating Muslims into secular society. Similar laws are under discussion throughout Europe.

A full discussion of *l'affaire du foulard*, or the "headscarf affair," lies outside my scope (see, e.g., Auslander 2000; Scott 2007). But two points touch on Jewish clothing. First, public alarm about Muslims who fail to dress like proper citizens, as Sandar Gilman shows, echoes nineteenth-century arguments against the incorporation of Jews into European civil society (2006). Indeed, current efforts in the West to undress Muslim women, in a sense, recall former Russian and Polish edicts to dress Jews in the attire of citizenship.

Second, the Western vision of generic personhood actually takes root in early Christianity, specifically, the Apostle Paul's invective against distinctive Jewish practices. From this perspective, "secular" is a cipher for a particular religious identity universalized as the unmarked body of modern citizenship (see Boyarin 1994). In Quebec, for example, the Bouchard-

Taylor Commission—officially, The Consultation Commission on Accommodation Practices Related to Cultural Differences—released a report in 2008 on "reasonable accommodation" to religious and ethnic minorities. Among many suggestions to enhance "interculturalism" and secularism, the report proposed relocating the crucifix prominently displayed inside the parliament building—a proposal unanimously rejected by the national assembly.

Islamic headscarves, like modest attire and wigs worn by Orthodox Jewish women, engender multiple meanings. We can view these garments as defying certain features of modernity, such as individualism, secularism, and egalitarianism. "In our country," declared French president Sarkozy in a parliamentary address, "we cannot accept that women be prisoners behind a screen, cut off from all social life, deprived of all identity." But these garments may also express a thoroughly modern assertion of the individual's right in a secular nation-state to resist collective coercion (see also Gilman 2006: 2). This way, women dress for religion as much as they do for free choice and citizenship.

European Jews, despite echoes of their own historical experience, largely remain silent about contemporary debates over Muslim veils (see McGoldrick 2006). They do so for two reasons. First, Orthodox Jews in France generally send their children to private religious academies. The ban on conspicuous symbols pertained only to public schools. Second, Muslim anti-Zionism often results in violence against Jews in public schools—so much so that the education minister reported in 2003, "There is a trivialization of antisemitism that worries us." If Muslims attack yarmulkes, so goes this logic, why should Jews defend the *burqa*? Sometimes the two religious minorities dress together against the coercive claims of the state; at other times, they dress apart.

ONLINE MODESTY AND BOUNDARIES BLURRED AND RENEWED

The Internet, with its reputation for lurid photos, illicit trysts, and unseemly temptations, hardly seems like an appropriate venue for fostering religious decorum.

Cyberspace lacks any moral center—no limits, no censoring, no constraints on individualism. Compared to tzniut, the Web is nothing if not immodest.

Ironically, though, the Internet offers new opportunities for the promotion and marketing of modest apparel. Numerous online merchants offer conservatively tailored clothing to devout Jews, Muslims, and Christians. Tznius.com, for example, strives "to keep you beautiful, modest (tznius) and looking feminine!" Other online venders of modest Jewish dress include Kosher Clothing, Frum Fashion, Kosher Casual, Below the Knee, Tznius Children, Challah and Hats, and Modest World, "the first Rabbinical approved clothing store on the web!"

The idea of modest clothing may conjure unstylish frumpiness. But many Hasidic and Orthodox women display keen awareness of contemporary fashions and thoroughly participate in consumerism (Levine 2003: 51). They dress for and against the wider society. Thus at FrumButWithIt.com, "tznius and fashion come together." Likewise, Funky Frum is "the place to shop for chic modest apparel … that won't compromise your femininity and contemporary sense of style" (www.funkyfrum.com). In Israel, a glossy new Haredi lifestyle and consumerism magazine, *Stylish*, showcases fashion tailored to modest sensibilities.

Many Hasidic women cultivate and internalize a self-image of royalty. They see disciplined refinement as befitting a Jew's regal soul (Fader 2007: 161). A hallmark of this etiquette—polite speech, stately bearing, modest clothing—is the lack of pollution by the crassness of the wider, non-Jewish world. Yet, ironically, these Jewish "royal souls," as Hasidic women say, are drawn to expensive clothing and jewelry (Fader 2009: 164–66). Of course, a devout Jewish woman truly needs no such finery and, indeed, the very concept of tzniut stresses inner, not outer, beauty. Hasidic women's clothing thus evidences a tension between Gentile-coded ostentation and Jewish simplicity and grace—that is, writes Fader, between "the material and spiritual" (2009: 3).

A unique genre of modest apparel for Orthodox women is the Sabbath or Shabbos robe, a "long, loose, comfortable, but especially beautiful robe or dress which you can slip into quickly before candle-lighting and, wear all Shabbat night … the ultimate in convenience, comfort, and elegance" (http://justrobes. co.il/what-shabbos-robes.php). The Shabbos Robe exemplifies religious modesty, "with sleeves down to the wrist and hemmed at the ankles" (www.larobes. com). But it is also an eminently practical garment for devout women who rush from work on Friday afternoons to buy groceries, cook, dress the kids for synagogue, and prepare the home for the Sabbath— all before sunset. "They look like an evening gown," said one proprietor, "but fit like a jumpsuit." This distinctively Jewish garment also, in this respect, represents archetypal modern values such as efficiency, pleasure, and consumerism.

Some Orthodox women shop for modest apparel at well-known retailers such as Land's End, Coldwater Creek, Talbots, and J. Jill. A now defunct website, Tznius Shopper, posted links to Wal-Mart and Sears (www.tzniusshopper.com). But they offered this caveat: "We have no control over the pictures that they use to show their clothing, and some of them show non-tznius necklines and sleeves or show models wearing slacks rather than skirts." Most readers will likely find the suggestion of glimpsing taboo eroticism in a Sears catalog delightfully quaint. This aside, Tznius Shopper portrayed a classic tension in Euro-American society between ethnic identity and acculturation—between a "Torah-observant lifestyle," in other words, and generic consumerism.

Another blurred vestimentary boundary in cyberspace is perhaps best illustrated by Biblical Garden Clothing Collection (www.biblicalgarden. com). This online vendor, which caters to Orthodox Jewish women, stocks the typical array of modest garb. Hence, they do not sell pants, shorts, skorts, sheer fabrics, slit-skirts, clingy knits, and solid reds. Despite this, Biblical Garden subscribes to a broad, politically conservative vision of modesty that seemingly works against Jewish religious particularism. The website posts links to Mormon Chic, Crowned With Silver ("For the Modern Christian Woman With an Old-Fashioned Heart!"), and Ladies Against Feminism. From the latter, you can click on Future Christian Homemakers, ExWitch Ministries ("God Answers Knee Mail"), TheologicallyCorrect.com ("TRUTH …

not Tolerance"), and a T-shirt company with designs such as "Patriarch in Training" and "I ♥ Obeying My Husband." Many Christian clothiers, in fact, despite the appearance of interfaith dialogue in the guise of consumerism, endorse Jewish conversion and Messianic Jews (e.g., Jews for Jesus). The latter wear yarmulkes, tefillin, and prayer shawls but also accept the divinity of Jesus or Yeshua, thus complicating any straightforward definition of Jewish identity (Kollontai 2004). Zipporah's Thimble, for example, offers attire for "Jewish, Messianic and God fearing communities … in line with the final authority of the Torah" (www. zipporahsthimble.com). Modest attire encloses religious Judaism but also, in a pluralistic world, blurs this boundary.

The Web hosts a multitude of Christian clothing shops with names like She Maketh Herself Coverings, The King's Daughters, Lilies of the Field, Vessels of Mercy Dress Shoppe, Modest Prom, and Mennonite Maidens. Several online retailers specialize in the white temple attire required by the Mormon Church, such as Dressed In White, Heavenly Delight, and White Elegance. Muslims seeking modest apparel, too, can shop online (e.g., Al Hannah Islamic Clothing, Artizara, Barakallah.com, Jelbab.com, DesertStore. com, and MuslimClothing.com). Many of these stores, like comparable Jewish shops, strive to offer women modest yet trendy attire—"styled … for a new generation" (www.shukronline.com), or "fun and funky" (www.rebirthofchic.com). IKEA, the international home furnishing company based in Sweden, now issues through the Hijab Shop in England an official headscarf for its Muslim employees (www. thehijabshop.com). In deference to veiling, some Islamic retailers use faceless mannequins or suitably crop the photos of their models. Mannequins are no less controversial to Haredi Jews. A "modesty brigade" in Tel Aviv insisted on the placement of scarves atop the mannequins in a wig shop (Berkovic 1999: 51–52). The proprietor initially refused, then agreed to a compromise. The wigs remain uncovered. But the Styrofoam mannequins now wear unfashionable eyeglasses.

Several online Islamic retailers specialize in modest swimwear. The wonderfully named Burqini (www.

ahiida.com) and Bodikini (www.bodykini.com) fuse performance-enhancing fabrics to Koranic morality, exposing only the face, hands, and feet. Similarly, Princess Modest Swimwear of Jerusalem sells athletic attire for "Christian, Jewish, Muslim, Druze, Atheist and all other modest dressers" (www.princessmodestswimwear. com). Aqua Modesta manufactures a four-piece, quick-drying, opaque swimsuit for Orthodox women that includes a long skirt with a sewn-in brief, lined sports bra, and three-quarter-sleeve top (www.aquamodesta. net). SeaSecret (www.seasecret.biz) also offers "kosher swimwear." Here, again, we see Jewish clothing blurring boundaries between devout communities and between interfaith orthodoxy and wider secular pursuits.

CONCLUSION

Since at least the seventeenth century, when boys dressed in new outfits for their bar mitzvah ceremonies (Pollack 1971: 61), Jews have looked to rites of passage to celebrate their worldly success. In the 1940s, American clothiers started peddling the "bar mitzvah suit" as a secular counterpart to matching sets of prayer shawls and tefillin (Joselit 1994: 93, 102). Today, reports *The Boston Globe*, the purchase of this outfit often rivals the actual ritual in significance. "If there's one *bat mitzvah* fashion imperative," declared *The Jewish Week* recently, "it's The Dress." The total cost of a bar/bat mitzvah party in the exclusive suburb of Scarsdale, according to *The New York Times*, can now reach upward of one million dollars. The rabbis rejected impoverishment and applauded the beautification of ritual. But is this what they had in mind?

Even devout women embrace the very consumerism their codes of modesty seemingly decry. Eligible brides go "*shidduch* [matchmaking] shopping" for glamorous clothing in anticipation of arranged dates with potential husbands (Berkovic 1999: 53). These Orthodox Jews are no less "on show," writes Landau, than young women in secular society (1992: 261). Indeed, Haredi women may dress in several expensive gowns and housecoats on the Sabbath and holidays (Heilman 1976: 54–57; Landau 1992: 274). *Frum* hardly eclipses fashion.

Much of the contemporary rationale for tzniut concerns, to repeat, the distinction between inner and outer beauty. Tzniut presents Jewish women as "minds and souls" dressed for a higher calling, not as erotic objects devoted to "self-display" (Manolson 1997: 39). Modesty enables women to reclaim their bodies and sexuality and shelters them against the inevitable "self-loathing" that arises from comparison with the impossible, fantasized standards of secular beauty (Safran 2007: 46). Tzniut also lends a woman "control over when, where, and to whom she reveals her attractiveness" (Feldman 2003: 152). Thus viewed, tzniut upholds the feminist ideal of empowerment and honesty.

Additionally, say devout Jews, tzniut protects the sanctity of femininity and motherhood. Traditional Judaism, we have seen, sees women as the bearers of life. Women are therefore holier than men, and so need of layers of protection, much like Torah scrolls, which Jews enwrap in fabric cloaks (Shapero 1987: 102–03). Judaism also likens women to royalty, we have seen. For this reason, women's clothing advertisements in Yiddish newspapers often employ regal imagery—say, "Large selection of hostess dresses for the Queen of the Seder" (Shapero 1987: 104–05). Modest garb is a gift in this view, not a burden.

Viewed from another angle, however, tzniut appears as a form of religious fanaticism—worse, an ideological effort to dress patriarchy in a pleasing rhetorical coat. Wigs, long hems, below-the-elbow sleeves, and high collars, like Muslim headscarves and burkinis, constitute an *anti*-fashion that rightly belongs, if anywhere today, at the margins of normal citizenship. But tzniut, as we have seen, works as much through fashion, advertising, the Internet, and consumerism even as it challenges these very modern pursuits. It thus seems best to view modest apparel for Jewish women as part of a wider, irresolvable conversation about gender, identity, and assimilation that both resists and accommodates modernity.

PART 7

MAKING GLOBAL FASHION

PART INTRODUCTION

Fashion is a loaded term. For those who follow its ebbs and flows, its endless breaks and repetitions, fashion may promise continual self-invention. Through fashion, you can become anything you want—a dapper gentleman, a dashing hooligan, an international man of mystery. You can leave your background behind, give in to a process of continual becoming and re-becoming. But for others, in fact for the majority of us, fashion is less a promise than a command. Buy the latest thing that everyone's wearing! Keep up with the trends! Don't let the rest of the world leave you behind! It is a command that not everyone can fulfil, and for many, it begins to nag, eating away at one's sense of self until one is compelled to take action. Fashion is the great failed promise of the capitalist dream.

But don't start thinking that fashion is just one monolithic thing. It is not a fixed structure imposed from on high. It is less a "system," as Roland Barthes (1985) famously described it, than it is a process. It unfolds. It evolves. It takes shape through the actions of millions of people, with their own stakes, hopes, and dreams, operating from different vantage points throughout the globe. Fashion, the chapters in this part of the reader emphasize, is a diverse collection of practices.

The chapters in this part of the reader describe fashion from a variety of vantage points: Indonesia, Vietnam, Tehran, New York, China. They look at how differently-positioned actors, operating within the global fashion industry, vie for positions within that industry.

Carla Jones and Ann Marie Leshkowich kick off this section by asking what happens when Asian fashion becomes fashionable outside of Asia. They look at the global trends that draw from Asian influences, and how those trends are shaping the ways people in Asia imagine and evaluate their own traditional clothing. For Jones and Leshkowich, fashion is a fluid, amorphous thing, taking shape through the practices of real people in real locations worldwide, not a system imposed from above. And yet, not everyone has an equal part to play in fashion's evolving game, with no clean slate to start from. Asian designers and consumers must contend with the structural advantages of a global fashion industry still centered in New York, London, Paris, and Milan. And they must contend with the way the Western world sees them, an "Orientalizing" gaze they increasingly turn back on themselves, whether to reaffirm or reject.

In his chapter, Alexandru Balasescu argues that a similar process is at work in Tehran. "Ideas about modernity, tradition, and the West," he writes, "are reworked according to the aesthetic approaches of each designer" (p. 311). These are not stable entities, structuring local practice in a fixed or predictable way. They are emerging constructs, shaped through ongoing practice. Balasescu describes the varied ways these categories are negotiated through the work of two, very different Tehran-based designers.

Stephanie Sadre-Orafai continues the emphasis on fashion as practice in her chapter on fashion image production in New York City. Over the course of four years, Sadre-Orafai embedded herself into the fashion industry, interning first at an ethnic women's lifestyle magazine and then at several model casting agencies, where she observed firsthand the way fashion industry workers reframe the bodies of fashion models "as media"

(p. 324). Fashion industry image producers, she argues, are "part of a broader set of cultural practices of typification, classification, and performance" (p. 320). They produce, and reproduce, various ethnic categories through the practice of casting and representing. Such workers in representation, she shows, "can both undo and reinscribe the explanatory power of categories of social difference" (p. 324), and yet they most often do the latter, conforming to the standards and expectations on an industry that sells carefully-controlled novelty through reference to prefabricated ethnic types.

The field of fashion production, this section iterates again and again, is racialized through and through. French designers sell fantasies of exoticized Asian others. New York modeling agents lend ambiguous ethnic bodies to New York brands trying to show off how "edgy" they are. And the racialization of fashion extends to the distribution of labor. In New York City, where the majority of high-end designers continue to be white, the manufacture of their garments is still disproportionately done by Asians, whether Bangladeshi women crammed into a Dhaka sweatshop, or Korean immigrants in one of several shrinking American garment districts. Christina Moon's contribution to this volume traces her own journey through the global fashion industry, starting in the production houses of New York City. "In a world of fashion I had always imagined as full of glamour, luxury, and beauty," she writes, "I saw an underworld of capitalist logics, abstract economics, and exploited labor" (p. 326). Inequality is intrinsic to fashion. Its business model depends on it. Its logic of continuous trend-chasing requires it.

That doesn't mean, however, that those lower-down in the fashion hierarchy are content to stay there. Jianhua Zhao's chapter continues the theme of disparities in the global fashion industry by concentrating on the manufacture of garments in China. China has become an indispensable player in the global fashion industry, the leading provider of skilled labor for the sewing and construction of clothing. And yet, despite the "Made in China" label adhered to so many garments, China's role in fashion is virtually erased. They provide the anonymous laborers of fashion, the silent, invisible hands at work. Creators of Chinese fashion labels, working in collaboration with the Chinese government, are now investing a great deal of time and energy in changing that. They are working to transform China from a center of manufacturing to a fashion center, i.e., a place where fashion is dreamed up and marketed. For in today's fashion industry, it is those who do intellectual labor who count. Those who do the actual work of producing clothes are barely even an afterthought.

It is hard to look at the global textile and apparel industry today and see it as anything other than regressive. It is a relic of the colonial era, creating a stark bifurcation between the global north, who design, sell, and market clothes, and the global south, who manufacture them. Plus, it is an environmental disaster in the making, the second-most polluting industry in the world after fossil fuels. The carbon costs of fashion's global production and distribution are immense. The costs to our waterways, filled with toxic dyes and additives from the manufacturing process, are difficult to overestimate. Despite decades of environmentalist rhetoric, the environmental costs of fashion only continue to worsen. The popularity of fast-fashion brands, such as H&M, Forever 21, and Zara, is driving the costs of our clothes down and accelerating our rate of consumption, and more importantly, waste production. We buy and discard more clothes than ever before, even while paying less for them, driving what critics call a "race to the bottom." Fashion brands are not numb to this problem, but increasingly aware of fashion's "true costs." Some, as Sharon Hepburn discusses in her chapter, are beginning to market themselves as an alternative. Brands like Patagonia, an "eco-conscious" sportswear company based in California, market themselves as "slow fashion," producing nontoxic, durable garments meant to last and be used for years, rather than discarded for the next trend. The marketing of Patagonia urges consumers to consume less, to only buy what they need and to make sure they choose what they buy wisely. Of course, Patagonia would like to provide that one garment that consumers choose. And herein lies the contradiction behind slow-fashion brands like Patagonia: they base the solution to consumption in more consumption. Hepburn describes the marketing strategy of brand's like Patagonia as "greenwashing," a kind of saturating of a brand's meaning with goodness and holism. When consumers buy Patagonia they feel like they are taking meaningful action: helping to save waterways, contributing to the bounty of the great outdoors, declaring themselves to be "eco-warriors" fighting the good fight on behalf of the planet. It's almost enough to forget that one is still participating in the very production one's consumption is imagined to critique. The greenness of Patagonia is thus a "complicated greenness," just as every promise fashion has ever made has been complicated. No easy solutions to the global textile and apparel industry's status quo emerge. The anthropologists in this section seek to elucidate for us just how deep its problems run.

33

THE GLOBALIZATION OF ASIAN DRESS:
Re-orienting fashion or re-orientalizing Asia?

Carla Jones and Ann Marie Leshkowich

Fashion icon Princess Diana wears a salwar-kameez, or Punjabi suit, as flashing cameras record her latest fashion statement. A *New York Times* fashion spread heralds the arrival of "Indo-chic," a haute couture interpretation of Vietnamese peasant and elite clothing. A savvy entrepreneur in Jakarta commissions rural Batak weavers to make items that will be marketed as "ethnic chic" in high-end boutiques in Indonesia and abroad.

Meanwhile, an Indonesian professional woman wonders whether her custom-made power suit will make the right impression at an interview. A Hong Kong designer wants to experiment with traditional styles, but worries, quite rightly, that the international fashion press will dismiss him as merely a Chinese designer. Korean feminists don *hanbok* in an impromptu fashion show for their colleagues at an international women's conference. And Vietnamese state propaganda posters include colorfully dressed ethnic minority women as signs of the modern nation's diversity and liberal acceptance of different traditions.

During the 1990s, Asian fashion became a noticeable global trend, changing the way that people inside and outside Asia think about and practice dress. First and most visibly, fashion elites and celebrities on the global stage embraced particular elements of Asian style for the world to see. Although present throughout the 1990s, the passion for so-called Asian chic occurred in waves. An initial peak in 1992/93 coincided with

the release of high-grossing Asian or Asian-themed films, such as *M. Butterfly, Indochine, Heaven and Earth,* and *The Wedding Banquet.* Janet Jackson and Madonna produced music videos inspired by Asian images, a Chinese nightclub for the former, and what director Mark Romanek described as a "Zenned-out minimalism" for the latter (Corliss 1993: 69). A second peak occurred in 1997/98, a period in which David Tang held a splashy opening for his Shanghai Tang boutique on New York's Madison Avenue, *Memoirs of a Geisha* topped best-seller lists, and the Dalai Lama became a celebrated pop-culture figure heralded at star-studded benefit concerts to Free Tibet. Throughout the decade, stylistic inspirations and cultural practices from Asia were so prevalent that they had become mainstream, even as they retained an exotic flair. As one American fashion columnist describes the trend, "Now everybody and his mom are 'into' acupuncture, organic vegetables and yoga. Meanwhile … sarong skirts and kimono jackets have become part of the working vocabulary of American fashion designers. The Tweeds catalog touts 'the pristine appeal of yoga pants' and Eddie Bauer calls attention to 'the unique mandarin collar' on a white cotton shirt" (McLaughlin 1998).

Second, while North Americans and Europeans explored the exotic yet familiar allure of mandarian collars, Asian men and women confronted the mundane, but increasingly complicated, dilemma of what clothes to make, sell, buy, and wear. As Asian

Adapted from Carla Jones and Ann Marie Leshkowich, "Introduction: The Globalization of Asian Dress: Re-Orienting Fashion or Re-Orientalizing Asia?" in *Re-Orienting Fashion: The Globalization of Asian Dress,* edited by Sandra Niessen, Ann Marie Leshkowich, and Carla Jones (Oxford: Berg, 2003), pp. 1–48.

economies flourished, then crashed and began to recover, Asians of different classes, ethnicities, and genders faced the decision of whether they should wear Western or Asian clothing. The former offered a neutrality of appearance and the hope that one might become an unmarked member of a modern international community in which Western suits, pants, shirts, skirts, and dresses are standard fare, but at the possible price of a loss of individual or ethnic identity. The latter seemed to celebrate that identity, while at the same time marking the wearer as Other, as not fully at home in the centers of power and normative Western fashion, even as those norms appeared to embrace Asian aesthetics. In between these two poles lay myriad options for combining, reinterpreting, and adapting clothing to make more particular statements about the wearer's identity and position, with each possibility carrying both costs and benefits.

Third, theses decisions were reinterpreted by Asian states seeking to craft visions of national unity for domestic and international audiences by juxtaposing stylized images of modernity, gender, and ethnicity, often in ambivalent or contradictory ways. States such as Singapore, Vietnam, China, and Indonesia touted versions of Asian modernity in which economic prosperity could coexist with, or even be achieved through, commitment to traditional values. Tourist posters echoed this juxtaposition by luring travelers with images of colorful customs, pristine religions, and unique sites, all conveniently accessible through modern cities and airports. In most cases, women clad in traditional dress visually symbolized this timeless, exotic Asian-ness.

Far from being separate, these three aspects of the globalization of Asian dress are intimately linked and interdependent. Princess Diana's donning of the salwaar-kameez was possible because the garment, worn by South Asian migrants, had become a visible presence on London streets. In wearing this outfit, Diana valorized it as an element of international fashion, and this in turn made fashion-conscious South Asian British women, both elite and middle-class, even more eager to be seen in it. The Indonesian woman choosing a power suit turned to a national fashion press for advice about what international looks

were "in." She also, however, took care to adapt these styles in accordance with local informal and personal standards of what was then considered appropriate and attractive. In both cases, the supposedly global and local in Asian dress are intertwined, interdependent, and mutually determining.

While the global interest in Asian dress might seem to open new democratic forms of cross-cultural exchange, the processes through which Asian dress has been globalized and celebrated within and outside Asia are also profoundly Orientalizing and feminizing. Even as the cross-fertilization of Asian and Western styles is changing the way people throughout the world think about and practice dress, the dress styles and dress practices associated with Asia and Asians have been consistently reworked through processes that might be called "homogenized heterogeneity": their differences are identified, assessed, and appropriated, purportedly with the goal of deciding where Asian dress fits into the global pantheon of clothing configurations. The result, however, is that no matter what form these fashions may take and no matter how praised they may be by fashion elites located in the centers of power, they get defined as somehow lesser than, somehow Other to, and somehow more feminized than their perennial Western foil. Asian styles may be reorienting global fashion, but the very same globalization process that has garnered international attention for Asian dress are re-Orientalizing Asia and Asians.

DRESSING, GENDERING, AND ORIENTALIZING THE COLONIAL SUBJECT

What are the conditions that have positioned dress, both in Asia and as read by outsiders, as marked Other or feminine? What factors shape current interpretations of how Asians choose to dress, and of styles that appear to be Asian in global cities, be they Jakarta or New York? Addressing these questions requires a historical perspective. We find that colonial discourse and domination linked dress to specific kinds of meanings, meanings that continue to circulate in the contemporary era. Edward Said's analysis of Orientalism ([1978] 1994) provides a compelling frame for understanding these dynamics. Said argues that imperialism created ideologies and representations of fundamental opposition between groups labeled East and West. This enterprise entailed defining and categorizing what the Orient was, a feat of knowledge production accomplished through scholarly research, "exotic travels," and mass-mediated images such as postcards and exhibitions. When combined with direct military force, colonial-era Orientalism as a way of seeing and knowing facilitated domination by Othering and feminizing colonized peoples, casting them as timeless, exotic, passive, or oppressed, but always fundamentally different from and inferior to those in the West. Orientalist discourse sometimes established Western superiority by baldly defining Others as unrepentant savages or backward races. At other times, however, Said finds that the discourse operated more subtly. For example, Orientalist scholars, including archaeologists, historians, and ethnographers, conducted extensive research to identify the charming or valuable aspects of a group's heritage. Their "discoveries" were then celebrated in ways that suggested that the people to whom these traditions belonged were ignorant of their worth and hence in need of Western masters to teach them about themselves.

Building on Said, we argue that the effects of the creation of Orientalist categories and modes of discernment are particularly striking for matters of style in Asia. Through Orientalism, differences in appearance and clothing were often read by the colonizers as indexes of deeper differences, even as the colonizers' discursive categories created the reality they supposedly described. Knowing what styles were fashionable in the metropole, collecting items from natives who were unaware of the value of their own cultural charms, enforcing dress codes among settlers, or critiquing native dress styles as imitative of the West or backwardly bare all served to make style an important terrain for negotiations over power. While some European colonial powers in Asia were met with forms of undress that they read as charmingly simple or disturbingly exposed, others were presented with sophisticated forms of civilization and appearances that took considerable discursive work to critique. Reducing these varied forms of difference to simply bad or

excessive style attempted to contain the threat of moral and political conflict. While we do not suggest that all forms of colonial rule were uniform or monolithic, we are interested in how a shared concern with matters of culture, and by extension matters of appearance and dress, served to cement apparently natural differences between colonizer and colonized. These discourses continue to shape readings of dress practices today, so that even when Asian dress is celebrated, such moves perpetuate a script of a dominant, knowledgeable West and an inferior, ignorant Orient. Four themes—race, gender, tradition, and imitation—show particularly well how ideas about dress and difference in several Asian colonial-era contexts were reworked, dropped, and picked up again in ways that made these ideas seem natural.

First, racial difference was read from dress practices under conditions of rule, both in the colonies and in Europe. For example, Emma Tarlo's research argues that British colonial rule, and Indian nationalism later, relied on strategic uses of masculine dress (1996). Tarlo describes how British colonials saw the Indian dhoti as emblematic of the savage and effeminate Indian male: savage because the item left the torso and lower legs unclad, and effeminate because the draped fabric more closely resembled the voluminous shirring of European women's dress than the more tailored straight lines of men's suits. That the dhoti could be so associated with racial inferiority shaped later nationalist rhetoric such that, as Partha Chatterjee has argued, Indian men seeking an alternatively modern Indian national culture felt they had no choice but to wear the European-style suit (1993).

Not all critiques of racial inferiority were made on the basis of bodily exposure or simplicity of fabric. Elaborate and luxurious garments could similarly be read as morally suspect forms. A striking example is that of Chinese silks. Early European explorers described Chinese court culture and trade in silks as impressively civilized. The silk trade from multiple Chinese dynasties to Rome and later to Northern and Western Europe was the result of the greater Chinese ability to produce fine fabrics, and of the European desire for a luxurious textile, for both men and women. Yet the drape and sheen of silk also eventually took on an effeminacy associated with the perceived decadence of Chinese culture. As a result, by the beginning of the eighteenth century, Europeans no longer found silk an appropriately masculine fabric for men's clothes (Honour 1961: 31; Steele and Major 1999: 71). Precisely because of such distinctions between morally upright, Utilitarian Western dress and sumptuous, decadent native clothing, Asian elites sometimes held on to elaborate styles or developed even more luxurious ones. This could serve as a silent protest against colonial attempts to usurp their power or as an attempt literally to fashion themselves as still possessing that power. According to Jean Gelman Taylor, this was the case in the Dutch East Indies during the mid- to late nineteenth century (1997). As aristocratic and royal families' material power decreased, males donned increasingly elaborate clothing. Aristocratic women were likewise important elements symbolizing this now fading power, as they were photographed in ever more restrictive and sumptuous clothing associated with "tradition," such as the wrapped sarong.

Second, and linked to this, we see that native women were deemed needy of rescue from native culture and native men precisely because of their supposed connection to tradition. Colonial discourse found in native women a particularly attractive symbol for justifying rule, thereby making gender a salient factor in debating cultural differences. Colonialism in its Orientalist form inscribed privilege as masculine, and masculinity as European. The European male was young, virile, clean and fully clothed, often in a suit (cf. Smith 1995; Tarlo 1996; Wilson 1985). In turn, the colonized male was dehumanized, represented as either brutishly male or effeminate. In this struggle over political power, native women served as particularly fertile symbolic terrain. In some versions of Orientalist logic, proof of the native male's backwardness could be found in his treatment of native women, as measured against a universal index of civilizations. As Frantz Fanon argued about colonial fascination with the veil in Algeria, the struggle over women's appearance had high stakes, "wrenching her free from her status … shaking up the [native] man" (1965[a]: 39). Much of the rhetoric justifying colonial conquest rested in the liberation of native women from the tyranny of native

men. In colonial India, Partha Chatterjee argues that the civilizing mission of British conquest was based on eradicating "barbarism" evidenced by a whole canon of "traditions" which oppressed Indian womanhood (1993: 118). Bound feet provided a similar rationale for expanding Western presence in China. This "curious erotic custom" (Levy 1966) served nicely as evidence that Chinese elite culture was actually barbarism masquerading as sophistication (Fan 1997; Steele and Major 1999; Wang 2000).

Third, colonial relations configured dress and gender in ways that affected nationalist movements and subsequent postcolonial states, through claims to "tradition." This process began before actual independence in many cases. To continue with examples from Chatterjee's research, once "tradition" was linked to women in colonial rhetoric, an indigenous bourgeoisie that was in large part the invention of colonial policies had little choice but to resist subjugation on the same terms, that is, over the treatment of women. Women became the boundary for marking colonizer from colonized. As a result, they came to stand for two highly stylized senses of the nation: the traditional essence requiring defense from outside contamination, and the internally different Other, the one that made the nation aware of itself. An imagined middle-class native woman was recast, not as evidence of Indian backwardness, but as the repository of a superior Indian "tradition." For example, Bengali men, acting in the outer material world of business and politics, had little choice but to wear European-style clothing. However, Bengali women were increasingly encouraged by Bengali men to preserve and present local culture through the use of "traditional" dress, i.e., the sari. Bengali women were therefore charged with upholding tradition through avoiding adoption of European manners or styles "such as the blouse, the petticoat, and shoes" (Chatterjee 1993: 122).

Fourth, and finally, even though new nationalist movements found it necessary to adopt forms of European style while seeking political legitimacy, they nonetheless sought to distinguish themselves from direct mimicry of European styles. Consistent with the Orientalist narrative, however, "native" attempts at approximating and reworking colonizers' styles could never fully succeed, no matter how hard one strove. Such attempts typically failed on two levels: first, in the eyes of the fellow colonized and, second, in those of the colonizers. Emma Tarlo describes how Indian men who chose to wear a European-style suit were initially ridiculed by their fellow class and ethnic peers. Similarly, Vicente Rafael documents how Filipino elites who dressed in European suits to participate in the American census were branded traitors in nationalist plays (2000). To colonizers, such attempts appeared as failed imitations, proof that natives were incapable of originality. Racial difference not only endured in spite of one's dress, clothing made it even more evident. Yet as Homi Bhabha argues (1997), mimicry is never complete, it is never a direct reinscription of the dominant narrative. For example, Dipesh Chakrabarty has suggested that while colonial Indian women's magazines promoted companionate marriage and orderly, clean homes, which might appear to imitate European styles, they nonetheless did not wholly endorse colonial models of ideal womanhood (1992). Rather, such magazines profiled women who did imitate European women (such as by wearing a blouse and skirt, or by playing tennis) as comical, absurd or tragic. In fact, new forms of national femininity were seen as selectively rejecting European femininities as hypersexual, consumerist, and inappropriate to newly forming national cultures.

While the themes of race, gender, tradition, and imitation emerged and were elaborated upon in different configurations in particular historical settings, all colonial Orientalisms shared key features. First, they were the result of unequal and sometimes violent contact between colonizing and local populations. Second, they rested on a constant script of difference and superiority. Viewing the world as having distinct and opposing cultures, evident in part by the unique and perhaps antithetical ways that people dressed, was an appealing frame for interpreting social, political, and stylistic encounters in the colonial era. The fact that conditions of colonial subjugation and domination not only facilitated but required the success of such dominant discourses may make them seem irrelevant to the current era, in which the world is supposedly being brought closer together under global exchanges of ideas and money. Yet, the very same Orientalist logic that cast Asia as feminine or women's dress as traditional in the colonial era continues to have salience today, under the apparently new guise of globalization.

GLOBALIZATION AND THE PRODUCTION OF FEMINIZED LOCALS

On the surface, colonial Orientalism and contemporary globalization seem quite different. The former drew its authority from the careful study and institutionalization of difference in order to compartmentalize the world into discrete and unequal regions. The latter, with its increase in the frequency, quantity, and importance of flows of people, things, capital, and ideas around the globe, seems to rest on breaking down barriers to draw us into common channels of communication and community. Looking deeper, however, scholars began in the 1990s to suggest that globalization is as productive of difference as it is of similarity. In addition, we find that these differences depend on many of the same discursive tropes of race, gender, tradition, and imitation that were previously deployed in colonial contexts. To explore the construction and effects of such rhetoric, we consider in detail one example of gender stereotypes: an image of women as timeless exemplars of localized tradition marginal to global processes. Not only is such a description empirically inaccurate, but its continued prevalence in both popular culture and scholarly accounts suggests that globalization itself needs to be explored as a gendered process producing and reproducing conceptions of a feminized, local Other.

When anthropologists first began considering globalization in the 1970s and 1980s, their foremost concern was to determine whether these processes were hurting or helping the supposedly local producers of local cultural traditions that had constituted their traditional object of study. The first round of evidence fueled critiques of globalization as neo-imperialist processes that incorporated people, often forcibly, into international capitalist structures. Images of a world drinking Coca-Cola and donning Levi's jeans encapsulated the threat of homogenization: an erasure of local distinctions and conformity in cultural practices in which people would look the same, act the same, and use the same goods. Although scholars concerned about homogenization sought to liberate peoples around the globe from colonial and neo-colonial domination, they shared the colonial-era supposition that the adoption of Western products or styles by non-Western peoples was an unreflexive, uncritical, and problematic form of imitation involving a rejection of their traditional cultures. Whether those traditional cultures were being derided by colonials as backward or lauded by leftist scholars as authentic expressions of ethnic identity and history, "culture" in both views seemed an essential feature bequeathed to a group as a racial or genetic inheritance that they could abandon only at their peril.

By the 1990s, anthropologists and other scholars of globalization found reason to be optimistic about the fate of cultural heterogeneity. First, as part of a broader turn toward the study of consumption practices, many noted that when products are used in different contexts, even products as synonymous with American corporate capitalism as Levi's jeans (Ong 1987), Coca-Cola (Miller 1997[b]), and McDonald's (Watson 1997), their meanings are transformed. Second, in the 1990s, the growing desire among Euro-American populations for clothing and other items of "ethnic chic," a development with which we began this introduction, suggested that globalization allowed for multidirectional cultural exchange. Young Malaysian girls working in electronics factories may be discarding sarongs in favor of jeans (Ong 1987), but trendsetters within the society where the jeans originated were now freely experimenting with those sarongs. Far from dying or fading away, diversity under globalization seemed to be more mobile and hence more widely appreciated.

Rather than the either/or paradigm of homogeneity versus heterogeneity, a rich assortment of studies focusing on cross-cultural consumption now suggests that globalization is producing what David Howes refers to as a "multiplicity of possible local-global articulations" (Howes 1996: 6). Such studies also argue that these articulations are the result of encounters negotiated on unequal terrain. What we have, then, is what might be described as *homogenized*

heterogeneity. Difference is appreciated, but it is also characterized and commodified globally through flows of knowledge, money, and people structured in accordance with relations of power. In the process, difference is transformed. Its edges are smoothed and its contours are flattened so that it fits more neatly into its assigned pigeonhole in the global display of culture. Certain groups and activities thus come to embody "tradition" more than others, a move that seems to reflect appreciation for diversity, but that can also position the groups in question as Other to global modernity.

Just as colonial Orientalisms depended on the discursive work of ruling classes and scholars, the contemporary production of homogenized heterogeneity rests on the definitional work of new kinds of global economic, social, and cultural elites. Ulf Hannerz (1996) has described one such elite class: the relatively well-off, educated, and globally sophisticated "cosmopolitans" whose passionate pursuit of the new and diverse drives the creation of global culture. At the opposite end of the spectrum are locals: those whose orientation remains rooted in everyday experiences and local frames of reference.

While being a cosmopolitan or local may seem an empirical affair, these statuses in fact depend as much on ideological orientations for apprehending the world as on concrete, measurable factors such as income, education, or consumption preferences. According to Hannerz, cosmopolitans may move around the world in clearly transnational projects, but they can also remain at home and consume the diversity of food, clothing, movies, art, etc. that global processes bring to their doors. Meanwhile, locals can travel and yet retain a fundamentally local perspective. Determining which passengers on an international jet flight or which diners at a local "ethnic" restaurant are or are not cosmopolitan thus rests on trying to fathom the intentions and perspectives motivating their actions. This feat is often accomplished through associative logic in which intention is ascribed based on the observed or presumed tendencies of others with whom one appears to share characteristics, most commonly gender, race, ethnicity, class, place of residence, religion, and education. Unfortunately, such an endeavor is prone to stereotyping. Ulf Hannerz's discussion of locals is instructive in this regard. He is noteworthy among prominent theorists of globalization for his attention to the concrete details of human actors' experiences. Nevertheless, in trying to characterize those experiences, he risks reproducing stereotypes about the local and traditional—stereotypes that in this case have much to do with gender.

As an example of a transnationally mobile local, Hannerz cites a 1985 *International Herald Tribune* article describing Nigerian market women's regular travels between Lagos and London (Harden 1985). By wearing loose-fitting clothes, they were able to smuggle products in both directions: outbound, they strapped dried fish to their thighs and upper arms; on the return flight, they carried frozen fish sticks, dehydrated milk, and baby clothes. Hannerz characterizes such acts as not cosmopolitan: "The shopping trips of Lagosian traders and smugglers hardly go beyond the horizons of urban Nigerian culture, as it now is. The fish sticks and baby clothes hardly alter structures of meaning more than marginally" (1996: 103). No matter where they go—and these particular traders go quite far—locals retain a fundamentally insular perspective.

The example of Nigerian traders caught our attention, primarily because their gender and the gendered nature of the commodities they carried (baby clothes, milk, and fish used in meal preparation) leapt off the page in what was otherwise a gender-neutral discussion of how people locate themselves as privileged cosmopolitans. Why, we wondered, did these internationally mobile women and their imported goods seem so obviously local? What further meanings were deployed by categorizing people and their activities in this way? What does this suggest about globalization as a gendered and gendering process?

An initial answer may be that associations between women, the traditional, and the local seem obvious. Indeed, in societies around the world, women *are* often held up as the bearers of tradition, as inculcators of cultural values through their roles in childrearing, and hence as somehow more connected to the space of home. As described above, many of these ideologies were explicitly deployed by colonial regimes and anticolonial nationalist movements. The problem

is that anthropologists, since Sherry Ortner (1974) and others (Collier 1974; Rosaldo 1974) explored the question of whether and why women appear to be universally subordinated, have tended to treat these characterizations, not as concrete and accurate descriptions of fact, but as discourses, as symbolic representations of the world and how it is gendered. By assuming the meaning of gendered activities, we not only miss the opportunity to interrogate how globalization processes construct gender, but risk further reproducing and naturalizing problematic gender stereotypes that a priori dismiss certain types of people, activities, and positions as insignificant.

How might an analysis of globalization as gendered and gendering complicate the claim that Nigerian women traders are not cosmopolitan? To start, it requires looking beyond stereotypes of women, domesticity, and locality to explore the broader context shaping the Lagos—London baby clothes trade. The newspaper article cited by Hannerz provides rich detail about this: how short-lived affluence during the 1970s oil boom, subsequent hard-currency shortages, government import restrictions, an overvalued exchange rate, and price controls on airline tickets combined to create strong Nigerian demand for imported goods and the opportunity to acquire them through extralegal measures (Harden 1985). The vibrant trade that resulted involved not just women, but men, many of them well-connected bureaucrats, and not just baby clothes and foodstuffs, but electronics, parrots, automotive parts, cosmetics, and consumer electronics. As for the baby clothes, they might be seen in Nigeria as the height of modern style, in large part because they come from a place as powerful and exotic as London. Smugglers thus may be crucial mediators through which elites and others in Lagos acquire the material goods literally to fashion themselves (and, in this case, their children) as cosmopolitans conversant with global heterogeneity. Dehydrated milk might carry the same sort of associations; we know, for example, that much to the dismay of public health officials who promote the nutritional and hygienic superiority of breast milk, dehydrated milk and baby formula have spread quickly around the world precisely because of their mass appeal as emblems of modernity.

Within this broader context, it becomes hard not to see Nigerian traders and the items in which they traffic as intimately implicated in processes of globalization. The only way to know for sure what the items carried by the traders represent is to trace these items, their histories, and their meanings, and to look at who creates, transports, sells, and consumes them, and why. That this may not seem necessary reflects just how taken-for-granted are the associations between women, the local, and the traditional.

We have focused on one example because we find it to be illustrative of what feminist scholars have critiqued as a widespread "masculinist" tendency in studies of globalization in which women are either entirely absent or assumed to occupy subordinate positions. Aihwa Ong (1999), Kamala Visweswaran (1994), Dorinne Kondo (1997), and Carla Freeman (2001) have noted similar problems in the work of Arjun Appadurai (1990, 1996) and David Harvey (1989). The critiques tend to focus on the authors' abstraction of global processes so that they become unmarked and ungendered. This amounts to an erasure of how gender and other factors unequally shape access to processes of cultural production and material accumulation. In different ways, these critiques suggest that, far from being a statement of fact or essential identity, whether one is mobile, global, and transnational, or nonmobile and local is a historical development, emerging through the particularities of political economy, social stratification, and gender roles and ideologies. To put it succinctly, whether one is male or female, with all that may imply in a given cultural context, shapes how one experiences and participants in globalization.

While critiquing theories of globalization for not paying sufficient attention to women is significant, we find that this risks distracting us from the potentially radical implications of gender analysis. Simply looking at women is not enough. Rather, we must focus on processes of gendering that, as Gayle Rubin (1975) has argued, divide the world so that spheres of human activity and knowledge become conceived of as masculine and feminine in ways that valorize or constrain that activity. Citing female traders as an example of the local in an increasingly global world not only erases these particular women from globalization,

but replicates gendered categories that define the local as feminine and Other to globalization processes. What's more, it is not just women who get assigned to the feminized local realm, but all who traffic in what can be defined as locally meaningful goods.

This discursive move should seem familiar to students of Orientalism: a realm of the world gets defined as feminine and Others to a more masculine and powerful subject in ways that confirm that subject's mastery of or superiority to the Other. Through such gendering processes, globalization reworks and perpetuates the Orientalist philosophies developed with colonialism. To the extent that theorists of globalization do not explicitly unpack these associations, they reproduce and legitimate them, much as Said claims an earlier generation of Orientalist scholars defined their object of study in ways that confirmed this region's Otherness and lent credence, however unintended, to colonial domination. When these gendering moves occur today on the global stage within the already feminized realms of fashion and Asian culture, the associations become all the more insidious and powerful. It is to these issues of contemporary Orientalism that we turn below.

CONTINUING ORIENTALIST LEGACIES THROUGH FASHION

During the 1990s, several prominent and stereotypical images of Asia coexisted comfortably in the cultural landscape of Europe and North America. In terms of style, we saw the proliferation of trendy "Oriental" lifestyle elements described in romantic prose designed to conjure up visions of a timeless, exotic, spiritual, and mysterious land. Geopolitically, there was the specter of a Chinese military apparatus and government actively rejecting Western democracy. Another image was of the Asian businessman, often Japanese or Chinese, wielding a cell phone and briefcase as he traveled the region making the deals that propelled the Asian Economic Miracle. Spending the money generated by that miracle was the brand-conscious female consumer of luxury goods who slavishly followed trends that originated in Europe or the United States. And behind these images was the specter of subservient Asian women, in myriad forms:

from uncomplaining yet overworked factory laborers, to demure and subservient geishas, to oppressively veiled Pakistani Muslim women, and hypersexual Thai prostitutes.

These images are rife with contradictions: a spiritual Asia, a superficial Asia focused on consumption, an economically and militarily powerful Asia, an oppressed Asia, a demure Asia, an erotically charged Asia. Why can such dramatically different stereotypes as these comfortably coexist in Western minds? While these images reference particularly modern features of globalization—transitional factories, global fashion, mass consumption, international capitalism, and sex tourism—the assumptions, viewpoints, and discursive moves through which these images are produced are by no means new. Contemporary ways of knowing and representing the Oriental Other as timeless, exotic, untouched, dangerous, passive, inscrutable, or oppressed are the legacies of earlier Orientalist frameworks developed to understand and subjugate Asia. Although much of this occurred under colonial domination, a period that has now ended in its formal sense, these categories of difference continue to have enormous explanatory appeal in the current era of globalization and the uncertainty that it has created about Western political, military, and economic dominance. As Orientalist logics circulate to counter this uncertainty, they are also subtly reworked to take account of new realities and thus produce new contours of difference. We see this as occurring in three ways. First, the masculine threat posed by Asian economic and military strength is reworked to seem androgynous or feminine. Second, diverse Asian cultures and histories are reduced to mere stylistic flourishes and hence feminized as part of the preserve of fashion. Third, Asian women are described as unambiguously oppressed and rendered passive, either by global capital or by their own traditions. As such, they are seen to be in need of rescue by enlightened Westerners.

During the 1990s, the two most threatening images of Asia circulating in North America and Western Europe centered on Asian economic and military prowess. These were usually rendered as a Japanese corporate powerhouse ready to outcompete Euro-American industry and a Chinese military machine capable of rejecting and defeating the forces of Western democracy. Even so, the images provoking such panic contained ready-made possibilities for neutralizing the threat. The Japanese businessman with his suit and cell phone, as Dorinne Kondo points out (1997), was rendered not as hypermasculine, but as anonymous and effeminate. He was no longer a threat to the West, but an unsuccessful mimic of it, either a corporate drone who did what he was told or a duplicitous, unethical competitor. Similarly, Chinese soldiers seemed less men than machines who followed orders and marched in step, not because of an affirmative commitment to country, but because they valued life differently and unquestioningly followed orders. In such ways, even images of a masculine Asia become rhetorically rendered as androgynous, passive, and perhaps even feminine.

The second dimension of contemporary Orientalist discourses of Asia is that of Asia as a source of exotic style. It strikes us as not coincidental that at the same time as the Asian Economic Miracle and Chinese military might sparked Orientalist anxiety in the West, Asian chic became all the rage in international fashion. This version of Asia has been a sort of utopian and euphoric embrace of elements of particular Asian traditions that now have come to stand for an undifferentiated Asia. From haute couture collections such as John Galliano for Christian Dior, which in 1997 featured bright reinterpretations of the Chinese cheongsam, to renditions of rice bowls and chopsticks aimed at the American middle class by mass retailers such as Pottery Barn and Pier One, Asian-ness has been reduced from a potentially threatening and unmanageable Other to a mere fashion statement. This process of glossing certain items as generically Asian alters the meanings and practices associated with them and erases their specific cultural and national origins. Asian chic is something that, while aesthetically appealing to many, is ultimately a trend: something simply to be consumed and then moved beyond.

We are not suggesting that a conspiracy of fashion-industry power brokers negotiated with global political and economic leaders to create a solution to perception of a Yellow Peril lapping at American shores. But neither would such a conscious collusion have been necessary, for that is the power of discourse. Strikingly, the end to the "miracle" of Asian dominance in the late twentieth century came at the hands of foreign-currency investors as many of the region's currencies collapsed in 1997. Yet just as the painful economic crisis affected more and more Asian countries through 1998 and 1999, so did the cachet of dressing and decorating in an Asian style increase in North America and Europe. Asia is indeed an invented construction, something that says more about an unmarked West than it does about any particular culture or nation in the region called Asia, but it is nonetheless a very real construction. It has become a commodified identity that corporations can define and sell as an invented yet racialized style.

That the threat to Western superiority posed by Asian business, military, and cultural strength was countered by reducing Asia to a style statement on the terrain of fashion—an industry with fascinating gendered connotations—suggests this move to be an emasculating or feminizing one. As a privileged site of production, fashion—particularly "high fashion" or haute couture—is a powerful sphere of cultural production. Nonetheless it is imagined as a feminized world. Its target audience is primarily female. Its constituents are thought to consume excessively and to be uncritically enthusiastic about personal decoration—charges disproportionately leveled at women. The world of fashion appears obsessed with surface appearances over hard, cold realities such as finance. Even though the high-fashion world is populated by men, the most successful designers are assumed to be homosexual (i.e., not fully masculine), and those who do engage in heterosexual relationships are greeted with raised eyebrows as the exceptions that prove the rule.

These impressions continue in spite of the fact that garment industries have been touted as the first step toward globalizing a developing economy, a move whose dependence on a supposedly docile feminine workforce might be seen as implying a contrast to the clearly masculine character of global industry.

Anthropological studies of female factory laborers provide clear support for the ways that industrial regimes consciously draw upon patriarchal ideologies to control their labor force, often colluding with national governments and workers' families to keep young women in line and their appetites, both material and sexual, under control (Ong 1987; Salaff [1981] 1995; Wolf 1992). In material and symbolic terms, then, laborers in the fashion industry are subject to a gendered system of production in which they are the passive, feminized mass to be ordered and controlled by what would seem to be gendered as the masculine structure of industrial production. But, material production is different from cultural production, and it is on the discursive level that fashion is feminized.

When the idea of "Oriental" style is added to the already feminized field of fashion, the discursive production of gender becomes all the more complicated and powerful. The striking proliferation of things "Oriental" at the precise moment that Asia appeared to enter global circuits of wealth and power clearly calls for critical analysis for what it reveals about continued Orientalisms in the West. It also raises the much less apparent, but perhaps more provocative, question of what happens when these styles, reverberate back to the sites from which they are imagined to have come.

The case of Princess Diana's donning of the salwaar-kameez mentioned above provides a useful example. A garment that had been worn by North Indian and Pakistani women for generations was suddenly deemed "fashion" by British socialites, not just because Princess Diana was a person whose every fashion choice was followed closely but because it made sense in a comfortable Orientalist logic. In this way, a cultural form that had been invisible to Western consumers was made chic through the recognizing and expert eye of an outsider. The garment had to cross a border to become "fashion," in a way that it could never have been while South Asian women wore it, and the only person capable of taking it across that border was a privileged celebrity and outsider. Another effect of the garment's journey was to make it seem newly chic to those very women who had always worn it in their everyday lives. The irony for them, however, was that pride in their garment's new fashionability could be interpreted through Orientalizing logic as a kind of enlightenment, a consciousness about the value of their garment that could only come from the Western fashion establishment telling them what was precious in their cultural heritage and what was not. The effect, then, was that these very women could appear to be imitating Western fashions even as they were said to be wearing their own traditional clothing.

This brings us to the third aspect of Orientalizing discourses about Asia, namely the ways in which notions of Asian style reinforced preexisting images of an essentialized, feminized Oriental Other powerless both at home and on the job. Even as critiques of Orientalism are commonplace within the academy, images of the voiceless, agency-less, victimized Asian woman still hold enormous explanatory power. One such example can be found in anti-globalization movement rhetoric that focuses almost unproblematically on the docility of the Asian female sweatshop worker, reproduced as an often mute symbol for a transnational movement. The campaign has been effective in linking global brand names, like Nike and Reebok, to images of poor underage women working in transnational factories. Such images are based on the material reality of harsh factory-floor working conditions. Yet the extent to which such campaigns have been able to raise general public consciousness about these issues has also been the result of discursive work. Representations of docile factory women, even as they call attention to very real circumstances of exploitation, confirm long-standing Western stereotypes of the subservient Asian woman.

So compelling are discourses of victimization and passivity that they readily explain other Asian women's behavior, even when those behaviors occurs in dramatically different contexts or at opposite ends of the class spectrum. Passiveness, and the oppression it implies, thus come to be read as a function of an essential cultural or national identity, rather than as the result of limited material power. A few additional examples will clarify this. In contrast to the docile factory laborer toiling in the trenches of production, it would be tempting to see the image of the consuming wealthy Asian woman as an important corrective. Yet even this stereotype is often read as an expression of a peculiar cultural essence. Although luxury fashion lines in Europe earn a significant portion of their revenues from sales in Asian markets, those consumers

are interpreted as blindly following the dictates of a fashion system or obeying mass group tastes. Rather than shopping to articulate a unique personal identity, as Western consumers might sympathetically be read, such women are imagined as selfishly and unreflexively seeking status (or face) through acquisition of Western luxury goods. Similarly, images of oppressed Asian women coexist comfortably in Western media with stereotypes of the savvy but restrained sexuality of the kimono-clad geisha, popularized in Arthur Golden's 1997 Novel *Memories of a Geisha*. The geisha was celebrated as nostalgic proof of the gentility and eroticism of Asian femininity, something Western women lack. At the same time, it implied a critique of the brutality of a society that would develop such an institution.

Images of passivity and oppression therefore work not only to erase striking cultural contradictions among various stereotypes, but also to make class differences seem less visible. Asian women's oppression is explained as a function of their being Asian and female—their essential national and cultural identities—not as a function of an often highly limited access to resources that might produce that oppression.

Asian women are thus not simply modern producers or traditional consumers, but a mix of all simultaneously. The very same women who may be oppressed by harsh labor conditions, low pay, and coercive regimes of labor discipline on the factory floor may choose to use part of their wages to purchase fashions through which they craft themselves as members of a new generation less beholden to traditional strictures on feminine decorum. Or, they may use their paychecks to purchase newly chic "traditional" outfits. As liberating as these sartorial statements may be, they can also carry prices: the disapproving scrutiny of others for challenging standards of feminine modesty, the material reality that Third World money spent in mass consumption tends to flow back to First World corporations, or the erasure of agency due to the assumption that wearing kimonos (or salwaar-kameez or sarong or hanbok or cheongsam or ao dai) is just something that Japanese (or South Asian or Indonesian or Korean or Chinese or Vietnamese) women do. Making sense of these choices and their ramifications requires charting how and why particular people are acting through both agency and constraint, and to understand the dialectical relationships between these characteristics. One way to do this, we suggest, lies in combining insights from performance theory and practice theory.

THE PRACTICE OF PERFORMANCE

Choosing what clothing to make, sell, or consume are all acts of performance because they provide an opportunity to display oneself to others in ways that can register one's actual or desired identity along a variety of lines—class, occupation, gender, sexual preference, race, ethnicity, religion, age, marital status, educational level, location of residence, etc. As such, performing difference or alliance through dress is simultaneously an act of politics and of self-making. Judith Butler has argued, based on the work of Michel Foucault, that performance is always more than the pure outward expression of an inner, essential self. Rather, such a self does not exist. It is precisely through performing that identities are made under conditions of unequal access to power and resources. As such, it is a constitutive and political act (1990).

The metaphor of performance proliferated in academic circles in the 1990s because it resonated with fantasies of self-making, of rejecting prefabricated identities and challenging constraints by becoming who we want to be. If identity were simply a performance, then recognizing that it was not based on anything material or essential offered the possibility for reinvention. These reinventions could be obvious or, more importantly, quite subtle. Even as people appeared to be performing the roles assigned to them, they might add little touches of irony or parody that could highlight just how constructed, just how much of a charade the whole affair was. If these points could be recognized as such, then the arbitrariness of identity would be exposed in ways that might allow for even more autonomous self-creation through role-play. This was a particularly strong thread in Butler's thinking about sex and gender. As Rosalind Morris claims, "By asserting that the body assumes its sex in the culturally mandated practices of everyday life, the theory of gender performativity offers the possibility of re-

styling that body in non-normative and occasionally subversive ways" (Morris 1995: 573). Performativity seemed the newest chapter in scholars' ongoing "romance of resistance" (Abu-Lughod 1990).

It is in the very metaphor of performance, however, that problems with this approach to dress and identity arise. Ironically, theorists who took as their point of departure the constraints and expectations that demand that we behave in certain ways may have underestimated just how constraining this context could be. While performativity emphasizes playing at roles, performance in fact is highly structured work. Performers require costumes, roles, and scripted lines and movements that they then memorize and enact before a critical audience. None of these is created by or dependent solely on the performer. Even improvised performances interact with audience expectations; they may challenge or startle us, but they do so by engaging us through shared understandings. All performances thus depend on preexisting conditions and meanings with which one may be able to play, but not without significant limitations. We may choose to dress in a certain way in an attempt to achieve a more privileged identity, but whether that performance is perceived by other people as believable, as "real," and hence whether we are recognized and validated as the person we wish to be, depends on how we have been previously classified. The task becomes to identify how these internally and externally produced constraints emerge, and how they affect performances.

This is precisely what practice theory has sought to do. One of the main goals of practice theory, as outlined by Bourdieu ([1972] 1977, [1979] 1984) and de Certeau (1984) is to show how social and cultural structures become translated and enacted through individual daily practices, such as habits of speech, physical mannerisms, or dress, and taste in art, music, or literature. As such, practice theory shares performance theory's emphasis on how abstract social and cultural categories become expressed and reproduced through individual actions. According to Rosalind Morris (1995), it was precisely this shared concern and the already established appeal of practice theory that provided fertile ground for the proliferation of performance theory in the 1990s.

We see in the two theories, however, a crucial difference in the weight they give to preexisting constraints. Intended as a corrective to structuralism that would allow for improvisation, uncertainty, and individuality in social life, practice theory nonetheless seems to depict people as trapped in structures that they helplessly reproduce. For example, Bourdieu ([1979] 1984) convincingly shows that class is not simply economic, but social and cultural. His discussion of social and cultural capital gained currency mostly because it squared with the fluidity of late twentieth-century life, in which people of the same income may be perceived as having different class status depending on their family backgrounds, education, clothing choices, and preferences for art, music, reading, etc. At the same time, however, practice theory risks making these class distinctions seem static; class status may not be the result simply of income, but it can be calculated, almost arithmetically, by taking account of how education and social connections shape taste. Little room is afforded for individual choice or idiosyncrasy, the very factors that practice theory hoped to address.

We have, then, two theories designed to track how social and cultural forms get reproduced and reworked through individual role-play. One (practice theory) risks reducing people to the sum total of their socially and culturally defined roles. The other (performance theory) overemphasizes the notion of play in "role-play" in an attempt to focus on the artificiality of identity, the agency of the individual performer, and the potential subversiveness of even the most banal practices of dress and self-display. What is needed is a synthesis of the two: an attention to *performance practices* that tracks the constraints shaping and limiting identity creation and subversion. Even if we view the performance of self as stemming from conscious choice, we must recognize that our desire to be a certain way is not entirely self-generated, nor can we determine the outcome. The desire to perform emerges within the concrete circumstances of our existence and the way that existence has been characterized by others, and it is often with those others that the success of the performance, in the eyes of both performer and audience, is debated and determined. As such, even the performance of desired identity can feel mandatory, and its effects can be ambiguous.

Projecting these concerns outward to the international stage, we suggest that by analyzing the articulations of transnational capital and human activity as performance practices, women's actions can be seen as neither the result of a totalizing Orientalist gaze from a Western fashion industry, nor the enacting of postcolonial national scripts, nor the unproblematic expression of self. Yet the extent to which practices of dress performance are intended or received as political or resistant acts depends on the audience(s). Acts that may seem resistant in a local context can take on alternative and less radical meanings in a global context, and vice versa. Given the weighty discursive legacy of Orientalism, its reworking through globalized economic and cultural structures, and the gendering processes associated with both, self-Orientalizing and internal Orientalizing emerge as reasonable, yet highly fraught, modes for individual and state-sponsored performances of gender and national identity on the domestic and international stages.

INTERNAL AND SELF-ORIENTALIZING AS NATIONAL AND PERSONAL STRATEGIES

Ruhlen's research on Korean feminists' use of the hanbok in local and international contexts (Ruhlen 2003) provides a rich example of how wearing an item of supposedly traditional dress can be seen by the wearers as expressing pride in national identity. Such moments can serve to reify and make all the more natural the comfortable link between nation and gender. At the same time, the specific instances Ruhlen describes raise a complication: what do we make of a feminist, one who in many ways wishes to challenge Korean traditions, wearing an item so associated with tradition?

If the image of a feminist wearing traditional clothing seems contradictory, that may be precisely the point, for it communicates the sense that women are, as Norma Alarcón, Caren Kaplan, and Minoo Moallem have argued, "both of and not of the nation" (Alarcón et al. 1999: 13). Because women are seen as fodder for symbols, they can simultaneously be imagined as essentially maternal and iconic of a national body, yet also different, citizens who must prove their worth through high-stakes performances of identity. The stakes become even higher in a context of globalization and transnational exchange that seems to challenge or at least destabilize that identity. Thus, while transnational exchanges in wealth or ideas appear to facilitate a well-meaning transnational feminism, these representations are still grounded in, and reinscribe, national affiliations. Orientalizing gazes, both across and within national boundaries, can serve local national goals. The feminist clad in traditional garb reinterpreted as a modern fashion statement provides Koreans unsure about their status within a globalized economy with a reassuring image that even as things change, the core of national identity remains in Korean hands.

Orientalist rhetoric is therefore co-opted, but also further elaborated, in local Asian contexts in ways that are specific to differences in power and gender, yet also serve the nation. Two forms in particular have been identified by scholars: internal Orientalism and self-Orientalism. Finding ways to interpret how each of these strategies shapes the intentions, context, and effects of Asian women's various dress choices requires that we attend not only to the oppressive institutions that benefit from their choices, but to the self-making and nation-making consequences of those decisions.

Several authors studying postcolonial and nationalist conditions in Asia have described forms of "internal Orientalism." Geraldine Heng and Janandas Devan (1992) describe an "internalized Orientalism" in the patriarchal Singaporean state that identifies those elements *within* the nation that prevent it from fully achieving a state of development that can prove it has "arrived" on the international front. In this case, those segments of the population charged with dragging down national success are consistently classed, raced, and gendered. Through a 1980s "debate" on marriage and reproductive choices, poor women of color were blamed for preventing the national success of Singapore.

Louisa Schein defines a second form of "internal Orientalism" within China. While exoticized Others are often deployed by states as a sort of exotic color

that will lure sightseers, the Chinese state, according to Schein, creates a fuller spectrum of exoticized Other that has little to do with international tourism or global politics. Rather, Schein describes how the Chinese state and urban Han Chinese have created a domestic narrative of Otherness about ethnic minorities that casts the Miao ambivalently as both backward and "titillating" (2000: 101). Their proximity to nature is evidence of lack of civilization but also of erotic simplicity. Not surprisingly, the symbol of ethnic identity that serves so malleably as both positive and negative is the ethnic woman, usually dressed in colorful, ethnically identifiable clothing.

In both examples, states seeking to position themselves as civilized, strong, and worldly do so through rhetorics of self-assessment that locate progress disproportionately with certain groups and displace the blame for limitations onto clearly identifiable Others. Much as colonial states justified their rule by defining the problems of the races they sought to control as a natural feature of those races and hence one they were powerless to address themselves, modern Asian nations often identify the Other within. They do so both to rationalize economic, social, or cultural obstacles and to establish the nation, usually dominated by ethnic majority groups, as the appropriate vehicle to address those problems by civilizing the internal Other or, at the very least, constraining it.

This brings us to a second form of Orientalism that has been identified by contemporary scholars of Asia, that of self-Orientalizing. If Orientalism has an ambivalent array of meanings, then claiming control over representations of exoticism can appear to reverse the imbalance of power between the West and the Rest. Just as national discourses of internal Orientalizing allow Asian states to seize control over the process of defining who is Other, so can producing and consuming an exoticized image of one's own cultural identity be a technique for asserting discursive control that can seem to turn the negative narrative of Western Orientalism on its head.

The Asian Values debate in insular Southeast Asia has been a particularly energetic case of such work. One example is that of the Singaporean state, which has invested deeply in creating and embracing a neo-Confucian identity. The campaign, headed by Prime Minister Lee Kuan Yew in the 1980s and picked up by other regional leaders in the 1990s, excavated and celebrated a narrow interpretation of Confucianism as the shared transnational heritage of all successful Asians. Part of the appeal of this rhetoric to leaders and many citizens was that it inverted the colonial-era accusation that Confucian philosophy might prevent full development (e.g., Marx's Asiatic Mode of Production, or Max Weber's argument that Confucianism was too hierarchical to allow flexible change). The Singaporean strategy has been to promote a version of Confucianism that not only instills pride in the Singaporean population for its "tradition" but provides the cultural rationale for a patriarchal state and its tactics in generating a skilled and globally attractive labor force. According to Aihwa Ong (1991, 1997), such self-Orientalist narratives are often told by national male leaders to attract foreign investors by depicting female workers as having a racially and culturally specific ability to do repetitive physical work for long hours. In this way, the now familiar refrain on the docility of Asian women workers is the result, not just of Western stereotyping, but of well-documented official investment rhetoric by Asian governments to perpetuate those stereotypes.

These self-Orientalizing moves highlight the problematic politics through which conditions of domination are resisted, yet reproduced. This can occur even when one consciously intends to combat Orientalisms. Dorinne Kondo (1997) calls such attempts "counter-Orientalisms" and uses this term to describe the ways in which Japanese fashion designers mobilize stereotypes of Asian-ness to question difference. Their efforts, however, rest on a form of self-Orientalizing that ultimately reinscribes differences. Part of Kondo's discussion concerns an ad campaign for the Japanese Suit, a garment produced by Rei Kawakubo's line Comme des Garçons in the late 1980s and marketed especially to Japanese businessmen. The ads, according to Kondo, sought to counter negative global images of Japan and Japanese masculinity, ranging from military defeat in the Second World War to the emasculation of contemporary Japanese men that we described above. The ads do so by evoking emotionally laden images of a particularly Japanese masculinity that is spiritual, harmonious, authentic, and forward-looking, even as it has been marked and Orientalized. All of this is then declared embodied in a Japanese Suit designed to appeal to conservative businessmen who might otherwise be wary of "fashion." Kondo reads the ads as doing two things at once. On the one hand, the ad campaign offers a way for Japanese men to create an affirmative masculinity that arms them against Western dominance. On the other hand, this masculinity is reactive, in that it is established on a terrain in which Japan is perpetually positioned as effeminate and inferior. The campaign plays on this fact, for in attempting to convince potential customers of the very need for such a thing as a Japanese Suit, it reinforces Japanese men's insecurities by implying the unsuitability of the British suit for their racialized bodies and identities. The Japanese Suit is thus intended to counter Orientalist depictions of Japan, at the very same time as its successful evocation of consumer desire rests on and confirms Japanese men's anxieties about being inferior mimics of Western capitalist powers.

Internal and self-Orientalizing are never simply unidirectional moves by elites against the disempowered. Just as indigenous bourgeoisies used selective strategies of "tradition" and "modernity" to resist colonial identities, so too are postcolonial populations selectively embracing elements of exoticism that serve their own purposes of self-orienting. Gender can figure centrally in this regard around questions of both masculinity and femininity. While Kondo focuses on images of Japanese manhood, the complicated conditions of who is Orientalizing whom and why similarly preclude easy interpretations of victimization or domination in representations of Asian women. Women's choices to attempt counter-Orientalisms by playing with images that might otherwise be seen as if one were Orientalizing oneself contrast with stereotypes of passive, docile Asian women, while nonetheless still reinscribing difference. It is here that our dual focus—first, on Asian states' internal Orientalizing practices through images of clothed women; and, second, on mid-level, feminized Asian actors' self- and counter-Orientalizing dress practices—becomes particularly instructive.

CONCLUSION

The globalization of Asian dress, both in terms of the spread of Asian style throughout the world and in terms of the growing prevalence of other forms of dress in Asia, has been accomplished through Orientalist ways of knowing, particularly the construction of an opposition between a modern, masculine West and a traditional, feminine Orient. Interest in Asian style during the 1990s may have stemmed from a genuine desire for cultural appreciation or a recognition of the growing global power of Asian economies, but it tended to reduce heritage and difference to a feminized, essentialized, and unthreatening accent or an exotic flair.

By looking at the practice of Asian dress performances, we can explore the decisions Asians, within and outside of Asia, make in ways that highlight the agency in their creation of self, while at the same time exploring the constraints on those choices—constraints typically posed by preexisting discourses and positions. We can also look at the ramifications of those choices, particularly the circumstances under which the highly fraught strategies of self-Orientalizing and internal Orientalizing succeed or fail in garnering material and symbolic power for those who deploy them.

34

HAUTE COUTURE IN TEHRAN:
Two faces of an emerging fashion scene

Alexandru Balasescu

Focusing on *haute couture* production in Tehran, this article uses two designers' careers to illustrate different understandings of fashion in the city. Ideas about modernity, tradition, and the West are reworked according to the aesthetic approaches of each designer. Mobility and modernity are discursively and materially linked in and by fashion design practices, as they simultaneously negotiate the tensions between state restrictions and consumer desires for fashion and bodily mobility.

LONG-TERM DYNAMICS

To understand the contemporary Iranian fashion scene it is necessary to have an idea of the country's sartorial history and its link to political change. Throughout most of the twentieth century, a policy of sustained modernization was pursued, mainly understood as Westernization. The Constitutional Revolution of 1904–6 and the formation of the first Iranian parliament were signs of the beginning of this new era. The commercial classes from the *bazaar* and the *shi'i* clergy were the main actors in this movement. The adoption of the Constitution in 1906 created a new political landscape. The political class's desires to construct a modern society brought about a series of reforms designed to give a modern look to Iranian society. Key to this aim was laws that targeted *men's* attire. The first law, in 1923, concerned the obligation for government employees to wear Iranian-made clothes during office hours.

After he visited Turkey in 1934 and met Kemal Ataturk, Reza Shah became determined to accelerate his reforms towards modernization and to generalize the wearing of Western attire. Some women of the upper classes and at the court were already wearing European hats and were participating in public gatherings. In 1935 a decree forbade the wearing of the veil in schools both for students and teachers. In the same year women were required to appear uncovered when dealing with the public administration (Baker 1997: 185). In 1936, Reza Shah promulgated a law forbidding veil wearing in public spaces. For many women, this law meant confinement to their homes. At the same time, various new regulations on women's behavior came into use under the guise of training in "good manners," prescribing a mode of behavior that embodied "veiling in the absence of the veil." Before women could participate in public their bodies needed to be disciplined (Najmabadi 1993).

After the forced abdication of Reza Shah, in September 1941, many women resumed veiling. Under the pressure of the *ulama* (the religious authorities), who had partially regained influence, Muhammad Reza, the new Shah, abrogated the law forbidding the veil. Nevertheless, the years of forced unveiling left a deep mark on the society. Veiling habits became not only indicators of education and class difference, but also the means by which such differences were constructed, through the limitations on behavior and mobility that they imposed. For the entire period of forced unveiling, access to education was practically

Adapted from Alexandru Balasescu, "Haute Couture in Tehran: Two Faces of an Emerging Fashion Scene," *Fashion Theory* 11, nos. 2/3 (2007): 299–317.

impossible for women coming from traditional social environments.

The Islamic Revolution erupted in the late 1970s as civil unrest. Whereas the Shah's policies, including dress regulations, were associated with Westernization, after the first violent repression of the regime's opponents on September 8, 1978, wearing non-Western style clothing was interpreted as spontaneous resistance against the Shah. However, with the installation of the new government led by Ayatollah Khomeini, women working in governmental positions were required to wear a form of covered dress. In the Spring of 1980 big demonstrations against head coverings swept Tehran. A period of unrest followed. On March 13, 1980, the Ayatollah announced publicly that women should consider it a moral duty to wear the chador (all-enveloping cloak). The restoration of shari'a law on May 30, 1981, established a punishment of imprisonment for up to one year for all women, Muslim or not, who did not cover sufficiently in public.

For the period that follows, studies about women's dress in Iran are scarce, the subject itself being a delicate one. Notable is Fariba Adelkhah's book, Revolution under the Veil (1991), which shows how the veiling policy had the effect of empowering a large number of women, who were now able to attend schools and become educated without the pressure of their families restricting their mobility outside the home. This increased social mobility among the lower classes, and contributed to the formation of a new middle class, attuned to Islamic sensibilities.

TIME AND FASHION IN TEHRAN

In Tehran I was fortunate enough to meet many of the most famous local designers. The designers I interviewed formed part of a cosmopolitan network, with links to capital cities around the world, such as Paris and London. According to the designers' accounts, and the opinions of some of their clients, there are no more than ten to twelve well-known designers in Tehran. Following a brief overview that outlines the main characteristics of haute couture in Tehran, I will focus in particular on the workshops and the production strategies of two designers in more detail.

References to the "traditional" and "the modern" will appear throughout this article, as the interviewees used them. I will point out how these categories refer to a specific aesthetic and mode of clothing use that contribute to the system of distinction in the urban environment of Tehran. Contemporary designers emphasize the modern aesthetics of the body's mobility, but this does not necessarily mean embracing "Western styles" of clothing for reasons I will discuss later. There are "modern" ways of looking at tradition, such as modern uses of "traditional clothes"; simultaneously, there are "not so modern" ways of wearing modern. Western-style clothes. As will become evident, being modern in Iran also means being attuned to the sensibilities and the aesthetic preferences of the upper classes.

In Tehran, one may easily find tailors ready to cut clothes to measure. In Enghelab Street between its intersection with Vali Asr and the Ferdousi Square there is a long series of tailors' shops for men. Zaratousht Street, west of Vali Asr is the well-known textile quarter, and there are also tailors for both men and women in this neighborhood. These shops usually offer their clients suits and dresses, cut to measure, that are copied directly from Western fashion magazines. They are open to the public all year around and are very much considered to be part of the fashion scene.

There is also a special category of fashion designers, who can be considered, along with the ready-to-wear boutiques, as the generators of the aesthetic canons of Tehran's urban style. While it is hard to speak of a well-established fashion industry in Tehran, there are constitutive elements of such an industry in the form of workshops belonging to local designers, and the development of brand names. An incipient fashion advertising industry, which includes fashion photography, is also part of this emerging fashion scene.

Most of the designers try to offer collections every season, but this is never guaranteed. Different reasons, often personal, may prevent a designer from being able to do this. The shows usually start in the early afternoon and last late into the night, with the men joining towards the end. Sometimes women model the designs, usually friends or relatives of the designer. Every designer I talked to told me that they did not have a fixed date for their presentations. Less constrained by competition than fashion designers in Paris and London, or by the capitalist acceleration of production and the fever of searching for the "newest, hottest, hippest" look, the designers organize their creations and sales in a less rigid time framework. Family events or religious celebrations frequently play a major role in scheduling events. Working in this flexible timeframe, the designers of Tehran develop individualistic approaches to an emerging industry.

MAHLA: FASHION AS BUSINESS

Unique in the Tehrani fashion scene is Mahla who organized two public fashion shows in Tehran during my fieldwork, one in January 2001, the second scheduled initially for August 18–22, 2003; a death in her family two weeks before the show caused her to postpone the event to September 30. Mahla also has a permanent strategy of model recruitment. She recruits her models by herself, among her daughters' friends, and on the street. If she sees somebody she likes, she introduces herself and her work, and invites the potential model to come to her workshop with a guardian, usually the mother. Over a cup of tea in her workshop, Mahla explains the nature of the employment, presents her journal, and asks if the girl would be available for modeling.

Mahla lives in the wealthy northern part of Tehran in a salubrious apartment decorated in baroque style, juxtaposing faux Louis XVI furniture, wonderful miniatures, and paintings dating from the Qajar period. There was also a display of thirteen early-twentieth-century dolls, presenting the costumes of different regions of Iran. Next to the dolls, textiles and fabrics from the same Qajar period were displayed. When I visited her apartment there were flowers and a number of evening dresses arranged on the big dining table. Two young women, covered with floral *chadors* were looking at the dresses. They were sisters, students of Mahla, who had come from Kerman (a city about 1,000 km southeast of Tehran) for a short visit accompanied by their mother.

From two small incidents that occurred during my visit one can get a sense of the nuances of how a public fashion designer deals with the issue of bodily exposure in Iran. On the first of these occasions, three visitors were covered with *chadors*, but Mahla and the photographer who accompanied me did not wear any head covering. After obtaining permission, I began photographing the scene. At one point, I took a photograph of Mahla and one of her students. After the flash went off, Mahla angrily told me "Look, look, I don't have a headscarf!" Then she retracted and said, "Oh, you are not a journalist, it's OK."

At some point in our conversation, one of Mahla's two daughters entered the room and asked for permission to "go out." I was surprised to recognize her as one of the models in the photographs of the Tehran fashion show in 2001. She was dressed in a nicely cut gray overcoat, *pateff* trousers, with a white scarf over her shoulders. I asked permission to take her picture. She asked, "would you like it with or without my scarf on my head?" I answered, "Anyway you feel comfortable." "I don't care," her daughter replied. To this, Mahla reacted strongly: "You should care, dear, you should care, because you are Muslim." In further meetings with Mahla, I realized that she is not somebody who is particularly invested in *russari* (headscarf) wearing. Another incident, while at her studio, confirmed this impression. While carrying some dresses to her car, she forgot to put her scarf on. She came back laughing radiantly at this incident.

In fact, her reaction to my photo shoot and her insistence on her daughter wearing the *russari* may be explained through the contextual conditions of these incidents. My camera represented a possible exposure to a larger public view, creating a different regime of dress than the context of our private meeting. The social position of Mahla as a *public* fashion designer did not permit her to expose herself publicly other than in conformity with the Islamic rules of dress. At that time, her fashion journal was still under the surveillance of the censorship commission. In addition, she was trying to receive approval from the Commission of Islamic Guidance for a new public fashion show. During the second incident, in the back alley of her studio, the risk of public exposure was less and she was able to enjoy a small act of everyday resistance.

On one occasion Mahla showed me *Lotous*, which calls itself *the first Persian fashion quarterly journal.*

Edited by her own fashion house, it mainly presents her own designs. The first issue appeared in January 2003. The second was scheduled to appear in March. Due to *ashoora*, which took place in March 2003, the journal appeared three months later, in June. *Lotous* fashion magazine is an important means of advertising in a society where women's clothing advertisements are rare. Though there are billboards all over Tehran advertising various products, clothing is very seldom their focus. Only men's clothing is advertised, while billboards about women's clothing appear only when Mahla has her public fashion shows. Officially, following *shari'a* moral rules, bodies are not to be shown in their entirety, especially women's bodies. So, commodities are advertised using photos of the objects themselves, and sometimes displaying part of the body like eyes or hands. They are usually accompanied by bilingual texts (Farsi and English), and sometimes parts of the body, like eyes, or hands. Due to these regulations, *Lotous* has had a difficult birth. In order to be able to publish this locally produced fashion magazine, Mahla needed to develop a strategy. She registered the journal as a journal for professional use, officially dedicated to those involved in the fashion industry. It is the first post-Revolution magazine showing the faces of Iranian fashion models and Mahla was initially concerned that it may not be accepted for this reason. In the past, photographs of female models had their faces erased, sometimes with paint. Likewise, the plastic female mannequins in shop windows lack facial features, or the upper half of their heads altogether. By contrast, the male mannequins have distinctly drawn features, painted eyes and hair, and individual facial expressions (see Balasescu 2006).

During our first extended conversation, Mahla showed me her manner of working. She did not feel the need to draw, but rather cut straight into the fabric. Like other designers, Mahla employs tailors to stitch the clothing. She works with fifteen employees, most of them students in the art and design faculty at the University of Tehran.

Besides ready-to-wear collections, Lotous house also provides uniforms for air hostesses, universities, schoolteachers, and schoolgirls, and for Hotel Dariush on Kish Island. In this respect, Lotous house is unique in Tehran, being the only design house that produces for clientele on this scale, and that plays such an important role in constructing a public image. It also benefits from occasional international press coverage. The public show in January 2001 was heavily commented on in the European press, and the second issue of *Lotous* magazine has been covered in the *Financial Times Europe* (March 17, 2003). The article took the usual journalistic approach of presenting Iranian fashion as if it were in the "Dark Ages." Temporal and historical references were used to suggest that Iran was lacking, or lagging behind, modernity.

Other designers in Tehran characterize Mahla's manner of working as industrial. Some see her more as a businesswoman than a designer. The new economic conditions, partly determined by the global networks in which local designers are embedded, creates a distinction between designers who prefer to keep their craft small in size (often explained as an artistic preference), and those dedicated to business—Mahla's case belonging to the latter category.

Many of Mahla's designs are adaptations of regional or historical dresses, (the Turkman style and the Qajar period are her favorite sources of inspiration). The main products are tunics and overcoats, with embroidered borders around the collar and at the end of the sleeves. She also produces evening dresses. In relating to the public at large, Mahla legitimates her work by reference to national history. When I asked her about the name of her brand. Mahla said:

> Lotous. Lotous is the name of the magazine, and Lotus is a flower, and it is Iranian. It is a symbol of the ancient religion, the Zoroastrian. It is the symbol of the three precepts: Good deeds, good talking, and good thinking.

The name of Mahla's brand is one of the multiple instances of tradition, more precisely pre-Islamic history, being invoked as an underlying principle by the contemporary stylist. The first issue of her magazine starts with an editorial entitled "Dress is the Living Museum of the Country." Modern dress, in her vision, is something that must be conceived in direct relation with history.

The governmental restrictions are also taken into account in this equation. It is interesting that, in her view, national identity and Islam are separate from one another. In her interpretation, history and national identity belong to the pre-Islamic era, while Islam is identified with the current governmental political orientation.

Many authors observe that members of the Iranian diaspora and the upper classes in Iran use Zoroastrianism as the referent in their claim to both national history and modern secularism. In modern Iran, during the Constitutional Revolution (1906) and in the post-Constitutional period, Zoroastrian intellectuals shaped the secular current of thought in Iran, and created a form of opposition to the clerics (Bayat-Philipp 1981). *Shi'i* officials in turn identified Zoroastrianism with negative influences from the West. The two poles of identity construction are constantly used in different configurations of power, depending on the historic moment. While during the Pahlavi dynasty Zoroastrianism became the major official landmark of national identity, after the Islamic Revolution, officials emphasized Iran's Islamic identity. In this dialectical dynamic, many who left Iran during or after the Islamic Revolution are likely to reorient themselves towards Zoroastrianism in their claims to Iranian national identity. Also, some local forms of resistance are expressed through the recuperation of Zoroastrianism.

Mahla's aesthetic and commercial strategies are now easier to understand. The choice of Lotous (a Zoroastrian symbol) as the brand of the fashion house somehow distances it from the Islamic regulation, while the products in themselves (at least the ones destined for the public) meet the requirements of the government. "Mixing culture with modernity" is both responding to the requirements of the Islamic government and meeting the consumers' desires for fashion, elegance, and "modern dress." In her discourse, "culture" refers both to Muslim and to Zoroastrian traditions, depending on the context. Mahla calls her eveningwear "modern dress" or "Western dress" interchangeably, thus using the generally accepted symbolic geography that equates the West with modernity.

PARISSA: THE PRIVILEGE OF EXOTICISM

Unlike Mahla, Parissa, who lives in the same area of northern Tehran, cuts almost exclusively "Iranian style" designs. She does not use a label or brand name because, she says, "everybody knows me."

Parissa's own style of dress has been her source of inspiration. She used to wear, and she still does, clothes inspired by traditional designs from different regions of Iran. This was, she says, a response to the clothing restrictions imposed after the Islamic Revolution, and the dominance of black and dark brown that followed for outer dress in urban areas.

> I used to wear a little bit of rustic things. And everybody kept saying, "oh, how beautiful that is!" I mean every village woman was wearing such things, but wearing them out in big cities ... was very unusual. They were quite Islamic, long skirts, and covers ... but colorful you know, like the village women, full of colors and everything.

The "fashion effect" of her clothing was based on its dislocation between the geographic and symbolic borders of the rural and the urban. In Tehran the terms "village" (*dahat*) and "villager" (*dahatie*) are used to designate an inferior social position, along with the term *amalleh* (worker). There is a significant difference between the two terms. *Amalleh* designates a low-class person, living and dwelling in an urban area; *dahatie* are people who belong to rural settings. While in villages their presence is considered "natural," and therefore justified, in the urban setting the villagers constitute an illegitimate presence. The privilege of the upper class resides in disregarding these symbolic hierarchies and the capacity to appropriate rural objects, commodities, and dress. While the "villager" is discursively stuck in his or her social and geographic position, and at best laughed at in urban settings, those in a privileged position can appropriate rural clothing as a privilege of power. In Tehran, this appropriation and the parallel diffusion of modern taste amongst the lower classes results in the progressive outmoding of things previously considered modern (that is, Western-inspired commodities) amongst the elite.

Uses of language related to fashion products mark this distinction in a similar way. While women from the middle classes and many young fashionable women prefer to use the French-inspired term *manto*, the intellectuals and the upper classes employ the Farsi word *roopoosh* for the same item of clothing. The recuperation of tradition among upper classes in Tehran may be interpreted at first glance as a nationalist reflex, combined with a revindication of pre-Islamic origins. While Mahla explicitly describes this tendency in her *Lotous* editorials, the role of Western aesthetic models and taste should not be underestimated. All of these designers are close to European expatriates in Iran, mostly working at the embassies. For European expatriates or tourists, Joomeh Bazaar, the Friday Flea Market, where one can find, among other handicrafts, Turkman textiles, is one of the main centers of attraction. Their taste is also appropriated by local Iranian friends. I do not mean to imply that designers make traditionally inspired dress solely because their foreign friends like them. But it should not be overlooked that many of their clients began to like and appreciate those clothes once foreigners (Europeans) showed interest in them. Joomeh Bazaar is one of the few public spaces in Tehran (alongside hotels and fashionable restaurants) where one can hear foreign languages spoken, and frequently see foreigners. In other words, Joomeh Bazaar provides a cosmopolitan flavor in an all too homogenous Tehran, offering alternative aesthetic visions and tastes.

There is a similarity in the power relation and social hierarchy established between urban centers and rural areas and between center and periphery on a global level. Exotic or rural-inspired clothing (e.g. the 2002 "savage tendency" in fashion) styled in Paris and signed by famous fashion houses identify their wearers as avant-garde, rather than marking them in ethnic terms. Without the brand name, the same kind of clothing, which may have been the source of inspiration for a stylist, identifies the wearer in ethnic terms if worn in an ethnically marked neighborhood of Paris. It may also place him or her in a socially disadvantageous position, de-legitimizing his or her presence in the public space (see Niessen[, Jones and Leshkowich] 2003).

Parissa sees her "ethnic dress" as something different from fashion. Asked what fashion is to her, she replied:

> What I am not doing. I am not up to date with fashion, I mean I make some clothes and things like this, which are never up to date, and never out of date, you know … Fashion for me is something that is changing all the time … something that in two-three years you cannot wear anymore.

Temporal references are at the core of the distinction between fashion and apparently unchanging dress. In fact, Parissa's clothes do gradually change in style, form, and color, but not with the speed of the fashion seasons in Paris. While browsing her portfolio, I could see how she has reworked styles over two decades.

The style of Parissa's creations closely follows the forms and cuts of the nineteenth-century Qajar period, merged with a series of modifications in order to make them more "wearable" or practical. That means, in her own terms, reducing the quantity of the fabric used in each dress and closing up holes that some dresses used to have under the armpits, in other words, adapting the clothes to a *mobile body* that needs to move continuously, a *modern body* circulating in an urban environment.

> They were wearing trousers made from so much fabric, and the skirt was what, fifteen meters. It's not so practical to drive and to walk around in, not with the life we lead now … So I used less material, fifteen meters is reduced to three meters …

The strength of Parissa's style resides in her ability to combine colors and motifs that suggest the "Iranian tradition," while at the same time appealing to a certain type of clientele. Her formulation of what constitutes "Iranian tradition" is particularly interesting. Parissa takes biannual trips to India, Delhi or Karachi, where she buys saris *en gross* from local producers. The retail price is very low. Parissa takes the laces and borders of the saris back to Tehran. In Tehran she buys fabric of foreign provenance, European or Asian, from vendors on Zartoosht Street. She chooses them for their quality and colors, not for their place of production. Once at home, she combines colors, fabric types, and borders, and decides on the model of dress she wants to make (for example a tunic, a two-piece Turkman-style cut or an evening dress). Once a week, her tailor comes to her house, discusses the models with her, and together they cut the material according to Parissa's measurements.

> He [the tailor] is living downtown. Usually he understands what I want, after twenty years of working together. If he does not, I will draw it for him. But actually I mostly tell him; I put the material on myself and tell him exactly what I want. With drawing alone, he does not get it.

In this process of creation, there are no designs, no standard patterns, no tracing paper involved. The combination of Indian borders, European or Asian fabrics, and innovative cuts and color mixing, gives birth to the Iranian style clothing for which Parissa is so well known among fashion consumers and for which she is recognized in Tehran and in the diaspora.

Dress can be an important way of coping with nostalgic feelings. Many of Parissa's clients are part of the Iranian diaspora from Southern California. August is a popular month for visiting the home city, and an occasion for renewing one's wardrobe: "Well, they usually come in the summer to see their families, and when they go back they buy 2–3 dresses … " What attracts them to her work is the symbolic link her designs create with their homeland.

> They like my colors because they are a little unusual, but at the same time the styles are Iranian, so when they are living outside and they feel a little nostalgic, they wear these clothes.

In the case of Parissa's creations, dress is a prompter for times past, and spaces lost. Mahla's claim that "dress is a living museum" comes to live in the actions of Parissa's clients who preserve the color and forms of Iranian dress even if the material comes from various other geographic locations. What makes her dress "Iranian" is the intersection between the style, the place of production, and the use and meanings that the clients attach to the clothes. Used as a mnemonic device, invested with the power to evoke particular spaces, Parissa's clothing appears to traverse the ephemera of fashion.

Although emotionally invested in by the clients, this style sets Parissa at a commercial disadvantage, since the clothes she makes do not meet the commercial logic of fashion. On the contrary, she says:

> [Fashion] it is something that in two–three years you cannot wear anymore. You have to throw it out, or leave it for another twenty years [and] maybe it comes back again. But my clothes are always there. And this is the problem. Because they never get out of fashion, people don't keep on buying them. If they have four or five dresses, they can wear them all their life. It hurts my pocket.

While in Paris or other Western locations, "ethnic" styles are incorporated into the fashion system, following the rhythm of going in and out of fashion, the clients' use of Parissa's creations, even in Western locations, do not participate in this logic. The 2003 Summer collections in Paris suggested Oriental embroideries, including those of Iranian provenance. But Parissa's clothes escape the ephemera of the fashion system through their use as a depository of memory among the Iranian diaspora.

Nevertheless, Parissa's elevated prices compensate for this commercial disadvantage. As a consequence of her prices and styles, Parissa has a well-defined category of clients: high-class established ladies from Tehran or the diaspora, young theater and film actors, and various artists from Tehran.

Nostalgia and atemporal aesthetics merge in the taste of Parissa's clients from across the borders. However, the local clients' preference for the "ethnic style" has different resonance and meaning. Here, it is associated more with the avant-garde, people who have the courage to bring elements of older styles into the new. Playing with time, as well as playing with geographical locations (as Parissa does with her "rustic style") is the privilege of the few, and adds prestige to the object, be it dress or some other commodity that attains some sort of timeless added value. Nevertheless, in her discourse, Parissa makes a clear distinction between the fashionable and the eternally elegant.

The dynamics of taste in Tehran follow patterns that are familiar elsewhere. As anywhere in the world, easily and light-heartedly bringing the past into the present also affirms one's separation from it, one's ability to play easily with those categories without feeling linked to them more than through a privileged relation. In this sense Tehran is not a place with a particularly "deviant" dynamic, but is an interconnected city, attuned to the dynamics of global fashion, but retaining its local particularities.

35

RECASTING FASHION IMAGE PRODUCTION:
An ethnographic and practice-based approach to investigating bodies as media

Stephanie Sadre-Orafai

Growing up as a teenager in the mid-1990s, and living far away from any global fashion capital, images were the most accessible point of entry for me into the world of fashion. Alongside posters of my favorite musicians, I adorned the walls of my bedroom with pages I tore from fashion magazines like *Allure, Elle*, and *Harper's Bazaar*. While certain models appeared across several of spreads, unlike the musicians on my wall, I neither paid much attention to who they were, nor imagined what their working lives were like. I just liked the moods and feelings their images evoked—the exotic locations, the gilded makeup, the gritty styling of the shoots. It all felt very urban and glamorous, far from my daily life in Tennessee. On weekends I watched *Fashion File*, the Canadian news digest show hosted by Tim Blanks and syndicated in the United States on E! Entertainment Television. The program profiled designers and featured footage from runway presentations in New York, Paris, and Milan, including interviews with editors, stylists, and other audience members. This was before the explosion of fashion reality TV in the early to mid-2000s that aggressively packaged backstage access in a new interactive formula to teach viewers how to see and articulate their own aesthetic through modes of direct and vicarious participation (see Sadre-Orafai 2012). In the 1990s, televised fashion programs still portrayed the industry as an elite and guarded institution, amplifying the celebrity status of those who worked within it.

While I continued to be an avid reader of fashion magazines throughout college, as I pursued a degree in anthropology and studied the relationship between race and popular culture, I never thought I would work on the industry academically, let alone in it. Yet in 2002, when I moved to New York City for graduate school, I took the opportunity to write a seminar paper on the rising popularity of "ethnically ambiguous" models, visually and textually decoding coverage of the trends in women's fashion magazines. My professor liked the paper, but suggested that I "go to a photo shoot" to see how the images were "actually produced" to make my analysis more anthropological. This seemed like a daunting task. While fashion images are accessible in public spaces, the sites of their production seemed, at best, endlessly receding: the higher one ascended the fashion hierarchy, the more exclusive these spaces became. As members of an elite industry with their own means to narrate and shape the stories told about them, fashion insiders seemed to have no incentive for allowing an anthropologist to study and analyze their practices firsthand. Yet, this exhortation spurred me to start what became a four-year, multi-sited ethnographic study of fashion image production.

In this chapter, I describe my entry into the field, first in 2003 at an ethnic women's lifestyle magazine, and then in 2004, 2006, and 2007 at a series of other sites, including modeling and casting agencies, and

Adapted from Stephanie Sadre-Orafai, "Recasting Fashion Image Production: An Ethnographic and Practice-Based Approach to Investigating Bodies in Media," in *Fashion Studies: Research Methods, Sites, and Practices*, edited by Heike Jenss (London: Bloomsbury, 2016), pp. 101–16.

the experiences that challenged my assumptions about the fashion industry: first, about how the industry worked, and second, how best to study its dynamics. As I will describe, these encounters pushed me to find new frameworks and approaches for analyzing the various sites, practices, and individuals involved in producing fashion images, particularly casting, which, for the purposes of my research, I define broadly as the recruitment, selection, development, and marketing of models. As I followed models through the multiple circuits of discovery and development—from open calls and go-sees to the sets of photo shoots and editorial offices of magazines—I tracked both models' and casting professionals' everyday lived experiences, as well as the social lives of the images they collaboratively produced together. In this process, I discovered that more than images were being produced in these interactions.

Narrating my route through these multiple field sites, I demonstrate how a series of seeming foreclosures and false starts led to insights that helped me reframe the object of my research: from the production of fashion images to the production of what I call *bodies as media*. This reorientation allowed me to focus on not just the visual aspects of fashion image production, but also the embodied, relational, and affective dimensions, including the socialization of models and casting professionals into the industry. By focusing on how each group learned to relate to their bodies as mediums for communicating both aesthetic discernment and display, I foreground how what is typically considered preproduction can be analyzed as its own production process.

Importantly, this shift unfolded from both practical and theoretical concerns that were directly connected to my ethnographic and practice-based approach. As I moved from the photo department of an ethnic women's lifestyle magazine and a struggling boutique modeling agency to a leading casting firm and top high fashion women's modeling agency, my thinking about fashion was shaped by both my combined research and employment in the industry and unlikely comparisons outside of it. In addition to drawing on my own socialization into the industry, I looked for inspiration beyond fashion to think about how

casting and modeling were part of a broader set of cultural practices of typification, classification, and performance. This helped me decenter both the fashion industry and published fashion image as the primary points of reference for understanding casting practices, enabling me to explore their broader ramifications and resonance. While the story I tell in this chapter is necessarily autobiographical, and as such, somewhat idiosyncratic, as most research processes are, it nevertheless reveals fault lines young fashion studies scholars are likely to face as they traverse fashion sites and practices, particularly those concerned with image production.

FROM WORKING ON FASHION TO WORKING IN FASHION

While *bodies as media* would eventually become the organizing framework for my analysis, I began with a more concrete object of study: fashion image production. As such, one of the first challenges I faced was figuring out how to access not just a one-off photo shoot, but a site (or series of sites) where I could regularly engage in observations, conversations, and practices alongside fashion image producers. While I debated how to make this happen, I took a summer internship in the editorial department of an academic press that had offices in midtown Manhattan. There I met postcollegiate editorial assistants roughly my age that had either interned at or knew someone who worked at a magazine. While none of these contacts directly led me to a field site, they introduced me to online resources, including Ed2010.com, for finding magazine internships.

That fall I applied widely, seeking positions at both men's and women's titles, niche and mainstream publications, and in a range of departments. In October 2003, I landed a photo internship at *Candy*, an ethnic women's lifestyle magazine with offices in the Flatiron district of Manhattan. Gina, the newly hired photo editor, explained that given the small size of the magazine's staff, the internship would be more like an assistant position. I would help organize contacts, proof and distribute call sheets, research stock photo requests, and assist on set.

The photo department seemed like an ideal place to explore my early research questions, which were largely practical: How are the images created? What does the editing process look like? Who makes which decisions? What kinds of considerations go into the process? Who are the most significant actors? What are their structural roles and relationships? While being on set was exciting, I found the office we shared with the two-person fashion department to be more revealing. There, I saw how ideas for fashion and beauty stories were developed, from the initial concept and collection of visual references, to finding the right creative team to execute it, to editing the resulting images for publication. While I did not have access to editorial staff meetings, I could listen to the informal conversations between Gina and other editors as they discussed plans for stories from selecting models and locations to finding the right photographer and creative team for the story concepts. I found that these exchanges often hinged on processes of mediation and translation, as well as the logistics of both.

About two months into my internship, just as I was getting down the rhythms of the photo department, the magazine folded. At a company-wide staff meeting at 4:00 p.m., the CEO made the announcement that the publisher had filed for bankruptcy protection citing the loss of its major financial backer. Earlier that day the staff had been finalizing the February 2004 issue, scheduled to be sent to the printer in less than two weeks: layouts were being edited, stock images secured, and last-minute fact-checking completed. The CEO announced that the December/January issue already on newsstands would be the last to be published.

And so I thought my time in the fashion world had ended abruptly. All of the stories I had worked on while at *Candy* were never published. At the time I felt as if this limited the potential of my analysis. I would not be able to track how the decisions and production practices I witnessed translated into a media artifact with its own social life and circulation. It felt incomplete. Originally my plan had been to factor the decisions made in the production process into my visual analysis of the final published work. It was not until later in my fieldwork that I realized this kind of comparison was not only

unnecessary, but that it obscured something key about the preproduction process itself.

I spent the next few months trying, unsuccessfully, to find another magazine internship. Frustrated, I broadened my search to include other kinds of fashion production sites, looking to Craigslist for leads. I ended up at Flair, a struggling boutique modeling agency, in April 2004. The agency was a small, one-room office space with a couch and two workstations. Max, the owner and head booker, explained that Flair filled a void in the market: ethnically diverse models. While he represented a handful of white models, most were black, Asian, or of mixed race. This, he explained, was both a personal mission and shrewd business decision. These models, he said, had a difficult time finding representation because of racism in the industry. While demand for white models was greater, he felt that there was an underserved client need for nonwhite models. If he took a chance and developed them, he could exploit this gap and build a niche.

While the staff of *Candy* was small, at Flair, it was often just Max and me in the office, with models stopping by to pick up cards or have their portfolios updated. Initially, I thought the small size and marginal status of the agency would make it an outlier, an inaccurate representation of the "real" fashion industry. Yet, it provided a unique opportunity for me to be socialized into the role of an agent with all of its attendant expectations. During the 17 months I spent there, moving from cold-calling and sending packages to clients to scouting and developing models, to actually booking them on editorial and campaign jobs (albeit small and less prestigious ones), my own socialization into the industry as a worker, not just as a researcher, became a valuable source of data. Through the trial-and-error process of learning a new skill and being fully responsible for it, I gained a better sense of the demands and pressures of working as a modeling agent.

One of my most significant lessons was learning how important it was to find the right language to describe a model and how images alone were never enough. Clients needed a narrative, either about the model's backstory or heritage, to bolster their perception about his or her suitability for a job (see Sadre-Orafai 2008).

This narrative work we did with clients dovetailed with the discursive work of development, where Max and I used stories about other models and clients to teach new models how to relate to their bodies and personas as malleable and marketable resources.

Aside from working closely with Max, I also developed friendships with some of the models, getting to know what was going on in their lives and how they saw the process, what frustrated them about it, and what kind of futures they imagined for themselves in and beyond the industry. I learned about rates and the kinds of ratios of both models and clients that agencies needed to be successful, or at least profitable, which we were always struggling to achieve. More than anything, though, I saw the incredible amount of work that went into creating just the possibility for published fashion images: the invisible, uncredited labor of modeling agents, which from an analytic standpoint could only be discussed as brokering images, not producing them. Resolved, I sought a way to reframe this work as productive. Going forward, casting and model development became two parts of a single, unified process.

WITHIN AND BEYOND FASHION

Moving from preliminary to primary fieldwork in 2006, I faced a familiar dilemma. While I knew casting and development were the central practices I wanted to examine, I was unsure how to access the more mainstream and high-end agencies. Somewhat naively I thought that since I was now a doctoral candidate with research funding—both sources of external validation for my ability to carry out the research and the importance of the project—I could engage these sites without having to work at them. Initially, I targeted two casting directors: Phillip, a close friend of Max and former modeling agent who worked on mostly commercial projects; and Jeremy, a vocal advocate for multicultural casting with a range of high fashion and commercial clients.

Both responded warmly to my emails and agreed to meet, extending offers to let me sit in on a few castings. They were frank in their assessment of the industry: Jeremy explained that while the same creative teams often worked on commercial and editorial projects, they were less likely to use nonwhite models for editorial jobs. He dealt with this cognitive dissonance by taking a long view of his client relationships, and worked to foster mutual trust and respect, so that he could push his clients to go beyond the industry status quo.

While both Jeremy and Phillip were supportive, neither of their agencies became a tenable field site: there were scheduling conflicts with Phillips agency, and Jeremy's business partner thought that the idea of being observed was "too weird." Both, however, gave me contacts of a few "like-minded" people who might be interested in helping. As I tried to set these new contacts and my old networks into motion, I also sent formal invitations to dozens of magazine bookings editors, casting agents, and directors of modeling agencies to participate in what I described as a research study on "multiculturalism and casting." Despite the impressive New York University letterhead, these failed to produce much interest. The exception was a tense meeting with a litigious model agency director in July. Initially sympathetic to the project, during the course of our forty-five-minute discussion she declared that it was too "dangerous" and would "get me killed," before accusing me of surreptitiously recording our conversation when I reached into my bag for a pen. While I found several individuals willing to talk about issues of race and casting "off the record," arranging for regular observations over the course of several months seemed nearly impossible.

So as summer came to an end and with it the rush of the New York Fashion Week, I returned to engaging these sites as I had before, by applying for internship positions—exchanging my free labor for access. After a handful of interviews in September, I began working at a photo agency in Soho. In addition to representing photographers and hair and makeup artists, the agency also had two producers on staff who occasionally held castings. While one producer was friendly, the other was decidedly not. I quickly realized that the castings at the agency neither occurred frequently enough, nor could I access them easily. I started looking for another internship almost immediately.

A month later, I began working at LVX, a leading fashion casting agency where I happily stayed for eleven months. LVX had a range of commercial, runway, editorial, and advertising clients and cast both models and "real people," or nonprofessional models. There were four full-time employees on staff, as well as a handful of interns and occasional freelancers and scouts. Because of the scale of the agency's business and open layout of its floor plan, I was able to see and participate in dozens of casting interactions each day, as well as editing sessions that led up to client presentations.

Before arriving at LVX I had not considered "real people" to be a meaningful category for my research. Yet, seeing the volume of nonprofessional models that came through the agency and the kinds of jobs for which they were booked, I quickly revised my perspective. I saw how the market for "real people" functioned as a disincentive for modeling agencies to represent a wider range of types. Indeed, I even found a handful of models from Flair in the agency's "real people" files. "Real people" provided a stopgap for the lack of racial, ethnic, and body diversity on high fashion agency boards. Clients' reasons for requesting "real people" were equally revealing. While some were looking for "edgier" or more authentic models, others saw it as a cost-saving strategy. This put the decline in models' rates following 9/11, which, in 2006 had not yet recovered, in sharp relief. Indeed, the more I explored this market, the more I realized how the category "real people" helped constitute the boundaries of the category "model" itself.

Viewing "real people" from the casting agents' perspectives, I also saw how the category posed different kinds of logistical issues, when compared to casting professional models. Agents needed to be able to find specific types with limited time and financial resources. To this end, they worked with scouts to collaboratively produce geographies of types in the city, which were based on their own experiences and ideas about where one might find particular types. They also devised research-based strategies for finding "real people" through associations or their own social networks. I found that these methods resonated with other kinds of embodied organizational memories based on experience, hunches, and shared wisdom, such as the low-tech profiling practices of law enforcement officers and other state agents (see Sadre-Orafai 2016).

By positioning casting practices like street scouting and booking photography beyond the frame of fashion, I was able to observe them more sharply as not just visual preproduction, but as knowledge-producing practices. This allowed me to challenge the idea that images—even casting photographs—were the primary outcome of these interactions. Instead, I found that casting agents' expertise centered more on producing knowledge about individuals, bodies, and types. And in so doing, they elaborated and refined theories of mediation—how people's appearances could be entextualized in different kinds of commercial contexts and made meaningful, as well as the limits of these translations. Just as narratives were important for securing jobs for models at Flair, casting agents drew on personal details from both "real people" and professional models to convince clients and one another about their suitability for particular jobs.

Four months into my internship at LVX, agents helped me arrange a concurrent position at DCM, a high-end women's modeling agency. DCM was a compelling site for all the reasons LVX was not. Whereas the agents at LVX emphasized the importance of "diversity," DCM had a de facto ban on nonwhite models, arguing that there was not enough of a client demand at the highest end of the market. Echoing Jeremy and Max's critiques, when pressed about the lack of diversity on their board, agents at DCM would say, "Black girls: twice the work, half the money." This was in early 2007—the height of the "Prada exclusive," where newly discovered models were booked for the high profile show and barred from appearing on other designers' runways, and the popularity of young, Eastern European models (Luu 2013). Many of these models lasted only a few seasons, leading to more aggressive scouting and high rates of turnover on editorial boards. Development in this context was necessarily compressed.

Unlike at Flair, I was not socialized into an agent role at DCM. This allowed me to focus on the interactions between models and agents, rather than my own experiences doing this work. While there were similarities between development practices I saw at Flair and those at DCM, because of the strength of the latter's reputation, barriers to entry for its models were much lower. Instead of just seeking any booking, agents were more selective in how they managed models' careers. While other agencies took six months to a year to develop a new model—building her experience through smaller editorial jobs and less prestigious runway and advertising work—at DCM, development started at the top and unfolded in just a few months. Justin, a junior agent, explained that many of the big-name photographers wanted to shoot models first, so to have models learn by doing work at a lower level, even if it was published or paid, ultimately hampered their careers. Yet, because the stakes were higher, agents at DCM were more conservative with the kinds of models they took on, vetting them with specific high-end clients in mind.

These practices led to a reproduction of the industry status quo and helped explain the lack of diversity on their board. It also pointed to the multiple layers of mediation and refraction involved in producing models' bodies as media. More than just cultivating models' bodies as abstract, ideally mutable surfaces, development practices at DCM revealed the impact already existing infrastructure has on not just channeling but actively shaping the seemingly neutral terms by which models are developed. Looking to media studies more broadly helps sharpen this point. As Raymond Williams writes, concerning the inevitability of broadcast television: "This predestination, however, when closely examined, proves to be no more than a set of particular social decisions, in particular circumstances, which were then so widely if imperfectly ratified that it is now difficult to see them as decisions rather than as (retrospectively) inevitable results" ([1975] 2005: 15). That is, while we may subscribe to ideologies concerning the neutrality of certain media forms, these ideas are outcomes of specific sociohistorical, political, cultural, and material actions. Placing models' development in this broader context allows us to deconstruct with more precision the cumulative effect of repeated selections that value some bodies as

more malleable and conducive forms of media than others. It shows how abstract categories have material effects.

CONCLUSION

By working at DCM and LVX at the same time, I was able to directly compare the two sides of producing models' bodies as media at the highest level of the industry. In thinking through my framework of bodies as media, I drew inspiration from anthropologist Janelle Taylor's concept "surfacing the body interior" which she uses to describe "the range of practices and processes that both materialize bodily surfaces as significant sites with broader orders, and surface that which lies hidden beneath them" (2005: 742) calling attention to the political, ethical, and social implications of the connections between mediation and appearances. Drawing on science studies and practice-based social theory, Taylor proposes that anthropologists approach "the body neither as an object nor as a text, nor only as a locus of subjectivity, but rather as a contingent configuration, a surface that is made but never in a static or permanent form" (Taylor 2005: 747). In doing so, she highlights the fluidity of both bodies and bodily surfaces amid the fixity with which we encounter them. More than just pointing to the idea that bodies are expressive mediums, Taylor highlights how, like most media forms, we ignore their mediating function in our focus on the content of their messages.

Paying attention to potential rupture, dynamism, and production of bodily surfaces—even in situations of reproduction, like at DCM—demonstrates how, despite the assumption that fashion relies on rigid categories of difference, it is a process that unfolds in looser ways that can both undo and reinscribe the explanatory power of categories of social difference. By attending to casting and model development as a single process, one can see how a practice-based, ethnographic approach can provide important insights that are not observable through a focus on publicly circulated media or on their material or economic production alone. Instead, bringing together discursive, visual, and embodied practices, it becomes possible to view the multiple ways casting professionals and models collaboratively produce models' bodies as legible types and forms that rely on existing visual referents and expectations, but are also malleable in their performance and perception. These practices, while firmly rooted within the fashion industry, have connections and analogues beyond it—from profiling practices in the context of law enforcement to the performance and management of perception in everyday interaction.

36

ETHNOGRAPHIC ENTANGLEMENTS:
Memory and narrative in the global fashion industry

Christina H. Moon

For the past ten years, I have been studying the global fashion industry through the labor of its cultural workers, including designers, design students and interns, sample makers, factory owners, clothing wholesalers, and sewers, among many others, who play a powerful role in the making of fashion. My field sites included several different design firms in New York and Los Angeles, a multinational design corporation, a high-end fashion company, and a mass fashion wholesale company, which took me to the varied spaces of the fashion industry: design studios, factories, corporate offices, and fashion runway shows across New York, Los Angeles, Paris, Hong Kong, Guangzhou, and Seoul. Though I arrived in New York in 2005 as a wide-eyed graduate student, lured to the city by the glamour and glossy images made by a rapidly transforming media apparatus in the global fashion industry, I left with the realization that the cultural labor of migrating subjects—immigrants and their children—had played an enormous role in transforming cities like New York, Paris, and Milan into the global fashion capitals we have come to know today. This is a thread found throughout my work; much of my research explores the working lives of these subjects, not just sewers but fashion workers, who not only perform new kinds of creative work for the industry (particularly in design), but who also form the social ties that connect design capitals and manufacturing landscapes in clothing throughout the world.

In this chapter, I explore "how it is I got there" in my initial research on the New York fashion industry of the mid-2000s: how I arrived at the research sites and subjects that make up my studies on the global fashion industry, and what implications ethnographic practice might have in drawing out new research questions and conclusions (and possibilities) for the study of fashion. It was not until the very act of writing up my research findings did I realize the importance of what my "methods" were, and how my own practice of going about and collecting information through ethnographic research—the interpretive and subjective practice of personally embedding oneself in the fashion world—would ultimately shape the kind of "global fashion industry" I would observe, interpret, and depict in written, documentary representation. In a world of fashion I had always imagined as full of glamour, luxury, and beauty, I saw an underworld of capitalist logics, abstract economics, and exploited labor. The ethnographic practice of talking to and being among communities of fashion workers enabled me to illuminate an industry run on relationships and old-world ties and connections. These were the intimate and affective sides to global connections driving the technology and innovation within the global fashion industry, often excluded in socioeconomic and political histories of fashion.

MAPPING THE GLOBAL COMMODITY CHAIN OF FASHION

As a student of the social sciences, I had inherited sociological maps of the industry, a global fashion

Adapted from Christina Moon, "Ethnographic Entanglements: Memory and Narrative in the Global Fashion Industry," in *Fashion Studies: Research Methods, Sites, and Practices*, edited by Heike Jenss (London: Bloomsbury, 2016), pp. 66–82.

industry that was imagined as a "global commodity chain" and "system of aesthetic cultural production" that produced regimes of "circulating values" and emerging "markets." The theoretical model of a global commodity chain, consisting of "nodes" and "points" in a network of labor and production processes, would have as the end result a finished commodity, and explained how a commodity was produced in a "transnational and global context" (Applebaum and Gereffi 1994; Bair 2005; Bonacich and Applebaum 2000; Gereffi and Korzeniewicz 1994). With the introduction of trade laws including the General Agreement on Trade and Tariffs (GATT), the North America Free Trade Agreement (NAFTA), and the Multifiber Trade Agreement (MTA), academics eagerly sought to apply this theoretical model of the 1990s to the fashion industry, one of the first industries to experience the increasingly *global* spatiality of its apparel firms and the development of transnational links in production processes (see Bonacich et al. 2004; Gereffi and Korzeniewicz 1994; Gereffi[, Spener, and Bair] 2002). At the same time, social and cultural theorists began to expand this literature with perspectives on the "social life of things" (Appadurai 1986)—the global commodity chain's complimentary analysis: seeking to humanize the anonymous sphere of capitalist commerce as described by economists, they increased the focus on exploring subject/object relations in the object's valorization processes, attempting to trace the whole life history of objects. Curiously, both concepts appeared at a time in the 1990s when academic scholars had begun to make claims that the primary site to study "modern capitalist economies" had shifted from sites of production to sites of consumption. Soon, studies across the social sciences would predominantly focus on the study of moving commodities, material culture, and consumption processes (Appadurai 1986; Bourdieu [1979] 1984; Carrier 1994, 1997; Miller 1986, 1995[b], 1996, 1998, 2001). It was now possible to study entire histories of objects from origins, states of becoming, circulation in trade, and meaning-making in consumption: radical approaches to the study of objects and commodities in circulation, which greatly inspired generations of ethnographers to explore the global breadth of industry through the analytical

unit of the commodity (Hart 2007). In time, the burgeoning field of fashion studies would produce scholarship on the production of fashion cultures and economies (Entwistle 2009), the making of fashion cities (Breward and Gilbert 2006), emergent fashion markets, consumerism and spatiality (Aspers 2010), fashion production and business practices (Blaszczyk 2008), and the making of sustainable fashion systems in a globalizing world (Black 2012).

In 2005, I thought that I too would go out into the world and trace the "object of fashion" through its Marxist, socioeconomic categories of production as a global commodity chain. Like sugar, cars, and Coca-Cola, I too would track fashion's multiple stages of becoming, like the "T-shirt travels" in its making, through the realms of production, distribution, and consumption beyond the borders of nation (Rivoli 2009). On a more humanistic level, I would analyze the different kinds of social and cultural worlds that the object moved back and forth in, exploring how the object gained cultural value, life history, and a whole biography of its own.

From cotton to fabric, from garment to fashion, into a system of symbolic meanings, I would then explain the hierarchical structures of a global fashion world and its fashion capitals, and the accumulation of cultural value as the object "becoming" through these worlds. Yet, although this would tell me something about the object itself, its cultural value, states of becoming, and political economy—there seemed to be *no people* in these mappings, neither the room for their complicated affectations and attachments for this world, nor the very contingencies that come along with all the nuances of global encounters in the making of fashion. As the cultural historian Michael Denning notes, "Maps are ways of conceiving totalities, understanding boundaries," yet maps are also "points of view—no single map tells us all we might want to know" (Denning 2004).

NARRATIVE TRAVERSING

From a practical perspective, I had no clue where I would begin to go "ethnographically." Where would I go to begin to study and track such an imagined, real, and transforming thing called the global fashion industry? An industry that changes day by day, minute by minute? I would have to "embark" on a field site and physically take myself there and so, I simply chose New York because it was the closest "global fashion capital" for me, a nice antidote to the quiet graduate life I had lived while at New Haven. On my first day of "field research" I found myself in the Garment District on 39th street, the very cultural heart of fashion history in the United States, and the geographical center of its commerce.

Here I was immediately confronted with the fleeting images and the sensory rush of a bustling neighborhood, full of people going on about their ordinary workday. It felt so different to be staring at some schematic of a supply chain in fashion—claimed objective representations of a global commodity chain that I had read about and imagined from the academic literature—to an actual physical place full of sounds, colors, images, smells, experiences, and human interactions. The ephemerality of everyday life and the cultural meaning it produced came at one as a full assault on the senses that bombarded in real time and lived experience, and every passing moment seemed to be full of possibilities, of potential interactions with different people, thick and detailed descriptions, fleeting thoughts, illuminations, with communicating signs abounding. These sudden moments of thought and feeling would go against all that I thought could be described, archived, or categorized all that I had ever found to be surefooted and confident, all that I had considered as "research." Here, I would have to talk to people, have all sorts of awkward and intimidating interactions and encounters, and have to acknowledge my own subjective positioning in light of an overwhelming anthropological history of modernist critique built on ethnocentrism, relativism, and "data collection." How would any of these theoretical models and concepts I had learned about, particularly the global commodity chain, guide me through any of this: gaining "access," getting people to talk to me, making and developing relationships, and then, later on, the personal entanglements, attachments, and investments that would influence the decisions I made as I went about the research? How would "methodology" guide

me through the fragmented pieces of "data" presented by people, their nonlinear stories, the scattering of their memories and various social histories, narratives that I would collect in the most haphazard ways? While theoretical models explained "how the industry worked" as an operational system, a fashion world rendered stable as sense, order, and function, what of the muddy and intimate locations that come along in global connections and field work? What of people, their relationships, the nuances and details that make up their working lives in fashion, their silences, ambivalences, and their stories? Would any of this even count as research? I had begun my own interactive process and politics of "traversing," as the anthropologist James Clifford (1997) once put it, and my field sites looked nothing like what I prepared myself to look for; there weren't any objective "nodes" of a global commodity chain, but instead just a bunch of stories.

I spent days in field research, not knowing whom I would talk to next. In an industry full of people who constantly told me that "time is money," it was impossible to expect anyone to have the time to call me, a random person, back. This went against the assumption that doing ethnography at "home" would be something of an easier task for myself as an "anthropologist." There seemed to be an underlying assumption that I would gain access to "deeper" levels of information and knowledge because I was using my own native language of English, my familiarity with "American cultural practices," because I ostensibly belonged to the same "ethnic categories" as some of my potential informants ("Asian"), and because I had embarked on field research in my "own backyard" (Nader 1972). It became immediately clear, however, how difficult it would be to get anyone in fashion to talk to me at all—I was trying to get in on the "inside" of an exclusive world full of overworked people, too busy to talk. Though I made lists of potential contacts before arriving in the field, making "cold-calls" to strangers who did not know me, to trace a commodity chain was just not a practical way to maneuver within this industry, which ultimately said something larger about the way it actually works. I found early on that there needed to be a reason for somebody to call me back, beyond the fact that I was a graduate student doing research for my dissertation.

STICKY EVOCATIONS: PRACTICES OF THE PERSONAL

My first route into the New York fashion industry came from my family's own personal contacts, specifically, from my parents' church in Hackensack, New Jersey, where so many of the young women from the Korean congregation were either students attending fashion design schools, or working for fashion companies in New York. While one interview came from a church friend working for Michael Kors, another came from a close friend, who works in Los Angeles's San Pedro Mart, designing and wholesaling clothes to Macy's, Urban Outfitters, and Nordstrom. Even my own parents' two closest sets of friends had something to say about fashion: one couple made their livelihood as clothing wholesalers in Korea, Argentina, and then New York, and another worked as a seamstress at a dry cleaning business for most of her working life. The global apparel trade was also tied to my father's oldest friend in the United States, a man who opened the first Korean restaurant on 32nd Street in Manhattan's Koreatown in 1983, selling classic Korean oxtail soup to the Korean laborers working and sewing in neighboring garment district factories. From my own personal networks, among those I grew up with, it seemed that everyone had something to say about fashion, clothing, and its meaning in their lives. And so, it seemed not a surprise that, while standing in the Garment District on that first day of field research, I had my own memory of "New York Fashion" from my own childhood. These memories would become embedded in the note-taking, observational, ethnographic narrative of my research:

The smell of paint, the sight of my mother hunched over, painting jewelry with colorful enamel paint.

My parents ran a small workshop first in the New York Garment District painting custom jewelry. In fact, the very first job my mother ever had in the U.S. after emigrating from Korea in the late 1960s, was working for a Jewish jewelry manufacturer in the district. Sponsored by her aunt, she had come to New York to study art and found a job mixing paint as a paint colorist for a factory. After working for this factory for four years, she learned all she needed to know about the business to start her own and, after meeting my father, a chemistry student sponsored by an American missionary in post-war Korea, they began their own business as a husband and wife team painting and wholesaling custom jewelry to local New York department stores. It seems to have been fate-with my father's understanding of chemical properties and my mother's sense of color, the two experimented with epoxy glue and paint and created jewel-tone colored enamels that, when applied to cheap metals, gave the illusion of expensive jewels.

Their small workshop was located in the Garment District and from the orders they filled, they made enough money to buy their first home in suburban New Jersey. Yet, just as soon as they began to make money, they began to look for ways out of the business. They worried that the toxic smell of paints would affect my mother's pregnancy with my brother. They could not afford the rising cost of wage labor, business was fast changing and jewelry could be made and painted for cheaper costs in other countries. Eventually, my parents closed their workshop and moved their operations into the basement of our family home, where they worked and painted along with all the other Korean friends they had in the neighborhood.

Heading down the basement steps I see my mother sitting alongside other Korean women, hunched over under fluorescent lights. They roll pieces of plastic cellophane into cone tubes, fill these tubes with brightly colored epoxy paint, and squeeze the paint out onto the jewelry. I help out by laying out the wooden rods, gently placing the painted earrings, belt buckles, rings out for drying. Our weekends are spent driving into the city to drop off the orders in the Garment District.

At first I thought it was a coincidence, but now I see it is no coincidence at all, that the field sites of my research had emerged from deep pools of sentiment and attachment, recognition, and memory among the subjects I interviewed. Neither did I realize that these memories of the Garment District, the childhood church friends who were now studying or working in fashion, the friends of family working as clothing traders or sewers, and even my parents' own paths in migrating to the United States and their factory work, were part of a history of ramifications of U.S. Cold War interventions in Asia, the industrialization of Asian nations through garments, the migration of postcolonials to the metropoles, with dreams of their children becoming Americans and fashion designers. They were part of this history that saw the rise of global fashion capitals and the development of new fashion culture industries in need of designers not just in New York City, but across Asia and in global cities around the world. I had thought "ethnographic field work" would lead me to a more glamorous, fashionable, and "contemporary" research site. Yet, here I was, knee-deep in the past, grappling with these intimate pulls and memories of the fashion and garment histories of my own family I was using "theories" and "methods" that had not equipped me to navigate any of these sticky subjective evocations—how conducting field research not only implicated my subjects' complex identities, but also spoke to my own shifting identities as a researcher.

I had come to the global fashion industry as an "outsider," as an "analyst"—*I was there to study it.* Yet, I was already unknowingly predisposed to its complicated histories and networks. The subject/object relationship of former ethnographies had not accounted for my own shifting interactions, positions, advocacies, and investments in my research, which would ultimately affect the conceptualization of my story. "The field" is not an empty site, never cleared or even a clearing, but mired in sentiment, drenched in memory, already being shaped as history, fictively produced and made. In an industry whose characterizations swing from the detached impersonal, anonymous realms of capitalist modes of production, to the unattainable objects and images of a glamorous fashion, it is ethnographic practices of the personal—relationships of familiarity and recognition, often intimate and affective ones—which would ultimately shape conceptualizations of the field sites and subjects.

Beyond family and friends, the only other way I was able to make contacts in "search of subjects" was through work and the intimate encounters of everyday labor. I offered my work for free to various companies, which gave me the opportunity to intern, be socialized into and work alongside people who I eventually interviewed and developed relationships with. Working for a minimum of a three-month period for each company, my relationships with people were forged in the daily routines and habitual repetitions of work, and those I worked closely with introduced me to other people and their already existing relationships, alliances, and networks. Although there were those who were genuinely interested in my research on the rise of New York as a global fashion capital during the 1990s and 2000s, in most cases, people called me back as an altruistic gesture toward their friend, who had introduced me in the first place, maintaining an important personal relationship (whether business or friendship) with that other person, whom they often regarded in high esteem. And strangely, by meeting people in this manner, I too would become a part of the social mesh, attachments, and networks that describe the industry.

By relying on other people's relationships, I didn't have much control over who I would be able to talk with next. I worried most days that the research had no focus around a singular "subject" that could be defined by an ethnic group or occupation. Anthropologists within the last 20 years have challenged this subject-other relationship, yet there still exists the persistent idea that subjects must be "defined," no matter how loosely by group, community, class formation, identity, social occupation, or racial and ethnic affiliation (Behar 1993, 1996; Behar and Gordon 1995; Clifford 1988[c], 1997, 2003; Clifford and Marcus 1986; Fabian 2014; Strathern 1988, 1999). The "subjects of my study," however, were not an already given or determined group of people as outlined in an abstract of a research proposal. They were subjects who only "emerged" through other people's introductions and relationships, as I made my way through the field research. The process, in its entirety, seemed to resemble more a scattered unfolding of inarticulate intuitions and sensings, rather than a definitively outlined plan with a "control group" and "set location of fieldwork." This method of interviewing might be recognized as the "snowball" effect, but as a metaphor this term neglects the idea that the relationships formed led me to interviews with other people (Agar 1996). "Relationships" do not lead to other interviews via "momentum," but through work, labor, friendship, time, and most especially trust. Consequently, my study did not become a study of "Korean fashion designs," and the subjects of this study were not "Asian American fashion designers," using the kind of nation-bound or identity-framing that has dominated anthropological literature on fashion for the last two decades; the people I spent time with could not be reduced to such simple categories as nation, race or ethnicity, colonizer/colonized, exploiter/exploited, fashion worker/garment worker, capitalist/laborer, and so on. Furthermore, I was not sure if this band of individuals could even be considered a "community" at all—how were, for instance, fashion designers, fashion students, technical designers, curators, PR agents and marketers, sweatshop activists, rehabilitated garment workers, and migrant sewers a community of subjects? Further, could a "community" exist transnationally, globally, or even as a cultural diaspora? I spent most of my days feeling unsure, worried about how to define the subjects of my study and how to make sense of it all.

Even more confusing was my being surrounded by "informants"—fashion designers, interns, PR agents, curators at museums, fashion business owners, factory managers, sewers, etc.—who were their own ethnographers seeking maps into the industry. Just as I was trying to understand the way the industry worked, they too were in the same sort of obsessive project of trying to imagine, interpret, accumulate information, and track the fashion industry's transformations and moves. In a strange role reversal, I found myself surrounded by people who were constantly trying to mine me, "the anthropologist," "the supposed expert," for more "inside" information or connections to "get in on the inside" of a fashion world and industry that I believed they were already on the inside of. I found it surprising that even those I believed to be at the top of some perceived hierarchy of the fashion world, never came to believe themselves to be at the "center" of it all. No one I spent time with felt themselves to be completely "in it," instead they felt they were not

positioned where they desired to be, and were always on the search to "penetrate" this fashion world even further. This confusion forced me to question the whole project on how to "get in on the inside of" anything at all, the project of finally knowing anything, "it," the object of study, "the way the world works" to some known degree or the end goal. Trying to depict "what this was" in texture and density, would only highlight the futile project of seeking some sort of truth value, and the "inevitable failure to represent or capture some sort of absolute real" (Stewart 1996: 22). As I moved through the field research, I had come to realize that, just as I followed and documented the complexity of their interpretations, I too was tracking and documenting my own interpretative moves in fashion.

I had become interested in the concrete or contingent relationships of people, what made up the "excesses" or "stuff" that made up their lives, the vivid stories, silences, the complicated social matrixes in which the "cultural" and "culture" emerged from—the ambivalences that had no place on a global commodity chain of fashion (Gaonkar and Povinelli 2003: 385). I was less interested in using a language of objects in circulation operating within static systems or closed totalities in distant field sites under total observation, and more interested in exploring the social practices and processes of the people participating in these global fashion worlds and industries. I wanted to begin not with how "things" were fashioning "networks" in circulation, but with how "people" formed and fashioned "relationships" in the constant making of those things, as well as the modes of attachment they affectively felt toward these complex fashion imaginaries.

MAKING SENSE OF IT ALL: OUTCOMES AND ARTIFACTS OF DISCUSSION

And so in New York, I began work as an intern for a large multinational fashion design company located on Seventh Avenue, spending my days in and out of the Garment District running errands. In this alluring center of it all, my first interviews came not from famous fashion designers, but from a group of security guards in an old industry building, many of whom had greeted factory owners in the front lobbies of district buildings for 10, 20, or 30 years. Unlike the newspaper articles that tracked the "death of the district" through the listing of statistics, these subjects narrated instead the changes of a neighborhood as they had witnessed it—through the disappearance of the garment factory owners who once used to be their employers. My inability to gain access to the more glamorous ends of the global fashion industry, led to another research site that witnessed the effects of deindustrialization among the Garment District from the "survivors"—from factory owners to security guards. They never relayed their stories as a chronology of trade laws, but rather as palpable experiences, haunting tales, and district folklore. It was, for them, the closing down of shops, the disappearance of sewers, the nuanced changes to the daily rituals of work, the physical and geographical transformations to the street—the tangible imprints of a lived experience through a changing neighborhood and industry, of a changing people and place.

My errands in the district as a low-rung intern included dropping off and picking up samples at local factories, and I thought it curious that the majority of local factories were owned by immigrants from Korea and China, who had come to dominate district factory production throughout the 1990s. I met one such factory owner who spoke to me because I was Korean American. He told me about growing up in the countryside in Korea during the 1960s: having left school at fourteen to work in sewing factories, as an adult he sewed the clothes at American multinational companies like Nike and Reebok, and eventually made his way to New York, working as a tailor in the 1990s. After saving up money, he now runs his own sample-making factory in the Garment District, creating the runway collections for the fashion designer Marc Jacobs. While the history of the Garment District is often told as a Jewish and Italian history of America, its most recent history includes these Korean and Chinese immigrants (Chin 2005; Soyer 2004; Waldinger 1986). Their personal histories intimately tie histories and processes of other places to the New York Garment District in time and space, and their work has powerfully redefined the value of the clothing in the district today—they make *not* garments, but runway samples. Their emergence, alongside the rise of New

York Fashion Week, shows that they have played, not a peripheral, but a central role in making New York into a global fashion capital. These same questions could be raised about global fashion weeks and cities around the world, looking at what the impact of these seemingly marginal/peripheral communities had on the making of these cities globally. In New York and Milan, immigrants from China are responsible for sample-making and garment work (see Ross 2004). In Paris's Le Sentier, West African immigrants dominate the garment trade (see Green 1997).

During my internships at several design firms, I worked as free labor in both the "front of the house," among design teams, public relations agents, and secretaries; and at the "back of the house" among production managers, patternmakers, sewers, and other interns. In the front of the house, I was surrounded by beautiful women who came dressed to the nines for work each day, hired to manage the appearances, impressions, and aesthetics of the company. From their styles of dress to their attitudes, to even the way they answered the phones, the labor of these fashion workers was performative in that they presented a smoothly run, "effortless," and "no sweat" operation. In their acts of self-effacement, their labor was to perform that no labor was involved—making me wonder why, when it comes to labor, it is often imagined as manual and masculine, and why the work of these fashion workers across the industry would not be considered labor at all. It was just one example of the "cultural discount" (including my own culturally discounted free labor as an intern) that pervaded the culture industries of New York. From fashion, architecture, design, media, and technology, these industries relied heavily on a free or highly casualized workforce who accepted nonmonetary rewards "as compensation for their work thereby discounting the cash price of their labor" (Ross 2009: 80).

In the back sample room, I worked among sample makers and interns who cut, sewed, and created the runway collections for New York Fashion Week and found everyday acts of communality and collective creativity in the making of runway collections. Though I originally thought that the internship would get me closer to the iconic namesake designer and the hidden, creative design practices behind her work, I watched instead an entire collective of workers design, creatively interpret, and communally produce fashions that were brandished under the designer's singular name. While I witnessed how labor is obscured with the brandishing of the label, I also found an environment that challenged the kind of "corporation" often depicted by discourse produced by the anti-sweatshop movement. Rather than a one-dimensional, anonymous, all-powerful, and unyielding entity that overshadows any possible form of political subjectivity, this multinational design corporation could be understood as the workplace setting for thousands of fashion's cultural workers.

The interns working in the back sample room were students attending either Parsons School of Design or the Fashion Institute of Technology (FIT) and surprisingly, in entirety, were students from Korea. I would learn that they were part of the post-1997 IMF crisis call for globalization, a new middle class and elite who wanted to send their students abroad for the prestige of a foreign degree, the chance to learn English language skills, get the experience of working for famous American fashion companies, with the opportunity to make powerful alumni connections upon their return to Asia. New York design schools greatly benefited from this migration of design students from industrializing manufacturing nations looking to "value up" the fashion chain and spur on fashion economies (see Tu 2011).

On their encouragement, I enrolled for a semester in the design school, which I nearly hopelessly failed, and listened to students tell me about how fashion brought them to New York, gave them the opportunity to live in this creative center of the world, where one could hone one's English, the language of globalization, graduate with an American brand-name degree, and tap into privileged alumni networks that would get them design jobs in Korea. While in New York, these design students provided substantial service to Seventh Avenue design companies: they made up a significant workforce of interns and designers—a conveniently free, casualized, temporary workforce of designers in the United States on "training" visas. Many of these designers planned to go back to Korea to develop new fashion and design culture industries the government had since poured

revenue into—I learned that Korea was undergoing its own deindustrialization. This became just another example of the sticky intersections between labor, capital, and migration among globalizing institutions— schools and corporations—in the socialization, training, and recruitment of new workers into new global professional fields of fashion design.

While at design school, I met many Asian American students who had grown up in and around garment districts in New York, Los Angeles, and San Francisco, with families who had worked in some aspect of the rag trade. Not wanting to go into the corporate world of American bridge-wear, the everyday clothing sold in department stores, I met many in search of more creative outlets, wanting to start their own businesses in fashion. I followed one such Asian American designer to Los Angeles, who planned to "revamp" her parents' ailing wholesale company—she hoped to combine her design skills with their 30 years of manufacturing knowledge in South America and China, to make the kind of fast fashion clothing that would sell to powerful corporate retailers in the Americas. While those in the high-end designer fashion world in places like Paris or New York would never consider this informal market of cheaply priced clothing on the eastern edge of the LA garment district as a place that makes fashion designs, the clothing designed in this part of the neighborhood made up a majority of all women's fast fashions sold in department stores, corporate retail outlets, and boutiques across the United States. The story became even more compelling when I realized that the fashions were designed and distributed by immigrant wholesalers and their children who designed, many of whom have multiple identities—ethnically Korean, born in Brazil, raised in America, and who've graduate from places like Parsons, who worked in this one area, in this one neighborhood, and for the most part down on one street (see Moon 2014).

CONCLUSION: RELATIONSHIPS OF RECOGNITION

In this thing called the global fashion industry, each field site, interview, person met, and invitation, appeared through affective and personal realms and connections. The memories, personal histories, stories, partnerships, and alliances—these relationships of recognition—shaped who I would speak to and where and what my field sites were, a "multi-sited" project which would lead to other cities and places. These relationships of affection guided me through these fashion worlds and industries, bringing me to transnational frameworks (in other times, in other spaces) of encounter and exchange, making visible the highly contingent character to fieldwork that is left unmentioned in "research" as well as the shifting dimensions of what we consider to be a "field site."

If we are to understand the recent transformations in the fashion industry and therefore in global capitalism, whether it is the changes to material culture, design and aesthetic landscapes, the shifts in our nuanced sensory experiences of time, image, touch, space, the body, and materiality through fashion, perhaps "being there" would help to get us to the intimacies and contingencies of work and life among fashion's cultural workers, locations to be further explored in fashion studies. How do these subjects shape visual culture and the aesthetic material landscapes of fashion? How have their practices altered our experience of life and of fashion? How are their work relationships and imaginaries of the fashion world embodied in the everyday experience of banal materiality? Their stories, meanings, desires, relationships resonate in everyday material cultural forms, making their way into the objects, aesthetics, and practices that have cultured our world. It is this deeply complex, intimate, socializing realm that I am grasping to have an understanding for—that buried space where we might see the relationship between forms of work and forms of art, and fashion. That space from which labor transforms into the unbearable lightness of beautiful, material forms.

37

MAKING CLOTHES FOR INTERNATIONAL MARKETS:
A clothing perspective on globalization

Jianhua Zhao

THE STORY OF A STEELERS JERSEY

The winter of 2005 was a joyful time for Pittsburgh Steelers' fans, because their team did the almost impossible. It went into the postseason as a wild card team and upset all the stronger teams on the road and was on its way to win the Super Bowl. The joy spread far beyond Pittsburgh and the United States. Mr. Zeng Gang, a contact and friend of mine who lives in Shanghai, China, and works in the business of international garment trade, was so excited for me that he sent me a Steelers jersey via FedEx. The Steelers jerseys, as I was told by Zeng Gang, were in high demand and mine was a sample for the follow-up orders from Reebok (merged with Adidas since 2006), the sportswear giant that makes jerseys for the National Football League (NFL) in the United States.

My Steelers jersey arrived just in time for the Super Bowl XL game, which was held in Detroit, Michigan, on February 5, 2006. As newly converted fans of the Steelers, my wife and I decided to go to a sports bar to watch the game in Pittsburgh. Right after lunch, we headed out for a bar, and I was wearing my brand-new Steelers jersey sent to me by Zeng Gang from Shanghai. After a few failed attempts for bars in nearby neighborhoods, which were fully booked, we luckily secured a table without a reservation in a sports restaurant/bar at Waterfront, a booming area for shopping and recreation in Pittsburgh. Our table was in a converted dining area where the restaurant had temporarily installed a big flat-screen TV to accommodate viewers of the game. The game was scheduled to begin in the evening. Like most people in the restaurant, we spent hours in the afternoon watching commercials and the warm-up shows, chatting, and drinking over snacks. By "people," I mean Steelers fanatics: They were all decked out in black and gold jerseys similar to mine.

Watching the 2006 Super Bowl game in a Pittsburgh sports restaurant is one of my most memorable Super Bowl experiences. Without a doubt, my experience was enhanced by the Steelers jersey made by Zeng Gang's suppliers in China. The jersey marked me as "one of us"—the Steelers fans, or as they call it, a member of the "Steelers nation." It helped to create a common frame of reference in which social distinctions outside this context or frame did not matter. The common frame—the Steelers team—was what brought everyone together. Consequently it facilitated a "bond"—the feeling of being an equal member of the Steelers nation—among the viewers in the restaurant, despite that many of whom were strangers. From my experience of watching the Super Bowl game in the sports restaurant, the most meaningful aspects of the jersey to me as a consumer were the black-and-gold pattern and the Steelers' logo; had I worn a Seahawks jersey, my experience in the restaurant would conceivably have been very different. Those most meaningful components of the Steelers jersey (to consumers like me) are controlled by the Steelers organization, marketed by the NFL, and licensed by the NFL to Reebok (both the NFL

Adapted from Jianhua Zhao, "Making Clothes for International Markets: A Clothing Perspective on Globalization," in *The Chinese Fashion Industry: An Ethnographic Approach* (London: Bloomsbury, 2013), pp. 132–52.

and Reebok also have their own logos on the jersey). All three organizations are based in the United States and are familiar to U.S. consumers. What the U.S. consumers may or may not know is that their NFL jerseys (as well as over one-third of their entire wardrobe) are made in China. The country of origin of their jerseys and other garments is usually marked on a small tag hidden from view. As the saying goes, out of sight, out of mind; it does not seem to matter to them where their jerseys come from. This is because unlike the logos of the Steelers, the NFL, and Reebok, the country of origin of their jerseys does not hold any symbolic meaning to them. In fact, this observation seems to be applicable to most U.S. consumers with regard to their views toward their clothes; nobody seems to care where their clothes are made.

The hidden tag inside our clothes that indicates the country of origin, however, is not only the material evidence of the interconnections of the global apparel industry, but also reflects the way in which the global fashion apparel industry is structured. For example, my China-made Steelers jersey clearly demonstrates the connection between the Chinese clothing industry and the United States, but at the same time, the story of the Steelers jerseys also shows that the symbolic meanings of the garments are disconnected from the producers in China. In order to understand the apparent contradictions inherent in the export of Chinese made garments, this chapter examines the patterns in which the Chinese apparel industry is connected to the global fashion industry. I argue that the contradiction between the material connection between U.S. consumers and Chinese producers and the disconnection of meaning of the garments between the two are caused by the uneven power between Chinese suppliers and U.S. corporate buyers on the one hand, and the power imbalance between China and the United States on the other hand. Using a network analysis, this chapter offers a new perspective on globalization from the vantage point of clothing. In what follows, I will discuss the current pattern of garment trade between the United States and China. Then, I will examine the international trade regimes that regulate U.S. textile and clothing

imports. This is to be followed by an analysis of the 2005 trade dispute between the United States and China concerning textile and apparel products and the implications of its resolution. Finally, I will explore what the transnational movement of Chinese made clothing can tell us about globalization. To start, let me explain why and how garments consumed in the United States (and most Western countries) are made elsewhere in the world.

"AN IMPERFECT INDUSTRY"

The apparel industry (as well as the textile industry) has been closely connected to industrialization and modernization since the Industrial Revolution started in Britain in the eighteenth century. Yet, no matter how advanced the technologies have become over the years, one of the key operations of the industry remains the same; it requires human operators sitting behind sewing machines to stitch the garments. Consequently, labor is one of the major components of the cost of the garments, and worse yet, a flexible cost. To reduce costs, the apparel industry in the United States (as well as in Britain and other developed countries) constantly seeks to exploit cheap labor both at home and abroad. The labor-intensive nature of and exploitation of labor in the apparel industry led Joanne Entwistle to call it "an imperfect industry" (2000[a]: 212). The labor-intensive but not capital or technology-intensive nature of the apparel industry also means that the cost or barrier of entry is low, so much so that the apparel industry is frequently a major means for developing countries such as China to kick off their industrialization process and grow their economy. Consequently, the need for the U.S. apparel industry to outsource its labor-intensive manufacturing in order to reduce the cost of labor is met with the need for China (and other developing countries) to develop their economy.

U.S. apparel firms' strategy to outsource their manufacturing operations to developing countries where cheap labor is abundant is a part of the broad shift in the U.S. economy from Fordism or Taylorism, which emphasizes vertical integration and economy of scale, to a mode called post-Fordist flexible accumulation, which emphasizes horizontal integration and economy of scope (Harvey 1989: 45; Kilduff 2005; Piore and Sabel 1984). Though the outsourcing of textile manufacturing from the United States to an international destination has become significantly pronounced since the 1970s, the U.S. textile and apparel manufacturers' search for cheaper labor began within its borders as they relocated their operations from the north to the south (Collins 2003). As U.S. firms' (and Western firms in general) search for cheap labor turned to international destinations, a trend of intensified transnational flow of goods and capital grew, which became known as globalization. As a beneficiary of this trend, China has become a major destination of sourcing for U.S. importers and retailers since the 1990s. However, this shift to China is but a continuation of a pattern of production that started in earlier decades in Japan, then Hong Kong, South Korea, and Taiwan (Bonacich and Waller 1994: 21–2). The dominant pattern in which China (and other East Asian NICs [Newly Industrialized Countries]) manufactures and exports garments to the United States (and the West in general) is called a "full-package" production, in which the Chinese fashion professionals play a significant role. Once again, the example of the NFL jersey can serve as an illustration.

In 2004, Zeng Gang was an international trade agent in Shanghai, representing an international trade firm based in San Francisco, which would receive orders from Reebok, the licensee of the NFL apparel products. Generally speaking, Zeng Gang would receive designs from Reebok, which he would then take to his suppliers in neighboring provinces and ask them to produce some preliminary samples. After the samples were finished, Zeng Gang would send Reebok the finished samples along with their FOB [Free on Board or Freight on Board] prices for confirmation. At that point, based on the qualities and quoted prices of the preliminary samples, Reebok would decide the number of styles and quantity for each style it would order from Zeng Gang's company. Once the decisions were made, Reebok would send Zeng Gang's company the orders along with the letter of credit and feedback on the chosen samples. Upon

receipt, Zeng Gang would go back to his suppliers with the samples and feedback from Reebok and instruct them to make a second batch of revised samples. Then, he would send the revised sample to Reebok for further confirmation (several revisions may take place if necessary). Once the samples—at this stage they are called *dahuoyang*, meaning samples for mass production—were confirmed, Zeng Gang and his suppliers would buy the appropriate fabric and start mass producing the garments. Before and during mass production, Reebok might request to inspect the suppliers' factories to ensure compliance with quality, safety, and labor standards at the facilities, in which case Zeng Gang would accompany Reebok representatives to the factories. Should Reebok identify issues of noncompliance with their standards in a factory, the factory would generally be given a reasonable amount of time to rectify those issues; in rare cases, Reebok could demand that Zeng Gang replace the supplier with a different one. In most cases, the mass production process would proceed as scheduled. Zeng Gang would then send a quality assurance agent, who was professionally trained in fashion design, to the factory for quality control and to ensure that the production schedule would be adhered to. After all the garments were finished and packaged in floor-ready condition, they would be inspected by a quality assurance company designated by Reebok to certify that the quality of the garments met Reebok's requirements. After that, the merchandise would be shipped to the port in Shanghai, and Zeng Gang would facilitate Chinese Customs clearance and a shipping company designated by Reebok would load the goods onto a boat en route to the United States. At that point, Zeng Gang's job would be done, and his company would be able to cash the letter of credit from Reebok (and his suppliers would in turn cash the letter of credit from his company). Yet, once the merchandise arrived in the United States, Reebok would conduct another round of quality inspection. Should the results be inconsistent with the terms set in their agreement, Reebok could request compensation from Zeng Gang's company, which they would generally honor because it would mean the end of business from Reebok if they didn't. In fact, in order to attract more business from

Reebok (because of the large quantities of its orders), Zeng Gang and his suppliers did more than they were asked to do in recent years. They began to offer their own designs (thanks to the work of the anonymous designers working in the factories) and send them to Reebok along with the samples based on Reebok's designs. On two occasions, their designs in fact won orders from Reebok.

The pattern of international trade between foreign corporate buyers and Chinese garment manufacturers through trade agents like Mr. Zeng is perhaps the most common practice in the Chinese clothing export sector.

However, there are also many trades that are conducted without trade agents. For example, some large U.S. buyers (large retailers or branded marketers) that have their own sourcing agents or offices in China usually buy from Chinese manufacturers directly. Similarly, many large Chinese garment manufacturers have their own international trade department, and would also like to cut out the middlemen as much as they can. However, neither party—large U.S. buyers with sourcing capacity in China and large Chinese manufacturers with in-house trading capacity— excludes trade through middlemen, and both have to rely on them as supplements to their existing businesses. For example, although Wal-Mart had its own sourcing center in Shanghai, they ordered from a trading company based in Beijing in 2004. An agent from the Beijing firm, whom I accompanied, went to Zhejiang province in order to locate the right manufacturer to fill the order. With or without trade agents, the services demanded by the U.S. buyers from the Chinese suppliers are largely the same—a full-package production service. A full-package production entails the suppliers being responsible for buying the fabrics and other inputs, making the samples, modifying the samples as needed, mass-producing the garments (which includes many processes), finishing and packaging, clearing Chinese Customs, and delivering floor-ready products to the shipping company. In other words, the Chinese suppliers are not just responsible for production, but also parts of product development, supply chain management, quality control, and logistics.

With respect to product development, there are various levels of participation by Chinese suppliers. At the highest level, foreign buyers would source finished products developed and produced by Chinese suppliers entirely. These foreign buyers tend to be smaller and the products tend to be generic. Though not yet a common trend, some foreign companies hire Chinese designers to develop products and then order them from Chinese manufacturers. At the medium level, Chinese suppliers would develop some products in addition to the product designs that they receive from foreign buyers, as Mr. Zeng Gang and his suppliers did for Reebok. This trend is becoming increasingly common in China today. At the lowest level, the Chinese suppliers would be involved in producing the samples for mass production based on designs or prototypes from the buyers. In the export of garments from China to the United States (and the West in general), the medium and lowest levels of participation by Chinese suppliers in product development are the most common types, especially when the garments are name-brand products. These different types of full-package production provided by Chinese suppliers are very different from the *maquiladora* or assembly production model in Mexico and Latin America, in which U.S. buyers merely outsource the assembly processes to Mexican or Latin American suppliers driven by specific tariff benefits offered by the U.S. government (Blair and Gereffi 2003: 152).

Although Chinese suppliers participate in product development as well as supply chain management, quality control, and logistics in addition to the production of the garments, they are considered original equipment manufacturers (OEMs), whereas their U.S. buyers are the original brand manufacturers (OBMs). In the case of the Steelers jerseys, the Steelers organization, the NFL, and Reebok can all claim varying degrees of "ownership" of the meaningful symbols, i.e., the design patterns and logos/brands. By their ownership of the symbolic components or brands of the jerseys, they—as represented by Reebok—are the OBM. Zeng Gang's suppliers, the Chinese manufacturers of the jerseys, are the OEMs. This distinction between the U.S. buyers and Chinese manufacturers is critical, because it means that the

OBM buyers control the most lucrative components and processes of the garments—the brand, the designs, the distribution, and marketing—whereas the OEM suppliers are in charge of the low-value-added processes of assembly and packaging. Despite the increasing participation by Chinese suppliers in the higher-value-added processes such as product design, supply chain management, and logistics, they cannot charge any premium for the additional services they provide; they are simply providing more services for minimum or no cost to the OBM buyers. For example, Zeng Gang and his suppliers could not demand that Reebok pay for the product development cost of the additional samples they made on their own for Reebok, not to mention demanding profit-sharing for those designs; they bore the cost themselves in the hope of getting more orders from Reebok. This indicates that no matter how much contribution the Chinese suppliers make to the development of the products, they have no claim to the most valuable components of the garments, i.e., the designs and brands (as reflected in my Steelers jersey). Moreover, because they have no access to the U.S. consumers and cannot participate in the marketing of the goods, they cannot map any meaning onto the garments at the site of consumption. The most meaningful components of the garments are firmly in the control of the OBM buyers and completely alienated from the Chinese manufacturers, to whom the garments are simply a means of livelihood. The alienation of the Chinese producers from the "meanings" of the garments they export is one of the key features of the "imperfect" global apparel industry. This imbalance of power between the Chinese suppliers and the U.S. corporate buyers is also reflected in the price of the garments—what the Chinese suppliers charge the U.S. corporate buyers, usually the FOB price, is only in the range of 20 to 25 percent of the U.S. buyers' retail price. That is to say, the U.S. buyers' retail price would have a 400 to 500 percent markup.

The power imbalance between Western corporate buyers (the OBMs) and Chinese producers (the OEMs) is often explained by a global commodity chain perspective (Gereffi and Korzeniewicz 1994). A commodity chain refers to "a network of labor and production processes whose end result is a finished commodity" (Hopkins and Wallerstein 1986: 159). Gereffi and Korzeniewicz's notion of "global commodity chains" (GCCs) extends Hopkins and Wallerstein's idea to a context that is characterized by economic globalization. According to Gereffi and Korzeniewicz, the global apparel industry consists of "buyer-driven commodity chains," by which they mean it is an industry in which "large retailers, brand-named merchandisers, and trading companies play the pivotal roles in setting up decentralized production networks in a variety of exporting countries, typically located in the third world" (1994: 97). By contrast, in a "producer-driven commodity chain," large transnational corporations play the central roles in coordinating production networks (including backward and forward linkages), which is "most characteristic of capital- and technology-intensive commodities such as automobiles, aircraft, semiconductors, and electrical machinery" (1994: 7). By characterizing the global apparel industry as "buyer-driven commodity chains," Gereffi and Korzeniewicz not only point out the interconnections of the global apparel industry, but also highlight the imbalance of power between the OBM buyers and OEM manufacturers.

Though "buyer-driven" and "producer-driven" commodity chains illustrate the different degrees of control over production in the two types of commodity chains, frequently the lead firms in both types of commodity chains are large corporations based in the West. Even though in a buyer-driven commodity chain, such as those in the global apparel industry, the OEM manufacturers in developing countries have a high degree of control over the production processes, they are subordinate to large Western OBM buyers. If an OEM supplier does not yield to the demands of the OBM, the OBM can simply replace it with another OEM supplier. In a capital- or technology-intensive producer-driven chain, a Western lead firm would have even greater control over its suppliers, regardless of whether they are in a developing country or not. The general pattern of the imbalance of power between the lead firms in the West and the suppliers in developing countries in the global commodity chains mirrors the imbalance of power in the global political economy, in which Western countries have far greater influence than the developing countries do. In fact, the global political-economic order shapes the structure and flow in the global commodity chains of clothing, which is especially evident in the international trade treaties and regimes pertaining to textiles and apparel. Though the hidden tag in our clothes that indicates the country of origin is practically meaningless to the U.S. consumers and the OBM buyers, it is critical for the United States to identify and regulate its imports of clothing.

IMPERFECT INTERNATIONAL TRADE REGIMES

Although U.S. corporations (as well as consumers) benefit from outsourcing the production of garments, such acts also result in job losses in the United States, particularly in southern states such as North Carolina, South Carolina, and Georgia, where the textile and apparel industries are concentrated. To prevent job losses in the textile and apparel industries, the U.S. worker and labor unions, plus relevant interest groups, have aligned with local and federal politicians and made the textile and apparel industries one of the industries most protected against imports in the United States.

In the 1950s, the United States instituted protective measures such as the Voluntary Export Restraint (VER) against imports of Japanese cotton products. However, this measure failed because it actually led to a dramatic increase of imports from Hong Kong and Taiwan. In the 1960s, the Kennedy administration tried to remedy the shortcomings of the VER by instituting the Short Term Arrangement (STA) on Cotton Textiles and later the Long Term Arrangement (LTA) on Cotton Textiles, in order to expand the restrictions on imports of cotton products from Japan to other U.S. trading partners. But the STA and the LTA also failed because the textile and apparel industries quickly shifted from cotton products to wool and man-made fibers that were not restricted by those trade regimes. The continued loss of jobs in the U.S. textile and apparel industries led to further expansion of protection. In 1974, the United States successfully negotiated an international treaty called the Multi-fiber Arrangement (MFA), which allowed the United States (as well as Western Europe and Canada) to restrict textile and apparel imports from

developing countries to limited quantities adjustable only on an annual basis. The quota system of the MFA was the most comprehensive and longlasting protective trade regime against U.S. imports of textile and apparel products.

The MFA was an unfair trade agreement from the beginning, and it clearly violated the principles of the General Agreement on Tariffs and Trade (GATT), the dominant international trade regime since World War II, which included most countries in the world as members (socialist countries such as China were not members of the GATT). As acknowledged by the U.S. International Trade Commission, the MFA departed from the GATT specifically in two respects: "(1) they [the quotas] were applied on a country-specific basis, in contradiction of the nondiscrimination obligation (all GATT members be treated equally when any trade measures are applied), and (2) they contradict the general principle of reducing or avoiding absolute quantitative limits" (USITC 2004: 8). Developing countries, whose clothing exports were unfairly restricted by quotas assigned by importing Western countries such as the United States and Britain (Japan and Australia did not adopt the MFA), attempted repeatedly to eliminate the MFA through multilateral negotiations under the framework of the GATT, and such efforts became a major agenda of the "Uruguay Round" (1986–1994). In 1994, an agreement was reached between developing and developed countries under the framework of the GATT that the MFA quota system would be gradually phased out over a ten-year period and completely removed by January 1, 2005. As the GATT was superseded by the World Trade Organization in 1995, the agreement was replaced by the WTO Agreement on Textiles and Clothing (ATC) with the same goal of phasing out the MFA in ten years (Scott 1998). As a member of the WTO (since December 2001), China was supposed to enjoy the full benefit of quota-free export of textile and apparel products to the United States in 2005 when the new trade regime of the ATC went into effect. However, when China negotiated with the United States in 1999 for its accession to the WTO, the United States (the European Union later followed suit) added a safeguard clause specific to textile and apparel products called

Paragraph 242 in the bilateral agreement, which allows the U.S. government to impose temporary quotas on U.S. imports of textile and clothing from China until December 2008 if such imports from China have caused "the existence or threat of market disruption" (Paragraph 242 of The Working Party Report on China's Accession to the WTO). Like the MFA, Paragraph 242, which specifically targets textile and apparel imports from China (but not from other countries), unfairly privileges the United States and violates the fair trade and nondiscrimination principles of the WTO, and contradicts the ATC agreement that aims to eliminate import quotas. Indeed, the contradiction between Paragraph 242 and the ATC became the source of a heated trade dispute between the two countries in 2005.

THE UNITED STATES–CHINA TEXTILE AND APPAREL TRADE DISPUTE IN 2005

By January 2005, under the ATC, all U.S. quotas on the imports of textile and clothing products were eliminated, which resulted in a dramatic surge of U.S. imports of textile and apparel products from China. Several product categories increased over 100 or even 1000 percent from a year earlier. The surge was caused in part by the rising U.S. demand for Chinese textile and apparel products and in part by the sudden elimination of all quotas, compounded by the fact that the U.S. government withheld quota restrictions on the majority of the product categories until the end of 2004 rather than lifting them gradually as they had agreed to in the 1994 GATT agreement (US GAO 2005: 10). Obviously, China was unable to demand that the United States live up to its responsibility under the agreement either. Nevertheless, the surge of U.S. imports of Chinese textile and clothing was reported widely by the U.S. media as a "flood" and "threat" (e.g., Barboza and Becker 2005). On April 6, 2005, seven petitions were filed by American Manufacturing Trade Action Coalition (AMTAC), National Council of Textile Organizations (NCTO), National Textile Association (NTA), and the labor union UNITE HERE, requesting the U.S. government to take safeguard actions against the importation of seven categories of Chinese textile and clothing products. On May 13, the Committee for the Implementation of Textile Agreements (CITA) of the U.S. Department of Commerce invoked Paragraph 242 and initiated threat-based safeguard quotas against the importation of three categories of textile and clothing products of Chinese origin. Five days later, CITA decided to impose safeguard quotas limiting the importation of four more categories of Chinese-made textile and clothing products, citing Paragraph 242 (http://otexa. ita.doc.gov). Since then, a lengthy and heated textile and apparel trade dispute has broken out between the United States and China.

Soon after the U.S. decision on limiting Chinese textile and apparel imports, the two governments followed the procedure under the WTO agreement and began consultation and negotiation. While the U.S. government cited Paragraph 242 in the bilateral agreement to justify its decisions, the Chinese government invoked its rights as a member of the WTO and the quota-free trade agreement of the ATC that both sides signed as members of the WTO. The two sides were so adamant in their positions that it took eight rounds of consultation and negotiation for the two governments to finally reach a resolution, far exceeding the three-month period of consultation stipulated in Paragraph 242. The negotiation process took so long that some categories of Chinese products had already exceeded the limits of the quotas set by the safeguard measures and were subsequently withheld by U.S. Customs before the bilateral agreement was reached. At the same time, however, U.S. Customs did not reject entry of those over-quota goods outright, as the U.S. government did not declare the safeguard measures permanent and continued to negotiate with the Chinese government even after the three-month consultation period ended. On November 8, 2005, both sides reached a broad-based compromise agreement, the terms of which included: China to accept quotas on 34 categories of textile and apparel products exporting to the United States from 2005 through 2008, much broader than the existing 19 product categories under temporary safeguard restrictions; and the United States to raise the percentage of annual increase of its importation of the Chinese textile and apparel products in those categories from 7.5 percent (as stipulated in Paragraph 242) to between 10 and 17 percent from 2005 through the end of 2008 (when all the quotas on Chinese textile and clothing imports would be finally lifted). The United States also agreed to allow entry of the Chinese-made products withheld by the U.S. Customs due to overage of the quota limits, with an understanding that the quantity exceeding the new annual quota limits would be half "subsidized" by the United States, with the other half counted toward the quotas of those product categories for the following year.

Similar to previous protectionist trade regimes, the new agreement between the United States and China is far from a fair trade agreement. Above all, the privilege of the United States is protected by Paragraph 242, and the final bilateral agreement is by and large an enforcement of Paragraph 242, albeit with more generous quotas. Just as the U.S. OBM buyers have the upper hand over Chinese OEM suppliers, the United States clearly has the upper hand over China in the trade agreement, which may be attributable to the fact that the United States is buying more from China than the other way around.

However, the fact that the United States has the upper hand does not explain why it exercises that power. Evidently, it is not in everyone's interests to limit clothing imports from China because the U.S. quotas on Chinese-made garments become added costs to the garments. The U.S. corporate buyers (importers, retailers, and branded marketers) would be better off without the extra costs of the quotas, and so would the U.S. consumers. Why, then, were the "voices" of the U.S. corporate buyers and consumers, let alone those of the Chinese suppliers, not "heard" by the U.S. government? Apparently, the global apparel chains do not just involve Chinese suppliers, the U.S. corporate buyers and consumers, but also other stakeholders, including domestically based manufacturers and workers in the United States (as well as manufacturers in other developing countries). It was their voices that were heard loud and clear by the U.S. government. To understand why the U.S. government adopted the protectionist policies it did, we have to examine the different positions and interests within the U.S. textile and apparel industries, and how these diverse interests are played out in U.S. politics.

IMPLICATIONS FOR CHINESE SUPPLIERS

The power imbalance between the United States and China, as reflected in the trade regime, and in particular the bilateral trade agreement in 2005, had profound implications for Chinese garment manufacturers and trade agents. As a whole, they are highly diverse and unorganized, and other than calling on the Chinese government for help, there was little they could do to influence U.S. trade policies. The nearly six-month trade dispute between China and the United States in 2005 was especially long for them. Representing their interests as well as the interests of the roughly 19 million workers employed in the Chinese textile and apparel industries, the Chinese government negotiated hard with its U.S. counterpart in the bilateral trade dispute in 2005. In the end, the Chinese government gave in to U.S. pressure and signed the new agreement that was largely favorable to the United States in exchange for a stable trade environment. In many ways, however, the resolution did not come as a surprise. First of all, the existence of the discriminatory clause of Paragraph 242 against China essentially framed the resolution. Second, in terms of trade with the United States, China was and is a net exporter to the United States. There were simply not enough bargaining chips at the disposal of the Chinese government. Third, aside from the interests in the textile and apparel industries, China also received pressure from the United States on other issues such as intellectual property rights and currency appreciation. The Chinese government had to balance the interests of the textile and apparel industries with the other interests. Moreover, the way in which the 2005 Sino-U.S. trade dispute was resolved should not be taken as an isolated incident; on the contrary, it reflects a broad pattern in the bilateral relationship in which the United States generally sets the terms. In the final analysis, the Sino-U.S. trade dispute in 2005 serves as a reminder that the United States remains the dominant power in the global political economy, which circumscribes the international trade in clothing.

Having no hope of getting help from the Chinese government, Chinese manufacturers and exporters had to deal with the fallout from the trade dispute on their own. Many of them were afraid to take new orders from the United States for fear of heavy losses during the prolonged negotiation period between the U.S. and Chinese governments. For those who did, they tried to beat others to the "finish line," i.e., U.S. Customs, to ensure that their goods would be there before the quota limits were reached. To do so, many of them did the otherwise unimaginable—they shipped their "cheap" products in the safeguarded categories by air instead of by sea, bearing the hefty shipping costs in order to avoid potentially even bigger losses (*Nanfang Daily*, 07/04/05). Mr. Zeng Gang, the trader of my Steelers jersey, shipped the order of the NFL jerseys when the quota of that category was over 90 percent filled in the fall of 2005. He was worried sick and prayed for ten days that his shipment would not be rejected by U.S. Customs.

Evidently, what the Steelers jerseys mean for Zeng Gang and his suppliers—a means of livelihood and a source of worry—has no bearing on the ways in which U.S. consumers use the garments. They are unable to map any symbolic meaning onto the garments at the site of consumption in the United States (or other Western countries) because of the uneven power between them and the OBM buyers. At the same time, the export of the garments, on which the Chinese suppliers' livelihood is dependent, is structured and regulated by international trade regimes that are shaped by the power imbalance between China and the United States. These characteristics of the export of garments from China to the United States support my argument that clothing offers a unique perspective on globalization.

CONCLUSION

In this chapter, I focused on the global connections of the Chinese clothing industry by looking at the exportation of Chinese-made garments to the United States. The export of Chinese-made garments illustrates the global connections of the Chinese apparel industry. At the same time, the meanings of the garments as constructed by U.S. consumers, like that of my Steelers shirt, were disconnected from the Chinese producers. I argue that the apparent contradiction inherent in the global flow of Chinese-made garments is caused by Western OBM buyers' control over Chinese OEM suppliers on the one hand and the imbalance of power between the United States and China on the other hand. The two types of power are layered over the Chinese-made garments. While the power of the OBMs renders the "made in China" tag invisible, the power of the state makes its existence essential to regulate the global movement of the garments. Although this chapter only focused on the export of Chinese-made garments to the United States, this pattern of trade resulting from the workings of these two types of power can be identified in the exports of Chinese garments to other Western countries as well.

I will conclude this chapter with a current development in the apparel industry in Shanghai. As the temporary quotas on apparel imports from China ended in the United States and the EU in 2008, Chinese-made garments are now traded in a quota-free environment. However, this does not mean that the Chinese OEM suppliers will no longer face any restrictions on their exports to the United States or the EU. The United States could use product-specific safeguard measures against Chinese imports until 2013 according to its WTO agreement with China (the same privilege applies to other WTO members including the EU). In addition, the United States could use other instruments such as anti-dumping duties against the surge of Chinese imports. Should the United States declare China as a currency manipulator, then the United States could target imports from China with more tariffs. All these pose external risks to Chinese manufacturers and exporters. In addition, there are also internal factors that would dampen the prospects for Chinese manufacturers and exporters, chief among which are the rapid appreciation of Chinese currency against the dollar and the euro and rising labor and land costs. In the past few years, Mr. Zeng Gang moved his office three times due to the rising cost of rent, from downtown to a suburban district, and then to a suburban county in Shanghai. As the export business has become increasingly sandwiched by falling demand and rising costs, Mr. Zeng opened a factory and became a true OEM supplier not just for international corporate buyers, but also for the domestic name-brand companies.

Though formal businesses like Mr. Zeng's remain the mainstream in the Chinese apparel industry, a new and disturbing trend has emerged in Shanghai. Experienced workers would quit their jobs and start their own underground, informal, and "homework" style businesses as subcontractors, repeating what happened in the United States and Great Britain in earlier decades (e.g., Bao 2001; Phizacklea 1990). The "imperfect" apparel industry is poised to become even more sinister in China.

38

IN PATAGONIA (CLOTHING):
A complicated greenness

Sharon J. Hepburn

I first looked through a Patagonia catalog in 1992, while doing anthropological fieldwork on tourism in Nepal. I prefer leisurely strolls to extreme sports, and summed up my first experience perusing the catalog as seeing images of "people doing incredibly stupid things, in incredibly expensive clothing." Nonetheless, I have since come to appreciate the clothing, and—like many others—have sought out the new catalog each season at my local outdoor store. They receive 500 copies of each season's catalog, and those do not last long: "We contact a few customers, then word gets out and they are gone," the store manager told me. That is remarkable for a city of 70,000 people (many unemployed), where most retail chains have closed over the past two decades, and where there is neither mountain nor surf in sight. The catalog itself is a desirable item, as the company found when they became concerned about the environmental impact of its production. A Patagonia Vice President of world retail told me that the company have encouraged "Patagoniacs" to return the catalogs for recycling, offering one dollar off a purchase for each returned. "But," he said "what we didn't realize is that people want to keep them." I am surprised at their surprise, because indeed, people do keep them. I lost my own collection of forty or so during an office move, but had no trouble locating a collection to work from: a friend lent me his collection of issues going back to 1988, which he hauled over in a box weighing over 10 kilos. For those who want more, in 1999 Patagonia published a coffee table book, *Patagonia:*

Notes from the Field (Gallagher 1999), of representative photos and "field reports" (see below), and a second book in 2010 called *Unexpected: 30 Years of Patagonia Catalogue Photography* (Sievert and Ridgeway 2010), which displays 100 photos selected from the 60,000 or so submitted for consideration each year (over the past decade at least).

The appeal and messages of the catalog are at the heart of the conundrums the company and consumers face. Patagonia explains (advertises?) their philosophy of minimal consumption and environmental protection in the catalog, which is styled such that "it's hard to tell if a catalog from Patagonia is magazine or a booklet selling merchandise" (Diamond 2005). Yvon Chouinard, cofounder of the company, feels the catalog is the company's "bible for each selling season" and is crucial as a vehicle "to share and encourage a particular philosophy of life, of what undergirds the image" (2005: 150). The environmental philosophy is presented alongside gripping narratives and stunning photos that often depict a view of nature comparable to that of the sublime aesthetic in Western literature and art, in which nature incites delicious fear, in which humans are tested, consoled, and experience transcendence. According to Chouinard, most people trying to describe a Patagonia catalog "start with the photographs" which use "Brilliant clarity and color" to convey "a boundless sense of nature and adventure … with … humans … a small detail in the face of immense nature" (1999: 11). Chouinard named the company for

Adapted from Sharon J. Hepburn, "In Patagonia (Clothing): A Complicated Greenness," *Fashion Theory* 17, no. 5 (2013): 623–45.

the place at the south end of South America, a place, he says, with a name which brings up "romantic visions of glaciers tumbling into fjords, jagged windswept peaks" (2005: 38) and he thought it a suitable name to attach to clothing designed to protect people in extreme sports in those extreme physical conditions, to protect people who envision themselves as small in—but transformed by—immense nature. The presentation of these two discourses—of conserving nature through minimal, responsible consumption, and of a particular view of nature and human experience—take up about 45 percent of the catalog space, and juxtaposing this to the goods for sale has a paradoxical effect: it increases consumption of goods produced by a company that asks us to reconsider consumption. Chouinard acknowledges that when this content is decreased to show more product, sales actually drop. We will return to this point at the end.

My task here is to chart the path of Patagonia to their present point, and to say that despite their protestations, they produce ecofashion, even "slow" fashion (after Clark 2008). They provide (relatively) sustainably produced clothing that does what fashion in general does: it lets a person express their style and taste in dress, and express aspects of how they situate themselves within discourses such as those of gender, class, taste, and various social issues. In this case what people wearing Patagonia clothing—the people moved by the popular catalog—are at least in part expressing are values regarding nature, to be sustained, but also as a place of transformation. Perlman (1987: 53) quotes Chouinard telling his corporate colleagues in 1986, "I'll tell you why people buy Patagonia clothing—to show off," and that whoever their actual customer may be, Chouinard says, "What we are very carefully controlling is who our customers *imagine* our customers to be." Reading that it could be imagined Patagonia applies generous amounts of "greenwash." But here in fact is a mixture of true intent, business acumen, and CEO swagger. For this article I will assume Patagonia's genuine intent to carry out responsible capitalism, but in any case, intent is not the only issue here. We—or the Patagonia company, or any genuinely intentioned eco-business—are left with the paradox that is perhaps unavoidable in an economy in which what Marx

([1867] 2007) called "enigmatic" or "mystical" quality (i.e. cultural meaning) is added to the functional value of products, as it is in capitalist economies, and including during times when sustainable production is an economic as well as ethical imperative (Beard 2008: 449).

SPORTSWEAR FOR UNCOMMON—NOT FASHIONABLE—PEOPLE

Patagonia is not interested in "fashion" but they explicitly insist their product be of high quality, and implicitly, increasingly, want it to look good, and not be "ordinary." And they do claim their ability "to make function and technical integrity look way cool" (2001 Holiday catalog: 16). In the early 1980s they moved away from the norm of the industry by making clothes in colors other than the rust, tan, or forest green that dominated the outdoor clothing industry. Says Chouinard, "we drenched the Patagonia line in vivid color … teal, French red, mango, seafoam, and iced mocha," moving the "still rugged" clothing from "bland-looking to blasphemous" (2005: 54). It was this bold coloring, not just the technical clothing line, that set the company on the path to its present fortunes. Chouinard admits that the new profits were driven by "fashion consumers" as well as the outdoor community. He knew that growth was mostly from the "non-technical" part of the line, and admits that he "worried that our image might become too soft and sports-wear oriented" (Chouinard 2005: 66). This worry was indirectly conveyed to catalog readers through the narratives, which came to be called "field reports," narratives not about the clothes for sale, but about what you did in them, and why, and the ethical issues of production. These field reports continue to be a primary vehicle through which the company consciously weaves and reweaves of the threads of their self-image and creed, which consumers are implicitly welcomed to participate in as they read. In a catalog produced in 1981, when the new "blasphemous" colors were introduced, a production manager Roger McDivitt wrote of his consternation when he got a telex from a "women's sportswear buyer … (who) … wanted to know if we would make the

Stand Up Shorts in Women's sizing in a 'non-ugly' color." McDivitt tells the reader that felt like he had been "cold-cocked" because "What the hell was sports-wear" and laments that his "equipment for alpinists' world was in pastel jeopardy" (Chouinard 2005: 36).

Thus, while moving towards providing for the desires of a broader clientele, who could sustain the company, Patagonia reminds the reader that they would really rather not be doing that. And the trends in the catalog photos show an interesting progression in attitudes towards customers, with ordinary folks (most of the clientele) becoming less common, and people having transformative experiences in vast, dangerous, humbling nature becoming more common. The earlier catalogs had more ordinary people doing ordinary things—the *real* core customer perhaps—riding horseback, gardening, tending children, or standing around with friends. The early catalogs point to nature, and adventure could be had in many ways, and found in many places, not just in wild, untamed wilderness. An early catalog encourages the reader to wave if they see a guy wearing the Patagonia (bomber-style, non-technical) jacket while he is working a garbage truck, because "he is one of us." One could, back then, do common things yet still be someone who was "one of us" uncommon people.

Through the 1990s the catalogs increasingly demonstrate a different aesthetic and conception of nature. This decision to stress some sports (extreme sports) and ways of being in nature (and not others) was a conscious strategy. For example, in directing the trajectory of the company's image, Chouinard continues the same attitude that had him separate clothes from his climbing equipment company: he did not want to soften the image. He says they could not use images of "sallow-skinned backpackers trudging over the Appalachian Trail" because "That's too safe" (Chouinard 2005: 152). Instead, the field reports make clear what kind of people they are writing about, and these are not people collecting garbage, or walking the Appalachian Trail. For example, in writing about approaches to part of the Colorado River dam, Ellen Meloy (1999: 85) presents herself and her Navajo companions (marked by sweat and dust and toil) as

being unlike the tourists who took the easy way to a destination (who look tidy and refreshed).

When developing a line of women's water-sport clothing, the idea of a bikini being associated with Patagonia was too dissonant for Chouinard, and so he founded the offshoot company "Water Girl USA" to accommodate hapless females who want good-looking, functional clothes to cover and protect themselves with when doing water sports (Chouinard 2005: 149). In case the selective presentation and labeling is not enough, Patagonia catalog authors regularly, explicitly, tell the reader that using these clothes for non-extreme activities is something they are, indulgently, turning a blind eye to. The narrator of the 2004 Spring catalog (p. 3), for example, tells the reader that they know some people wear Patagonia climbing clothes for things other than rock climbing, which is a "sacred" sport. They allow that if you are using them for say, yoga, "Well, fine," but if it is going further adrift, like for Pilates, then "We don't want to know."

PATAGONIA SPORTSWEAR TODAY: ELEGANCE AND SEX-FLEECE

Patagonia sportswear today is presumably for those times you are not hanging in mid-air in immense nature, when you are not traveling in "extreme" destinations, or otherwise not in situations other—ordinary—people would want to escape from. The clothes are, presumably, for when you are working to sustain your "dirtbag" life, or for when you (like me, perhaps) simply need to be ready for the conditions you might face when, say, carrying your laptop down to a coffee shop (for which Patagonia now has numerous options, including a US$69 "barista tote," in three colors). And the sportswear is, the 2001 Spring catalog advises, for when you have "had enough haute couture."

Yet, the range has moved far beyond pastel toilet seat cover jackets. And the authors of the catalog do not shy away from using words like "elegant" and "classy" when describing a man's hemp shirt (2001 Spring catalog: 7). They entice with the idea of a sex-like experience with a Micro D-Luxe fleece pullover, which they call "the *Kama Sutra* of microdenier fleece" (1997 Winter catalog: 26), and ask you to imagine "the softest thing you can think of … don't be shy, you know … what it is … and imagine it against your skin" (1999 Fall catalog: 76) as it "caresses the senses" (2001 Holiday catalog: 32). Nor do the catalog authors ignore that people want to look good, and so the catalog reader is reassured, for example, that "You'll like the body-slimming drape of these … shorts" (2001 Spring catalog: 34), and that a work shirt is "so becoming you'll feel better the minute you put it on" (2001 Holiday catalog: 35), and that though you wear "Double Duty" durable canvas pants, they have a "sexy" low rise (2001 Holiday catalog: 37).

Take, for example, the 3-in-1 Tres Jacket that I purchased myself (at a 75 percent off end-of-season sale). This jacket is a sartorial world away from eco-dress-ish, chunky, box-quilted down jackets, toilet seat covers, or Scottish cagoules. The outer shell is "waterproof/breathable," being made of the "technical" H2No fabric with Deluge DWR (durable water repellent) finish. The underarm zips are certainly useful, as is the snap-on hood, the "high, zip-through stand-up collar that opens flat for venting," and the "zippered and secure" welted hand-warmer pockets to hold my "essentials." And there are nice comfort details like soft fabric at the chin so that I do not feel the abrasion of the zip or technical fabric, and soft lining in the hood, which looks to me like the "*Kama Sutra* fleece" noted above, and yes, it feels nice on the skin. There are princess seams back and front "for contouring." The reversible zip-in 600-fill premium European goose-down liner, which can also be worn alone as a vest, is beautiful. The vest's soft but highly durable fabric is all-recycled polyester, but looks and feels like silk. One side has (flattering) chevron-shaped quilting, and the reverse side has delicate pintucks and shirring (such as one normally sees on a blouse, or lingerie) on the front and back at waist level, "for feminine fit and flair." Like most Patagonia garments, it is impeccably stylish in a particular kind of way. To me it is beautifully designed, functional, and appears to be made to rigorous quality standards, and I like that it is (I'm told) ethically "sound." Patagonia would say this is not "fashion," but I hardly mind.

DRESSED FOR SUBLIME EXPERIENCES

The narratives and photos in the catalogs, those bibles for each season, create an image of what Patagonia would have you doing: you would be engaging in extreme sports, in vast nature, or preserving that nature, and—either way—having transformative experiences. The images and narratives, and the affect they produce have cultural roots in the sublime aesthetic, prominent in literature and art of the Victorian period in particular. In this, nature was not pretty and beautiful, nor the source of physical sustenance; instead, nature was immense, fearful, even ugly. Nature is where one could be tested through struggle, and experience a transcendence of mere daily existence, in the "aesthetics of the infinite" (Nicolson 1959). The experience of the sublime affects the mind "with a sense of overwhelming grandeur or irresistible power" (*The Oxford English Dictionary*, http://www.oed.com/). It is a "rapturous terror," a "delectable horror," a "delicious shudder" (Bangs 2008), an "agreeable kind of horror" (Addison 1743: 300), an experience of dangerous, awesome power, which is relished for itself, and for what it does to you. Victorian novelist Mary Shelley in *Frankenstein*, for example, tells how the "sublime and magnificent scenes" of the Alps "elevated me from all littleness of feeling" and "subdued and tran-quilized" grief (Shelley 1823: 197). Poet Elizabeth Barrett Browning delights in the scenery of the Alps, but in some places for her "it was like standing in the presence of God when He is terrible … I think I never saw the sublime before" (Browning 1851, cited in Clubbe and Giddey 1982: 19). Poet Thomas Gray talks about the "sacred terror" and "severe delight" of the Alps in his 1739 journey (Nicolson 1959: 19). Travel and other writing about Patagonia (the place) over the past few centuries echo these themes (Nouzeilles 1999; Penaloza 2004). In his cultural history of Patagonia (the place) Moss writes that this is "the perfect landscape of the imagination: faraway, without form and void, but crisscrossed by storylines and legendary pathways." He says that these storylines, from Darwin though Chatwin and beyond, create "the world's poetic refuge, the chthonic hope for all who are forced to live in cramped, man-made spaces" (Moss 2008: 283), and the name evokes "a degree of risk or difficulty, a notion of being somewhere on the periphery of modern communications" (Moss 2008: 253), a place where modern man can find redemption in awe and fear inspiring nature. The name (of the place) Patagonia "brings to mind," says Chouinard (noted above), what is in fact the landscape of the sublime, including "romantic visions of glaciers tumbling into fjords, jagged windswept peaks" (2001 Holiday catalog: 23) and so he named his clothing company after it.

The Patagonia catalog carried this sublime aesthetic through to the present in their advocacy of the experience of fear and bliss, in intense measure, as a road to transformation. Looking at the dominant themes of the images of the catalog, supported by narratives, we see/read about man (indeed, mostly *man*) pitted against immense nature, fearful, tested, and surviving transformed, removed from mundane life and transported to some other realm.

Chouinard puts this experience of self-testing through the risk of death at the forefront of the narrative he gives of his own life in extreme sports. In his film *180 Degrees South, Conquerors of the Useless* (Malloy 2010) he describes "dirtbags" such as himself who live for their sports, and who thereby, hopefully, become better people. This includes, and perhaps requires, risking death. He describes his own routes up the face of El Cap in the 1960s, which were "over-hang the whole way … don't know if you could get down if you got stuck." It was, he says, like "guys who ride the big waves," you "could just die," that the "fear of the unknown is the greatest fear of all … but we just went for it." He mocks people who are escorted up Everest for US$80,000, "CEOs and plastic surgeons" who even get their "sleeping bag laid out with a chocolate on top," because "the whole purpose of climbing something like Everest is to effect some kind of spiritual and physical gain, but if you compromise the process you're an asshole when you start and an asshole when you get back." The compromiser has relative ease and relies on others; a true sportsman, a Patagoniac, tests themselves in extreme situations in nature, faces fear with self-reliance, and emerges spiritually and physically transformed.

These themes are repeated in the field report narratives in the catalogs, juxtaposed to either the goods for sale, or the "awe-inspiring" photos of small man in immense nature. Barry Blanchard (1998 Fall catalog: 5), for example, describes "freaking out" and feeling "impend-ing doom" as he finds himself in the "fully psycho" act of hanging in air off an ice wall, and relates how he saved himself and named the route "Burning in Water, Drowning in Flame," feeling good as he had "personal evolution" that day through this unexpected but welcomed challenge, and his survival of risk in nature. Jonathan Copp (2005 Winter catalog 2005: 32) describes a climb that extended into the night in difficult conditions, in which he was himself "entombed in animal fear" and sees his friends and notices "a hell-bent look in their eyes, like smoldering embers" when they realize their predicament, and that "the real suffering had only just begun." Of course, they survived, renewed and transformed. Adam Chamberlain (2003 Winter catalog: 2) talks of "bodies pushed way past exertion" to feel what, he says, you feel in the mountains, "aware, humble, joyous:" bodies challenged in nature, for sublime experience.

John Long (2010 Spring catalog: 3) describes being "tied to a stake half a mile up a rock face, too late to go down with the only crack dead-ended just ahead" and in this dire situation in nature he notes, "we could not escape ourselves," and they were "Shriveled with fear … only when we surrendered to the hateful gale … and the whole glimmering catastrophe could we experience the freedom we had sought all along … we were fashioned out of mud and hail." Long describes this transformation through being small man suffering against nature, as "chasing an age-old dream" of humanity to go to a "fantastic elsewhere" in nature. That fantastic elsewhere would be within the sublime experience, born of fear, and awe of nature. Sarah Marlarey (1999: 74), a rare female field report author, describes her transformation from blossom-adorned bride to "brown, dirtbag climber." She is scared during an unforeseen climb in the dark, yet, though "Numb, exhausted, shorn" she is "pure—an animal using old instincts … (as she kicks out) … blindly against the near vertical gully of rock and ice." In this time of fear and danger, she notices the arc of stars moving in the clear night sky, "so fast it's almost dizzying" and—struck by the sublime—she is "no longer afraid."

ENVIRONMENTAL POLICIES AND PRACTICES

Patagonia is well known for its commitment to wilderness conservation and sustainable practices. The company reviews their policies at all levels—from offices, to cafeterias, to factories—to assess and minimize environmental impact. Employees can have two months away from work with pay each year to do an internship related to the environmental ideals of the company (Esposito 2009: 203; Haas and Hartman 1995; McSpirit 1998). There is no doubt that the company works far beyond what Simon and Alagoma refer to as the "truncated notions of environmental citizenship" (2013: 325) in government educational programs such as Leave No Trace: Patagonia considers not only the "traces" left in rock faces and campsites, but also the traces left in the environment by the production and consumption cycle. Doug Tompkins, a one-time partner of Chouinard (and founder of Esprit clothing, and North Face outdoor clothing), and his wife used most of their profits to buy up wilderness in Patagonia (the place, not the company), which they are donating to the Chilean government and people to create nature sanctuaries (Robbins 2011). One percent of all Patagonia sales, or profits (whichever is higher) go to environmental projects.

Well in advance of most other companies, Patagonia calculated the environmental impact of producing the fabrics they used (Hartman and Haas 1995; Hartmann 2008). Synchilla, the fleece they have been making since 1985 came out on top, being made entirely from recycled bottles these days. They found cotton to be the most polluting, as were most "natural" source textiles, as is often the case (Scaturro 2008: 470). In response, Patagonia started to use only organic cotton, absorbing a large portion of the extra cost. These tales of corporate practice and commitment are told in the catalog, alongside "field reports." Sometimes they *are* the field report. And the consumer reading the catalog reads these on pages opposite superbly beautiful and evocative photographs of small man in immense nature, and turning the page she can find the Patagonia products for sale.

DILEMMAS OF DREAMS, DESIRE, AND DEMAND

Thomas (2008: 533) explains the notion of "greenwash": just as white-wash covers up things we would rather not see, greenwash is a marketing ploy, to be or to profess to be green, simply because it sells and some consumers want greenness, or want to be seen to be wanting it. Patagonia is known as a company that aims to use sustainable practices. Say Conley and Freidenwald-Fishman in *Marketing That Matters*, Patagonia's openness about the pollution they cause "created a high level of trust among its employees and managers" (2006: 177) and presumably among customers too. In *Companies with a Conscience* (1994), Scott and Rothman include Patagonia as one of the twelve companies examined that "make a difference." Whether or not Patagonia's narratives are greenwash, it is hard to deny that greenness helps sell their product, and perhaps that, as Corbett argues more pointedly, the narratives actually help "work around any guilt related to consumerism" while encouraging people to pile up more of the "latest and greatest outdoor stuff" (2006: 111). And they can feel fashionable while they do that, as green can indeed be "the New Black" (Prothero[, McDonagh, and Dobscha] 2010; Winge 2008).

But it is—I argue now—a double greenness: it is not only the greenness of production processes to protect nature, but also greenness as a more ethereal, aesthetic quality with parallels in Western literary discourses, that links the wearer with images of the sublime *in* nature, and the sublime experience *of* nature. But the irony is that this very aesthetic, at the heart of how Patagonia displays their goods in the catalog, quite likely, very likely, inspires people to buy the product, whether for doing extreme sport, or going to the coffee shop. As Chouinard intended, who the catalog reader believes their fellow customer is, and what they represent, encourages a feeling of affinity—or desired affinity—that can inspire a purchase.

While the product is made in an environmentally conscientious way, it is still a product being bought, which had to be made, and it took resources to do so. And we must ask—as Patagonia asks us to—was that purchase necessary?

Returning to my Tres Jacket described above, for example, I have a few questions to ask of myself, and the company with the "cleanest line" policy. This is "non-technical" clothing (it is not to climb a rock face in, after all) that nonetheless benefits from the technology of technical clothing. Looking at it, it is hard to say "this is necessary, and it's the cleanest line for the purpose." That is, for my purposes.

The question I would ask, adopting the company's ethos, is "is this the cleanest line for what I do and need?" and "do I really need all that?" Am I traveling in Siberia, yet must still look smart for the unexpected invitation to an embassy dinner? Must I look good but still be ready for whatever happens should I make a traverse of the frozen food aisle at the supermarket? That last line may seem frivolous and mocking, but Patagonia evokes a similar range of activity. And so I am asking, does my jacket need to be, as a different jacket was described, "as functional on a mixed route as in a movie line" (1998 Fall catalog: 15)? The bigger question is how many people do actually need all that? Not many, I would say. And even much (or all) of the "technical" clothing can be worn as non-athletic wear, as the maligned sportswear, and it often is. Even though the clothing might be the cleanest line for the extreme sports person, what does that phrase mean, if the garment provides far more than what the average purchaser needs? What worth or need if, as one Patagonia executive admits in an interview, the average customer, like me, "might not be pushing the product to the edge" (Lenson 1994: 4).

And then the question comes, what else am I—and 1,000s of others—buying here? The answer should be clear by now, but Chouinard himself tells us the answer. The catalog yields more sales when there is a particular balance of text, photo, and product. If the text and dramatic images of nature and extreme sportsmen falls away, "ironically" the sales drop. Although the opposite of what Chouinard claims to want, this juxtaposition with the full knowledge of what proportions increase sales, facilitates creating "addiction" to the product, says Todor, giving Patagonia's strategy as an example of an effective technique to get customers "hooked" on your product (Todor 2007: 99). So it is safe to say that (some, many, or all) people are buying what is conveyed in the images/writing when they buy their Patagonia clothing.

Or, put another way, if they buy more when there are more of the images/writing, then the latter spurs them on to buy: it creates desire for something, not just the goods for sale, but those things linked imaginatively with them, produced just for the kind of person who writes or the person/place depicted in the field reports.

I am not saying anything is, necessarily, intentional "greenwash" here. My point is that a conundrum is almost unavoidable in a capitalist, consumer society. The very effort to educate consumers, demonizing excess consumption, can, when tied to an ideal and an attractive product, encourage people to buy things they otherwise would not. If people are to buy things beyond what they absolutely need, they are buying the material object, but also the magical property of the commodity. When that product is imbued with the mana of "eco-consciousness," "saving wilderness," and "transcendence in nature," as well as "the kind of thing a fit, adventurous and ethical person would wear," then the company is caught—in a phrase from the decade the company was born in—in a catch 22.

At this time, Schumacher's (1973) phrase and title "small is beautiful" became a widely used term and book in thinking about what work, production, and business should be, and the *Whole Earth Catalog* guided the spirit of consumption for some of the new reflexive eco-conscious consumers (Binkley 2003). Other businesses founded in the same era, such as The Body Shop, were also motivated to curb consumer excess, and the founders of such businesses were—like Chouinard and friends—in some way finding a way to make a living while "dropping out." Clothing linked to this counterculture episteme of the 1970s, such as tie-dye shirts and rope sandals ("eco dress," after Winge 2008: 512) gave a visual cue to a worldview, of "naturalness," and caring about "the ecology" (Welters 2008), but the garments were not linked to any particular function except cover. In contrast, the early sartorial choices of climbers were old shirts from thrift stores, etc., and the products Chouinard later sold to replace or supplement them were tied to a different passion, the passion for climbing. The early Chouinard products made no visual statement about ecology in general, and certainly a jacket made of fabric intended for a toilet seat cover—while it could say "use what's available, be frugal"—it also did not scream "minimalism" or "protect the earth," or "wear natural fabrics." In fact the fabric radiated fakeness, but if it were read as a statement, it would be read as some sort of empathy with the outdoor activities, of being in nature, or of looking like you were prepared to be there, whether or not you ever were. The early Patagonia company stayed close to the values of "use what's necessary," in clothes and other things, but do not waste your time or money on pointless things. But at that time they had no overtly expressed concern with ecological issues as such. Through the early 1990s until the present, as explained above, Patagonia increasingly wove this concern with the environment into their production practices and catalog narratives. Joining with the earlier indexing of the clothing with "being in nature," Patagonia effected what I am here calling a double greenness, that of "green" practices, combined with a particular vision of wilderness, these two linked by a re-creation (through images and narratives) of a sublime mythology with a few centuries of literary and artistic precedents.

Patagonia has green practices, but if these (combined with actual need) at times (or often) fail to justify the purchase, there is the image or idea of greenness, wilderness, and personal transcendence within it—this, the "magic" of this particular commodity—to sell it. And the magic the clothing at least potentially does—for people who are insiders, unique, uncommon—is that it reaffirms for them, and projects to others in the know, an affinity with certain ideals, of lifestyle, linked with a vision of nature. It goes beyond save the planet, and save humanity, so that we can survive and not wipe out the very things we need to survive; it goes beyond the image of nature as fragile and in danger of destruction; it calls to nature as a source of redemption, as an antidote to society, and a place of spiritual transformation.

This double greenness sells Patagonia clothing, but in doing so it becomes what I would call a *complicated* greenness. If people buy the clothes pictured in juxtaposition to the two discourses of greenness, then these are at least in some part selling them, and therein lie the seeds of the contradiction, and thus, complication. Winge (2008) argues that ecofashion allows people to wear clothing that is ethical while still

being able to express their style and taste. Patagonia—despite its protestations—is indeed ecofashion: it is "ethical" but allows people to express style, taste, and ethical commitments, or even allows people to create their image as a person having those commitments, whether or not they do. As such, like any other item of clothing— whether dress or fashion—Patagonia clothing is a medium to mark particular kinds of taste tied to class and other social markers.

In his 2012 book *The Responsible Company: What We've Learned from Patagonia's First 40 Years*, Chouinard (and Stanley) lay out an inspiring (to me) manifesto for responsible capitalism. In 2012 they posted an advertisement in *The New York Times* on Black Friday (the biggest shopping day of the year in the USA) saying "Don't Buy This Jacket," encouraging people to not buy what they don't need. In 2013 Patagonia's webpage explaining their Common Threads Initiative aimed at sustainable consumption, flatly states that "Everything we make—everything anyone makes—costs the planet more life than it gives back" (Patagonia.com 2013), a stronger version of Patagonia's earlier "everything we do pollutes" (Conley and Freidenwald-Fishman 2006: 177). And a Patagonia Vice President of world retail told me, acknowledging the dilemma, that his job requires him to fly all over the world, and Chouinard flies down to Patagonia (the place) to fly-fish a few times a year: don't buy the jacket but do fly the gas-consuming plane to go where you might sell it, or might have worn it. In his 2012 manifesto Chouinard states his faith that customers of all consumer goods will insist on environmental laws becoming more restrictive, and even that investors in all businesses will be demanding high levels of environmental accountability, and that to "compete, a company will have to be at least as responsible as its competitors" (Chouinard and Stanley 2012: 35). This might be true for some (Casadesus-Masanell et al. 2009), but it is perhaps touchingly optimistic given how many people struggle to provide basic subsistence for their families, even in countries called "affluent." In the end, even the best-intentioned capitalists and consumers trying to sort out these issues are left with this complicated greenness, as even in their best attempts to dispel the magic of the commodity, they recast the spell that creates it.

PART 8

THE AFTERLIVES OF DRESS AND FASHION

PART INTRODUCTION

Design clothes. Get them manufactured. Market them. Distribute them to stores for purchase. That may be the end of a brand's involvement with an item of clothing, but that is not the end of the story. Our clothes lead lives after we are done with them. The brands we wear take on unanticipated new meanings. This concluding section of the book explores the afterlives of dress and fashion, the complex, often unsanctioned and illegal ways that clothes, logos, and fashion-related intellectual property circulate after their production and sale.

Karen Tranberg Hansen's chapter looks at the transnational second-hand clothing trade, with Zambia as her ethnographic case study. She explains what happens to our clothes when we donate them to charities, the new circuits they travel through, the new lives they lead. "Our used garments," she writes, "arrive in Zambia and enter into a local dress universe in which their meanings are redefined" (p. 357). Discarded shirts and jeans are repurposed, artfully put together according to local norms and practices, in ways that often play with, or challenge extant cultural scripts. Like other authors in this volume, Hansen emphasizes the agency of dress consumers, putting clothing to use for their own ends. Any American or European fantasy about starving African youth, wearing whatever hand-me-down little league T-shirt needs to be abandoned. The second-hand clothing consumers Hansen describes are discerning. They have specific tastes and interests. They make the clothes imported from elsewhere a part of their world. They do not become some peripheral outpost of ours.

This emphasis on agency runs through this section, as anthropologists who have studied the way fashion is taken up in particular regional contexts are often struck by its social dynamism and cultural specificity. Even outright imitation, claims Philomena Keet in her article on Japanese denim brands, can be agentive. In reproducing the look, cut, and feel of American denim jeans with almost preternatural precision, Japanese denim brands have made themselves into sought after cultural objects in Japan and well beyond. But are these jeans "authentic?" Or mere copies of cultural objects from elsewhere? Keet challenges the very question as ethnocentric, depending on a Western, and specifically Euro-American construction of authenticity in which authenticity requires an object to have originated in a particular place, time, or context. For Japanese jeans aficionados, on the other hand, authenticity is a function of faithful reproduction. Japanese denim is authentic *because* it is an accurate copy. Its successful imitation is the grounds for its evaluation by its consumers and the justification for the high price tag its commands.

Magdalena Craciun takes this critique even further to challenge the very basis upon which Western-imposed, intellectual property laws are written and reinforced. The notion of the "fake" fashion brand, she says, depends upon a romanticized Western notion about unique, "original" works, produced by inspired, solitary individuals, who forged the work from the contents of their inner being. A product is "authentic" to the extent that it can be traced directly back to this inner being. Originality, as a concept with real legal consequences, thus depends upon a dubious metaphysical concept. It also depends upon the erasure of sociality from the creative process and a willful ignorance of the power dynamics operating between people and places. In the brand, such logic reaches its apotheosis. Brands signify authenticity, demarcate originality, even when garments carrying a brand were made in sweatshops halfway around the world from their initial design. The modern trademark, the sign of the brand, serves more to cover up an object's origins, to construct a myth around its production, than to elucidate anything meaningful about how it was made or where it comes from. And as such, it is weapon number one in the fight against copycats and pirates, themselves typically marginal producers in the developing world. The very idea of original and fake, then, serve to reinforce power differences between the centers of the fashion world—New York, Milan, Paris, London—and everywhere else.

It is these power discrepancies with which Brent Luvaas's chapter on do-it-yourself (DIY) streetwear brands in Indonesia is specifically concerned. In Indonesia, where many of the most iconic Western clothing labels' signature products are physically manufactured, young Indonesians are producing their own clothing lines which remix and rework the trademarks of those brands. To do so, argues Luvaas, is to take symbolic possession over the companies outsourcing their labor to Indonesia, to claim that Nike, the Gap, and Ralph Lauren are not just "made in Indonesia," but themselves Indonesian products. The cut and paste, design strategy of Indonesian streetwear brands, Luvaas writes, "is not just a quick and easy method of producing images, though it is certainly that; it is also a tactic of global re-positioning, a rewriting of the power relationships embedded in neoliberal capitalism" (p. 386).

The unsanctioned circulation of garments, trademarks, and brands should thus not be read as some crisis in global capitalism, the authors in this concluding section of the reader imply, nor some critical malfunction that needs to be fixed in order to keep trade free and fair. Rather, the circulation of fashion beyond the control of the corporations who claim ownership over it should be a cause for hope. Fashion is not a fixed system. It is not a well-oiled machine. It breaks down. It skips gears. It is taken apart and reconstructed in various ways. And these reconstructions—these fissures in the smooth functioning of the machine—instill fashion with life. They lend it meaning. They inscribe it with purpose. They keep companies from dominating the discourse. Fashion is a living, evolving thing precisely because it does not work the way fashion brands would have it work. It is beyond any one company's control. It is beyond a single imposed system of meanings. Perhaps "fakes," "copies," and other varieties of cultural appropriation are not the problem, but one part of the solution, decentering the West as the power hub of fashion and opening the field of fashion production to a much broader set of social actors.

39

OTHER PEOPLE'S CLOTHES?
The international second-hand clothing trade and dress practices in Zambia

Karen Tranberg Hansen

World-wide exports of second-hand clothing from North America and Europe have expanded rapidly in recent years, with spectacular import increases in sub-Saharan Africa over the last two decades. Such clothing is given many names in the countries that import it. It was called *Vietnam* in Kivu in the eastern part of the former Zaire in the 1970s, and *calamidades* in Mozambique in the 1990s. It is known by local terms that mean "dead white men's clothes" in Ghana, "died in Europe" in northwestern Tanzania (Weiss 1996: 138), and "shake and sell" in Senegal (Heath 1992: 28). In East Africa it is called *mitumba*, which is Swahili for "bale." In Malawi, it is *kaunjika*, which in Nyanja/Chewa means "to pick," while in Zambia *salaula* means in Bemba "selecting from a pile in the manner of rummaging."

The significance of these references to the West's clothing surplus depends on the case at hand and the economic and cultural politics of its time. What matters in Zambia is the way *salaula* names how people deal with clothing, selecting, and choosing garments to suit both their clothing needs and desires. Their concern with cutting a fine figure struck anthropologists in the past (Mitchell 1956; Richards [1939] 1969; Wilson 1941–42) and their active preoccupations with clothing, style, and fashion continue to do so today. Because of the many influences on which clothing practices draw, Zambian dealings with clothing—both new and used, for of course they implicate one another—

offer a particularly rich case for exploring some of the complex interactions between the local dress scene and its insertion in a variety of larger contexts.

Clothing, style, and fashion are important topics of everyday conversation in Zambia. The dressed bodies of persons of importance are the subjects of intense scrutiny and comment, as is the appearance of casual bystanders. Above all else, dress sensibilities in Zambia are visual and sensual. Created in performance, the aesthetic effect of the dressed body is a particular *look* that people strive to produce. The clothing competence they bring to bear on this process is extensive. Poor and rich, women and men, adolescent and adult, they all want to look "outstanding," "unique," or "exclusive." The meanings of clothes do not inhere in the garments themselves, but are attributed to them in ongoing interaction. That is to say that how clothing is construed and how it matters has a lot to do with the context in which it is worn. Even then, because individual dress practice does not always conform to widespread norms, the body surface easily becomes a battleground where questions about dress and its acceptability are tested.

On the pages that follow, I map out some of these processes in relation to Zambia, pointing to complex dialectics between the local clothing scene and its location in a larger context that includes other African countries, the West, Asia, and the mass media, among many other things. I begin with history, hinting at

Adapted from Karen Tranberg Hansen, "Other people's clothes? The international second-hand clothing trade and dress practices in Zambia," *Fashion Theory* 4, no. 3 (2000): 245–74 enduring entanglements between the second-hand clothing trade and current clothing consumption in the Zambian case. Then I sketch some contours of the international second-hand clothing trade and note some of its different dynamics across Africa. Next I turn to Zambia and the clothing consumption practices that have arisen around the rapidly growing import of second-hand clothing since the middle to late 1980s. I draw from research I have conducted since the early 1990s on the entire circuit of the international second-hand clothing trade from the point of sourcing in the West to the point where our used garments arrive in Zambia and enter into a local dress universe in which their meanings are redefined (Hansen 2000).

THE SECOND-HAND CLOTHING TRADE

In much of the West today, second-hand clothing makes up fringe, or niche, markets. Income distribution, purchasing power, affordable mass-produced garments and apparel, and concerns with fashion have reduced the need for large segments of the population to purchase used clothing. But well into the nineteenth century, used clothing constituted the effective market for much of the population except the very rich. Still in many countries in the Third World today, where the cost factor is enormously important, second-hand clothing is both desired and needed. While grinding poverty and deteriorating purchasing power as a result of prolonged economic decline in most of the countries of sub-Saharan Africa since the 1970s help explain why this region is the world's largest import market for the lowest-quality used clothing, economics and poverty do not adequately account for the popularity of a commodity like *salaula* in Zambia. As I point out briefly below, the history of the second-hand clothing system of provision feeds into and sharpens popular sensibilities of clothing consumption.

Past and present, the export trade in used clothing has been closely linked to the costs of domestic garment manufacture in a process on which historians have begun to throw light (Lemire 1997; Perrot (1981) 1994; Roche (1989) 1996). A detailed historical tracing of this trade is difficult because of the very nature of second-hand clothing consumption, which tends to

exhaust the material evidence of its own past through extensive wear. Until well after the beginning of ready-made garment production, clothes went through many lives, passed down, resold or exchanged for other goods, altered or mended, and resewn before they reached the final phase of their journey and were recycled as rags into paper. "The success of the second-hand clothes trade can only be commemorated," suggests the costume historian Madeleine Ginsburg, "by their absence from museum collections of material survivals. [But it] would be an injustice to pay a similar complement to its history, of interest in its own right and as an aspect of the garment history" (1980: 121).

By 1600, if not earlier, the second-hand clothing trade flourished in major European cities, concentrated in specifically located markets, stores, and pawnshops. The abandonment of guild regulations and sartorial dress rules increased the demand for fashionable clothing, much of which was satisfied from the second-hand clothing market (Lemire 1991a). Itinerant "old clothes men" traded across the countryside in a process through which garments continued to change hands (Lemire 1997: 75–93). From the mid-eighteenth century on, the availability of more affordable cotton and wool fabrics began gradually reducing home markets in second-hand clothing at the same time as early mass producing tailoring firms made new clothing more affordable (Lemire 1991b).

Like any other commodity in demand, second-hand clothing was sourced and traded across vast distances. By the first half of the eighteenth century the Netherlands and London were centers for the wholesale trade in used clothes, with exports to Belgium, France, and South America. The export trade reached the colonies as well, including North America and Africa. By the late nineteenth century in Paris, reasonably priced ready-wear competed so effectively with second-hand clothes that the used clothing trade became limited to exports, especially to colonial Africa (Perrot [1981] 1994: 71).

The profitable potential of the second-hand clothes market in colonial Africa was seized after the two World Wars, when surplus army clothing was exported by used clothing dealers in America and Britain and on the Continent. The availability of army clothing and men's work clothing from the early production of ready-wear are among the reasons why the histories of second-hand clothing consumption in Africa are distinctly gendered. Men's greatcoats and jackets came first, and only in the inter-war period did women's wear begin to enter used clothing consignments for export. But the substantive growth of the African second-hand clothing export market is a phenomenon postdating the Second World War, a product both of supply and demand: a vast surplus of still wearable used clothing in the West, and growing desires and needs for clothes in Africa, where socioeconomic transformations catapulted more and more Africans into new markets as consumers.

THE CHARITABLE CONNECTION

Developments in the export trade in second-hand clothing since the Second World War have depended to a great extent on the clothing collection activities of major charitable organizations who supply both domestic and foreign second-hand clothing markets. The charities have a long, and changing, involvement with second-hand clothing. In both Europe and the United States at the end of the nineteenth century, philanthropic groups collected and donated clothes to the poor (Ginsburg 1980: 128). In the period after the Second World War, shifts in income distribution and growing purchasing power enabled more consumers than ever before to buy not only new, but more, clothes, including fashions and styles oriented toward specific niches, for example, teenage clothing, corporate and career dressing, and sports and leisure wear. Such dress practices produced an enormous yield of used, but still wearable, clothes, some of which ended up as donations to charity.

Many charitable organizations began emphasizing store sales in the late 1950s, among them the Salvation Army, for which the sale of used clothing was the largest single source of income in the United States by the 1960s (McKinley 1986). The charitable organizations dominated the second-hand clothing retail scene in the 1960s and 1970s. During the 1980s, they were joined by a variety of specialist second-hand clothing stores that began to appear operating on a for-profit basis, with names, in the Chicago area, like Crowded Closet, Flashy Trash, Hollywood Mirror, Hubba Hubba, Bewitched, and Strange Cargo. Although most of the specialty resale stores cater to women, some stock garments for both sexes, and there are stores for children's clothing as well. Men's stores are beginning to appear—for example, Gentlemen's Agreement on the Upper East Side of Manhattan (*New York Times*, 14 December 1997, p. B14) and Second Time Around, in the middle of Boston's Newbery Street (*Wall Street Journal*, 20 January 1997, p. 1 and p. 6). Some stores operate on a consignment basis, selling "gently worn" designer clothes both for women and men; others source in bulk from commercial second-hand clothing vendors, or both.

Rarely featuring words like "used," "second-hand" or "thrift" in their names, most of these recent stores target specific consumers, for example, young professionals who may want high-quality clothes at modest prices or young people keen on retro and vintage fashion, punk, and rave styles (McRobbie 1989). There is a vigorous resale market for designer clothes in specialty stores whose customers buy designer labels to wear as "investment dressing," much as collectors buy art (*New York Times*, 4 June 1996, p. B11). And "thrift shopping" appears to have developed a new allure, providing pastime activity for vintage connoisseurs who are on the look-out for rare finds (*New York Times*, 28 September 1997, Travel section p. 27). Some of these businesses donate garments that do not sell well "to charity," and some also dispose of their surplus at bulk prices to commercial second-hand clothing dealers.

The charitable organizations are the largest single source of the garments that fuel today's international trade in second-hand clothing. Because consumers in the West today donate much more clothing than the charitable organizations can possibly sell in their thrift shops, the charitable organizations resell their massive overstock at bulk prices to commercial second-hand clothing dealers. While the spectacular increase in second-hand clothing exports to Africa since the mid-1980s has taken place alongside the growth of the international humanitarian aid industry, this export is less about charity than it is about profits. In fact, used clothing as outright donations in crisis and relief situations plays a very minor role in an export process that is overwhelmingly commercial.

The second-hand clothing trade is an unusual industry with peculiar problems that arise from the uneasy relationship between "charity" and commercial interests and the ways that each of these is organized. In the West today, the second-hand clothing trade both in domestic and foreign markets is dominated by non-profit charitable organizations and private textile recycling/grading firms, often family-owned. Its financial side has largely eluded public scrutiny. Thriving by an ethic of giving in the West, the major charitable organizations look like patrons in a worldwide clothing donation project. Yet the major charitable organizations routinely sell a large proportion of their donated clothing, between 40 and 75 percent depending on whom you talk to, to textile recyclers. Their extensive interactions with textile recyclers/graders add a commercial angle to their dealings about which there is little substantive knowledge. What is more, growing environmental concerns in the West in recent years have enhanced both the profitability and respectability of the rag trade and given its practitioners a new cachet as textile salvagers and waste recyclers.

From across the United States and northwestern Europe the textile recyclers/graders truck the used clothing they purchase in bulk from the charitable organizations to warehouses/sorting plants near major port cities. "Used clothing" includes not only garments but also shoes, handbags, towels, sheets, blankets, and draperies. The clothes are sorted by garment type, fabric, and quality before being compressed into bales. The standard weight is 50 kilograms; yet some firms also compress bales of much larger weights, usually of unsorted clothing. The clothes are often sorted under poor work conditions by poorly paid workers, some of whom are recent immigrants from countries where the clothes will be sold. The bottom quality goes to Africa, and medium quality to Latin America, while Japan receives a large portion of top-quality items, among which brand-name denim jeans and sneakers are in popular demand.

This sketch of some of the shifting contours of the second-hand clothing trade appears to explain its dynamics with reference to the history of clothing manufacture, first tailor-made and then factory-produced garments. But it is also, and in the longer haul, a cultural story about consumption and about the importance of clothing, both new and old, to modern sensibilities, embodying new social and cultural abilities to discriminate. In the process, clothing has become an important agent of social change (Martin 1994).

WORLD EXPORTS AND IMPORTS

The second-hand clothing trade constitutes an immense, profitable, but barely examined world-wide commodity circuit that exports millions of dollars' worth of used clothing abroad. It grew more than sixfold over the last one and a half decades, from a value of US $207 million in 1980 to US $1,410 million in 1995 (UN 1996: 60). The United States is the world's largest exporter in terms of both volume and value, followed by Germany, the Netherlands, Belgium-Luxembourg, and Japan. Between 1990 and 1995 alone, United States world-wide exports of this commodity doubled, from a value of US $174 million to US $340 million (UN 1996: 60).

The countries of sub-Saharan Africa are the world's largest second-hand clothing destination, receiving in 1995 close to one-fourth of total world exports, worth US $379 million, up from US $117 million in 1990 (UN 1996: 60). There are several Asian countries among the large net importers of second-hand clothing, including Pakistan, Singapore, India, and Hong Kong. The large importers include such Middle Eastern countries as Syria and Jordan, as well as Malaysia and several countries in Latin America. Sizeable exports go not only to developing countries but also to Japan, the Netherlands, and Belgium-Luxembourg, which all engage in both import and re-export of this commodity.

African used-clothing markets undergo quick changes not only because of civil strife and war but also because of legislation guiding the entry or prohibition of second-hand clothing imports. Monetary policies affecting exchange rates and the very availability of foreign exchange influence the ability of local wholesalers to import. Some countries have at one time or the other banned imports, among them the Côte d'Ivoire, Nigeria, Kenya, and Malawi. Some countries have restrictive policies, for example South Africa, which only allows import of second-hand clothing for charitable purposes rather than for resale. Some small countries like Benin, Togo, and Rwanda before its civil wars, are large importers and active in transshipment and re-export. And although second-hand clothing imports are banned in some countries, there is a brisk transborder trade in this commodity.

AFRICAN SECOND-HAND CLOTHING MARKETS

Second-hand clothing exporters need local knowledge not only about the political climate, import rules, tariffs, and currency regulations but also about clothing consumption practices in the various African countries. Some exporters have lived in Africa, and those who have not make on-site visits to familiarize themselves with local clothing markets. From the African end, wholesalers feed back information to their contacts in North America and Europe about which garments do and do not sell well.

Exporters need to reckon with considerable regional variation in Africa's clothing markets. In Muslim-dominated North Africa, for example, used clothing constituted only 7 percent of total garment imports in 1980 compared to 33 percent in sub-Saharan Africa (Haggblade 1990: 508–9). Tunisia is an exception to this with large imports, probably due to long practices of re-export (Van Groen and Lozer 1976).

Local dress conventions differ in terms not only of religious norms but also of gender, age, class, and region, informing cultural norms of dress practice and influencing what types of garments people will wear and when. Briefly, in several countries in West Africa, distinct regional dress styles that are the products of long-standing textile crafts in weaving, dyeing, and printing today co-exist with styles of dressing introduced during the colonial period and after. In Nigeria and Senegal, for example, second-hand clothing has entered a specific niche. Although people from different socioeconomic groups, not only the very poor, now purchase imported second-hand clothing

and use it widely for everyday wear, Senegalese and Nigerians commonly follow long-standing regional style conventions on important occasions, dressing with pride for purposes of displaying locally produced cloth in "African" styles (Denzer 1997: 10–12; Heath 1992: 21, 28). This is much in contrast to Zambia, where such textile crafts hardly existed and where people from across the socioeconomic spectrum except at the very top are dressing in the West's used clothing. What is more, people in Zambia have been wearing Western-styled clothing since the early twentieth century, in fact for so long that they have made it their own. As a result, references to the West are not very helpful when explaining local dress conventions. Last but not least, there are invented dress "traditions." In Mobuto Sese Seko's Zaire, for example, the "authenticity" code forbade men from wearing Western coats and ties and women from wearing jeans. His successor, President Laurent Kabila of the Democratic Republic of the Congo, is conservative in matters of women's dress. One of his first edicts after assuming power in 1997 was to ban women's wearing of jeans and miniskirts (*The Post*, 22 July 1997, p. 10).

THE *SALAULA* MARKET IN ZAMBIA

Zambia's second-hand clothing trade dates back to the colonial period, when imported used clothes reached Northern Rhodesia—as Zambia was called then—from across the border with the Belgian Congo, now the Democratic Republic of the Congo. Direct importation of this commodity was prohibited in Zambia during the first decades after independence in 1964. When restrictive import and foreign exchange regulations were relaxed in the middle to late 1980s, the second-hand clothing trade grew rapidly. The name *salaula* came into use at that time.

Second-hand clothing consignments destined for Zambia arrive by container ships in the ports of Dar es Salaam in Tanzania, Durban in South Africa, and Beira in Mozambique, from where they are trucked to wholesalers' warehouses in Lusaka, the capital. Lusaka is the hub of the *salaula* wholesale trade, though some firms have up-country branches. At the warehouse, marketeers, vendors, and private individuals purchase bales of *salaula*. They in turn distribute and sell their goods in urban and rural markets, hawk them in the countryside, and transfer them in rural exchanges in return for produce, goats, chicken, and fish. Today, in Zambia's urban and provincial markets, the *salaula* sections are many times larger than the food sections. *Salaula* is also sold from private homes in urban middle- and high-income residential areas, and some traders bring second-hand clothing to city offices and institutions like banks to sell on credit to employees who receive monthly paychecks.

The explosion of Zambia's *salaula* market has provided an income source for traders and created ancillary economic activities in repair, alteration, and support services for many others, including mature women and men, and a growing number of out-of-school youth, especially young men. In effect, in Zambia's declining economy, the *salaula* trade has created work opportunities for people who never held formal-sector jobs and for retrenched employees from both the public and private sectors. It also serves as a sideline for people who are seeking to extend their meagre earnings from jobs elsewhere. But above all, the *salaula* trade has made a profusion of clothing available from which dress-conscious consumers can purchase just the garments they want. "Watch Lusaka," suggested one writer. "All who are gorgeously attired mostly get their clothes abroad." Lusaka's so-called boutiques, he went on "have become rather like museums ... neither Lusaka's Cairo Road nor the Kamwala shopping area is the place to look. You have a better chance at the second-hand clothes dealer, the flea market or even the city centre market dealer who jaunts between Lusaka and Johannesburg" (*Times of Zambia*, 26 August 1995, p. 4). He might have added what people in Zambia readily will tell you, namely that "three-fourths" of the population "shops from *salaula*." My survey observations about clothing consumption practices across class in Lusaka in fact confirm that popular impression.

ZAMBIAN CLOTHING PROFILES

What influences consumers in Zambia when they go about acquiring *salaula*? There is much more at stake in buying *salaula* than a mere exchange of cash, or barter, for clothes. Just as wholesalers of *salaula* are selective when ordering clothing consignments from the West to retail in local markets, so are consumers in their purchase of garments. Vital dimensions of the demand side are cultural taste and style matters. Indeed, consumption is hard work that may be understood through the practices and meanings consumers bring to bear on how they acquire and use things (de Certeau 1988: 30–1).

When shopping from *salaula*, consumers' preoccupations with creating particular looks are inspired by fashion trends and popular dress cultures from across the world. Negotiating both clothing needs and desires, consumers are influenced by a variety of sources when they purchase garments. They draw on these influences in ways that are informed by local norms about bodies and dress. Above all, clothing consumption implicates cultural norms about gender and authority. Local notions of what to wear when and how to present the dressed body construct dress practice in Zambian terms that influence how people dress in garments from *salaula*. Clothing consumers speak of these terms in the language of tradition. Because this is a made up tradition, it is subject to change. That is why the normative terms for how to dress delineate rather than determine how people dress, leaving room for idiosyncratic and provocative dress practices as well.

To flesh out the normative aspects of Zambian dress practice I asked the persons I interviewed to describe both a well-dressed woman and a well-dressed man and to explain what made people look not well-dressed. These questions followed discussions of their favorite types of clothes and what they did not like to wear and why. In fact, the two sets of questions complemented one another. The descriptions of well-dressed persons were remarkably uniform across the different residential areas in which I interviewed, constituting what amounts to a culturally dominant notion of how to dress—in effect, a dress code. Questions about hairstyles, makeup, and accessories supported these notions as well. Only in *apamwamba* (a Nyanja term, meaning literally "those on the top") households and women-headed households with ample economic means were these notions occasionally challenged. Some young adults also challenged, or wanted to challenge, these norms that circumscribed their clothing desires.

The composite clothing profiles of a well-dressed woman and a well-dressed man have much in common. The adult dress profile of both sexes is tidy, with smooth lines and careful color coordination. It is loosely fitting rather than tight. "Too many" different garments, colors, and fabrics distort the smooth profile, making the person look disheveled, and drawing undue attention to the dressed body. Women's moderate use of jewelry and make-up, and the hairstyles of both sexes enhance the total look to make it appear natural rather than artificial. In short, dress should complement the body structure and display it to its advantage.

For both sexes, these formal dress profiles convey notions about respectability and maturity, and of being in charge. Regardless of urban or rural residence, the accepted notion of how to dress makes adult men insist on suits, ties, long-sleeved shirts, and when of a certain age, hats for their public ensemble. Leather shoes, not boots, sneakers, or sandals, mark the man as properly put together. And irrespective of occupation and location, adult women insist on skirts below the knee, short-sleeved loose blouses or dresses, on top of which a *chitenge* (a wrapper of colorful printed cloth) can be worn if necessary and, when of a certain age, head-scarves; shoes with heels, not sandals, and certainly not sneakers, are part of their ensemble in public. But on the matter of how to present the dressed body the clothing profiles of women and men differ significantly. Women must cover their "private parts," which in this region of Africa includes their thighs. This means that dress length, tightness, and fabric transparency become issues in interactions with men and elders both at home and in public.

The active concern with cutting a good figure on Zambian terms is evident in the hard work of *salaula* consumption. That work includes shopping in the market, where consumers gather information on the availability of specific garments/styles and screen and sort products while they skillfully work their way through the piles of *salaula*, checking both for quality and style. They turn garments inside out to examine if the sewing is neat and whether there are rips or other flaws in the fabric. But the work of consumption extends far beyond the market. A well-dressed person is well-kempt herself, and her clothing is well kept. Producing the smooth, tidy clothing profile involves processes that easily escape the gaze of the casual observer or traveler, who sees *salaula* only as the West's cast-offs. The desire to be well turned out, even if the garments are second-hand, makes clothes-conscious Zambians insist on immaculate ensembles whose elements are carefully laundered and ironed. For this reason, the faded and torn jeans that are part of *salaula* bales imported from the United States are particularly unpopular. The desire to look spick and span prompts careful scrutiny of fabric quality to ascertain that colors of printed fabrics will not run in washing. Fading in sunlight is an issue as well. Most households do their laundry in cold water using strong detergents containing bleach, and clothes are usually hung up in the sunlight to dry. This is why color fastness and fabric quality are important issues in identifying clothes that are durable and will keep their good looks. And everyone pays great attention to shoes, commonly carrying a piece of cloth under the waist of a *chitenge* wrapper in their handbags or their pockets to remove Lusaka's dust when entering public buildings and private homes.

The attraction of *salaula* to clothing-conscious Zambian consumers goes far beyond the price factor and the good quality for money that many of these garments offer. Above all, *salaula* makes available an abundance and variety of clothes that allow consumers to make their individual mark on the culturally accepted clothing profile. But the fact that we can identify Zambian terms for acceptable dress does not mean that everyone dresses alike. Nor does the desire to dress in "the latest" produce passive imitation and homogeneity. It is precisely the opposite effect consumers seek to achieve from *salaula* and that they find missing from much store-bought clothing: uniqueness. What they want are clothes that are fashionable rather than common. One of the women I interviewed in a high-income area put it this way when explaining why she shopped from *salaula*: "I don't want to wear what everyone else is wearing." "Clothes from *salaula* are not what other people wear," said another woman, explaining why they are viewed as "exclusive."

The desire for uniqueness, to stand out, while dressing the body on Zambian terms, produces considerable variations in dress in public workplaces and offices. Women never wear the same dress to work every day, according to their own reports, but rotate their garments and make new combinations of dresses and skirts. Their rotation occasionally includes dresses in a cut and style that in the West might be considered to be cocktail or evening wear. They may wear a *chitenge* dress to work as well, something rarely seen in the 1980s. In some banks and private firms, women wear suited uniforms, but have a "free dress" day once a week when they dress with their own sense of style.

Men work hard to achieve uniqueness in clothing presentation, too. Suits are worn in Zambia across a much wider range of the white-collar and civil service ranks than in the midwestern United States, for example. Civil servants rotate their immaculately kept suits, including older suits that wear the marks of time but always are crisply pressed. Young male bank tellers and clerical workers vary their suited look by wearing different types of shirt, tie and handkerchief combinations. Some men also wear jewelry, such as necklaces, tie-pins, bracelets, and rings, which they rotate. In fact men's suits are worn so commonly in Lusaka's downtown that, unlike in Harare, in neighboring Zimbabwe, you hardly ever encounter an adult Zambian man wearing shorts in public there.

Because notions of proper dress are context-dependent, their constraining effects may be temporarily put aside. This is the case on the urban disco and evening entertainment scene, which in the 1990s often displayed miniskirts and tight and transparent women's garments. Men who attend such events dress in designer jeans and trousers. And some could very occasionally be seen wearing the very high-waisted trousers inspired by Zairean rumba musicians. Specially styled jackets go with such trousers, adorned with a variety of inserted contrastive fabric or special collar, button, and pocket details. The majority of those who can afford to attend such events are of *apamwamba* background, the only group, as I suggested above, with an effective choice in the clothing market.

Last but not least, both play, idiosyncrasy, and pragmatics enter into how some people dress. I met many young men trading in the *salaula* markets who enjoyed dressing in a striking manner in garments they took a liking to. Examples include one young man who wore what looked like a hospital orderly's white uniform topped by a pink *peignoir*. Another young man dressed proudly in a church elder's purple gown. Dress practices such as these are not so much deliberate attempts to develop personal style distinctions as they are examples of the playfulness of young men who relish dressing up and showing off. This attitude of delight is also evident in the red nail polish that some young male street vendors paint on some, or all, of their fingers. "It looks good, we like it," they will tell you. What is more, the Zambian clothing scene is full of what to the Western eye may appear as unorthodox or incongruous styles, such as men wearing combinations of women's clothing, including coats, sweaters, and shorts, and women wearing men's dust coats and jackets. Such dress practices do not represent deliberate cross-dressing, but reflect the differential availability of women's and men's seasonal garments in the *salaula* consignments. Such clothing efforts are pragmatic aims at combining, for example, cold weather garments or work clothes from what is available from *salaula*.

OTHER PEOPLE'S CLOTHES?

In everyday talk in Zambia, few would think of blaming the West for affecting clothing consumption whether new or old, and there is no suggestion of *salaula*'s being the flip side of Western fashion. In fact, people here rarely use the category "the West." Instead they talk about the "outside," which includes neighboring countries in the region, as well as Hong Kong and the United States. Or they invoke the "well developed countries" or "the donor countries." This is not surprising since, after all, in the postcolonial era, especially from the mid-1970s on, "development" has been the principal avenue through which "the West" has affected their lives. They also use terms that emerge in the context of specific encounters, for instance the United States, the United Kingdom or India. Their narratives employ changing idioms of time and place that are indicative of the varying types of exposure to the world beyond home among the generations who grew up prior to and after independence.

What the West is, above all, is an imagined place, associated with power, wealth, and an abundance of consumer goods that surpass most local products in quality and style. From it comes, for example, via American youth subculture, the hip-hop and rap-inspired style of young male street vendors in Zambia. Yet women's two-piece outfits are not American-derived, but influenced rather by British and South African fashions. Distinctions between Zambian styles and dress styles in America, Britain, South Africa, and elsewhere obscure dynamic relationships and influences that cross such boundaries, producing creative tensions that energize the everyday world of dress practice. There is a multiplicity of heritages at work here, with complex dialectics between local and foreign influences, and between what is considered to be "the latest" and what is current, in a reconfiguration process that generates distinct local clothing consumption practices.

The popularity of *salaula* as an element of dress practice in a developing country like Zambia offers interdisciplinary scholarship on dress and popular culture several important insights. First of all, dress conventions in Zambia are the outcomes of multiple interactions that engage style-conscious individuals with influences from many different parts of the world. Prominent in the dress practices I have described in this article are inspirations from across the African continent, particularly in women's dress, through processes that are establishing what is beginning to look like a pan-African fashion system in its own right. The second insight concerns matters of cultural taste and style that are embedded in a complex host of local social and cultural processes. These processes have worked themselves out differently across the generations, by class, and, as I have shown here, particularly by gender. This insight adds a startling twist to conventional assumptions about gender and dress that have tended to attribute late twentieth-century concerns with style and fashion to women. For in the case of Zambia, adolescent girls and adult women have far less scope for experimentation with clothing than men, for whom local society allows more room to move with fashion. And the last but not the least compelling insight arising from this study of second-hand clothing consumption is that being poor and being a discriminating consumer arc not mutually exclusive.

40

MAKING NEW VINTAGE JEANS IN JAPAN:
Relocating authenticity

Philomena Keet

INTRODUCTION—MAKING JEANS, RENDERING AUTHENTICITY

This paper will look at the production and consumption of premium "vintage" denim in Japan, arguing that high-end Japanese jeans, through various production and marketing strategies, resolve the "authenticity anxiety" (Taylor Atkins 2000: 31) of trying to be authentic Japanese individuals through an originally American cultural product. This has had a rather peculiar consequence of more general interest to those following the trajectories of contemporary denim. These local issues have led to a broader shift in the geographical authenticity of "new" vintage jeans away from America to Japan, such that even American jeans brands, for example cult brand PRPS, stake their claim to "being real" partly through the use of Japanese denim. While this seems to go against notions of authenticity being concerned with origins, it seems odd that one country can effectively appropriate the forms of authenticity for another. These Japanese jeans also show how authenticity can be perceived differently between and within cultures.

Much of this research was carried out during the summer and autumn of 2009 during two stays in the town of Kojima in west Japan, which is known as the locus for artisanal production of denim, as well as through related national magazines and jeans shops in Tokyo. In Kojima I interviewed staff at shops-cum-showrooms and various jeans-related factories.

While considering the connoisseur consumer, this paper is therefore biased towards the producers of denim and jeans for the purpose of investigating how Japanese denim products are rendered as authentic through manufacturing processes, sales talk and advertising. As Moeran (1997) found with the pottery produced in rural Japan, the physicality of the final jeans product was not always as important as the mechanisms by which it was created. I will argue that this is true for the jeans described in this paper and will focus on the manufacturing processes and how the final jeans product is planned in two Kojima-based companies.

Following the idea that authenticity is socially constructed (Peterson 1997) and not inherent to an object, I will look at how denim production companies in Japan have been successful at "rendering authenticity" (Gilmore and Pine 2007) through such authenticating strategies (Taylor Atkins 2000) as employing old machines no longer used in America and now-defunct time-consuming techniques. Premium or high-end jeans are characterized variously by being high-quality denim, better fitting, produced on a small scale and designed and retailed for over US$100 a pair (sometimes much more). Within this, there is a category of vintage reproduction jeans that are not judged so much on objective quality but by factors such as stitch color and the presence of "hidden rivets." The popularity of vintage jeans is part of a larger trend in Japan's oversaturated markets for making consumption

Adapted from Philomena Keet, "Making New Vintage Jeans in Japan: Relocating Authenticity," *Textile: The Journal of Cloth and Culture* 9, no. 1 (March 2011): 44–61.

decisions on the basis of the opportunities a commodity presents for achieving personal authenticity (Lindholm 2008).

Authenticity belongs to the "set of values that includes sincere, essential, natural, original, and real" (Lindholm 2008: 1) and as such is defined against what is fake, replica, copy, artificial. While the authentic holds a true and real relationship to some origin and/or content (it is what it "purports to be" Lindholm 2008: 2) the degree to which these correspondences are significant may differ between cultures, giving rise to variation in what is considered to be authentic. In particular, cultures that have historically very different philosophical backgrounds to that in the "West" may conceive of "authenticity" somewhat differently. Vann (2006) found, for example, that fake and genuine goods in Vietnam were classified in a way that did not fit with international intellectual property laws. Hendry suggests that in Japan, authenticity lies not only in a unitary correspondence to the "real thing" (honmono) but can also be experienced through faithful replication (2000). This is crucial in understanding how Japanese replicas of American vintage jeans have become highly sought after, not only in Japan but throughout the world.

Japan has become a new locale of authenticity for denim but what does authenticity mean in the case of denim? Jeans are inextricably associated with America (despite the fact that the denim material and name "jeans" both originate in Europe). Levi's 501xx vintage models attract the highest premiums, and the older the better. The 501 style, still in production today, has the longest history of any jeans cut in the world. Although there have been changes over the century or so since it first came into existence, it remains the model of genealogical authenticity for any denim lover.

When searching for the most authentic newly produced jeans (which is necessary due to the rarity of such vintage pairs), however, Japanese denim fans choose these "super jeans" (Izuishi 1999: 244) that are assembled in Japan using denim woven in Japan over their American counterparts. I will look at how certain Japanese jeans companies come to portray themselves as, and be seen as, more or less authentic than others, particularly with respect to the "original"

American brands. As I will argue, there is also a move towards greater personal authenticity such that jeans are made for maximum "fit" to the wearer as well as being rendered as genealogically or correspondently authentic. First I will look at the history of jeans in Japan, and how the domestication of American jeans led eventually to the production of authentic Japanese "super denim."

HISTORY OF JAPANESE DENIM

The first jeans available for purchase in Japan were second-hand jeans obtained from the American occupation forces, to be found first in Kobe and Tokyo's Ueno around 1946. Known as "G.I. pants" (ji-ai pantsu), they were abbreviated to "G-pan": jeans are still known by this moniker in present day Japan. Being second hand, they were soft and worn, but invariably available in sizes that were too big for many of the young people who hankered after them. The charismatic founder of Japanese jeans brand Evisu, Yamane, tells a story of his first experience trying to get hold of a pair of these G-pan. As a young middle-school boy he wondered what G-pan meant: "I'll never forget the shop assistant saying 'It means G.I. pants.' Those words sent shivers down my spine" (Yamane 2008: 30).

Jeans therefore made a somewhat eventful entrance to Japan: they were not thought of as fashionable but rather represented a worn, hardy, work-wear type of antifashion or jitsuyouhin (literally "utility goods"). However, at the same time, having been actually worn by these G.I.s, they came infused with all the mixed feelings of resentment and exoticism towards these American occupants. It was perhaps this streak of "the enemy" in the very fabric of the G-pan that was so affecting to Yamane and others.

While G-pan were available from the beginning of the Occupation era, it was not until the mid-1960s that Japan really started to produce its own denim. The background to this development is a confluence of geography, population and industrial changes, factors that all came together with a particular company, Maruo (Sugiyama 2009). Based in the small town of Kojima in the prefecture of Okayama, west Japan, the company, later known as Big John, was one of many in the region that were producing school uniforms, but the first to switch to making jeans. On finally producing their first pairs, they had trouble selling them: Japanese customers would not buy such starchy and stiff trousers. They started to pre-wash the jeans; Japan was therefore one of the first countries in which denim washing processes developed. Other companies started to follow Big John, including their main, and now far more successful, rivals— Edwin. Edwin managed to gain the rights to sell Levi's and Lee in Japan, and thus the Japan jeans market expanded rapidly in the 1970s and 1980s. Japan started to make its own machines for the industrial weaving and stitching of denim.

Up until the 1990s, most jeans that were made in Japan played down their origin and used marketing and production strategies that affiliated them with America, almost masquerading as American brands. Indeed Edwin (supposedly named "Edo-win" as a challenge to their west Japan rivals) has frequently used Brad Pitt in its advertising and was commonly thought of as an American brand. Big John was well known for being the first Japanese denim brand but with such a name the cultural references are obvious.

Starting in the 1980s but continuing into the 1990s, the burgeoning denim scene in Japan led to a quest by both producers and consumers to find a "better," more authentic pair of jeans from amongst the variety and quantity of denim being produced. "The early 1990s saw jeans spread as everyday wear, but it was also a period in which the value of old jeans that used to be worn as work wear was re-established," states the website of the Japan Jeans Association (www.best-jeans.com, accessed December 2009). Pairs of vintage Levi's were sought out and brought back to Japan from thrift shops in America and Europe and were scientifically and systematically analyzed. The threads were unraveled and subject to tests that revealed their thickness, density and other physical properties. The discrepancies between the lettering on the rivets, the back patches, the stitching and so on of different years were carefully documented and recorded. Eventually guides were produced that would allow one to date a vintage pair of Levi's to a particular year.

At this point the locus of the "real thing" was very firmly placed in these old American Levi's, and many of them were bought by … eager to discover and replicate the … they were so highly evaluated. Studio … if not the first then one of the first pair… jeans," their D01 model. A pamphlet pro… their 30th anniversary in 2009 describes then… the antithesis of the rationalism always sought by the motherland" (Lightning 2009a: 27), pointing to the craftsmanship and tradition that the company had learnt from Europe. Years after the more niche Studio D'artisan, mainstream brand, Edwin came out with the oxymoronically named "New Vintage" range in 1994. Natural indigo was reintroduced because chemical indigo dyes did not produce the fading that was a mark of vintage jeans (Taussig 2008).

The history of jeans in Japan seems to illustrate perfectly the image of Japan as a nation that copies, domesticates and improves (Cox 2008; Taylor Atkins 2000; Tobin 1992). There is a hint in these accounts that Japan falls short in innovation, which is as mistaken for jeans as it is for the Sony Walkman (Du Gay *et al.* 1997). Japan was an innovator of denim distressing techniques and washing in particular (Sugiyama 2009). In the Studio D'artisan brochure, it says of the 1980s that "people appeared who were trying things out that couldn't be done in the motherland, America" (Lightning 2009a: 27). It is because emerging jeans brands were able to combine innovative Japanese know-how with what they had learnt about "original" vintage denim that they could forge for themselves a "new authenticity."

KOJIMA AS AUTHENTICATING STRATEGY

The town of Kojima has become an important authenticating strategy in itself for many of these premium Japanese denim brands. It is written about in tourist literature and denim promotional material as the "birthplace" of jeans (*ji-nzu no hassyouchi*). Tourism within Japan is strongly linked to regional specialties and souvenirs and, like the rice spoons (*shamoji*) of Miyajima (Daniels 2001), denim gains a certain spirituality from its association with Kojima, spreading the "fame" of Kojima as it is consumed throughout the country. "The place where D'artisan jeans are born, the denim Mecca Kojima" runs one headline in a pamphlet. The national train company, JR West, produces a pamphlet about a "jeans bus" that takes denim tourists around Kojima's showrooms, museums and shops. Television programs see celebrities traveling to Kojima to get a pair of order-made jeans that they distress themselves. There is much truth in this image: Kojima is a place whose extensive network of small enterprises that grew around its uniform production industry, specializing in sewing, fasteners and so on, lent themselves well to the production of denim (Sugiyama 2009). The small size of the enterprises (there was a saying that in Kojima you could throw a stone and hit a company president), and the well-connected network they formed meant that about ten years ago it was easy for small, innovative makers to conduct their own jeans experiments. It certainly formed the nucleus of independent jeans production in particular. Kojima is romanticized as the location of these special old shuttle looms, the place where *aizome* (dyeing from Japanese indigo plants) craftsmen (*shokunin*) work and so on. While this was true a decade or so ago, the town's current situation reveals a somewhat different picture.

The jeans bus is a regular bus that follows the normal route with images of jeans daubed on its sides. The Betty Smith Jeans Museum is closed by default but, on the rare occasion a visitor arrives, a lady rushes across to unlock the door and switch on the lights and video presentations. The most popular attraction in Kojima remains the old house of the salt pioneer, Nozaki. There are old looms in Kojima but even jeans that are assembled and/or washed and distressed there usually get their denim material from Fukuyama, further west. There are some more senior craftsmen remaining, but for the most part "super jeans" are more likely to be sewn up in a small factory staffed by young Chinese women workers. Production sites are closing down all the time.

Like the Onta potters (Moeran 1997) who are propelled towards more individually based modes of production despite their show of solidarity, the Kojima image of craft locale is at odds with its current situation in which the network of smaller producers is breaking down and giving way to larger companies that take manufacturing orders as well as having their own brands. Kojima is a somewhat lackluster jeans Mecca, but for the super denim cognoscenti it remains an important signifier of quality. This authentically rendered image of Kojima has helped to relocate some of the jeans authenticity of America to this other "birthplace."

TWO KOJIMA JEANS MAKERS

There are dozens of "super jeans" companies who specialize in "Made in Japan" new vintage denim, many of whom are based in Kojima, such as Momotaro Jeans. These makers are regularly listed in book-style magazines that are published perhaps on a yearly basis as special editions, like the Lightning magazine series of "denim books" (for example, Lightning 2009b).

I will look at one of the key "super jeans" companies, Studio D'artisan, hereafter shortened to D'artisan but known affectionately by its fans as D'arti (*daruchi*). The firm is based in Osaka, but the factory where all the washing and distressing is done is in Kojima.

I will compare the authenticating strategies used by D'artisan with those of another very small maker, Tuki, based in Okayama not far from Kojima. Both are concerned only with making what they regard to be the best products they can, without pandering to the demands of their customer base. This is an authenticating discourse that distances the companies from profit motives and from making their discerning customers from feeling like they are being "sold to." While both brands are concerned with achieving a certain authenticity, the form that authenticity takes and the strategies used to render it are very different, showing how denim/jeans authenticity is multivalent and possible to render in a number of ways.

STUDIO D'ARTISAN

Studio D'artisan was founded early in the history of Japanese denim in 1969 from a desire to reproduce vintage denim using Japanese materials and techniques, including the *aizome* indigo dyeing that had flourished in Japan for centuries. The man who started it, Takagi, was studying abroad in Europe where he would forage in local bazaars and markets for old jeans and military garb. There are suggestions that Takagi was the first to think of making reproduction vintage jeans that matched the classics in shape and texture. "He's the one that came up with it all," said Mr. Fujiwara, the current president of the company. The French name, translating as "craftsman's studio" encapsulates an idea held of a European craftsman, operating separately and less commercially than his American jeans industry counterpart. Now, D'artisan's core customers range from 18 to 60 years old, with some of the older clientele having patronized the brand for much of its history. Most D'artisan jeans are just under 20,000 yen, roughly US$200, with many costing significantly more, especially if they have been subject to washing and other "processing" (*kakou*).

"Now, vintage jeans are accepted without question, but at the time [thirty years ago] it was only D'artisan who were focusing on *aizome* dyeing and who took up jeans in a real (*honkakuteki*) way" states D'artisan's thirtieth anniversary booklet (Lightning 2009a: 26). But there is a clear paradox here. How can you newly "make" vintage? Why is it not called, more accurately "reproduction" vintage? Second-hand vintage Levi's are distinguished by calling them *furugi*, literally old clothes. "Vintage refers to the type of material—it's the narrow-width fabric" explains Fujiwara. By making the denim fabric on old shuttle looms similar to the ones that produced the original jeans of the early twentieth century (in many cases on the very same looms used over fifty years ago), "vintage-ness," a key element of authenticity, can be literally woven into the new jeans. In a slight departure from the loss of aura via mechanical reproduction (Benjamin 1992), the "vintage" aura of these jeans has been reinstated through production techniques, which though mechanical, are sufficiently outdated to pass as "original." Hendry (2000) finds the same creation of authenticity can be achieved by using the same methods to make a new copy that were used to make an old original in the case of a replica of Shakespeare's house that was built for a theme park in Japan.

The replica was, she argued, more authentic than the original old house since it was a faithful copy that furthermore was unsullied by the passage of time. The same can be said for D'artisan jeans.

Weaving denim from old shuttle looms rather than modern projectile ones not only takes more time to produce a length of a narrower width fabric but it leaves a characteristic edge that is not frayed, called "selvedge."

This selvedge denim is one of the strategies used by not only D'artisan, but by many of these smaller companies and more recently, following Japan's lead, by global high-fashion brands, in the rendering of historical authenticity. However, the majority of D'artisan jeans are not made from such selvedge denim, getting their denim instead from Fukuyama: in fact only the SP-006 selvedge model is advertised as a "Made in Kojima" model. So what of all the other non-selvedge D'artisan jeans? How do they come to bear the patina of authenticity? D'artisan jeans have features that are literally copied from vintage models: the width of the belt loops, the color of the stitching (also done on old machines), even the leather patch features two pigs (the D'artisan logo) pulling apart a pair of jeans, in a blatant homage to Levi's two horses. The sales techniques of the shop assistants in the D'artisan shops emphasize these features. As Fujiwara explained: "The staff take time to explain the difference between the various jeans to customers. Whether it's one- or non-wash, how it was woven, how it was stitched, how it was dyed, how the jeans will change once you wear them, whether they'll shrink after you wash them or not …" While calling to attention the high "craftsmanship" that goes into producing D'artisan jeans, the sales patter also incorporates the concept that the jeans must not only be authentic in themselves but authentic to the wearer, the customer. Do they suit not only your body shape, but your overall appearance and *funiki* (atmosphere, aura)? Like all of these strategies, this is not unique to D'artisan and some brands claim to go so far as to actually dissuade customers from buying their jeans if a fitting proves less than satisfactory. This stems from the same refusal to be seen to be interested in profit at the expense of craft and quality. "Our stance is just to make good things and have them recognized by our customers" said Fujiwara, denying they have a market whose tastes they actively target.

This rationale echoes the ideal of *chokkan* (direct perception) that was central to Yanagi's concept of *mingei* (folk art) (Moeran 1997). It implies a universal aesthetic that if the self is subsumed, can be recognized as "good" or "beautiful" by anybody. Moeran shows however that this *chokkan* is not achieved in practice and that there is no inherent aesthetic standard in these jeans but a set of values that derive from recreating the features, and importantly, by the same methods (the old shuttle loom for example) as early "original" jeans.

Denim is perhaps unique in being the only fabric whose resultant garments we are happy to buy when they show obvious signs of wear and tear (Miller and Woodward 2007). On a visit to the shop in Tokyo and later the factory in Kojima, D'artisan's president was always most animated when excitedly showing me the qualities of these particular jeans. He presents them to me, exclaiming: "These are new (*shinpin*)." This is indeed surprising as not only were they faded and worn, as is common for pre-distressed jeans, but they were also incredibly soft and malleable. An attempt to stand them up resulted in the waist concertinaing into the frayed ankles with barely any starchy resistance. "We process them until the point that they would rip if we did it anymore" says Fujiwara. Indeed there are no holes in the main body of the denim, although the bottoms were frayed, and a semicircle was completely worn away at the heel as if someone had been walking around for years in these jeans, which were too long for them.

He was clearly very proud of this achievement and would not reveal all of the methods he used to get them so soft. "These don't just look like vintage jeans," he said, "they feel like them." These jeans cost a good couple of hundred dollars more for the privilege of having them not just aesthetically, but texturally processed to a mock pre-worn state. Jeans in their "original" state, as work wear (*jitsuyouhin*), demanded the presence of being faded, frayed and torn. As a result of the softness of vintage Levi's, softness became a marker of authenticity in itself that has been pursued to extremes here. D'artisan have produced by mechanical means denim that not only looks like its historical precedent but feels probably softer than any vintage jeans would have done through merely wearing them, working in them and washing them for years.

This pair of new jeans has been subject to various processes all taking time and money in their execution and development in order to look and feel as much like a pair of original, early twentieth-century jeans in their *jitsuyouhin* worn state. That is, their authentic value derives from their particularly faithful visual and tactile reproduction of an original, not in their genealogical or essential relationship to the original itself. Like the Shakespeare house, in fact, they are better than the original, precisely because they come in the state of being soft and worn-in, something that the original can only achieve through the passage of time. The great enthusiasm that continues amongst Japanese denim enthusiasts for vintage Levi's 501xx shows that the original remains highly privileged as a locus of authenticity in Japan, but when they cost over a thousand dollars, a pair of pre-worn jeans made using similar techniques and with a similar aesthetic satisfies the desire for authenticity at a lower cost.

DENIM FANS—SATISFYING YOUR SELF

So far I have considered how jeans producers attempt to render authenticity in their products. They claim that they do not target particular markets but it is clear from their continued existence that there is a market for these authentically rendered jeans. Who comprises this market, and why, if they are spending an average of US$200 plus on jeans, do they not choose to spend the same amount on more widely recognized and status-bestowing high-fashion designer jeans?

I first came across the term *denimu maniakku* when talking to an employee of Kojima-based premium denim maker Nola, named Nakajima. He was telling me about his company's jeans, which are not dissimilar in many ways to D'artisan's (and the large majority of other small makers that feature in the same denim special issues). Giving me what was surely a version of his sales patter, he proudly showed me the old machine that they used for the stitching, on display in their Kojima shop-cum-showroom. He explained that only jeans stitched on such old machines acquired real diagonal "puckering" on the hems. Continuing with the "authentic" features of the jeans, he told me to press down on the area around the pocket, pointing out the presence of rivets that, despite being invisible, were significant in their mere presence. What kind of person would be impressed by an invisible feature? Who would care about puckering, which is not a feature that makes the jeans any better to wear, or necessarily better to look at? *Mania no hito* was the answer: obsessive fans, cognoscenti, or denim "geeks" (*otaku*). Not wishing to make them sound as if they are slightly unhinged, I will refer to them as fans, not maniacs (as would be the literal translation), although the term *maniakku* includes the elements both of strong liking for jeans (fans) and deep knowledge about them (cognoscenti).

The shop assistant himself admitted to being such a fan. "Us mutual fans (*mania doushi*) will look back at each other's jeans if we pass in the street" he says. "If often happens to me." These fans can identify a pair of these "super jeans" at a mere glance from factors such as the fabric quality and color, the presence of selvedge, the fit, distressing patterns and of course the labels and back-pocket stitching.

On the day I met him, Nakajima was wearing a pair of jeans that were a loose, wide fit. The denim was crisp, starchy, a deep blue and had a slight surface sheen. The hems were turned up and the selvedge on display. There was no red thread: "we use beige thread, it's more natural." I asked how long he had been wearing that pair. "Since April 1" he replied, with unexpected precision. Nakajima, like his fellow denim fans, treats the wearing of jeans with as much interest and care as they do their selection for purchase.

> I have been wearing them every day since then, and haven't washed them yet. The last pair I wore for 11 months without washing, but then my baby threw up on them so I had to. I stopped wearing them then. I still have them, folded up and put away. I wanted to wear them for a year precisely, as I did with the pair prior to that. I plan to wear them again at some point in the future.

The point of wearing each identical pair for a fixed period of time was that they ended up with a shape, wear, color and feel that were all "unique to yourself" (*jibun senyou*). "Your face (*kao*) comes out through them" he added. With one pair he experimented by washing them every three months, in order to compare them with a pair that was not washed at all.

It is not only how often you wear and wash your jeans that is of concern to the denim fan but also how you wash them. The Lightning "Denim Book" guide (2009b) has a few pages at the front where they ask denim fans: "What brand denim are you wearing? What do you like about them? How long have you been wearing them? How often do you wear them? How do you wash them?" The answers to the last question include "I don't; normally; with special denim wash; and water only."

Studio D'artisan is one of the best-known brands that attracts these denim fans. When it opened its first shop in Tokyo, a queue of fans had formed outside. People had come from as far as Japan's northern island, Hokkaido. There is at least one D'artisan customer who owns over a hundred pairs, according to the president. "These denim fans are a small slice of the pie. There are fewer and fewer people who think 'If it's not like this, it's no good.'" One of the biggest consumer stories of 2009 in Japan was the rise of ultra-cheap (*gekiyasu*) jeans, meaning under around US$10. But the consensus seems to be that if these small makers can keep their core customers of *denim maniakku*, then their continuation and that of Kojima will be possible.

The main demographic of these "Made in Japan" premium jeans are men over thirty-five years of age: they have both the disposable income to treat themselves to a pair of jeans that will last and they have passed the adolescent and young adult periods of experimenting with and being interested in changing fashions. A stance that many of these jeans makers take is that they are not in the "fashion" business. They seem to say that whereas fashion is volatile and superficial, their products are perceived as historically grounded, stable and "real." Harada, once more, does not hold this attitude: just as he is not interested in linking his jeans to an authentic past, he does not see his products as separate from fashion. There is a timelessness, a constancy about this conception of authenticity. He reasons that there are two types of people who are interested in vintage jeans and their new repro-counterparts: teenagers and young adults, and men approaching middle age and over. The former category research, buy and wear these jeans as part of the larger project of finding themselves as Harada did when he was a university student; the latter category choose their jeans and wear them as a result of having graduated from this youthful process and having settled into their own style. A more negative view would hold that these are another breed of *otaku* who wear these repro-vintage jeans because they have no confidence in participating in "fashion." Rather than spending money on an expensive pair of jeans that mark them out as being "of the moment," they spend money on a pair that gives them the satisfaction of having the best craftsmanship quality and something that is as close to the "real thing" as they can get. The purchase and wearing results in "self satisfaction" (*jiko manzoku*) as Nakajima put it. Brands like D'artisan and Tuki are barely known except outside these fan circles, so if there are status symbols at all it is only to the wearer. The search for the *honkakuteki* pair of "super jeans" is an inward-facing act, a project that works on the self, rather than the relatively outward-facing act of buying a well-known high fashion pair of jeans.

CONCLUSION

Anxiety has been recently reevaluated as key to many fashion decisions made by individuals (Woodward 2007). There is anxiety over expected social responses to one's sartorial appearance and the anxiety about negotiating the balance between fitting in to a collective as well as standing out as an individual. Where vintage jeans in Japan are concerned, I argue that there is another anxiety that begs for resolution: "authenticity anxiety." Taylor-Atkins (2000) formulated the term to describe the dilemma he saw that Japanese jazz musicians had of having to be authentic through imitating the West: they were in the "awkward position of trying to authenticate themselves with reference to two very different standards—that of 'jazz' and that of 'Japanese culture'" (Taylor-Atkins 2000: 31). Not merely copying the *otehon* of vintage Levi's, but also "domesticating" (Tobin 1992) them through the strategies raised in this paper, has made it possible to express a Japanese identity through the American cultural product of jeans. This is not an anxiety that presents itself to all Japanese jeans wearers but it seems to affect the category of denim "maniacs," who are mostly men over thirty.

The "new vintage" super jeans of this paper support the Japanese version of authenticity that lies not in an original but in a copy achieved by using the same methods as those used to create the original (Hendry 2000; Moeran 1997). New models based on vintage Levi designs are not conceived of as inauthentic fakes but as faithful copies that, in being new, are even better than the real thing, the blemished original. The distressing processes achieve an even more perfect copy in that the jeans are rendered not as fashion but as worn work wear, in keeping with their original purpose. Non-distressed denim allows a different dimension of "real-ness" to be achieved through complicated wearing patterns that produce a pair of jeans that is unique to your body, authentic to your "self." In this way, in a saturated marketplace where consumption choices allow many "optional identities" (Lindholm 2008) personal authenticity is sought and achieved through wearing in a pair of these "super jeans."

This concern with rebranding (almost debranding) denim in terms of craft rather than fashion, and appealing to the wearer as holding the authentic owner relationship to the jeans over and above the company brand is typical of an increasing concern with authenticity in Japan. Japan, the "Empire of the Signs" (Barthes 1982) is often seen as an epitome of the postmodern society with all its free-floating symbolism: it follows that amongst this indiscriminate market where seemingly anything goes, there is an opposite movement that is obsessed in finding amongst this what is most "real."

A pair of blue jeans, like jazz (Taylor Atkins 2000), is a kind of "universal language"—so universal, in fact, as to be even "blindingly obvious" (Miller and Woodward 2007) and "culturally odourless" (Iwabuchi 2002), being easily domesticated globally despite their American origins. Whilst "blindingly obvious" in much of everyday life, these "super jeans" are the result of taking even the most obvious aspects of jeans—the stitching, rivets and so on—

and making them extraordinarily significant. The passionate investigation and pursuit of quality by many Japanese denim cognoscenti has resulted in an "exceptional authenticity" being successfully rendered for "Made in Japan" premium jeans. This authenticity, established fully in the 1990s in Japan, is now recognized globally, resulting in a slew of global high and quality fashion brands, ranging from the cult PRPS to Paul Smith, Dior and Savile Row tailors, using the "Made in Japan" quality as an authenticating strategy of their own.

41

FAKE BRANDS

Magdalena Craciun

FAKE

In the common understanding, a *fake* is something other than that which it is claimed or presumed to be. "To deem an object inauthentic is to assert that it is not, despite claims to the contrary, an example of an identified class of objects, or not the creation of an identified person or group" (Handler 2001: 964). This understanding implies an intention to deceive: this object is produced and displayed with the intention of making someone believe it is indiscernibly identical with another object. Fakes have presumably always existed (Benjamin [1936] 1999; Schwartz 1996). Moreover, the existence of these objects has probably never been regarded with moral indifference (Grafton 1990; Johns 2009). However, with the advent of modernity—and in response to various cultural conceptualizations, epistemological developments, technological changes, commercial interests, and legal elaborations that gained prominence during this period—their presence has become even more problematic.

This section disentangles the complex set of concepts, interests, and concerns that operates within the common understanding of fake. It also points out that the ways authenticity and inauthenticity are intimately bound up in each other's histories are rarely mentioned in this common understanding.

ORIGINAL, COPY, AND FAKE

The fake is the opposite of the original, that is, a unique work produced by an inspired, solitary, creative, and unique author. The powerful cultural figure of the author is a Romantic creation. Romanticism attributed substance to certain persons and things, at the expense of other persons and things. The received history of the notion of the author locates its first articulations in Wordsworth's self-presentation as a poet who exercises his genius and produces an original work and Young's theoretical emphasis on originality as the defining element of literary composition and his criticism of the mere mastery of composition rules that predominated in classical literature (Woodmansee 1984). The original works the author creates owe their individuality solely to their creator. The source of inspiration is located in the author's inner reality. Authored works are creations ex nihilo, entirely new matter brought into being by the genius of the creator, endowed with the same unique qualities their creator possesses (Trilling 1972). The notion of the author transcends the cultural boundaries of Romanticism: the author becomes the "agent of original self-definition" and the "paradigm case of the human being" (Taylor 1991: 62). This history tends to forget episodes that demonstrate the way the, Romantic notion of author is constructed with reference to its shadow, the forger. In eighteenth-century Britain, for example, in a period when literary forgeries proliferated, the Romantic idea of the author as the originator of a work was also articulated in response to the practice of forgery (Russett 2006). Moreover, Romantic writers used these literary productions as sources of inspiration and even modeled the figure of the Romantic poet upon the tragic life and death of a young forger, Chatterton,

Adapted from Magdalena Craciun, "The Elusive Nature of Inauthenticity: Manufacture and Trade in Fake Branded Garments in Turkey," in *Material Culture and Authenticity: Fake Branded Fashion in Europe* (London: Bloomsbury, 2013), pp. 18–71.

whom they nevertheless condemned and placed on the very margin of the literary canon (Groom 2007). Partial as it is, this received history carries the Romantic component of the common understanding of fake.

In the Romantic understanding, an *original* is a singular work that expresses an author's unique inner reality. In contrast, a copy, even a perfectly imitated copy, is an empty, soulless thing. What is lost is the sense of a direct connection with the author's inner being. A copy is similar to a translation, that is, "something of the original is both added to and erased in the copy" (McClean 2002: 22). A copy resembles a quotation, that is, it shows "what we are to respond to rather than being what we are to respond to" (Danto 1973: 13). A copy has no value of its own and exists only because the original has value and is, therefore, worth copying. Moreover, copies are incomplete, inaccurate, crude, and clumsy versions executed in inferior materials. In this way, copying, a venerated tradition especially in the education of artists, is reconceptualized to fit the Romantic emphasis on originality and authenticity (Baudrillard 2001). The act of copying is considered a second-rate activity, a failure of creativity, a mere demonstration of technical proficiency and imitative ability, and a "simple repetition without any addition of personality or work that would deposit the trace of an original self" (Frow 2003: 59). Therefore, in this Romantic understanding, the original and the copy are placed in a hierarchical relationship, with the original as the valorized term and the copy as the discredited term.

There have been numerous attempts to eliminate the conceptual distance between the original and the copy. Much of twentieth-century art was marked by such disputes, and its exemplary moments involved "radical renunciation(s) of originality" (Frow 2003: 59). Different artists questioned the notion of original and experimented with copying, appropriation, ready-mades, pastiche, paraphrase, parody, and homage (McClean and Schubert 2002). Intentional or not, forgers also brought their contribution to this critique. The ideological message of forgery was conveyed by forgeries that were indiscernible from the original to the naked eye. These objects undermined the belief in the artist's ability to create unique works. Even after they were disclosed and removed from collections, these objects continued to raise the question of whether authenticity mattered aesthetically (Dutton 1983; Jones 1992; Radnóti 1999). These practices aimed to demonstrate that the copy was the "*underlying condition of the original*" and that the original and the copy "mutually sustain each other" (Krauss 1981: 58, 64; emphasis in the original). Nevertheless, "despite the elite artist's loss of belief in the artistic myth, the conventions of authenticity have not been dispensed with" (Lindholm 2008: 24) and remain at the core of contemporary culture.

Moreover, there have been numerous instances in which the proclaimed aesthetic and material distance between the original and the copy has been questioned. As modernity became the "age of mechanical reproduction" (Benjamin [1936] 1999), and as modern individuals began to embrace the "culture of the copy" (Schwartz 1996) and to delight in the deluge of copies, these developments conspired to blur the line between the original and its copy. However, the somewhat paradoxical response to the development of modern reproductive technologies is a preoccupation, if not obsession, with the original. Latour and Lowe state, for example, that "paradoxically, this obsession for pinpointing originality increases proportionally with the availability and accessibility of more and more copies of better and better quality … No copies, no original" (2010: 278). The Romantic distinction between the original and the copy has remained at the center of contemporary culture.

In the dominant understanding, the mutual constitution of these concepts is not mentioned. In this understanding, original and copy are caught up in a hierarchical relationship, with a yawning gap interposed between them. The culturally and materially inferior copy stands as "the discredited part of the pair, the one that opposes the multiple to the singular, the reproducible to the unique, and the fraudulent to the authentic" (Krauss 1981: 58).

The fake is placed on an even lower position. In the Romantic understanding, the author is the sole origin of his or her works. In contrast, the faker copies someone else's work or imitates someone else's style, signs his or her work with that author's name, and tries to pass it off as an original. The fake, conceals its biography, mimics the biography of the original, and attempts to replace it. The fake simultaneously draws on and subverts the authority called upon to authorize its existence and to give it value. This intention to deceive has always been condemned. However, the fake becomes an even more serious threat when it is understood as prejudicing a right.

The criminalization of the fake begins with the conceptualization of knowledge as property. The notion of intellectual property was articulated during the disputes between authors, publishers, and book pirates that raged in the book trade in the early modern period. Rose (1994) points out that the notion emerges through the articulation of the Romantic theory of authorship and Locke's theory of labor. Locke argues that an individual, as the proprietor of his or her own person, is also the owner of the products of his or her labor. The right of property in the products of one's labor is declared a just reward for one's labor and a natural right, prior to any social regulation. During these disputes, Lockean ideas about real property were translated to the cause of literary property. Woodmansee (1984) and Gaines (1991) stress that this articulation is not an inevitable theoretical outcome: it was realized, at that time and later, not so much through logical affinity, but interested rhetorical shifts. These disputes served as a background against which an agreement was reached: artistic and literary works were to be understood as intellectual properties owned by their individual originators. The law recognized and granted rights in this new type of property. A consequence of this legal elaboration was the criminalization of fake, because this prejudices the right of the author and, therefore, owner of the original. In this way, the hierarchical opposition between original and copy/fake has been not only culturally defined, but also legally regulated.

AUTHORED AND AUTHORIZED OBJECTS

The legal notion of intellectual property was further refined to serve a wide range of interests, not only in the domain of culture, but also in the realm of commerce.

As a consequence, the notion of fake was enlarged to refer to not only fraudulently authored objects, but also unauthorized copies.

This pragmatic reformulation was articulated around two crucial notions in the Romantic thinking, that is, the notions of original and copy. Intellectual property law began to operate with a particular notion of originality and an enlarged concept of original. Romantic theory distinguished between the original and the copy. Intellectual property law maintained this distinction; however, it protected creative efforts of many types and recognized many works as originals, regardless of whether they were unoriginal, banal, or even imitative. "A kind of doubleness" was put at work in the legal concept of originality. "[T]he law retained the connotations of artistic creativity and the ideal of the singular work. [However] 'creativity' came to refer simply to the work's point of origination, not to the unique, soul-invested nature of the work itself" (Gaines 1991: 58). This reduction of originality to the blunt fact of origin was realized through a tautological shift in the discourse: "[A]ll works of authorship are original. Why? Because they originate with authors" (Gaines 1991: 63). The uneasy coexistence of these partially overlapping notions of authenticity has ever since been concealed in the legal discourse.

Moreover, intellectual property law began to use a nuanced category of the copy. Romantic theory discredited copying, in any form, licit or illicit. Intellectual property law encouraged and, simultaneously, policed coping in the legal context, an authored work was conceived as the source of its authorized copies. In the accusatory legal context, the unauthorized copy was presented as the outcome of a clandestine act of intellectual trespassing carried out for base motives. A copy needed not be identical to amount to an infringement. In this way, intellectual property law provided generative conditions for sanctioned processes of duplication and prohibitive obstacles for unauthorized processes of reproduction (Geismar 2005). This legal framework has ever since distinguished between authorized, legitimate and, thus, authentic, and unauthorized, illegitimate and, therefore, inauthentic copies.

This pragmatic reformulation was a response to the growth of trade and the development of more integrated, dynamic, and commoditized economies in which the implementation of novel ideas and technologies became crucial. "The Romantic image of the individuated author as creative genius, autonomously creating works characterised as embodiments of personal originality, provided ideological support for the legal institution of fictions that denied and obscured market forces" (Coombe 1998: 255). "Intellectual property is justified on the basis that it provides an incentive for future productive activity, or that it acknowledges and represents the sovereignty of the individual over their thoughts and ideas" (Moor 2007: 96). Intellectual property claims, rights, and restrictions were developed in different European countries and the United States beginning in the eighteenth century. These laws aimed to construct authors and owners and regulate reproductive activities. They offered (limited) monopoly rights over knowledge to its primary or "entitled" producers. They granted the rights to materialize and, thereby, control knowledge and to capitalize on the attendant profit that the circulation of this knowledge and of the products that materialized it could afford. These laws also ruled that the unauthorized reproduction of the products that materialized this protected knowledge could potentially pose an economic threat to its primary or "entitled" producers and, as a consequence, criminalized the unauthorized duplication and the resulting unauthored and unauthorized objects. These laws "constitute a political economy of mimesis in capitalist societies" (Coombe 1998: 206). The forms of abundance that industrial development made possible have been locked into this particular conceptual framework.

Today these laws are hegemonic in markets and courts of law around the world. The major vehicles for protecting intellectual property—and for deciding which objects fall outside the legitimate domain and are, thus, fakes—are patent, copyright, and trademark. Patents are applied to inventions, copyright is used to protect literary and artistic creations, and trademark is used to protect the qualities that distinguish the products of a company from those of others. Copyright

and patent promote profits generated from new works and inventions, whereas trademark protects and perpetuates existing monopolies (Moor 2007). This legislation has spread to virtually any country with aspirations of taking part in the global economy. International pressure is so strong that countries that refuse to enact such laws or fail to enforce them find themselves on the receiving end of serious trade sanctions. Moreover, the introduction of this legislation is often portrayed as a matter of democracy and progress, and countries that refuse or lag behind are frequently described as politically and culturally "backward" states (Lippert 1999).

In this pragmatically refined conceptualization of intellectual property, authored and authorized objects materialize knowledge over which individuals and corporations are given property rights. Fraudulently authored and unauthorized objects infringe on these rights and are consequently criminalized.

THE MATERIALITY OF INAUTHENTICITY

In the modern period, anxieties about the authenticity of objects have found resolution in an objectivist understanding of authenticity as inherent in materiality and in the development of scientific methods for the investigation of materiality.

In other periods, the authenticity of objects was evaluated through different methods. Relics, for example, were evaluated in relation to the biography of the person who offered the object or the biography of the object itself. In the first case, it was important to know who this priestly individual was, for he or she could transform certain objects into sacramental artifacts through specific invocations. The substance and methods of creation of these objects were completely irrelevant. In the other case, the connection with a saint and the story of the acquisition were important. The value of these objects lay precisely in their substance. However, relics were not man-made, but recuperated from the cadavers and possessions of venerated saints (Geary 1986; Lindholm 2002).

In the modern context, when man-made objects became so important, the craze for collecting spread throughout society, and technologies for multiplication began to develop, the identification of objects as authentic or inauthentic became crucial as regards their financial value. In this period, when objective observation and experimentation were increasingly valorized over received opinion (Jaffé 1992), the authenticity of objects began to be conceptualized as an objective and measurable attribute inherent in their very materiality. Consequently, it could be established scientifically through an investigation into the essence of these objects in terms of date of creation, materiality, authorship, workmanship, primary context, function, and use.

The development of this understanding was not only a response to the practical problems that confronted especially the market for art and antiquities, but also an extension of the notion of individualism. With the advent of modernity, the medieval worldview of a cosmic order ordained and encompassed by God was replaced by individualism. This was a worldview that allowed individuals to locate ultimate reality within themselves. They were conceived as fixed and bounded entities, each with its own unique internal essence (Handler 1986). Their truth could be discovered through an investigation or self-investigation of their inner beings. This way of conceptualizing the individual was extrapolated to the material world. Artifacts were also conceived as stable, fixed, and self-contained entities, autonomous from their context and audience (Jones 2010). Their ultimate reality, that is, their authenticity, was inherent in their materiality. The truth of objects could be discovered through a scientific investigation into their essence.

In this way, the fear that objects could no longer be guaranteed by their authors, owners, or authorizing institutions was countered by the theory that deception could not be denied forever, inscribed as it was in the very materiality of the object. The fake could always be identified. Something in its materiality eventually betrayed its true nature. Inauthenticity was declared an attribute of materiality. This objectivist understanding of the authenticity of objects remains hegemonic in contemporary institutions such as the art market, museums, markets, and courts of law, that is, in institutions in which authenticity has commercial value (Handler 2001).

However, the materiality of inauthenticity is not always brought to the foreground. Depending on circumstances and interests, it might be very well be pushed to the background. There are instances in which materiality must be investigated. In this case, the aim is to denigrate an individual object. Inauthenticity is inscribed in materiality, but it is not necessarily inferior. There are other instances in which materiality ought to be rejected a priori as inferior. In this case, the aim is to create and denigrate a category of objects. A discursive strategy through which this aim might be achieved involves lumping together all types of inauthentic objects as the same kind of immoral thing.

There is a huge variety of inauthentic objects, ranging from forgeries of art and luxury objects, themselves extraordinary objects, to the ubiquitous fake brands of today, unofficial copies as banal as the official ones. There are significant differences between these objects, in terms of knowledge, craftsmanship, and technology that go into their production. There are also significant differences in terms of the morality associated with their presence: art forgeries, fake branded garments, and fake medication do not pose the same moral dilemmas.

In the dominant discourse, the different types of inauthentic object are often treated interchangeably. Ideas elaborated for the condemnation and exclusion of a type of inauthentic object are used for the condemnation and exclusion of other types of inauthentic objects. The reasoning behind this is that all types of inauthentic objects represent transgressions against identity, property, morality, and the authority of the law (Baines 1999; Haywood 1987; Malton 2009). Therefore, all types of inauthentic objects are—and should be—equally condemned as inferior products of dubious morality.

In brand discourse the inverse of this strategy is the lumping together of all types of authentic objects, be they art objects or branded commodities, in one category. This is achieved through interested omissions of the conceptual difference between authenticity as originality and authenticity as origin and of the material differences between various types of authentic objects. In this discourse, brand is the equivalent of a signature (Frow 2003).

BRAND

In the simplest understanding, *brand* is a mode of mediation between producers and consumers. Brands are usually associated with the development of modern capitalism (Carrier 1995). However, Wengrow argues that theoretically they can appear in any large-scale economy, for they represent a way of coping with the "reality of living in a community … formed and sustained through the circulation of impersonal objects," a reality specific not only to modern capitalist societies (2008: 21). Earlier discussions of brand tend to focus on the more traditional function of brand, which approximates the function of the trademark in legal discourse. Brand identifies the origin and/ or ownership of the commodities to which its name and logo are affixed (Manning 2010). At the same time, brand functions as a guarantee of quality and consistency, and an index of the goodwill associated with the source of commodities. Names and logos are, therefore, "visible or materialised goodwill" (Foster 2008b: 79). More recent discussions of brand present it in financial terms—as an "intangible asset," a "wealth generator" whose value increases, or at least does not decrease, with use—and in legal terms—as a protected form of intellectual property (Moor 2007). Moreover, almost all recent accounts see brand as incorporating far more than a name and a logo and proclaim that brand embodies "relationships," "values," and "feelings" (Fournier 1998; Nakassis 2012). They focus, to use Foster's (2005) words, not only on trademarks of production, but also on lovemarks of consumer loyalty. In the present account, the notion of brand is further unpacked through a focus on production and consumption, and the complex set of concepts, interests, and concerns that link them, and through an analysis of brand as a legally protected form of property.

For a long period in the modern history of brand, branded commodities organized the processes of production: developments and improvements in printing, papermaking, packaging, and manufacturing technologies of various sorts have been linked with the requirements of standardization and presentation (Moor 2007). More recently, the brand itself organizes production. Lury points out that brand has acquired a new *productive* role in the contemporary global economy. Brand has become "a mechanism—or medium—for the co-construction of supply and demand … an abstract machine for the reconfiguration of production" (2004: 27–28). Innovation in product design as well as the management of corporate extension are organized around the brand. This change is related to the recognition of brand as a valuable intangible asset, whose already existent reputation diminishes the risks associated with product innovation and corporate growth. To make her point clearer, Lury employs the punning opposition between brand as logo ("the sign or slogans that mark brands") and brand as *logos* ("the kind of thought or rationality that organizes the economy") (2004: 5).

This shift has coincided with a more general transformation within developed economies, in which the creative components of the production process of branded commodities are carried out and organized in the company and the manufacturing components are outsourced to smaller companies, usually from less developed economies (Gereffi 1999). The mass production of branded clothes incorporates millions of workers from all over the world (and in many cases forces them to work in appalling conditions) (Klein 1999; Schneider 2006). Among the many consequences of this way of organizing the production of branded commodities, two are mostly relevant for the present discussion. The first regards the ability of the brand to index the product. In the contemporary economy, brand acts as a transferable form of property that can operate entirely through licensing and without any involvement or regulation of product quality. Manning points out that in this context "it becomes debatable whether trademarks indicate any specific source at all or whether they even act as guarantees of quality relative to, for example, the actual locus of production" (2010: 37). Beebe is even more categorical, entirely rejecting this possibility: "the modern trademark does not function to identify the true origin of goods. It functions to obscure that origin, to cover it with a *myth* of origin" (2008: 52, quoted in Manning 2010: 37). Although authenticity (as origin) remains a constitutive element of brand discourse, as corporations increasingly produce their commodities in poorer parts of the world, the brand is increasingly distanced from the site of production and cannot entirely guarantee the product. The second consequence regards the capacity of brand to index the producer. Throughout the modern and contemporary history of brand, its actual producers have been almost always erased from sight. This is more the case today, when branded commodities are "worldly things" (Foster 2008a), produced in locations with cheap and docile labor forces, circulated through complicated commodity chains, and consumed in another, more affluent place. The actual places of production, and the working conditions, are often a matter of secrecy (Klein 1999). Brand has not been so much an index of a producer, but rather a means to create, consolidate, and unify a prosthetic personality, that is, the modern corporation (Mazzarella 2003).

Brand does not only organize production, but also harnesses consumption. "The creation of value for many consumer products … depends not only upon the extraction of surplus value from the labour of the producer, but also from the meaningful use to which the consumer puts the product" (Foster 2005: 10). Brand is designed to perform not only a functional, but also a symbolic role. Brand singularizes commodities and adds a touch of extraordinariness to what is, in many cases, an ordinary mass-produced object. In the brand discourse, this aim is often achieved through an overlapping of the notions of authenticity as origin and authenticity as originality/uniqueness. However, uniqueness is often claimed at the level of brand, and not of the product, in many cases mass-produced commodities similar to those produced by other companies. Moreover, brand capitalizes on human propensity for forging deep or, equally valid, shallow affective connections with things. Furthermore, brand appropriates people's social productivity, that is, their production of themselves and of their social relationships. Finally, brand makes use of culture in the sense that it works with people's imaginaries and practices of common social worlds and insinuates itself into these webs of meanings. Brand management is a concerted effort to shape and control consumers' associations with and uses of brands. Arvidsson argues

that the purpose of brand management is to guide consumers' investment of affect and to make sure this guidance unfolds in a way that guarantees the reproduction of a distinctive brand image and, thus, strengthens brand equity. In his words, "for consumers, brands are means of production … For Capital, brands are a means of appropriation" (2006: 93–94). This belief in the importance of brand-consumer relationship as a site of value creation is at the core of contemporary brand management.

However, this is how brand *ideally* functions. Despite considerable efforts to cultivate brand identities and to keep consumers' associations within the boundaries of these carefully crafted identities, brand may not always work in the ways intended. In practice, there are instances in which the desired reattachment of objects to people is achieved, and consequently, capitalized upon. In these cases, consumers "pay [monopoly] rent for the use of a brand that has become entangled with their particular biographies and passions" (Foster 2008a: 19). There are also instances in which consumers invest brands with meanings and put them to uses not conceived by their owners.

Consumption plays a crucial role in the determination of what brands come to represent for consumers. Miller (1987) argues that consumption is a form of human creativity in industrialized societies through which individuals appropriate commodities and pursue projects of self-fabrication denied to them in the realm of production. Various studies have illustrated this theoretical proposition in relation to the consumption of branded commodities and the articulation of individual and social projects. Miller (1998) shows that food brands are mobilized to define and enact particular relationships within a family. These brands might become so entangled into these relationships that they are finally rendered essential and indispensable. They come to objectify family values and relationships. Skeggs (1997) describes ways in which knowledge of brand names and of their class connotations as well as actual consumption of branded garments are used in processes of social distinction. Brand becomes a means that people of lower background employ to construct "respectability." In their study of secondhand consumption practices,

Gregson and Crewe (2003) present the profound dislike of more middle-class consumers of branded commodities and their derision of the attempts of other consumers to acquire cultural capital in objectified forms through brands. Rausing (2002) points out that Estonians consume expensive foreign branded commodities to demonstrate that they have returned to "normality," that is, they are no longer forced to be citizens of the Soviet Union. Appadurai (1996) emphasizes that deterritorialized populations might use brands from their places of origin to acquire a sort of ontological security and brands from their new locations to demonstrate to themselves and others their successful integration into their new home.

Moreover, there are instances in which brand itself is harnessed by the unauthorized producers of fake brands, a process brand owners try to control through the legal apparatus of intellectual property laws. Brand is a legally protected form of property, mainly under trademark law. This is a late addition to the intellectual property legislation. Initially, the trademark was not considered a form of intellectual property, as it did not involve the creation of something new, but the use of preexistent linguistic and material forms. Sherman and Bently (1999) argue that in the premodern period creative labor was the organizing principle of intellectual property laws. Copyright, designs, and patents were distinguished in terms of the quality and, later, quantity of the creative labor embodied in the works in question. Toward the end of the nineteenth century, in the context of rapid economic development and in response to a growing preoccupation with objectivity, calculability, and stability, this organizing principle was no longer appropriate. Registration became a prerequisite for the protection of nearly all forms of intellectual property. This eliminated the necessity to distill and measure elusive creativity, offered indisputable proofs of origin and ownership, and "ensured that intangible property was placed in a format which was stable yet indefinitely repeatable" (Sherman and Bently 1999: 182). Copyright, designs, and patents were "still differentiated in terms of their relative 'value.' The main difference was that value now tended to mean the economic value of the property rather than, as had been the case previously, the quality or quantity of the mental labour embodied in the property in question" (Sherman and Bently 1999: 194). The early claim that the trademark could not be included in the intellectual property system because it was noncreative became therefore obsolete. Its economic value allowed the trademark to be conceptualized and protected as a form of intellectual property.

The law prevents the "dilution" of the brand's semiotic distinctiveness, protects investment in design and marketing, and safeguards the brand owner from unfair forms of competition. The law also protects the consumer from being "confused" or deceived as to the origin, ownership, and quality of branded commodities. However, in the past decades, there has been a growing tendency in the law to favor the "dilution" rather than the "confusion" definition of trademark infringement, therefore to protect the companies rather than the consumers' interest in the identification of the origin and content of the branded commodity (Lury 2004). In addition, the brand owner has been redefined as a "quasi-author" who "creates" the meanings attached to the brand (Coombe 1998). This emphasis on the trade-related aspects of trademark law is evident in the recent agreements on international trade, for example the Agreement on Trade-Related Aspects of Intellectual Property Rights (TRIPS) and the Anti-Counterfeiting Trade Agreement (ACTA) (Blakeney 2009; Grosse Ruse-Khan 2008). These changes reflect legislative efforts to respond to, and simultaneously support, the growing importance of brands in the global economy. "All commentators agree that a brand consists of much more than a brand name—but they also agree that without a protected brand name, a brand does not exist" (Moore 2003: 336). Trademark law is particularly important in the present context, when names, signs, and designs are believed to play a greater role in identifying the brand in the minds of consumers and, therefore, in carrying the values the brand is supposed to contain. This law protects a company's profits by excluding other individuals or companies from using these names, signs, and designs and, consequently, capitalizing on the value they are expected to produce.

FAKE BRAND

In the legal understanding, a fake brand is the outcome of an act of counterfeiting, that is, the "unauthorized copying of the trademark, labels or packaging of goods on a commercial scale, in such a way that the get-up or lay-out of the cover, label or appearance of the goods closely resemble those of the original" (Sodipo 1997: 126). Infringement is judged on the basis of substantial similarity, but is often a question of degree, as an infringing object need not be literally identical to a protected object. Nevertheless, the law draws a sharp line between the authentic and the fake, the genuine and the counterfeit. Authentic commodities are those whose brand names and logos truthfully signify a corporate origin. In contrast, fake brands are inauthentic because they

> misrepresent the relationship between an object
> and its creator or producer. Corporations and
> international IPR organizations argue that,
> because counterfeits misrepresent that proprietary
> relationship, their production and sale violate
> companies' intellectual property and damage their
> good names. Further, they claim that counterfeiters
> deceive consumers into buying goods that are
> not what they appear, and, more seriously, cause
> consumer injuries and deaths. (Vann 2006: 287)

The disruptive potential of fake branded commodities is objectified in their very materiality. The slipshod versions, the so-called obvious fakes, diminish the exclusive appeal of branded commodities and affect carefully constructed brand identities. The higher-quality versions, the so-called real fakes, which might have been produced in the same factories and/or with the same materials as the originals, reveal the size of the premium the brand owner charges. These objects undermine claims of authenticity, originality, uniqueness, and quality in the brand discourse and dissipate the value of brand itself, not only of particular branded commodities. "These brazen simulacra … expose a conceit at the core of the culture of Western capitalism: that its signifiers can be fixed, that its editions can be limited, that it can franchise the platonic essence of its mass-produced modernity" (Comaroff and Comaroff 2006: 13).

Different factors might have contributed to the production of counterfeits. One factor is the nature of branded commodity. Counterfeiting might be seen as "a natural outgrowth of the fact that intellectual property law seeks to create a false scarcity in categories of things which, by their very nature, are relatively cheap and easy to produce" (Moor 2007: 101). Another factor is the nature of brand economy. Counterfeiting might be seen as an inevitable consequence of the current divisions in the global economy. In many cases, this illegitimate production shadows the legitimate production of branded commodities as an unwanted consequence of the outsourcing of the manufacture of branded commodities in low-wage countries. Badly paid manufacturers harness the value of brand and use the infrastructure of the global brand economy. Moreover, counterfeiting might be interpreted not only a pragmatic response to present conditions, but also as a defiant response that reflects past and present realities. Sodipo (1997) points out that many of the regulations contained in the current intellectual property legislation were originally imposed in the colonies to protect the interests of the colonizers. In addition, in the former colonies, economic and social exclusion, access to technologies of reproduction and authentication, and lax legal systems have prompted many to engage in daring and dangerous activities. These places have become manufacturing sites for fakes of every conceivable sort. In these places, deception has become a means of production. However, this is not so much about defying authority, but about "creating a sort of authority for oneself" (Siegel 1998: 57, quoted in Comaroff and Comaroff 2006: 14). In brief, when the focus is on its production, a fake brand conjures up either an accusation or a "badge of honour" (Dent 2012).

The consumption of counterfeited commodities might be explained in different ways too. It is linked to the perceived inability of brand/trademark to indicate origin and to guarantee quality and consistency. The counterfeit is just a commodity like any other for consumers who ceased to believe in this promise of brand and have few rights to redress should the branded commodities change or deteriorate. Another explanation relates the consumption of fake brands to unsatisfied demands. Branded commodities are desired by many consumers, but hard to acquire because of their prohibitive prices. In these conditions, the social value of branded goods is met by their unauthorized versions. However, their consumers are rarely the "confused" or "deceived" individuals portrayed in intellectual property legislation. The dominant perspective on the consumption of fake brands adds a pejorative dimension to this explanation and is largely indifferent to the issue of confusion.

This links the consumption of fake brands to status emulation and disparages it. Envious consumers do not have the means to emulate and go for the fakes. At work here is the cultural denigration of the copy/fake and the social derision of the person of lesser means who imitates the taste of his or her social superiors. In brief, when the focus is on its consumption, a fake brand is conceived either in appreciative terms, as savvy consumption, or in derisive terms, as emulation.

In the past decades, counterfeiting seems to have proliferated tremendously. However, official reports might exaggerate the dimensions of this phenomenon. When reading the alarming statistics, one should also keep in mind the ways corporations and governments estimate the dimensions of this phenomenon. The assessment of the amount of money lost to business through these illegal activities is rather peculiar, for there is no guarantee that the consumers of the unauthorized copies, if not tempted with commodities at a much lower price, would have otherwise bought the authorized versions at the original price (Blakeney 2009; Sodipo 1997). This logic is more illustrative of corporate greed at the prospect of how much money can be made if everyone buys a company's legitimate products and is used to justify corporate demand for drastic intervention from national governments and international organizations.

The fierce battle against counterfeiting is mainly carried out in the poorer parts of the world (Comaroff and Comaroff 2006) (as well as in poorer parts of the Western world) (Stoller 2002). To naturalize a muscular response, counterfeiting is often equated with illicit activities such as banditry, drug trafficking, and terrorism, in a rhetoric that effortlessly brings economic security and national and international security together on the basis of vague allegations rather than concrete proofs.

CONCLUSION

The chapter has unpacked the notion of fake brand and has demonstrated why we are encouraged to think about fake branded commodities in a particular way. This has developed in relation to the notions of fake, brand, and fake brand and the attendant interests and concerns that shaped their conceptualization. Moreover, this unpacking has revealed the importance of the law as arbiter of what is a fake brand. Furthermore, it has emphasized the role accorded in these elaborations to the materiality of objects placed or forced into the categories of fake, brand, and fake brand.

This conclusion spells out what we are encouraged to think about fake brands and the people who engage with them. These objects are considered inferior material forms. The people who engage with them are derided as self-deceivers and condemned as deceivers of others. The fake-ness (criminal activity) of the fake brand is pushed to the forefront and vigorously condemned; its brand-ness (materiality) is declared insignificant. Powerful institutions, from courts of law to governmental agencies and international trade organizations, circulate this basic set of assumptions all over the world and attempt to command people's apprehension of materiality and to socialize people not to engage with these objects and in these activities.

In short, these studies demonstrate that we live in a world unevenly circumstanced by this dismissive and condemnatory conceptual framework. Perhaps against the pretention of universalism with which this conceptual framework, especially in the form of intellectual property legislation, is circulated around the world, anthropologists seem more preoccupied to analyze instances in which the assumptions about objects and people encapsulated in this framework are not recognized, or they are contested or simply ignored. On the whole, this body of literature concurs with more general theoretical insights into the multiple and contradictory articulations between global and local in the modern world (Miller 1995[b]; Sykes 2009).

42

ON CUTTING AND PASTING:
The art and politics of DIY streetwear

Brent Luvaas

GRAPHIC MANIPULATION

Adhari Adegreden Donora (Ade) and I sat in the cramped backroom of Reddoor distro in Yogyakarta, Indonesia, amid toppling-over stacks of plastic-sheathed T-shirts, some American indie rock band blaring over the loudspeakers, while he hunched over the computer and tinkered with a new design. So far he had etched out a bright yellow telephone with the "paintbrush" tool of Corel Draw. It was an old-fashioned phone, clunky and cumbersome, and Ade had most likely never used one like it. It had that picturesque, nostalgic quality common to phones in movies or high school drama productions, a phone archetype. Beneath it, he had spelled out in a bold black font the name of the clothing label he sold through the shop: "FireFighter Fight!"— as much an exclamation as a name. He was now using the "shape" tool to construct a black, spiral telephone chord out of small, overlapping circles. "Naïve," he told me, laughing, pointing out the commonality between his own mouse drawn-efforts and the kind of anti-skill conceptual art emerging out of New York in the 1980s.

The final motif might become the graphic on a T-shirt. It might become the print pattern of a blazer or a hooded sweat jacket. It might be the singular logo placed strategically over the right breast of a sweater. More likely it will become nothing at all, one of many discarded visual ideas, left in the archives of the "Document" folder of Ade's PC.

Ade and I had become good friends over the last several months. This, however, was the first time I had watched him work. I wanted to know more about his process of constructing images, and I asked him a number of technical points, about what software he uses (Corel Draw, sometimes Adobe Photoshop or Illustrator), where he gets his images (websites, Japanese fashion magazines, French design books). It was important stuff, and I wanted to record it in a more formal way.

"When do I get to interview you?" I asked.

Ade hesitated. "As what?"

I was a bit confused by Ade's response, thinking the answer was obvious. So I asked him in return, "What do *you* mean?"

"Well, as the manager of Reddoor?" he explained. "Or as a student?"

No, as a designer.

Ade grimaced and reflected for a moment before responding. "If you want to interview a designer, you should interview someone else. I'm not a designer at all. I don't really design anything. I'm more of a graphic manipulator." He used the English term, then added the Indonesian translation "*manipulator grafis.*" It is a term Ade is particularly fond of. It shows up in his designs, peppers his speech, steps in as a descriptive term for the pieced together look of his compositions. But it's not as if Ade doesn't know how to design. In fact, at the time of this research he was enrolled in one

Adapted from Brent Luvaas, "On Cutting and Pasting: The Art and Politics of DIY Streetwear," in *DIY Style: Fashion, Music, and Global Digital Cultures* (London: Berg, 2012), pp. 104–23.

of the top design programs in the country. He knows the foundations of design inside and out. He's just not all that interested in design as it's most commonly conceptualized, making pretty little pictures that help sell products.

Ade was raised by a conservative Muslim family in Riau, a relatively wealthy region in Sumatra. He grew up comfortably middle class and could have gone on to any number of professional positions in Riau's booming oil industry, but that was never really Ade's thing. He had always liked to draw, to paint, to create things with his mind and his hands. His parents discouraged him from thinking of art as a career option, though, and Ade never really gave it serious consideration. They would have preferred something more practical for him, economics, perhaps, or engineering. Those are the two fields, Ade told me, that Indonesian parents tend to want their children to go into.

Ade said it never really occurred to him that he could even make a career out of art until his sister moved to Yogyakarta and recommended to their parents that they send him to ISI (Institut Seni Indonesia, the Art Institute of Indonesia) to study design. She convinced them that he could live a comfortable, respectable life as a designer. There are plenty of opportunities in that field these days, as the Indonesian economy adapts to the global marketplace and expands its cultural sector, and besides, Ade would have his sister to look after him in Yogya and keep him from getting into too much trouble. His parents eventually gave their consent.

ISI, it turns out, was a good place for Ade, but not for the reasons his parents or sister had in mind. He discovered punk at ISI, gothic fashion, and indie rock. He learned about radical European art movements like Surrealism, Dadaism, and Situationism; got involved with the House of Natural Fiber, "an informal creative community of collaborative expression" (www.natural-fiber.com/about.html); and began taking part in large media installations that involved lots of flashing lights, disorienting imagery, and music made from scraping metal and amplifying cellphone frequencies.

Ade quickly lost any interest he once might have had in the textbook variety of design work. Instead, he pursued design as experimentation and critique. It became for him part of a larger project of visual "education," of "waking up" the Indonesian populace, as he liked to put it, challenging their thinking about the aesthetic universe they occupy. It is hardly a revolutionary concept for an art academy design program, but it felt new to Ade, an approach to design based more on the desire to communicate than to sell.

In his design work, Ade attempts to lure in his viewers with familiar imagery, then present to them something different from what they expected, something incongruous, even disconcerting. He borrows from a repertoire of dislocated imagery: innocuous woodland creatures, fire-breathing dinosaurs, cartoon aliens, and in keeping with the name of his clothing label, anything having to do with firefighting (Dalmatians and fire hydrants, flames and hoses).

But there is always something slightly off about this work, some uncomfortable juxtaposition (see Hebdige 1979) that challenges the innocuousness of what he is depicting. One of his favorite motifs involves a simple image of a deer with its antlers missing from its head. A single antler protrudes from the creature's nose like a unicorn's horn. It looks clumsy, its weight unevenly distributed, as if it is about to fall over. A number of his pieces also involve firefighters, those public servants who (presumably) protect us from harm. Ade's firefighters, however, tend to be monstrous, anonymous figures hidden behind gas masks and helmets. In Ade's work, the dangerous is rendered harmless. The harmless, in turn, becomes grotesque.

The term "graphic manipulation," then, has more than one meaning here. It refers to the manipulation of existing graphics, the collaging, that is, of sampled materials, and to the "graphic" nature of such manipulation, its underlying violence, its subversion of visual forms. And it also refers to the more practical aspects of Ade's fashion production. For him, the design of garments themselves happens elsewhere, with limited direction from him. His design work is almost purely graphic in orientation, composed on a computer and delivered to production houses in digital format. It challenges the very notion of what fashion design means, makes it far simpler, far more accessible, a practice available to anyone with a computer and access to pirated software, in other words, to pretty much everyone Ade knows. It should come as no surprise, then, that so many people Ade knows are themselves designers.

In this chapter, I discuss the art and politics of Indonesian DIY streetwear design such as Ade's, the way indie designers like him construct compositions out of existing graphics and forge new relationships with both fashion production and global commerce in the process. Cut and paste, I argue, is not just a quick and easy method of producing images, though it is certainly that; it is also a tactic of global re-positioning, a rewriting of the power relationships embedded in neoliberal capitalism. Designers such as Ade, I suggest, sample materials from those more powerful others—corporations, political bodies, designers with established cachet—who exert such a fundamental influence over the ways they imagine and relate to everyday life. And in so doing, they take possession over those institutions, put their own stamp on them, and make them their own. They infuse the branded imagery of global commerce with a new democratic potency, a new dynamic sociality.

THE GLOBAL ASCENDANCE OF STREETWEAR

The reduction of fashion to graphics is, of course, no Indonesian innovation. Designers like Ade proudly trace their aesthetic lineage back through a canon of streetwear labels out of California, New York, and, more recently, London, Vancouver, and Tokyo, for whom the graphic T-shirt remains the most significant, and frequently employed, medium. As Carbone and Johnson (2011) point out in their recent "Oral History of the Graphic T-shirt," the history of streetwear itself is largely the history of graphic manipulation, repurposing existing imagery for the design of boards, T-shirts, and sneakers. Born out of the subcultural intersections of surfing, skateboarding, punk, and hip hop, streetwear's roots lie in the ethnically diverse and stylistically eclectic Southern Californian surf scene of the late 1970s and early 1980s. It soon expanded to New York, where the budding hip hop scene helped launch it into public visibility. Early brands like Powell Peralta, Santa Cruz, and perhaps most influential of all, Stüssy, converted board art to T-shirt art, transposing one

graphic medium onto another (Carbone and Johnson 2011; Sims 2010; Vogel 2007). As they did so, they emphasized the graphic element as the central visual focus of a garment, erasing the authorial contributions of the garment's designers, and consigning non-graphic creative production to the unglamorous position of manual labor. The graphic *was* the fashion, an innovation that not only played to the strengths of a board designer, but also appealed to the punk-influenced DIY ethos of the surf and skate community. Not everyone could design clothing, but most people can put some sort of image together, either by drawing or spraypainting, or at least through collaging some moderately novel composition. Streetwear designers did all of the above, and as they became more and more influential figures in the world of international fashion, they became a greater and greater challenge to the fashion industry as usual.

According to Paul Mittleman of the long-lived Southern California streetwear company Stüssy, streetwear borrowed the DIY tactics of both punk and hip hop (in Carbone and Johnson 2011). Designers cut and pasted from popular culture, remixed the logos of well-known brands, "mixed and matched" from innumerable subcultural sources (Fujiwara, as cited in Sims 2010: 117), and took to regularly satirizing those staples of couture that had come to represent the state of fashion worldwide. Says Bobby Hundreds of the respected Los Angeles streetwear line The Hundreds, "Stüssy was founded upon parody. The line was a direct rip-off of high-end fashion lines, but [Shawn Stüssy] brought it to the street level" (Fujiwara, as cited in Sims 2010). The original Stüssy logo was based on Chanel's. Later renditions referenced Louis Vuitton, Commes des Garçons, and Avenue B.

And it wasn't just fashion that the early streetwear scene took on. Los Angeles label Freshjive created brand parodies of Tide, the laundry detergent giant, along with Special K cereal and 7–Eleven convenience stores. Fellow Los Angeles label X-Large borrowed from video game companies, pulpy old Hollywood films, and major fast food franchises. Fuct took from science fiction films and sports paraphernalia, Obey from professional wrestling and mainstream newspapers. When surf and skate brands Quicksilver,

Volcom, Stüssy, and Obey became international names, their fellow streetwear designers took from them, too, lumping together the former scene mainstays with the rest of corporate capitalism that they saw as so fundamentally opposed to their scene's own way of doing business. Parody became a strategy of brand distinction, a way of distancing themselves from capitalism as usual. This was street level anti-fashion, a declaration of sartorial independence.

Of course, that sense of independence from mainstream capitalism was perhaps always a bit more gestural than actual, as much a part of streetwear's brand appeal as its politics. Streetwear labels are in the apparel industry, too, after all, selling garments— albeit in smaller batches than major fashion labels— and tailoring their goods to changing markets. Style journalist Josh Sims estimates that streetwear is now one of the world's biggest clothing sectors, with sales in the billions of U.S. dollars per year. Sims is no doubt lumping together athletic clothing goliaths such as Nike, Adidas, and Puma with smaller brands such as Mooks and Mecca, but it nonetheless begs the question of just how "outside" streetwear labels can claim to be. Plus, for decades now, respected streetwear labels such as AKA, Undefeated, and Alife have partnered with athletic giants such as Nike, Adidas, and Puma to produce limited-edition shoes of their own. The conceptual distinction between streetwear and ready-to-wear is getting more and more difficult to maintain.

This is especially true as couture brands, from Paul Smith to Commes des Garçons, borrow continually from streetwear in their designs. Early streetwear labels may have appropriated imagery from couture brands, but clearly the influence goes both ways. This is largely because of the street credibility brands such as Obey, Undefeated, and A Bathing Ape are perceived to have by couture labels, and it also speaks to the decline in the brash confidence of couture to manufacture global trends. Where once the fashion world presumed to hold a monopoly on popular taste, to forge the new looks of the moment by tailoring the wardrobes of the elite and letting them "trickle down" (Aspelund 2009) to the masses, today, fashion much more often goes in the opposite direction, "bubbling up" (Polhemus 1994;

Sims 2010) from "the streets." Begin.. with Yves Saint-Laurent, the top houses of ... have looked to urban streetwear for inspiration for their designs (Aspelund 2009; Polhemus 1994), co-opting elements of subcultural style (the "Beat" style, famously, for Saint-Laurent; punk for Jean-Paul Gautier and Betsey Johnson; mod for John Galliano and Mary Quaint; goth, industrial, and steam punk for Alexander McQueen) and re-interpreting them as couture. While the grand couturiers of yesteryear prided themselves on setting the standards for elite fashion, conjuring, as if from nothing, the hot new looks for tomorrow, today's designers attempt to predict what fashions will sell tomorrow by carefully scrutinizing what the cool kids already have on. These days, many brands prefer the street-tested product to the unproven experiment. They employ "coolhunters" (Gladwell 2000) to track down the latest trends, borrow from youth styles, and check out what the small streetwear labels are selling in New York, London, and Tokyo. "High fashion and street fashion are now blended," claims Jake Burton, creative director of the extreme sports clothing label of the same name. "The irreverence of street is now demanded at the highest levels of fashion" (cited in Vogel 2007: 49–50).

The Indonesian indie scene, for its part, first encountered streetwear brands like Stüssy, Juice, and Volcom through surf shops that popped up in Bali and other major surf destinations in Indonesia in the mid-1980s, and then again through the Australian clothing chain Planet Surf, who, by the mid-1990s had established outlets at malls throughout urban Indonesia. By the time it reached them, streetwear was already inextricably caught up in international couture, part of the same markets, the same systems of status production and distinction. And yet it retained something of its countercultural cachet. Streetwear both linked its customers with a larger world of transnational commerce and differentiated them from it. It captured something of the hipster's ambivalence and ambiguity. Streetwear was both *fashionable* and yet not *fashion*, per se. That was no doubt its appeal to middle-class self-professed rebels like Ade, and it should come as no surprise that when young aspiring designers like him started their own labels in the

...they would borrow ...e approach to design.

...ned the term *bricolage* to describe ...he concrete" (Lévi-Strauss 1966), wh... ...individual "makes do with 'whatever is at h... to conduct a number of diverse tasks (Lévi-Strauss 1966: 17). The bricoleur, he explains, constructs works out of available materials, whether they were intended for this purpose or not. Unlike "the engineer," who constructs from raw materials "conceived and procured for the purpose of a project" (Lévi-Strauss 1966), the bricoleur puts existing things to new purposes. The engineer creates; the bricoleur tinkers. And this is not just tinkering for the sake of tinkering. The bricoleur "speaks through the medium of things" (Lévi-Strauss 1966: 21), makes meaning out of assemblage.

Since Lévi-Strauss developed the concept, bricolage has been packaged and repackaged for use by a variety of social theorists. Anthropologists, in particular, have made heavy use of the concept, employing it for a diverse range of theoretical tasks, from describing how educators design instructional curricula (Hatton 1989; Wagner 1990) to accounting for the hodgepodge religious rituals of colonial subjects (Chao 1999). At its most banal, bricolage in these texts simply refers to how people put pieces of things together to form a complex whole. At its most extravagant, bricolage is no less than the dynamic subversion of dominant forms.

The way cultural theorists have used bricolage has tended to lie somewhere between these two extreme poles. On the one end, is the position most closely associated with Hebdige (1979), Clarke (1976), and the Centre for Contemporary Cultural Studies (CCCS) in Birmingham, England. These cultural studies theorists used the concept of bricolage to describe the aesthetic practices of working-class subcultures of the 1960s and 1970s. Such theorists argued that subcultural practitioners challenge the hegemony of the dominant (read, bourgeois) culture not through explicit acts of resistance, but "obliquely" through style (Hebdige 1979: 17). They take everyday items associated with respectability and upward-mobility, a business suit or a school girl uniform, for instance, and deconstruct them through their personal attire, juxtapose them with incongruous elements, or sometimes even literally rip them apart and reassemble them with precarious materials like safety pins or duct tape. In the process, the appropriated materials take on new resonance and significance. They become dissociated from their original context and come to signify group solidarity, rebellion against the "mainstream," and self-imposed marginality. Hebdige thus read punk and mod fashions as forms of "semiotic guerilla warfare" (Eco 1972), attempts to "disrupt and reorganize meaning" (Hedbige 1979: 106). For him and others within the CCCS, bricolage was a method of aesthetic subversion, an act of visual resistance in line with the tradition of Surrealist collage.

At the other end of the pole is the more pessimistic position assumed by a certain brand of poststructuralist thinker, most notably Derrida (1980), who sees nothing particularly resistant or subversive in the practice. For Derrida, bricolage is not only quite prosaic and ordinary, but in fact the only kind of aesthetic practice possible. He takes issue with Lévi-Strauss's juxtaposition between the bricoleur and the engineer, claiming that since every act of linguistic communication entails the structuring elements of syntax and lexicon, all discourse is already bricolage. For Derrida, then, bricolage is little more than business as usual.

My own understanding of bricolage as a cultural practice lies somewhere in between Hebdige and Derrida. I am sympathetic with claims by Derrida that the logic of bricolage is intrinsic to human linguistic practice, but I would argue that his use of the term fails to recognize a significant qualitative difference between compositions that base their value on their perceived originality, and compositions whose assembled nature is a deliberate, and meaning-laden aspect of their value. Bricolage of the latter sort, I would argue, can be, and often is, fundamentally transformative, rendering explicit what would otherwise be unacknowledged, hidden, or even outright denied in one's work. Similarly, I share Hebdige's belief that bricolage can serve as a potent mechanism for reworking dominant meanings, but I would argue that the emphasis on bricolage as resistance misses the more complex positionalities it often enacts, namely, the ambivalence and "in-betweenness" of contemporary consuming subjects.

The rest of this chapter will consider examples of bricolage put into practice by Indonesian indie streetwear designers and attempt to develop a more useful conception of the term for our times, one that maintains critical aspects of both of these two bodies of argument without being reducible to either one. Ade and other Indonesian indie designers' graphic manipulation, I demonstrate, is a variety of bricolage that speaks volumes about the state of contemporary cultural production, the social meaning and value of fashion, and the position of Indonesian youth in the larger global economy.

PASTICHE AND THE LOGIC OF LATE CAPITALISM

Examples of bricolage are all around us. Hip hop musicians routinely sample from 1970s soul hits and 1950s bop. DJs lay down raga beats over turn of the century gospel. Hollywood directors such as Quentin Tarantino and Robert Rodriguez construct their storylines out of recycled B-movie plots. And tens of thousands of teenagers from around the world piece together YouTube video montages out of television clips and radio hits. This is not just cultural production as usual; it is a particular moment in cultural production, a moment where producers expose, and indeed glory, in their products' assembled quality. Their meaning is derived by their very lack of originality, their deliberate intertextual nature.

Indonesian indie fashion designers, for their part, engage in bricolage through the computer-age methodology of digital "cut and paste." Sometimes cutting and pasting in this context means using the "cut" tool on Corel Draw or Adobe Photoshop to extract an exact copy from a digital image found on a website, then the "paste" tool to apply it to the "canvas" of one of these programs. Sometimes, however, it is done less directly. A designer will scour the Internet for appropriate materials and then attempt to reproduce the images found using the electronic paintbrush and shape tools of Corel Draw.

If, however, the source image is too intricate to recreate on as clumsy a program as Corel Draw, a designer may sketch the image out on paper first and then scan it onto their computer. Or, if he or she is not particularly good at drawing, there are a couple of other possible solutions. Hamid Ariwinata of Triggers Syndicate has his "more-talented" friends sketch out those images he can't quite get right himself. Other designers take digital pictures of the images from which they sample, or print out, images they want and trace them with white paper and a pencil. Some even trace directly off the computer screen.

Like the bricoleurs Lévi-Strauss discusses in *The Savage Mind*, these DIY designers assemble and disassemble, and combine and recombine, instead of creating something wholly from scratch. They tinker with the images they locate through the World Wide Web, put a new spin on them, and remake them for a local audience.

Jameson has attributed the prevalence of such practices of assemblage and recombination in contemporary society to the cultural logic of late capitalism. Aesthetic production, he argues, has become deeply, and irretrievably, integrated into commodity production—that is, "the frantic economic urgency of producing fresh waves of ever more novel-seeming goods [from clothing to airplanes], at ever greater rates of turnover" (Jameson 1991: 4). The result is a cultural tendency toward "pastiche"—Jameson's version of bricolage—an aesthetic with no allegiances, no hidden meanings, and no qualms about borrowing from anything and everything in a continual quest to incite customers to buy. Pastiche, Jameson claims, makes all aesthetics equivalent, mere fodder for capitalist exploitation. It is like parody in that it draws from other peoples' work, but it differs from parody in that is devoid of its "ulterior motives." It is "amputated of satiric impulse" (Jameson 1991: 17), all glossy surface with nothing underneath. It is, he concludes, little more than "a neutral practice of mimicry" (Jameson 1991).

That Indonesian indie fashion design is integrated with commodity production is difficult to deny. Designers sell their work, and they do so in an increasingly competitive environment, in which standing out (*tampil beda*) is of critical importance. The quest for new visual ideas is ongoing, and as Dendy Darman of the Bandung-based streetwear brand Unkl347 explains, quite urgent. In Indonesia, he told me, "Ideas only last for about a month." Due to widespread piracy, "Things get stale quickly here." "Outside of the country," he went on, "if you come up with something new, it can last a year or so, but here, after a month, everyone's already wearing it." Bigger companies, he explained, will create a design, and if it does well, sell it continually until it stops selling, but Unkl347 doesn't have that luxury. They only print a design once, with limited editions, before moving on to something else. They have to stay continually fresh or risk becoming irrelevant. Cutting and pasting speeds up the process of design production, makes it quick and easy to crank out new products.

Ahmad Marin of fellow Bandung label Monik/Celtic tells a similar story to Dendy's. "In design," he tells me "I don't think about how to follow people, but how to innovate, innovate, innovate. That is the key, I think, if you are running [a] design or [other] creative business. You must change change change change. Adapt adapt adapt adapt." And that's exactly what his company does. Every season of Monik/Celtic's products have their own tone, theme, and look. They stray into a number of directions from bright and cheerful to dark and gloomy, but they are always distinctly current.

Marin goes to great lengths to keep it that way, taking annual trips to Singapore, Malaysia, and beyond to survey the world of international streetwear and look for new directions for his company to go. He describes his company's design concept (*konsep*) as "simple" or "pop," but for Marin this can mean any number of things, depending on what's happening in streetwear more generally. It can mean disco rabbits, dancing robots, Little Red Riding Hoods making their way through an enchanted forest, owls and unicorns, towering Godzillas, or miniature poodles.

His work is about as close to Jameson's notion of pastiche as any designer's I encountered in Indonesia. It borrows from anywhere and everywhere, other places and other times, from the disco 1970s of New York to the demure Victorian era of England, without any

consistent allegiances or affiliations. It mimics other popular brands, pieces together divergent imagery into a range of designs for sale at distros across the nation. And there is no doubt something "schizophrenic" (Deleuze and Guattari 1996) about this work, the way it seems to flit from one idea to another, as does the postmodern subject of poststructuralist thought.

But Monik/Celtic's work remains immediately recognizable to other Indonesian designers. It has a crisp, clean quality to it, a look that retains its simplicity even as it scavenges from diverse sources. Moreover, despite its schizophrenic content, there is a perspective that emerges from the work. And it's not that of the generic capitalist manufacturer trying to cash in on a trend. Marin, like most designers in the archipelago nation, fervently denies that money has ever been a motivating factor in what he does. His push comes from somewhere else: a desire to set himself and his company apart, a desire to matter in the international arena, to help put Indonesia on the fashion map, not just as a manufacturer of other company's designs, but a design center in its own right. It is, in other words, a perspective on global fashion put forward by someone on its periphery.

STUCK IN THE MIDDLE

Anthropologist Lila Abu-Lughod has argued that we can "use resistance as a *diagnostic* of power" (Abu-Lughod 1990: 42). Following the lead of Foucault ([1978] 1990), she suggests that the appearance of resistance itself helps shed light on where power relations lie, gives us a sense of where to look for inequalities and forms of domination. Where there is resistance, there is power, and vice versa. Perhaps the same can be said of cutting and pasting. Where acts of bricolage take on a self-consciously assembled quality, we can be reasonably certain that some sort of power discrepancy is in place. Sometimes, cut and paste serves to reinforce that discrepancy, as is clearly the case with the Indonesian state's appropriation of regional cultural practices. Other times, it challenges it, undermining the authority of the borrowed image or text and re-positioning the appropriator in a new relationship with what is appropriated.

In the case of DIY fashion design, finding the demarcating lines of power is fairly easy. Unkl347, Monik/Celtic—and for that matter, FireFighter Fight!—are tiny companies by world standards, run by a bunch of skaters and surfers from a poverty-stricken industrializing nation, with no real expectations of "making it big." They are small fish in a big sea, even if in Indonesia's fashion scene, they are about as big as brands can get. The source companies from which designers borrow, meanwhile, tend to be major players in the international economy, brands such as Nike, Xerox, and Converse; media companies such as Twentieth Century Fox, Sony, and Viacom. Their products are all over Indonesia, whereas Unkl347 and Monik/Celtic, after ten or so years of relative success at home, have barely managed to begin selling their products in Singapore and Malaysia. The hundreds of other independent clothing companies in the archipelago nation are not doing nearly that well.

This is not a case of literal domination, though. These brands have little direct power over Indonesian designers. Rather, these transnational companies compose a matrix of global brands that assert more and more dominion into the daily lives of Indonesian youth. They dominate the aesthetic landscape of Indonesia, its roadways, its malls, its billboards, its television stations and its Internet content. These brands are all around them, and compose the very fabric of contemporary life. "They are who we are," Dendy told me.

Modern life has become so deeply saturated with international brands that they are integral to the very way contemporary youth conceive of themselves. And not only in the sense that Appadurai delineates, offering glimpses into new "possible lives" (Appadurai 1996: 53), but in the sense of establishing a measure of their own deprivation, a recognition of how little they have in comparison to similarly situated youth in other places. Dendy, Marin, and Ade are comfortably middle class. They are not the poorest of the poor by any means, but they are not the richest of the rich, either. They have a relatively decent economic position by Indonesian standards and are well educated, but by world standards are barely middle class. And these are the most successful among indie designers. The vast majority of them remain well below the poverty line by the reckoning of any industrialized nation. They may be able to afford a cell phone (or two) and a motorbike, but, like Ade, they still tend to live in bleak, student housing units well after graduation, many surviving on less than US$2 a day.

The young Indonesian designers I met while carrying out my fieldwork do their best to live a cosmopolitan lifestyle, of fast food and designer clothes, imported music and fashion, albeit while maintaining something of an ironic, hipster positionality in relation to all these things, but even for Dendy and Marin, their access is still limited. Most young people involved in the Indonesian indie scene can't afford cable television or subscriptions to foreign magazines. Very few have ever left the country. Many don't even own a TV, most don't own a computer, and they still get most of their music through swapping MP3s and burning CDs. Most of them have to rent Internet access by the hour, or share computers with friends and colleagues to keep costs down. This can make cutting and pasting a painfully slow process.

Indonesian indie designers, then, are both empowered and constrained by their middle-class status. They have more money than the average Indonesian, with some degree of access to personal computers, the Internet, foreign media, and the resources of production. But they retain a marginal position in the global economy, particularly the global fashion economy, where Indonesia remains merely an anonymous manufacturing base for outsourced production. They occupy an uncomfortable middle ground between "here" and "elsewhere," the "traditional" and the "modern," the "first" and the "third" world. They can observe global youth cultures from afar, but they are not yet full participants within them. It is a frustrating position, and it speaks volumes about why Indonesian designers do the kind of work they do.

DESIGNER VANDALISM

Bricolage like Ade's, Marin's, and Dendy's simply can't help but take a stand. It always positions its practitioner in some sort of new relationship with that which it reproduces. In the most basic sense, bricolage of this sort involves a reconstitution of the consumer as a producer. Ade, for instance, has placed himself within a pantheon of internationally recognized designers by appropriating their work within his own.

And sometimes, this re-positioning through cut-and-paste takes on an explicitly oppositional stance, as well. Consider, for example, Unkl347's "Xerox" logo design. It features their "bowl" logo, very familiar to many young Indonesians, disintegrating into pixilated dots. This is a blatant imitation of Xerox's trademark "X," but just in case you missed the reference, the designers at Unkl347 printed the word "Xerox" beneath the image. The effect is jarring. The viewer recognizes the symbol of one brand exhibiting characteristics of another. It creates a momentary visual confusion. Unkl347 appears to have morphed into another brand. They have possessed it, taken it over. And in the process, the world's biggest supplier of copying machines has become little more than a copy itself. They are image fodder for some tiny Indonesian company. They are fair game.

This is distro-label design at its closest to "culture jamming" (Lasn 1999), to anti-commercial agit-prop launching visual tirades against the tyranny of the market. This is designer *détournement* (Debord 1995), "the theft of aesthetic artifacts from their [original] contexts and their diversion into contexts of one's own devise" (Marcus 1989: 168). Like the streetwear designs that inspired it, it turns a corporate logo into a form of personal expression.

This work is irreverent, satirical, even occasionally biting in its commentary. But it is not exactly critique. Its relationship with what it reworks and remixes is much more complex than that. Dendy's work often displays a peculiar reverence for the very thing he appropriates. It pays homage, even as it denies a company's singular right to control its own images. Take another example from Unkl347's collection. In this design, the 347 bowl logo is faded and cracked, some of its resolution lost as in a Xerox transfer. Below the logo is written, this time in past-tense verb form, "XEROXED," with the "ED" highlighted. Here, Unkl347 seems to be doing a couple of things: (1) Acknowledging their own debased position in relationship to a global company, their own status as something of a cheap copy; and (2) converting

a global brand into a transitive verb, something to be done, carried out, enacted, performed. For Dendy, to Xerox is to take hold of, to make something one's own. It is a tactic of the disenfranchised and left behind. Unkl347 may be a copycat company, they proclaim through this design, but it is a company that turns that status into a term of empowerment.

Unkl347 want their customers to know they took their material from somewhere else, and they make their methodology explicit, often visually cite their sources. "We even go so far as to acknowledge it [in our designs] so that people know," says Dendy. One of their designs, for instance, features an almost exact copy of the album cover for "Goo" by the New York art punk band Sonic Youth. A young, modish couple in bowl cuts and sunglasses smoke cigarettes while they lounge in each other's arms. Beside the image, the original handwritten words "I stole my sister's boyfriend" have been replaced with "I stole my Sonic Youth."

Through such work, Dendy and other designers like him engage in what could be called brand vandalism, or "brandalism" (Moore 2007), tagging corporate logos and foreign album covers the way urban gangs mark their territory in the inner city, and declaring in the process the world of international commerce their own home turf. Designers like Dendy contest the very hegemony of transnational corporations over youth trends, taking their designs for their own and manipulating them for their own purposes. They declare the cultural products of transnational capitalism as public domain, rejecting the very idea that such imagery are the exclusive property of their producers at all. Dendy takes recognizable corporate logos and prints his own brand name over them. Ade takes his images from design books, online pamphlets and brochures, and manipulates them for his own use. These designers routinely take other designers' work, chop them up and reassemble them, then put their own stamp on them. And they do so openly, without embarrassment or shame.

One of Ade's creations, for instance, an asphalt-gray hooded sweatshirt he wears all the time, features a series of repeated yellow silhouettes of his favorite mangled, unicorn-deer motif. In the center of the shirt is a bold yellow caption reading "YOU ARE graphic manipulator TARGET." No one, Ade seems to be announcing with his design, is safe from graphic manipulation. But unlike Dendy or Hamid, Ade does not let his viewer know who the target of his attack is. The source material of his work remains anonymous. Authorship is denied.

WE ARE THE BRANDS WE CONSUME

Anthropologists have found resistance in nearly every nook and cranny of contemporary lives (Abu-Lughod 1990; Brown 1996). Inspired by such influential thinkers as De Certeau (1984) and Scott (1985), we have had a long, and well-documented, love affair with "the romance of resistance" (Abu-Lughod 1990). But despite a rather large body of critiques against the over-use of the concept, talk of resistance continues to pop up all over the place in ethnographic work. We have yet to come up with an alternative explanation sufficient for making sense of such deconstructive acts of bricolage that are becoming increasingly common in the Information Age (Castells 2000), the remixes of popular songs, the mash-ups and video collages that animate the Internet, and the cut-and-paste designs of Indonesian indie streetwear.

There is, I would argue, an element of resistance to what distro-label designers do, sometimes explicit, sometimes more subtle, but we have to be careful about assigning resistance too liberally to youth aesthetic practice. Indie designer resistance is always an ambivalent resistance, what Kondo, following Hutchens, has termed "complicitous critique" (Kondo 1997). Indie designers uphold, often even glorify, the source material of their designs. Unkl347's Xerox logo, for instance, both takes over the international brand and declares the brand something worth taking over. Dendy's work is often deeply reverential of what he borrows from.

Just as an emphasis on bricolage as an expression of the cultural logic of late capitalism misses a great deal of its subtlety, to call such work "resistant," then, also misses the mark. The principle motivation of designers like Dendy, Marin, and Ade is not so much critiquing the source material from which they borrow as with asserting a kind of ownership over it, appropriating

commercial imagery in efforts to reproduce themselves as active global citizens. Sometimes, the reconstituted aesthetic objects they produce take on subversive meanings, as in Dendy's Xerox design. Sometimes, they work to reproduce or reinforce an existing meaning, as in Hamid's tributes to the giants of heavy metal. The most compelling feature of indie fashion bricolage, then, is not its utility as a mode of resistance, but the way it re-positions individuals in relationship to those materials from which they sample. Bricolage is a means of claiming and asserting authority over cultural forms produced by other, generally (though not always) more powerful social actors in other places and other times. It is a technology of cultural production, and what it produces is not only a new set of meanings in association with a borrowed image or idea, but a new relationship between that image and its bricoleur.

Deleuze and Guattari, in their seminal, and notoriously opaque work *Anti-Oedipus*, describe bricolage as "the ability to rearrange fragments continually in new and different patterns or configurations" (1996: 7). It is, for them, a form of production that grafts production onto production that indeed carries out the productive project indefinitely, forever forestalling the possibility of conclusion. In bricolage, there is no end-product to be finally consumed. And there is no clear distinction between production and consumption, either; there is only a continual cycle of production and reproduction. Bricolage, then, thwarts any stabilization of the relations of production into a hierarchy of producer and consumer. It muddies the water, complicates and complexifies, and restores a fluid, frenzied nature to the activity of production. And for this reason, bricolage is the key productive activity of the contemporary "schizophrenic" subject, Deleuze and Guattari's idealized "nomadic" agent, who refuses to be pinned down and resists being fully integrated into any one regime of power.

When we see bricolage in this light, as a productive practice that maintains the activity of production indefinitely, that instills it with a vital sociality, a continual cultural revision, it becomes fairly easy to understand why aesthetic forms that privilege bricolage have become so widespread in our global capitalist era. It is not simply that borrowing from other sources makes capitalism more efficient or provides ready-made models for greedy manufacturers. Rather, bricolage has become so widespread because it empowers consumers—the driving force of late capitalism—to be more than simply consumers. It weaves them into a massive web of dynamic producer/consumers, cultural remixers, and DIYers, and furthers a fundamentally inclusive process of production. Technologies like Corel Draw, or mash-up programs on the Internet give consumers a means of asserting more direct control over what they consume: to affect it, contribute to it, or simply take some sort of direct ownership over it.

Cut-and-paste techniques complicate the very notion of innovation itself, the conceit of originality, independence, and creative autonomy. They may not threaten the smooth functioning of the capitalist economy, or even the continuation of global corporate domination of apparel design and manufacture, but they do challenge the power relationships operating within it. They destabilize the distinctions between producer and consumer, designer and knock-off artist, creator and remixer, and ultimately, global and local.

BIBLIOGRAPHY

Abaza, Mona. 2007. "Shifting Landscapes of Fashion in Contemporary Egypt." *Fashion Theory* 11(2–3): 281–97

Ableman, Paul. 1982. *Anatomy of Nakedness*. London: Orbis.

Abrahams, Roger D. 1976. *Talking Black*. Rawley, MA: Newbury House.

Abu-Lughod, Lila. 1990. "The Romance of Resistance: Tracing Transformations of Power Through Bedouin Women." *American Ethnologist* 17(1): 41–55.

Addison, Joseph. 1743. *Remarks on Several Parts of Italy etc. in the Years 1701, 1702, 1703*. The Hague: Henry Scheurleer.

Adelkhah, Fariba. 1991. *La revolution sous le voile. Femmes islamiques d'Iran* (Revolution under the Veil). Paris: Karthala.

Agar, Michael H. 1996. *The Professional Stranger. An Informal Introduction to Ethnography*. San Diego, CA: Academic Press.

Ahl al-Shaykh, His Eminence Shaykh Mohammed Ibn Ibrahim. 2000. *Judgement about Gender Mixing. Followed by Fatwas Important for Women*. Riyadh: Dar Ibn al-Athir.

Ahmed, Leila. 1992. *Women and Gender in Islam: Historical Roots of a Modern Debate*. New Haven, CT: Yale University Press.

Alarcón, Norma, Caren Kaplan, and Minoo Moallem. 1999. "Introduction: Between Woman and Nation." In Caren Kaplan, Norma Alarcón, and Minoo Moallem (eds), *Between Woman and Nation: Nationalisms, Transnational Feminisms and the State*. Durham, NC: Duke University Press.

Allen, Charles. 1976. *Plain Tales from the Raj*. London: Macdonald Futura.

Allen, Charles. 1980. *Tales from the Dark Continent*. London: Macdonald Futura.

Allen, Robert C. 1991. *Horrible Prettiness: Burlesque and American Culture*. Chapel Hill, NC: University of North Carolina Press.

Allerton, Catherine. 2007. "The Secret Life of Sarongs: Manggarai Textiles as Super-skins." *Journal of Material Culture* 12(1): 22–46.

Almagor, Uri. 1985. "A Tourist's 'Vision Quest' in an African Game Reserve." *Annals of Tourism Research* 12(1): 31–48.

Alvi, Sajida, Homa Hoodfar, and Sheila McDonough, eds. 2003. *Muslim Veil in North America: Issues and Debates*. Toronto: Women's Press.

Ames, David. 1955. "The Use of a Transitional Cloth-Money Token among the Wolof." *American Anthropologist* 57(5): 1016–24.

Amin, Qasim. (1899) 1992. *The Liberation of Women*, trans. Samiha Sidhom Peterson. Cairo: American University of Cairo Press.

Anderson, Benedict. 1991. *Imagined Communities*. Revised ed. London: Verso Press.

Appadurai, Arjun. 1986. "Introduction: Commodities and the Politics of Value." In Arjun Appadurai (ed.), *The Social Life of Things*, pp. 3–63. Cambridge: Cambridge University Press.Appadurai,

Appadurai, Arjun. 1990. "Disjuncture and Difference in the Global Cultural Economy." *Public Culture* 2(3): 1–24.

Appadarai, Arjun. 1993. "Consumption, Duration and History." *Stanford Literature Review* 10(1–2): 11–33.

Appadurai, Arjun. 1996. *Modernity at Large*. Minneapolis: University of Minnesota Press.

Appadurai, Arjun, ed. 1986. *The Social Life of Things: Commodities in Cultural Perspective*. Cambridge: Cambridge University Press.

Appadurai, Arjun and Carol Breckenridge. 1988. "Why Public Culture?" *Public Culture* 1(1): 5–9.

Applebaum, Richard and Gary Gereffi. 1994. "Power and Profits in the Apparel Commodity Chain." In Edna Bonacich, Lucie Cheng, Norma Chinchilla, Nora Hamilton, and Paul Ong (eds), *Global Production:*

The Apparel Industry in the Pacific Rim, pp. 42–62. Philadelphia, PA: Temple University Press.

Arvidsson, Adam. 2006. *Brands: Meaning and Value in Media Culture*. Oxford: Routledge.

Ashmore, Sonia. 2010. "Hippies, Bohemians and Chintz." In Christopher Breward, Philip Crang, and Rosemary Crill (eds), *British Asian Style: Fashion & Textiles Past & Present*. London: V&A Publishing.

Aspelund, Karl. 2009. *Fashioning Society: A Hundred Years of Haute Couture by Six Designers*. New York: Fairchild Publications.

Aspers, Patrik. 2010. *Orderly Fashion: A Sociology of Markets*. Princeton, NJ: Princeton University Press.

Auslander, Leora. 2000. "Bavarian Crucifixes and French Headscarves: Religious Signs and the Postmodern European State." *Cultural Dynamics* 12(3): 283–309.

Baba, Naïm Ahmat. 2003. "Un cellulaire pour la frime." *Tel Quel* 13: 13.

Baillie, John. 1832. Extracts from the Journal of Rev. John Baillie, New Lattakoo, September 30, 1830. *Transactions of the Missionary Society*, April 1832; contained in *Quarterly Chronicle of Transactions of the London Missionary Soceity, in the Years, 1829, 1830, 1831, and 1832*, 4: 442–48.

Baines, Paul. 1999. *The House of Forgery in Eighteenth-Century Britain*. Aldershot: Ashgate.

Bair, Jennifer. 2005. "Global Capitalism and Commodity Chains: Looking Back, Going Forward." *Competition and Change* 9(2): 153–80.

Baker, Patricia. 1997. "Politics of Dress: The Dress Reform Laws of 1920–1930s Iran." In Nancy Lindisfarne-Tapper and Bruce Ingham (eds), *Languages of Dress in the Middle East*, pp. 178–93. Richmond: Curzon.

Bakhtin, Mikhail. 1981. *The Dialogic Imagination. Caryl Emerson and Michael Holquist*, trans. and ed. Michael Holquist. Austin: University of Texas Press.

Bakhtin, Mikhail M. 1982. *The Dialogic Imagination: Four Essays*, ed. M. Holquist. Austin: University of Texas Press.

Balasescu, Alexandru. 2006. "Faces and Bodies: Gendered Modernity and Fashion Photography in Tehran." *Gender and History* 17(3): 737–68.

Banerjee, Mukulika and Daniel Miller. 2003. *The Sari*. Oxford: Berg.

Bangs, Richard. 2008. *Quest for the Sublime: Finding Nature's Secret in Switzerland*. Birmingham, AL: Menasha Ridge Press.

Bao, Xialon. 2001. *Holding Up More Than Half the Sky: Chinese Women Garment Workers in New York City, 1948–92*. Chicago: University of Chicago Press.

Barber, Karin. 1991. *I Could Speak Until Tomorrow: Oriki, Women and the Past in a Yoruba Town*. Washington, DC: Smithsonian Institution Press.

Barboza, David and Elizabeth Becker. 2005. "Free of Quota, China Textiles Flood the U.S". *New York Times*, March 10. www.nytimes.com/2005/03/10/business/worldbusiness/free-of-quota-china-textiles-flood-the-us.html (accessed Septmber 5, 2018).

Barth, Henrik. 1857. *Travels and Discoveries in Noth and Central Africa*. New York: Harpers and Brothers.

Barthes, Roland. 1967. *Systeme de la Mode*. Paris: Editions du Seuil.

Barthes, Roland. 1982. *Empire of Signs*, trans. Richard Howard. New York: Hill & Wang.

Barthes, Roland. 1983. *The Fashion System*. Berkeley: University of California Press.

Barthes, Roland. 1985. *The Fashion System*. London: Jonathan Cape.

Baudrillard, Jean. (1973) 1975. *The Mirror of Production*. St Louis: Telos.

Baudrillard, Jean. 1988. *Selected Writings*. Stanford, CA: Stanford University Press.

Baudrillard, Jean. (1968) 1996. *The System of Objects*, trans. James Benedict. London: Verso.

Baudrillard, Jean. 2001. "Simulations." In Richard Kearney and David M. Rasmussen (eds), *Continental Aesthetics. Romanticism to Postmodernism. An Anthology*, pp. 411–30. Oxford: Blackwell.

Bayat-Philipp, Mangol. 1981. "Tradition and Change in Iranian Socio-Religious Thought." In Michael E. Bonine and Nikki Keddie (eds), *Modern Iran. The Dialectics of Continuity and Change*, pp. 37–58. Albany: State University of New York Press.

Bayat, Asef. 2007. "Islamism and Politics of Fun." *Public Culture* 19(3): 433–459.

Bean, Susan S. 1989. "Gandhi and Khadi, the Fabric of Indian Independence." In Annette B. Weiner and Jane Schneider (eds), *Cloth and Human Experience*, pp. 355–76. Washington, DC: Smithsonian Institution Press.

Beard, Nathaniel Dafydd. 2008. "The Branding of Ethical Fashion and the Consumer: A Luxury Niche or Mass-market Reality?" *Fashion Theory* 12(4): 447–68.

Beck, Rose Marie. 2000. "Aesthetics of Communication: Texts on Textiles (Leso) from the East African Coast (Swahili)." *Research in African Literatures* 31(4): 104–24.

Beck, Ulrich and Elisabeth Beck-Gernsheim. 1995. *The Normal Chaos of Love*. Cambridge: Polity Press.

Beebe, Barton. 2008. "The Semiotic Account of Trademark Doctrine and Trademark Culture." In Graeme B. Dinwoodie and Mark D. Jamis (eds), *Trademark Law and Theory: A Handbook of Contemporary Research*, pp. 42–64. Cheltenham: Edward Elgar.

Behar, Ruth. 1993. *Translated Woman: Crossing the Border with Esperanza's Story*. Boston, MA: Beacon Press.

Behar, Ruth. 1996. *The Vulnerable Observer: Anthropology That Breaks Your Heart*. Boston, MA: Beacon Press.

Behar, Ruth and Deborah Gordon, eds. 1995. *Women Writing Culture*. Berkeley: University of California Press.

Bell, Enid Moberly. 1947. *Flora Shaw (Lady Lugard DBE)*. London: Constable.

Bell, Quentin. 1949. *On Human Finery*. New York: A. A. Wyn.

Ben-Amos, Paula Girshick. 1980. *The Art of Benin*. London: Thames & Hudson.

Bendixsen, Synnøve. 2013. "'I Love My Prophet': Religious Taste, Consumption, and Distinction in Berlin." In Emma Tarlo and Annelies Moors (eds), *Islamic Fashion and Anti-Fashion: New Perspectives from Europe and North America*, pp. 272–90. London: Bloomsbury.

Benedict, Ruth. 1931. "Dress." In Edwin R. A. Seligman (ed.), *Encyclopedia of Social Science*, vol. 5, pp. 235–37. New York: Macmillan Co.

Benjamin, Walter. 1992. *Illuminations*. London: Fontana.

Benjamin, Walter. (1936) 1999. "The Work of Art in the Age of Mechanical Reproduction." In Walter Benjamin, *Illuminations*, pp. 217–52. London: Pimilco.

Berkovic, Sally. 1999. *Straight Talk: My Dilemma as a Modern Orthodox Jewish Woman*. Hoboken, NJ: Ktav.

Bernstein, Basil. 1975. *Class, Codes, and Control*. New York: Schocken Books.

Berry, E. 1941. *Mad Dogs and Englishmen*. London: Michael Joseph.

Bhabha, Homi. 1997. "Of Mimicry and Man: The Ambivalence of Colonial Discourse." In Frederick Cooper and Ann Stoler (eds), *Tensions of Empire: Colonial Cultures in a Bourgeois World*, pp. 152–60. Berkeley: University of California Press.

Bhachu, Parminder. 2004. *Dangerous Designs: Asian Women Fashion the Diaspora Economies*. London: Routledge.

Binkley, Sam. 2003. "The Seers of Menlo Park: The Discourse of Heroic Consumption in the 'Whole Earth Catalog.'" *Journal of Consumer Culture* 3(3): 283–313.

Birkett, Dea. 1989. *Spinsters Abroad*. Oxford: Basil Blackwell.

Black, Sandy, ed. 2012. *The Sustainable Fashion Handbook*. London: Thames and Hudson.

Blair, Jennifer and Gary Gereffi. 2003. "Upgrading, Uneven Development, and Jobs in the North American Apparel Industry." *Global Networks* 3(2): 143–69.

Blakeney, Michael. 2009. "International Proposals for the Criminal Enforcement of Intellectual Property Rights: International Concern with Counterfeiting and Piracy." *Intellectual Property Quarterly* 1: 1–26.

Blanchard, Barry. 1998. "Field Report: Evolving." *Patagonia* [Catalog] Fall, 5.

Blaszczyk, Regina Lee, ed. 2008. *Producing Fashion: Commerce, Culture, and Consumers*. Philadelphia: University of Pennsylvania Press.

Blier, Suzanne. 1987. *The Anatomy of Architecture*. Cambridge: Cambidge University Press.

Bloch, Maurice. 1991. "Language, Anthropology and Cognitive Science." *Man* 26(2): 183–98.

Boesen, Elisabeth. 2008. "Gleaming Like the Sun: Aesthetic Values in Wodaabe Material Culture." *Africa* 78(4): 582–602.

Bogatyrev, Petr. 1971. *The Functions of Folk Costume in Moravian Slovakia*. The Hague: Mouton.

Bohannan, Paul J. 1956. "Beauty and Scarification Amongst the Tiv." *Man* 56(129): 117–21.

Bonacich, Edna and Richard P. Appelbaum. 2000. *Behind the Label: Inequality in the Los Angeles Apparel Industry*. Berkeley: University of California Press.

Bonacich, Edna, Lucie Cheng, Norma Chinchilla, Nora Hamilton, and Paul Ong, eds. 2004. *Global Production: The Apparel Industry in the Pacific Rim*. Philadelphia, PA: Temple University Press.

Bonacich, Edna and David V. Waller. 1994. "The Role of U.S. Apparel Manufacturers in the Globalization of the Industry in the Pacific Rim," In Edna Bonacich, et al. (eds), *Global Production: The Apparel Industry in the Pacific Rim*, pp. 21–41. Philadelphia, PA: Temple University Press.

Boser-Sarivaxévanis, Renée. 1975. *Recherche sur L'histoire des textiles traditionnels tissés et teints de l'Afrique occidentale*. Basel: Verhandlungen der Naturforschenden Gesellschaft.

Bosman, Willem. 1705. *A New and Accurate Description of the Coast of Guinea*. London.

Bourdieu, Pierre. (1972) 1977. *Outline of a Theory of Practice*, trans. Richard Nice. Cambridge: Cambridge University Press.

Bourdieu, Pierre. (1979) 1984. *Distinction: a social critique of the judgment of taste*, trans. Richard Nice. Cambridge, MA: Harvard University Press.

Bourdier, Jean-Paul. 1991. "Houses of Light: Rural Mosques of Senegal and Mali." *MIMAR: Architecture in Development* 39: 61–67.

Bowen, Elenore Smoth. 1964. *Return to Laughter: An Anthropological Novel*. Garden City, New York: Published in collaboration with the American Museum of Natural History by Doubleday.

Bowlby, Rachel. 1985. "Modes of Shopping: Mallarmé at the Bon Marché." In N. Armstrong and L. Tennenhouse (eds), *The Ideology of Conduct: Essays on Literature and the History of Sexuality*. New York: Methuen.

Boyarin, Daniel. 1994. *A Radical Jew: Paul and the Politics of Identity*. Berkeley: University of California Press.

Boyer, Ruth. 1983. "Yoruba Cloths with Regal Names." *African Arts* 16: 42–45, 98.

Braddock, Sarah E. and Marie O'Mahoney. 1999. *Techno Textiles: Revolutionary Fabrics for Fashion and Design*. London: Thames and Hudson.

Braham, Peter. 1997. "*Fashion: Unpacking a Cultural Production*." In Paul du Gay (ed.), *Production of Culture/Cultures of Production*, pp. 119–76. London: Sage Publications.

Breckenridge, Carol A., ed. 1995. *Consuming Modernity: Public Culture in a South Asian World*. Minneapolis: University of Minnesota Press.

Brenner, Suzanne. 1996. "Reconstructing Self and Society: Javanese Muslim Women and the Veil." *American Ethnologist* 23(4): 673–98.

Brett-Smith, Sarah. 1989. *Fruitful Death: Minianka Women's Shrouds*. Paper presented at the Eighth Triennial of the Arts Council of the African Studies Association, Washington, DC.

Brett-Smith, Sarah. 1990–91. "Empty Space: The Architecture of Dogon Cloth." *RES. Anthropology & Aesthetics* 19–20:162–77.

Breward, Christopher. 1995. *The Culture of Fashion: A New History of Fashionable Dress*. Manchester: Manchester University Press.

Breward, Christopher. 1999. *The Hidden Consumer: Masculinities, Fashion and City Life* 1860–1914. Manchester: Manchester University Press.

Breward, Christopher and David Gilbert, eds. 2006. *Fashion's World Cities*. Oxford: Berg.

Breward, Christopher, Philip Crang, and Rosemary Crill. 2010. *British Asian Style: Fashion & Textiles Past & Present*. London: V&A Publishing.

Bronner, Leila Leah. 1993. "From Veil to Wig: Jewish Women's Hair Covering." *Judaism* 42(4): 465–77.

Brown, Erica. 2003. "'A Crown of Thorns': Orthodox Women Who Chose Not to Cover Their Hair." In Lynne Schreiber (ed.), *Hide and Seek: Jewish Women and Hair Covering*, pp. 178–95. New York: Urim.

Brown, Michael F. 1996. "On Resisting Resistance." *American Anthropologist* 98(4): 729–35.

Browning, Elizabeth Barrett. 1851. Letter to John Kenyon.

Broyde, Rabbi Michael J. 1991. "Tradition, Modesty and America: Married Women Covering their Hair." *Judaism* 40(1): 79–87.

Buck, Elizabeth. 1993. *Paradise Remade: The Politics of Culture and History in Hawai'i*. Philadelphia, PA: Temple University Press.

Burchell, William J. 1822–24. *Travels in the Interior of Southern Africa*. 2 vols. London: Longman, Hurst, Rees, Orme, Brown & Green. Reprinted, 1967; Cape Town: Struik.

Burke, Timothy. 1996. *Lifebuoy Men, Lux Women: Commodification, Consumption, and Cleanliness in Modern Zimbabwe*. Durham, NC: Duke University Press.

Butler, Judith. 1990. *Gender Trouble: Feminism and the Subversion of Identity*. New York: Routledge.

Caldwell, John. 1976. *The Socio-Economic Explanation of High Fertility: Papers on the Yoruba Society of Nigeria*. Canberra: The Australian National University.

Callaway, Helen. 1987. *Gender, Culture and Empire*. London: Macmillan.

Callon, Michel. 1986. "Some Elements of a Sociology of Translation: Domestication of the Scallops and the Fishermen of St. Brieuc Bay." In John Law (ed.), *Power, Action and Belief: A New Sociology of Knowledge?* pp. 196–223. London: Routledge.

Campbell, Colin. 1995. "*The Sociology of Consumption*." In Daniel Miller (ed.), *Acknowledging Consumption: A Review of New Studies*, pp. 96–126. London: Routledge.

Campbell, Colin. 1996. "The Meaning of Objects and the Meaning of Actions: The Sociology of Consumption and Theories of Clothing." *Journal of Material Culture* 1(1): 93–106.

Campbell, Colin. 1997. "Shopping, Pleasure, and the Sex War." In Pasi Falk and Colin Campbell (eds), *The Shopping Experience*, 166–76. London: Sage.

Campbell, John. 1822. *Travels in South Africa…Being a Narrative of a Second Journey…*, 2 vols. London: Westley. Reprinted 1967; New York: Johnson Reprint Corporation.

Cannon, Charlie. 1989. Trance-portation: Neo-Shamanism in Contemporary America. Honors Thesis, Department of Anthropology, Wesleyan University.

Carbone, Bradley and Noah Johnson. 2011. "An Oral History of the Graphic T-Shirt." In *Complex*, Vol. 2011: www.complex.com.

Carmichael, A. C. 1969. *Domestic Manners and Social Condition of the White, Coloured, and Negro*. London: Manning and Smithson, London House Yard.

Carrel, Barbara Goldman. 1999. "Hasidic Women's Head Coverings: A Feminized System of Hasidic Distinction." In Linda B. Arthur (ed.), *Religion, Dress, and the Body*, pp. 163–79. Oxford: Berg.

Carrier, James G. 1992. "Occidentalism: The World Turned Upside Down." *American Ethnologist* 19(2): 195–212.

Carrier, James, ed. 1994. *Gifts and Commodities: Exchange and Western Capitalism since 1700*. London: Routledge.

Carrier, James G. 1995. *Gifts and Commodities: Exchange and Western Capitalism since 1700*. London: Routledge.

Carrier, James, ed. 1997. *Meanings of the Market: The Free Market in Western Culture*. Oxford: Berg.

Carreira, António. 1968. *Panaria Cabo-Verdiano-Guineense: Aspectos históricos e sócio-económicos*. Lisbon: Junta de Investigacoes do Ultramar.

Casadesus-Masanell, Ramon, Michael Crooke, Forest Reinhardt, and Vishal Vasishth. 2009. "Households' Willingness to Pay for 'Green' Goods: Evidence from Patagonia's Introduction of Organic Cotton Sportswear." *Journal of Economics and Management Strategy* 18(1): 203–33.

Castells, Manuel. 1996. *The Rise of the Network Society*. Oxford: Blackwell Publishers.

Castells, Manuel. 2000. *The Information Age: Economy, Society and Culture*, vol. 1. Malden, MA: Blackwell Publishers Inc.

Castiglione, Baldassare. (1528) 1953. "The Courtier." In Burton A. Milligan (ed.), *Three Renaissance Classics: The Prince, Utopia, The Courtier*, trans. Sir Thomas Hoby, 1851. New York: Scribner.

Chakrabarty, Dipesh. 1992. "Postcoloniality and the Artifice of History: Who Speaks for 'Indian' Pasts?" *Representations* 37 (winter): 1–26.

Chamberlain, Adam. 2003. "Winter Road Trip." *Patagonia* [Catalog] Winter, 2.

Chamberlin, Eric Russell. 1967. *Everyday Life in Renaissance Times*. New York: Capricorn Books.

Chao, Emily. 1999. "The Maoist Shaman and the Madman: Ritual Bricolage, Failed Ritual, and Failed Ritual Theory." *Cultural Anthropology* 14(4): 505–34.

Chapin Norman A. 1983. "Curing among the San Blas Kuna of Panama." Unpublished PhD thesis, University of Arizona.

Chatterjee, Partha. 1993. *The Nation and Its Fragments: Colonial and Postcolonial Histories*. Princeton, NJ: Princeton University Press.

Chin, Margaret M. 2005. *Sewing Women: Immigrants and the New York City Garment Industry*. New York: Columbia University Press.

Chouinard, Yvon. 1999. "Introduction." In Nora Gallagher (ed.), *Patagonia: Notes from the Field*, pp. 8–11. San Francisco, CA: Chronicle Books.

Chouinard, Yvon. 2005. *Let My People Go Surfing: The Education of a Reluctant Businessman*. New York: Penguin Group.

Chouinard, Yvon and Vincent Stanley. 2012. *The Responsible Company: What We've Learned from Patagonia's First 40 years*. Ventura, CA: Patagonia Books.

Christiansen, Connie Carøe. 2013. "Miss Headscarf: Islamic Fashion and the Danish Media." In Emma Tarlo and Annelies Moors (eds), *Islamic Fashion and Anti-Fashion: New Perspectives from Europe and North America*, pp. 225–40. London: Bloomsbury.

Clark, Hazel. 2008. "SLOW + FASHION—an Oxymoron—or a Promise for the Future …?" *Fashion Theory* 12(4): 427–46.

Clark, Hazel and Alexandra Palmer, eds. 2004. *Old Clothes, New Looks. Second Hand Fashion*. Oxford: Berg.

Clarke, Alison. 1999. *Tupperware: The Promise of Plastic in 1950's America*. Washington, DC: Smithsonian Institution Press.

Clarke, Alison. 2000. "'Mother swapping': The Trafficking of Nearly New Children's Wear," In Peter Jackson, Michelle Lowe, Daniel Miller, Frank Mort (eds), *Commercial Cultures*. Oxford: Berg.

Clarke, John. 1976. "The Skinheads and the Magical Recovery of Community." In Stuart Hall and Tony Jefferson (eds), *Resistance through Ritual: Youth Subcultures in Postwar Britain*, pp. 99–102. Birmingham: University of Birmingham.

Clifford, James. 1988a. "On Ethnographic Authority." In James Clifford (ed.), *The Predicament of Culture: Twentieth-Century Ethnography, Literature, and Art*, pp. 21–54. Cambridge, MA: Harvard University Press.

Clifford, James. 1988b. "Histories of the Tribal and the Modern." In James Clifford (ed.), *The Predicament of Culture: Twentieth Century Ethnography, Literature, and Art*, pp. 189–214. Cambridge, MA: Harvard University Press.

Clifford, James. 1988c. *The Predicament of Culture: Twentieth-Century Ethnography, Literature, and Art*. Boston, MA: Harvard University Press.

Clifford, James. 1997. *Routes: Travel and Translation in the Late Twentieth Century*. Cambridge, MA: Harvard University Press.

Clifford, James. 2003. *On the Edges of Anthropology: Interviews*. Chicago: Prickly Paradigm Press.

Clifford, James and George E. Marcus, eds. 1986. *Writing Culture: The Poetics and Politics of Ethnography*. Berkeley: University of California Press.

Clubbe, John and Ernest Giddey. 1982. *Byron et la Suisse, Universite De Lausanne Publications de la Faculte des Lettres*. Geneva: Librarie Droz S. A.

Cohen, A. and John L. Comaroff. 1976. "The Management of Meaning: On the Phenomenology of Political Transactions." In Bruce Kapferer (ed.), *Transaction and Meaning: Directions in the Anthropology of Exchange and Symbolic Behavior*, pp. 87–108. African Studies Association, vol 1. Philadelphia, PA: Institute for the Study of Human Issues.

Cohen, Erik. 1985. "The Tourist Guide: The Origins, Structure, and Dynamics of a Role." *Annals of Tourism Research, Special Edition. Tourist Guides: Pathfinders, Mediators, and Animators* 12(1): 5–29.

Cohn, Bernard S. 1983. "Representing Authority in Victorian India." In Eric Hobsbawm and Terence Ranger (eds), *The Invention of Tradition*. Cambridge: Cambridge University Press.

Cohn-Bendit, Daniel and Gabriel Cohn-Bendit. 1968. *Obsolete Communism: The Left-Wing Alternative*, trans. Arnold Pomerans. New York: McGraw-Hill.

Cole, Jennifer. 2008. "Fashioning Distinction: Youth and Consumerism in Urban Madagascar." In Jennifer Cole and Deborah Durham (eds), *Figuring the Future: Globalization and Temporalities of Children and Youth*, pp. 99–124. Santa Fe, NM: School for Advanced Research Press.

Cole, Jennifer and Deborah Durham. 2008. "Introduction: Globalization and the Temporality of Children and Youth." In Jennifer Cole and Deborah Durham (eds), *Figuring the Future: Globalization and the Temporalities of Children and Youth*, pp. 3–23. Santa Fe, NM: School for Advanced Research Press.

Cole, Jennifer and Deborah Durham, eds. 2008. *Figuring the Future: Globalization and the Temporalities of Children and Youth*. Santa Fe, NM: School for Advanced Research Press.

Collier, Jane Fishburne. 1974. "Women in Politics." In Michelle Zimbalist Rosaldo and Louise Lamphere (eds), *Woman, Culture, and Society*. Stanford, CA: Stanford University Press.

Collins, Jane L. 2003. *Threads: Gender, Labor, and Power in the Global Apparel Industry*. Chicago: University of Chicago Press.

Comaroff, Jean. 1985. *Body of Power, Spirit of Resistance*. Chicago: University of Chicago Press.

Comaroff, Jean. 1994. "Les vieux habits de l'empire: faconner le sujet colonial." *Anthropologie et Societes* 18(3):15–38.

Comaroff, Jean. 1996. "The Empire's Old Clothes: Fashioning the Colonial Subject." In David Howes (ed.), *Cross-cultural Consumption: Global Markets, Local Realities*, pp. 19–39. London: Routledge.

Comaroff, Jean and John L. Comaroff. 1987. "The Madman and the Migrant: Work and Labor in the Historical Consciousness of a South African People." *American Ethnologist* 14(2): 191–209.

Comaroff, Jean and John Comaroff. 1997. *Of Revolution and Revelation: Volume Two*. Chicago: University of Chicago Press.

Comaroff, John L. and Jean Comaroff. 2006. "Law and Disorder in the Postcolony: An Intoduction." In John L. Comaroff and Jean Comaroff (eds), *Law and Disorder in the Postcolony*, pp. 1–56. Chicago: University of Chicago Press.

Conklin, Beth A. 2007. "Ski Masks, Veils, Nose-rings and Feathers: Identity on the Frontlines of Modernity." In Elizabeth Ewart and Michael E. O'Hanlon (eds), *Body Arts and Modernity*, pp. 18–35. Wantage: Sean Kingston Publishing.

Conley, Chip and Eric Freidenwald-Fishman. 2006. *Marketing That Matters: 10 Practices to Profit Your Business and Change the World*. San Francisco, CA: Berrett-Koehler Publishers.

Conroy, Marianne. 1998. "Discount Dreams: Factory Outlet Malls, Consumption, and the Performance of Middle-Class Identity." *Social Text* 54(1): 63–83.

Coombe, Rosemary J. 1998. *The Cultural Life of Intellectual Properties: Authorship, Appropriation, and the Law*. Durham, NC: Duke University Press.

Copp, Jonathan. 2005. "Field Report: Les Droites." *Patagonia* [Catalog] Winter, 32.

Corbett, Julia B. 2006. *Communicating Nature: How We Create and Understand Environmental Messages*. Washington, DC: Island Press.

Cordwell, Justine M. and Ronald A. Schwarz, eds. 1973. *The Fabrics of Culture: The Anthropology of Clothing and Adornment*. The Hague: Mouton Press.

Corliss, Richard. 1993. "Pacific Overtures." *Time*, September 13, 68–70.

Corrigan, P. 1995. "Gender and the Gift: The Case of the Family Clothing Economy." In Stevi Jackson and Shaun Moores (eds), *The Politics of Domestic Consumption*. London: Prentice Hall.

Cort, Louise. 1989. "The Changing Fortunes of Three Archaic Japanese Textiles." In Annette B. Weiner and Jane Schneider (eds), *Cloth and Human Experience*, pp. 380–415. Washington, DC: Smithsonian Institution Press.

Cox, Rupert, ed. 2008. *The Culture of Copying in Japan*. Abingdon: Routledge.

Cragg, Violet. n.d. "Violet in Nigeria, by Herself and Margaret Kerrich." Manuscript. Rhodes House, Oxford.

Crane, Diana. 2000. *Fashion and Its Social Agendas: Class, Gender and Identity in Clothing*. Chicago: University of Chicago Press.

Crawley, Ernest. 1931. *Dress, Drink, and Drums: Further Studies of Savages and Sex*. London: Methuen and Co.

Crill, Rosemary. 2010. "Trading Materials: Textiles and British Markets." In Christopher Breward, Philip Crang and Rosemary Crill.

Csordas, Thomas J. 1994. "Introduction: The Body as Representation and Being-in-the-World." In Thomas J. Csordas (ed.), *Embodiment and Experience: The Existential Ground of Culture and Self*, pp. 1–24. Cambridge: Cambridge University Press.

Culler, Jonathan. 1975. *Structuralist Poetics*. London: Routledge and Kegan Paul.

Cummingham, Hugh. 1980. *Leisure in the Industrial Revolution*. London: Croom Helm.

Dalby, Liza. 1993. *Kimono: Fashioning Culture*. New Haven, CT: Yale University Press.

Daniels, Inge. 2001. "The Fame of Miyajima: Spirituality, Commodification, and the Tourist Trade in Souvenirs in Japan." PhD thesis, University College London.

Danto, Arthur C. 1973. "Artworks and Real Things." *Theoria* 39(1–3): 1–17.

Darish, Patricia. 1989. "Dressing for the Next Life: Raffia Textile Production and Use Among the Kuba of Zaire." In Annette B. Werner and Jane Schneider (eds), *Cloth and Human Experience*, pp. 118–42. Washington, DC: Smithsonian Institution Press.

Darwin, Charles. 1859. *The Origin of Species*. New York: The Modern Library.

Darwin, Charles. 1871. *The Descent of Man, and Selection in Relation to Sex*. New York: The Modern Library.

Darwin, Charles. (1872) 1955. *The Expression of Emotions in Man and Animals*. New York: Greenwood Press.

Davidoff, Leonore and Catherine Hall. 1987. *Family Fortunes: Men and Women of the English Middle Class*, 1780–1850. Chicago: University of Chicago Press.

Dávila, Arlene. 2003. "Ethnicity, Fieldwork, and the Cultural Capital that Gets Us There: Reflections from U.S. Hispanic Marketing." *Aztlan* 28(1): 145–61.

De Certeau, Michel. 1984. *The Practice of Everyday Life*, trans. Steven Randall. Berkeley: University of California Press.

De Certeau, Michel. 1988. The Practice of Everyday Life, trans. Steven Kendall. Berkeley: University of California Press.

De Kadt, Emanuel. 1979. *Tourism—Passport for Development?" Perspective on the Social and Cultural Effects of Tourism in Developing Countries*. Published for the World Bank and UNESCO. New York: Oxford University Press.

De Vault, M. 1991. *Feeding the Family: The Social Organization of Caring as Gendered Work*. Chicago: University of Chicago Press.

Debord, Guy. 1995. *The Society of the Spectacle*, trans. Donald Nicholson-Smith. New York: Zone Books.

Deeb, Lara. 2006. *An Enchanted Modern: Gender and Public Piety in Shi'i Lebanon*. Princeton, NJ: Princeton University Press.

Deleuze, Gilles and Félix Guattari. 1996. *Anti-Oedipus: Capitalism and Schizophrenia*. Minneapolis: University of Minnesota Press.

Deloitte. 2008. *Analyse af beklædningsbranchen—tendenser og ud-fordringer*. Copenhagen: Deloitte.

Denning, Michael. 2004. *Globalization in the Age of Three Worlds*. New York: Verso.

Dent, Alexander S. 2012. "Understanding the War on Piracy, or, Why We Need More Anthropology of Pirates." *Anthropological Quarterly* 85(3): 659–72.

Denzer, LaRay. 1997. "The Garment Industry under SAP with a Special Case Study on Ibadan." Unpublished paper presented in workshop on SAP and the Popular Economy. Development Policy Centre, Ibadan, Nigeria. August.

Derrida, Jacques. 1980. "Structure, Sign, and Play in the Discourse of the Human Sciences." In Jacques Derrida, *Writing and Difference*, pp. 278–94. New York: Routledge.

Derrington, Shivani. 2010. "Wardrobe Stories." In Christopher Breward, Philip Crang, and Rosemary Crill (eds), *British Asian Style: Fashion & Textiles Past & Present*. London: V&A Publishing.

Di Leonardo, Micaela. 1987. "The Female World of Cards and Holidays: Women, Families, and the Work of Kinship." *Signs: Journal of Women in Culture and Society* 12(3): 440–53.

Diamond, Ellen. 2005. *Fashion Retailing: A Multi-channel Approach*, vol. 1. Upper Saddle River, NJ: Prentice-Hall.

Dicken, Peter. 1998. *Global Shift: Transforming the World Economy*, 3rd edn. New York: Guilford Press.

Diderot, Denis. (1796) 1926. "Supplement to Bougainville's Voyage." In *Rameau's Nephew and Other Works*, trans. Wilfred Jackson, pp. 117–59. London: Chapman and Hall.

Doob, Leonard W. 1961. *Communication in Africa, a Search for Boundaries*. New Haven, CT: Yale University Press.

Douglas, Mary. 1966. *Purity and Danger: An Analysis of the Concepts of Pollution and Taboo*. London: Routledge & Kegan Paul.

Douglas, Mary and Baron Isherwood, eds. 1979. *The World of Goods*. London: Allen Lane.

Douny, Laurence. 2011. "Silk-embroidered Garments as Transformative Processes: Layering, Inscribing and Displaying Hausa Material Identities." *Journal of Material Culture* 16(4): 401–15.

Douny, Laurence. 2013. "Wild Silk Wrappers of Dogon: Wrapping and Unwrapping Material Identities." In Susanna Harris and Laurence Douny (eds), *Wrapping & Unwrapping the Body: Archaeological and Anthropological Perspectives*. Walnut Creek, CA: Left Coast.

Drucker, Peter. 1965. *Cultures of the North Pacific Coast*. San Francisco, CA: Chandler.

DTB. 2008. *Årsberetning 2007*. Herning: Dansk Textil & Beklædning.

Du Gay, Paul, Stuart Hall, Linda Janes, Hugh Mackay, and Keith Negus. 1997. *Doing Cultural Studies: The Story of the Sony Walkman*. Milton Keynes: Open University.

Duncombe, Jean and Dennis Marsden. 1999. "Love and Intimacy: The Gendered Division of Emotion and 'Emotion Work'." In Graham Allan (ed.), *The Sociology of Family Life*, pp. 91–110. Oxford: Blackwell.

Dunlap, Knight. 1928. "The Development and Function of Clothing." *Journal of General Psychology* 1(1): 64–78.

Dupont Company. 1952. *Dupont: The Autobiography of an American Enterprise*. Wilmington, DE: E. I. du Pont de Nemours and Company.

Durham, Deborah. n.d. *Village of Devilthorns/Village of Lights: Liberalism and Cultural Identity in an African Democracy*. Unpublished manuscript. Sweet Briar College, Sweet Briar, VA.

Durham, Deborah. 1995a. "The Lady in the Logo: Tribal Dress and Western Culture in a Southern African Community." In Joanne B. Eicher (ed.), *Dress and Ethnicity*, pp. 183–94. Oxford: Berg Publishers.

Durham, Deborah. 1995b. "Soliciting Gifts and Negotiating Agency: The Spirit of Asking in Botswana." *Journal of the Royal Anthropological Institute*, n.s., 1(1): 111–28.

Durham, Deborah and James W. Fernandez. 1991. "Tropical Dominions: The Figurative Struggle over Domains of Belonging and Apartness in Africa." In James W. Fernandez (ed.), *Beyond Metaphor: The Theory of Tropes in Anthropology*, pp. 190–210. Stanford, CA: Stanford University Press; Durham, NC: Duke University Press.

Durkheim, Emile. 1964. "The Dualism of Human Nature and Its Social Conditions." In Kurt Wolff (ed.), *Essays on Sociology and Philosophy*, pp. 325–40. New York: Harper and Row.

Dutton, Dennis. 1983. *The Forger's Art: Forgery and the Philosophy of Art*. Berkeley: University of California Press.

Dwyer, Claire. 2010. "From Suitcase to Showroom: British Asian Retail Spaces." In Christopher Breward, Phillip Crill, and Rosemary Crang (eds), *British Asian Style: Fashion & Textiles Past & Present*. London: V&A Publishing.

Eco, Umberto. 1972. "Towards a Semiotic Inquiry into the Television Message." *Working Papers in Cultural Studies* 3: 103–21.

Edwards, Douglas R. 1994. "The Social, Religious, and Political Aspects of Costume in Josephius." In Judith Lynn Sebesta and Larissa Bonfante (eds), *The World of Roman Costume*, pp. 153–59. Madison: University of Wisconsin Press.

Egan, R. Danielle. 2003. "Eyeing the Scene: The Uses and (Re)uses of Surveillance Cameras in an Exotic Dance Club." *Critical Sociology* 30(2): 299–319.

Eicher, Joanne B. 2000. "The Anthropology of Dress." *Dress* 27(1): 59–70.

Eicher, Joanne B., ed. 2010. *Encyclopedia of World Dress and Fashion*, 10 vols, continuing online 2011. New York: Oxford University Press. (Also published as *Berg Encyclopedia of World Dress and Fashion*. Oxford: Berg).

Eicher, Joanne B. 2015. "Subtle and Spectacular: Dressing in Kalabari Style." In Paula Rabinowitz and Cristina Giorcelli (eds), *Habits of Being 4: Excess and Quotidian*, pp. 262–81. Minneapolis: University of Minnesota Press.

Eicher, Joanne B. 2016. "Editing Fashion Studies: Reflections on Methodology and Interdisciplinarity." In Heiki Jenss (ed.), *Fashion Studies: Research Methods, Sites and Practices*, pp. 198–214. London: Bloomsbury.

Eicher, Joanne B. and Mary Ellen Roach-Higgins. 1992. "Definition and Classification of Dress: Implications for Analysis in Gender Roles." In Ruth Barnes and Joanne Eicher (eds), *Dress and Gender: Making and Meaning*, pp. 8–28. Oxford: Berg.

El-Guindi, Fadwa. 1981. "Veiling Infitah with Muslim Ethic: Egypt's Contemporary Islamic Movement." *Social Problems* 28(4): 465–85.

El-Guindi, Fadwa. 1999a. "The Anthropology of Dress." In Fadwa El-Guindi, *Veil: Modesty, Privacy and Resistance*, pp. 49–76. Oxford: Berg.

El-Guindi, Fadwa. 1999b. *Veil: Modesty, Privacy and Resistance*. Oxford: Berg.

Ellinson, Rabbi Getsel. 1992. *Women and the Mitzvot. Vol. 2. The Modest Way*. New York: Feldheim.

Entwistle, Joanne. 2000a. *The Fashioned Body. Fashion, Dress and Modern Social Theory*. Cambridge: Polity Press.

Entwistle, Joanne. 2004. "From Catwalk to Catalog: Male Fashion Models, Masculinity, and Identity." In Helen Thomas and Jamilah Ahmed (eds), *Cultural Bodies: Ethnography and Theory*, pp. 55–75. Maiden, MA: Blackwell.

Entwistle, Joanne. 2006. "The Cultural Economy of Fashion Buying." *Current Sociology* 54(5): 704–24.

Entwistle, Joanne. 2009. *The Aesthetic Economy of Fashion: Markets and Value in Clothing and Modelling*. London: Bloomsbury Academic.

Errington, Shelly. 1990. "Recasting Sex, Gender, and Power: A Theoretical and Regional Overview." In Jane Monnig Atkinson and Shelly Errington (eds), *Power and Difference: Gender in Island Southeast Asia*, pp. 1–58. Stanford, CA: Stanford University Press.

Esposito, Mark. 2009. *Put Your Corporate Social Responsibility Act Together*. Mustang, OK: Tate Publishing.

Europa World Year Book. 1999. vol. 1. London: Europa Press.

Evans, Nancy H. 1976. "Tourism and Cross-Cultural Communication." *Annals of Tourism Research* 3(4): 189–98.

Evans-Pritchard, Edward E. 1968. *The Nuer*. Oxford: Oxford University Press.

Ewen, Stuart. 1988. *All Consuming Images: The Politics of Style in Contemporary Cultures*. New York: Basic Books.

Fabian, Johannes. 2014. *Time and the Other: How Anthropology Makes Its Object*. New York: Columbia University Press.

Fader, Ayala. 2007. *A Ritual Garment: Bringing Up the Next Generation of Hasidic Jews in Brooklyn*. Princeton, NJ: Princeton University Press.

Fader, Ayala. 2009. *Mitzvah Girls: Bringing Up the Next Generation of Hasidic Jews in Brooklyn*. Princeton, NJ: Princeton University Press.

Fadzillah, Ida. 2005. "The Amway Connection: How Transnational Ideas of Beauty and Money Affect Thai Girls' Perceptions of Their Future Options." In Sunaina Maira and Elisabeth Soep (eds), *Youthscaps: The Popular, the National, the Global*, pp. 85–102. Philadelphia: University of Pennsylvania Press.

Fan, Hong. 1997. *Footbinding, Feminism and Freedom: The Liberation of Women's Bodies in Modern China*. London: Frank Cass.

Falk, Pesach Eliyahu. 1998. *Modesty: An Adornment for Life*. New York: Feldheim.

Fanon, Frantz. 1965b. *Les damnés de la terre*. Paris: Maspero.

Fanon, Frantz. 1986. *Black Skin White Masks*. London: Pluto Press.

Fader, Ayala. 2009. *Mitzvah Girls: Bringing Up the Next Generation of Hasidic Jews in Brooklyn*. Princeton, NJ: Princeton University Press.

Faurschou, Gail. 1990. "Obsolescence and Desire: Fashion and the Commodity." In Hugh J. Silverman (ed.), *Postmodernism: Philosophy and the Arts*, pp. 234–59. London: Routledge.

Feeley-Harnik, Gillian. 1989. "Cloth and the Creation of Ancestors in Madagascar." In Annette B. Weiner and Jane Schneider (eds), *Cloth and Human Experience*, pp. 75–118. Washington, DC: Smithsonian Institution Press.

Feldman, Jan. 2003. *Lubavitchers as Citizens: A Paradox of Liberal Democracy*. Ithaca, NY: Cornell University Press.

Ferguson, Charles A. 1959. "Diglossia." *Word* 15(2): 325–40.

Ferguson, James. 2002. "'Of Mimicry and Membership', Africans and the 'New World Society'." *Cultural Anthropology* 17(4): 551–69.

Fernandes, Leela. 2006. *India's New Middle Class: Democratic Politics in an Era of Economic Reform*. Minneapolis: Minnesota University Press.

Finkelstein, Joanne. 1991. *The Fashioned Self*. Philadelphia: Temple University Press.

Flügel, John Carl. 1930. *The Psychology of Clothes*. London: The Hogarth Press.

Foley, Brenda. 2002. "Naked Politics: Erie, PA v the Kandyland Club." *NWSA Journal* 14(2): 1–17.

Forge, Anthony. 1970. "Learning to See in New Guinea." In Philip Mayer (ed.), *Socialization: The Approach from Social Anthropology*, pp. 269–91. London: Tavistock.

Forster, Edward Morgan. (1910) 1992. *Howard's End*, ed. O. Stallybrass. London: Penguin Books. (Reset and reprinted from the Abinger Edition, 1975).

Fortis, Paolo. 2010. "The Birth of Design: A Kuna Theory of Body and Personhood." *Journal of the Royal Anthropological Institute*, n.s., 16(3): 480–95.

Fortis, Paolo. 2014. "Artefacts and Bodies among Kuna People from Panama." In Elizabeth Hallam, Tim Ingold (eds), *Making and Growing: Anthropological Studies of Organisms and Artefacts*, 89–106. Farnham: Ashgate.

Foster, Robert J. 2005. "Commodity Futures: Labour, Love, and Value." *Anthropology Today* 21(4): 8–12.

Foster, Robert J. 2008a. "Commodities, Brands, Love and Kula: Comparative Notes on Value Creation." *Anthropological Theory* 8(1): 9–25.

Foster, Robert J. 2008b. *Coca-Globalization. Following Soft Drinks from New York to New Guinea*. New York: Palgrave Macmillan.

Foucault, Michel. (1977) 1995. *Discipline and Punish*. New York: Vintage.

Foucault, Michel. (1978) 1990. *History of Sexuality*, vol. 1. New York: Vintage.

Fourneau, J. and L. Kravetz. 1954. "Le pagne sure la Côte de Guinée et au Congo du XVe siècle à nos jours." *Bulletin de l'Institute d'Etudes Centrafricaine* 7–8:5–22.

Fournier, Susan. 1998. "Consumer and their Brands: Developing Relationship Theory in Consumer Research." *Journal of Consumer Research* 24(4): 343–73.

Fowler, Marian. 1987. *Below the Peacock Fan*. Ontario: Penguin Books, Canada.

Fox, Richard Wightman and T. J. Jackson Lears. 1983. "Introduction." In Richard Wightman Fox and T. J. Jackson Lears (eds), *The Culture of Consumption: Critical Essays in American History*, 1880–1980, pp. ix–xvii. New York: Pantheon.

Fox-Genovese, Elizabeth. 1987. "The Empress's New Clothes: The Politics of Fashion." *Socialist Review* 17(1): 7–30.

Frank, Katherine. 1986. *A Voyager Out*. Boston, MA: Houghton Mifflin.

Frank, Katherine. 2002a. *G-Strings and Sympathy: Strip Club Regulars and Male Desire*. Durham, NC: Duke University Press.

Frank, Katherine. 2002b. "Stripping, Starving, and Other Ambiguous Pleasures." In Merri Lisa Johnson (ed.), *Jane Sexes It Up: True Confessions of Feminist Desire*, pp. 171–206. New York: Four Walls Eight Windows.

Freeman, Carla. 2001. "Is Local: Global as Feminine: Masculine? Rethinking the Gender of Globalization." *Signs* 26(4): 1007–37.

Freud, Sigmund. 1950. *Totem and Taboo*. New York: W. W. Norton & Co.

Freudenberger, Herman. 1973. "Fashion, Sumptuary Laws and Business." In Gordon Wills and David Midgley (eds), *Fashion Marketing: An Anthropology of Viewpoints and Perspectives*, pp. 137–47. London: Allen & Unwin.

Friedman, Andrea. 1996. "'The Habitats of Sex-Crazed Perverts': Campaigns against Burlesque in Depression-Era New York City." *Journal of the History of Sexuality* 7(2): 203–38.

Friedman, Jonathan. 1994. "The Political Economy of Elegance: An African Cult of Beauty." In Jonathan Friedman (ed.), *Consumption and Identity*, pp. 167–89. Chur: Harwood Academic Publishers.

Frow, John. 2003. "Singnature and Brand." In Jim Collins (ed.), *High-Pop: Making Culture into Popular Entertainment*, pp. 56–74. Oxford: Blackwell.

Fuglesang, Minou. 1994. *Veils and Videos: Female Youth Culture on the Kenyan Coast*. Stockholm: Stockholm Studies in Social Anthropology.

Gaines, Jane M. 1991. *Contested Culture: The Image, The Voice, and the Law*. Chapel Hill: University of North Carolina Press.

Gaitskell, Deborah. 1990. "Devout Domesticity? A Century of African Women's Christianity in South Africa." In Cheryl Walker (ed.), *Women and Gender in Southern Africa to 1945*. London: James Currey.

Gallagher, Nora. 1999. *Patagonia: Notes from the Field*. San Francisco, CA: Chronicle Books.

Gamble, David P. 1967. *The Wolof of Senegambia*. London: International African Institute.

Gandoulou, Justin-Daniel. 1984. *Entre Paris et Bacongo*. Paris: Centre Georges Pompidou, Collection "Alors".

Gandoulou, Justin-Daniel. 1989. *Dandies à Bacongo: Le culte de l'élégance dans la société congolaise contemporaine*. Paris: L'Harmattan.

Gaonkar, Dilip Parameshwar and Elizabeth A. Povinelli. 2003. "Technologies of Public Forms: Circulation, Transfiguration, Recognition." *Public Culture* 15(3): 385–98.

Gates, Henry Louis, Jr. 1988. *The Signifying Monkey*. Oxford: Oxford University Press.

Geary, Patrick. 1986. "Sacred Commodoties: The Circulation of Medieval Relics." In Arjun Appadurai (ed.), *The Social Life of Things: Commodities in Cultural Perspective*, pp. 169–94. New York: Cambridge University Press.

Geismar, Haidy. 2005. "Reproduction, Creativity, Restriction. Material Culture and Copyright in Vanuatu." *Journal of Social Archaeology* 5(1): 25–51.

Gell, Alfred. 1998. *Art and Agency: An Anthropological Theory*. Oxford: Oxford University Press.

Genovese, Eugene D. 1974. *Roll, Jordan, Roll: The World the Slaves Made*. New York: Pantheon.

Gereffi, Gary. 1999. "International Trade and Industrial Upgrading in the Apparel Commodity Chain." *Journal of International Economics* 48(1): 37–70.

Gereffi, Gary and Miguel Korzeniewicz, eds. 1994. *Commodity Chains and Global Capitalism*. Westport, CT: Praeger; Westport, CT: Greenwood Press.

Gereffi, Gary, David Spener, and Jennifer Bair, eds. 2002. *Free Trade and Uneven Development: The North American Apparel Industry after NAFTA*. Philadelphia, PA: Temple University Press.

Gibbins, Keith. 1971. "Social Psychological Theories of Fashion." *Journal of the Home Economics Association of Australia* 3: 3–18.

Gibbins, Keith and Anthony Schneider. 1980. "Meaning of Garments." *Perceptual and Motor Skills* 51(1): 287–91.

Giddens, Anthony. 1991. *Modernity and Self-Identity*. Cambridge: Polity Press.

Giddens, Anthony. 1992. *The Transformation of Intimacy: Sexuality, Love and Eroticism in Modern Societies*. Cambridge: Polity.

Gilfoy, Peggy. 1987. *Patterns of Life: West African Strip-Waeving Tradtions*. Washington, DC: National Museum of African Art.

Gillette, Maris. 2000. "What's in a Dress? Brides in the Hui quarter of Xi'an." In Deborah S. Davis (ed.), *The Consumer Revolution in Urban China*, pp. 80–107. Berkeley: University of California Press.

Gilman, Sander L. 2006. *Multiculturalism and the Jews*. New York: Routledge.

Gilmore, James H. and B. Joseph Pine. 2007. *Authenticity: Contending with the New Consumer Sensibility*. Boston, MA: Harvard Business School Press.

Ginsburg, Madeleine. 1980. "Rags to Riches: The Second-Hand Clothes Trade 1700–1978." *Costume* 14(1): 121–35.

Givens, David B. 1977. "Shoulder Shrugging: A Densley Communicative Expressive Behavior." *Semiotica* 19(1–2): 13–28.

Gladwell, Malcolm. 2000. *The Tipping Point: How Little Things Can Make a Big Difference*. New York: Back Bay Books/Little Brown and Company.

Goffman, Erving. 1979. *Gender Advertisements*. Cambridge, MA: Harvard University Press.

Gökansel, Banu and Anna Secor. 2013. "Transnational Networks of Veiling-Fashion between Turkey and Western Europe". In Emma Tarlo and Annelies Moors (eds), *Islamic Fashion and Anti-Fashion: New Perspectives from Europe and North America*, pp. 157–67. London: Bloomsbury.

Golden, Arthur. 1997. *Memoirs of a Geisha*. New York: Alfred A. Knopf.

Golding, F. D. 1942. "Wild Silkworms of Nigeria." *Farm & Forest* 3: 35–40.

Göle, Nilufer. 1996. *The Forbidden Modern: Civilization and Veiling: Critical Perspectives on Women and Gender*. Ann Arbor: University of Michigan Press.

Gondola, Ch. Didier. 1999. "Dream and Drama: The Search for Elegance among Congolese Youth." *Africa Today* 42(1): 23–48.

Goody, Esther N., ed. 1982. *From Craft to Industry: The Ethnography of Proto-Industrial Cloth Production*. Cambridge: Cambridge University Press.

Gow, Peter. 1999. "Piro Designs: Painting as Meaningful Action in an Amazonian Lived World." *Journal of the Royal Anthropological Institute* 5(2): 229–46.

Gow, Peter and Margherita Margiotti. 2012. "Is There Fortune in Greater Amazonia?" In Giovanni Da Col and Caroline Humphrey (eds), *Cosmologies of Fortune: Luck, Vitality and the Contingency of Daily Life. Social Analysis*, vol. 56, Special Issues 1–2, pp. 43–56.

Grafton, Anthony. 1990. *Forgers and Critics: Creativity and Duplicity in Western Scholarship*. Princeton, NJ: Princeton University Press.

Gramsci, Antonio. 1971. *Selections from the Prison Notebooks*, ed. and trans. Quentin Hoare and Geoffrey N. Smith. London: Lawrence and Wishart.

Green, Nancy. 1997. *Ready to Work, Ready to Wear: A Century of Industry and Immigrants in Paris and New York*. Durham, NC: Duke University Press.

Gregson, Nicky and Louise Crewe. 2003. *Second-Hand Cultures*. Oxford: Berg.

Groom, Nick. 2007. "Romanticism and Forgery." *Literature Compass* 4(6): 1625–49.

Grosse Ruse-Khan, Henning. 2008. "A Pirate of the Caribbean? The Attractions of Suspending TRIPS Obligations." *Journal of International Economic Law* 11(2): 313–64.

Gullestad, Marianne. 1990. "Doing Interpretive Analysis in a Modern Large Scale Society: The Meaning of Peace and Quiet in Norway." *Social Analysis* 29: 38–61.

Haas, Erika J. and Harvey Hartman. 1995. "Patagonia Struggles to Reduce Its Impact on the Environment." *Total Quality Environmental Management* 5(1): 1–7.

Haggblade, Steven. 1990. "The Flip Side of Fashion: Used Clothing Exports to the Third World." *Journal of Development Studies* 26(3): 505–21.

Hall, Dennis. 2001. "Delight in Disorder: A Reading of Diaphany and Liquefaction in Contemporary Women's Clothing." *Journal of Popular Culture* 34(4): 65–74.

Hall, Stuart and Tony Jefferson. 1976. *Resistance through Rituals: Youth Subcultures in Post-War Britain*. London: Hutchinson.

Halliday, Michael A. K. 1976. "Anti-Languages." *UEA Papers in Linguistics* 1: 15–45.

Halls, Zillah. 1973. *Coronation Costume and Accessories 1685–1953*. London: Her Majesty's Stationery Office.

Hammerich, Paul, ed. 1993. *Magasin på tværs i 125 år*. Copenhagen: Gyldendal.

Handler, Richard. 1986. "Authenticity." *Anthropology Today* 2(1): 2–4.

Handler, Richard. 2001. "Anthropology of Authenticity." In Neil J. Smelser and Paul B. Baltes (eds), *International Encyclopedia of the Social and Behavioural Sciences*, pp. 936–67. Oxford: Pergamon.

Handley, Susannah. 1999. *Nylon: The Manmade Fashion Revolution*. London: Bloomsbury.

Hanna, Judith L. 1998. "Undressing the First Amendment and Corseting the Striptease Dancer." *Drama Review* 42(2): 38–69.

Hanna, Judith L. 1999. "Toying with the Striptease Dancer and the First Amendment." In Stuart Reifel (ed.), *Play and Culture Studies*, Vol. 2, *Play Contexts Revisited*, pp. 37–56. Stamford, CT: Ablex.

Hannerz, Ulf. 1989. "Notes on the Global Ecumene." *Public Culture* 1(2): 66–75.

Hannerz, Ulf. 1990. "Cosmopolitans and Locals in World Culture." *Theory, Culture, and Society* 7(2–3): 237–51.

Hannerz, Ulf. 1992. *Cultural Complexity: Studies in the Social Organization of Meaning*. New York: Columbia University Press.

Hannerz, Ulf. 1996. *Transnational Connections*. London: Routledge.

Hannerz, Ulf. 2004. *Foreign News: Exploring the World of Foreign Correspondents*. Chicago: University of Chicago Press.

Hansen, Karen Tranberg. 2000. *Salaula: The World of Secondhand Clothing and Zambia*. Chicago: University of Chicago Press.

Hansen, Karen Tranberg. 2004a. "Dressing Dangerously: Miniskirts, Gender Relations, and Sexuality in Zambia." In Jean Allman (ed.), *Fashioning Africa: Power and the Politics of Dress*, pp. 166–85. Bloomington: Indiana University Press.

Hansen, Karen Tranberg. 2004b. "The World in Dress: Anthropological Studies of Clothing, Fashion, and Culture." *Annual Review of Anthropology* 33: 369–92.

Hansen, Karen Tranberg. 2005. "Getting Stuck in the Compound: Some Odds Against Social Adulthood in Lusaka, Zambia." *Africa Today* 51(4): 3–16.

Hansen, Karen Tranberg, ed. 2008. *Youth and the City in the Global South*. Bloomington: Indiana University Press.

Hansen, Karen Tranberg. 2009. "Youth, Gender, and Secondhand Clothing in Lusaka, Zambia: Local and Global Styles." In Eugenia Paulicelli and Hazel Clark (eds), *The Fabric of Cultures: Fashion, Identity, and Globalization*, pp. 112–27. New York: Routledge.

Harden, Blaine. 1985. "Flying Smugglers Supply Nigerians." *Washington Post*, October 10, A29.

Hart, Keith. 2007. "A Short History of Economic Anthropology." *The Memory Bank, A New Commonwealth Ver 5.0.*, November 9. Available online: http://thememorybank.co.uk/2007/11/09/a-short-history-of-economic-anthropology/ (accessed August 19, 2018).

Hartman, Harvey and Erika J. Haas. 1995. "Patagonia Struggles to Reduce Its Impact on the Environment." *Environmental Management* 5(1): 3–7.

Hartmann, Patrick. 2008. "Virtual Nature Experiences as Emotional Benefits in Green Product Consumption: The Moderating Role of Environmental Attitudes." *Environment and Behavior* 40(6): 818–42.

Harvey, David. 1989. *The Condition of Postmodernity*. Oxford: Basil Blackwell.

Hattersley, Alan F. 1952. "The Missionary in South African History." *Theoria* 4: 86–88.

Hatton, Elizabeth. 1989. "Lévi-Strauss's 'Bricolage' and Theorizing Teacher's Work." *Anthropology & Education Quarterly* 20(2): 74–96.

Haywood, Ian. 1987. *Faking It: Art and the Politics of Forgery*. Brighton: Harvester.

Heaphy, Brian. 2007. *Late Modernity and Social Change: Reconstructing Social and Personal Life*. London: Routledge.

Heath, Deborah. 1992. "Fashion, Anti-fashion, and Heteroglossia in Urban Senegal." *American Ethnologist* 19(1): 19–33.

Hebdige, Dick. 1979. *Subculture: The Meaning of Style*. London: Routledge.

Heilman, Samuel. 1976. *Synagogue Life: A Study in Symbolic Interaction*. Chicago: University of Chicago Press.

Heilman, Samuel. 1992. *Defenders of the Faith: Inside Ultra-Orthodox Jewry*. New York: Schocken Books.

Helmstadter, Richard J. 1992. "The Reverend Andrew Reed (1787–1862): Evangelical Pastor as Entrepreneur." In Richard W. Davis and Richard J. Helmstadter (eds), *Religion and Irreligion in Victorian Society: Essays in Honor of R.K. Webb*. New York: Routledge.

Hendrickson, Ann Alfhild (Hildi). 1994. "The 'Long' Dress and the Construction of Herero Identities in Southern Africa." *African Studies* 53(2): 25–54.

Hendrickson, Carol. 1996b. "Selling Guatemala: Maya Export Products in US Mail Order Catalogs." In David Howes (ed.), *Cross-cultural Consumption: Global Markets, Local Realities*, pp. 106–25. London: Routledge.

Hendry, Joy. 2000. *The Orient Strikes Back*. Oxford: Berg.

Heng, Geraldine and Janandas Devan. 1992. "State Fatherhood: The Politics of Nationalism, Sexuality, and Race in Singapore." In Andrew Parker, Mary Russo, Doris Sommer, and Patricia Yaeger (eds), *Nationalism and Sexualities*. New York: Routledge.

Henkin, Rabbi Yehuda. 2003a. "Contemporary Tseni'ut." *Tradition* 37(3): 1–48.

Henkin, Rabbi Yehuda. 2003b. "More on Women's Hair Covering." *Tradition* 37: 148–51.

Hepburn, Sharon. 2000. "The Cloth of Barbaric Pagans: Tourism, Identity, and Modernity in Nepal." *Fashion Theory: the Journal of Dress, Body, and Culture* 4(3): 275–301.

Herman, Gary. 1971. *The Who*. London: Studio Vista.

Herzfeld, Michael. 1993. "In Defiance of Destiny: The Management of Time and Gender at a Cretan Funeral." *American Ethnologist* 20(2): 241–55.

Heussler, Robert. 1968. *The British in Northern Nigeria*. London: Oxford University Press.

Hevia, James. 1995. *Cherishing Men from Afar: Qing Guest Ritual and the Macartney Embassy of 1793*, Durham, NC: Duke University Press.

Hirschfeld, Larry. 1977. "Art in Cunaland: Ideology and Cultural Adaptation." *Man*, n.s., 12(1): 104–23.

Hobsbawm, Eric. 1983. "Introduction: Inventing Traditions." In Eric Hobsbawm and Terence Ranger (eds), *The Invention of Tradition*, pp. 1–14. Cambridge: Cambridge University Press.

Hobsbawm, Eric and Terence Ranger. 1983. *The Invention of Tradition*. Cambridge: Cambridge University Press.

Hochschild, Arlie. 1989a. "The Economy of Gratitude." In David D. Franks and E. Doyle McCarthy (eds), *The Sociology of Emotions: Original Essays and Research Papers*. Greenwich, CT: JAI Press.

Hochschild, Arlie. 1989b. *The Second Shift: Working Parents and the Revolution at Home*. New York: Viking.

Hodge, Robert and Gunther Kress. 1988. *Social Semiotics*. Ithaca, NY: Cornell University Press.

Holland, Samantha. 2004. *Alternative Femininities*. Oxford: Berg.

Hollander, Anne. 1994. *Sex and Suits: The Evolution of Modern Dress*. New York: Alfred A. Knopf.

Hollway, Wendy. 1984. "Gender Difference and the Production of Subjectivity." In Stevi Jackson and Sue Scott (eds), *Feminism and Sexuality: A Reader*. Edinburgh: Edinburgh University Press.

Honour, Hugh. 1961. *Chinoiserie: The Vision of Cathay*. New York: Harper and Row.Holman

Holman, Rebecca H. 1980a. "A Transcription and Analysis System for the Study of Women's Clothing Behavior," *Semiotica* 32(1–2):11–34.

Holman, Rebecca. 1980b. "Clothing as Communication: An Empirical Investigation." In Jerry C. Olson (ed.), *Advances in Consumer Research*, vol. 7, pp. 372–77. Ann Arbor, MI: Association for Consumer Research.

Holman, Rebecca. 1981. "Apparel as Communication." In Elizabeth C. Hirschman and Morris B. Holbrook (eds), *Symbolic Consumer Behavior*, pp. 7–15. Ann Arbor, MI: Assocaition for Consumer Research.

Holub, Emil. 1881. *Seven Years in South Africa: Travels, Researches, and Hunting Adventures, between the Diamond-Fields and the Zambesi (1872–79)*, 2 vols, trans. Ellen E. Frewer. Boston, MA: Houghton Mifflin.

Hoodfar, Homa. 1991. "Return to the Veil: Personal Strategy and Public Participation in Egypt." In Nanneke Edclift and M. Thea Sinclair (eds), *Working Women: International Perspectives on Labor and Gender Ideology*, pp. 104–24. New York: Routledge.

Hopkins, Terence and Immanuel Wallerstein. 1986. "Commodity Chains in the World-Economy Prior to 1800." *Review* 10(1): 157–70.

Horton, Robin. 1960a. *The God as Guests: An Aspect of Kalabari Religious Life* (Special Publication). Lagos: Nigeria Magazine Press.

Horton, Robin. 1960b. "New Year in the Delta." *Nigeria Magazine*, No. 67, December, 256–95.

Horton, Robin. 1965. *Kalabari Sculpture*. Lagos: Nigerian National Press.

Howe, James. 1998. *A People Who Would Not Kneel: Panama, the Unites States and the Kuna*. Washington, DC: Smithsonian Institution Press.

Howe, James. 2009. *Chiefs, Scribes, and Ethnographers: Kuna Culture from Inside and Out*. Austin: University of Texas Press.

Howell, Georgina. 1975. *In Vogue: Six Decades of Fashion*. London: Allen Lane.

Howes, David. 1996. "Introduction: Commodities and Cultural Borders." In David Howes (ed.), *Cross-Cultural Consumption: Global Markets, Local Realities*. London: Routledge.

Hughes, Isaac. 1841. "Missionary Labours among the Batlapi." *The Evangelical Magazine and Missionary Chronicle* 19: 522–23.

Hunt, Nancy R. 1990. "'Single Ladies on the Congo'. Protestant Missionary Tensions and Voices." *Women's Studies International Forum* 13(4): 395–403.

Ingold, Tim. 2000. "*Making Culture and Weaving the World*." In Rupert Graves-Brown (ed.), *Matter, Materiality and Modern Culture*, pp. 50–71. London: Routledge.

Ingold, Tim. 2007. "Materials against Materiality." *Archaeological Dialogues* 14(1): 1–16.

Irvine, Judith T. 1974. "Caste and Communication in a Wolof Village." PhD diss., Anthropology Department, University of Pennsylvania.

Ivaska, Andrew M. 2004. "Anti-Mini Militants Meet Modern Misses: Urban Style, Gender, and the Politics of 'National Culture' in 1960s Dar es Salam." In Jean Allman (ed.), *Fashioning Africa: Power and the Politics of Dress*, pp. 104–21. Bloomington: Indiana University Press.

Iwabuchi, Koichi. 2002. *Recentering Globalization: Popular Culture and Japanese Transnationalism*. Durham, NC: Duke University Press.

Izuishi, Shouzou. 1999. *Kanbon buru- ji-nzu*. Tokyo: Shinchousha.

Jackson, Michael. 1989. *Paths toward a Clearing*. Bloomington: Indiana University Press.

Jackson, Stevi. 1996. "Heterosexuality as a Problem for Feminist Theory." In Lisa Adkins and Vicki Merchant (eds), *Sexualizing the Social: Power and the Organization of Sexuality*. London Macmillan.

Jaffé, David. 1992. "Peiresc and New Attitudes to Authenticity in the Seventeenth Century." In Mark Jones (ed.), *Why Fakes Matter: Essays on Problems of Authenticity*, pp. 157–73. London: British Museum Press.

Jakobson, Roman. 1971. "Language in Relation to Other Communication Systems." In *Selected Writings of Roman Jakobson*, vol. 2, pp. 52–84. The Hague: Mouton.

Jakobson, Roman and Morris Halle. 1956. *Fundamentals of Language*. The Hague: Mouton.

James, Deborah. 1996. "'I Dress in This Fashion': Transformations in *Sotho* Dress and Women's Lives in a Sekhukhuneland Village, South Africa." In Hildi Hendrickson (ed.), *Clothing and Difference*, pp. 34–65. Durham, NC: Duke University Press.

Jameson, Frederic. 1991. *Postmodernism, or The Cultural Logic of Late Capitalism*. Durham, NC: Duke University Press.

Jamieson, Lynn. 1998. *Intimacy: Personal Relationships in Modern Society*. Cambridge: Polity.

Janson, Tore and Joseph Tsonope. 1991. *Birth of a National Language: The History of Setswana*. Gaborone, Botswana: Heinemann Botswana.

Jeffrey, Craig. 2010. *Timepass: Youth, Class, and the Politics of Waiting in India*. Stanford, CA: Stanford University Press.

Jeffries, Charles. 1949. *Partners for Progress: The Men and Women in the Colonial Service*. London: George C. Harrap.

Johns, Adrian. 2009. *Piracy: The Intellectula Property Wars from Gutenberg to Gates*. Chicago: University of Chicago Press.

Johnson, Marion. 1974. "Cotton Imperialism in West Africa." *African Affairs* 73(291): 178–87.

Johnson, Merri Lisa. 1999. "Pole Work: Autoethnography of a Strip Club." In Barry Dank and Roberto Refinetti (eds), *Sex Work & Sex Workers: Sexuality & Culture*, vol. 2, pp. 149–57. New Brunswick, NJ: Transaction.

Jones, Carla and Ann Marie Leshkowich. 2003. "Introduction: The Globalization of Asian Dress: Re-orienting Fashion or Re-orienting Asia?" In Sandra Niessen, Ann Marie Leshkowich and Carla Jones (eds), *Re-orienting Fashion: The Globalization of Asian Dress*. Oxford: Berg.

Jones, G. I. 1963. *The Trading States of the Oil Rivers: A Study of Political Development in Eastern Nigeria*. London: Oxford University Press.

Jones, Mark. 1992. *Why Fakes Matter: Essays on Problems of Authenticity*. London: British Museum Press.

Jones, Mark. 2010. "Negotiating Authentic Objects and Authentic Selves. Beyond the Deconstructing of Authenticity." *Journal of Material Culture* 15(2): 181–203.

Joselit, Jenna Weissman. 1994. *The Wonders of America: Revinventing Jewish Culture* 1880–1950. New York: Henry Holt.

Jury, Mark and Dan Jury, producers and directors. 1987. *Bizarre Rituals: Dances Sacred and Profane*. Videocassette, 83 minutes. Gorgou Video.

Kaplan, Marion A. 1991. "The Making of the Jewish Middle Class: Women, Family, and Identity." In Marion A. Kaplan (ed.), *Imperial German,* 1618–1945, pp. 173–251. Oxford: Oxford University Press.

Keane, Webb. 2005. "The Hazards of New Clothes: What Signs Make Possible." In Susanne Küchler and Graeme Were (eds), *The Art of Clothing: A Pacific Experience*, pp. 1–16. London: UCL Press.

Keesing, Roger M. 1989. "Creating the Past: Custom and Identity in the Contemporary Pacific." *The Contemporary Pacific* 1(1/2): 19–42.

Keesing, Roger M. 1992. *Custom and Confrontation: The Kwaio Struggle for Cultural Autonomy*. Chicago: University of Chicago Press.

Keller, Manfred. 1955. "*The Story of Living Fibers.*" In General Foods Corporation (ed.), *The Power of an Idea*, pp. 121–43. Portland, ME: The Bond Wheelwright Co.

Kilduff, Peter. 2005. "Patterns of Strategic Adjustment in the U.S. Textile and Apparel Industries since 1979." *Journal of Fashion Marketing and Management* 9(2): 180–94.

Kiliçbay, Bariş and Mutlu Binark. 2002. "Consumer Culure, Islam and the Politics of Lifestyle. Fashion for Veiling in Contemporary Turkey." *European Journal of Communication* 17(4): 95–511.

King, Lindsay M. and Russell T. Clement. 2012. "Style and Substance: Fashion in Twenty-First-Century Research Libraries." *Art Documentation: Journal of the Art Libraries Society of North America* 31(1) Spring: 93–107. Published by The University of Chicago Press on behalf of the Art Libraries Society of North America.

Kirk-Greene, Anthony H. M. 1955. "Those were the Days." *Corona* 7(3): 108–11.

Kirk-Greene, Anthony H. M. 1978. "On Governorship and Governors in British Africa." In L.H. Gann and Peter Duignan (eds), *The Rulers of British Africa*, 1870–1914. London: Croom Helm.

Klein, Naomi. 1999. *No Logo: Taking Aim at the Brand Bullies*. New York: Picador Press.

Klopper, Sandra. 1987. "You Need Only One Bull to Cover Fifty Cows: Zulu Women and 'Traditional' Dress." *African Studies Seminar Paper*, 213. University of Witswatersrand.

Kollontai, Pauline. 2004. "Messianic Jews and Jewisj Identity." *Journal of Modern Jewish Studies* 3(2): 195–205.

Kondo, Dorinne. 1992. "The Aesthetics and Politics of Japanese Identity in the Fashion Industry." In Joseph J. Tobin (ed.), *Re-made in Japan: Everyday Life and Consumer Taste in a Changing Society*, pp. 176–203. New Haven, CT: Yale University Press.

Kondo, Dorinne. 1997. *About Face: Performing Race in Fashion and Theater*. London: Routledge.

Krapf-Askari, Eva. 1965. "The Social Organization of the Owé." *African Notes* 11(3),April, 9–12.

Krapf-Askari, Eva. 1966. "Time and Classifications: An Ethnographic and Historical Case-Study." *Odu* 11(2),January, 3–18.

Krauss, Rosalind. 1981. "The Orginality of the Avant-garde. A Postomodernist Repetition." *October* 18: 47–66.

Krauss, Samuel. 1970. "The Jewish Rite of Covering the Head." In Joseph Gutmann (ed.), *Beauty and Holiness: Studies in Jewish Customs and Ceremonial Art*, pp. 420–67. New York: Ktav.

Kress, Gunther and Robert Hodge. 1979. *Language as Ideology*. London: Routledge and Kegan Paul.

Kreutzinger, Helga. 1966. *The Eri Devils in Freetown Sierra Leone*. Acta Ethnologica et Linguistica 9. Vienna: Verlag Osterreichische Ethnologische Gesellshaft.

Kriedte, Peter, Hans Medick and Jurgen Schlumbohm, eds. 1981. *Industrialization before Industrialization*. Cambridge: Cambridge University Press.

Kroeber, Alfred L. 1919. "On the Principle of Order in Civilization as Exemplified in Changes in Fashion." *American Anthropologist*, n.s., 21(3): 262–63.

Kroeber, Alfred L. and Jane Richardson. 1940. "Three Centuries of Women's Dress Fashions: A Quantitative Analysis." *Anthropological Records* 5(2): 111–53.

Küchler, Susanne. 1988. "Malangan: Objects, Sacrifice, and the Production of Memory." *American Ethnologist* 15(4): 625–37.

Küchler, Susanne. 2003. "Rethinking Textile: The Advent of the 'Smart' Fiber Surface." *Textile: The Journal of Cloth and Culture* 1(3): 262–73.

Küchler, Susanne. 2010. "Materials and Design." In Alison J. Clarke (ed.). *Design Anthropology*, pp. 130–42. Vienna: Springer.

Küchler, Susanne and Daniel Miller, eds. 2005. *Clothing as Material Culture*. Oxford: Berg.

Küchler, Susanne and Graeme Were. 2003. "Clothing and Innovation: A Pacific Perspective." *Anthropology Today* 19(2): 3–5.

Küchler, Susanne and Graeme Were. 2005. *The Art of Clothing: A Pacific Experience*. London: UCL; Portland, OR: Cavendish.

Kuper, Hilda. 1973. "Costume and Identity." *Comparative Studies in Society and History* 15(3): 348–67.

Lamb, Venice and Judith Holmes. 1980. *Nigerian Weaving*. Hertingfordbury: Roxford Books.

Landolphe, Jean Francois. 1823. *Mémoires du Capitaine Landolphe, rédigés sur son manuscrit par J.S. Quesne*. Paris: Bertrand.

Landau, David. 1992. *Piety and Power. The World of Jewish Fundamentalism*. New York: Hill and Wang.

Landau, Melanie. 2008. "Re-Covering Women as Religious Subject: Reflections on Jewish Women and Hair-Covering." *The Australian Journal of Jewish Studies* 22: 52–74.

Langer, Susanne K. 1942. *Philosophy in a New Key*. Cambridge, MA: Harvard University Press.

Larymore, Constance. (1908) 1911. *A Resident's Wife in Nigeria*, 2nd edn. London: George Routledge.

Langmore, Diane. 1989. "The Object Lesson of a Civilized, Christian Home." In Margaret Jolly and Martha Macintyre (eds), *Family and Gender in the Pacific: Domestic Contradictions and the Colonial Subject*. Cambridge: Cambridge University Press.

Lasn, Kalle. 1999. *Culture Jam: How to Reverse America's Suicidal Consumer Binge—And Why We Must*. New York: Harper Collins.

Latour, Bruno. 2005. *Reassembling the Social. An Introduction to Actor-Network-Theory*. Oxford: Oxford University Press.

Latour, Bruno and Adam Lowe. 2010. "The Migration of the Aura or How to Explore the Original Through its Facsimilies." In Thomas Bartschere and Roderick Coover (eds), *Switching coldes. Thinking Through Digital Technology in the Humanities and the Arts*, pp. 275–98. Chicago: University of Chicago Press.

Latour, Bruno and Steve Woolgar. (1979) 1986. *Laboratory Life: The Construction of Scientific Facts*, 2nd edn. Princeton, NJ: Princeton University Press.

Laver, James. 1969. *Modesty in Dress, an Inquiry into the Fundamentals of Fashion*. London: Heinemann.

Law, John. 2004. *After Method. Mess in Social Science Research*. London: Routledge.

Law, John and Annemarie Mol, eds. 2002. *Complexities. Social Studies of Knowledge Practices*. Durham, NC: Duke University Press; Routledge.

Layne, Linda L. 1989. "The Dialogics of Tribal Self-Representation in Jordan." *American Ethnologist* 16(1): 24–39.

Lears, T. J. Jackson. 1983. "From Salvation to Self-Realization: Advertising and the Therapeutic Roots of the Consumer Culture, 1880–1930." In Richard Wightman Fox and T. J. Jackson Lears (eds), *The Culture of Consumption: Critical Essays in American History, 1880–1980*, pp. 3–38. New York: Pantheon.

Leilund, Helle. 2007. "Dragter og tekstiler på Nationalmuseet." In Carsten U. Larsen and Bente Gammeltoft (eds), *Nationalmuseets Arbejdsmark 1807–2007*, pp. 325–40. Copenhagen: Nationalmuseet.

Leith-Ross, Sylvia. 1983. *Stepping Stones. Memoirs of Colonial Nigeria, 1907–1960*. London: Peter Owen.

Lemire, Beverly. 1991a. *Fashion's Favourite: The Cotton Trade and the Consumer in Britain, 1660–1800*. Oxford: Oxford University Press.

Lemire, Beverly. 1991b. "The Nature of the Second-Hand Clothes Trade: The Role of Popular Fashion and Demand in England, *c.* 1700–1850." In CISST (ed.), *Per una storia della moda pronta: problemi e ricerche*, pp. 107–16. Atti del V Convegno Internazionale del CISST, Milan, February 26–28, 1990.

Lemire, Beverly. 1997. *Dress, Culture and Commerce: The English Clothing Trade before the Factory, 1660–1800*. New York: St Martin's Press.

Lemonnier, Pierre. 1992. *Elements for an Anthropology of Technology*. Ann Arbor: Museum of Anthropology, University of Michigan.

Lenson, Barry. 1994. "Patagonia's Environmental Marketing—A Boomer Paradigm?" *Boomer Report*, April, 4.

Leshkowich, Ann Marie. 2000. "Tightly Woven Threads: Gender, Kinship, and 'Secret Agency' among Cloth and Clothing Traders in Ho Chi Minh City's Ben Thanh Market." PhD diss., Harvard University, Cambridge, MA.

Lèvi–Strauss, Claude. 1963. "Structural Analysis in Linguistics and Anthropology." In *Structural Anthropology I*, trans. Claire Jacobson and Brooke Grundfest Schoepf, pp. 31–54. Harmondsworth: Penguin Books.

Lèvi -Strauss, Claude. 1966. *The Savage Mind*. Chicago: University of Chicago Press.

Levine, Donald. 1985. *The Flight from Ambiguity*. Chicago: University of Chicago Press.

Levine, Stephanie Wellen. 2003. *Mystics, Mavericks, and Merrymakers: An Intimate Journey Among Hasidic Girls*. New York: New York University Press.

Levtzion, N. and J. F. P. Hopkins, eds. 1981. *Corpus of Early Arabic Sources for West African History*. Cambridge: Cambridge University Press.

Levy, Ariel. 2006. *Female Chauvinist Pigs: Women and the Rise of Raunch Culture*. New York: Free Press.

Levy, Howard. 1966. *Chinese Footbinding: The History of a Curious Erotic Custom*. New York: W. Rawls.

Lewin, Lauri. 1984. *Naked Is the Best Disguise: My Life as a Stripper*. New York: William Morrow.

Li, Xiaoping. 1998. "Fashioning the Body in Post-Mao China." In Anne Brydon and Sandra Niessen (eds), *Consuming Fashion: Adorning the Transnational Body*, pp. 71–89. Oxford: Berg.

Liebmann, James A. 1901. "Briton, Boer and Black in South Africa." In *British Africa*, British Empire Series, vol. 2. London: Kegan Paul, Trench, Trubner. (First edition, 1899.)

Liechty, Mark. 2003. *Suitably Modern: Making Middle-Class Culture in a New Consumer Society*. Princeton, NJ: Princeton University Press.

Liechty, Mark. 2006. "Building Body, Making Face, Doing Love: Mass Media and the Configuration of Class and Gender in Kathmandu." In Todd Joseph Miles Holden and Timothy J. Scrase (eds), *Medi@sia: Global Media/tion In and Out of Context*, pp. 25–43. New York: Routledge.

Liepe-Levinson, Katherine. 1998. "Striptease: Desire, Mimetic Jeopardy, and Performing Spectators." *Drama Review* 42(2): 9–37.

Lightning, ed. 2009a. *Studio D'artisan 30th Anniversary Book*. Tokyo: Ei Publishing.

Lightning, ed. 2009b. *The Denim Book*. Tokyo: Ei Publishing.

Lind, Charlene. and Mary E. Roach-Higgins. 1985. "Fashion, Collective Adoption, and the Social-Political Symbolism of Dress." In Michael R. Solomon (ed.), *The Psychology of Fashion*, pp. 183–92. Lexington, MA: Heath and Co.

Lindholm, Charles. 2002. "Authenticity, Anthropology, and the Sacred." *Anthropological Quarterly* 75(2): 331–38.

Lindholm, Charles. 2008. *Culture and Authenticity*. Oxford: Blackwell.

Lipovetsky, Gilles. 1994. *The Empire of Fashion: Dressing Modern Democracy*, trans. Catherine Porter. Princeton, NJ: Princeton University Press.

Lippert, Owen. 1999. *Competieive Strategies for the Protection of Intellectual Property*. Vancouver: Fraser Institute.

Littlewood, Roland. 1985. "An Indigenous Conceptualization of Reactive Depression in Trinidad." *Psychological Medicine* 15(2): 275–81.

Livingstone, David. 1857. *Missionary Travels and Researchs in South Africa, etc.* London: J. Murray.

Lloyd, Peter. 1953. "Craft Organization in Yoruba Towns." *Africa* 23(1): 30–44.

Long, John. 2010. "Out of Mud and Hail." *Patagonia* [Catalog] Spring, 3.

Lovelace, Earl. 1981. *The Dragon Can't Dance*. London: Longman.

Lukose, Ritty. 2005. "Consuming Globalization: Youth and Gender in Kerala, India." *Journal of Social History* 38(4): 215–35.

Lurie, Alison. 1981. *The Language of Clothes*. New York: Random House.

Lury, Celia. 2004. *Brands: The Logos of the Global Economy*. London: Routledge.

Luu, Phong. 2013. "Russell Marsh: Model Maker." *Telegraph*, March 16, Available online: http://fashion.telegraph.co.uk/columns/phong-luu/TMG9933193/Russell-Marsh-Model-maker.html (accessed September 1, 2014).

Luvaas, Brent. 2012. *DIY Style: Fashion, Music, and Global Digital Cultures*. London: Berg.

Luvaas, Brent. 2016. *Street Style: An Ethnography of Fashion Blogging*. London: Bloomsbury.

Lyttleton, K. S. 1892. *How to Pack, How to Dress, How to Keep Well on a Winter Tour of India (for Ladies)*. London: E. Stanford.

Macfarlane, Alan. 1987. *The Culture of Capitalism*. Oxford: Blackwell.

Mack, John. 1989. *Malagasy Weaving*. London: Shire.

Mackenzie, John. 1871. *Ten Years North of the Orange River: A Story of Everyday Life and Work among the South Adrican Tribes*. Edinburgh: Edmonston & Douglas.

Mackenzie, John. 1883. *Day Dawn in Dark Places: A Story of Wanderings and Work in Bechuanaland*. London: Cassell. Reprinted 1969, New York: Negro Universities Press.

Mackenzie, John. 1975. *Papers of John Mackenzie*, ed. Anthony J. Dachs. Johannesburg: Witwatersrand University Press.

MacLeod, Arlene. 1991. *Accommodating Protest: Working Women, the New Veiling, and Change in Cairo*. New York: Columbia University Press.

MacMillan, Margaret. 1988. *Women of the Raj*. London: Thames and Hudson.

Mafela, Lily. 1994. "Domesticity: The Basis for Missionary Education of Batswana Women to the End of the 19th Century." *Botswana Notes and Records* 26: 87–93.

Magubane, Bernard. 1971. "A Critical Look at Indices Used in the Study of Social Change in Colonial Africa." *Current Anthropology* 12(4–5): 419–45.

Mahmood, Saba. 2005. *The Politics of Piety. The Islamic Revival and the Feminist Subject*. Princeton, NJ: Princeton University Press.

Mains, Geoffrey. 1984. *Urban Aboriginals: A Celebration of Leathersexuality*. San Francisco, CA: Gay Sunshine Press.

Maira, Sunaina and Elisabeth Soep, eds. 2005. *Youthscapes: The Popular, the National, the Global*. Philadelphia: University of Pennsylvania Press.

Makhlouf, Carla. 1979. *Changing Veils. Women and Modernization in North Yemen*. Austin: University of Texas Press.

Malinowski, Bronislaw. (1929) 1987. *The Sexual Life of Savages in North-Western Melanesia*. Boston, MA: Beacon Press.

Malinowski, Bronislaw. (1922) 2014. *Argonauts of the Western Pacific*. New York: Routledge.

Malloy, Chris, director. 2010. *180 Degrees South: Conquerors of the Useless*. Documentrary. 85 minutes. Santa Monica, CA: Woodshed Films.

Malton, Sara. 2009. *Forgery in Nineteenth-Century Literature and Culture: Fictions of Finance from Dickens to Wilde*. New York: Palgrave Macmillan.

Mandle, Jay R. and Joan D. Mandle. 1988. *Grass Roofs Commitment: Basketball and Society in Trinidad and Tobago*. Pakersburg: Caribbean Books.

Mani, Bakirathi. 2003. "Undressing the Diaspors." In Nirmal Puwar and Parvati Raghuram (eds), *South Asian Women in the Diaspora*, 117–36. Oxford: Berg.

Mann, Kristin. 1986. *Marrying Well*. Cambridge: Cambridge University Press.

Manning, Frank E. 1973. *Black Clubs in Bermuda: Ethnography of a Play World*. Ithica NY: Cornell University Press.

Manning, Paul. 2010. "The Semiotics of Brand." *Annual Review of Anthropology* 39: 33–49.

Manolson, Gila. 1997. *Outside/Inside: A Fresh Look at Tzniut*. Southfield, MI: Targum.

Marchand, Roland. 1985. *Advertising the American Dream*. Berkeley, Los Angeles: University of California Press.

Marchand, Roland. 1998 *Creating the Corporate Soul: The Rise of Public Relations and Corporate Imagery in American Big Business*. Berkeley: The University of California Press.

Marcus, George E. 1998. *Ethnography Through Thick and Thin*. Princeton, NJ: Princeton University Press.

Marcus, George E. 1999. "Critical Anthropology Now: An Introduction." In George E. Marcus (ed.), *Critical Anthropology Now*, pp. 3–28. Santa Fe, NM: School of American Research Press.

Marcus, Greil. 1989. *Lipstick Traces: A Secret History of the Twentieth Century*. Cambridge: Harvard University Press.

Margiotti, Margherita. 2009. "Kinship and the Saturation of Life among the Kuna of Panamá." PhD thesis, University of St Andrews, Fife.

Marks, Shula. 1989. "Patriotism, Patriarchy and Purity: Natal and the Politics of Zulu Ethnic Consciousness." In Leroy Vail (ed.), *The Creation of Tribalism in Southern Africa*, pp. 215–40. Berkeley: University of California Press.

Marlarey, Sarah. 1999. "The Secrets of the Night." In Nora Gallagher (ed.), *Patagonia: Notes from the Field*, p. 74. San Francisco, CA: Chronicle Books.

Marmorstein, Emile. 1954. "The Veil in Judaism and Islam." *Journal of Jewish Studies* 5(1): 1–11.

Martin, Phyllis M. 1994. "Contesting Clothes in Colonial Brazzaville." *Journal of African History* 35(3): 401–26.

Marx, Karl. (1867) 1977. *Capital: Volume I*. New York: Vintage.

Marx, Karl. (1867) 2007. *Capital: A Critique of Political Economy. Vol. 1, Part 1, The Process of Capitalist Production*. New York: Cosimo.

Marx, Karl. 1967. *Capital: A Critique of Political Economy*. 3 vols. New York: International Publishers.

Masquelier, Adeline. 1996. "Mediating Threads: Clothing and the Texture of Spirit/Medium Relations in *Bori* (Southern Niger)." In Hildi Hendrickson (ed.), *Clothing and Difference: Embodied Identities in Colonial and Post-colonial Africa*, pp. 66–94. Durham, NC: Duke University Press.

Masquelier, Adeline. 2005. "The Scorpion's Sting: Youth, Marriage, and the Struggle for Social Maturity in Niger." *Journal of the Royal Anthropological Institute* 11(1): 59–83.

Masquelier, Adeline. 2008. "When Female Spirits Start Veiling: The Case of the Veiled She-Devil in a Muslim Town of Niger." *Africa Today* 54(1): 39–64.

Masquelier, Adeline. 2009. *Women and Islamic Revival in a West African Town*. Bloomington: Indiana University Press.

Mason, Michael. 1970. "The Jihad in the South: An Outline of the Nineteenth Century Nupe Hegemony in North-Eastern Yorubaland and Afenmai." *Journal of the Historical Society of Nigeria* 5(2): 193–209.

Matsuo, Hiroshi. 1970. *The Development of the Javanese Cotton Industry*. Occasional Paper 7. Tokyo: Institute of Development Economics.

Matumo, Augustine. 1989. "Fired for Ikalanga?" *The [Botswana] Guardian*, March 17, 1, 7.

Mauss, Marcel. 1966. *The Gift*. London: Cohen and West.

Mauss, Marcel. 1973. "Techniques of the Body," trans. Ben Brewster. *Economy and Society* 2(1): 70–88.

Mazzarella, William. 2003. "'Very Bombay': Contending with the Global in an Indian Advertising Agency." *Cultural Anthropology* 18(1): 33–71.

McCallum, Cecilia. 2001. *Gender and Sociality in Amazonia: How Real People are Made*. Oxford: Berg.

McClean, Daniel. 2002. "Introduction." In Daniel McClean and Karsten Schubert (eds), *Dear Images: Art, Copyright and Culture*, pp 10–45. London: Ridinghouse/ICA.

McClean, Daniel and Karsten Schubert, eds. 2002. *Dear Images: Art, Copyright and Culture*. London: Ridinghouse/ICA.

McCloud, Aminah B. 1995–96. "American Muslim Women and U.S. Society." *Journal of Law and Religion* 12(1): 51–59.

McCracken, Grant. 1982. "Politics and Ritual Sotto Voce. The Use of Demeanor as an Instrument of Politics in Elizabethan England." *Culture* 2(2): 53–62.

McCracken, Grant. 1988. *Culture and Consumption*. Bloomington: Indiana University.

McCracken, John. 1977. *Politics and Christianity in Malawi 1875–1940: The Impact of the Livingstonia Mission in the Northern Province*. Cambridge: Cambridge University Press.

McGoldrick, Dominic. 2006. *Human Rights and Religion: The Islamic Headscarf Debate in Europe*. Portland, OR: Hart Publishing.

McGovern, Mike. 2010. "This is Play: Popular Culture and Politics in Côte d'Ivoire." In Anne-Maria Makhulu, Beth A. Bugenhagen, and Stephen Jackson (eds), *Hard Work, Hard Times: Global Volatility and African Subjectivities*, pp. 69–90. Berkeley: University of California Press.

McGranahan, Carole. 2013. "Conference Chic, or, How to Dress Like an Anthropologist." [Blog] *Savage Minds*, November 20. Available online: https://savageminds.org/2013/11/20/conference-chic-or-how-to-dress-like-an-anthropologist/ (accessed August 20, 2018).

McKinley, Edward H. 1986. *Somebody's Brother: A History of the Salvation Army's Men's Social Service Department 1891–1985*. Lewiston, NY: Edwin Mellen Press.

McKinney, Ellen and Joanne. B. Eicher. 2009. "Unexpected Luxury: Wild Silk Textile Production among the Yoruba of Nigeria." *Textile: The Journal of Cloth and Culture* 7(1): 40–55.

McLaughlin, Patricia. 1998. "Capricious." Phillynews.com. Available online: http://interactive.phillynews.com/sunmag/712/style.shtml (accessed June 25, 2002).

McRobbie, Angela. 1989. "Second-Hand Dresses and the Role of the Ragmarket." In Angela McRobbie (ed.), *Zoot-Suits and Second-Hand Dresses: An Anthology of Fashion and Music*, pp. 23–49. London: Macmillan.

McRobbie, Angela. 1994. *Postmodernism and Popular Culture*. London: Routledge.

McRobbie, Angela. 1998. *British Fashion Design: Rag Trade or Image Industry*. London: Routledge.

McSpirit, Kelly. 1998. "Sustainable Consumption: Patagonia's Buy Less, But Buy Better." *Corporate Environmental Strategy* 5(2): 32–40.

Mears, W. Gordon A. n.d. "The Bechuana Mission or the Advance of Christianity into the Transval and the Orange Free State." *Methodist Missionaries*, no. 4. Rondebosch, Cape Town: The Methodist Missionary Department.

Meloy, Ellen. 1999. "Feral Hunger." In Nora Gallagher (ed.), *Patagonia: Notes from the Field*, p. 85. San Francisco, CA: Chronicle Books.

Mernissi, Fatima. 1987. *Beyond the Veil: Male-Female Dynamics in a Modern Muslim Society*. Bloomington: Indiana University Press.

Messing, S. D. 1960. "The Non-Verbal Language of the Ethiopian Toga." *Anthropos* 55(3/4): 558–60.

Michaels, Walter Benn. 1987. *The Gold Standard and the Logic of Naturalism*. Berkeley: University of California Press.

Michelman, Susan. O. and Joanne B. Eicher. 1995. "Dress and Gender in Kalabari Women's Societies." *Clothing and Textiles Research Journal* 13(2): 121–30.

Miller, Daniel. 1987. *Material Culture and Mass Consumption*. Oxford: Basil Blackwell.

Miller, Daniel. 1994. *Modernity—An Ethnographic Approach*. Oxford: Berg.

Miller, Daniel. 1995a. *Acknowledging Consumption: A Review of New Studies*. London: Routledge.

Miller, Daniel. 1995b. "Consumption and Commodities." *Annual Review of Anthropology* 24: 141–61.

Miller, Daniel. 1996. *Capitalism and Mass Consumption*. Oxford: Berg.

Miller, Daniel. 1997a. *Capitalism: An Ethnographic Approach*. Oxford: Berg.

Miller, Daniel. 1997b. "Coca-Cola: A Black Sweet Drink from Trinidad." In Daniel Miller (ed.), *Material Cultures*. London: University College London Press.

Miller, Daniel. 1997c. "How Infants Grow Mothers in North London." *Theory, Culture and Society* 14(4): 67–88. London: Sage.

Miller, Daniel. 1998. *A Theory of Shopping*. Ithaca, NY: Cornell University Press.

Miller, Daniel. 2001. *Dialectics of Shopping*. Chicago: University of Chicago Press.

Miller, Daniel. 2005. "Introduction." In Susanne Küchler and Daniel Miller (eds), *Clothing as Material Culture*, pp. 1–19. Oxford: Berg.

Miller, Daniel and Sophie Woodward. 2007. "A Manifesto for the Study of Denim." *Social Anthropology* 15(3): 335–51.

Miller, Daniel and Sophie Woodward, eds. 2010. *Global Denim*. Oxford: Berg

Miller, Daniel and Sophie Woodward. 2012. *Blue Jeans: The Art of the Ordinary*. Berkeley: University of California Press.

Mintz, Jerome R. 1992. *Hasidic People: A Place in the World*. Cambridge, MA: Harvard University Press.

Mintz, Sidney. 1986. *Sweetness and Power. The Place of Sugar in Modern History*. New York: Viking.

Mitchell, James Clyde. 1956. *The Kalela Dance*. Rhodes-Livingstone Papers no. 27. Manchester: Manchester University Press.

Moeran, Brian. 1997. *Folk Art Potters of Japan*. Richmond: Curzon.

Moffat, Mary. 1967. "Letter to a Well-Wisher." *Quarterly Bulletin of the South African Libary* 22: 16–19.

Moffat, Robert. 1825. "Extracts from the Journal of Mr. Robert Moffat." *Transactions of the Missionary Society* 33: 27–29.

Moffat, Robert. 1834. "Extracts from a Letter from Rev. R. Moffat." [Kuruman or Lattakoo (?)].

Moffat, Robert. 1842. *Missionary Labours and Scenes in South Africa*. London: John Snow. Reprinted, 1969; New York: Johnson Reprint Corporation.

Mol, Annemarie. 2002. *The Body Multiple: Ontology in Medical Practice*. Durham, NC: Duke University Press.

Moon, Christina. 2014. "Slow Road to Fast-Fashion." *Pacific Standard*, March 17. Available online: www.psmag.com/business-economics/secret-world-slow-road-korea-los-angeles-behind-fast-fashion-73956 (accessed August 20, 2018).

Moor, Liz. 2007. *The Rise of Brands*. Oxford: Berg.

Moore, Elizabeth Anne. 2007. *Unmarketable: Brandalism, Copyfighting, Mocketing, and the Erosion of Integrity*. New York: The New Press.

Moore, Sally Falk. 1994. "The Ethnography of the Present and the Analysis of Process." In Robert Borofsky (ed.), *Assessing Cultural Anthropology*, pp. 375–76. New York: McGraw-Hill.

Moore, Kathleen M. 2007. "Visible Through the Veil: The Regulation of Islam in American Law." *Sociology of Religion* 68(3): 237–51.

Moore, Robert E. 2003. "From Genericide to Viral Marketing: On 'Brand'." *Language & Communication* 23(3–4): 331–57.

Moors, Annelies. 2004. "Islam and Fashion on the Streets of San'a, Yemen." *Etnofoor* 16(2): 41–56.

Moors, Annelies. 2009. "Islamic Fashion in Europe: Religious Conviction, Aesthetic Style, and Creative Consumption." *Encounters* 1(1): 175–201.

Morris, Rosalind. 1995. "All Made Up: Performance Theory and the New Anthropology of Sex and Gender." *Annual Review of Anthropology* 24: 567–92.

Morrison, Toni. 1987. *Beloved*. New York: Knopf.

Moss, Chris. 2008. *Patagonia: A Cultural History*. Oxford: Oxford University Press.

Moyer, Eileen. 2003. "Keeping Up Appearances: Fashion and Function Among Dar es Salam Street Youth." *Etnofoor* 16(2): 88–105.

Mukerji, Chandra. 1983. *From Graven Images: Patterns of Modern Materialism*. New York: Columbia University Press.

Mundy, Martha. 1983. "San'a Dress, 1920–75." In R. B. Serjeant and Ronald Lewcock (eds), *San'a': An Arabian Islamic City*, pp. 529–41. London: World of Islam Festival Trust.

Murra, John. 1989. "Cloth and Its Function in the Inka State." In Annette Weiner and Jane Schneider (eds), *Cloth and Human Experience*. Washington: Smithsonian Institution Press.

Mutawakil, Antelak al-. 2001. "Self-Liberation and National Struggle in Yemeni Women's Early Short Stories." *Al-Masar* 3(3): 13–28.

Nader, Laura. 1972. "Up the Anthropologist-Perspectives Gained from Studying Up." In Dell Hymes (ed.), *Reinventing Anthropology*, pp. 285–311. New York: Pantheon Press.

Naji, Myriem and Laurence Douny. 2009. "Editorial: The 'Making' and 'Doing' of the Material World: French Anthropology of Techniques Revisited." *Journal of Material Culture* 14(4): 411–32.

Najmabadi, Afsaneh. 1993. "Veiled Discourse, Unveiled Bodies." *Feminist Studies* 19(3): 487–518.

Nakassis, Constantine. 2012. "Brand, Citationality, Performativity." *American Anthropologist* 114(4): 624–38.

Nansen, Christiania. 1890. *Paaski over Grönland*, trans. H. M. Gepp as *The First Crossing of Greenland*, 2 vols. London, 1890.

Nash, Jeffrey E. 1977. "Decoding the Runner's Wardrobe." In James P. Spradley and David W. McCurdy (eds), *Conformity and Conflict: Readings in Cultural Anthropology*, 3rd edn, pp. 172–85. Boston, MA: Little, Brown, and Co.

Navaro-Yashin, Yael. 2002. "The Market for Identities: Secularism, Islamism, Commodities." In Deniz Kandiyoti and Ayse Saktanber (eds), *Fragments of Culture. The Everyday of Modern Turkey*, pp. 221–54. New Brunswick, NJ: Rutgers University Press.

Neich, Roger. 1982. "A Semiological Analysis of Self-Decoration in Mount Hagen, New Guinea." In Ino Rossi (ed.), *The Logic of Culture*, pp. 214–31. South Hadley, MA: J. F. Bergin.

Newell, Sasha. 2005. "Migratory Modernity and the Cosmology of Consumption in Côte D'lvoire." In Lillian Trager (ed.), *Migration and Economy: Global and Local Dynamics*, pp. 163–90. Walnut Creek, CA: AltaMira.

Nicolson, Marjorie Hope. 1959. *Mountain Gloom and Mountain Glory: The Development of the Aesthetics of the Infinite*. Ithaca, NY: Cornell University Press.

Nicolson, Nigel. 1977. *Mary Curzon*. London: Weidenfeld and Nicolson.

Niessen, Sandra. 2009. *Legacy in Cloth, Batak Textiles of Indonesia*. Leiden: KITLV Press.

Niessen, Sandra, Carla Jones and Ann Marie Leshkowich, eds. 2003. *Re-Orienting Fashion: The Globalization of Asian Dress*. Oxford: Berg.

Nilan, Pam and Carles Feixa, eds. 2006. *Global Youth? Hybrid Identities, Plural World*. New York: Routledge.

Niven, Rex. 1982. *Nigerian Kaleidoscope*. London: C. Hurst.

Noble, David F. 1977. *America by Design: Science, Technology and the Rise of Corporate Capitalism*. New York: Alfred A. Knopf.

Nordenskiöld, Erland. 1938. *An Historical and Ethnological Survey of the Cuna Indians*. Göteborg: Etnografiska Museet.

Nørgaard, Mads, ed. 2002. *Modeleksikon: Fra couture til kaos*. Copenhagen: Politikens Forlag.

Norris, Lucy. 2005. "Cloth that Lies: The Secrets of Recycling in India." In Susanne Küchler and Daniel Miller (eds), *Clothing as Material Culture*, pp. 83–105. Oxford: Berg.

Northcott, William C. 1961. *Robert Moffat: Pioneer in Africa, 1817–1870*. London: Lutterworth Press.

Nouzeilles, Gabriela. 1999. "Patagonia as Borderland: Nature, Culture, and the Idea of the State." *Journal of Latin American Studies* 8(1): 35–48.

Nunley, John. 1980. "Aesthetic Symbolism and Behavior in Freetown Masquerades." Paper delivered at The African Dress and Textile Symposium, University of Minnesota.

Nyamnjoh, Francis B. 2004. "Globalization, Boundaries, and Livelihoods: Perspectives on Africa." *Identity, Culture, and Politics* 5(1/2): 37–59.

O'Barr, William M. 1994. *Culture and the Ad: Exploring Otherness in the World of Advertising*. Boulder, CO: Westview Press.

Ọbáyẹmí, Adé. 1978a. "An Archaeological Mission to Akpaa." *Confluence* 1: 60–67.

Ọbáyẹmí, Adé. 1978b. "The Sokoto Jihad and the 'O-kun' Yoruba: A Review." *Journal of the Historical Society of Nigeria* 9(2): 61–87.

O'Connor, Kaori. 2004a. "Lycra, Babyboomers and the Immaterial Culture of the New Midlife: A Study of Commerce and Culture." PhD diss., University College London. (A book drawn from this thesis is currently in preparation).

O'Connor, Kaori. 2004b. "Material Culture, Capitalism and Social Change at Home." *Anthropology Matters* 2 (November).

Obeyesekere, Gananath. 1981. *Medusa's Hair: An Essay on Personal Symbols and Religious Experience*. Chicago: University of Chicago Press.

Ong, Aihwa. 1987. *Spirits of Resistance and Capitalist Discipline*. Albany: State University of New York Press.

Ong, Aihwa. 1990a. "Japanese Factories, Malay Workers: Class and Sexual Metaphors in West Malaysia." In Jane Atkinson and Shelley Errington (eds), *Power and Difference: Gender in Island Southeast Asia*. Stanford, CA: Stanford Press.

Ong, Aihwa. 1990b. "State versus Islam: Malay Families, Women's Bodies, and the Body Politic in Malaysia." *American Ethnologist* 17(2): 258–76.

Ong, Aihwa. 1991. "The Gender and Labor Politics of Postmodernity." *Annual Review of Anthropology* 20: 279–309.

Ong, Aihwa. 1997. "Chinese Modernities: Narratives of Nation and Capitalism." In Aihwa Ong and Donald Nonini (eds), *Undergrounded Empires: The Cultural Politics of Modern Chinese Transnationalism*, pp. 171–202. New York and London: Routledge.

Ong, Aihwa. 1999. *Flexible Citizenship*. Durham, NC: Duke University Press.

Ortner, Sherry B. 1974. "Is Female to Male as Nature is to Culture?" In Michelle Zimbalist Rosaldo and Louise Lamphere (eds), *Woman, Culture, and Society*, pp. 68–87. Stanford, CA: Stanford University Press.

Ortner, Sherry B. 1995. "Resistance and the Problem of Ethnographic Refusal." *Comparative Studies in Society and History* 37(1): 173–93.

Osteen, Mark, ed. 2002. *The Question of the Gift*. London: Routledge.

Overing, Joanna and Alan Passes, eds. 2000. *The Anthropology of Love and Anger: The Aesthetics of Conviviality in Native Amazonia*. London: Routledge.

Packard, Randall M. 1989. "The 'Healthy Reserve' and the 'Dressed Native': Discourse on Black Health and the Language of Legitimation in South Africa." *American Ethnologist* 16(4): 686–703.

Parker, Ann and Avon Neal. 1977. *Molas: Folk Art and the Kuna Indians*. Wilkes-Barre, MA: Wilkes-Barre Publishing.

Pastoreau, Michel. 2001. *The Devil's Cloth*. New York: Columbia University Press.

Peake, Robert Edmund. 1984. "Tourism and Alternative Worlds: The Social Constuction of Reality in Malindi Town, Kenya." PhD diss., School of Oriental and African Studies, University of London.

Peel, John D. Y. 1983. *Ijeshas and Nigerians*. Cambridge: Cambridge University Press.

Peigler, Richard S. 2004. "The Silk Moths of Madagascar." In J. Claire Odland, Bennet Bronson, and Chapurukha M. Kusimba, (eds), *Unwrapping the Textile Traditions of Madagascar*, pp. 154–63. Chicago, IL: Field Museum; Los Angeles, CA: UCLA Fowler Museum of Cultural History.

Pemberton, John. 1994. *On the Subject of "Java."* Ithaca, NY: Cornell University.

Penaloza, Fernando. 2004. "A Sublime Journey to the Barren Plains: Lady Florence Dixie's across Patagonia (1880)." *Limina* 10: 81–97.

Perani, Judith. 1989. "Northern Nigerian Prestige Textiles." In Beatae Engelbrecht and Bernhard Gardi (eds), *Man Does Not Go Naked*, pp. 65–81. Basel: Museum für Völkenkunde.

Perani, Judith and Norma H. Wolff. 1999. *Cloth, Dress, and Art Patronage in Africa*. Oxford: Berg.

Perani, Judith and Norma H. Wolff. 1992. "Embroidered Gown and Equestrian Ensembles of the Kano Aristocracy." *African Arts* 25(3): 70–81, 102–04.

Perham, Margery. 1960. *Lugard. The Years of Authority*. London: Collins.

Perlman, Eric. 1987. "Dreams for Sale: Catalogues for People Who May Not Want to Buy Things." *Backpacker*, January, 52–54.

Perniola, Mario. 1989. "Between Clothing and Nudity." In Michel Fehrer (ed.), *Fragments for a History of the Human Body*, vol. 2, pp. 237–65. New York: Zone.

Perrot, Philippe. (1981) 1994. *Fashioning the Bourgeoisie: A History of Clothing in the Nineteenth Century*, trans. Richard Bienvenu. Princeton, NJ: Princeton University Press.

Peterson, Richard A. 1997. *Creating Country Music: Fabricating Authenticity*. Chicago: University of Chicago Press.

Phelan, Peggy. 1993. *Unmarked: The Politics of Performance*. New York: Routledge.

Philip, Robert. 1828. *Researches in South Africa: Illustrating the Civil, Moral, and Religious Condition of the Native Tribes*, 2 vols. London: James Duncan. Reprinted 1969, New York: Negro Universities Press.

Phizacklea, Annie. 1990. *Unpacking the Fashion Industry: Gender, Racism and Class in Production*. London: Routledge.

Picton, John. 1995. *The Art of African Textiles: Technology, Tradition and Lurex*, exhibition catalog. London: Barbican Art Gallery.

Picton, John and John Mack. 1979. *African Dress II: A Select and Annotated Bibliography*. East Lansing, MI: African Studies Center.

Piercing Fans International Quarterly. 1996. Special Issue: "The Tribal Aesthetic", no. 47.

Pinney, Christopher. 2001. "Piercing the Skin of the Idol." In Christopher Pinney and Nicholas Thomas (eds), *Beyond Aesthetics: Art and the Technologies of Enchantment*, pp. 157–80. Oxford: Berg.

Pinney, Christopher. 2006. "Four Types of Visual Culture." In Christopher Tilley, Webb Keane, Susanne Küchler, Michael Rowlands, and Patricia Spyer (eds), *Handbook of Material Culture*, pp. 131–45. London: Sage Publications.

Piore, Michael J. and Charles F. Sabel. 1984. *The Second Great Divide: Possibilities for Prosperity*. New York: Routledge.

Polakoff, Claire. 1982. *African Textiles and Dyeing Techniques*. London: Routledge.

Polhemus, Ted. 1978. *Fashion and Anti-Fashion*. London: Thames and Hudson.

Polhemus, Ted. 1989. "Style Groups: The New Ethnicities." Seminar paper, Oxford University.

Polhemus, Ted. 1994. *Streetstyle: From Sidewalk to Catwalk*. London: Thames and Hudson.

Polhemus, Ted. 1996. *Style Surfing: What to Wear in the 3rd Millennium*. London: Thames and Hudson.

Pollack, Herman. 1971. *Jewish Folkways in Germanic Lands (1648–1806)*. Cambridge, MA: MIT Press.

Prothero, Andrea, Pierre McDonagh, and Susan Dobscha. 2010. "Is Green the New Black? Reflections on a Green Commodity Discourse." *Journal of Macromarketing* 30(2): 147–59.

Puwar, Nirmal. 2002. "Multi-cultural Fashion … Stirrings of Another Sense of Aesthetics and Memory." *Feminist Review* 71: 63–87.

Radnóti, Sandor. 1999. *The Fake: Forgery and Its Place in Art*. Lanham, MD: Rowman & Littlefield.

Rafael, Vicente. 2000. *White Love and Other Events in Filipino History*. Durham, NC: Duke University Press.

Ranger, Terence. 1983. "The Invention of Tradition in Colonial Africa." In Eric Hobsbawm and Terence Ranger (eds), *The Invention of Tradition*. Cambridge: Cambridge University Press.

Rausing, Sigrid. 2002. "Re-Constructing the Normal: Identity and the Consumption of Western Goods in Estonia." In Ruth Mandel and Caroline Humphrey (eds), *Markets and Moralities: Ethnographies of Postsocialism*, pp. 127–42. New York: Berg.

Read, James. 1850. "Report on the Bechuana Mission." *Evangelical Magazine and Missionary Chronicle* 28: 445–47.

Renne, Elisha P. 1995. *Cloth That Does Not Die: The Meaning of Cloth in Bunu Social Life*. Seattle: University of Washington Press.

Richards, Audrey I. (1939) 1969. *Land, Labour and Diet in Northern Rhodesia*. Oxford: Oxford University Press.

Richardson, Jane, and Alfred L. Kroeber. 1940. 'Three centuries of women's dress fashions: A quantitative analysis' *Anthropological Records* 5(2): 111–53.

Richardson, Miles. 1974. "Images, Objects, and the Human Story." In Miles Richardson (ed.), *The Human Mirror: Material And Spatial Images of Man*, pp. 3–14. Baton Rouge: Louisiana State University Press.

Rivoli, Pietra. 2009. *The Travels of a T-Shirt in the Global Economy: An Economist Examines the Markets, Power and Politics of the World Trade*. Hoboken, NJ: John Wiley & Sons.

Roach, Mary Ellen and Joanne B. Eicher. 1965. *Dress, Adornment and the Social Order*. New York: John Wiley and Sons.

Roach, Mary Ellen and Joanne B. Eicher. 1973. *The Visible Self: Perspectives on Dress*. Prentice Hall.

Roach, Mary Ellen and Joanne B. Eicher. 1979. "The Language of Personal Adornment." In Justine M. Cordwell and Ronald A. Schwartz (eds), *The Fabrics of Culture*, pp. 7–23. The Hague: Mouton.

Roach, Mary Ellen and Kathleen E. Musa. 1980. *New Perspectives on the History of Western Dress*. New York: Nutriguides Inc.

Robbins, Jim. 2011. "When the Rich Go Wild." *Condé Nast Traveller* 46(9): 51–65.

Robinson, Dwight E. 1976. "Fashions in Shaving and Trimming of the Beard; The Men of the Illustrated London News, 1842–1872." *American Journal of Sociology* 81(5): 1133–41.

Roche, Daniel. (1989) 1996. *The Culture of Clothing: Dress and Fashion in the Ancien Regime*, trans. Jean Birrell. Cambridge: Cambridge University Press.

Rooks, Noliwe M. 1996. *Hair Raising: Beauty, Culture, and African American Women*. New Brunswick, NJ: Rutgers University Press.

Rosaldo, Michelle Zimbalist. 1974. "Woman, Culture, and Society: A Theoretical Overview." In Rosaldo, Michelle Zimbalistand Louise Lamphere (eds), *Woman, Culture, and Society*, pp. 17–42. Stanford, CA: Stanford University Press.

Rosaldo, Renato. 1989. *Culture and Truth: The Remaking of Social Analysis*. Boston, MA: Beacon Press.

Rose, Kenneth. 1969. *Superior Person: A Portrait of Curzon and his Circle in Late Victorian England*, London: Weidenfeld and Nicolson.

Rose, Mark. 1994. *Authors and Owners: The Invention of Copyright*. Cambridge, MA: Harvard University Press.

Rosenblatt, Daniel. 1996. "'*Ko Titirangi te Maunga …*' ('Titirangi is the Mountain …'): Urban *Marae* and the Construction of Maori Community in Auckland." Paper presented at the 25th Annual Meeting of the Association for Social Anthropology in Oceania, Kona, Hawai'i, February.

Rosenfeld, Lawrence B. and Timothy G. Plax. 1977. "Clothing as Communication." *Journal of Communication* 27(2): 24–31.

Ross, Andrew. 2004. *Low Pay, High Profile: The Global Push for Fair Labor*. New York: The New Press.

Ross, Andrew. 2009. "No Collar Labor in America's 'New Economy.'" *Socialist Register* 37: 76–87.

Rowlands, Michael. 1994. "The Material Culture of Success: Ideals and Life Cycles in Cameroon." In Jonathan Friedman (ed.) *Consumption and Identity*, pp. 147–66. Chur: Harwood Academic Publishers.

Rowlands, Michael. 2011. "Of Substances, Palaces, and Museums: The Visible and the Invisible in the Constitution of Cameroon." *JRAI* 17(1): S23–S38.

Rubin, Arnold. 1988b. "The Tattoo Renaissance." In Arnold Rubin (ed.), *Marks of Civilization: Artistic Transformations of the Human Body*, pp. 233–62. Los Angeles: Museum of Cultural History, UCLA.

Rubin, Gayle. 1975. "The Traffic in Women: Notes on the 'Political Economy' of Sex." In Rayna R. Reiter (ed.), *Toward an Anthropology of Women*, pp. 157–210. New York: Monthly Review Press.

Rubin, Israel. 1972. *Satmar: An Island in the City*. Chicago: Quadrangle.

Ruhlen, Rebecca N. 2003. "Korean Alterations: Nationalism, Social Consciousness, and 'Traditional Clothing.'" In Sandra Niessen, Ann Marie Leshkowich, and Carla Jones (eds), *Re-Orienting Fashion: The Globalization of Asian Dress*, pp. 117–38. Oxford: Berg.

Russell, Elnor. 1978. *Bush Life in Nigeria*. Privately published.

Russett, Margaret. 2006. *Fictions and Fakes: Forging Romantic Authenticity, 1760–1845*. Cambridge: Cambridge University Press.

Rutledge H. 1966. *Milestones in the Du Pont Company's Textile Fibers History and Some Important Industry Dates*. Wilmington, DE: Textile Fibers Department, E. I. du Pont de Nemours and Co.

Ryder, Alan Frederick C. 1965. "A Reconsideration of the Ife-Benin Relationship." *Journal of African History* 6(1): 25–37.

Ryder, Alan Frederick C. 1969. *Benin and Europeans, 1485–1897*. New York: Humanities Press.

Sacks, Harvey. 1985. "The Inference-Making Machine: Notes on Observability." In Teun A. van Dijk (ed.), *Handbook of Discourse Analysis: Discourse Analysis in Society*, pp. 13–23. Orlando, FL: Academic Press.

Sadre-Orafai, Stephanie. 2008. "Developing Images: Race, Language, and Perception in Fashion-model Casting." In Eugenie Shinkle (ed.), *Fashion as Photograph: Viewing and Reviewing Images of Fashion*, pp. 141–53. London: I.B.Tauris.

Sadre-Orafai, Stephanie. 2012. "The Figure of the Model and Reality Television." In Joanne Entwistle and Elizabeth Wissinger (eds), *Fashioning Models: Image, Text, and Industry*, pp. 119–33. London: Berg.

Sadre-Orafai, Stephanie. 2016. "Mug Shot/Head Shot: Danger, Beauty, and the Temporal Politics of Booking Photography." In Jo Turney (ed.), *Fashion Crimes: Dressing for Deviance*. London: I.B.Tauris.

Safran, Rabbi Eliyahu. 2007. *Sometimes You Are What You Wear! An Argument for Tzniut—Modesty*. Bloomington, IN: Xlibris.

Sahlins Marshall. 1976. *Culture and Practical Reason*. Chicago: University of Chicago Press.

Sahlins, Marshall. (1988) 1994. "Cosmologies of Capitalism: The Trans-Pacific Sector of the 'World System.'" In Nicholas B. Dirks, Geoff Eley, and Sherry B. Ortner (eds), *Culture, Power, History*, pp. 412–57. Princeton, NJ: Princeton University. Press.

Sahlins, Marshall. 1989. "Cosmologies of Capitalism: The Trans-Pacific Sector of the World System." *Proceedings of the British Academy for 1988*, vol. 74, pp. 1–51.

Sahlins Marshall. 1994. "*Goodbye to Triste Tropes: Ethnography in the Context of Modern World History*." In Robert Borofsky (ed.), *Assessing Cultural Anthropology*, pp. 377–95. London: McGraw-Hill.

Sahlins, Marshall. 1996. "The Sadness of Sweetness: The Native Anthropology of Western Cosmology." *Current Anthropology* 37(3): 395–428.

Said, Edward. (1978) 1994. *Orientalism*. London: Vintage.

Salaff, Janet W. (1981) 1995. *Working Daughters of Hong Kong*. New York: Cambridge University Press.

Salim, Degla. 2013. "Mediating Islamic Looks." In Emma Tarlo and Annelies Moors (eds), *Islamic Fashion and Anti-Fashion: New Perspectives from Europe and North America*, pp. 209–24. London: Bloomsbury.

Salvador, Mari Lyn. 1976. "The Clothing Arts of the Cuna of San Blas, Panama." In Nelson H. H. Graburn(ed.), *Ethnic and Tourist Art: Cultural Expressions from the Fourth World*, pp. 165–82. Berkeley: University of California Press.

Salvador, Mari Lyn. 1978. *Yer Dailege! Kuna Women's Art*. Albuquerque, NM: Maxwell Museum of Anthropology.

Salvador, Mari Lyn, ed. 1997. *The Art of Being Kuna: Layers of Meaning among the Kuna of Panama*. Los Angeles: UCLA Fowler Museum of Cultural History.

Sanders, Clinton R. 1988. "Drill and Frill: Client Choice, Client Typologies, and Interactional Control in Commercial Tattoo Settings." In Arnold Rubin (ed.), *Marks of Civilization: Artistic Transformations of the Human Body*, pp. 219–32. Los Angeles: Museum of Cultural History, UCLA.

Sandıkcı, Özlem and Güliz Ger. 2002. "In-between Modernities and Postmodernities: Investigating Turkish Consumptionscape." In Susan Broniarczyk and Kent Nakamoto (eds), *Advances in Consumer Research*, vol. 29, pp. 465–70. Salt Lake City, UT: Association for Consumer Research.

Sandıkcı, Özlem and Güliz Ger. 2005. "Aesthetics, Ethics and the Politics of the Turkish Headscarf." In Suzanne Küchler and Daniel Miller (eds), *Clothing as Material Culture*, pp. 61–82. Oxford: Berg.

Sandıkcı, Özlem and Güliz Ger. 2007. "Constructing and Representing the Islamic Consumer in Turkey." *Fashion Theory* 11(2/3): 189–210.

Sapir, Edward. 1931. "Fashion," *Encyclopaedia of the Social Sciences*, 6, pp. 139–44. New York: Macmillan.

Saunders, Nicholas J. 2002. "The Colours of Light: Materiality and Chromatic Cultures of the Americas." In Andrew Jones and Gavin MacGregor (eds), *Colouring the Past: The Significance of Archaeological Research*, pp. 209–26. Oxford: Berg.

Saussure, Ferdinand de. 1966. *Course in General Linguistics*. New York: McGraw Hill.

Savigliano, Marta. 1995. *Tango and the Political Economy of Passion*. Boulder, CO: Westview.

Scalway, Helen. 2010. "South Asian Patterns in Urban Space." In Christopher Breward, Philip Crang, and Rosemary Crill (eds), *British Asian Style: Fashion & Textiles Past & Present*. London: V&A Publishing.

Scaturro, Sarah. 2008. "Eco-tech Fashion: Rationalizing Technology in Sustainable Fashion." *Fashion Theory* 12(4): 469–88.

Schapera, Isaac. 1947. *Migrant Labour and Tribal Life: A Study of Conditions in the Bechuanaland Protectorate*. London: Oxford University Press.

Schapera, Isaac. 1952. "The Ethnic Composition of the Tswana Tribes." In *Monographs on Social Anthropology*, no. 11. London: London School of Economics and Political Science.

Schein, Louisa. 2000. *Minority Rules: The Miao and the Feminine in China's Cultural Politics*. Durham, NC: Duke University Press.

Scheld, Suzanne. 2007. "Youth Cosmopolitanism: Clothing, the City, and Globalization in Dakar, Senegal." *City and Society* 19(2): 232–53.

Schneider, Jane. 1980. "Trousseau as Treasure: Some Contradictions of Late Nineteenth-Century Change in Sicily." In Eric B. Ross (ed.), *Beyond the Myths of Culture: Essays in Cultural Materialism*, pp. 323–56. New York: Academic Press.

Schneider, Jane. 1987. "The Anthropology of Cloth." *Annual Review of Anthropology* 16: 409–48.

Schneider, Jane. 1988. "European Expansion and Handcrafted Cloth: A Critique of Oppositional Use-value vs. Exchange-value Models." *Journal of Historical Sociology* 1(4): 431–38.

Schneider, Jane. 1989. "Rumpelstiltskin's Bargain: Folklore and the Merchant Capitalist Intensification of Linen Manufacture in Early Modern Europe." In Jane Schneider and Annette Weiner (eds), *Cloth and Human Experience*. Washington: Smithsonian Institution Press.

Schneider, Jane. 1994. "In and Out of Polyester: Desire, Disdain and Global Fibre Competitions." *Anthropology Today* 10(4): 2–10.

Schneider, Jane. 2006. "Cloth and Clothing." In Christopher Tilley, Webb Keane, Susanne Küchler, Michael Rowlands, and Patricia Spyer (eds), *Handbook of Material Culture*, pp. 203–20. London: Sage Publications.

Schneider, Jane and Annette Weiner. 1986. "Cloth and the Organization of Human Experience." *Current Anthropology* 27(2): 178–84.

Schreiber, Lynne, ed. 2003. *Hide and Seek: Jewish Women and Hair Covering*. New York: Urim.

Schumacher, Ernst. 1973. *Small Is Beautiful: A Study of Economics as if People Mattered*. London: Blond & Briggs.

Schwarz, Hillel. 1996. *The Culture of the Copy: Striking Likenesses, Unreasonable Facsimiles*. New York: Zone Books.

Schwarz, Ronald A. 1979. "Uncovering the Secret Vice: Toward an Anthropology of Clothing and Adornment." In Justine M. Cordwell and Ronald A. Schwarz (eds), *The Fabrics of Culture*, pp. 23–46. The Hague: Mouton Press.

Scott, James C. 1985. *Weapons of the Weak: Everyday Forms of Peasant Resistance*. New Haven, CT: Yale University Press.

Scott, Joan Wallach. 2007. *The Politics of the Veil*. Princeton, NJ: Princeton University Press.

Scott, Mary and Howard Rothman. 1994. *Companies with a Conscience: Intimate Portraits of Twelve Firms that Make a Difference*. New York: Carol Publishing Group.

Scott, Robert. 1998. "U.S. Trade Policies for the Textile and Apparel Industries: The Political Economy of the Post-MFA Environment." In Alan V. Deardoff and Robert M. Stern (eds), *Constituent Interests and U.S. Trade Policies*, pp. 145–60. Ann Arbor: University of Michigan Press.

Seif, Jennifer. 1995. "Engendering Christian Life in Natal: The Zulu Mission of the American Board, 1835–1900." MA thesis, Department of Anthropology, University of Chicago.

Severi, Carlo. 1993. *La Memoria Rituale: Folliae Immagine del Bianco in una Tradizione Sciamanica Amerindia*. Florence: La Nuova Italia.

Shapero, Miriam. 1987. "The Dress System of Traditional Jewry." Unpublished rabbinic thesis, Hebrew Union College-Jewish Institute of Religion, Graduate Rabbinic Program, New York.

Shapiro, Marc. 1990. "Another Example of 'Minhag America.'" *Judaism* 39(2): 148–54.

Shaw, Margaret. 1974. "Material Culture." In W. D. Hammond-Tooke (ed.), *The Bantu-speaking Peoples of Southern Africa*. London: Routledge & Kegan Paul.

Shelley, Mary. 1823. *Frankenstein or the Modern Prometheus*, 2 vols, vol. 1. London: G. & W. B. Whittaker.

Shenon, Philip. 1993. "The Mist Off Perfume River." *New York Times*, November 21.

Sherman, Brad and Lionel Bentley. 1999. *The Making of Modern Intellectual Property Law: The British Experience, 1760–1911*. Cambridge: Cambridge University Press.

Sherzer, Dina and Joel Sherzer. 1976. "Mormaknamaloe: The Cuna *Mola*." In Philip Young and James Howe (eds), *Ritual and Symbol in Native Central America*, pp. 21–42. Eugene: University of Oregon.

Showalter, Elaine. 2001. "Fade to Greige." *London Review of Books* 23(1): 37–39.

Shukla, S. 2001. "Locations for South Asian Diasporas." *Annual Review of Anthropology* 30: 551–72.

Sider, Gerald M. 1986. *Culture and Class in Anthropology and History*. Cambridge: Cambridge University Press.

Siegel, James T. 1998. *A New Criminal Type in Jakarta: Counter-Revolution Today*. Durham, NC: Duke University Press.

Sievert, Jane and Jennifer Ridgeway, eds. 2010. *Unexpected: 30 Years of Patagonia Photography*. Ventura, CA: Patagonia.

Silverstein, Michael. 1976. "Shifters, Linguistic Categories, and Cultural Description." In Keith H. Basso and Henry A. Selby (eds), *Meaning in Anthropology*, pp. 11–55. Albuquerque: University of New Mexico Press.

Silverstein, Michael. 1981. "Metaforces of Power in Traditional Oratory." Paper presented to the Department of Anthropology, Yale University, New Haven, CT.

Simmel, Georg. (1904) 1971a. "Fashion." In Donald N. Levine (ed.), *On Individuality and Social Form*, pp. 294–323. Chicago: University of Chicago Press.

Simmel, Georg. (1904) 1971b. "How Is Society Possible?" In Donald N. Levine (ed.), *On Individuality and Social Forms*, pp. 6–22. Chicago: University of Chicago Press.

Simmel, Georg. (1904) 1971c. *On Individuality and Social Forms*, ed. Donald N. Lavine. Chicago: University of Chicago Press.

Simmel, Georg. 1950a. "Adornment." In *The Sociology of Georg Simmel*, ed. and trans. Kurt H. Wolff, pp. 338–44. New York: Free Press.

Simmel, Georg. 1950b. *The Sociology of Georg Simmel*, ed. and trans. Kurt H. Wolff. New York: Free Press.

Simmel, Georg. 1955. *Conflict and The Web of Group-Affiliations*, trans. Kurt H. Wolff and Reinhard Bendix. New York: The Free Press.

Simmel, Georg. 1957. "Fashion." *American Journal of Sociology* 62(6): 541–58.

Simmel, Georg. 1988. *Kinship and Class in the West Indies.* Cambridge: Cambridge University Press.

Simon, Gregory L. and Peter S. Alagona. 2013. "Contradictions at the Confluence of Commerce, Consumption and Conservation; or, an REI Shopper Camps in the Forest, Does Anyone Notice?" *Geoforum* 45: 325–36.

Sims, Josh. 2010. *Cult Streetwear.* London: Laurence King.

Skeggs, Beverly. 1997. *Formations of Class and Gender: Becoming Respectable.* London: Sage.

Skoggard, Ian. 1998a. *The Indigenous Dynamic in Taiwan's Postwar Development: The Religious and Historical Roots of Entrepreneurship.* Armonk, NY: M. E. Sharpe, Inc.

Skoggard, Ian. 1998b. "Transnational Commodity Flows and the Global Phenomenon of the Brand." In Anne Brydon and Sandra Niessen (eds), *Consuming Fashion: Adorning the Transnational Body*, pp. 57–71. Oxford: Berg.

Skov, Lise. 2003. "Fashion-nation: A Japanese Globalization Experience and a Hong Kong Dilemma." In Sandra Niessen, Ann Marie Leshkowich and Carla Jones (eds), *Re-orienting Fashion: The Globalization of Asian Dress*, pp. 215–42. Oxford: Berg.

Slater, Don. 1997. *Consumer Culture and Modernity.* New York: Polity Press

Smith, Andrew. 1939–40. *The Diary of Dr. Andrew Smith, 1834–1836*, 2 vols, ed. Percival R. Kirby. Cape Town: Van Riebeeck Society.

Smith, Carol. 1995. "Race-Class-Gender Ideology in Guatemala: Modern and Anti-Modern Forms," *Comparative Studies in Society and History* 37(4): 723–49.

Smith, Fred. 1982. "Fratha Dress." *African Arts* 15: 36–42, 92.

Smith, Valene L. ed. 1989. *Hosts and Guests: The Anthropology of Tourism*, 2nd edn. Philadelphia: University of Pennsylvania Press.

Sodipo, Bankole. 1997. *Piracy and Counterfeiting: GATT, TRIPS and Developing Countries: 5.* International Economic Development Law. London: Kluwer Law International.

Somerville, William. (1802) 1979. *William Somerville's Narrative of His Journeys to the Eastern Cape Frontiers and to Lattakoe, 1799–1802*, ed. Edna and Frank Bradlow. Cape Town: Van Riebeeck Society.

Soyer, Daniel. 2004. *A Coat of Many Colors: Immigration, Globalization, and Reform in New York City's Garment Industry.* New York: Fordham University Press.

Ṣóyínká, Wolé. 1988. *Aké: The Years of Childhood.* Ibadan: Spectrum.

Spitzer, Leo. 1974. *The Creoles of Sierra Leone.* Madison: University of Wisconsin Press.

St. Augustine. (1467) 1984. *City of God.* Harmondsworth, Middlesex, England: Penguin.

Stanley, Liz. 1992. *The Auto-biographical I.* Manchester: Manchester University Press.

Steele, Valerie. 1991. "The F Word." *Lingua Franca: Journal of Academic Life* 1(April): 17–20.

Steele, Valarie and John Major. 1999. *China Chic: East Meets West.* New Haven, CT: Yale University Press.

Steiner, Christopher B. 1985. "Another Image of Africa: Toward an Ethnohistory of Cloth Marketed in West Africa, 1873–1960." *Ethnohistory* 32(2): 91–110.

Stephen, Lynn. 1991. "Cultures as a Resource: Four Cases of Self-Managed Indigenous Craft Production in Latin America." *Economic Development and Cultural Change* 40(1): 101–30.

Stephen, Lynn. 1993. "Weaving in the Fast Lane: Class, Ethnicity, and Gender in Zapotec Craft Commercialization." In June Nash (ed.), *Crafts in the World Market: The Impact of Global Exchange on Middle American Artisans*, pp. 25–59. Albany: State University of New York Press.

Stewart, Kathleen. 1996. *Space On the Side of the Road: Cultural Poetics in an "Other" America.* Princeton, NJ: Princeton University Press.

Stoller, Paul. 1995. *Embodying Colonial Memories: Spirit Possession, Power, and the Hauka in West Africa.* New York: Routledge.

Stoller, Paul. 2002. *Money Has No Smell: The Africanization of New York.* Chicago: University of Chicago Press.

Strachey, Lytton. (1918) 1948. *Eminent Victorians.* Middlesex: Penguin Books.

Strasser, Susan. 2000. *Never Done: A History of American Housework.* New York: Owl Books/Henry Holt and Company.

Strathern, Marilyn. 1988. *The Gender of the Gift.* Berkeley: University of California Press.

Strathern, Marilyn. 1999. *Property, Substance and Effect. Anthropological Essays on Persons and Things.* London: Athlone Press.

Strega, Linda. 1985. "The Big Sell-Out: Lesbian Femininity." *Lesbian Ethics* 1(3).

Sugiyama, Shinsaku. 2009. *Nihon no buru-ji-nzu monogatari*. Okayama: Kibito.

Sundstrom, Lars. 1974. *The Exchange Economy of Pre-Colonial Tropical Africa*. New York: St. Martin's Press.

Suryakusama, Julia. 2001. "The Kebaya As Identity, Expression and Oppression." *Latitudes* 3: 71–73.

Sykes, Karen. 2009. *Ethnographies of Moral Reasoning: Living Paradoxes of a Global Age*. New York: Palgrave Macmillan.

Tambiah, Stanley J. 1985. "A Performative Approach to Ritual." In Stanley J. Tambiah (ed.), *Culture, Thought, and Social Action*, pp. 123–66. Cambridge, MA: Harvard University Press.

Tarlo, Emma. 1996. *Clothing Matters: Dress and Identity in India*. Chicago: University of Chicago Press; London: Hurst.

Tarlo, Emma. 2010a. "The South Asian Twist in British Muslim Fashion." In Christopher Breward, Philip Crang, and Rosemary Crill (eds), *British Asian Style: Fashion & Textiles Past & Present*. London: V&A Publishing.

Tarlo, Emma. 2010b. *Visibly Muslim: Fashion, Politics, Faith*. Oxford: Berg.

Taussig, Michael T. 1993. *Mimesis and Alterity: An Alternative History of the Senses*. New York: Routledge, Chapman and Hall.

Taussig, Michael. 2008. "Redeeming Indigo." *Theory, Culture and Society* 25(1): 1–15.

Taylor, Charles. 1991. *The Ethics of Authenticity*. Cambridge, MA: Harvard University Press.

Taylor, Janelle S. 2005. "Surfacing the Body Interior." *Annual Review of Anthropology* 34: 741–56.

Taylor Atkins, E. 2000. "Can Japanese Sing the Blues?" In Timothy J. Craig (ed.), *Japan Pop*. New York: Eastgate.

Teunissen, José. 2005. "Global Fashion Local Tradition: On the Globalisation of Fashion." In Jan Brand and José Teunissen (eds), *Global Fashion Local Tradition: On the Globalisation of Fashion*, pp. 8–21. Arnhem: Terra.

Thoi Trang Tre (New Fashion). 1994–97. Various issues.

Thomas, Nicholas. 1992. "The Inversion of Tradition." *American Ethnologist* 19(2): 213–32.

Thomas, Nicholas. 2003. "The Case of the Misplaced Ponchos: Speculations Concerning the History of Cloth in Polynesia." In Chloë Colchester (ed.), *Clothing the Pacific*, pp. 79–96. Oxford: Berg.

Thomas, Sue. 2008. "From 'Green Blur' to Ecofashion: Fashioning an Eco-Lexicon." *Fashion Theory* 12(4): 525–40.

Thompson, E. P. 1967. "Time, Work-Discipline, and Industrial Capitalism." *Past and Present* 38(1): 56–97.

Thompson, Robert F. 1983. *Flash of the Spirit*. New York: Vintage Books.

Tice, Karin E. 1995. *Kuna Crafts, Gender, and the Global Economy*. Austin: University of Texas Press.

Tilley, Christopher. 2006. "Theoretical Perspectives. Introduction." In Christopher Tilley, Webb Keane, Susanne Küchler, Michael Rowlands and Patricia Spyer (eds), *Handbook of Material Culture*, pp. 60–74. London: Sage Publications.

Tobin, Joseph J. 1992. "Introduction: Domesticating the West." In Joseph J. Tobin (ed.), *Re-made in Japan*. New Haven, CT: Yale University Press.

Tobin, Joseph J., ed. 1992. *Re-made in Japan*. New Haven, CT: Yale University Press.

Todor, John I. 2007. *Addicted Customers: How to Get Them Hooked on your Company*. Martinez, CA: Silverado Press.

Towner, John. 1985. The Grand Tour: A Key Phase in the History of Tourism. *Annals of Tourism Research* 12(3): 297–334.

Tremlett, Horace M. 1915. *With the Tin Gods*. London: Bodley Head.

Trilling, Lionel. 1972. *Sincerity and Authenticity*. London: Oxford University Press.

Trouillot, Michel-Rolph. 1982. "Motion in the System: Coffee, Color, and Slavery in Eighteenth-Century Saint Domingue." *Review* 5(3): 331–88.

Tu, Thuy Linh Nguyen. 2011. *The Beautiful Generation: Asian Americans and the Cultural Economy of Fashion*. Durham, NC: Duke University Press.

Turner, Terence. 1969. "Tchikrin, A Central Brazilian Tribe and its Symbolic Language of Bodily Adornment." *Natural History* 78(October):50–59, 80.

Turner, Terence. 1979a. "Kinship, Household, and Community Structure among the Kayapó." In David Maybury-Lewis (ed.), *Dialectical Societies*, pp. 179–214. Cambridge, MA: Harvard University Press.

Turner, Terence. 1979b. "The Social Skin." In Jeremy Cherfas and Roger Lewin (eds), *Not Work Alone: A Cross-Cultural Study of Activities Superfluous to Survival*, pp. 112–40. London: Temple Smith.

Tylor, Edward B. (1871) 1958. *Primitive Culture*. New York: Harper and Brothers.

Tyrrell, Barbara H. 1968. *Tribal Peoples of Southern Africa*. Cape Town: Books of Africa.

Ucko, Peter J. "Penis Sheaths: A Comparative Study." In *Proceedings of the Royal Anthropological Institute of Great Britain and Ireland for 1969*, pp. 24–67.

al-'Umran, Ahmad. 2001. *The Crown of Chastity. The Hijab, Its Rulings and Its Virtues*. Riyadh: Dar Ibn al-Athir.

United Nations (UN). 1996. *1995 International Trade Statistics Yearbook 1994. Vol. II: Trade by Commodity*. New York: United Nations.

Urry, John. 1990. *The Tourist Gaze: Leisure and Travel in Contemporary Societies*. London: Sage.

US Government Accountability Office (GAO). 2005. "U.S.-China TradeL Textile Safeguard Procedures Should Be Improved." Report to Congressional Committees.

US International Trade Commission (USITC). 2004. *Textile and Apparel: Assessment of the Competitiveness of Certain Foreign Supplies to the U.S. Market*, vol. 1. Washington, DC: US International Trade Commission.

Usra, Marfat Bint Kamil. 2001. *Valuable Advices about Women's Transgressions in Dress and Ornaments*. Riyadh: Dar Ibn al-Athir.

Vale, V. and Andrea Juno. 1989. *Re/Search #12: Modern Primitives, An Investigation of Contemporary Adornment and Ritual*. San Francisco: Re/Search Publications.

Van Groen, Barth and Piet Lozer. 1976. *La Structure et l'organisation de la friperie à Tunis*. Groupe d'études Tunis. Amsterdam: Université Libre Amsterdam.

Vann, Elizabeth F. 2006. "The Limits of Authenticity in Vietnamese Consumer Markets." *American Anthropologist* 108(2): 286–96.

Veber, Henne. 1996. "External Inducement and Non-Westernization in the Uses of the Ashéninka Cushma." *Journal of Material Culture* 1(2): 155–82.

Veblen, Thorstein. (1899) 1994. *The Theory of the Leisure Class: An Economic Study of Institutions*. New York: B. W. Huebsch.

Vertovec, Steven. 2007. "Super-diversity and Its Implication." *Ethnic and Racial Studies* 29(6): 1024–54.

Vilaça, Aparecida. 2007. "Cultural Change as Body Metamorphosis." In Carlos Fausto and Michael Heckenberger (eds), *Time and Memory in Indigenous Amazonia: Anthropological Perspectives*, pp. 169–93. Gainsville: University of Florida Press.

Visweswaran, Kamal. 1994. *Fictions of Feminist Ethnography*. Minneapolis: University of Minnesota Press.

Vogel, Steven. 2007. *Streetwear: The Insider's Guide*. San Francisco: Chronicle Books.

Vološinov, Valentin N. (1929) 1973. *Marxism and the Philosophy of Language*. Cambridge, MA: Harvard University Press.

Vom Bruck, Gabriele. 1997a. "Elusive Bodies: The Politics of Aesthetics among Yemeni Elite Women." *Signs* 23(1): 175–214.

Vom Bruck, Gabriele. 1997b. "A House Turned inside out. Inhabiting Space in a Yemeni City." *Journal of Material Culture* 2(2): 139–73.

Waggoner, Catherine E. 1997. "The Emancipatory Potential of Feminine Masquerade in Mary Kay Cosmetics." *Text and Performance Quarterly* 17(3): 256–72.

Wagner, Jon. 1990. "'Bricolage' and Teachers' Theorizing." *Anthropology & Education Quarterly* 21(1): 78–81.

Waldinger, Roger. 1986. *Through the Eye of the Needle: Immigrants and Enterprise in New York's Garment Trades*. New York: New York University Press.

Wallerstein, Immanuel. 1974. *The Modern World System*. New York: Academic Press.

Wang, Ping. 2000. *Aching for Beauty: Footbinding in China*. Minneapolis: University of Minnesota Press.

Warnier, Jean-Pierre. 2006. "Inside and Outside: Surfaces and Containers." In Christopher Tilley, Webb Keane, Susanne Küchler, Michael Rowlands and Patricia Spyer (eds), *Handbook of Material Culture*, pp. 186–96. London: Sage Publications.

Waterbury, Ronald. 1989. "Embroidery for Tourists: A Contemporary Putting-Out System in Oaxaca, Mexico." In Annette B. Weiner and Jane Schneider (eds), *Cloth and Human Experience*, pp. 243–71. Washington, DC: Smithsonian Institution Press.

Watson, James L., ed. 1997. *Golden Arches East*. Stanford, CA: Stanford University Press.

Weber, Max. 1978. *Economy and Society*, trans. Guenther Roth and Claus Wittich. Berkeley: University of California Press.

Weber, Max. (1904–05) 1985. *The Protestant Ethic and the Spirit of Capitalism*, trans. Talcott Parsons. London: Counterpoint.

Weiner, Annette B. 1985. "Inalienable Wealth." *American Ethnologist* 12: 210–27.

Weiner, Annette B. 1989. "Why Cloth? Wealth Gender, and Power in Oceania." In A. Weiner, J. Schneider (eds), *Cloth and the Human Experience*. London: Smithsonain Institute Press.

Weiner, Annette B. 1992. *Inalienable Possessions: The Paradox of Keeping while Giving*. Berkeley: University of California Press.

Weiner, Annette B. and Jane Schneider, eds. 1989. *Cloth and Human Experience*. Washington, DC: Smithsonian Institution Press.

Weinstein, Deena. 1989. "The Amnesty International Concert Tour: Transnationalism as Cultural Commodity." *Public Culture* 1(2): 60–65.

Weiss, Brad. 1996. "Dressing at Death: Clothing, Time, and Memory in Buhaya, Tanzania." In Hildi Hendrickson (ed.), *Clothing and Difference: Embodied Identities in Colonial and Post-Colonial Africa*, pp. 133–54. Durham, NC: Duke University Press.

Weiss, Brad. 2009. *Street Dreams and Hip Hop Barbershops: Global Fantasy in Urban Tanzania*. Bloomington: Indiana University Press.

Weiss, Susan. 2009. "Under Cover: Demystification of Women's Head Covering in Jewish Law." *Nashim: A Journal of Jewish Women's Studies & Gender Issues* 17: 89–115.

Welters, Linda. 2008. "The Natural Look: American Style in the 1970s." *Fashion Theory* 12(4): 489–510.

Wengrow, David. 2008. "Prehistories of Commodity Branding." *Current Anthropology* 49(1): 7–34.

Wesley, John. 1986. *The Works of John Wesley*, vol. 3, ed. A. C. Outler. Nashville: Abingdon Press.

Westermarck, E. (1891) 1922. *The History of Human Marriage*, vol. 1. New York: The Allerton Book Company.

Wilk, Richard. 1990. "Consumer Goods as Dialogue about Development." *Culture and History* 7: 79–100.

Wilk, Richard. 1995. "Learning to Be Local in Belize: Global Systems of Common Difference." In Daniel Miller (ed.), *Worlds Apart*, pp. 110–33. London: Routledge.

Wilkinson, R. H. 1970. "The Gentleman Ideal and the Maintenance of a Political Elite". In P. W. Musgrave (ed.), *Sociology, History, and Education*. London: Methuen.

Williams, Howard. 1887. "First Experiences in the Kuruman District." *Chronicle of the London Missionary Society*, March, 110–17.

Williams, Raymond. (1975) 2005. *Television: Technology and Cultural Form*, ed. Ederyn Williams. London: Routledge.

Williams, Raymond. 1977. *Marxism and Literature*. Oxford: Oxford University Press.

Williams, Rosalind. 1982. *Dreamworlds: Mass Consumption in Late Nineteenth Century France*. Berkeley: University of California Press.

Williamson, Janice. 1992. "I-less and Gaga in the West Edmonton Mall: Toward a Pedestrian Feminist Reading." In David H. Currie and Valerie Raoul (eds), *The Anatomy of Gender: Women's Struggle for the Body*. Ottawa: Carleton University Press.

Willis, Justin. 1993. *Mombasa, the Swahili, and the Making of the Mijikenda*. Oxford: Clarendon Press.

Willoughby, William C. 1899. "Our People: What They Are Like and How They Live." *News from Afar: LMS Magazine for Young People*, n.s., 15(6): 84–86.

Wilson, Elizabeth. 1985. *Adorned in Dreams: Fashion and Modernity*. London: Virago Press.

Wilson, Godfrey. 1941. *An Essay on the Economics of Detribalization in Northern Rhodesia*, Part 2. Rhodes-Livingstone Papers 6. Manchester: Manchester University Press.

Wilson, Godfrey. 1941–42. *An Essay on the Economics of Detribalization, Vols 1 and 2*. Rhodes-Livingstone Papers nos. 5 and 6.

Winge, Theresa M. 2008. "'Green Is the New Black': Celebrity Chic and the 'Green' Commodity Fetish." *Fashion Theory* 12(4): 511–24.

Winstone, H. V. E. 1978. *Gertrude Bell*. London: Jonathan Cape.

Wittgenstein, Ludwig. 1978. *Philosophical Investigations*. Berkeley: University of California Press.

Wolf, Arthur P. 1970. "Chinese Kinship and Mourning Dress." In Maurice Freedman (ed.), *Family and Kinship In Chinese Society*, pp. 189–208. Stanford, CA: Stanford University Press.

Wolf, Diane. 1992. *Factory Daughters*. Berkeley: University of California Press.

Wolf, Eric R. 1982. *Europe and the People without History*. Berkeley: University of California Press.

Wolf, Roberta and Schlachter Trudy. 2000. *Millennium Mode: Fashion Forecasts from 40 Top Designers*. New York: Rizzoli.

Woodmansee, Martha. 1984. "The Genius and the Copyright: Economic and Legal Conditions of the Emergence of the 'Author'." *Eighteenth-Century Studies* 17(4): 425–48.

Woodward, Sophie. 2005. "Looking Good, Feeling Right: Aesthetics of the Self." In Susanne Küchler and Daniel Miller (eds), *Clothing as Material Culture*, pp. 21–39. Oxford: Berg.

Woodward, Sophie. 2007. *Why Women Wear What They Wear*. Oxford: Berg.

Woolf, Virginia. (1938) 1986. *Three Guineas*. London: The Hogarth Press.

Wroblewski, Chris. 1989. *Skin Shows: The Art of Tattooing*. London: Virgin.

Yamane, Hidehiko. 2008. *Tateoti: Evisu the Photobook*. Tokyo: Ei Publishing.

Yamani, May. 1997. "Changing the Habits of a Lifetime: The Adaptation of Hejazi Dress to the New Social Order." In Nancy Lindisfarne-Tapper and Bruce Ingham (eds), *Languages of Dress in the Middle East*, pp. 55–67. Richmond: Curzon.

Yelvington, K. (Forthcoming). "Gender and Ethnicity at Work in a Trinidadian Factory." In J. Momsen (ed.), *Caribbean Women*. London: Macmillan.

Young, Iris Marion. 1980. "Throwing Like a Girl: A Phenomenology of Feminine Body Comportment Motility and Spatiality." *Human Studies* 3(2): 137–56.

INDEX